Handbook of Research Methods in Experimental Psychology

**Blackwell Handbooks of Research Methods in Psychology**

Created for advanced students and researchers looking for an authoritative definition of the research methods used in their chosen field, the *Blackwell Handbooks of Research Methods in Psychology* provide an invaluable and cutting-edge overview of classic, current, and future trends in the research methods of psychology.

- Each handbook draws together 20–25 newly commissioned chapters to provide comprehensive coverage of the research methodology used in a specific psychological discipline.
- Each handbook is introduced and contextualized by leading figures in the field, lending coherence and authority to each volume.
- The international team of contributors to each handbook has been specially chosen for its expertise and knowledge of each field.
- Each volume provides the perfect complement to non-research based handbooks in psychology.

*Handbook of Research Methods in Industrial and Organizational Psychology*
Edited by Steven G. Rogelberg

*Handbook of Research Methods in Clinical Psychology*
Edited by Michael C. Roberts and Stephen S. Ilardi

*Handbook of Research Methods in Experimental Psychology*
Edited by Stephen F. Davis

*Handbook of Research Methods in Developmental Psychology*
Edited by Douglas M. Teti

# Handbook of Research Methods in Experimental Psychology

*Edited by*

## Stephen F. Davis

**Blackwell**
Publishing

© 2003, 2005 by Blackwell Publishing Ltd
except for editorial material and organization © 2003, 2005 by Stephen F. Davis

BLACKWELL PUBLISHING
350 Main Street, Malden, MA 02148-5020, USA
9600 Garsington Road, Oxford OX4 2DQ, UK
550 Swanston Street, Carlton, Victoria 3053, Australia

The right of Stephen F. Davis to be identified as the Author of the Editorial Material in this
Work has been asserted in accordance with the UK Copyright, Designs, and Patents Act 1988.

First published 2003
First published in paperback 2005 by Blackwell Publishing Ltd

1   2005

*Library of Congress Cataloging-in-Publication Data*

Handbook of research methods in experimental psychology / edited by
Stephen F. Davis.
        p. cm. – (Blackwell handbooks of research methods in psychology)
Includes bibliographical references and index.
    ISBN 0-631-22649-4 (hbk. : alk. paper) – ISBN 1-4051-3280-9 (pbk. : alk. paper)
    1. Psychology–Research–Methodology.   2. Psychology, Experimental–Research–
Methodology. I. Davis, Stephen F. II. Series.

    BF76.5.H35 2003
    150'.7'24–dc21

                                                                2003001710

ISBN-13: 978-0-631-22649-9 (hbk. : alk. paper) – ISBN-13: 978-1-4051-3280-0 (pbk. : alk. paper)

A catalogue record for this title is available from the British Library.

Set in 10.5/12.5 pt Adobe Garamond
by Graphicraft Ltd, Hong Kong
Printed and bound in the United Kingdom
by TJ International, Padstow, Cornwall

The publisher's policy is to use permanent paper from mills that operate a sustainable forestry
policy, and which has been manufactured from pulp processed using acid-free and elementary
chlorine-free practices. Furthermore, the publisher ensures that the text paper and cover board
used have met acceptable environmental accreditation standards.

For further information on
Blackwell Publishing, visit our website:
www.blackwellpublishing.com

# Contents

# Contributors

**Brenda J. Anderson**, Department of Psychology and the Program in Neurobiology and Behavior, SUNY at Stony Brook

**Scott A. Bailey**, Department of Psychology, Texas Lutheran University

**Lewis Barker**, Department of Psychology, Auburn University

**W. Robert Batsell, Jr**, Department of Psychology, Kalamazoo College

**Melissa Burns**, Department of Psychology, Texas Christian University

**William Buskist**, Department of Psychology, Auburn University

**E. J. Capaldi**, Department of Psychological Sciences, Purdue University, Indiana

**Stephen F. Davis**, Department of Psychology, Emporia State University

**C. James Goodwin**, Department of Psychology, Wheeling Jesuit University

**Heather E. Gorby**, Department of Psychology, SUNY at Stony Brook

**Richard J. Harris**, Department of Psychology, University of New Mexico and American Society of Radiologic Technologists

**Henry E. Heffner**, Laboratory of Comparative Hearing, Department of Psychology, University of Toledo

**Rickye S. Heffner**, Laboratory of Comparative Hearing, Department of Psychology, University of Toledo

**Jeffrey S. Katz**, Department of Psychology, Auburn University

**Roger E. Kirk**, Department of Psychology and Neuroscience, Baylor University, Texas

**Daniel P. McCloskey**, Department of Psychology, SUNY at Stony Brook

**David Matsumoto**, Department of Psychology, San Francisco State University

**Richard L. Miller**, Department of Psychology, University of Nebraska at Kearney

**Mauricio R. Papini**, Department of Psychology, Texas Christian University

**David G. Payne**, Vice Provost and Dean of the Graduate School, Binghamton University

**Robert W. Proctor**, Department of Psychological Sciences, Purdue University, Indiana

**Jesse E. Purdy**, Department of Psychology, Southwestern University, Texas

**Bryan K. Saville**, Department of Psychology, Stephen F. Austin State University, Texas

**Steven J. Schapiro**, Department of Veterinary Sciences, University of Texas M. D. Anderson Cancer Center

**Lauren Fruh VanSickle Scharff**, Department of Psychology, Stephen F. Austin State University, Texas

**H. R. Schiffman**, Department of Psychology, Rutgers University, New Jersey

**Randolph A. Smith**, Department of Psychology, Ouachita Baptist University, Arkansas

**Despina A. Tata**, Department of Psychology, SUNY at Stony Brook

**Deanne L. Westerman**, Department of Psychology, Binghamton University

# PART I

*Historical Roots and Future Trends*

# CHAPTER ONE

# Psychology's Experimental Foundations

## C. James Goodwin

When the fledgling American Psychological Association (APA) held its third annual meeting at Princeton University in December of 1894, a major item of business for the 22 attendees was the ratification of the organization's first Constitution. It was a modest document – seven "Articles" that filled less than a page in the published report. Article 1 is worthy of note as a way to begin this Handbook's opening chapter, because it concerned the basic nature of the emerging academic discipline of psychology. It described the principal object of the Association as "the advancement of psychology *as a science*. Those eligible for membership are engaged in this work" (Cattell, 1895, p. 150, italics added). This statement did not mark the origins of the attempt to make psychology "scientific," but it provided a clear statement of the values held by the early leaders of academic psychology in the United States.

Recognition of the scientific status for this newly emerging field did not happen overnight, of course – declaring one's discipline to be a science does not by itself bring about such standing. Indeed, the status of psychology was an important issue throughout the late nineteenth and early twentieth century, with some insisting that psychology would always be a subdiscipline of philosophy, while others argued that psychology could be reduced to physiology. The ambiguity of psychology's disciplinary identity is illustrated by what happened to Princeton psychologist James Mark Baldwin in the early 1890s. He ordered the two-volume set of Alexander Bain's famous psychological treatises, and when it arrived Baldwin protested the import duty of $25, referring to a law that allowed scientific books to be imported duty-free. The official reply from the government was that its experts had determined that the books were "in no way scientific" (quoted in O'Donnell, 1985, p. 132).

One way to convince others (even government "experts" perhaps) that one's field is scientific is to apply recognized scientific methods to the questions of interest, and that is precisely what the early psychologists did, borrowing methodology from physiologists (e.g., psychophysics and reaction time) or creating new strategies (e.g., mental tests and mazes). The purpose of this opening chapter is to examine the origins and early evolution of the efforts to incorporate scientific methodology into the pursuit of knowledge about mind and behavior. I have organized the chapter around four broad categories of research methodology, each with its roots in the nineteenth century. These categories I have labeled:

- Measuring the mind – a brass instrument psychology;
- Looking inward – "questionaries" and the era of introspection;
- Assessing individual differences – the mental testing movement;
- Observing behavior – the legacy of comparative psychology.

After describing the methods associated with each of these categories, I will close the chapter with a brief description of the manner by which the early psychologists were trained to become psychological scientists.

## Measuring the Mind – A Brass Instrument Psychology

Experimental psychology's earliest methods were developed to measure and shed light on the nature of such basic cognitive processes as sensation, perception, attention, and memory. The story is well known, and began in Germany in the second half of the nineteenth century with the creation of research laboratories and through the work of such familiar names as Fechner, Helmholtz, Wundt, Ebbinghaus, Müller, and Külpe. The traditional starting point for experimental psychology is considered by some to be the publication of Fechner's *Elements of Psychophysics* ([1860] 1966), and by others to be the founding of Wundt's laboratory at Leipzig in 1879. As E. G. Boring elegantly wrote, however, "History is continuous and sleek, [and famous people and events] are the handles that you put on its smooth sides" (1963, p. 130). Thus, experimental psychology did appear suddenly. Throughout the nineteenth century, philosophers, physiologists, and physicists were asking related questions about human mental processes and behavior, and a conviction that recognizably scientific methods could be applied to psychological phenomena developed gradually.

It was Wundt, however, who made this evolving belief about a scientific psychology explicit, and he did so in the Preface to his two-volume *Principles of Physiological Psychology* ([1874] 1904), stating in no uncertain terms: "The book which I here present to the public is an attempt to mark out a new domain of science" (p. v). Shortly after publishing his *Principles*, Wundt was appointed to Leipzig, and within a few years he established a laboratory and began to fulfill the promise of his bold statement. Using equipment borrowed from physiologists and physicists, work in Wundt's laboratory centered on topics that he considered amenable to strict experimental control; for the most part, this meant research on basic sensory processes. To learn about the so-called "New Psychology," students came from all over Europe and also from abroad (especially the United States – see the final section of this chapter). Americans studying in Europe returned home to create their own laboratories, influenced by the Leipzig model but with their own special character. By the turn of the twentieth century, there were about 40 such labs in the United States and they constituted approximately 80 percent of the psychology laboratories worldwide (Benjamin, 2000).

In Wundt's laboratory, attention focused initially (i.e., in the 1880s) on the methodologies associated with psychophysics and reaction time. As the American psychologist James McKeen Cattell, Wundt's assistant in the mid-1880s, described it in a letter to his parents, work in the lab researched "two departments – the relation of the internal stimulus to the sensation, and the time of mental process" (cited in Sokal, 1981, p. 156). The former concerned the determination of sensory thresholds, using psychophysical methods first outlined by Fechner, and the latter involved reaction time and the famous "complication" method, by which times for mental events were inferred from differences in reaction time for tasks that varied in their degree of mental complexity.

*Psychophysics*

By the time Wundt's laboratory was producing original research, the psychophysics methodology first standardized by Fechner had already been in use for 20 years and physiologists (e.g., Ernst Weber) had been studying sensory thresholds for an even longer period. It had been Fechner's genius to find a way to quantify sensation by relating sensory qualities to measured changes in the physical stimulus, and while many of his concepts were already under fire in the mid-1880s (e.g., the psychological equality of just noticeable differences), the methods he developed were in widespread use to investigate the two main problems of psychophysics – the problem of detection and the problem of difference. The first problem dealt with the question of how much of a stimulus had to be present in order for it to be just barely noticed and the second problem concerned how different two stimuli had to be before they could be just barely distinguished.

Psychophysics research in the late nineteenth century involved refining Fechner's methods, and using these methods either to classify sensory qualities or test the limits of empirical relationships such as Weber's Law. For instance, a study by Fullerton and Cattell (1892) examined a common psychophysics task – making judgments about the relative weights of two objects – and suggested refinements in the psychophysics method of constant stimuli. Fullerton and Cattell found that when people were allowed to use the judgment "equal" when deciding about the weight of two objects, in addition to the normal judgments of "heavier" and "lighter," they tended to overuse the "equal" choice. When the researchers forced their judges to guess which was heavier, after they had initially made an "equal" choice, the subjects were more often right than wrong. This led to the recommendation that when performing the weight-comparison task using the method of constant stimuli, people should only be allowed to give judgments of "heavier" or "lighter"; the "equal" judgment should be eliminated.

The use of psychophysics methodology to identify sensory qualities was a prime activity in the Cornell laboratory of E. B. Titchener during the 1890s. Titchener, British in nationality but Germanic in temperament, was committed to identifying the basic elements of human conscious experience, at least early in his career, and he relied heavily on the study of difference thresholds to advance his cause. He believed that any time someone could consistently distinguish between two stimuli it meant that two distinct conscious experiences had been identified. In studies involving color vision, for instance, Titchener would ask his participants (or "observers" as they were often called at the time) to judge the smallest possible differences among color patches of varying wavelengths, brightnesses, and degrees of saturation. By this process, Titchener (1896) counted literally thousands of distinct sensory qualities.

One final example of research using psychophysical methods illustrates an important point about the values held by most American experimentalists. In contrast with Wundt (German) and Titchener (German in spirit), who both thought of laboratory work primarily as basic research, American researchers were by their nature pragmatic, and much of their research had an applied tinge to it. A fine example of this is the doctoral dissertation of Edmund Sanford, who earned his degree at Johns Hopkins in the late 1880s under G. Stanley Hall, and directed the laboratory at Clark University in the 1890s (Goodwin, 1987). Sanford's (1888) project used psychophysics methodology to examine "the relative legibility of the small letters" (p. 402). Using a device of his own creation, Sanford presented each of the 26 letters "without natural sequence" (p. 404; that is, he knew about what today we would call counterbalancing) at varying distances until they passed a recognition threshold. His results were complicated, but he found, for example, that wide letters (e.g., "o") were more legible than narrow ones (e.g., "i") and that confusions frequently occurred among similar letters (e.g., "e" and "o"). The important point in the present context is that the research shows a typical strategy among American experimental psychologists – they liked to produce research with potential usefulness. In Sanford's case, the outcome had implications for the decisions made by journal editors about font type and size and similar decisions made by those developing an important new technological advance at the time – the typewriter.

*Reaction time*

Because of their desire to legitimize the "New Psychology" as scientific, the early experimental psychologists were much enamored of reaction time methodology, developed in the late 1860s by the Dutch physiologist F. C. Donders. It seemed to offer great promise as a means to measure, with some precision, the duration of specific types of mental activities. Donders reasoned that if nerve impulses take a measurable amount of time (and Helmholtz's famous experiments had shown just that), and if mental activity depends on nerve impulses, then it ought to be possible to measure various mental processes by measuring the amount of time taken to complete certain tasks.

Most of Cattell's work at Leipzig used reaction time methodology, and he strongly defended the use of this tool in a letter to his parents. As an aside, this letter should resonate with all experimental psychologists doing basic research who have tried to explain their work to their parents. Cattell wrote:

> I determine the time required by simple mental processes – how long it takes us to see, hear, or feel something – to understand, to will, to think. You may not

consider this so very interesting or important. But if we wish to describe the world – which is the end of science – surely an accurate knowledge of our mind is more important than anything else . . . if one thinks that knowledge for its own sake is worth the pursuit, then surely a knowledge of mind is best of all. (cited in Sokal, 1981, p. 125)

Cattell eventually became strongly interested in individual differences in reaction time, but this focus developed after he left Leipzig (Sokal, 1987). While working in Wundt's laboratory, he completed a number of studies examining various factors affecting reaction time. One of them, completed with his German colleague Gustav Berger, is a perfect illustration of the reaction time logic (Cattell, 1886). With Cattell and Berger alternating in the roles of experimenter and observer, they first established their basic reaction times – the amount of time taken to lift a finger from a depressed telegraph key upon perceiving a colored light. Next, they determined what they referred to as "perception time" and "will time." In perception time, they would see a red light or a blue one, but would respond only when the light was blue. In will time, two hands and two keys were involved – one to be lifted if the light was red and the other for blue. Perception time added the mental event of color discrimination, and will time added to the discrimination the choice of which hand to use. Hence, by subtracting out the various times, the mental events of choice and discrimination could be measured. Adding mental tasks to the basic reaction time "complicates" the process; hence, the reaction time experiment was sometimes known as the complication experiment.

A great deal of effort went into reaction time methodology, even though it was soon determined that the subtraction logic of Donders, with its assumption that mental events combine in a simple additive fashion, was oversimplified. Reaction time was also influenced by such factors as the intensity and duration of the stimulus, which sense was stimulated, whether attention was on the sensory aspect of the task or the motor aspect, and the attributes of the person completing the task (i.e., the individual differences that became of interest to Cattell). Although no modern researcher believes that specific types of mental events are being precisely measured in a reaction time study, the method remains widely used today for testing predictions about mental activity – more complicated acts should take longer than simpler ones. For instance, our knowledge of visual imagery relies heavily on the prediction that reaction times should increase when stimuli are presented at different degrees of angular rotation (Shepard & Metzler, 1971).

*A brass instrument psychology*

Before concluding this section, there are several important points to be made. First, completing both psychophysics and reaction time studies required extremely sophisticated apparatus. In a threshold study for hearing, for instance, auditory stimuli of precise frequencies had to be presented; in a complication experiment, exact response times had to be recorded. As mentioned above, the early experimentalists borrowed liberally from the other sciences, especially when it came to devices for presenting stimuli (e.g., tuning forks) and devices for measuring the passage of time (chronographs). The apparatus pieces often included components made of brass, leading the American psychologist/ philosopher William James to refer to the entire enterprise of experimental psychology, somewhat sarcastically, as a "brass instrument" psychology.[1] A consequence of the necessity for complicated apparatus was that researchers had to be competent mechanics and knowledgeable about the operation of the chronographs, pendulums, kymographs, and other devices that populated the late nineteenth-century laboratory. Indeed, Cattell once commented that not only was it necessary to know something about physics to be an experimental psychologist, one practically had to be an original investigator in physics (Sokal, 1981, pp. 151–2). In the study on letter detection described above, I mentioned that Sanford devised the apparatus. This situation was a common occurrence and Sanford was just one of many experimentalists who had a talent for apparatus building (Goodwin, 1987). Thus, the idea that mechanical aptitude is an essential attribute for an experimental psychologist derives from this time.

A second point about research in the era of brass instruments was that the studies typically included data from very few individuals, often no more than three or four. Furthermore, data from all participants would be reported separately rather than in the form of summary statistics. This was understandable – inferential statistical analyses (e.g., analysis of variance) had not yet been invented. The normative research strategy was to control conditions very carefully, collect data from those very familiar with laboratory procedures, and then present the results for each of the participants, with the hope that a similar outcome would occur for each. That is, the additional participants served the purpose of *replication* and the logic was identical to that used much later for research in the Skinnerian tradition – small N, tight control, data reported for each subject.

The final point, an extension of the one just made, was that the roles of experimenter and research participant were not as sharply delineated as they became by the middle of the twentieth century (Danziger, 1980). In fact, most experimentalists played both roles within the same study. In Cattell's reaction time study, for instance, Cattell and Berger had an equal level of authority, alternating in the roles of data gatherer and data source. Research at this time, then, was more of a collaborative effort among peers than it later became, when "experimenter" with a capital "E" collected data from "subjects" with a small "s."

## Looking Inward – "Questionaries" and the Era of Introspection

One way to discover what a person is thinking about, or to measure a person's knowledge or attitudes, is to ask the person directly. Although fraught with the dangers of a variety of biasing effects, self-reports have been and continue to be an important data source for experimental psychologists. The origins of self-report methodology in psychology lie in the creation of questionnaires, or "questionaries" as they were first called, and in the use of the method of introspection. Questionaries were first used by Charles Darwin and his cousin Francis Galton, and then popularized by the American psychologist G. Stanley Hall. Introspection was actually several methods, not one, and has a complex history that is usually oversimplified to the extreme in textbook accounts. The introspection that characterized work in Wundt's laboratory, for instance, bore virtually no similarity to the introspection conducted in Titchener's lab.

## Questionaries

Galton is normally credited with being the originator of the survey method, but his cousin also used the technique when compiling information for his well-known book on emotion, *Expressions of the Emotions in Man and Animals* (Darwin, 1872). Interested in evaluating the extent of universality in emotional expression, Darwin sent sets of questions to correspondents around the globe, in effect completing the first cross-cultural study of emotion. The questions on the survey (today we would think of them as good examples of leading questions) mainly concerned the specific forms of various facial expressions of emotion, as is clear from the following examples from his list of questions:

> Is astonishment expressed by the eyes and mouth being opened wide, and by the eyebrows being raised? . . .

> Is contempt expressed by a slight protrusion of the lips and by turning up the nose, and with a slight expiration? (Darwin, 1872, pp. 15–16)

Most of the responses to these and similar questions were "yes," regardless of culture, and Darwin used the data to bolster his evolutionary theory of emotional expression.

Galton used surveys to support his beliefs about the inheritance of intelligence and to investigate the nature of imagery. In the first study, he surveyed members of the British Royal Society who excelled in scientific fields, asking them questions about the origins of their interest in science (e.g., "How far do your scientific tastes appear innate?") (cited in Forrest, 1974, p. 126). The replies helped to strengthen Galton's conviction that intelligence, in this case of the scientific variety, was more a matter of "nature" than it was of "nurture."[2] He did concede that nurture played a role, however, especially concerning the focus of one's intellectual activity – he used his cousin's experiences on the HMS *Beagle* to illustrate the point (Fancher, 1996). In his study of imagery, Galton wished to determine the extent to which people used visual imagery, and the nature of the images. He asked his respondents to imagine their breakfast table that morning and to report the image's clarity, whether the objects were "well defined," and the quality of the colors in the image. He was surprised to discover that the scientists in his survey reported little use of imagery, but that women and children seemed capable of vivid images (Goodwin, 1999).

In the United States, it was Clark University's G. Stanley Hall who most vigorously promoted the use of surveys, or "questionaries." Hall was a man of widely divergent interests, but with an abiding belief that the theory of evolution should inform all theorizing in psychology (Ross, 1972). This conviction led him to promote a "genetic" psychology, a psychology that examined both phylogenetic and ontogenetic human development. The former is illustrated by his willingness to encourage work in comparative psychology at Clark, and the latter made him a pioneer in the study of child and adolescent development. A part of his research on child development, begun in the 1880s when he taught at Johns Hopkins University, included the use of surveys to reveal, for example, "The contents of children's minds" (Hall, [1883] 1948). Hall sent his survey to schoolteachers in the Boston area and they collected data from more than 200 children who were just beginning school. He was taken aback by their lack of knowledge, reporting, for example, that 75 percent did not know what season of the year they were currently experiencing, 88 percent did not know what an island was, and 91 percent could not locate their ribs (Hall, [1883] 1948). Hall also noted that children raised in the country were more knowledgeable than those raised in the city. Having grown up on a farm, Hall did not find this result surprising – at a time when the United States was still largely rural, many people shared Hall's belief that "city life is unnatural, and that those who grow up without knowing the country are defrauded of that with-out which childhood can never be complete or normal" (p. 261). Encouraged by the quantity of information from this questionary, Hall became enamored of the method. Between this early survey and 1915, Hall created and compiled data from 194 questionaries related to child development (Ross, 1972).[3]

One last point about Hall's questionary research is that it represents a clear departure from the type of laboratory research described earlier in this chapter. In particular, by involving large numbers of people and summarizing their data in the form of percent-ages, Hall's work contrasted with the typical laboratory study that intensively studied just a few individuals, with data reported for each individual. Hence, the questionary studies represented an early form of research that eventually created pressure to incor-porate statistical analysis into the results of research.

*Introspection*

As mentioned above, traditional textbook accounts provide a distorted view of this famous method. As it is usually described in introductory psychology texts, it is depicted as hopelessly subjective and as a methodology that psychology had to jettison before it could become truly an "objective science." As with most distorted historical accounts, there is a germ of truth in this description, but the real story of introspection is infinitely more complex. First, it was several methods, not one; second, those researchers using it were well aware of the perils and took complicated steps to avoid the problems with the method; third, although its heyday was in the years prior to World War I, it remained a widespread tool long after John Watson (1913) thought he had written its obituary in his so-called "behaviorist manifesto" of 1912.

It was mentioned earlier that Wundt believed laboratory research to be appropriate for investigating certain types of problems that could be brought under tight experi-mental control. Specifically, he believed that the lab was the best place for investigating the attributes of immediate conscious experience. The simple example of temperature illustrates the contrast between immediate experience and what was called "mediate" or mediated experience (Goodwin, 1999). When we examine an outside thermometer from inside our house, the temperature outside is not being experienced by us directly, but is being mediated by the instrument. To have an immediate conscious experience of temperature is to experience it directly by going outside. It was the latter experience that interested Wundt and he was acutely aware of the essential problem of studying such an experience. In contrast with mediated experience, which can meet the scientific criterion of objectivity (i.e., two observers can agree on a thermometer reading), immediate experience is private. To deal with the problem of subjectivity, Wundt made a distinction between what he called self-observation (*Selbstbeobachtung*) and internal perception (*innere Wahrnehmung*). As Danziger (1980) pointed out, later descriptions of Wundt's work confused the two terms and translated both as "introspection." By self-observation, Wundt meant the traditional and commonsense meaning for introspection – a detailed reflection on one's experiences in life, an activity known to philosophers for ages. By internal perception, Wundt meant a more precise process of responding immediately to some specific event. In Wundt's lab, self-observation was not allowed because it was too susceptible to bias; internal perception was the method of choice. What this amounted to in practice was a simple verbal report given by a highly trained observer reacting in a tightly controlled laboratory experiment. These reports were "largely limited to judgments of size, intensity, and duration of physical stimuli" (Danziger, 1980, p. 247), that is, to the kinds of responses found in psychophysics and reaction time experiments. Wundt was highly critical of a later form of introspection, developed by his student Oswald Külpe at his laboratory at Würzburg, and championed by another of his students, E. B. Titchener of Cornell.

Titchener's version of self-report came to be known as "systematic experiment introspection." Similar to what Wundt meant by self-observation, and rejected by him for that reason, it involved experiencing some experimental task, then giving a detailed account of the mental processes that occurred during the event. A one-minute experimental task, for example, might be followed by a four-minute detailed description of the experience. Titchener was not unaware of the difficulties with such a method – there was great potential for bias, reporting what one expected to experience, and there was the obvious problem of memory. Titchener believed the problem of bias could be solved by keeping the tasks relatively simple, maintaining tight experimental control, and through an extensive process of repeating the task, both within and between subjects. As for memory, Titchener (1909, p. 22) recognized that introspection was in fact retrospection. To ease the memory load he borrowed a technique from Külpe's Würzburg lab – fractionation (Goodwin, 1999). This involved breaking a complex task into subtasks, doing an introspective analysis for each, and then combining the results. Finally, Titchener insisted that his introspectors be highly trained, becoming, in effect, introspecting machines. A sufficiently high level of training would insure, he believed, that introspective accounts would flow automatically, without the intervention of interfering thoughts that could bias the description. In Titchener's words, the trained introspectionist "gets into an introspective habit, . . . so that it is possible for him, not only to take mental notes while the observation is in process, without interfering with consciousness, but even to jot down written notes, as the histologist does while his eye is still held to the ocular of the microscope" (Titchener, 1909, p. 23).

The systematic experimental introspection envisioned by Titchener no longer exists, but some idea of what it was like can be gleaned from published reports of research using the method. A good example is the doctoral dissertation of Karl Dallenbach, a student of Titchener's and later a colleague on the Cornell faculty. Dallenbach's (1913) study was a complex series of experiments on the phenomenon of attention. One experiment examined the limits of attention, using a divided attention task not unlike the methodology used by mid-century cognitive psychologists. Dallenbach's three observers faced a difficult challenge. On a table in front of them were two metronomes, each set to a different speed. The primary task was to keep track, for both metronomes combined, of the total number of beats between coincident beats. At the same time, they had to complete one of several concurrent tasks, such as adding numbers. After doing this for 60 or 90 seconds, the observer stopped and gave an introspective description. Here is a portion of the transcript of one of these accounts:

> The sounds of the metronomes, as a series of discontinuous clicks, were clear in consciousness only four or five times . . . , and they were especially bothersome at first. They were accompanied by strain sensations and unpleasantness. The rest of the experiment my attention was on the adding, which was composed of auditory images of the numbers, sometimes on a dark grey scale which was directly ahead and about three feet in front of me. This was accompanied by kinaesthesis of eyes and strains in chest and arms. When these processes were clear in consciousness the sounds of the metronomes were very vague or obscure. (Dallenbach, 1913, p. 467)

This task was only one of several in a series of studies completed by Dallenbach for his dissertation – in fact, over the course of a year, his observers completed a total of more than 1,400 different introspective trials. As with the brass instrument research mentioned above, data were reported for all three observers throughout the study. There were a number of conclusions about the limits of attention, most confirmed in more modern research. The research also supported Titchener's general ideas about the elements of immediate conscious experience. He believed these fundamental elements to be sensation, images, and affective states (Titchener, 1909). If you reread the introspective account, you can see all three of these elements ("strain sensations," "auditory images," "unpleasantness").

Titchener's system of psychology, usually called structuralism because of its emphasis on identifying the basic structure of human conscious experience, fell into disfavor in the 1920s and eventually passed from the scene after his death in 1927. Part of the reason was that despite Titchener's care, introspection's problems with preconceived bias were never satisfactorily solved. More important, Titchener's system was out of step with the important need for practical applications that characterized American psychology in its early years. Indeed, a strong case can be made that the fall of structuralism and the rise of behaviorism had more to do with the latter's practical appeal than the former's methodological inadequacies. Behaviorism promised improvements in life (e.g., in child rearing, in education, in industry), whereas structuralism promised little more than a catalog of sensory qualities. Nonetheless, it is important to recognize that experimental psychology owes E. B. Titchener a large debt of gratitude. As the prototype of a positivist approach to psychology, nobody else in psychology's early years was more adamant

than Titchener about the value of basic science and the importance of systematic laboratory research in the search for understanding the human condition (Tweney, 1987). And
whereas his particular form of systematic experimental introspection has long passed
from the scene, cognitive psychologists today routinely ask participants to "think out
loud," with their verbal reports subjected to "protocol analyses" (Ericsson & Simon,
1993) that are not too far removed from the kinds of content analysis that Titchener
used when drawing conclusions from his introspective accounts.

## Assessing Individual Differences – The Mental Testing Movement

At first glance, it might seem odd to see mental testing as one of the categories of
experimental methodology described in this chapter. Rather, it would seem that such a
discussion would belong in a handbook on psychological assessment that emphasized
correlational research. Experimental psychology has to do with general laws arrived at
through systematic experimentation, it would be argued, whereas mental testing concerns individual differences, determined through correlational analysis. Now this distinction might be a reasonable one, and it is largely taken for granted today, but it was not
a distinction made by psychology's pioneers. In fact, the first clear separation between
what Cronbach (1957) called psychology's two disciplines, experimental and correlational, did not occur until the 1930s and the publication of *Experimental Psychology*
(1938) by Columbia's Robert Woodworth, sometimes called the "Columbia Bible"
because of its widespread influence on the training of experimental psychologists (Winston,
1990). Woodworth was the first to contrast what he referred to as the experimental and
correlational methodologies. And in making the distinction, he was the first to use the
terms "independent" and "dependent" as they are currently used to describe the variables
that are manipulated and measured, respectively, in an experimental study. An important consequence of the difference between experiments and correlations, according to
Woodworth, was that causality could be inferred from the first but not the second, an
argument that now routinely appears in all methodology texts, even if it oversimplifies
several hundred years of arguments over the nature of causality.

As Winston (1990) has convincingly argued, prior to Woodworth's distinction
between experimental and correlational methods, most early American psychologists
would have included mental testing under the general heading of "experiment." The two
editions of Boring's famous history, appearing before (1929) and after (1950)
Woodworth's book, illustrate the Columbia psychologist's influence on the status of
mental testing methodology. In the first edition, Boring considered the mental test "in a
way experimental" (1929, p. x), primarily on the grounds that such tests were developed
and validated using scientific methods and that much of the testing involved tasks
similar to those used in other laboratory situations (e.g., reaction time). In the second
edition, showing the Woodworth effect, Boring decided that mental testing research
was not really experimental, arguing that such research didn't manipulate independent
variables; rather, "the primary variable is a difference of persons" (Boring, 1950, p. 571).
Considering the era encompassed by this chapter (i.e., earlier than Boring's first edition),

it is not inappropriate to consider the early history of mental testing as part of "psychology's experimental foundations."

Readers should look elsewhere for a comprehensive history of mental testing (e.g., Fancher, 1985). My intent here is to focus on the Galton/Cattell tradition, because it is closest to the other methodological traditions described in this chapter. In particular, the Galton/Cattell approach was largely characterized by the adaptation of brass instrument technology to the study of individual variation.

Mental testing originated with Galton's attempts to measure individual differences in a variety of traits in humans. In part, this work reflected his general curiosity about individual variation, but he also had evolution in mind. A cornerstone of his cousin's theory was that individual variation produced some variants that were more adaptable than others, and natural selection resulted in the survival and reproduction of these successful variants. For Galton, intelligence fit this model perfectly – intelligence varied widely, was a trait that facilitated human survival, and the most intelligent people would therefore survive and pass their ability along to the next generation. Galton also saw no reason why natural selection could not be helped along by judicious selective breeding. As he rather crudely put it, just as race horses and dogs could be selectively bred for certain traits, "so it would be quite practicable to produce a highly-gifted race of men by judicious marriages during several consecutive generations" (Galton, [1869] 1891, p. 1).[4] Such a program requires a technique for determining who is gifted (i.e., for measuring variation in intelligence), and this consideration led to his program of mental testing. His tests included physical measurements (height, weight, arm span, etc.) and measures that were more psychological, but concentrated on simple sensory/motor tasks (e.g., color discrimination, reaction time). These tasks might not seem related to our current notions of intelligence, but Galton, showing the effects of traditional British empiricist thinking, argued that if the mind depended on information from the senses, then "the more perceptible our senses are of difference, the larger is the field upon which our judgment and intelligence can act" (Galton, [1883] 1965, p. 421).

Galton was never quite able to affect who married whom in Great Britain, but his ideas about mental testing had a profound effect on the American psychologist James McKeen Cattell. We have already seen that Cattell was a prominent student of Wundt's in the mid-1880s and knowledgeable about experimental methodology and brass instrument technology. After completing his degree at Leipzig, however, Cattell spent some time studying medicine in Great Britain and got to know Galton. He was immediately captivated by Galton's approach to testing, and when Cattell returned to the United States in 1889, he brought Galton's program with him. Teaching first at the University of Pennsylvania for two years, then at Columbia for the rest of his career, Cattell became testing's strongest advocate, at least during the 1890s. In 1890 he published a description of 10 such tests, and in the article's title, coined the term "mental test" (Cattell, [1890] 1948).

Like Galton, Cattell relied heavily on tests of simple sensory capacity and judgment. His training in Wundt's laboratory and his familiarity with brass instruments clearly influenced his choice of specific tests, with half of his tests involving either psychophysical methods (absolute threshold for pain, difference thresholds for weights, and two-point thresholds) or reaction time (for sound and for the time taken to move one's hand 50 cm). He also tested grip strength, color naming, the ability to bisect a line, the ability to judge the passage of 10 seconds, and the ability to repeat a string of letters.

Initially at least, Cattell's approach was purely inductive – his main goal was to collect as much data as he could, assuming, like the good inductionist, that some general principles about mental life would eventually emerge. As he wrote in his mental tests article, the new field of psychology could not "attain the certainty and exactness of the physical sciences, unless it rest[ed] on a foundation of experiment and measurement (Cattell, [1890] 1948, p. 347). In short, before psychology can be of use in any way, precise measurement of psychological phenomena must already be demonstrated. Cattell did suggest that the tests might eventually be "useful in regard to training, mode of life, or indication of disease" (p. 347), but his primary goal was simply to collect as much data as possible.

A modest functional purpose for his testing program began to emerge after Cattell went to Columbia. By the mid-1890s he had convinced the authorities at Columbia to test all the incoming freshmen, arguing that the outcome might help "to determine the condition and progress of students, the relative value of different courses of study, etc." (cited in Sokal, 1987, p. 32). The project eventually led to a study by Cattell's student Clark Wissler, and the Wissler study brought about the demise of the Galton/Cattell approach to mental testing. In brief, Wissler, ([1901] 1965) decided to use the new statistical tool of correlation to examine the relationship among the tests and, more importantly, to see if the tests' scores were associated in any way with success at Columbia. If they were, of course, this would make the tests useful in the same way that SAT and ACT tests are used today – as admissions tools. As you might guess from the nature of the testing program, however, Wissler found no correlation between Cattell's mental tests and student grades at Columbia. Sensory capacity, reaction time, and grip strength simply didn't predict performance in the classroom. Wissler even found that how well a student did in gym class was a better predictor of classroom performance than Cattell's tests.

The Galton/Cattell approach to mental testing did not survive the Wissler study, and was soon replaced by a more effective strategy being developed at the same time in Paris by Alfred Binet. The Binet tests, which assessed higher mental processes more closely associated with school performance, were imported to the United States by Henry Goddard and institutionalized by Lewis Terman as the Stanford–Binet test. Yet the kinds of mental tests advocated by Cattell did not entirely disappear with the Wissler debacle, as other experimental psychologists used them for more specialized purposes. For instance, Lightner Witmer, who succeeded Cattell at the University of Pennsylvania and was also a student of Wundt's, used Cattell-like tests when he developed his famous clinic in the late 1890s. Witmer used the tests to help diagnose and treat children with a variety of school-related problems, some of which we would call learning disabilities today (McReynolds, 1987). Carl Seashore, another psychologist trained in brass instrument experimental methodology, developed a series of auditory discrimination tests (i.e., psychophysics) that became well known as an assessment tool for predicting musical ability (Sokal, 1987).

## Observing Behavior – The Legacy of Comparative Psychology

Like the mental testing category, this final set of methodological strategies has its roots in Darwinian theory. Darwin himself can be considered one of the original comparative psychologists. In his book on emotions, mentioned earlier in the description of the origins of survey methodology, Darwin (1872) supported his evolutionary theory of emotional expression by making comparisons between humans and other species. Other British naturalists soon followed Darwin's lead, studying animals for clues about the evolution of human mental processes and behaviors. These included George Romanes, a friend and protégé of Darwin, Douglas Spalding, and Conwy Lloyd Morgan, the best known of the three. Romanes' highly detailed catalog of animal behavior, published in 1882 as *Animal Intelligence* ([1882] 1886), used the term "comparative psychology" for the first time. Spalding systematically investigated instincts and made observations of what would later be called imprinting and critical periods (Boakes, 1984). Morgan became the most prominent of the British comparative psychologists, and with his famous "canon" of parsimony, corrected what he saw as an excessive amount of anthropomorphism in the work of Romanes and other contemporaries (Morgan, 1895). However, it is incorrect to report, as is often done in textbook histories, that Morgan's goal was to substitute a mechanistic approach to animal behavior for Romanes' more intentionalist account. Although Morgan urged interpretive caution, he believed that some degree of anthropomorphism was inevitable when studying animal behavior and that a number of species exhibited higher mental processes (Costall, 1993). Nonetheless, behaviorists later used Morgan's ideas to support their argument that when attempting to understand behavior, one should always look for simpler, more mechanical explanations. This logic, of course, was congenial with behaviorism's cornerstone assumption that simple conditioning processes underlie much of behavior, animal and human.

The early comparative psychologists studied animal behavior both in the animal's natural world and in the laboratory. Although questions about the evolution of consciousness and other human traits motivated much of this research, many researchers studied animal behavior simply for the purpose of understanding the behavior of a particular species (Dewsbury, 2000). Whatever the purpose, studying animal behavior, especially in the confines of the laboratory, clearly required methods that were different from those needed to study humans, a problem that led to the development of a variety of laboratory techniques that were more observational and behavioral than those of the brass instrument, self-report, and mental testing categories already considered. Those studying animal behavior learned, by necessity, to develop very precise skills of direct observation and to define the topics of interest in terms of behaviors being observed. That is, they developed an understanding of the need for what eventually came to be called operational definitions long before the term "operationism" existed. These behavioral methods were developed for a wide variety of species and ranged from detailed observations of naturally occurring behaviors in the field to laboratory studies involving such devices as puzzle boxes and mazes. The latter device has a long and venerable history as one of psychology's cornerstone methods.

## Maze-learning methodology

In a book that is organized for the most part by such traditional research topics as memory, association, transfer of training, and attention, it is significant that Robert Woodworth's *Experimental Psychology* (1938) has an entire chapter devoted to "maze learning." The inclusion is an indication of the importance of this method for psychology's history, and a case can be made that the maze is the first piece of apparatus created by psychologists, and not borrowed from other disciplines such as physiology (Goodwin, 1991).

Although Thorndike was watching baby chickens escape from maze-like devices at about the same time (late 1890s), credit for creating the maze as an apparatus goes to Clark University's Willard Small (Goodwin, 1999). With his colleague Linus Kline, Small was studying the rat's "home-finding" ability. On the suggestion of Clark's laboratory director, Edmund Sanford, Small built three 6 ft × 8 ft mazes, using the same design as that of England's famed Hampton Court maze, but adjusting it to a rectangular pattern. He then tested a number of rats, observing their behavior as they learned the maze. Although he was unable to measure the progress of learning with any precision (e.g., he left the rats in the maze overnight), he was able to draw some conclusions that were later supported by others (Small, 1901). For instance, he tested several blind rats and found that their performance did not differ from sighted animals. This outcome led him to conclude that vision was unimportant for learning and that the rats learned the maze primarily through their kinesthetic sense. John Watson later made a similar argument as a result of the maze studies he completed at Chicago with Harvey Carr (Carr & Watson, 1908; Watson, 1907). It is also worth noting that although maze-learning studies have sometimes been held up as an example of the artificiality of laboratory research, Small decided to use mazes because he was deliberately trying to simulate the rat's normal underground tunneling environment as much as possible (Miles, 1930).

Small's conclusions about maze learning are less important than the fact that he created an experimental methodology that was soon widely copied. The Hampton Court design was adapted for work with other species, even sparrows (Porter, 1904), and other maze designs quickly proliferated. By the mid-1920s, for example, Warner and Warden (1927) counted more than 100 different maze patterns in use. This diversity in fact created a problem – studies designed to examine the same phenomenon often yielded different results when different mazes were used. This dilemma in turn led to a great deal of research on "maze reliability," and one of the purposes of the Warner and Warden article was to propose a standardized maze (which failed to become popular). Maze reliability also became a major research topic in Edward Tolman's laboratory (e.g., Tolman & Nyswander, 1927).

In the early years of maze research, during a time when research in psychology tended to concentrate on basic mental processes, and with much of the work devoted to the study of sensation and perception, research focused on the issue of which of the rat's senses were essential for maze learning to occur. Small made a start with his blind rats, and Carr and Watson (Watson, 1907) more systematically ruled out other senses (e.g., smell). This elimination was accomplished surgically, in a study that was flawless methodologically, but aroused the ire of antivivisectionists, the early twentieth-century version of the animal rights movement (Dewsbury, 1990). By the time Woodworth published his chapter on maze learning in 1938, however, it was widely recognized that maze learning involved considerably more than a rat stringing together a sequence of motor movements, in response to sensory cues of some kind. By then, interest had shifted away from the question of which senses enabled a rat to learn a maze (no clear consensus was ever reached) and toward more general issues of learning. Instead of being the main center of attention, then, the maze became a means to the end of settling larger questions about the nature of learning. Maze studies became the cornerstone of debates between followers of Tolman and Hull, for instance, as they battled over such issues as whether rats could develop "cognitive maps" of their environment. Today, mazes are not nearly as popular as they once were, but they remain useful in studies designed to examine various aspects of learning, memory, spatial ability, and in pharmacological research as a means to test various drug effects.

## Training Experimentalists – From the Drill Course to the Columbia Bible

Becoming a competent experimental psychologist in the late nineteenth and early twentieth century was a daunting task. Whether interested in psychophysics, reaction time, questionaries, introspection, mental testing, or maze learning, students had to be knowledgeable in philosophy, physiology, and physics, as well as in the emerging new discipline of scientific psychology, and they had to be able to create, build, manage, and repair the apparatus that populated the laboratories where they learned their craft.

As mentioned at the outset of the chapter, a substantial number of American students learned about the new laboratory psychology by traveling to Germany and studying either at Wundt's laboratory in Leipzig or one of the other labs that developed in imitation of Wundt. Benjamin, Durkin, Link, Vestal, and Accord (1992), for instance, estimated that no fewer than 33 Americans earned their doctoral degrees under the tutelage of Wundt. In the German university, students did not take "courses" in research methodology, as we would think of them today. Rather, they learned how to do research by participating in ongoing projects and eventually developing projects of their own. As described by Titchener (1898), the student at a German university "gets his training by serving as 'versuchsobject' for his seniors, and the training varies as the investigations in progress vary. If he desires to repeat the classic experiments in any particular field, he must do so on his own account" (p. 313). In short, the training was hardly standardized and students essentially learned science by doing science. This approach was consistent with the German educational philosophy of the time (i.e., *Wissenschaft*), one that emphasized academic freedom and the creation of new knowledge through original research.

Several universities founded in the United States in the late nineteenth century deliberately incorporated the German philosophy of education (e.g., Johns Hopkins in 1876, Clark University in 1889), but the training of experimentalists took on a character that was distinct from the German model. In the American universities, the research function of the laboratory was supplemented by a pedagogical function – what came to be known as the "drill course." Typically lasting for a year, these courses did not produce original research; instead, they concentrated on a deliberate process of acculturation, shaping students to share the values held by those advocating the new scientific psychology. In actual practice, students in the drill courses replicated classic experiments (e.g., psychophysics, reaction time), learned how to maintain and use the often complicated apparatus, discovered how to introspect or observe with precision, and in general became converts to the belief that psychological phenomena could be understood by using scientific methods. The drill course originated at the graduate level, but gradually worked its way into the undergraduate curriculum.

The presence of drill courses created a need for a textbook to guide both instructors and students. The first one, written by Edmund Sanford in the 1890s, can be considered the first text of laboratory psychology written in the English language, and it is significant to the extent that it helped standardize the training of experimental psychologists (Goodwin, 1987). Sanford initially published the text in installments in the *American Journal of Psychology* in the early 1890s, and then combined the articles into *A Course in Experimental Psychology I: Sensation and Perception* (1894).[5] The book contained 239 practice experiments to familiarize students with the basic laboratory methods involved in the study of sensation and perception. There was also a 57-page chapter on "suggestions for apparatus" that included numerous drawings and practical tips on construction, maintenance, and where to purchase some of the standard pieces.

Sanford's text was widely used in the 1890s but it is largely forgotten today because of its replacement – the massive four-volume set of manuals written by E. B. Titchener in the period 1901–5. Titchener's manuals were arguably his most important work; they played a major role in the scientific training of hundreds of experimental psychologists, and they can be instructive even today. The manuals are divided into two categories, qualitative and quantitative experiments. In the qualitative experiments (Titchener, 1901), students, working in pairs and alternating the roles of experimenter and observer, would experience various sensory and perceptual phenomena, then respond to a series of questions designed to elicit introspective information. For instance, in a study on olfaction, students smelled several scents, then responded to questions about the extent to which the smells either mixed to form a new scent or resulted in one smell overwhelming the other. In the quantitative experiments (Titchener, 1905), students worked through a series of psychophysics and reaction time experiments. Because Titchener recognized that instructors might need as much help as students when working their way through the drill course, he published separate instructor's manuals and student texts, and the former were twice the length of the latter.

In addition to creating a need for texts, the drill course also had an effect on the design of apparatus, especially when drill courses became popular at the undergraduate level. Instructors were understandably nervous when novices were in the vicinity of expensive research apparatus, so a need developed for less sophisticated pieces (Evans, 2000). Another of Sanford's contributions, for instance, was a simple chronoscope for reaction time studies. It was not as accurate as the famous Hipp chronoscope, but it was easy to use and its accuracy (to 1/100th second)[6] was sufficient for drill course purposes. Its $15 price tag was not cheap at a time when faculty salaries averaged about

$1200–$1500 (Goodwin, 1987), but with their accompanying necessities (e.g., batteries), Hipp chronoscopes cost considerably more, about $170 (Sanford, 1893).

The drill course became a standard part of the psychology curriculum, but as the twentieth century stretched into its second and third decade, psychological knowledge and research methodology expanded far beyond the basic sensory and perceptual studies that made up the bulk of these courses and their accompanying manuals. At Columbia University, starting in 1905, Robert Woodworth began organizing his laboratory exercises into a set of sheets that he distributed to students. These eventually became a 225-page mimeographed "textbook" of experimental psychology, and ultimately the 1938 "Columbia Bible" that was described earlier in this chapter. Over the next 20 years, this book and its second edition, coauthored with Harold Schlosberg (Woodworth & Schlosberg, 1954), had no serious competition as the means by which students learned about experimental psychology. Winston (1990) estimated that as many as 100,000 students learned about experimental psychology from the Woodworth books.

As mentioned in the section of this chapter on mental testing, the major legacy of the Woodworth text is the distinction now routinely made between experimental and correlational research, and within experimental research, the distinction between independent and dependent variables. Yet the bulk of the text was made up of chapters summarizing the content areas of experimental psychology. It wasn't until the 1960s that textbooks in experimental psychology took on the format that is most commonly seen today – chapters devoted to teaching the process of completing research and describing various research designs, rather than summarizing the outcome of those procedures.

It has now been more than a century since the fledgling American Psychological Association published their modest constitution, in which they proposed "the advancement of psychology as a science" as their principal objective. The architects of this constitution set out to build on the momentum started in Germany to create a new way of looking at psychological phenomena – a scientific way. As will be demonstrated by the remaining chapters in this Handbook, these past 100 years have rather dramatically increased our knowledge of causes of behavior and the operations of the mind.

## Notes

1.  To say that James disliked the "New Psychology" of the laboratory would be an understatement. Referring to the type of research described in this section of the chapter, James wrote that such experimental methodology

    > taxes patience to the utmost, and could hardly have arisen in a country whose natives could be *bored*. Such Germans as Weber, Fechner, Viervordt, and Wundt obviously cannot; and their success has brought into the field an array of younger experimental psychologists, bent on studying the *elements* of the mental life, dissecting them out from the gross results in which they are embedded, and as far as possible reducing them to quantitative scales. (James, 1890, p. 192, italics in the original)

2.  Incidentally, Galton described this research in a book that he titled *English Men of Science: Their Nature and Nurture* (1874). Although Galton was not the first to use the terms

"nature" and "nurture," his use of the words in the title marks the point when this issue began to be referred to as the "nature–nurture" issue.

3. Hall's enthusiasm was not widely shared. In a letter to Clark University's librarian, L. N. Wilson, Titchener wrote: ". . . you probably have no idea of the sort of contempt in which Hall's methods . . . are in general held in psychology. . . . Whenever his questionary papers get reviewed, they get slightingly reviewed" (quoted in Goodwin, 1999, p. 165). Among other things, Titchener was reacting to the lack of precision in Hall's method. Relying on teachers to present the surveys, often in oral form, opened the door for a variety of biases. In a similar and somewhat prophetic vein, William James once expressed concern about questionaries becoming "among the common pests of life" (1890, p. 194).

4. This line of thought led Galton to coin the term "eugenics."

5. Sanford never managed to complete a second volume, which was to cover such topics as attention, memory, and other cognitive processes.

6. The Hipp chronoscope was accurate to 1/1000th of a second (Evans, 2000).

## References

Benjamin, L. T., Jr (2000). The psychology laboratory at the turn of the 20th century. *American Psychologist, 55*, 318–21.

Benjamin, L. T., Jr, Durkin, M., Link, M., Vestal, M., & Accord, J. (1992). Wundt's American doctoral students. *American Psychologist, 47*, 123–31.

Boakes, R. (1984). *From Darwin to behaviourism: Psychology and the minds of animals.* New York: Cambridge University Press.

Boring, E. G. (1929). *A history of experimental psychology.* New York: Century.

Boring, E. G. (1950). *A history of experimental psychology* (2nd edn.). Englewood Cliffs, NJ: Prentice-Hall.

Boring, E. G. (1963). Fechner: Inadvertent founder of psychophysics. In R. I. Watson & D. T. Campbell (eds.), *History, psychology, and science: Selected papers by Edwin G. Boring, Harvard University* (pp. 126–31). New York: Wiley.

Carr, H. A., & Watson, J. B. (1908). Orientation in the white rat. *Journal of Comparative Neurology and Psychology, 18*, 27–44.

Cattell, J. McK. (1886). The time taken up by cerebral operations. *Mind, 11*, 220–42.

Cattell, J. McK. ([1890] 1948). Mental tests and measurements. *Mind, 15*, 373–81.

Cattell, J. McK. (1895). Proceedings of the third annual meeting of the American Psychological Association. *Psychological Review, 2*, 149–72.

Costall, A. (1993). How Lloyd Morgan's canon backfired. *Journal of the History of the Behavioral Sciences, 29*, 113–22.

Cronbach, L. J. (1957). The two disciplines of scientific psychology. *American Psychologist, 12*, 671–84.

Dallenbach, K. M. (1913). The measurement of attention. *American Journal of Psychology, 24*, 465–507.

Danziger, K. (1980). The history of introspection reconsidered. *Journal of the History of the Behavioral Sciences, 16*, 241–62.

Darwin, C. (1872). *The expression of the emotions in man and animals.* London: Murray.

Dewsbury, D. A. (1990). Early interactions between animal psychologists and animal activists and the founding of the APA committee on precautions in animal experiments. *American Psychologist, 45*, 315–27.

Dewsbury, D. A. (2000). Issues in comparative psychology at the dawn of the twentieth century. *American Psychologist, 55*, 750–3.

Ericsson, K. A., & Simon, H. A. (1993). *Protocol analysis: Verbal reports as data*. Cambridge, MA: MIT Press.

Evans, R. B. (2000). Psychological instruments at the turn of the century. *American Psychologist, 55*, 322–5.

Fancher, R. E. (1985). *The intelligence men: Makers of the I.Q. controversy*. New York: Norton.

Fancher, R. E. (1996). *Pioneers of psychology* (3rd edn.). New York: Norton.

Fechner, G. T. ([1860] 1966). *Elements of psychophysics*. New York: Holt, Rinehart & Winston.

Forrest, D. W. (1974). *Francis Galton: The life and work of a Victorian genius*. New York: Taplinger.

Fullerton, G. S., & Cattell, J. McK. (1892). On the perception of small differences. *University of Pennsylvania Philosophical Series, No. 2*. Philadelphia: University of Pennsylvania.

Galton, F. (1874). *English men of science: Their nature and nurture*. London: Macmillan.

Galton, F. ([1869] 1891). *Hereditary genius*. New York: Appleton.

Galton, F. ([1883] 1965). Galton on mental capacity. In R. J. Herrnstein & E. G. Boring (eds.), *A sourcebook in the history of psychology* (pp. 421–3). Cambridge, MA: Harvard University Press.

Goodwin, C. J. (1987). In Hall's shadow: Edmund Clark Sanford (1859–1924). *Journal of the History of the Behavioral Sciences, 23*, 153–68.

Goodwin, C. J. (1991, August). *Maze learning as method: Origins and early development*. San Francisco: American Psychological Association.

Goodwin, C. J. (1999). *A history of modern psychology*. New York: Wiley.

Hall, G. S. ([1883] 1948). The contents of children's minds. In W. Dennis (ed.), *Readings in the history of psychology* (pp. 255–76). New York: Appleton-Century-Crofts.

James, W. J. (1890). *Principles of psychology*. Boston: Henry Holt.

McReynolds, P. (1987). Lightner Witmer: Little-known founder of clinical psychology. *American Psychologist, 42*, 849–58.

Miles, W. R. (1930). On the history of research with rats and mazes: A collection of notes. *Journal of General Psychology, 3*, 324–37.

Morgan, C. L. (1895). *An introduction to comparative psychology*. London: Walter Scott.

O'Donnell, J. M. (1985). *The origins of behaviorism: American psychology, 1870–1920*. New York: New York University Press.

Porter, J. P. (1904). A preliminary study of the English sparrow. *American Journal of Psychology, 15*, 313–46.

Romanes, G. J. ([1882] 1886). *Animal intelligence*. New York: D. Appleton.

Ross, D. (1972). *G. Stanley Hall: The psychologist as prophet*. Chicago: University of Chicago Press.

Sanford, E. C. (1888). The relative legibility of the small letters. *American Journal of Psychology, 1*, 402–35.

Sanford, E. C. (1893). Some practical suggestions on the equipment of a psychological laboratory. *American Journal of Psychology, 5*, 427–38.

Sanford, E. C. (1894). *A course in experimental psychology. I. Sensation and perception*. Boston: D. C. Heath.

Shepard, R. N., & Metzler, J. (1971). Mental rotation of three-dimensional objects. *Science, 171*, 701–3.

Small, W. S. (1901). Experimental study of the mental processes of the rat. II. *American Journal of Psychology, 12*, 206–39.

Sokal, M. M. (ed.) (1981). *An education in psychology: James McKeen Cattell's journal and letters from Germany and England, 1880–1888*. Cambridge, MA: The MIT Press.

Sokal, M. M. (1987). James McKeen Cattell and mental anthropometry: Nineteenth-century science and reform and the origins of psychological testing. In M. M. Sokal (ed.), *Psychological testing and American society, 1890–1930* (pp. 21–45). New Brunswick, NJ: Rutgers University Press.

Titchener, E. B. (1896). *An outline of psychology.* New York: Macmillan.

Titchener, E. B. (1898). A psychological laboratory. *Mind, 7,* 311–31.

Titchener, E. B. (1901). *Experimental psychology: A manual of laboratory practice. Vol. 1: Qualitative experiments. Part 1: Student's manual. Part 2: Instructor's manual.* New York: Macmillan.

Titchener, E. B. (1905). *Experimental psychology: A manual of laboratory practice. Vol. 2: Quantitative experiments. Part 1: Student's manual. Part 2: Instructor's manual.* New York: Macmillan.

Titchener, E. B. (1909). *A text-book of psychology.* New York: Macmillan.

Tolman, E. C., & Nyswander, D. B. (1927). The reliability and validity of maze-measures for rats. *Journal of Comparative Psychology, 7,* 425–60.

Tweney, R. D. (1987). Programmatic research in experimental psychology: E. B. Titchener's laboratory investigations, 1891–1927. In M. G. Ash & W. R. Woodward (eds.), *Psychology in twentieth-century thought and society* (pp. 35–57). Cambridge, UK: Cambridge University Press.

Warner, L. H., & Warden, C. J. (1927). The development of a standardized animal maze. *Archives of Psychology, 15* (whole #92).

Watson, J. B. (1907). Kinesthetic and organic sensations: Their role in the reactions of the white rat to the maze. *Psychological Review Monograph,* Supplements, 8 (whole #33).

Watson, J. B. (1913). Psychology as the behaviorist views it. *Psychological Review, 20,* 158–77.

Winston, A. S. (1990). Robert Sessions Woodworth and the "Columbia Bible": How the psychological experiment was redefined. *American Journal of Psychology, 103,* 391–401.

Wissler, C. ([1901] 1965). Clark Wissler (1870–1947) on the inadequacy of mental tests. In R. J. Herrnstein & E. G. Boring (eds.), *A sourcebook in the history of psychology* (pp. 442–5). Cambridge, MA: Harvard University Press.

Woodworth, R. S. (1938) *Experimental psychology.* New York: Holt.

Woodworth, R. S., & Schlosberg, H. (1954). *Experimental psychology* (2nd edn.). New York: Holt.

Wundt, W. ([1874] 1904). *Principles of physiological psychology* (5th edn.). (E. B. Titchener, trans.). New York: Macmillan.

# CHAPTER TWO

# Current and Future Trends in Experimental Psychology

## E. J. Capaldi and Robert W. Proctor

Psychology, since its earliest days, has emphasized the use of experimental methods. As a scientific discipline, the field of psychology is usually dated to 1879, when the first laboratory devoted to experimental investigation of psychological phenomena was established by Wilhelm Wundt. A major factor allowing psychology to be a scientific discipline has been its emphasis on the experimental method and control of environmental variables. With some exceptions, it is generally accepted that the scientific approach provided by experimental methodology offers a more objective method than others for establishing facts and evaluating alternative explanations. Experimental methods are indispensable to the establishment of useful theory.

Another widely accepted view is that a primary goal of science is the development of theory. This view is accepted not only by experimental psychologists, but also by all varieties of other scientists and by philosophers and historians of science. A scientific theory may be regarded as a set of interrelated laws that serve to explain and describe relationships among a circumscribed set of empirical phenomena. As for the role of theory in science, Neal Miller, an experimental psychologist of exceptional accomplishment, said the following: "Pure empiricism is a delusion. A theorylike process is inevitably involved in drawing boundaries around certain parts of the flux of experience to define observable events and in the selection of the events that are observed" (Miller, 1959, p. 200).

A view similar to Miller's was voiced recently by Edward O. Wilson, an evolutionary biologist and a founder of sociobiology, in his best-selling book, *Consilience*. According to Wilson, "Nothing in science – nothing in life, for that matter – makes sense without theory" (1999, p. 56). A final example of a prominent individual who emphasizes the importance of theory in science is Thomas Kuhn, arguably one of the most prominent philosophers of science in this or any other time. Kuhn, in his monumentally influential book, *The Structure of Scientific Revolutions*, stated,

In the absence of a paradigm or some candidate for a paradigm, all of the facts that could possibly pertain to the development of a given science are likely to seem equally relevant. As a result, early fact-gathering is a far more nearly random activity than the one that subsequent scientific development makes familiar. (Kuhn, 1962, p. 15)

For now, let us identify Kuhn's notion of paradigm with theory; later on, we will define paradigm and related concepts more rigorously.

There are many elements that go into the development of adequate scientific theory. One of the more important elements, methodology, is the topic of this chapter. Methodology may be defined as a procedure for making scientific decisions about empirical or theoretical matters. Essentially, we shall be concerned with the conditions that must be met in the creation of adequate methodology. Rather than offering formal considerations for the construction of methodology at this point, let us consider a straightforward example from the history of science that exemplifies important factors that go into the creation of methodology. Although it is not generally realized, one of the great methodological advances in the history of science involved Galileo's invention of the telescope in the sixteenth century. At the time of the telescope's invention, it was generally accepted that only direct sensory experience could be relied upon to produce useful science (see Chalmers, 1999). The telescope was at odds with that methodological rule because, of course, sensory experience was indirect in the sense that the telescope intervened between the objects and the senses. Galileo's report that the heavens were not as generally assumed at that time was disputed by his critics as unacceptable because his evidence involved the indirect sensory experience provided by the telescope. Note that Galileo's critics were reasonable in the sense that they could have been correct: nature could have been so organized that only direct sensory experience can be trusted. Of course, subsequent experience had shown that this is not the case. Much, if not most, of science involves experience as revealed through various instruments. Our senses provide only a minuscule part of the information needed to construct useful science. As Wilson has said in *Consilience*,

> In the ultimate sense our brain and sensory system evolved as a biological apparatus to preserve and multiply human genes. But they enable us to navigate only through the tiny segment of the physical world whose mastery serves that primal need. Instrumental science has removed the handicap. Still, science in its fullness is much more than just the haphazard expansion of sensory capacity by instruments. The other elements in its creative mix are classification of data and their interpretation by theory. Together they compose the rational processing of sensory experience enhanced by instrumentation. (Wilson, 1999, p. 56)

Clearly, accepting indirect experience as a major means for constructing science was one of the more monumental methodological changes in the history of science. But consider how it came about. No amount of rational thinking, no matter how well and deeply done, could cause one to accept the data as revealed by the telescope. It is intuitively obvious that rational considerations simply are not adequate for this purpose. There is only one way that the data provided by Galileo's telescope could be justified, and that is by experience. In other words, if the indirect data provided by the telescope resulted in the creation of useful theory, then on that basis it could be justified. A prime message of this chapter is that the development of adequate methodology ultimately depends on how useful that methodology proves to be in revealing empirical and theoretical relationships. In brief, the ultimate justification of methodology is empirical.

## Alternatives to Scientific Methodology: Postmodernism

There are numerous types of social scientists, including psychologists, who reject experimentation and other objective methodologies of the sort accepted within academic, or mainstream, psychology. These individuals, who may be characterized as postmodernists, favor a variety of alternative methodologies that are said to be superior to the more traditional scientific methods employed in mainstream psychology (Smith, Harré, & Van Langenhove, 1995). Another salient feature of the postmodernist approach is that it is employed not merely in connection with psychology, but with all sorts of intellectual activity in general, as for example, literature, the law, morality, and philosophy (see Alcock, 2001; Wilson, 1999). In our opinion, postmodernism cannot be ignored.

Some examples of the methodologies recommended by postmodernists include hermeneutics, deconstruction, narrative, dramaturgy, and hypothetical data rotation. Postmodernists go under several labels, as, for example, contextualists and social constructionists (Capaldi & Proctor, 1999). A characteristic of postmodernists in general is the idea that all knowledge is personal. This is a form of relativism. Relativism is the idea that the validity of any point of view is dependent upon the specific context in which it is embedded. That is to say, there are no universally valid statements. It appears that postmodernists are united in employing a form of radical empiricism that rejects general theoretical statements. Wilson (1999) makes the following acerbic contrast between postmodernism and the Enlightenment, which gave rise to modern science. According to Wilson, "Postmodernism is the ultimate polar antithesis of the Enlightenment. The difference between the two extremes can be expressed roughly as follows: Enlightenment thinkers believe we can know everything, and radical postmodernists believe we can know nothing" (p. 44).

Capaldi and Proctor (1999) have indicated that some salient features of the postmodernist approach are as follows. Postmodernists of various stripes tend to believe that even minor differences between two situations result in considerable novelty. Given this view, there is little hope of generalizing one experimental result to either another or to the real world. The view precludes the acceptance of lawful relationships, and essentially rules out science, which is simply viewed by postmodernists as one approach to knowledge among many, no better or worse. Some postmodernists adopt a position that has come to be known as underdetermination. According to the underdetermination thesis, a given body of evidence does not uniquely determine any theoretical position. Put somewhat differently, underdetermination suggests that an infinite number of theories is logically compatible with any specific body of evidence. Kitcher has suggested that scientists would react to this state of affairs as follows:

> The notion that theories are inevitably underdetermined by experience has become a philosophic commonplace. Scientists, however, sometimes greet this allegedly mundane point with incredulity. "It's hard enough," they complain, "to find *one* way of accommodating experience, let along many." And these supposed ways of modifying the network of beliefs are changes that no reasonable – sane? – person would make. There may be a *logical* point here, but it has little to do with science. (Kitcher, 1993, p. 247)

As an example of what Kitcher has in mind, an opponent of evolution might suggest that the fossil record was doctored by extraterrestrials to mislead human beings. Although this is logically possible, there is no evidence to support it and so scientists find little reason for believing it.

Relativists, and some others (e.g., Rychlack, 1981), suggest that theories are under-determined by evidence. Employing this logical gambit, relativists want to say that any theory is as good as any other theory. This is a case in which dependence on logic alone is misleading. As Laudan (1996) has indicated, there is little basis for accepting hypotheses merely because they are logically compatible with observations for which supporting evidence is lacking. As an example, it is possible that leprechauns live among us, but have yet to be observed. Few of us would want to believe in leprechauns on this basis. Capaldi and Proctor (1999) provide an extended discussion and analysis of the underdetermination thesis, demonstrating that in their view it has little relevance for understanding science.

## Postmodernist methods

In this section we explore some characteristics of some postmodernist methods. According to *deconstruction* (Derrida, 1978), texts have multiple meanings, none of which correspond to the intention of the author, who may not be aware of the meaning himself or herself. As may be seen, in contrast to science, which is interpersonal and seeks to avoid the subjective in making decisions about a theory, deconstruction is highly personal and seeks to emphasize subjectivism in reaching decisions.

*Narrative* (Sarbin, 1986) is the view that the world can be best understood as a story that has a beginning, middle, and end. According to this view, psychology has more to learn from poets, novelists, and playwrights than it does from a scientific approach. Shakespeare, it is held, is more relevant for understanding psychology than is Darwin. *Dramaturgy* (Harré, 2000) is a close relative of the narrative approach.

*Hypothetical data rotation* (Gergen & Gergen, 1991) involves at the outset the employment of orthodox procedures for developing an experiment. However, rather than actually conducting the experiment, the researcher follows other procedures. He or she begins by rotating hypothetical result patterns through the research design, considering the theoretical implications of each pattern. With each new pattern, the investigator is forced into theoretical explanation, each of which is capable of revealing the potential of each theoretical position. The rationale for this procedure is as follows: any conclusion reached by this method would be as good or as valuable as any conclusion reached by actually conducting the experiment, because the researcher will interpret the results of the actual experiment in terms of his or her own biases.

We conclude this section by indicating that, in our view, the postmodernist methods must be evaluated by the same criteria used to evaluate more traditional scientific methods. For example, postmodernist methods need to be evaluated empirically and, in the process, demonstrate that they are as useful for at least some purposes as more object-ive methodologies such as experimentation. Sadly, it is doubtful that postmodernists will accept this challenge (Capaldi & Proctor, 1999; Proctor & Capaldi, 2001a; Wilson, 1999).

## The Historical Development of Scientific Methodology

The distinctive feature of science, many agree, is its unique method, the scientific method. But what is identified as *the* scientific method today was not yesterday's, and it may not be tomorrow's. Major methodological principles in science, for example, the rejection of falsified theories, have often been justified employing logical-intuitive (foundationist) criteria. Thus conceived, the scientific method is held to be secure and trustworthy. However, if methodological statements are empirical statements, as we suggest, then they may not be as secure as many suppose. As Laudan, a prominent philosopher of science, has said, "There are those who would like to make methodology more secure than physics; the challenge rather is to show that it is as secure as physics" (1996, p. 141). In this section, we shall describe some of the major methodological changes that have occurred over the last few hundred years.

As we have seen, Galileo (1564–1642) was responsible for introducing the idea that indirect observations are desirable in science, even more so than more direct sensory experience. In his *Principia*, which was published in 1687, the great scientist Sir Isaac Newton recommended a methodological approach to science that would not be con-sidered entirely compatible with today's methodological mainstream. Newton, who was a follower of Sir Francis Bacon, suggested that induction was the principal method by which scientific fact and theory could be known. Induction, in this sense, means arriving at general statements by the careful study in isolation of many individual instances. Newton, along with his contemporaries, not only professed to accept induction as the method of science but also to reject the use of hypothesis testing. To Newton and one of his principal followers, the great Scottish philosopher Thomas Reid, hypotheses were not only not very useful, but they could very well be misleading as well. This point of view is well illustrated by the following remarks regarding the widely used hypothetical entity called aether, taken from the *Encyclopaedia Britannica* (1771), remarks that may well have been written by Reid:

Before the method of philosophizing by induction was known, the hypotheses of philosophers were wild, fanciful, ridiculous [ . . . ] Aether seems to be an exceedingly tractable sort of substance: Whenever the qualities of one body differ from those of another, *a different modification of aether* at once solves the phaenomenon. The aether of iron must not, to be sure, be exactly the same with the nervous aether, otherwise it would be in danger of producing sensation in place of magnetism. It would likewise have been very improper to give the vegetable aether exactly the same qualities with those of the animal aether; for, in such a case, men would run great risk of striking root in the soil, and trees and hedges might eradicate and run about the fields . . . It is impossible to gravel an aetherial philosopher. Ask him what questions you please, his answer is ready: – "As we cannot find the cause *any where* else; ergo, by dilemma, it must be owing to aether!" For example, ask one of those sages, What is the cause of gravity? he will answer, Tis *aether!* Ask him the cause of *thought,* he will gravely reply, "The solution to this question was once universally allowed to exceed the limits of human genius: But now, by the grand *discoveries* we have lately made, it is as plain as that three and two make five: – *Thought* is a mere *mechanical* thing, an evident effect of certain motions in the brain produced by the *oscillations* of a subtle elastic fluid called *aether!*" (*Encyclopaedia Britannica*, 1771, pp. 31, 34)

By the early nineteenth century, it became apparent to a number of natural scientists that unaided induction, particularly induction that eschewed the postulation of hypothetical entities, as indicated by the above quotation, could not be avoided in the construction of solid scientific theory. A major figure of this era was the great methodologist, William Whewell. Whewell's great contribution, essentially, was to indicate that the adequacy of a hypothesis could be determined by how well the hypothesis predicts. This gambit, if you will, that is, tying the adequacy of a hypothesis to its confirmed predictive consequences, was then and is today recognized as a major methodological advance. Another great methodologist, John Stuart Mill, did not agree with Whewell that prediction of new phenomena was more important, methodologically speaking, than the explanation of already existing phenomena, a matter we shall treat in more detail later. Hypothesis testing has been accepted as a major methodological innovation in science since the 1850s.

The first half of the twentieth century saw the introduction into science of two great approaches to the philosophy of science. One of these approaches was logical positivism, a view that combines empiricism (positivism) with symbolic logic. According to the logical positivists, all statements were of one of three types, synthetic, analytic, or nonsense. Synthetic statements are empirical ones such as "grass is green"; analytic statements are logical ones that are true by definition such as "all bachelors are unmarried." Statements that are neither analytic nor synthetic are nonsense. The nonsense category would include metaphysical statements and all others that were not verifiable empirically or demonstrable logically. Logical positivism had a tremendous influence on psychology during this period, particularly on behaviorism (see Bergmann & Spence, 1941, 1944). The second of these influential approaches, one that retains much of its influence even today, is that of Sir Karl Popper. Popper's famous methodological rule was that scientists should make every effort to falsify their hypotheses. Falsificationism is the view that is accepted today by many scientists from many fields.

In the second half of the twentieth century, two new developments in the philosophy of science appeared. We have already considered one of these developments, postmodernism, and the relativism to which it gave rise. The second great methodological development was that of naturalism. Naturalism is the view that all matters in science are to be decided in the same way, empirically. On this view, methodological statements are empirical statements and are to be evaluated in the same manner as any other empirical statement. For example, if one says that a major criterion for judging the adequacy of a theory is parsimony, the naturalist asks what the nature of the empirical evidence is supporting this view.

## Justifying Scientific Methods

There have been three general ways of justifying methodological principles in science: logical-intuitive, employing core background assumptions, and naturalism.

### *Logical-intuitive*

The historically oldest method, and one still used today, might be called *logical-intuitive*. As this label suggests, methodological statements have been evaluated in terms of whether or not they are logical and whether or not they appeal to intuition. As Laudan (1996) has said, in the early days of science, methodological disputes involved trading intuitions. Evaluating methods on the basis of their logical-intuitive appeal was a procedure employed by Newton and many other scientists in the succeeding centuries. Perhaps the most noteworthy use of the logical-intuitive procedures for evaluating methodology is that associated with Popper. As previously noted, Popper suggested that the appropriate methodological approach was that of attempting to falsify one's theory. In arriving at this methodological maxim, Popper simply employed his own intuition as to an appropriate approach to science. It seems not to be generally realized that Popper offered no defense of his falsification procedure beyond stating that it is the single best approach to conducting science. Popper admitted openly that his falsification principle was a convention and was not based upon any sort of additional reasoning or evidence (see Popper, 1959, p. 50). In essence, Popper was telling us how he thought science ought to be done.

### *Employing core background assumptions*

A second general approach to evaluating methodology is relatively recent. It consists of determining whether or not one's methodological dictums are consistent with one's more general core background assumptions. To date, these core background assumptions have been of two distinct types. On the one hand, we have the core background assumptions of Kuhn, which he has characterized as a paradigm established on the basis of scientific considerations. Kuhn defined the paradigm as consisting of a disciplinary matrix, for example, the shared education of scientists, together with specific exemplars from the discipline (e.g., F = ma). In Kuhn's view, paradigms are more basic than the methodological rules to which they give rise. Consequently, according to Kuhn, each paradigm would have its own distinctive set of methodological rules.

The second set of core background assumptions giving rise to distinct methodologies arise not so much from science as from general ontological considerations. As one example, a general ontological consideration of so-called contextualists is that novelty can arise at any time and thus is always to be expected. The idea is taken very seriously by many contextualists, who go so far as to suggest that specific laws that may be in force in one era may be replaced in another era by an entirely different set of laws. Another way in which novelty can arise is as follows. Some additional factor added to a particular set of already existing factors may modify those factors qualitatively so as to give rise to a completely novel situation. Obviously, if one accepts this position, experimental methods are not going to be seen as of much use (see, e.g., Jaeger & Rosnow, 1988). For example, anything isolated in the laboratory might be completely and qualitatively modified when applied in the real world, which allows additional factors to operate. This way of justifying methodology on the basis of one's ontology is characteristic of postmodernists in general. It is a point of view that, as we indicated earlier, leads to relativism.

### Naturalism

The most recently suggested procedure for evaluating methodology is that suggested by naturalism. As indicated, naturalism is the point of view that all matters, without exception, are to be settled as they are in science, that is, empirically. According to this view, methodological statements are empirical statements, and they are to be evaluated in the same way as other empirical statements. The pragmatic issue here is: does a particular methodological procedure better advance our interests than either some other methodological procedure or not employing that procedure at all? According to Larry Laudan, one of the leading naturalists, methodological rules express means–ends relations of the following sort: if one's goal is Y, then one ought to do X. More particularly, Laudan has suggested:

> If we can get evidence that following a certain rule promotes our basic ends better
> than any of its known rivals does, then we have grounds for endorsing the rule. If
> we have evidence that acting in accordance with a rule has thwarted the realization
> of our cognitive ends, we have grounds for rejecting the rule. Otherwise, its status
> is indeterminate. (Laudan, 1996, p. 136)

One of the major features of naturalism is that it suggests that to understand science fully we should seek to determine how science *is actually* practiced, rather than to employ the procedure of, say, Popper, which is to say how science *should be* practiced, given our intuitions. One of the earliest methods for determining how science is actually practiced was that employed by Kuhn (1962), which was to consult the historical record. Essentially, Kuhn examined a specific area of scientific activity in depth in an effort to determine what sort of empirical, methodological, and paradigmatic assumptions were being employed. Lately, the idea of determining how science should be practiced by examining the behavior of real scientists actually practicing science has caught on very substantially (see, for example, Klahr & Simon, 1999, 2001). Some of the procedures employed include observing scientists in their daily laboratory activity, reading the notebooks of scientists, and observing how nonscientists solve contrived problems of a scientific nature. Such procedures have used children (Samarapungavan & Wiers, 1997), as well as adults (Dunbar, 1994).

## Implications of a Naturalistic Approach to Methodology

In this section we consider some of the more important methodologies employed in science from the standpoint of a naturalistic approach. These include hypothesis testing, explanatory theory, promise, and the role of logic.

### Hypothesis testing

We begin by considering hypothesis testing, its strengths and weaknesses. Within experimental psychology, and, indeed, within science generally, hypothesis testing, the major methodological innovation introduced by Whewell, is widely considered to be *the* method of science (Proctor & Capaldi, 2001a, 2001b). We agree that hypothesis testing is one of the more important methodological innovations ever introduced into science, and it is inconceivable to us to conduct science in its absence. Hypothesis testing is clearly of major usefulness when well-formulated and testable hypotheses are explicitly stated and when the necessary experimental conditions for testing the hypotheses are realized. A great advantage to the hypothesis-testing approach to research is that we do not have to sit by passively waiting to observe some important phenomenon. Rather, we can act proactively, seeking to produce phenomena critical to evaluation of a hypothesis.

However, as with any empirical procedure, hypothesis testing has its limitations. A clear deficiency of the hypothesis-testing approach is that in the very initial stages of developing a theory it is fairly easy to subject it to procedures that have the capacity to disconfirm the theory. Another difficulty with hypothesis testing, taken too literally, is that it is difficult in practice to achieve a clear-cut test of a hypothesis. According to the Duhem–Quine thesis (Chalmers, 1999), one never tests a hypothesis in isolation. Rather, a number of other matters are under test, in addition to the hypothesis itself. These other matters include, to mention a few, the reliability of the testing equipment, whether the hypothesis has been validly derived from the theory, and whether auxiliary assumptions contained within the general theory are themselves valid. For each of the reasons given, and others beside, a disconfirmation of a hypothesis may not be due to the weakness of the hypothesis itself but to these other matters. A third difficulty with the hypothesis-testing approach is that experience teaches us that when experimental evidence disconfirms a hypothesis, scientists may not reject the hypothesis outright, but they may seek to rescue it by either modifying it or employing some additional auxiliary assumptions. Modifying disconfirmed hypotheses, rather than rejecting them outright, has often led to useful science (see Chalmers, 1999; Lakatos, 1970).

An outstanding example of such a hypothesis is the Rescorla–Wagner (1972) model. This model was originally formulated in order to explain a variety of phenomena in classical conditioning in animals. Although outstandingly successful at first, much subsequent data disconfirmed the model (see Miller, Barnet, & Grahame, 1995). On the basis of some classical conditioning findings, some investigators reasoned that human judgments of causality should follow many of the same rules isolated in animal classical conditioning. Not only did this turn out to be the case, but it was found that one of the better models for describing human causality judgments was the Rescorla–Wagner model. Given these circumstances, the Rescorla–Wagner model was modified in certain ways, which allowed it to explain human causality data, but without losing its fundamental character (Van Hamme & Wasserman, 1994). Essentially, then, a model that was disconfirmed by a variety of empirical observations was subsequently found to be useful by employing a slight, but effective, modification.

A fourth difficulty with hypothesis testing is that scholarship reveals that scientists seldom attempt to test hypotheses with the intention of falsifying them. More commonly, scientists attempt to employ conditions that will tend to confirm predictions of the hypothesis (Chalmers, 1999; Lakatos, 1976). A final difficulty with hypothesis testing, one emphasized in a number of sources (e.g., Chalmers, 1999; Kuhn, 1962), is that if failure to confirm a hypothesis were grounds for rejecting it, then all theories in science would be rejected because all theories are falsified by at least some observational data. What scientists appear to do in practice is to accept a theory that has the greatest explanatory potential together with the fewest problems (Holcomb, 1998; Kuhn, 1962; Laudan, 1996).

*Explanatory theory*

An explanatory theory is one that seeks to explain already known phenomena. A prime example of an explanatory theory is plate tectonics. Plate tectonics is a theory that explains continental drift and is widely accepted in geology. When Alfred Wegener (1924) first introduced the idea of plate tectonics, he did so exclusively on the basis of already known phenomena. Thus, plate tectonics was an exclusively explanatory theory at its inception. Interestingly, plate tectonics was accepted in Europe much earlier than in the United States. The reason is that Europeans did not emphasize hypothesis testing as much as it was emphasized in the USA (Laudan, 1996; Oreskes, 1999). The theory ultimately did become accepted in the USA, of course, but only later, when it was used to predict new phenomena as a result of hypothesis testing. This example illustrates the strengths and weaknesses of both explanatory theories and hypothesis testing. On the one hand, explanations of already known phenomena are capable of generating new insights. On the other hand, explanatory theories, unlike hypothesis-testing theories, tend to be passive in the sense that they may not provide us with phenomena critical to their evaluation. As indicated, this is one of the strengths of hypothesis testing, the

ability to seek out a critical phenomenon. However, if we demand that the only acceptable theories be based on hypothesis testing, then we may sometimes delay or overlook
significant new theories.

Brush (1989), in an important paper in the highly prestigious journal *Science*,
supplied empirical evidence that, under some conditions at least, explanation may be
considered as important as prediction to a relevant scientific community. Brush examined the published comments of most physicists several years after Einstein's predictions
concerning the bending of light were confirmed. Brush found that confirming the
prediction of the bending of light was not more valued than relativity theory's explanation of Mercury's orbit. To put the matter briefly, Brush found that in evaluating
Einstein's theory of relativity, almost all physicists valued the explanation of existing
phenomena as much as the prediction of new phenomena.

Historical analysis points to the importance of explanatory theories in science. Donovan,
Laudan, and Laudan (1992), employing historical analysis in which they and others
examined various scientific writings, provided numerous examples of important scientific theories originally suggested on the basis of explanation, rather than prediction. As
merely one example, Finocchario (1992), who examined Galileo's writings in detail,
suggested that Galileo's acceptance of Copernicus was based on the ability of that theory
to explain already known phenomena, rather than to predict new phenomena.

*Promise*

Kuhn (1962), on the basis of historical analysis, suggested that scientists often accept
a new theory on the basis of its promise for solving significant problems. This point of
view was recently emphasized by Greene (1999), a prominent physicist who is among
those attempting to develop string theory. Many physicists devote much time and effort
to developing string theory, which is commonly employed because it is one of the major
approaches to reconciling quantum mechanics and relativity theory. Interestingly, string
theory cannot produce at present a single verifiable prediction. Thus, as Greene indicates,
the considerable emphasis that physicists devote to string theory is on the basis of its
promise.

That promise as a factor in theory acceptance is not restricted to physics can be shown
by way of an example from psychology. Watson (1913) wrote a very famous paper in
which he suggested that a behavioral approach to psychology was more useful than a
structuralist approach, which was then currently popular. Watson admitted that he
could not do a better job of explaining some phenomenon than did the structuralists.
But he gave as the major reason for accepting behaviorism that it promised to be more
useful than structuralism for constructing adequate theory in psychology.

As Greene has said of the role of promise in science,

> The history of physics is filled with ideas that when first presented seemed com-
> pletely untestable but, through various unforeseen developments, were ultimately
> brought within the realm of experimental verifiability. The notion that matter is
> made of atoms, Pauli's hypothesis that there are ghostly neutrino particles, and the

possibility that the heavens are dotted with neutron stars and black holes are three prominent ideas of precisely this sort – ideas that we now embrace fully but that, at their inception, seemed more like the musings of science fiction than aspects of science fact. (Greene, 1999, p. 226)

## The role of logic

No one would deny that logic is relevant to judging the usefulness of scientific methodology. For example, no one would want to use a methodological principle that was self-contradictory. On the other hand, logic alone is an insufficient basis for arriving at useful methodological principles. As one example, Kuhn (1962) showed that the methodological principle supplied by the logical positivists and Popper to the effect that we should reject disconfirmed theories is unworkable, despite the fact that it sounds logically reasonable. Essentially, on the basis of the historical record, Kuhn showed that all theories are at all times incompatible with at least some phenomena. This is a particular problem early in the development of a theory. Thus, if we were to follow the methodological principle suggested by the logical positivists and Popper – that we reject theories that are disconfirmed by some evidence – no theory in the history of science would ever have come to be accepted. A particularly good discussion of these issues in relation to Newton's theory is to be found in Chalmers (1999).

Another example close to home of where logic has given way to an empirical analysis has been in connection with null hypothesis significance testing in psychology. One suggestion has been to ban the use of statistical significance tests because they possess logical inadequacies (Hunter, 1997). Recently, Krueger (2001) strongly disagreed with this view. He suggests that we continue to use null hypothesis significance testing despite its admitted logical difficulties. The essence of Krueger's position is that hypothesis testing has proved to be a very useful tool in the past and thus will likely prove to be useful in the future. Although Krueger did not profess to be a naturalist, his proposal that we continue to use null hypothesis empirical hypothesis testing because it is empirically useful is entirely consistent with the spirit of naturalism.

## Summary

The message of this chapter is that, of the three ways of establishing the usefulness of a scientific methodology – intuitive-logical, use of core background assumptions, and empirical, the empirical method is to be preferred. In suggesting this, it is not our intention to say that logic should be abandoned in the evaluation of methodology. But it sometimes happens that logical considerations and empirical considerations fail to agree. In such cases, empirical considerations may override logical ones, depending on a variety of circumstances.

What are the implications of suggesting that methodological statements are like theoretical statements? One implication is that methodological statements are to be evaluated in the same way as more obvious and recognized theoretical statements, that is to say, empirically. Several empirical methods for evaluating methodological statements have already been mentioned. These include examining the historical record, as did Kuhn (1962), and examining scientists as they go about their normal activities, as did Dunbar (1994). A second implication is that methodological statements are not to be considered as having a higher truth status than other empirical statements. A common, indeed almost universal, misconception among scientists is that methodological statements have a truth value greater than that of other empirical or theoretical statements. Indeed, as Laudan (1996) has suggested, the opposite may be the case, with specific theoretical statements being more secure empirically than many methodological statements because the theoretical statements have undergone more rigorous testing.

Third, like any theoretical statement, methodological statements may be more useful under some circumstances than under others. We would not expect psychological theories to explain physical phenomena. Similarly, experimentation, which is highly useful under a wide variety of conditions, is nevertheless not universally useful. For example, in the beginning stages of any investigation, the most useful procedures may be to simply observe phenomena of interest, to interrogate nature or individuals, and to use other less controlled methodological procedures. According to this line of reasoning, blanket statements concerning the usefulness of a particular methodology under any and all circumstances are to be regarded with considerable suspicion. As another example, hypothesis testing, certainly one of the great methodological advances in all of science, as indicated earlier, while of great usefulness under some circumstances, is of limited usefulness under others.

A fourth implication of considering methodological statements to be like theoretical statements is that they should be evaluated on a relative, rather than an absolute, basis. To cite a previously used example, it is sometimes useful in science to continue to employ theories that have suffered a variety of discomfirmations, such as the Rescorla–Wagner model. Another example is Krueger's (2001) recent recommendation that null hypothesis testing continue to be used, despite its logical weaknesses, because it leads to better scientific decision making than the alternative of not employing it. A key consideration in deciding to continue to employ an otherwise disconfirmed theory is whether a suitable alternative exists. If a better theoretical alternative exists, then we might be little troubled by abandoning the disconfirmed theory. We are perhaps justified in elevating the above statement to a prime methodological principle. That is to say, methodological evaluation, in common with theoretical evaluation, is seldom if ever an absolute matter. Rather, methodological evaluation, in common with theoretical evaluation, is almost always a relative matter.

A final useful comparison between specific scientific theories and methodological statements is to realize that they are similar in that both, based on accumulating evidence, may be modified or rejected. So, we should not think of scientific methods as static any more than we think of scientific theories as static. This view contains the hope that over time our scientific methods, like our scientific theories themselves, will become progressively more adequate. Although hypothesis testing is of central importance in experimental psychology, it is well to bear in mind that it may be augmented by other methods, even scientific methods that have yet to be introduced and developed.

# References

Alcock, J. (2001). *The triumph of sociobiology.* New York: Oxford University Press.

Bergmann, G., & Spence, K. W. (1941). Operationism and theory in psychology. *Psychological Review, 48,* 1–14.

Bergmann, G., & Spence, K. W. (1944). The logic of psychophysical measurement. *Psychological Review, 51,* 1–24.

Brush, S. G. (1989). Prediction and theory evaluation: The case of light bending. *Science, 246,* 1124–9.

Capaldi, E. J., & Proctor, R. W. (1999). *Contextualism in psychological research? A critical review.* Thousand Oaks, CA: Sage.

Chalmers, A. F. (1999). *What is this thing called science?* (3rd edn.). Indianapolis, IN: Hackett Press.

Derrida, J. (1978). *Of grammatology* (G. C. Spivak trans.). Baltimore: Johns Hopkins University Press.

Donovan, A., Laudan, L., & Laudan, R. (eds.) (1992). *Scrutinizing science: Empirical studies of scientific change.* Baltimore: Johns Hopkins University Press.

Dunbar, K. (1994). How scientists really reason: Scientific reasoning in real-world laboratories. In R. J. Sternberg & J. Davidson (eds.), *The nature of insight* (pp. 365–95). Cambridge, MA: MIT Press.

*Encyclopaedia Britannica* (1771). Edinburgh: C. Macfarquhar.

Finocchario, M. A. (1992). Galileo's Copernicanism and the acceptability of guiding assumptions. In A. Donovan, L. Laudan, & R. Laudan (eds.), *Scrutinizing science: Empirical studies of scientific change* (pp. 49–67). Baltimore: Johns Hopkins University Press.

Gergen, K. J., & Gergen, M. M. (1991). Toward reflexive methodologies. In F. Steier (ed.), *Research and reflexivity* (pp. 76–94). Newbury Park, CA: Sage.

Greene, B. (1999). *The elegant universe.* New York: Norton.

Harré, R. (2000). Acts of living. *Science, 289,* 1303–4.

Holcomb, H. R., III (1998). Testing evolutionary hypotheses. In C. Crawford & D. L. Krebs (eds.), *Handbook of evolutionary psychology* (pp. 303–34). Mahwah, NJ: Erlbaum.

Hunter, J. E. (1997). Needed: A ban on the significance test. *Psychological Science, 8,* 3–7.

Jaeger, M. E., & Rosnow, R. L. (1988). Contextualism and its implications for psychological inquiry. *British Journal of Psychology, 79,* 63–75.

Kitcher, P. (1993). *The advancement of science: Science without legend, objectivity without illusion.* New York: Oxford University Press.

Klahr, D., & Simon, H. A. (1999). Studies of scientific discovery: Complementary approaches and convergent findings. *Psychological Bulletin, 125,* 524–43.

Klahr, D., & Simon, H. A. (2001). What have psychologists (and others) discovered about the process of scientific discovery? *Current Directions in Psychological Science, 10,* 75–9.

Krueger, J. (2001). Null hypothesis significance testing: On the survival of a flawed method. *American Psychologist, 56,* 16–26.

Kuhn, T. S. (1962). *The structure of scientific revolutions.* Chicago: University of Chicago Press. (revised edn. published in 1970)

Lakatos, I. (1970). Falsification and the methodology of scientific research programmes. In I. Lakatos & A. Musgrave (eds.), *Criticism and the growth of knowledge* (pp. 91–196). New York: Cambridge University Press.

Lakatos, I. (1976). History of science and its rational reconstructions. In C. Howson (ed.), *Method and appraisal in the physical sciences* (pp. 1–39). New York: Cambridge University Press.

Laudan, L. (1996). *Beyond positivism and relativism: Theory, method, and evidence*. Boulder, CO: Westview Press.

Miller, N. (1959). Liberalization of basic S-R concepts: Extensions to conflict behavior, motivation and social learning. In S. Koch (ed.), *Psychology: A study of science, Vol. 2: General systematic formulations, learning, and special processes* (pp. 196–292). New York: McGraw-Hill.

Miller, R. R., Barnet, R. C., & Grahame, N. J. (1995). Assessment of the Rescorla–Wagner model. *Psychological Bulletin, 117*, 363–86.

Oreskes, N. (1999). *Rejection of continental drift*. New York: Oxford University Press.

Popper, K. R. (1959). *The logic of scientific discovery*. New York: Basic Books.

Proctor, R. W., & Capaldi, E. J. (2001a). Evaluation and justification of methodologies in psychological science. *Psychological Bulletin, 127*, 759–72.

Proctor, R. W., & Capaldi, E. J. (2001b). Improving the science education of psychology students: Better teaching of methodology. *Teaching of Psychology, 28*, 173–81.

Rychlak, J. F. (1981). *Introduction to personality and psychotherapy*. Boston: Houghton Mifflin.

Samarapungavan, A., & Wiers, R. W. (1997). Children's thoughts on the origin of species: A study of explanatory coherence. *Cognitive Science, 21*, 147–77.

Sarbin, T. R. (ed.) (1986). *Narrative psychology: The storied nature of human conduct*. New York: Praeger.

Smith, J. A., Harré, R., & Van Langenhove, L. (1995). *Rethinking methods in psychology*. Thousand Oaks, CA: Sage.

Van Hamme, L. J., & Wasserman, E. A. (1994). Cue competition in causality judgments: The role of nonpresentation of compound stimulus elements. *Learning and Motivation, 25*, 127–51.

Watson, J. B. (1913). Psychology as the behaviorist views it. *Psychological Review, 20*, 158–77.

Wegener, A. L. (1924). *The origins of continents and oceans* (3rd edn.) (J. G. A. Skerl, trans.). London: Methuen.

Wilson, E. O. (1999). *Consilience: The unity of knowledge*. New York: Vintage.

# PART II

*Research Designs, Methodological Issues, and Analytic Procedures*

# CHAPTER THREE

# Traditional Nomothetic Approaches

## Richard J. Harris

*Idiographic* versus *nomothetic*: Like most dichotomies, this one is – especially for psychologists – a false one. A purely idiographic study, delineating and attempting to "understand" a single individual (or a small collection of unique individuals) with no claim to, or attempt at, generalization beyond any single individual is an exercise in narcissism, not science. On the other hand, a purely nomothetic study describing the characteristics of large groups of individuals and predicting relations among group-level variables that do not hold (or are not even examined) for any single individual, may be a perfectly respectable application of sociology or economics, but it's not psychology.

Fortunately, psychologists do not really carry out purely idiographic or purely nomothetic studies, though some researchers may claim to do so. Even the most resolutely idiographic research finds an appreciative audience only because that audience can discern in the details of a single person's behavior, themes or principles that seem likely to hold for other people (perhaps including themselves) as well – just as one of the values that an adolescent boy can derive from reading *The Catcher in the Rye* is the discovery that his difficulty dealing with raging hormones is not unique.

Ironically, the deepest insight into what governs a single person's behavior emerges only when that behavior can be examined in the context of other people's behavior, as shown by the repeated finding of superiority of statistical over clinical prediction (Meehl, 1954; Grove & Meehl, 1996). An even clearer example of this same irony is provided by the many studies of paired-associate (PA) learning in which the one-element (all-or-none) learning model is supported (Atkinson, Bower, & Crothers, 1965, chapter 3). Although examining any single person's trial-to-trial progress through the PA list leads to observation of the eventual emergence of perfect performance, the string of inter-mingled errors and correct responses leading to that perfect performance is very noisy. This finding, together with the fact that the number of correct responses, summed across items, shows a strong upward trend (as more and more items enter the learned state) has the consequence that it is only when each item for a given person is lined up on the trial of last error, and these realigned sequences are combined across several persons, that it becomes clear that the backward learning curve is essentially flat – that is, that the learning process for single items for a single person is all-or-none, not gradual.

On the other hand, nomothetic researchers do have a tendency to describe the results of their group comparisons as though they applied to every individual (in the case of comparisons of pre- and post-treatment means) or to every pair of individuals exposed to the two different conditions. For instance, one of the most reliable findings in dissonance research from the late 1950s on is that of *postdecision spread*, an increase, once an irrevocable choice between two alternatives has been made, in the attractiveness of the chosen alternative and a decrease in the attractiveness of the rejected alternative. "Reliability" in this case actually refers to the consistency with which the difference between the chosen and rejected alternatives in *mean* attractiveness is statistically significantly greater postdecision than predecision – but the abstracts and discussion sections of the papers reporting this finding (as well as textbook summaries thereof) were invariably phrased with the same sort of apparent universality as the description I gave in the preceding sentence. I was therefore quite concerned when only about 60 percent of the subjects I ran in the early stages of my dissertation study (Harris, 1967) showed the predicted spread effect. Concerned, that is, until I began reading results sections of postdecision dissonance studies more carefully and examining original data where available. This 60 : 40 split between the percentage of individuals who showed a spread versus a shrinkage effect turned out to be quite typical.

In short, it is probably more necessary to remind "traditional nomothetic" researchers of the need to include individual-level analyses and explanations than it is to remind idiographically inclined researchers of the need to consider the generalizability of their findings across individuals. After all, the latter's audiences will test that generalization, whether the researcher does or not.

Nevertheless, "traditional nomothetic" methods have dominated psychological research over the decades, centuries, and now, millenia. All I have to do in this chapter is to summarize the methods described in a few hundred methodology textbooks and employed in a few hundred thousand research articles. All I can *realistically* hope to do is to provide a summary of the dimensions along which nomothetic approaches vary and the relations of these dimensions to the desiderata and disadvantages of the various methods, leavened by slightly more detailed discussion of a few methodological points I feel have been overlooked or given insufficient attention.

Almost nothing in this chapter (including my diatribe on the nonexistence of purely idiographic or purely nomothetic research) is original with me, and almost everything said here has been said better, more clearly, and certainly in more detail elsewhere – though most of my points are so multiply determined, having come from so many instructors, so many textbooks, so many discussion sections or footnotes, that my feeble attempts to cite sources will inevitably slight many researchers, methodologists, and philosophers of science who deserve better treatment. (I am, after all, the person who decried the lack of any test of the sphericity assumption in multivariate analysis of variance to an audience that included Huynh Huynh, the inventor and publisher of just such a test [Huynh & Feldt, 1970]; who presented a paper that essentially reinvented Gollob's [1968] FANOVA (factor-analytic variation) model as applied to multiple-*df* interactions; and who, after decades of teaching three-alternative logic for significance testing, finally got around to presenting papers on it at a couple of conferences, only to be informed by a true scholar, Bob Pruzek, that Henry Kaiser had presented that logic in a 1960 *Psychological Review* paper.)

## Dimensions of Traditional Nomothetic Research Methods

Let's begin by discussing some dimensions along which nomothetic approaches vary. Factorially combining those dimensions should then yield a taxonomy of nomothetic approaches. However, not all dimensions are relevant to all of the properties of designs that concern us, and the various dimensions are far from independent, so it will actually be more useful to examine multiple taxonomies constructed from subsets of dimensions.

### Dimension 1. Goal(s) of the research

Is this research intended to

1. Establish facts?
2. Generate hypotheses that explicate relations among facts?
3. Test causal hypotheses?

*Just the facts* Research designed to determine "just the facts" (which facts may include relations between variables, as well as distributions of and/or descriptive statistics for single variables) has many uses. Such research can be very useful in applied settings as a supplement to or corrective to anecdotal evidence. For example, staff at the American Society of Radiologic Technologists (ASRT; members produce the X-ray, CAT scan, PET, and MRI images for radiologists to interpret) had been receiving numerous calls complaining about the deterioration of the RT's workplace environment as a result of the shortage of RTs and attendant increases in workload. ASRT decided that it would be useful to document just how bad the situation had become and therefore commissioned an environmental scan of the radiographer's workplace environment. The results (ASRT, 2002) revealed a much higher level of satisfaction among RTs with their workplaces than the anecdotal evidence had suggested: the RTs' mean ratings of overall satisfaction with their current facility, with the radiology staff and the radiology department therein, with their job, and with the overall quality of radiologic patient care were all above 4 on the 5-point scale provided, and 74 of the 82 specific attributes they rated were given one of the top two ratings by more than half of the technologists. This is not to say that major efforts to address the areas of dissatisfaction aren't warranted, but the approach one takes to improving an already rewarding profession is apt to be somewhat different than the rescue effort one must mount to head off apocalypse.

This kind of research can also be useful in establishing quantitative parameters for decision making. For example, the leadership of a professional society may be convinced that requiring members of the national organization also to belong to their state affiliate society and vice versa will decrease national-society membership but increase state-society membership, but without good estimates of the magnitudes of (and a check on the presumed directions of) those two effects it would be very difficult to make a sound decision on whether or not to institute such a joint-membership policy.

Just-the-facts research can also be useful to academic/basic researchers in developing a corpus of basic findings for subsequent "mining" for unexpected (e.g., apparently contradictory) results that can stimulate the development of hypotheses, the revision of existing theories, and so forth. (This research is similar to, but distinct from, the middle level of this dimension, collection of data specifically to help understand a particular prior finding.)

Probably not finally, but the last use I came up with: just-the-facts research can be used to establish the ecological validity/generalizability of basic research. For instance, hypothesis-testing research may have determined that whether similarity of ethnicity or similarity of beliefs is the more important determinant of liking depends on the range of beliefs among the persons whose attractiveness is being evaluated. Whether the net effect in the "real world" is that ethnicity or belief is more important cannot be determined until the range of beliefs typically encountered in that real world has been assessed.

*Explicating the facts*    A classic example of this goal for research is Haire's (1950) study of the "real" reason(s) shoppers (predominantly housewives in that era) were reluctant to buy instant coffee (a new product at the time). When asked directly for their reasons, the overwhelming response was "doesn't taste as good" (as fresh-brewed coffee). Yet, taste tests consistently found that consumers were unable to discriminate reliably between fresh-brewed and instant coffee. Haire then took the less direct (projective?) approach of asking each of a number of shoppers to read a shopping list and then describe the person who had prepared that list. Half of the shoppers read a list that included a one-pound can of percolator coffee, while the other half read a list that included (embedded among a number of fillers common to both lists) a jar of instant coffee. "Nescafé Mom" was described as lazy, failing to plan household purchases well, a spendthrift, and a poor wife. Those participants so describing her did not themselves buy instant coffee. Haire's client then switched its ad campaign to emphasize how much more time you would have available to spend with your family if you weren't slaving over a hot percolator (sound familiar?).

*Testing hypothesized causal relations*    This goal is the primary engine driving basic research efforts. Hypotheses to be tested may come from hunches, from the process of attempting to understand (or refusing to take at face value) previous results, or via formal derivations from existing theories. To keep the derivation→operationalization→empirical test→theory assessment→theory revision or further derivation cycle (aka the hypothetico-deductive method) going full steam, hypotheses that are based on hunch or the extension of or reaction to previous results must eventually be integrated into a set of interconnected theoretical propositions.

Textbooks and courses on techniques for translating one's assumptions about behavior into formal, algebraic models that can then be used to derive research hypotheses that you know really do follow from your assumptions constitute a pair of vanishing species. My own recent (twice-a-decade) offerings of a seminar on mathematical psychology have used Wickens's (1982) text, the last 10 copies of which (doled out to and collected at the end of the semester from my students) Professor Wickens was able to provide me after it went out of print. Reasons for this decline include the incorporation of these techniques into substantive courses and textbooks dealing with particular areas of psychology (most notably, cognition and learning "broadly defined" – as we say at UNM when in the midst of a hiring process), and the less salutary substitution of structural equations modeling, computer simulation (especially neural network modeling), and verbal-intuitive models under the mistaken belief that they are just as effective as algebraic modeling at establishing what further hypotheses can or cannot be derived from one's assumptions. What appears to follow from verbally stated assumptions can be very different from their true implications (Harris, 1976); direction of causality must be built into, rather than derived from, structural equations models (James, Mulaik, & Brett, 1982); and computer simulation can demonstrate that a particular behavior follows from specific combinations of the numerical values of the various input parameters, but cannot establish that any particular behavior or relation between behaviors is a general consequence of one's assumptions.

## Dimension 2. Source of participants

1. Random sample from a well-defined population;
2. Random sample from an implicitly (circularly?) defined population;
3. Convenient sample.

A *random sample* from some population is one that is chosen in such a way that every member of the population to which the researcher wishes to generalize has an equal chance of being represented in the sample. This procedure does not preclude deliberately oversampling from relatively rare subpopulations, provided that subsequent descriptive statistics are weighted by the proportion of each subgroup in the population. Nor does it preclude hierarchical sampling procedures in which, for example, a random sample of states is selected, then a random sample of counties within each selected state is selected, then a random sample of census tracts within each county is selected, and so forth. (The advantage of such hierarchical sampling schemes is that complete enumeration of potential participants need only take place at the lowest level of the hierarchy.)

Ideally, researchers should define the population to which they wish to generalize and then devise a sampling scheme that will guarantee each member of the target population an equal chance of representation in the study. Many researchers, however, recruit participants from a readily available source – for example, an introductory psychology research-participation pool. If the selection of participants from that source is essentially random (e.g., if the topics and methods of the various experiments aren't revealed until after the student has signed up for a given session of a given study), then this group can be considered a random sample from an incompletely specified population whose characterization includes willingness to volunteer for initially undefined research studies.

Otherwise, the researcher has in hand a *convenient sample* (aka a "convenience sample," though that terminology has always seemed a bit ungrammatical to me) of at best uncertain external validity. For hypothesis-testing research, however, internal validity may be of much greater concern and is easily accomplished with convenient samples via random *assignment* (cf. dimension 4).

Textbooks on survey research (e.g., Dillman, 2000) or more specialized texts (e.g., Lehtonen & Pahkinen, 1995) can be consulted for detailed treatment of sampling procedures.

## Dimension 3. Levels of the independent variable(s) (IV)

1. Manipulated;
2. Simulated;
3. Measured;
4. What independent variable?

A *manipulated* independent variable is, obviously, one whose levels are established by the experimenter through differences in the way in which research participants are treated – for example, differences in the dosage level of a drug, differences in the difficulty or other features of the tasks they perform, differences in the order in which blocks of questions appear on the questionnaires mailed to them, or differences in the number of times they cross paths with various fellow participants as they move from station to station. A *simulated* independent variable shares with manipulated IVs differential treatment of participants, but relies on the cooperation of those participants to make the operational and conceptual definitions of the IV match up. For instance, participants may be asked to behave as though they have just been informed that their tumor is malignant (or, in another condition, benign), or as though large amounts of real money (rather than imaginary money or "points") hinge on their choices in an experimental game paradigm, or as though they are "real" prisoners or prison guards. Simulated IVs have a justifiably poor reputation, because the difference between how people believe they would behave and how they actually do behave in given situations can be dramatically different (cf., e.g., Milgram, 1963; Hofling, Brotzman, Dalrymple, Graves, & Bierce, 1966; Gallo, 1966), and no one has ever, to my knowledge, been able to develop a reliable method of predicting which situations will display minimal versus large discrepancies between simulated and actual behavior – though most social psychologists share the belief that the match is liable to be closer, the higher the manipulation is in *experimental* (vs. *mundane*) realism (Aronson, Brewer, & Carlsmith, 1985). A degree of simulation, however, is probably present in more studies than we prefer to admit, as when our results and the interpretation thereof hinge on participants behaving as though they really cared about the solutions to the tasks with which we present them. (I still fondly recall participant #114 from my dissertation study, who, after seven hours' worth of ratings of and paired comparisons among various long-playing albums, announced that he had been choosing randomly, waiting for the apparatus to start smoking or some other variant on the "whoops" paradigm to occur.)

A *measured* independent variable is one for which the participant's level is brought with him or her to the study and simply assessed (via observation or measurement) by the researcher. Indeed, designation of many measured variables (e.g., level of depression, satisfaction with one's job, choice of major, job description) as independent or dependent is determined by the intention or theoretical position of the researcher.

Finally, many studies (especially those with purely descriptive, just-the-facts goals) do not require the presence of any IV, nor the separation of the variables measured into independent and dependent categories.

## Dimension 4. Assignment of participants to levels of the IV(s)

1. Random;
2. Selection;
3. Measurement.

*Random assignment* involves the use of some mechanical procedure or algorithm (based, e.g., on a table of random numbers or the pseudo-random-number generator built into a statistical package) to determine to which level of a manipulated independent variable any given participant is to be exposed. Various constraints can be applied to the randomization procedure (e.g., every block of 12 successive participants must include three assigned to each of the four experimental conditions, or each participant in condition A is to be matched with a participant in condition B of about the same age), but a random process has to be involved at some point (e.g., after matching participants pairwise with respect to some battery of variables, flipping a coin to determine which of any given pair gets treatment 1). It is important to remember that the researcher's attempt to simulate a random-number table in assigning participants to conditions is unlikely to be successful, and that employing systematic assignment (1st participant to level 1, 2nd to level 2, 3rd to level 3, 4th to level 1, 5th to level 2, etc.) cannot be guaranteed to be an adequate approximation to random assignment.

*Selection* is usually self-selection (allowing participants to choose which treatment condition they wish to participate in or giving them veto power over the treatment to which they're initially assigned), but it can also arise through (nonrandom) selection by others, as when principals are allowed to determine which of their teachers will be asked to employ each of a number of curricula being compared.

When a *measured* (rather than manipulated or simulated) IV is employed, each participant's position on the IV is determined by her or his preexisting position on the IV (age, gender, occupation, etc.).

## Dimension 5. Number and timing of measurements vis à vis changes in IV(s)

These are the primary "tools of the trade" in designing experiments and (especially) quasi-experiments so as to counter various potential "threats to validity" – the marvelously apt phrase coined by Campbell and Stanley. For instance, the threat of measurement-induced change being mistaken for an effect of one's treatment can be countered by having one group of participants who are exposed to the treatment but are measured only posttest. The catalog of threats and design answers to same is far too long to be summarized in this chapter, but it is readily available in Campbell, Stanley, and Gage (1981) and in many subsequent research-design textbooks.

## *Dimension 6. Determination of scores on the dependent variable(s)*

What instrument or technique one uses to assess participants' behavior comes close to what most of us mean by a "research method," just as diagnostic and treatment methods are categorized by their technology: PET, MRI, microsurgery, progressive desensitization, and so forth. I will therefore defer discussing this dimension to the section on the relation between dimensions and methods.

## *Relations among dimensions*

As mentioned earlier, the above are hardly independent dimensions. The most obvious "for instance" is the relation between the goal of one's research endeavor (Dimension 3) and the way in which levels of the independent variable are determined and research participants assigned thereto (Dimension 4). If a researcher's goal is to test causal hypotheses, the true experiment (random assignment of participants to levels of a manipulated independent variable) is the gold standard – but clearly neither a guarantee of valid causal inference nor the only combination of those two design dimensions that can contribute to our confidence in a causal hypothesis. Although the oft-encountered statement that "correlation doesn't prove causality" is correct, neither does experimentation. Three kinds of evidence are needed to establish that $X$ causes $Y$:

1. Evidence that $X$ and $Y$ are correlated;
2. Evidence that changes in $X$ precede changes in $Y$;
3. Evidence ruling out alternative explanations of the form "$W$ causes both $X$ and $Y$."

Correlational research is just as good as true experiments at providing Type 1 evidence. Experiments have an advantage (but not a monopoly) in providing Type 2 evidence, because the manipulation of the IV and subsequent observation of consequences for scores on the dependent variable guarantees time precedence. (This situation does not, however, preclude mutual causation, because had we chosen instead to manipulate $Y$ we might well have observed consequent changes in $X$.) Where experiments gain their primary advantage over purely correlational research and over quasi-experiments is in providing Type 3 evidence by ruling out the whole set of third-variable alternative explanations of the form "subjects at level $i$ of the IV differ systematically from subjects at level $j$ of the IV in their average position on individual-difference variable $W$."

Researchers employing correlational and quasi-experimental designs (which share the absence of random assignment to levels of the IV) can eliminate particular individual-difference variables via statistical control, but a researcher can never be sure that there isn't an unexamined individual-difference variable generating a spurious correlation between the independent and dependent variables. This advantage of experimental designs is gained by random assignment to conditions and far outweighs in importance (for purposes of supporting causal hypotheses) the advantage of tighter control over conditions provided by the manipulated independent variable (as compared to statistical controls).

If the IV is manipulated, but random assignment is not employed, the design is a quasi-experiment; if the IV is established via measurement (which precludes random assignment) the design is correlational; and if there is no IV the research is purely descriptive. Thus Dimensions 3 and 4 combine factorially to yield a taxonomy of research designs varying in the strength of evidence they can provide for causal relations. Dimensions 1 and 2 are also strongly related, in that the utility of just-the-facts research (Level 1 of Dimension 1) is heavily dependent on the external validity of that research, so random sampling from a well-defined population will generally be required.

Dimension 5 is nearly independent of the other five dimensions, except that if scores on the dependent variable(s) are extracted from an archive, the researcher engaged in the data-mining operation will have no control over the position of the study yielding those data on the other five dimensions. Which brings us to the correspondence between the above six dimensions and particular methods employed in nomothetic research.

## Traditional Nomothetic Research Methods Related to Dimensions

Among many alternative organizing principles, one can order nomothetic research methods in terms of their obtrusiveness (the extent to which the data-collection procedure requires that the participants live up to their recently APA-conferred change of designation) as follows:

1. Mining of archives;
2. Direct observation;
3. Self-report;
4. Interventions.

### *"Mining" of archival data*

*Archival* data began life as observational or self-report data, but have been recorded and stored in a format that makes them accessible to researchers with no further involvement with the original participants. Examples include *census data, historical analyses*, and *meta-analysis*.

*Census data* are any set of data that provide a score on the dependent and independent variables for every individual in the population to which you wish to generalize. The most common approximations to census data are the decennial compilations of the United States Census, but the records of licensing bodies for various professions (e.g., physicians and allied health professionals) also come close to providing censuses of the population of individuals eligible to practice those professions. (There are always, of course, recording errors; time lags between the collection of data and current age, membership status, etc.; and failures or refusals to report all the information requested that prevent any set of archived data from meeting the strict definition of a census.) Census data usually provide only scores on IVs, but if the individual-case data are available (with personal identifying information suitably removed) data-mining researchers can provide their own analyses of relationships among these variables. Census data also seldom include scores on manipulated IVs, except possibly for information as to which of two or more forms of the data-collection instrument (e.g., the short versus the long U.S. Census questionnaire) a given individual responded to.

The systematic collection of psychological data is a historically recent phenomenon, so *historical analyses* that reach back more than a century and that attempt to generalize beyond single cases require considerable effort on the part of the researcher to develop coding schemes to translate historical documents into scores on independent (measured, rather than manipulated) and dependent variables. Even research spanning mere decades that relies on historical documents such as newspapers (e.g., to trace changes in attitudes toward various ethnic groups) or paintings (e.g., to trace changes in perceptions of physical attractiveness) often requires extensive *content analysis*. Excellent examples of the use of historical analyses for hypothesis-testing research are provided by Dean Simonton's (1980, 1984) studies of leadership.

*Meta-analysis* also mines data that have already been collected – usually by researchers other than the meta-analyst. The data are gleaned from published research reports and (where they can be obtained) raw data sets (usually unpublished, but provided by cooperative colleagues). The meta-analyst usually strives for a complete census of all studies of a given effect (i.e., of the relation between a particular conceptually defined independent and a particular conceptually defined dependent variable). Meta-analytic studies differ from traditional reviews of the literature ("Let's wait for the *Psych. Bull.* article" has been a common response to apparently conflicting results for at least the past five decades) in two major ways. First, the magnitude and variability of each effect is estimated, not by counting the number of studies achieving versus those failing to achieve statistical significance for that effect, but by combining effect size measures (e.g., a correlation or the mean difference, rather than the associated $p$ values) across the various studies. Second, these effect size measures are supplemented by scores on measures of the ancillary features of each study – the study's position on each of the six dimensions described earlier, measures of methodological quality (whether, e.g., any clinical assessments were "blinded"), and measures of any other aspect of the studies the meta-analyst suspects might interact with effect size. Effect size is then correlated with each of the ancillary variables and/or subjected to a regression analysis with those variables as predictors so as to tease out relevant interacting and intervening variables.

## Observation, obtrusive and unobtrusive

*Observation* refers to any recording of participants' responses by the researcher in a way that is out of the participant's control. This procedure can be as simple a matter as recording button presses or as complex as applying to participants' ongoing behavior a complex coding scheme requiring months of training. Observational techniques also vary in how obtrusive they are and, partly as a consequence, in the ethical issues they raise.

*Traces and direct coding of behavior* As mentioned in discussing dimension 5 above, observation involves the researcher's determining what score to assign to a particular aspect of the participant's behavior. Among the least obtrusive of observational methods is the use of *traces*, the residue left behind by a participant's behavior. These traces include erosion measures (e.g., carpet wear) to assess traffic flow through or the relative popularity of various items within museum exhibits or grocery stores (an inherently nomothetic set of measures if ever there was one), and "garbology," that is, gleaning evidence from trash receptacles as to, for example, alcohol consumption. Webb, Campbell, Schwartz, Sechrest, and Grove (1981) provide a downright entertaining catalog and discussion of a large number of trace measures. These and other unobtrusive (nonreactive) measures have the advantages of making it unlikely that we are dealing with simulated behavior (cf. Dimension 3 above) and of testing the generality of relations across a broader variety of measures.

*Direct observation of behavior* (without intervention via manipulated independent variables) involves developing a coding scheme to capture the practically or theoretically relevant aspects of the participants' behavior, training coders to apply this classification scheme, and then choosing or providing an appropriate setting (e.g., the local mall, a lab equipped with tape recorders and one-way mirrors, the parking lots of football stadiums) in which to observe relevant behavior. The coding scheme can be quite simple (as in "standing on the corner" 1–10 ratings of physical attractiveness, which proved in Berscheid, Dion, and Walster's (1971) freshman-dance study to be better predictors of liking for one's date than much more elaborate personality scales) or very complex (as in Bales's Interaction Process Analysis and Symlog systems; Bales, Cohen, & Williamson, 1979).

## Self-report

*Self-report* refers to situations where participants choose the words in which to describe their characteristics, their (usually past) behavior, and/or their intellectual and/or affective responses to stimuli. The researcher may limit the participants' responses to a set of fixed alternatives (as in ratings of their level of agreement with various statements) or may leave the participants free to put their responses in their own words.

*Scales* A *scale* is a set of items (usually questions or declarative statements), responses to which are intended to permit ordering individuals along a single conceptual dimension.

(Alternatively, a scale tapping a single conceptual *domain* – e.g., intelligence – may employ unidimensional *subscales* designed to assess logically independent, though not always uncorrelated, dimensions or factors that jointly define that domain – e.g., verbal, mathematical, spatial, numerical, and social intelligence.) The most commonly used scale is the single-item "scale" asking the participant to provide an overall self-evaluation of his or her position on the dimension – e.g., "On a scale from 1 (highly unfavorable) to 7 (highly favorable), how favorable are you towards fluoridation of municipal water supplies?" Such single-item scales provide no check on whether the underlying concept is unidimensional or multidimensional, nor do they provide checks on the internal consistency of participants' responses. Multiple-item scales come in a wide variety of forms, the best known being Likert scales (a mixture of items implying a position close to one end and items implying a position close to the opposite end of the conceptual dimension, with respondents indicating their level of agreement with or the applicability to themselves of each item by selecting one of three to seven response alternatives); Thurstone scales (items covering the full range of positions on the conceptual dimension, with the respondent indicating agreement with or the applicability of each item via a dichotomous agree/disagree or applies/doesn't apply response); and Guttman scales (items and response alternatives similar to Thurstone scales, except that the items are worded so that an individual whose true position on the underlying dimension is $x$ will endorse all items at position $x$ or lower but disagree with or disavow the applicability of all items at positions greater than $x$ – e.g., "If my child's temperature were ___ degrees above normal, I would call the doctor"). Many other scale formats have also been employed.

Any textbook on attitudes or on survey research will provide advice on scale construction, and compilations of existing scales – usually with accompanying information on studies of the scale's reliability and validity – are available both as appendices to methods textbooks (e.g., Miller, 1991) and as stand-alone volumes (e.g., Robinson, Rusk, & Head, 1968; Robinson, Shaver, & Wrightsman, 1991).

*Questionnaires and interviews* These present the participants with a highly structured set of stimuli in the form of specific questions or statements (with which the participants indicate level of agreement) about the issue at hand. The questions can be open-ended, asking the participants to respond in their own words, or can involve fixed alternatives from which the respondent is asked to choose – though "Other (Please specify ___ )" is often the last alternative. The order and wording of the questions can have a big impact on responses.

## Interventions

*Interrupted time series* Most research seeks a considerable excess of participants (cases, independently sampled units) over outcome variables and independent conditions, so as to have plenty of degrees of freedom (essentially, the difference between number of participants and number of parameters that must be estimated from the data) to employ in estimating within-condition variability and thereby provide more powerful discrimination among levels of the independent variable(s). However, there are a number of situations where the number of outcome measures far exceeds the number of independently sampled cases yielding scores on those measures. Perhaps the most common of these situations is the *interrupted time series* design, in which one or a few sampling units (e.g., an entire metropolitan area) is observed at several time points (e.g., the metropolis's drunken-driving arrests measured every week for a year) before and after the introduction of some intervention (e.g., more severe penalties for driving while intoxicated – DWI).

The traditional approach to assessing the direction and statistical significance of the difference between preintervention and postintervention behavior – carrying out a correlated- (paired-) means *t* test – suffers from two disadvantages. First, this test will have negative degrees of freedom and will thus be impossible to carry out unless we ignore the almost always substantial (auto)correlations among the various measures. Doing so, however, may grossly underestimate or grossly overestimate the true reliability of the pre–post difference. Second, if there is an overall trend across measurement conditions (e.g., if DWI arrests had been decreasing steadily over the weeks prior to the intervention), a substantial difference between preintervention and postintervention means is expected, even if the intervention has no effect whatever on the trend.

Both of these problems are dealt with by subjecting the series of measurements to a *time series analysis* (Benjamin, 2002; Glass, McGaw, & Smith, 1981). Time series analysis first searches for a mathematical model that fits the preintervention trend (sometimes linear, sometimes curvilinear, sometimes periodic) and that accounts for the autocorrelations among observations. This model can be used to (a) transform the observations to a smaller number of statistically independent measures to which standard statistical tests do apply and (b) generate the postintervention data points we would expect to see if the preintervention trend continued unchanged into the postintervention period – that is, if the intervention had no effect.

*True and quasi-experiments*   As mentioned in our discussion of relations among dimensions, true and quasi-experiments share the use of a manipulated IV. They differ in that true experiments assign participants to the levels of the IV(s) randomly, whereas quasi-experiments do not. For instance, one treatment (i.e., one level of the IV) may be administered to each of the members of a preexisting group (e.g., the students in a single classroom) whereas another group is exposed to a different treatment.

The true experiment provides the strongest evidence for a causal relation between an IV and a dependent variable, but any given true experiment is nevertheless always open to a number of challenges. The adequacy of the match between the operational and conceptual definitions of the IV (did telling the participants they were to receive electric shocks arouse *fear* or *anxiety*?) may be called into question. Or (unintentional) bias on the part of the research assistant recording participants' behavior may arise if the assistant is not kept blind as to which experimental condition a given participant has been exposed to. Or confounds between the experimental manipulation and other "nuisance" variables may be detected. (For example, the two therapists who administered the desensitization treatment may have been able to hold experimental sessions only in the morning, whereas the implosion therapists may have been available only for afternoon sessions.)

By far the most common deficiency of the true experiment, however, flows from its greatest strength: random assignment to the levels of the IV (usually in roughly equal numbers) may result in levels of the IV that are very atypical of "real world" settings and may thus yield results whose external validity is questionable. This situation is especially likely in factorial designs, where *combinations* of levels of the IVs may be produced that almost never occur together in the real-world setting to which the researcher would like to generalize. For example, we might randomly assign equal numbers of participants to each of the four combinations of each of the four combinations of gender (i.e., vita labeled as describing a male versus female faculty member) x discipline (i.e., whether the person described is said to be on the social work faculty or on the engineering faculty) and discover that recommended salaries are significantly higher for the female faculty members in both disciplines. Given, however, that female engineers are still rare and that engineering faculty command higher salaries than do social work faculty, it is likely that in most "real" US universities the mean female salary, averaged over all females in either school, is considerably lower than the mean male salary for the two disciplines. This difference between representation of combinations of IVs in the experiment versus in the real world can be corrected for – but only if the real-world proportions are known or can be established via descriptive just-the-facts research. Many research methods textbooks and chapters deal exclusively or primarily with the design of true experiments, so there should be no difficulty finding detailed treatment of, and advice with respect to, experimental designs.

As pointed out earlier, lack of random assignment leaves the *quasi-experiment* open to many more threats to validity (including internal validity) than the true experiment. The number one threat is that preexisting differences among the extant groups assigned to the different levels of the IV(s) or variables associated with the process by which participants are (often self-)selected for particular levels may be confounded with the experimental manipulation, thereby making it difficult to disentangle the effects of the manipulation from the effects of the selection process. Statistical controls can approximate the results that would have been obtained had the levels of the IV been equated for one or more of the possible confounding variables, but (a) these controls almost always assume linearity, and (b) one can never be sure that some unsuspected dimension of preexisting differences or a selection factor the researcher hasn't "covaried out" doesn't remain to bias (upward or downward) the effects of the experimental manipulation. Although thoughtful design (aided perhaps by the catalog of validity threats and the design elements that minimize them provided by Campbell, Stanley, & Gage, 1981) can help strengthen one's case in any one study, the primary tool for increasing confidence in the causal nature of the relation between a conceptually defined dependent variable and a conceptual IV that doesn't lend itself to random assignment (as well as independent/dependent pairs of variables that don't permit experimental manipulation at all) is replication by as many different researchers studying as many different participant populations and as many different operational definitions of the conceptual independent and dependent variables as possible. In other words, "wait for the *Psych. Bull.* article" (or the equivalent *Current Directions* or *Review of Personality and Social Psychology* meta-analytic review) is as valid a slogan as ever.

## Assorted Points about Nomothetic Approaches

Prepare for a passel of platitudes.

### *Don't be apologetic about the artificiality of experiments*

One of the most common lay criticisms of basic/laboratory/experimental studies (the three terms are of course far from synonymous) is that they require participants to respond to stimuli or combinations thereof that they are unlikely to encounter in their everyday lives, presented in settings that are similarly unusual – that is, they're "artificial." I share with many others a preference for thinking of this "artificiality" as a major *advantage* of the experimental method. We've had millennia to learn from observation of "everyday life," so collecting data on one more instance of a familiar combination of variables and settings is unlikely to lead to new understanding of behavior in those familiar settings. (Researchers employing participant observation routinely report that the power of immersion in a new unfamiliar environment to stimulate surprise at unexpected patterns and relations fades in at most a few months.) Using experimental manipulation to explore unusual combinations of IVs and settings provides us, then, with a much better chance of gaining new insights into behavior. Yes, it *is* unusual for social evidence (what others tell us we're seeing) to conflict with physical evidence (what our own senses tell us we're seeing), which is precisely why the Asch line-judgment paradigm was so effective at adjusting upward our estimate of the importance of social influence.

### *A little bit of algebraic modeling comes in very handy*

The common view of formal, algebraic modeling is that it's an exercise best left to the very late stages of a research program, after many years of data on a particular aspect of behavior have accumulated. However, relying on verbally stated assumptions and one's intuitions about the "obvious" implications of those assumptions to guide you through the early stages of your research in a given area can lead to the following.

*Reporting at face value results that are logically impossible* For instance, Leahey and Harris (1985, p. 287; cited in Hintzman, 1991, p. 41) claimed that "Men still have more partners than women do, and they are more likely to have one-night stands." But, as can readily be shown by filling the cells of a matrix with a 1 for every male (row $i$) who is a partner of a particular female (column $j$), the mean number of partners per male is identical to the mean number of partners per female times the ratio of total number of females to total number of males (a ratio that is close to 1.0 for most populations), so that Leahey and Harris must have had either a sampling problem or a gender difference in direction of reporting bias – *not* a true gender difference in number of partners.

*Reporting data as strongly confirming a theory that they actually firmly reject* For instance, Gerard (1964) proposed that, as a consequence of dissonance-reduction processes, a participant in the Asch line-judgment paradigm who conforms on one false-majority trial will, "all other things equal," conform on the next false-majority trial, whereas a participant who gives an independent judgment on one false-majority trial will also successfully resist conformity on the next trial. In short, and as Kiesler and Kiesler (1968) stated explicitly in their paperback text on conformity, Gerard asserts that $\Pr(C_{n+1}|C_n) = \Pr(I_{n+1}|I_n) = 1.0$. Gerard and the Kieslers both go on to say that this model implies a binomial distribution of conforming responses, which Gerard's data appeared to display. The Kieslers characterized these data as providing "strong support" for the theory. However, I pointed out (Harris, 1976) that these assumptions actually imply not just bimodality, but a two-point distribution such that *all* participants conform on either zero percent or 100 percent of the false-majority trials. This actual prediction from Gerard's assumptions was soundly *dis*confirmed by his data and by all other data collected in the line-judgment paradigm of which I'm aware.

*Reporting data as supportive of or as disconfirming a research hypothesis "derived" from your theoretical assumptions, when in fact that hypothesis does not necessarily follow from your theory* See Harris (1976) for details of another dissonance-based example, Brehm and Cohen's prediction of a greater postdecision spread effect for a decision between two attractive than between two unattractive alternatives (with relative attractiveness held constant), which prediction was taken seriously enough for Greenwald (1969) to take his finding of a curvilinear relation between absolute attractiveness and magnitude of the spread effect as a disconfirmation of dissonance theory. However, the monoticity assumptions of dissonance theory (which include the assumption, called into question recently by Haruki Sakai, 1999, that dissonance is a monotonic increasing function of the ratio of dissonant to consonant cognitions) are insufficient to yield the Brehm and Cohen prediction. Rather, those assumptions imply that, with relative attractiveness held constant, an increase in absolute attractiveness may lead to an increase, a decrease, or no change in dissonance (and the magnitude of the spread effect), depending on the details of the changes in number of positive and negative features of the chosen and rejected alternatives that yield the increase in absolute attractiveness. Because Greenwald was unaware of the dependence of the direction of change in dissonance on the aforementioned details, he didn't assess differences in positive and negative features separately, but only overall differences in attractiveness. We thus have no way of knowing *what* dissonance theory predicts for his data. Which leads us to the next point.

*The mistaken impression that your verbally stated assumptions are sufficient to account for the phenomena you're investigating may lead you to miss some fascinating actual implications of those assumptions and/or fail to collect data on variables that are crucial to knowing what results will be supportive of your assumptions* To take another gender-difference example, Hunt (1974; cited in Baron & Byrne, 1981) reported data purporting to show that, during one recent decade, about 90 percent of men versus only 40 percent of women engaged in premarital sex. Several studies have also reported that a higher percentage of men than of women engage in extramarital sex. These findings, unlike the claimed gender difference in number of partners discussed earlier, could logically hold in a population. However, if rates of premarital (heterosexual) sex are to be markedly higher for men than women, and ditto for extramarital sex, there must be a lot more divorced/widowed women coupling with never-married men than divorced/widowed men involved with never-married women. Had Hunt realized that his data contradicted the popular notion of "dirty old men" preying on single women he might have been motivated to probe more deeply (e.g., gathering data on the ages of the partners in premarital and extramarital sex) so as to tell if this reversal of myth actually holds or if the data instead reflect differential reporting biases for the two genders.

*Further, relying on the verbal-intuitive approach to generating your research hypotheses forfeits the positive benefits of the use of formal models* For instance, a research question posed at the University of New Mexico simply could not be answered meaningfully without the aid of a bit of algebraic modeling. One question was whether there is something inherently different about what groups see as fair ways of sharing losses as compared to the sharing of positive outcomes. The obvious test of this hypothesis would be to compare the allocation schemes groups adopt in a condition in which net outcome for the group is, say, +$80 to one in which net outcome is −$80. However, $80 is not only different from −$80 in sign but is also $160 more than −$80, and there is strong prior evidence that, for positive group outcome and with inputs (individual contributions to the group effort) held constant, the "rate of exchange" (the amount of additional outcome one is entitled to per dollar of additional contribution to the group) increases very nearly linearly as total group outcome increases. Our research hypothesis that the rate of exchange in a negative-group-outcome condition is higher than would be anticipated based on linear projection from the positive-sum-of-outcome conditions (because subjects give less weight to Adams' ratio formula in the negative-outcome condition, where it requires that the partners who contribute most suffer the greatest loss) can thus be expressed as a contrast among the mean rates of exchange in conditions differing only in total group outcome by (a) leaving the population means for those conditions as unknowns; (b) solving for the slope and intercept of the best-fitting straight line relating the population means for the positive-total-outcome conditions to the numerical magnitudes of those total outcomes; (c) "plugging in" the total group outcome for the negative-outcome condition to obtain the expected value of the rate of exchange in that condition if it is indeed governed by the same process, with the same weights, as are the positive-outcome conditions; (d) writing the algebraic statement that the actual population mean rate of exchange in the negative-outcome condition is higher than its expected, linear-projection value; and then (e) applying a bit of high school algebra to this statement to get it into the form, $\sum c_j \mu_j > 0$, which can then be tested as a standard contrast among the corresponding sample means. For instance, in an experiment involving total group outcomes of −$40, $40, $80, and $120, the contrast that tests this research hypothesis is $6\mu_{-40} - 11\mu_{40} - 2\mu_{80} + 7\mu_{120}$. Although this example may seem (and is) a rather involved, multistep path from conceptual to research hypothesis, it involves no mathematical skills beyond familiarity with the formulae for bivariate regression and a modicum of high school algebra.

I must admit that when I accepted the position of Director of Research at ASRT after more than 32 years in an academic department I anticipated little call for algebraic modeling in the primarily descriptive, just-the-facts survey research that the society most needs. I've found instead that situations constantly arise where the willingness (just about anyone reading this chapter has the ability) to put a problem into algebraic terms comes in very handy.

Yes, the means computed in a research report I was asked to critique took into account the fact that equal numbers of RTs were sampled from each state, regardless of the total number of RTs who practice there, but they weren't adjusted for the fact that additional large samples were obtained from each of 10 large metropolitan areas. How can we estimate the proportion of RTs in the affected states who work in, versus outside of, the oversampled metropolitan area, given that some of the RTs who report working in the metro area were a part of the random sample of all RTs in the state whereas other RTs were a part of the "special" sample restricted to the metro area? By solving a small set of simultaneous equations.

Yes, RTs who have used a new technology are more favorable towards that technology than RTs who have not yet used it – but is this because RTs become more favorable after being exposed to the technology, or because those RTs who had a favorable opinion before the technology "came in the door" lobbied for and got it, whereas those RTs who had a preexisting negative opinion lobbied against it successfully? Fortunately the questionnaire asked current users how much influence they had had in the decision to adopt the technology. A bit of algebra showed that, if the difference in favorability were entirely due to self-selection (and thus to preexisting attitudes, rather than to any postadoption change in attitudes), the percentage of noninfluential users who favor the technology should be closer to the percentage of nonusers (influential or not, because the question wasn't asked of nonusers) than to the percentage of influential users who favor it. Instead, the reverse was true, to a statistically significant degree.

An unpublished study of Internet usage by RTs conducted a few years ago asked respondents to rank order (in terms of importance) about 15 different reasons for getting on the Internet, omitting any that didn't apply to them at all. The table of results included the number of respondents assigning any number (rank) to a given reason, and the mean rank assigned by those respondents who assigned it a rank. Is there any way to compute from those two figures the mean rank a given reason would have achieved if we had, for each respondent, assigned all nonranked reasons the average of the unused rank orders? That's my next miniproject.

## Data analysis soap boxes

I've devoted about half of my teaching effort over the years to statistics courses at all levels, so it's hardly surprising that many of the points that I feel need emphasizing in discussions of research methods have to do with the analysis of the resulting data. I've been able to use the "soap boxes" provided by a couple of textbooks (Harris, 1994, 2001) to present more detailed arguments for these points than I have space for in this chapter, so I'll confine the present presentation to a recitation of the points with a minimum of supporting arguments.

*The role of statistical inference*  Null hypothesis significance testing (NHST) has had a lot of "bad press" in recent years, to the extent that an APA committee was formed to consider, among other aspects of data analysis, the proposition that NHSTs should be banned from APA journals. Harlow, Mulaik, and Steiger (1997) provide a comprehensive collection of position papers on both sides of the issue. My own "take" on the controversy is that most of the misuses of significance testing come from forgetting the straw-man character of the null hypothesis. There are no true null hypotheses (e.g., no two population means that are identical to 20 or 30 decimal places and no pair of real variables whose population correlation is exactly 0.00000 . . . ) except by construction (as in Monte Carlo studies in which random samples are drawn from artificial populations). We test the null hypothesis only because, if we can't rule out an effect size of zero, our confidence interval around the true population effect will include both positive and negative values, that is, we won't be able to say with sufficient confidence whether the population effect is positive or negative. NHST is thus *not* designed to tell us whether or not $H_0$ is true (we know a priori that it is not), but to tell us whether we have amassed sufficient evidence to be confident that the *sign* or *direction* of the population effect we're examining matches the sign or direction of that effect in our sample. Every significance test should therefore have *three* possible outcomes (not the two allowed for in most treatments of the logic of hypothesis testing): we conclude that the population effect is positive (based on a statistically significant positive sample effect), that the population effect is negative (statistically significant negative sample effect), or that we don't have enough evidence to be confident of the sign of the population effect (as indicated by a statistically nonsignificant sample effect).

Unfortunately the standard treatment of NHSTs as leading to only two possible conclusions (that the population effect is nonzero or that it might be zero in the case of two-tailed tests, that the population effect has the sign we predicted for it or that it might be zero or opposite to prediction in the case of one-tailed tests) forces the users who take two-valued logic seriously and who wish to be able to come to a conclusion about the sign of the effect they are testing to employ a one-tailed test and therefore abandon scientific method by declaring their hypothesis about the sign of the effect nondisconfirmable, no matter how strong the evidence against it.

*Consistency of overall follow-up tests*  The preceding discussion of NHST implicitly focused on single-degree-of-freedom tests involving a single correlation or the difference between a single pair of means. However, if the goal of NHST is to specify the sign or direction (in the population) of such single-*df* effects, what is the purpose of multiple-*df* tests such as the traditional overall *F*-ratio in analysis of variance (ANOVA)? It is to save us a large amount of possible wasted effort by telling us whether there are any statistically significant single-*df* effects to be found imbedded in the large (often infinite) number of possible comparisons among our means or correlations among our various measures. For instance, the traditional overall *F*-ratio is logically and algebraically equivalent to a test of the largest $F_{contr}$ obtainable for any contrast among our $k$ independent means (i.e., any test of $H_0$: $\Sigma c_j\mu_j > 0$ for any set of $c_j$s that sum to zero) when that largest possible contrast is tested against the Scheffé post hoc critical value. Thus, the overall $F$-ratio is statistically significant if and only if at least one contrast among our means is statistically significant by the Scheffé criterion and vice versa.

No such relation holds, however, between the overall $F$-ratio and the much more common follow up to a significant overall $F$, namely tests (using, e.g., the Tukey HSD cricital value) of only *pairwise* comparisons among our means. A researcher can have a statistically significant overall $F$ and yet no pair of means that are significantly different, or pairs of means that are statistically significant by the Tukey HSD critical value (which controls experimentwise alpha at the specified level for all $k(k-1)/2$ pairwise comparisons) and yet a nonsignificant overall $F$. If you are interested only in pairwise comparisons, then, you should begin your analysis with the Studentized range test (essentially a Tukey HSD test of the difference between the smallest and the largest sample means); and if you're interested only in the direction in which each of $k-1$ experimental conditions differ from a single control group, Dunnett's test applied to the largest such sample difference is the appropriate overall test with which to begin your analysis.

*The interpretation of multivariate analyses*  Briefly, a "truly" or "fully" multivariate analysis determines that linear combination or combination(s) of a set (or sets) of variables that maximizes the univariate statistic obtained when the linear combination is treated as a new variable in its own right and "subjected to" the univariate analysis. Thus, for instance, multiple regression finds that linear combination of a set of predictor variables that has the highest squared correlation with the outcome variable of any such linear combination. And multivariate analysis of variance finds that linear combination of a set of dependent variables that, when computed as a single score for each participant and treated as a new dependent variable in a standard, univariate ANOVA of differences among the means of your $k$ groups, yields a larger overall $F$ ratio than any other linear combination of the outcome variables.

The significance test for the deliberately maximized univariate statistic (e.g., multiple $R^2$, the squared multiple correlation between $Y$ and the *regression variate*, or Roy's GCR statistic, which is a monotonic transformation of the $F$ ratio for differences among the means on the *discriminant function*) must of course use a larger critical value than you would use if you were testing a single predictor or a single dependent variable, and even a larger critical value than the Bonferroni-adjusted critical value (the univariate critical value computed for an alpha equal to desired experimentwise alpha, divided by the number of univariate tests you would consider conducting) you would employ if you were to carry out a separate univariate analysis on each of the single variables in the set. (We can refer to this latter procedure as *multiple univariate analyses*.)

Clearly, then, any advantage of the fully multivariate analysis over multiple univariate analyses is lost (as is, indeed, any reason for carrying out the fully multivariate analysis at all) if your use of the multivariate technique is confined to carrying out the overall test, with follow-up tests and interpretations based on a series of univariate analyses on single variables. (This is, however, the most often recommended and the most often used approach to multivariate analysis of variance – an overall, multivariate test followed – if the overall test is statistically significant – by a univariate ANOVA on each dependent variable, usually without any adjustment of the alphas for these univariate tests.) If your interest is solely in how each variable in the set performs when used by itself, you will always have more powerful tests of the univariate "performance measures" if you skip the overall multivariate test and instead go straight to the univariate tests with Bonferroni-adjusted alphas. However, of course, doing so will forgo the possibility of identifying some linear combination of the variables (e.g., a particular pattern of scores on the various predictors) that far outperforms any single variable. (See Harris 2001, chapter 1 for a number of examples of such "multivariate gain.")

As you've no doubt noticed, this point is a straightforward extension of the earlier point (which was itself a rip-off of S. N. Roy's *union-intersection principle*) that researchers should match their overall test to the specific, single-*df* comparisons that are – or should be – the ultimate goal of your analyses. (Multivariate analysis of variance may seem like an exception, in that the discriminant function maximizes a multiple-*df* overall $F$ ratio. However, that shouldn't be the stopping point of the analyis. Rather, the researcher should then proceed to test particular contrasts among the means on the discriminant function or, better still, on simplified, less high-performance but more readily interpretable versions of the discriminant function. (See Harris, 2001, chapter 4, for details.)

*Univariate vs. multivariate approach to repeated-measure designs* There is a very large cottage industry in the production of methodological papers on the issue of whether and under what conditions the researcher should use the univariate versus the multivariate approach to analyzing a repeated-measures design. Invoking the principle that the researcher's overall test should be tailored to the specific comparisons that are your ultimate goal allows us to cut through this Gordian knot and come up with a clear answer: with very few exceptions, always use the multivariate approach.

Briefly, the univariate approach involves testing each contrast among the levels of your within-subjects factor against a common pooled error term, namely the mean square (MS) for the interaction between subjects and the within-subjects factor ($MS_{SxW}$ – often disguised in computer output under the label, $MS_{residual}$). The corresponding overall test is based on the maximum possible value that $F_{contr}$ achieves for any choice of contrast coefficients, namely $(p - 1)$ times $MS_W/MS_{SxW}$.

The multivariate approach, on the other hand, consists of testing each contrast among the levels of W against its variance across subjects – in essence, computing a score for each participant on the contrast (possible in a within-subjects design because each subject provides a score at each level of W) and then carrying out a single-sample $t$ test of the null hypothesis that the population mean score on the contrast is zero. Computationally, $F_{contr}$ under the multivariate approach (which is the default approach in SPSS and most other statistical packages nowadays) is computed as $SS_{contr}/$(normalized variance of this particular contrast), whereas the univariate approach computes it as $SS_{contr}/MS_{SxW}$. Moreover, $MS_{SxW}$ equals the average of the normalized variances of any set of mutually orthogonal contrasts, so it's clear that the univariate approach is strictly valid if and only if all contrasts have identical normalized variance – that is, all contrasts are equally consistent from subject to subject – whence comes the "sphericity test" reported by most statistical packages when performing a repeated-measures analysis.

The large majority of all papers on the univariate/multivariate approach issue have focused on the overall test. It is by now well known that the univariate approach's overall test is positively biased – often strongly so – whereas the multivariate approach's overall test is unbiased (provided that the usual normality and homogeneity of variance assumptions are met by each dependent variable and each linear combination thereof), yielding rejection of the overall null hypothesis about as often as the alpha level of the test says it should. A great deal of effort has been expended (successfully) in finding ways to "patch up" the univariate approach's overall test (by multiplying its numerator and denominator degrees of freedom by a fraction that shrinks as the normalized variances of different contrasts become more unequal) so as to yield about the right actual alpha level. (That's where the epsilon measures also reported by most statistical packages come into play.)

They shouldn't have bothered. The proper focus should be on tests of single-*df* contrasts among the levels of W. When not all of these contrasts have the same normalized variance (normalization consisting of using contrast coefficients whose squares sum to 1.0, so that we can meaningfully compare consistency of different variances from subject to subject), $MS_{SxW}$ will underestimate the variances of some contrasts and overestimate the variances of others, so that the resulting $F_{contr}$s will be (often grossly) overestimates of the true reliability of some contrasts and underestimates of others. "Shrinking" the degrees of freedom for all contrasts thus makes the discrepancy between nominal and actual alphas even worse for about half of the contrasts in any given set of orthogonal contrasts.

We have strong reasons for expecting the variances of different contrasts to be quite different in most situations. For instance, where the levels of W represent performance over trials, we expect the correlation between performance on trials 2 and 3 to be much higher than the correlation between performance on trials 3 and 20, and thus the variability of the trial 20–trial 3 difference to be much higher than the variability of the trial 3–trial 2 difference. And where most participants' profiles of scores across conditions have a common general shape but with highly variable parameters (e.g., linear but with great individual differences in slopes, as in most studies of schemes for allocating group outcomes equitably), the variance of scores on the contrast that taps the relevant pattern can be and often is hundreds of times higher than the variances of contrasts orthogonal to that pattern. Further, Monte Carlo studies have shown that degrees of departure from the sphericity assumption that are much too small to be detected by the available significance tests can nonetheless lead to severe inflation and deflation of the actual alphas for different contrasts.

Most importantly, the univariate approach's overall test, patched up or not, is a very poor guide to whether or not any contrasts among the levels of the within-subjects factor are statistically significant when tested correctly – that is, against their own variance across subjects. You can have a statistically significant univariate overall test but no statistically significant contrast or vice versa. The sometimes recommended compromise of employing a patched-up (epsilon-adjusted) univariate-approach overall test, followed by multivariate-approach tests of specific contrasts is thus useless – especially so if statistical significance of the univariate overall test is made a condition for proceeding to the tests of specific contrasts.

In other words, take what is very likely the default option in your statistical package and always use the multivariate approach to analyze your repeated-measures results.

## Whither Hence?

If you're an experienced researcher who just can't resist reading any and every discussion of research methods, curl up with any of the references with which you aren't already familiar. If you're a true novice coming to this Handbook and this chapter "honestly," curl up with a good general treatment of research methods (e.g., Dooley, 2001). If you're especially interested in experimental methods (and by now you of course know that this doesn't mean "untried and unproven" but instead refers to a combination of manipulation of and random assignment to the levels of one or more independent variables), Aronson, Brewer, and Carlsmith's (1985) treatment is a great starting place for further exploration.

## References

American Society of Radiologic Technologists (2002). *Environmental scan of the radiographer's work-place: Technologist vs. administrator perspectives, 2001.* Available at <http://www.radsciresearch.org/research/index.asp>.

Aronson, F., Brewer, M., & Carlsmith, J. M. (1985). *Experimentation in social psychology.* In G. Lindzey and E. Aronson (eds.), *Handbook of social psychology,* vol. 1 (3rd edn.) (pp. 441–86). New York: Random House.

Atkinson, R. C., Bower, G. H., & Crothers, E. J. (1965). *An introduction to mathematical learning theory.* New York: Wiley.

Bales, R. F., & Cohen, S. P., with Williamson, S. A. (1979). *SYMLOG : A system for the multiple level observation of groups.* New York: Free Press.

Baron, R. A., & Byrne, D. (1981). *Social psychology: Understanding human interaction* (3rd edn.) Boston: Allyn & Bacon.

Benjamin, K. (2002). *Regression models for time series analysis.* New York: Wiley.

Berscheid, E., Dion, K., Walster, E., et al. (1971). Physical attractiveness and dating choice: A test of the matching hypothesis. *Journal of Experimental Social Psychology, 7,* 173–89.

Campbell, D. T., Stanley, J. C., & Gage, N. L. (1981). *Experimental and quasi-experimental designs for research.* Boston: Houghton Mifflin.

Dillman, D. A. (2000). *Mail and internet surveys: The tailored design method* (2nd edn.) New York: Wiley.

Dooley, D. (2001). *Social research methods* (4th edn.) Upper Saddle River, NJ: Prentice-Hall.

Gallo, P. S., Jr. (1966). Effects of increased incentives upon the use of threat in bargaining. *Journal of Personality & Social Psychology, 4,* 14–20.

Gerard, H. B. (1964). Conformity and commitment to the group. *Journal of Abnormal & Social Psychology, 68,* 209–11.

Glass, G. V., McGaw, B., & Smith, M. L. (1981). *Meta-analysis in social research.* Thousand Oaks, CA: Sage. (Out of print, but available through Books on Demand <http://wwwlib.umi.com/bod>.)

Gollob, H. F. (1968). Confounding of sources of variation in factor-analytic techniques. *Psychological Bulletin 70*, 330–44.

Greenwald, H. J. (1969). Dissonance and relative versus absolute attractiveness. *Journal of Personality and Social Psychology, 11*, 328–33.

Grove, W. M., & Meehl, P. E. (1996). Comparative efficiency of informal (subjective, impressionistic) and formal (mechanical, algorithmic) prediction procedures: The clinical-statistical controversy. *Psychology, Public Policy, & Law, 2*, 293–323.

Haire, M. (1950). Projective techniques in marketing research. *Journal of Marketing, 14*, 649–56.

Harlow, L., Mulaik, S., & Steiger, J. (1997). *What if there were no significance tests?* Mahwah, NJ: Lawrence Erlbaum Associates.

Harris, R. J. (1967). *Stimulus sampling models of post-decision dissonance phenomena.* (Doctoral dissertation, Stanford University.) Abstract published in *Dissertation Abstracts 29* (1968): 674-A. Ann Arbor, Michigan: University Microfilms. ProQuest order # AAT 6811304.

Harris, R. J. (1976). The uncertain connection between verbal theories and research hypotheses in social psychology. *Journal of Experimental Social Psychology 12*, 210–19.

Harris, R. J. (1994). *An analysis of variance primer.* Itasca, IL: F. E. Peacock.

Harris, R. J. (2001). *A Primer of Multivariate Statistics* (3rd edn.) Mahwah, NJ: Erlbaum.

Hintzman, D. L. (1991). Why are formal models useful in psychology? In W. E. Hockley & S. Lewandowsky (eds.), *Relating theory and data: Essays on human memory in honor of Bennet B. Murdock* (pp. 39–56). Mahwah, NJ: Erlbaum.

Hofling, C. K., Brotzman, E., Dalrymple, S., Graves, N., & Bierce, C. (1966). An experimental study of nurse–physician relations. *Journal of Nervous and Mental Disease, 143*, 171–80.

Huynh, H., & Feldt, L. S. (1970). Conditions under which mean square ratios in repeated measurement designs have exact *F*-distributions. *Journal of the American Statistical Association, 65*, 1582–9.

James, L. R., Mulaik, S. A., & Brett, J. M. (1982). *Causal analysis: Assumption, models, and data.* Beverly Hills, CA: Sage.

Kaiser, H. F. (1960). Directional statistical decisions. *Psychological Review, 67*, 160–7.

Kiesler, C. A. & Kiesler, S. B. (1968). *Conformity.* Reading, MA: Addison-Wesley.

Lehtonen, R., & Pahkinen, E. J. (1995). *Practical methods for design and analysis of complex surveys.* New York: Wiley.

Meehl, P. E. (1954). *Clinical versus statistical prediction: A theoretical analysis and a review of the evidence.* Northvale, NJ: Jason Aronson, Inc.

Milgram, S. (1963). Behavioral study of obedience. *Journal of Abnormal & Social Psychology, 67*, 371–8.

Miller, D. C. (1991). *Handbook of research design and social measurement* (5th edn.). Newbury Park, CA: Sage.

Robinson, J. P., Rusk, J. G., & Head, K. B. (1968). *Measures of political attitudes.* Ann Arbor: University of Michigan Press.

Robinson, J. P., Shaver, P. R., & Wrightsman, L. S. (1991). *Measures of personality and social psychological attitudes.* Ann Arbor: University of Michigan Press.

Sakai, H. (1999). A multiplicative power-function model of cognitive dissonance: Toward an integrated theory of cognition, emotion, and behavior after Leon Festinger. In E. Harmon-Jones & J. Mills (eds.), *Cognitive dissonance: Progress on a pivotal theory in social psychology* (pp. 267–94). Washington, DC: American Psychological Association.

Simonton, D. K. (1980). Land battles, generals, and armies: Individual and situational determinants of victory and casualties. *Journal of Personality & Social Psychology, 38*, 110–19.

Simonton, D. K. (1984). Leader age and national condition: A longitudinal analysis of 25 European monarchs. *Social Behavior & Personality, 12*, 111–14.

Webb, E. J., Campbell, D. T., Schwartz, R. D. D., Sechrest, L., & Grove, J. B. (1981). *Nonreactive measures in the social sciences* (2nd edn.). Boston, MA: Houghton Mifflin.

Wickens, Thomas D. (1982). *Models for behavior: Stochastic processes in psychology.* San Francisco: W. H. Freeman.

# CHAPTER FOUR

# Traditional Idiographic Approaches: Small-N Research Designs

## Bryan K. Saville and William Buskist

Strolling through the stacks of psychology periodicals in any college or university library creates the distinct impression that there is an awful lot of scientific research going on in psychology these days. That impression is right on the money. Leafing through almost any of these journals leaves the impression that all of psychological research either involves survey research or between-groups designs. That impression is not entirely accurate for it overlooks a rigorous methodology that actually predates survey and between-group research in psychology and is still very much alive today. This kind of research is called small-N research and it is the mainstay for conducting studies in the field of psychology known as behavior analysis.

The small-N approach to research is characterized by in-depth study of a single or relatively few subjects under tightly controlled experimental conditions in which the independent variable(s) is repeatedly manipulated over successive trials or conditions and in which the dependent variable(s) is repeatedly measured. Sometimes small-N research is referred to as "single-subject research," but this designation is a misnomer because, more often than not, such research involves more than one subject. The small-N approach is used in basic research involving both human and nonhuman subjects where the goal is to understand basic behavioral processes, and in applied research in which understanding and changing maladaptive behaviors is the primary goal. In this chapter, we provide a brief history of small-N research, an overview of its core characteristics, and finally, a description of basic small-N designs.

# History of Small-N Experimental Designs

With the emergence of psychology as an independent discipline in the late 1800s, psychologists faced the daunting task of determining how best to go about uncovering the basic psychological processes in which they were interested. Early psychological researchers often borrowed their experimental and measurement methods from physical sciences, such as physiology and chemistry, and tended to employ small numbers of subjects. As Robinson and Foster (1979) noted, "The emphasis was on selecting one or two subjects, arranging some change in the subjects' situations (such as presenting new stimuli or problem-solving situations), and then carefully observing what happened" (p. 29). This approach characterized the first 50 years of experimentation in psychology.

Wilhelm Wundt, typically considered to be the founder of modern psychology, as well as the first proponent of structural psychology, used such an approach to examine the basic structures of the human mind. In general, Wundt asked small numbers of subjects to introspect regarding their feelings in the presence of different stimuli. Similarly, Hermann Ebbinghaus (1885) served as the only subject in his ground-breaking studies of human memory. In an attempt to control for the effects of previously learned material, Ebbinghaus developed the "nonsense syllable" and examined his ability to memorize and retain various combinations of those syllables under a variety of experimental conditions.

Edward L. Thorndike (1911) and Ivan P. Pavlov (1927) adopted similar experimental approaches in their early studies on learning with nonhuman subjects. Thorndike used a small number of cats and measured the time that it took them to escape from a puzzle box. He observed that the amount of time needed to escape followed a negatively accelerated pattern across trials. From these studies, Thorndike formulated the law of effect, a law that has retained its importance in psychology up through the present day. Pavlov, although initially concerned with studying digestion, turned his attention to a process that came to be known as classical or respondent conditioning. Using a small number of dogs as subjects, Pavlov paired a neutral stimulus (e.g., a sound) with a biologically relevant stimulus (e.g., food) and observed that, with repeated pairings, the neutral stimulus came to elicit the same response in the dogs as the biologically relevant stimulus. In short, the small-N approach to psychological experimentation was the dominant form of research methodology employed throughout the early 1900s.

## The ascendancy of large-N research

In the 1920s, though, the emphasis on small-N designs began to give way to another form of research methodology initially used by agricultural researchers. Ushered in by the publication of R. A. Fisher's (1925) *Statistical Methods for Research Workers*, psychologists began to tinker with the large-N (between-group) approach to experimentation. Whereas researchers using small-N methodology focused on changing stimulus conditions and observing differences in the behavior of one or a few subjects, those using large-N methodologies typically divided their subjects into two or more groups and compared the average performances across those groups. To control for potentially confounding variables, the experimenter randomly assigned subjects to either a control group or one or more experimental groups. The behavior of subjects in the experimental group(s) was typically measured twice, once during a pretest and then again after manipulation of the independent variable (IV). Similarly, the behavior of participants in the control group was also measured twice. In contrast, though, there was no manipulation of the IV between pretest and posttest measures for the control subjects. If a difference in behavior between members of the two groups was identified during posttest measures, the experimenter attributed that difference to the IV.

Another disparity between these two approaches was in the use of inferential statistics to identify changes in the dependent variable (DV) caused by manipulations of the IV. In contrast to small-N designs, large-N designs used, among others, the analysis of variance (ANOVA) statistic developed by Fisher to identify potential differences in behavior between control and experimental groups. These powerful statistical methods had a profound influence on the way psychological research was carried out and subsequently led to decreased use of small-N methodologies. In essence, psychological researchers came to believe that a large number of subjects and the use of inferential statistics were necessary to show convincingly the effects of the IV and to assure generalizability of their findings.

## Reemergence of small-N designs

The assumed switch from small-N to large-N designs was substantiated by E. G. Boring (1954). Boring analyzed three volumes – 1916, 1933, and 1951 – of the *Journal of Experimental Psychology* and found that, in 1916, not a single published study utilized large-N designs. In contrast, over 50 percent of the articles published in 1951 employed control groups and inferential statistics. Robinson and Foster (1979) also observed that the number of large-N studies published in two journals (*Psychological Review* and the *Journal of Experimental Psychology*) dramatically increased during the mid-1900s. Whereas the median number of subjects reported in these journals in 1916 was 10, this number had risen to 32 by 1975. Moreover, less than 3 percent of the published articles in these journals in 1975 used five or fewer subjects. Thus, although several well-known psychologists continued to advocate for the use of individual subjects (e.g., Sidman, 1960; Skinner, 1938), it is clear that, during the mid-1900s, the large-N approach became the dominant method of conducting psychological research and has remained so to the present.

However, in the 1960s, some psychologists began to question the utility of the large-N group approach to psychological experimentation. Robinson and Foster (1979) listed two primary reasons for the reappearance of small-N methodology: (a) the continued refinement of small-N designs since the appearance of Fisher's work, and (b) the increased need by psychologists for a means of dealing with a small number of subjects both in laboratory and applied settings. In comparison to the small-N designs used by psychologists in the early 1900s, the small-N designs used by modern-day researchers are considerably more proficient at isolating the impact of the IV. One only need examine methodology textbooks (e.g., Hersen & Barlow, 1976; Johnston & Pennypacker, 1993; Kazdin, 1982; Kratochwill, 1978; Lattal & Perone, 1998; Poling, Methot, & LeSage, 1995; Robinson & Foster, 1979; Sidman, 1960) and journals (e.g., *Journal of the Experimental Analysis of Behavior, Journal of Applied Behavior Analysis, The Psychological Record,* and *The Behavior Analyst*) devoted primarily to small-N designs to realize the relative sophistication of modern small-N designs.

Building on the early recommendations of Skinner (e.g., 1938), basic researchers began to view small-N methodology as a viable means of evaluating both human and nonhuman behavior. For example, psychologists interested in studying the details of responding under different schedules of reinforcement found small-N designs superior to large-N designs for elucidating these particulars (Ferster & Skinner, 1957). In addition, as researchers began to realize the prospect of applying their findings in an attempt to better the human condition, clinicians and other applied practitioners searched for an approach that could be used with a small number of subjects (e.g., Baer, Wolf, & Risley, 1968). Practicing clinicians, for example, seldom use large-N methodology to evaluate the efficacy of a treatment for their clientele. Furthermore, because large-N designs describe the "average subject," many researchers assert that these approaches tend to overlook variability that often emerges across subjects (e.g., Hersen & Barlow, 1976; Sidman, 1960). Consequently, as limitations of the large-N approach to psychological experimentation became better understood and the need for analysis of individual subjects emerged, the use of small-N designs increased.

## Characteristics of Small-N Designs

One way to describe the general characteristics of small-N designs is by comparing them with the typical characteristics of large-N designs. In general, these two approaches differ along five dimensions: (a) number of subjects used, (b) level of the IV experienced by subjects, (c) measurement of the DV, (d) methods of analyzing data, and (e) methods of generalizing the findings to others in the population (see Table 4.1).

### Number of subjects used

With large-N designs, the most common practice is to select 30 or more subjects and then randomly assign them either to the control group or one or more experimental groups. After experimental manipulation of the IV, group averages are calculated and compared statistically to determine whether a significant difference exists between or among groups.

In contrast, small-N designs characteristically employ fewer subjects, based on the idea that careful analysis of individual subjects will lead to a greater understanding of the general psychological principles that operate at the level of the individual. As B. F. Skinner believed, "it is more useful to study one animal for 1,000 hours than to study 1,000 animals for one hour" (Kerlinger & Lee, 2000, p. 547). Following Skinner's

**Table 4.1**    A comparison of small-N and large-N designs

| Characteristic | *Type of Design* | |
| --- | --- | --- |
| | *Small-N* | *Large-N* |
| 1.  Number of subjects used | Small number of subjects (i.e., fewer than 10) | Large number of subjects (i.e., more than 30) |
| 2.  Level of the IV experienced by subjects | All levels of the IV | One level of the IV |
| 3.  Measurement of the DV | Continuous and repeated measurement | Pretest and posttest |
| 4.  Methods of analyzing experimental data | Visual analysis | Statistical analysis |
| 5.  Methods of generalizing findings to others | Direct and systematic replication | Random selection and assignment of subjects |

(1938, 1953) canon, small-N advocates presume that the meticulous analysis of individual subjects allows researchers to identify and understand the variables that engender and maintain various psychological processes to a greater extent than does the measurement and subsequent comparison of group averages, which often do not accurately describe any one individual's behavior (Sidman, 1960). Traditional behavior analytic journals such as the *Journal of the Experimental Analysis of Behavior* and the *Journal of Applied Behavior Analysis* remain devoted to the early ideas championed by Skinner and other small-N adherents, and typically publish studies that employ small numbers of subjects (i.e., fewer than 10).

## Level of the IV experienced by subjects

A second characteristic that differentiates small-N designs from large-N designs is the level of the IV that is experienced by subjects. Because of the emphasis in large-N designs on random assignment of subjects to different experimental conditions, different levels of the IV are typically assigned to each of the different treatment conditions. For example, imagine that a researcher wishes to examine the effects of different styles of music on typing accuracy. The researcher might have one group type while no music is playing (the control group), a second group would type to classical music (Experimental Group 1), and a third group would type to country music (Experimental Group 2). Subsequently, the average number of correctly spelled words would be compared statistically to determine whether there was a significant difference across groups. A significant difference across groups would suggest that the type of music differentially affects typing accuracy.

Conversely, subjects in small-N designs customarily receive all levels of the IV. As such, individual participants would initially engage in a typing task while listening to no music (i.e., baseline). Following this condition, each participant would type to classical music (Condition 1). Next, each participant would experience baseline conditions a second time. Finally, each participant would complete the task while listening to classical music (Condition 2). The number of correctly spelled words by each participant under both baseline conditions would be compared to his or her own performance under Conditions 1 and 2. In addition, individual performances under each of these conditions would be compared to the performances of other participants responding under the same conditions. Thus, in contrast to the large-N approach, which entails intergroup and intragroup comparisons, small-N designs focus on intersubject and intrasubject comparisons. Hence, each participant automatically serves as his or her own baseline or control, and between-subjects variability can effectively be identified and controlled.

## Measurement of the DV

The third difference between large-N and small-N designs concerns measurement of the DV. Large-N designs generally only measure the DV once or twice during the course of a study (e.g., pretest and posttest). The influence of the IV on the DV is typically assessed only *after* all data are collected.

Small-N designs generally entail continuous or repeated measurements of the DV throughout the study. In our previous example, a researcher might alternate the no music condition with the two music conditions, exposing participants to the different conditions several times each, with typing accuracy measured during each condition. Thus, the researcher measures the DV continuously and repeatedly during the study, and a comparison of the effects of the IV could be analyzed across conditions.

Continuous or repeated measurements of the DV in small-N designs are advantageous for two reasons. First, continuous analysis may allow the researcher to identify and control confounding or secondary variables that may be affecting the DV. Controlling the effects of these secondary variables may serve to increase stability in the DV. Second, repeated measurement of the DV allows the researcher the luxury of manipulating the IV at a moment's notice in order to determine whether it, and not some other uncontrolled variable, is producing observed fluctuations in the DV.

## Methods of analyzing data

The fourth characteristic that differentiates large-N from small-N designs resides in the method used for data analysis. Typically, hypothesis testing via statistical analysis is used in large-N comparison group designs. Samples of subjects are randomly assigned to groups, the IV is manipulated, the DV measured, and group means calculated. Further statistical analyses are then run to determine whether observed differences across groups were due to chance or sampling error, or if they were produced by changes in the IV.

Finally, assumptions are made regarding whether similar patterns of responding would be observed in the population from which the samples were chosen.

In contrast, researchers using small-N designs often present data in the form of line graphs. Although statistical analyses have been advocated for use in small-N designs (e.g., Crosbie, 1993, 1999; Kazdin, 1976), visual analysis is typically used to identify whether disparities exist across conditions.

In general, compared to the pretest/posttest measures that are common with large-N designs, visual analysis of continuously measured data allows for the identification of minute-to-minute or session-to-session changes that may not be detected through statistical analysis. For example, in their early work on schedules of reinforcement, Ferster and Skinner (1957) used visual analysis of cumulative records to detect changes in individual response patterns that emerged under various schedules of reinforcement. Whereas statistical analysis would have been able to identify significant changes in the average number of responses across different schedules, visual analysis allowed Ferster and Skinner (1957) to observe the often-drastic differences in individual response patterns that appeared under different schedules of reinforcement.

Consider, for example, the typical patterns of responding in pigeons that emerge under variable-interval (VI) and fixed-interval (FI) schedules of reinforcement (Ferster & Skinner, 1957). Under VI schedules, most pigeons exhibit a steady and moderate rate of responding. In contrast, pigeons responding under an FI schedule emit few responses during the first part of the interreinforcement interval, but steadily increase their rate of responding as the time to reinforcement nears. If the average number of responses under both schedules is used as a comparative benchmark, faulty conclusions regarding the patterns of responding that appear under VI and FI schedules might easily be reached (i.e., responding under VI and FI schedules is similar). Conversely, visual analysis of responding clearly shows that responding under these schedules is different. Visual analysis allowed Ferster and Skinner (1957) to demonstrate that different schedules of reinforcement have different effects on behavior. Although no explicit rules exist for ascertaining significant effects through visual analysis (Sidman, 1960), it is generally accepted that visual analysis of continuously measured data provides a viable and effective alternative to statistical analysis (Johnston & Pennypacker, 1993; Lattal & Perone, 1998).

## Methods of generalizing findings

The final characteristic that distinguishes small-N designs from large-N designs is the way in which collected data allows researchers to generalize their findings. In general, it is believed that the average response emitted by a truly random sample of subjects chosen from the greater population will also be the most frequently observed response emitted by other members of the greater population, who were not explicitly studied. If subjects are randomly selected and assigned to different experimental conditions, comparative statements regarding the generalization of similar psychological principles to the greater population can be made with considerable confidence.

Small-N researchers rely on the *replication* of previously observed findings to generalize their findings to other subjects and settings. Small-N designs involve two types of replication: direct replication and systematic replication (Sidman, 1960). Direct replication entails the exact reproduction of a previous experiment – the same subjects, methodology, manipulation and measurement of variables, and so on. Often, small-N experimental designs include deliberate manipulations that are intended directly to replicate previous experimental conditions. For example, in the common ABAB experimental design, a baseline phase (A) is alternated with a second experimental phase (B) in which the IV is manipulated. Because each subject experiences both baseline and experimental phases twice, this design can be said to include the direct replication of previously observed experimental conditions. If similar results are obtained under the second B condition, then there is increased confidence that manipulation of the IV was, in fact, responsible for changes in the DV. Consequently, this sequence may lead to a better understanding of the behavioral processes operative at the level of the individual in any given situation.

Systematic replication involves the replication of a previous experiment or experimental condition, but one or more parameters of the experiment are systematically manipulated to determine how the DV of interest is affected. For example, in Ferster and Skinner's (1957) early work on schedules of reinforcement, nonhuman subjects (e.g., pigeons and rats) responding under an FI schedule of reinforcement typically emitted a "scalloped" response pattern. Systematic replications with human subjects, however, often failed to obtain similar results. Rather, human subjects characteristically emitted a low constant or high constant rate of responding (see Lowe, 1979). The application of behavior analytic principles in an attempt to solve socially significant problems is also largely based on the systematic replication of experiments initially conducted in the operant laboratory with nonhuman subjects (e.g., Baer, Wolf, & Risley, 1968; Cooper, Heron, & Heward, 1987). Thus, results from previous experiments serve as the baseline condition for subsequent experiments in which one or more variables of interest are manipulated and new cause–effect relations are identified.

Although we have presented the characteristics of small-N research designs by contrasting them with the general characteristics of large-N designs, we must emphasize that these disparate research designs do not necessarily constitute a clear dichotomy in psychological methodology. Rather, these designs may be seen as lying on opposing ends of a continuum, where characteristics of each design may merge if the experimental question requires some combination of small-N and large-N methodology. For example, consider the Martell and Willis (1993) study in which they divided subjects into two groups (a characteristic of large-N designs) and gave either positive or negative feedback about a third group's work performance, which was later viewed on videotape. Both the positive and negative feedback groups, however, observed members of the videotaped group engaging in both effective and ineffective work behaviors (a characteristic of small-N designs). This design allowed Martell and Willis (1993) to determine how a combination of two variables, type of feedback and type of work behavior, affected subjects' subsequent recall about the videotaped work performances.

In addition, recent debate concerning the use of statistical analyses with small-N designs has again surfaced in the psychological literature (e.g., the Fall 1999 issue of *The Behavior Analyst*). Although it is clear that small-N and large-N designs differ along several dimensions, researchers would do well to remember that the nature of their experimental questions ultimately determines which design is best suited for their particular purposes.

## Varieties of Small-N Designs

Similar to large-N designs, small-N designs come in several varieties, depending on the question the researcher is addressing. In this section we will discuss four types of small-N designs: ABA, ABAB, small-N designs with more than one IV, and multiple baseline designs. However, before we offer descriptions of these designs, we briefly review elements common to all types of small-N designs, regardless of their complexity.

### Common features of small-N designs

With a few exceptions, all small-N designs share four important features: continual monitoring of the DV, the inclusion of both baseline and treatment conditions, reversal of these conditions, and the use of stability criteria to determine when these conditions should be changed. It is these features, in addition to the use of a single or a few subjects, which distinguish small-N designs from their large-N counterparts.

*Continual monitoring of the DV* A hallmark of all small-N designs centers on the selection and monitoring of the DV. As Robinson (1981) articulated, the DV used in small-N studies should be objectively measurable, easily emitted over long durations by participants, and be sensitive to fluctuations or changes in the environment. Because small-N investigations typically extend over many days, and sometimes weeks or months, the DV is continually monitored, allowing the researcher to become very familiar with it and the variables of which it may be a function. It is this feature that clearly distinguishes small-N methodology from large-N methodology, which, as noted earlier, typically involves a single manipulation of the IV and a single or a few measurements of the DV.

*Baseline and treatment conditions* All small-N designs have at least two conditions under which participants perform. The condition in which the participant's behavior is measured in the absence of the IV is called the *baseline*. The purpose of this condition is to determine dimensions (i.e., frequency, duration, intensity, and/or latency) of this particular behavior as it occurs naturally. Once a stable measure of this behavior has been obtained, the researcher introduces the IV and records its effects on the behavior of interest. This condition is called the *treatment* condition. In the parlance of small-N researchers, the baseline condition is often referred as "A" and the treatment condition is called "B" (see Figure 4.1). In small-N designs that introduce a second IV, the second treatment condition is denoted as "C." In all small-N designs, the baseline serves as a control condition against which subsequent treatment conditions are compared.

*Reversal* Although there are certain circumstances in which small-N investigators use only a single baseline and a single treatment condition (AB or BA designs), the most

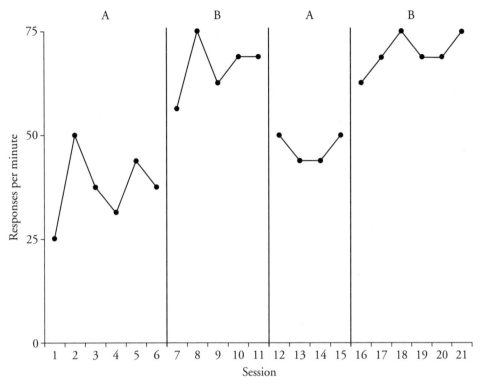

**Figure 4.1** General format of the ABA and ABAB designs.

rigorous small-N designs are those in which the baseline and treatment conditions are repeated or reversed. In essence, reversal designs are those in which replication of the baseline or treatment conditions or both are a built-in feature of the experimental design (e.g., ABA and ABAB designs). The chief advantage of using a reversal design, of course, is to ascertain that the IV is the variable that caused changes in the DV.

For example, suppose that in an ABA design, we find that during the treatment condition the DV increases relative to the first baseline. During the second baseline, the DV remains at those elevated levels. The failure to replicate the levels of the DV observed during the first baseline probably means that some other variable (or combination of variables), is responsible for the change in the DV relative to the first baseline.

*Stability criteria* Researchers determine the length of the baseline and treatment conditions according to specific *stability criteria* that are usually established prior to the start of the experiment. Stability criteria vary depending on the nature of the behavior under study and how it is to be measured. However, the keys to establishing a functionally useful stability criterion are twofold. First, no obvious upward or downward trend in responding should be present. Second, the amount of variability in behavior across the last several sessions (i.e., three or four sessions) of baseline or treatment is restricted to no more than 5 or 10 percent across those sessions. For example, suppose the DV in a small-N study is the emission of a particular behavior, for example, key-pecking in pigeons or talking (off-task) in schoolchildren, then we may adopt a stability criterion of 5 percent or less variability in the number of responses per given unit of time (sessions). If we are interested in some other dimension of behavior, for example, the number of correct responses emitted by participants in matching-to-sample task, then we set our stability criterion accordingly, in this case 5 percent or less variability in the number of errors made per session over five consecutive sessions.

Using stability criteria such as these means that baseline and treatment conditions often have no preset duration, although for practical reasons researchers often limit the number of sessions that participants spend in any one condition. Not all participants move through the study at the same pace. Indeed, unlike participants in large-N designs who all finish the study at about the same time, participants in small-N studies often require different amounts of time to complete the study.

## The ABA design

The most common type of small-N design is the ABA design. An ABA design involves first establishing a baseline (A), introducing the IV or treatment (B), and then discontinuing treatment during a return to baseline (A). The chief advantage to using an ABA design is that if behavior returns to the same or near the same levels as during the first baseline, then the investigator can be fairly certain, although not 100 percent positive, that the IV introduced during the treatment condition is responsible for any changes observed in the behavior during that condition.

As an example, suppose that we wish to develop an analog of human competition in the human operant laboratory. Accordingly, we place a pair of participants on independent fixed-interval 30 second (FI 30 sec) schedules of reinforcement in which the participant earns points later exchangeable for money. Under this schedule, the first response after 30 seconds have elapsed from the beginning of the experimental session, or after the last delivery of points, results in reinforcer delivery. Typically, humans respond at very low rates under this schedule (e.g., Lowe, 1979).

Once we have established a stable baseline, we introduce our IV – the competitive FI schedule. Under this schedule, the formerly independent FI schedules are now linked in such a way that the first participant who satisfies the requirement of the FI 30 sec schedule receives the points. The other person receives no points – only an indication that the points have been awarded to his or her competitor. Under this schedule, we find that both participants show dramatic and sustained increases in responding (Buskist, Barry, Morgan, & Rossi, 1984; Buskist & Morgan, 1987). After participants' behavior stabilizes under this schedule, we replace the competitive FI schedule with the independent FI schedule. Under this second baseline condition, both participants' behavior returns to baseline levels.

In this case, we have established that the competitive FI schedule is the likely cause of the increases observed in our participants' behavior. A powerful means of increasing our confidence that it was, in fact, the competitive FI schedule responsible for increasing subjects' responding is to use an ABAB design.

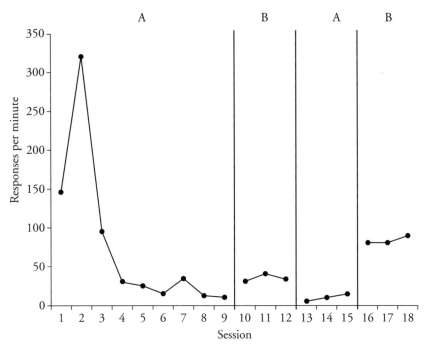

**Figure 4.2** Representative data from a subject who first responded under a regular FI schedule of reinforcement (the first A condition), followed by a competitive FI schedule (the first B condition) and then a repetition of both baseline (the second A condition) and treatment (the second B condition).
*Source*: After Buskist et al. (1984).

## The ABAB design

The only difference between the ABA design and the ABAB design is the addition of a second treatment condition following the second baseline. This addition seems like a small difference, but the payoff in including a second treatment condition is huge. If behavior is similar under both baselines, and increases (or decreases) in like fashion under both treatment conditions, the researcher's confidence in establishing a causal relation between the IV and DV is beyond question.

Figure 4.2 illustrates the results of the "FI competition" study described above but with a second treatment condition. Note that responding is similar during both baselines but increases during both treatment conditions, underscoring the powerful effects of the competitive FI schedule on human behavior.

Thus the chief advantage of the ABAB design over the ABA design is its potential to establish – indeed, guarantee – the existence of a causal relation between the IV and DV. Another advantage of the ABAB design is the opportunity it provides to use different levels of the IV. That is, it is possible to vary the amount or duration of the IV in the second treatment condition, thereby providing potentially useful information about how this manipulation of the IV differentially affects the DV.

The primary disadvantage of the ABAB design, of course, is that it requires more time (and possibly funds) to conduct because of the addition of the second treatment condition. In establishing a sound scientific basis for causality, though, this is a relatively small price to pay.

## Small-N designs with more than one IV

As in large-N designs, it is possible to examine the effects of two or more IVs and their potential interactions in the same study. In small-N designs, this feat is accomplished generally by presenting conditions in the following order: A-B-A-C-A-BC-A, with "C" representing a second IV. Using this sequence, the independent effects of each IV (B and C) on the DV are first determined and then their joint interaction (BC), if any, is examined. Before and after each IV condition – B, C, and BC – participants respond under baseline conditions, providing the customary control conditions already described above for the ABA and ABAB designs.

A unique example of a variation of a small-N design involving two IVs is provided in the research on competition above. In this study, Buskist and Morgan (1987) first placed pairs of participants under independent FI 30 sec reinforcement schedules. The low rate performance typical of humans responding under this schedule emerged. Next, the researchers introduced the competitive FI 30 sec described above, causing participants' responding to increase. Next, Buskist and Morgan introduced the second IV: half of the pairs of participants trained under a differential-reinforcement-of-rate responding (DRL) schedule; the other participants trained under a fixed-ratio (FR) schedule. The DRL participants soon emitted very low rates of responding and the FR subjects soon emitted high rates of behavior. The question these researchers addressed is whether these different kinds of training would differently affect responding under the competitive FI schedule. If so, then DRL subjects should show lower rates of competitive FI responding than they did under the earlier FI competition. In contrast, the FR subjects should show higher rates of responding than they did under the first FI competition. This is exactly what the researchers found (see Figure 4.3).

Although this study involved the manipulation of two IVs (the competitive FI schedule and for half of the participants, the DRL schedule; for the other half, the FR schedule), the researchers opted not to study the interactive effects of these IVs since it would be difficult, if not impossible, to expose subjects simultaneously to both the DRL and FR schedules. Nonetheless, by using this sort of small-N design, these researchers were able to determine that giving participants a particular history of noncompetitive responding influences their behavior in subsequent competitive conditions.

The primary advantage of this type of small-N design is the additional information it may yield about a second IV and its potential interaction with the other IV. Like the ABAB design, its primary drawback is additional time and effort required to run the experiment out to accommodate the sessions required for the additional baseline and treatment conditions.

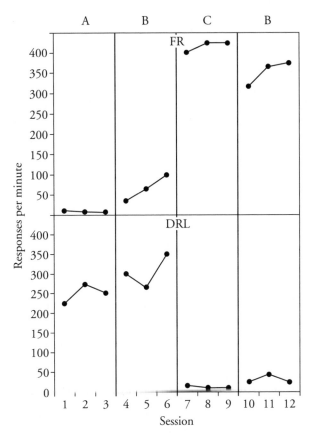

**Figure 4.3** Representative data from the two subjects each of whom responded under different treatment conditions after first being exposed to the original treatment condition (data are from the last three sessions in each condition). Upper panel: this subject first responded under a regular FI schedule followed by a competitive FI schedule. Next, this subject responded under an FR schedule followed by a return to the original competitive FI schedule. Lower panel: this subject first responded under a regular FI schedule followed by a competitive FI schedule. Next, this subject responded under a DRL schedule followed by a return to the competitive FI schedule.
*Source*: After Buskist and Morgan (1987).

## The multiple baseline design

The final type of small-N design that we will review is the multiple baseline design. In this design, more than one baseline is established before any treatment condition is introduced. This design is popular in the applied literature and is particularly useful when the researcher wishes to examine, or monitor, for example, more than one behavior in a particular subject or subjects. The multiple baseline design may also be used across settings or participants.

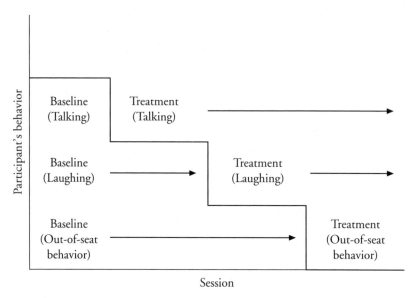

**Figure 4.4**   Schematic diagram of a multiple baseline design across three behaviors.

Consider, for example, a seven-year-old boy who consistently engages in three off-task behaviors: leaving his seat, talking to his neighbors, and laughing out loud for no apparent reason. The appropriate small-N approach to reducing these disruptive behaviors is the *multiple baseline across behaviors* design. We would begin by measuring the frequency of each of these behaviors under baseline conditions. However, the baseline for each behavior would be of progressively longer duration (see Figure 4.4). These baselines are established to determine if changes in any of these behaviors, not just the targeted behavior, are caused by the treatment. It may be that by attempting to change the initial targeted behavior, we discover that either or both of the other behaviors are also affected.

Once all three baselines are well established, we introduce a treatment condition in which only one of the behaviors is targeted for change, let's say, the child's being out of his seat; we arrange for some aversive stimulus – a firm "Return to your seat, Stephen" – to be delivered by the teacher, contingent on the child leaving his seat. However, we continue to measure all three behaviors. Should only the targeted behavior decline as a result of this treatment, then we may safely conclude that that treatment was successful in reducing that behavior but not the others. We then move on to the second behavior and eventually the third, using a different treatment protocol for each.

A primary advantage of the multiple baseline design is that it allows researchers to monitor how manipulation of the IV simultaneously affects a range of behaviors. After all, the behaviors we emit are not likely to be totally independent of one another. We might find in our example, for instance, that a particular treatment may reduce all three behaviors, even though delivery of the IV is contingent only on the child being out of his seat. In such a case, we say that the treatment effect generalized to the other two behaviors – talking and laughing out loud.

The chief disadvantage of the multiple baseline design is that it is generally follows an AB format – no reversal of conditions occurs. Without this feature, our confidence in establishing cause and effect relations is decreased.

## Small-N Designs: Some Final Thoughts

Small-N designs provide a powerful methodology for studying the behavior of individuals and the variables of which it is a function. Unlike large-N designs, data are not aggregated and behavior is not discussed in terms of how the "average" individual performs. Instead, the individual's behavior is discussed per se and without reference to the central tendencies of the group. Behavior is monitored carefully over extended periods, yielding a clear picture of the variables that may be operating at any given time and under any given circumstances to influence the frequency, intensity, duration, or latency of a given behavior. The built-in reversal of conditions characteristic of small-N designs provides the opportunity to replicate both manipulation of the IV and measurement of the DV, providing researchers the opportunity for within-subject control.

Nonetheless, small-N designs are not perfect designs. They generally require more time to conduct than large-N designs. Some critics question the generalizability of the results obtained in small-N studies. After all, how can small-N designs show that what applies to the individual also applies to the group to which that individual may belong? Small-N researchers retort that (a) including large number of subjects does not guarantee generalization of results, and (b) in small-N designs, generalizability occurs through the accumulation of data gathered across studies that systematically replicate one another. That is, generalization of results occurs when several studies, using different subjects behaving under slightly different conditions, yield consistent results.

In the final analysis, the decision whether to use a small-N design or a large-N design depends on the experimental question being addressed. If the question centers on determining how people *tend* to act, think, feel, or perceive in certain situations, regardless of whether the IV can be readily manipulated, then a large-N design may be the better design. If the question centers on how an individual behavior is affected precisely by a particular variable or variables that the researcher can readily manipulate, then a small-N design may be the more appropriate design.

## References

Baer, D. M., Wolf, M. M., & Risley, T. R. (1968). Some current dimensions of applied behavior analysis. *Journal of Applied Behavior Analysis, 1*, 91–7.

Boring, E. G. (1954). The nature and history of experimental control. *American Journal of Psychology, 67*, 573–89.

Buskist, W., Barry A., Morgan, D., & Rossi, M. (1984). Competitive fixed-interval performance in humans: Role of "orienting" instructions. *The Psychological Record, 34*, 241–57.

Buskist, W., & Morgan, D. (1987). Competitive fixed-interval performance in humans. *Journal of the Experimental Analysis of Behavior, 47*, 145–58.

Cooper, J. O., Heron, T. E., & Heward, W. L. (1987). *Applied behavior analysis.* New York: Macmillan.

Crosbie, J. (1993). Interrupted time-series analysis with brief single-subject data. *Journal of Consulting & Clinical Psychology, 61,* 966–74.

Crosbie, J. (1999). Statistical inference in behavior analysis: Useful friend. *The Behavior Analyst, 22,* 105–8.

Ebbinghaus, H. (1885). *Memory: A contribution to experimental psychology.* (H. A. Ruger & C. E. Bussenius, trans.). New York: Dover.

Ferster, C. B., & Skinner, B. F. (1957). *Schedules of reinforcement.* Englewood Cliffs, NJ: Appleton-Century-Crofts.

Fisher, R. A. (1925). *Statistical methods for research workers.* Edinburgh: Oliver & Boyd.

Hersen, M., & Barlow, D. H. (1976). *Single case experimental designs.* New York: Pergamon Press.

Johnston, J. M., & Pennypacker, H. S. (1993). *Strategies and tactics of behavioral research* (2nd edn.). Hillsdale, NJ: Lawrence Erlbaum Associates.

Kazdin, A. E. (1976). Statistical analyses of single-case experimental designs. In M. Hersen & D. H. Barlow (eds.), *Single case experimental designs* (pp. 265–316). New York: Pergamon.

Kazdin, A. E. (1982). *Single-case research designs: Methods for clinical and applied settings.* New York: Oxford University Press.

Kerlinger, F. N., & Lee, H. B. (2000). *Foundations of behavioral research* (4th edn.). New York: Harcourt College Publishers.

Kratochwill, T. R. (ed.) (1978). *Single subject research: Strategies for evaluating change.* New York: Academic Press.

Lattal, K. A., & Perone, M. (eds.) (1998). *Handbook of research methods in human operant behavior.* New York: Plenum Press.

Lowe, C. F. (1979). Determinants of human operant behavior. In M. D. Zeiler & P. Harzem (eds.), *Advances in analysis of behaviour: Vol. 1 Reinforcement and the organization of behaviour* (pp. 159–92). New York: Wiley.

Martell, R. F., & Willis, C. E. (1993). Effects of observers' performance expectations on behavior ratings of work groups: Memory or response bias? *Organizational Behavior and Human Decision Processes, 56,* 91–109.

Pavlov, I. P. (1927). *Conditioned reflexes: An investigation of the physiological activity of the cerebral cortex.* London: Oxford University Press.

Poling, A., Methot, L. L., & LeSage, M. G. (1995). *Fundamentals of behavior analytic research.* New York: Plenum Press.

Robinson, P. W. (1981). *Fundamentals of experimental psychology* (2nd edn.). Englewood Cliffs, NJ: Prentice-Hall.

Robinson, P. W., & Foster, D. F. (1979). *Experimental psychology: A small-N approach.* New York: Harper & Row.

Sidman, M. (1960). *Tactics of scientific research.* New York: Basic Books.

Skinner, B. F. (1938). *The behavior of organisms.* Englewood Cliffs, NJ: Appleton-Century-Crofts.

Skinner, B. F. (1953). *Science and human behavior.* New York: Macmillan.

Thorndike, E. L. (1911). *Animal intelligence: Experimental studies.* New York: Macmillan.

# CHAPTER FIVE

# The Importance of Effect Magnitude

## Roger E. Kirk

This chapter examines the role of measures of *effect magnitude* in psychological research. Measures of effect magnitude fall into one of three categories as shown in Table 5.1. The categories are (a) measures of effect size (typically, standardized mean differences), (b) measures of strength of association, and (c) other measures. The measures are used for three purposes: integrating the results of empirical research studies in meta-analyses, supplementing the information provided by null hypothesis significance tests, and determining whether research results are practically significant. Practical significance is concerned with the usefulness of results. Statistical significance, the focus of null hypothesis significance tests, is concerned with whether results are due to chance or sampling variability. Null hypothesis significance testing was developed between 1915 and 1933 by three men: Ronald A. Fisher (1890–1962), Jerzy Neyman (1894–1981), and Egon S. Pearson (1895–1980). Fisher, who was employed as a statistician at a small agricultural research station 25 miles north of London, was primarily responsible for the new paradigm and for advocating 0.05 as the standard significance level (Lehmann, 1993). Neyman was primarily responsible for introducing confidence intervals in the 1930s – an alternative approach to statistical inference (Cowles, 1989).

For over 70 years, null hypothesis significance testing has been the cornerstone of research in psychology. Cohen (1990) observed that "The fact that Fisher's ideas quickly became *the* basis for statistical inference in the behavioral sciences is not surprising – they were very attractive. They offered a deterministic scheme, mechanical and objective, independent of content, and led to clear-cut yes–no decisions" (p. 1307). In spite of these apparent advantages, null hypothesis significance testing has been surrounded by controversy. The acrimonious exchanges between Fisher and Neyman that began in 1935 set the pattern for the debate that has continued to this day (Box, 1978, p. 263). One of the earliest serious challenges to the logic and usefulness of null hypothesis significance testing appeared in a 1938 article by Joseph Berkson. Since then there has been a crescendo of challenges (Bakan, 1966; Carver, 1978, 1993; Cohen, 1990, 1994;

**Table 5.1** Measures of effect magnitude

| Measures of effect size | Measures of strength of association | Other measures |
|---|---|---|
| Cohen's (1988) $d$, $f$, $g$, $h$, $q$, $w$ | $r$, $r_{pb}$, $r^2$, $r_{pb}^2$, $R$, $R^2$, $\hat{\varepsilon}$, $\hat{\varepsilon}^2$, $\hat{\varepsilon}_{Y|\psi}^2$, $\eta$, $\eta^2$, $\eta_{mult}^2$, $\hat{\eta}_{Y|\psi}^2$, $\phi$, $\phi^2$ | Absolute risk reduction (ARR) |
| $D_{Mdn} = Mdn_1 - Mdn_2$ | Chambers' (1982) $r_e$ | Cliff's (1993) $p$ |
| $D_{\bar{X}} = \bar{X}_1 - \bar{X}_2$ | Cohen's (1988) $f^2$ | Cohen's (1988) $U_1$, $U_2$, $U_3$ |
| Glass's (1976) $g'$ | Contingency coefficient ($C$) | Doksum's (1977) shift function |
| Hedges's (1981) $g$ | Cramér's (1946) $V$ | Dunlap's (1994) Common language effect size for bivariate correlation ($CL_R$) |
| Mahalanobis's $D^2$ | Fisher's (1921) $Z$ | Grissom's (1994) probability of superiority (PS) |
| Rosenthal and Rubin's (1989) $\Pi$ | Friedman's (1968) $r_m$ | Huberty's (1994) $I$ |
| Tang's (1938) $\phi$ | Goodman & Kruskal's (1954) $\lambda$ & $\gamma$ | Logit $d'$ |
| Thompson's (2002) $d*$ | Hays's (1963) $\omega^2$, $\hat{\omega}_{Y|\psi}^2$ $\rho_I$, & $\rho_{IY|\psi}$ | McGraw & Wong's (1992) Common language effect size (CL) |
| Wilcox's (1996) $\hat{\Lambda}_{Mdn,orb}$ | Herzberg's (1969) $R^2$ | Number needed to treat (NNT) |
| Wilcox & Muska's (1999) $\hat{Q}_{.632}$ | Kelley's (1935) $\varepsilon^2$ | Odds ratio ($\hat{\omega}$) |
| | Kendall's (1963) $W$ | Preece's (1983) ratio of success rates |
| | Lord's (1950) $R^2$ | Probit $d'$ |
| | Rosnow, Rosenthal, & Rubin's (2000) $r_{alerting}$, $r_{contrast}$, $r_{effect\ size}$ | Relative risk (RR) |
| | Tatsuoka's (1973) $\hat{\omega}_{mult.c}^2$ | Relative risk reduction (RRR) |
| | Wherry's (1931) $R^2$ | Rosenthal and Rubin's (1982) Binomial effect size display (BESD) |
| | | Rosenthal & Rubin (1994) Counternull value of an effect size ($ES_{counternull}$) |
| | | Wilcox's (1996) Probability of superiority ($\lambda$) |

Falk & Greenbaum, 1995; Hunter, 1997; Meehl, 1967; Rozeboom, 1960; Schmidt, 1996; and Shaver, 1993).

In this chapter I examine some of the criticism of null hypothesis significance testing and describe ways to supplement the paradigm. The fifth edition of the *Publication Manual of the American Psychological Association* (2001) explicitly recognizes that null hypothesis significance tests and *p* values tell only part of the story.

> Neither of the two types of probability value [significance level and *p* value] directly reflects the magnitude of an effect or the strength of a relationship. For the reader to fully understand the importance of your findings, it is almost always necessary to include some index of effect size or strength of relationship in your Results section. . . . The general principle to be followed, however, is to provide the reader not only with information about statistical significance but also with enough information to assess the magnitude of the observed effect or relationship. (APA, 2001, pp. 25–6)

## Three Criticisms of Null Hypothesis Significance Testing

What are the major criticisms of classical null hypothesis significance testing? Three criticisms are frequently mentioned.

### Answering the wrong question

Cohen (1994) and others have criticized null hypothesis significance testing on the grounds that it doesn't tell researchers what they want to know (Berger & Berry, 1988; Carver, 1978; Dawes, Mirels, Gold, & Donahue, 1993; Falk, 1998). To put it another way, null hypothesis significance testing and scientific inference address different questions. In scientific inference, what we want to know is the probability that the null hypothesis ($H_0$) is true given that we have obtained a set of data ($D$); that is, $p(H_0|D)$. What null hypothesis significance testing tells us is the probability of obtaining these data or more extreme data if the null hypothesis is true, $p(D|H_0)$. Unfortunately for researchers, obtaining data for which $p(D|H_0)$ is low does not imply that $p(H_0|D)$ also is low. Falk (1998) pointed out that $p(D|H_0)$ and $p(H_0|D)$ can be equal but only under rare mathematical conditions. Researchers incorrectly reason that if the *p* value associated with a test statistic is suitably small, say less than 0.05, the null hypothesis is probably false. This form of deductive reasoning has been referred to by Falk and Greenbaum (1995) as the "illusion of probabilistic proof by contradiction." The logic underlying this form of reasoning has been examined by Falk and Greenbaum (1995) and Nickerson (2000). Associated with this form of reasoning are the incorrect, widespread beliefs that (a) the *p* value is the probability that the null hypothesis is true, and (b) the complement of the *p* value is the probability that the alternative hypothesis is true. Nickerson (2000) summarized other common misconceptions regarding null hypothesis significance testing including the beliefs that (a) a small $p$ value is indicative of a large treatment effect, (b) the complement of the $p$ value is the probability that a significant result will be found in a replication, (c) statistical significance is indicative of practical significance, (d) failure to reject the null hypothesis is equivalent to demonstrating that it is true, and (e) a small value of $p(D|H_0)$ implies that $p(D|H_1)$ must be large, where $H_1$ denotes the alternative hypothesis.

## *All null hypotheses are false*

A second criticism of null hypothesis significance testing is that it is a trivial exercise. As John Tukey (1991) wrote, "the effects of A and B are always different – in some decimal place – for any A and B. Thus asking 'Are the effects different?' is foolish" (p. 100). More recently, Jones and Tukey reiterated this view.

> For large, finite, treatment populations, a total census is at least conceivable, and we cannot imagine an outcome for which $\mu_A - \mu_B = 0$ when the dependent variable (or any other variable) is measured to an indefinitely large number of decimal places. . . . The population mean difference may be trivially small but will always be positive or negative. (Jones & Tukey, 2000, p. 412)

The view that null hypotheses are never true except those we construct for Monte Carlo tests of statistical procedures is shared by many researchers (Bakan, 1966; Berkson, 1938; Cohen, 1990; Harris, 1994, p. 21; Thompson, 1998). Hence, because type I errors cannot occur, statistically significant results are assured if large enough samples are used. Thompson (1998) captured the essence of this view when he wrote, "Statistical testing becomes a tautological search for enough participants to achieve statistical significance. If we fail to reject, it is only because we've been too lazy to drag in enough participants" (p. 799). It is ironic that a ritualistic adherence to null hypothesis significance testing has led researchers to focus on controlling the type I error that cannot occur because all null hypotheses are false while allowing the type II error that can occur to exceed acceptable levels, often as high as 0.50 to 0.80 (Cohen, 1962, 1969).

Rindskopf (1997) has argued that most researchers are not really interested in the possibility that the population effect is precisely zero, but rather in whether the effect is close enough to zero to be of no interest. This has led some researchers to suggest that instead of testing a point null hypothesis – for example, the effect is zero – researchers should test a range null hypothesis that involves designating a range of values that is considered effectively null (Serlin, 1993; Serlin & Lapsley, 1985, 1993; Yelton & Sechrest, 1986). According to Cortina and Dunlap (1997), the adoption of this strategy would rarely lead to a different outcome than current practice.

Other modifications to null hypothesis significance tests have been suggested. The traditional two-tailed test does not permit a conclusion about the direction of an effect, although most researchers do draw such a conclusion. Bohrer (1979), Harris (1994, 1997), and Kaiser (1960) have suggested a modification that permits conclusions about directionality. The modification, called a *three-outcome test*, consists of replacing the alternative hypothesis, say $H_1 : \mu_1 \neq \mu_2$, with two alternatives: $H_> : \mu_1 > \mu_2$ and $H_< : \mu_1 < \mu_2$. The modified test permits a researcher to conclude that $\mu_1 > \mu_2$ or $\mu_1 < \mu_2$ or, if the null hypothesis is not rejected, that the direction of the difference between $\mu_1$ and $\mu_2$ is indeterminate. Although the three-outcome test was recommended as early as 1960, Hunter (1997) reported that it has not found much acceptance. Recently, Jones and Tukey (2000) proposed a similar three-alternative conclusion procedure that eliminates the null hypothesis. It is too early to determine if their proposal will find favor among researchers.

Traditional one-tailed tests do not permit researchers to conclude that an effect is statistically significant if the direction of the effect is opposite to that predicted even though the test statistic would fall in the rejection region if the prediction were reversed. Braver (1975) and Nosanchuk (1978) described a modification of the alternative hypothesis that circumvents the problem. They pointed out that one- and two-tailed tests are the limiting cases of *split-tail* tests. In a split-tail test, $c \times$ (significance level) is allocated to the predicted tail of the sampling distribution of the test statistic where $c$ is a proportion and $(1 - c) \times$ (significance level) is allocated to the opposite tail. For example, if the alternative hypothesis states that $\mu_1 > \mu_2$, $c = 0.8$, and $\alpha = 0.5$, the upper boundary of the nonrejection region is the 96th percentile of, say, the $t$ distribution and the lower boundary the first percentile. The significance level is $(1 - 0.8)(0.05) + (0.8)(0.05) = 0.01 + 0.04 = 0.05$. In this example, evidence against the research hypothesis must be four times as strong under the null hypothesis before the researcher concludes that $\mu_1 < \mu_2$ than it has to be to conclude that $\mu_1 > \mu_2$. A traditional two-tailed test can be thought of as a special case of a split-tail test in which $c = 0.5$. If $c = 0.5$, the size of the two critical regions is the same. A one tailed test occurs when $c = 1$, resulting in infinite bias $[c/(1 - c)$ arbitrarily large] against concluding that the research hypothesis has placed the rejection region in the wrong tail. The choice of $c$ presumably reflects the researcher's prior subjective probabilities regarding the direction of the population difference. Values of $c > 0.5$, but $< 1$ are reasonable. The choice of $c = 1$ does not leave room for the possibility that the researcher's prediction could be wrong and is avoided in this approach. This modification, like the three-outcomes test has found little acceptance among researchers.

## Making a dichotomous decision from a continuum of uncertainty

A third criticism of null hypothesis significance testing is that by adopting a fixed level of significance, a researcher turns a continuum of uncertainty into a dichotomous reject–do not reject decision (Frick, 1996; Grant, 1962; Rossi, 1997; Wickens, 1998). A $p$ value only slightly larger than the level of significance is treated the same as a much larger $p$ value. Some researchers attempt to blur the reject–do not reject dichotomy with phrases such as "the results approached significance" or "the results were marginally significant." However, studies of the way psychologists interpret $p$ values find a "cliff effect" at 0.05 in which reported confidence in research findings drops perceptibly when $p$ becomes larger than 0.05 (Beauchamp & May, 1964; Rosenthal & Gaito, 1963, 1964). The adoption of 0.05 as the dividing point between significance and nonsignificance is quite arbitrary. The comment by Rosnow and Rosenthal (1989, p. 1277) is pertinent, "surely, God loves the .06 nearly as much as the .05."

## Beyond Null Hypothesis Significance Tests

These criticisms and others have led some researchers to call for a ban on significance testing (Carver, 1978; Hunter, 1997; Schmidt, 1996). Nickerson advocated a less radical position:

> [null hypothesis significance testing] is arguably the most widely used method of analysis of data collected in psychology experiments and has been so for a long time. If it is misunderstood by many of its users in as many ways as its critics claim, this is an embarrassment for the field. A minimal goal for experimental psychology should be to attempt to achieve a better understanding among researchers of the approach, of its strengths and limitations, of the various objections that have been raised against it, and of the assumptions that are necessary to justify specific conclusions that can be drawn from its results. (Nickerson, 2000, pp. 289–90)

It is clear that null hypothesis significance testing is open to criticisms, but then the alternatives are not perfect either.

Researchers want to answer three basic questions from their research (Kirk, 2001): (a) Is an observed effect real or should it be attributed to chance? (b) If the effect is real, how large is it? and (c) Is the effect large enough to be useful? The first question concerning whether chance is a viable explanation for an observed effect is usually addressed with a null hypothesis significance test. A significance test tells the researcher the probability of obtaining the effect or a more extreme effect if the null hypothesis is true. The test doesn't tell the researcher how large the effect is. This question is usually addressed with a descriptive statistic, confidence interval, and measure of effect magnitude. The third question concerning whether an effect is useful or practically significant is more difficult to answer. The answer requires a judgment that is influenced by a variety of considerations including the researcher's value system, societal concerns, assessment of costs and benefits, and so on. One point is evident, statistical significance and practical significance address different questions. In the following sections, I describe the advantages of confidence intervals relative to null hypothesis significance tests, the importance of reporting measures of effect magnitude, and the accumulation of knowledge through meta-analysis.

## Advantages of Confidence Intervals

Confidence intervals and null hypothesis significance tests are two complementary approaches to classical statistical inference. As Tukey pointed out, rejection of a null hypothesis is not very informative. We know in advance that the hypothesis is false. Tukey (1991) stated that rejection of a two-sided null hypothesis simply means that a researcher is able to specify the direction of a difference. Failure to reject means that the researcher is unable to specify the direction. Is this any way to advance psychological knowledge and theory building? I think not. How far would physics have progressed if their researchers had focused on discovering ordinal relationships?

A descriptive statistic and confidence interval provide an estimate of the population parameter and a range of values – the error variation – qualifying that estimate. A $100(1 - \alpha)\%$ confidence interval for, say, $\mu_1 - \mu_2$ contains all of the values for which the null hypothesis, $\mu_1 - \mu_2 = 0$, would not be rejected at $\alpha$ level of significance. Values outside the confidence interval would be rejected. An important advantage of a confidence interval is that it requires the same assumptions and information as a null hypothesis significance test, but the interval provides much more information. Instead of simply knowing the direction of a difference as in a significance test, a confidence interval also provides a range of values within which the population parameter is likely to lie. Furthermore, a descriptive statistic and confidence interval use the same unit of measurement as the data. This facilitates the interpretation of results and makes trivial effects harder to ignore. Confidence intervals and measures of effect magnitude are especially useful in assessing the practical significance of results. However, in spite of these advantages, confidence intervals rarely appear in psychology journals. What we see in the journals is a reject–nonreject decision strategy that doesn't tell researchers what they want to know and a preoccupation with $p$ values that are several steps removed from examining the data. Perhaps the recommendation in the fifth edition of the *Publication Manual of the American Psychological Association* will result in greater use of confidence intervals.

> The reporting of confidence intervals (for estimates of parameters, for functions of parameters such as differences in means, and for effect sizes) can be an extremely effective way of reporting results. Because confidence intervals combine information on location and precision and can often be directly used to infer significance levels, they are, in general, the best reporting strategy. The use of confidence intervals is therefore strongly recommended. (APA, 2001, p. 22)

## Measures of Effect Magnitude

### Effect size

In 1969 Cohen introduced the first effect size measure that was explicitly labeled as such. His measure, denoted by $\delta$, expresses the size of a population contrast of means, say $\psi = \mu_E - \mu_C$, in units of the population standard deviation,

$$\delta = \frac{\psi}{\sigma} = \frac{\mu_E - \mu_C}{\sigma},$$

where $\mu_E$ and $\mu_C$ denote the population means of the experimental and control groups and $\sigma$ denotes the common population standard deviation. The size of the contrast is influenced by the scale of measurement of the means. Cohen divided the contrast by $\sigma$ to rescale the contrast in units of the amount of error variability in the data.

What made Cohen's contribution unique is that he provided guidelines for interpreting the magnitude of $\delta$:

$\delta = 0.2$ is a small effect
$\delta = 0.5$ is a medium effect
$\delta = 0.8$ is a large effect.

According to Cohen (1992), a medium effect of 0.5 is visible to the naked eye of a careful observer. Several surveys have found that 0.5 approximates the average size of observed effects in various fields (Cooper & Findley, 1982; Haase, Waechter, & Solomon, 1982; Sedlmeier & Gigerenzer, 1989). A small effect of 0.2 is noticeably smaller than medium but not so small as to be trivial. A large effect of 0.8 is the same distance above medium as small is below it. These operational definitions turned Cohen's measure of effect size into a much more useful statistic. For the first time, researchers had general guidelines for interpreting the size of treatment effects. The guidelines are particularly useful for researchers working in uncharted territory, for example, assessing the performance of animals in a new apparatus. An effect size is a valuable supplement to the information provided by a $p$ value. A $p$ value of 0.0001 loses its luster if the effect turns out to be trivial. Effect sizes also are useful for comparing and integrating the results of different studies. This application is described later in the section on Cumulating Knowledge through Meta-analysis.

The parameters of Cohen's $\delta$ are rarely known. The sample means of the experimental and control groups are used to estimate $\mu_E$ and $\mu_C$. An estimator of $\sigma$ can be obtained in a number of ways. Under the assumption that $\sigma_E$ and $\sigma_C$ are equal, the sample variances of the experimental and control groups are pooled as follows

$$\hat{\sigma}_{Pooled} = \sqrt{\frac{(n_E - 1)\hat{\sigma}_E^2 + (n_C - 1)\hat{\sigma}_C^2}{(n_E - 1) + (n_C - 1)}}.$$

An estimator of $\delta$ is

$$d = \frac{\bar{Y}_E - \bar{Y}_C}{\hat{\sigma}_{Pooled}},$$

where $\bar{Y}_E$ and $\bar{Y}_C$ denote, respectively, the sample mean of the experimental and control groups and $\hat{\sigma}_{Pooled}$ denotes the pooled estimator of $\sigma$. Gene Glass (1976) in his pioneering work on meta-analysis recommended using the sample standard deviation of the control group, $\hat{\sigma}_C$, to estimate $\sigma$. He reasoned that if there were several experimental groups and a control group, pairwise pooling of the sample standard deviations could result in different values of $\hat{\sigma}_{Pooled}$ for each experimental–control contrast. Hence, the same size difference between experimental and control means would result in different effect sizes when the standard deviations of the experimental groups differed. Glass's estimator of $\sigma$ is

$$g' = \frac{\bar{Y}_{E_j} - \bar{Y}_C}{\hat{\sigma}_C},$$

where $\bar{Y}_{E_j}$ and $\bar{Y}_C$ denote, respectively, the sample means of the $j$th experimental group and control group. Larry Hedges (1981) used a different approach to estimate $\sigma$. He observed that population variances are often homogeneous, in which case the most precise estimate of the population variance is obtained by pooling the $j = 1, \ldots,$ $p$ sample variances. His pooled estimator

$$\hat{\sigma}_{Pooled} = \sqrt{\frac{(n_1 - 1)\hat{\sigma}_1^2 + \ldots + (n_p - 1)\hat{\sigma}_p^2}{(n_1 - 1) + \ldots + (n_p - 1)}} \qquad [1]$$

is identical to the square root of the within-groups mean square in a completely randomized analysis of variance. Hedges' estimator of $\delta$ is

$$g = \frac{\bar{Y}_{E_j} - \bar{Y}_C}{\hat{\sigma}_{Pooled}} \qquad [2]$$

According to Hedges (1981), all three estimators of $\delta - d$, $g'$, and g – are biased. He recommended correcting $g$ for bias as follows,

$$g_c = J(N - 2)g, \qquad [3]$$

where $J(N - 2)$ is the bias correction factor described in Hedges and Olkin (1985, p. 80). The correction factor is approximately

$$J(N - 2) \cong \left(1 - \frac{3}{4N - 9}\right).$$

Hedges (1981) showed that $g_c$ is the unique, uniformly minimum variance-unbiased estimator of $\delta$, and also described an approximate confidence interval for $\delta$:

$$g_c - z_{\alpha/2}\hat{\sigma}(g_c) \leq \delta \leq g_c + z_{\alpha/2}\hat{\sigma}(g_c) \qquad [4]$$

where $z_{\alpha/2}$ denotes the two-tailed critical value that cuts off the upper $\alpha/2$ region of the standard normal distribution and

$$\hat{\sigma}(g_c) = \sqrt{\frac{n_E + n_C}{n_E n_C} + \frac{g_c^2}{2(n_E + n_C)}}.$$

Cumming and Finch (2001) describe procedures for obtaining exact confidence intervals using noncentral sampling distributions. The procedures require the use of special statistical software.

Cohen's $\delta$ has a number of features that contribute to its popularity: (a) it is easy to understand and has a consistent interpretation across different research studies, (b) the sampling distributions of estimators of $\delta$ are well understood, and (c) estimators of $\delta$ can be readily computed from $t$ statistics and $F$ statistics with one degree of freedom that are reported in published articles. The latter feature is particularly attractive to researchers who do meta-analyses.

The correct conceptualization of the denominator of $\delta$ and its computation can be problematic when the treatment is a classification or organismic variable (Grissom & Kim, 2001; Olejnik & Algina, 2000). For experiments with a manipulated treatment and random assignment of participants to $j = 1, \ldots, p$ levels of the treatment, the computation of an effect size such as $g_c$ is relatively straightforward. The denominator of $g_c$ is the square root of the within-groups mean square. This mean square provides an estimate of $\sigma$ that reflects the variability of observations for the full range of the manipulated treatment. If, however, the treatment is an organismic variable such as gender, boys and girls, the square root of the within-groups mean square does not reflect the variability for the full range of the treatment because it is a pooled measure of the variation of boys alone and the variation of girls alone. If there is a gender effect, the within-groups mean square reflects the variation for a partial range of the gender variable. The variation for the full range of the gender variable is given by the total mean square and will be larger than the within-groups mean square. Effect sizes should be comparable across different kinds of treatments and experimental designs. Use of the square root of the total mean square to estimate $\sigma$ in the gender experiment gives an effect size that is comparable to those for treatments that are manipulated. The problem of estimating $\sigma$ is more complicated for multitreatment designs and designs with repeated measures and covariates. Olejnik and Algina (2000) provide guidelines for computing effect sizes for such designs.

There are other problems. The three estimators of $\delta$ assume normality and a common standard deviation. The value of the estimators is greatly affected by heavy-tailed distributions and heterogeneous standard deviations (Wilcox, 1996, p. 157). Considerable research has focused on ways to deal with these problems (Olejnik & Algina, 2000; Kendall, Marss-Garcia, Nath, & Sheldrick, 1999; Kraemer, 1983; Lax, 1985; Wilcox, 1996, 1997). Some solutions attempt to improve the estimation of $\delta$; other solutions call for radically different ways of conceptualizing effect magnitude. In the next subsection, I describe measures that are based on the proportion of variance in the dependent variable that is explained by the variance in the independent variable.

*Strength of association*

Another way to supplement null hypothesis significance tests is to provide a measure of the strength of the association between the independent and dependent variables. Carroll and Nordholm (1975) and Särndal (1974) describe a variety of measures of strength of association. Two popular measures are omega squared, $\omega^2$, for a fixed-effects treatment and the intraclass correlation, $\rho_I$, for a random-effects treatment. A fixed-effects treatment is one in which all treatment levels about which inferences are to be drawn are included in the experiment. A random-effects treatment is one in which the $p$ treatment levels in the experiment are a random sample from a much larger population of $P$ levels. For a completely randomized analysis of variance design, both omega squared and the intraclass correlation are defined as

$$\frac{\sigma_{Treat}^2}{\sigma_{Error}^2 + \sigma_{Treat}^2},$$

where $\sigma_{Treat}^2$ and $\sigma_{Error}^2$ denote, respectively, the treatment and error variance. According to Hays (1963), who introduced omega squared, $\omega^2$ and $\rho_I$ indicate the proportion of the population variance in the dependent variable that is accounted for by specifying the treatment-level classification, and thus are identical in general meaning. The parameters $\sigma_{Treat}^2$ and $\sigma_{Error}^2$ for a completely randomized design are generally unknown, but they can be estimated from sample data. Estimators of $\omega^2$ and $\rho_I$ are

$$\hat{\omega}^2 = \frac{SS_{Treat} - (df_{Treat})MS_{Error}}{SS_{Total} + MS_{Error}}$$

$$\hat{\rho}_I = \frac{MS_{Treat} - MS_{Error}}{MS_{Treat} + (n-1)MS_{Error}},$$

where $SS$ and $MS$ denote, respectively, sum of squares and mean squares, $df_{Treat}$ denotes the degrees of freedom for $SS_{Treat}$, and $n$ is the number of observations in each treatment level. Both omega squared and the intraclass correlation are biased estimators because they are computed as the ratio of unbiased estimators. In general, the ratio of unbiased estimators is itself not an unbiased estimator. Carroll and Nordholm (1975) showed that the degree of bias in $\hat{\omega}^2$ is slight.

Earlier I noted that the usefulness of Cohen's $\delta$ was enhanced when he suggested guidelines for its interpretation. Based on Cohen's (1988, pp. 284–8) classic work, the following guidelines are suggested for interpreting omega squared:

$\omega^2 = 0.010$ is a small association
$\omega^2 = 0.059$ is a medium association
$\omega^2 = 0.138$ or larger is a large association.

Sedlmeier and Gigerenzer (1989) and Cooper and Findley (1982) reported that the typical strength of association in the journals that they examined was around 0.06 – a medium association.

Omega squared and the intraclass correlation, like the measures of effect size, are not without their detractors. One criticism voiced by O'Grady (1982) is that $\hat{\omega}^2$ and $\hat{\rho}_I$ may underestimate the true proportion of explained variance. If, as is generally the case, the dependent variable is not perfectly reliable, measurement error will reduce the proportion of variance that can be explained. It is well known that the absolute value of the product-moment correlation coefficient, $r_{XY}$, cannot exceed $(r_{XX'})^{1/2} (r_{YY'})^{1/2}$, where $r_{XX'}$ and $r_{YY'}$ are the reliabilities of $X$ and $Y$ (Gulliksen, 1950, pp. 22–3). O'Grady (1982) also criticized measures of strength of association on the grounds that their value is affected by the choice and number of treatment levels. In general, the greater the diversity and number of treatment levels, the larger is the strength of association. Levin (1967) observed that omega squared is not very informative when an experiment contains more than two treatment levels. A large value of $\hat{\omega}^2$ simply indicates that the dependent variable for at least one treatment level is substantially different from the other levels. As is true for all omnibus measures, $\hat{\omega}^2$ and $\hat{\rho}_I$ do not pinpoint which treatment level(s) is responsible for a large value.

One way to address the last criticism is to compute omega squared and the intraclass correlation for two-mean contrasts as is typically done with Hedges' $g_c$. This solution is in keeping with the preference of many quantitative psychologists to ask focused one-degree-of-freedom questions of their data (Judd, McClelland, & Culhane, 1995; Rosnow, Rosenthal, & Rubin, 2000) and the recommendation of the *Publication Manual of the American Psychological Association*: "As a general rule, multiple degree-of-freedom effect indicators tend to be less useful than effect indicators that decompose multiple degree-of-freedom tests into meaningful one degree-of-freedom effects – particularly when these are the results that inform the discussion" (APA, 2001, p. 26). The formulas for omega squared and the intraclass correlation can be modified to give the proportion of variance in the dependent variable that is accounted for by the $i$th contrast. The formulas are

$$\hat{\omega}^2_{Y|\psi_i} = \frac{SS\hat{\psi}_i - MS_{Error}}{SS_{Total} + MS_{Error}}$$

$$\hat{\rho}_{IY|\psi_i} = \frac{SS\hat{\psi}_i - MS_{Error}}{SS\hat{\psi}_i + (n-1)MS_{Error}},$$

where $SS\hat{\psi}_i = \hat{\psi}_i^2 / \sum_{j=1}^{p} c_j^2 / n_j$ and the $c_j$s are coefficients that define the contrast (Kirk, 1995, p. 179). These two measures answer focused one-degree-of-freedom questions as opposed to omnibus questions about one's data.

A measure of strength of association that is popular with meta-analysts is the familiar product-moment correlation coefficient, $r$. The square of $r$ called the *coefficient of determination* indicates the sample proportion of variance in the dependent variable that is accounted for by the independent variable. The product-moment correlation and its close relatives can be used with a variety of variables:

| | |
|---|---|
| product-moment correlation | $X$ and $Y$ are continuous and linearly related |
| phi correlation, $\phi$ | $X$ and $Y$ are dichotomous |
| point-biserial correlation, $r_{pb}$ | $X$ is dichotomous, $Y$ is continuous |
| Spearman rank correlation, $r_s$ | $X$ and $Y$ are in rank form. |

The point-biserial correlation coefficient is particularly useful for answering focused questions. The independent variable is coded 0 and 1 to indicate the treatment level to which each observation belongs. Wilcox (1996) provides an excellent critique of this and other potentially useful measures of correlation.

Two categories of effect magnitude have been described thus far: measures of effect size and strength of association. Researchers differ in their preferences for the measures. Fortunately, it is a simple matter to convert from one measure to another. Conversion formulas are shown in Table 5.2. The omega squared and intraclass correlation formulas in the table are for a contrast. Also shown in Table 5.2 are formulas for converting the $t$ statistic into each of the measures of effect magnitude.

## Other measures of effect magnitude

Quantitative psychologists continue to search for ways to supplement the null hypothesis significance test and obtain a better understanding of their data. Most attention has focused on measures of effect size and strength of association. But as Table 5.1 shows, there are many other ways to measure effect magnitude. Some of the statistics in the "Other measures" column of Table 5.1 are radically different from anything described thus far. One such measure for the two-group case is the *probability of superiority*, denoted by PS (Grissom, 1994). PS is the probability that a randomly sampled member of a population given one treatment level will have a score, $Y_1$, that is superior to the score, $Y_2$, of a randomly sampled member of another population given the other treatment level. The computation of PS is straightforward: $PS = U/n_1 n_2$, where $U$ is the Mann–Whitney statistic and $n_1$ and $n_2$ are the two sample sizes. The value of $U$ indicates the number of times that the $n_1$ participants who are given treatment level 1 have scores that outrank those of the $n_2$ participants who are given treatment level 2, assuming no ties or equal allocation of ties. Dividing $U$ by $n_1 n_2$, the number of possible comparisons of the two treatment levels, yields an unbiased estimator of the population $Pr(Y_1 > Y_2)$. According to Grissom (1994), PS does not assume equal variances and is robust to nonnormality.

Another example of a different way of assessing effect magnitude is the odds ratio. It is applicable to the two-group case when the dependent variable has only two outcomes, say, success and failure. The term *odds* is frequently used by those who place bets on the outcomes of sporting events. The odds that an event will occur are given by the ratio of the probability that the event will occur to the probability that the event will not occur. If an event can occur with probability $p$, the odds in favor of the event are $p/(1 - p)$ to 1. For example, suppose an event occurs with probability $^3/_4$, the odds in favor of the event are $(^3/_4)/(1 - ^3/_4) = (^3/_4)/(^1/_4) = 3$ to 1.

The computation of the odds ratio is illustrated using the data in Table 5.3 where participants in experimental and control groups are classified as either a success or a failure. For participants in the experimental group, the odds of success are

$$Odds(\text{Success} | \text{Exp. Grp.}) = \frac{n_{11}/(n_{11} + n_{12})}{n_{12}/(n_{11} + n_{12})} = \frac{n_{11}}{n_{12}} = \frac{42}{8} = 5.2500.$$

For participants in the control group, the odds of success are

**Table 5.2** Conversion formulas for four measures of effect magnitude

| | $t$ | $g$ | $r_{pb}$ | $\hat\omega^2_{Y\mid\psi_i}$ | $\hat\rho_{1Y\mid\psi_i}$ |
|---|---|---|---|---|---|
| $g=$ | $t\sqrt{\dfrac{2}{n}}$ | | $\sqrt{\dfrac{r_{pb}^2\,df\,2n}{n^2(1-r_{pb}^2)}}$ | $\sqrt{\dfrac{2(\hat\omega^2-2n\hat\omega^2-1)}{n(\hat\omega^2-1)}}$ | $\sqrt{\dfrac{2(\hat\rho_1-n\hat\rho_1-1)}{n(\hat\rho_1-1)}}$ |
| $r_{pb}=$ | $\dfrac{t}{\sqrt{t^2+df}}$ | $\sqrt{\dfrac{g^2n^2}{g^2n^2+df\,2n}}$ | | $\sqrt{\dfrac{\hat\omega^2(1-2n)-1}{\hat\omega^2(1-2n)+df(\hat\omega^2-1)-1}}$ | $\sqrt{\dfrac{\hat\rho_1(1-n)-1}{\hat\rho_1(1-n)+df(\hat\rho_1-1)-1}}$ |
| $\hat\omega^2_{Y\mid\psi_i}=$ | $\dfrac{t^2-1}{t^2+2n-1}$ | $\dfrac{ng^2-2}{ng^2+4n-2}$ | $\dfrac{r_{pb}^2(df+1)-1}{r_{pb}^2 df+(1-r_{pb}^2)(2n-1)}$ | | $\dfrac{\hat\rho_1}{2-\hat\rho_1}$ |
| $\hat\rho_{1Y\mid\psi_i}=$ | $\dfrac{t^2-1}{t^2+n-1}$ | $\dfrac{ng^2-2}{ng^2+2n-2}$ | $\dfrac{r_{pb}^2(df+1)-1}{r_{pb}^2 df+(1-r_{pb}^2)(n-1)}$ | $\dfrac{2\hat\omega^2}{\hat\omega^2+1}$ | |

**Table 5.3**  Classification of participants

|  | Success | Failure | Total |
| --- | --- | --- | --- |
| Experimental group | $n_{11} = 42$ | $n_{12} = 8$ | $n_{11} + n_{12} = 50$ |
| Control group | $n_{21} = 28$ | $n_{22} = 22$ | $n_{21} + n_{22} = 50$ |
| Total | $n_{11} + n_{21} = 70$ | $n_{12} + n_{22} = 30$ |  |

$$Odds\,(\text{Success} \mid \text{Control Grp.}) = \frac{n_{21}/(n_{21} + n_{22})}{n_{22}/(n_{21} + n_{22})} = \frac{n_{21}}{n_{22}} = \frac{28}{22} = 1.2727.$$

The ratio of the two odds is the odds ratio, $\hat{\omega}$,

$$\hat{\omega} = \frac{Odds(\text{Success} \mid \text{Exp. Grp.})}{Odds(\text{Success} \mid \text{Control Grp.})} = \frac{n_{11}/n_{12}}{n_{21}/n_{22}} = \frac{n_{11}n_{22}}{n_{12}n_{21}} = 4.1$$

In this example, the odds of success for participants in the experimental group are 4.1 times greater than the odds of success for participants in the control group. When there is no association, the two rows (or two columns) are proportional to each other and $\hat{\omega} = 1$. The more the groups differ, the more $\hat{\omega}$ departs from 1. A value of $\hat{\omega}$ less than 1 indicates reduced odds of success among the experimental participants; a value greater than 1 indicates increased odds of success among the experimental participants. The lower bound for $\hat{\omega}$ is 0 and occurs when $n_{11} = 0$; the upper bound is arbitrarily large, in effect infinite, and occurs when $n_{21} = 0$.

The probability distribution of the odds ratio is positively skewed. In contrast, the probability distribution of the natural log of $\hat{\omega}$, $\ln \hat{\omega}$, is more symmetrical. Hence, when calculating a confidence interval for $\hat{\omega}$, it is customary to work with $\ln \hat{\omega}$. A $100(1 - \alpha)\%$ confidence interval for $\ln \omega$ is given by

$$\ln \hat{\omega} - z_{\alpha/2}\hat{\sigma}_{\ln \hat{\omega}} < \ln \omega < \ln \hat{\omega} + z_{\alpha/2}\hat{\sigma}_{\ln \hat{\omega}}$$

where $z_{\alpha/2}$ denotes the two-tailed critical value that cuts off the upper $\alpha/2$ region of the standard normal distribution and $\hat{\sigma}_{\ln \hat{\omega}}$ denotes the standard error of $\ln \hat{\omega}$ and is given by

$$\hat{\sigma}_{\ln \hat{\omega}} = \sqrt{1/n_{11} + 1/n_{12} + 1/n_{21} + 1/n_{22}}.$$

Once the end points of the confidence interval are found, the values are exponentiated to find the confidence interval for $\omega$. The computation will be illustrated for the data in Table 5.3 where $\hat{\omega} = 4.125$ to three places. A $100(1 - 0.05)\%$ confidence interval for $\ln \omega$ is

1.4171 − 1.96(.04796) < ln $\omega$ < 1.4171 + 1.96(.04796)
0.4771 < ln $\omega$ < 2.3571.

The confidence interval for $\omega$ is

$$e^{0.4771} < \omega < e^{2.3571}$$
$$1.6 < \omega < 10.5$$

We can be 95 percent confident that the odds of success for participants in the experimental group are between 1.6 and 10.5 times greater than the odds of success for participants in the control group. Notice that the interval does not include 1. The odds ratio is widely used in the medical sciences, but less often in psychology. Space limitations preclude an examination of other potentially useful measures of effect magnitude. The reader is referred to the excellent overview by Grissom and Kim (2001).

Before leaving this topic, I want to emphasize that important or useful results do not necessarily require large effect magnitudes. Prentice and Miller (1992) and Spencer (1995) provide examples of how small effect magnitudes can be both theoretically and practically significant. One needs to calibrate the magnitude of an effect by the benefit possibly accrued from that effect. In the next section, I illustrate the role of effect magnitude in the accumulation of knowledge.

## Cumulating Knowledge through Meta-analysis

For far too long, rejecting null hypotheses and obtaining small $p$ values have been the primary goals of many researchers. This overreliance on null hypothesis significance tests has, in effect, placed blinders on researchers. Consider a researcher who believes that a medication will improve the intelligence test performance of Alzheimer patients. He randomly assigns 20 patients to experimental and control groups and administers the medication to the experimental group and a placebo to the control group. In due time he administers an intelligence test to the patients and performs a $t$ test, $t(18) = 2.076$, $p = 0.052$. To his dismay, the $p$ value is larger than 0.05, which means that the null hypothesis cannot be rejected. What's wrong with this typical scenario? The researcher focused on the null hypothesis and $p$ value without asking whether the data supported the scientific hypothesis. Unfortunately, a result that is not statistically significant is interpreted as providing no support for the scientific hypothesis, even though the data are consistent with the hypothesis. Suppose that the mean for the experimental group is 13 IQ points above that for the control group. This information should make any rational researcher think that the data provides some support for the scientific hypothesis. In fact, the best guess that can be made is that the population mean difference is 13 IQ points. A 95 percent confidence interval for the population mean IQ difference indicates that it is likely to be between −0.2 and 26.2. The nonsignificant $t$ test doesn't mean that there is no difference between the groups in IQ; all it means is that the researcher cannot rule out chance or sampling variability as an explanation for the 13-point difference.

Suppose that instead of focusing on statistical significance, the researcher focused on what the data said about the scientific hypothesis. He computed an estimate of Cohen's $\delta$ using formulas [1] − [3] given earlier and obtained $g_c = 0.89$. If the 13-point difference

**Table 5.4**  Meta-analysis statistics for the Alzheimer experiment

|  | $n_E$ | $n_C$ | $g_c$ | $\hat{\sigma}^2(g_c)$ | $1/\hat{\sigma}^2(g_c)$ | $g_c/\hat{\sigma}^2(g_c)$ |
|---|---|---|---|---|---|---|
| Experiment 1 | 10 | 10 | 0.8893 | 0.2198 | 4.5502 | 4.0465 |
| Experiment 2 | 11 | 11 | 0.8245 | 0.1973 | 5.0692 | 4.1795 |
|  |  |  |  |  | 9.6194 | 8.2260 |

is not attributable to chance, it is a large effect. Anyone who has worked with intelligence tests would probably agree that 13 IQ points is a large effect. A 95 percent
confidence interval for the population effect size using formula [4] is from −0.03 to 1.8.
The data provide considerable support for the researcher's scientific hypothesis although
he cannot rule out chance sampling variability as a possible explanation for the difference. Will the results replicate, are they real? There is only one way to find out – do a
replication. Does the medication appear to have promise with Alzheimer patients? I
think so. Notice the difference in our reasoning process when we shift attention from
the *t* test and *p* value to deciding whether the data support our scientific hypothesis and
are practically significant.

The researcher, encouraged by the large effect size, decided to repeat the experiment.
This time 22 Alzheimer patients were available. In the second experiment, the mean of
the experimental group was 12 IQ points above the control group. A 95 percent confidence interval for the population mean difference is 0.5 to 24.5. Because the interval
includes zero, the null hypothesis for the second experiment cannot be rejected at the
0.05 level of significance. The effect size is $g_c = 0.82$; a 95 percent confidence interval for
the effect size is −0.05 to 1.7. To obtain an overall summary of the results of the two
experiments, the researcher performed a meta-analysis. The terms needed for the analysis
are shown in Table 5.4. In this example, the experiments share a common effect size but
have different sample sizes. Following Hedges and Olkin (1985, pp. 112–13), a weighted
mean of the effect sizes is

$$\bar{g}_c = \frac{\sum\limits_{i=1}^{k} g_{c_i}/\hat{\sigma}^2(g_{c_i})}{\sum\limits_{i=1}^{k} 1/\hat{\sigma}^2(g_{c_i})} = \frac{8.2260}{9.6194} = .86$$

with estimated variance $\hat{\sigma}^2(\bar{g}_c) = 1/\sum_{i=1}^{k} 1/\hat{\sigma}^2(g_{c_i}) = 1/9.6194 = 0.1040$. A 95 percent
confidence interval for the common effect size is

$$\bar{g}_c - 1.96(\hat{\sigma}(\bar{g}_c)) < \delta^* < \bar{g}_c + 1.96(\hat{\sigma}(\bar{g}_c))$$
$$0.2 < \delta^* < 1.5.$$

The researcher can be 95 percent confident that the common effect size is greater than
0.2 (a small effect) and less than 1.5 (a large effect). Because the interval does not

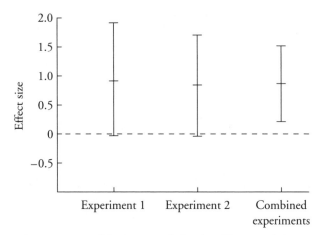

**Figure 5.1**   Ninety-five percent confidence intervals for the effect sizes ($g_c$).

include 0, the null hypothesis can be rejected at the 0.05 level of significance. A graphical summary of the two experiments and the meta-analysis is shown in Figure 5.1. The graph drives home the point that the medication is effective.

Although meta-analysis is typically used as a secondary data analysis strategy, this example shows that it also is a useful primary analysis strategy. It allows researchers to accumulate results over a series of studies to obtain a better evaluation of the scientific hypothesis. It is well known that a single study rarely provides a definitive test of a scientific hypothesis. The outcomes of a series of null hypothesis significance tests also can be accumulated. But the analysis techniques – "vote-counting" of reject–nonreject decisions and synthesis of $p$ values – are much less effective than meta-analysis. Meta-analysis has the added advantage of accumulating results in a manner that focuses on the effects of interest rather than $p$ values.

The Alzheimer example illustrates how measures of effect size, confidence intervals, meta-analysis, and graphs can supplement null hypothesis significance testing. Bayesian analysis is yet another way of supplementing null hypothesis significance testing. For an insightful comparison of this and other approaches, the reader is referred to Howard, Maxwell, and Fleming (2000).

It is time for researchers to avail themselves of the full arsenal of quantitative and qualitative statistical tools that are available. It is evident that the current practice of focusing exclusively on a dichotomous reject–nonreject decision strategy of null hypothesis testing can actually impede scientific progress. I suspect that the continuing appeal of null hypothesis significance testing is that it is considered to be an objective scientific procedure for advancing knowledge. In fact, focusing on $p$ values and rejecting null hypotheses actually distracts us from our real goals: deciding whether data support our scientific hypothesis and are practically significant. The focus of research should be on our scientific hypotheses, what data tell us about the magnitude of effects, the practical significance of effects, and the steady accumulation of knowledge.

# References

American Psychological Association (2001). *Publication Manual of the American Psychological Association* (5th edn.). Washington, DC: American Psychological Association.

Bakan, D. (1966). The test of significance in psychological research. *Psychological Bulletin*, 66, 423–37.

Beauchamp, K. L., & May, R. B. (1964). Replication report: Interpretation of levels of significance by psychological researchers. *Psychological Reports*, 14, 272.

Berger, J. O., & Berry, D. A. (1988). Statistical analysis and the illusion of objectivity. *American Scientist*, 76, 159–65.

Berkson, J. (1938). Some difficulties of interpretation encountered in the application of the chi-square test. *Journal of the American Statistical Association*, 33, 526–42.

Bohrer, R. (1979). Multiple three-decision rules for parametric signs. *Journal of the American Statistical Association*, 74, 432–7.

Box, J. F. (1978). *R. A. Fisher: The life of a scientist.* New York: Wiley.

Braver, S. L. (1975). On splitting the tails unequally: A new perspective on one- versus two-tailed tests. *Educational and Psychological Measurement*, 35, 283–301.

Carroll, R. M., & Nordholm, L. A. (1975). Sampling characteristics of Kelley's $\varepsilon^2$ and Hays' $\hat{\omega}^2$. *Educational and Psychological Measurement*, 35, 541–54.

Carver, R. P. (1978). The case against statistical significance testing. *Harvard Educational Review*, 48, 378–99.

Carver, R. P. (1993). The case against statistical significance testing, revisited. *Journal of Experimental Education*, 61, 287–92.

Chambers, R. C. (1982). Correlation coefficients from 2 × 2 tables and from biserial data. *British Journal of Mathematical and Statistical Psychology*, 35, 216–27.

Cliff, N. (1993). Dominance statistics: Ordinal analyses to answer ordinal questions. *Psychological Bulletin*, 114, 494–509.

Cohen, J. (1962). The statistical power of abnormal-social psychological research: A review. *Journal of Abnormal and Social Psychology*, 65, 145–53.

Cohen, J. (1969). *Statistical power analysis for the behavioral sciences.* New York: Academic Press.

Cohen, J. (1988). *Statistical power analysis for the behavioral sciences* (2nd edn.). Hillsdale, NJ: Lawrence Erlbaum.

Cohen, J. (1990). Things I have learned (so far). *American Psychologist*, 45, 1304–12.

Cohen, J. (1992). A power primer. *Psychological Bulletin*, 112, 115–59.

Cohen, J. (1994). The earth is round ($p < .05$). *American Psychologist*, 49, 997–1003.

Cooper, H., & Findley, M. (1982). Expected effect sizes: Estimates for statistical power analysis in social psychology. *Personality and Social Psychology Bulletin*, 8, 168–73.

Cortina, J. M., & Dunlap, W. P. (1997). On the logic and purpose of significance testing. *Psychological Methods*, 2, 161–72.

Cowles, M. (1989). *Statistics in psychology: An historical perspective.* Hillsdale, NJ: Lawrence Erlbaum.

Cramér, H. (1946). *Mathematical methods of statistics.* Princeton, NJ: Princeton University Press.

Cumming, G., & Finch, S. (2001). A primer on the understanding, use, and calculation of confidence intervals that are based on central and noncentral distributions. *Educational and Psychological Measurement*, 61, 532–74.

Dawes, R. M., Mirels, H. L., Gold, E., & Donahue, E. (1993). Equating inverse probabilities in implicit personality judgments. *Psychological Science*, 4, 396–400.

102    *Kirk*

Doksum, K. A. (1977). Some graphical methods in statistics. A review and some extensions. *Statistica Neerlandica, 31*, 53–68.

Dunlap, W. P. (1994). Generalizing the common language effect size indicator to bivariate normal correlations. *Psychological Bulletin, 116*, 509–11.

Falk, R. (1998). Replication – A step in the right direction. *Theory and Psychology, 8*, 313–21.

Falk, R., & Greenbaum, C. W. (1995). Significance tests die hard: The amazing persistence of a probabilistic misconception. *Theory and Psychology, 5*, 75–98.

Fisher, R. A. (1921). On the "probable error" of a coefficient of correlation deduced from a small sample. *Metron, 1*, 1–32.

Frick, R. W. (1996). The appropriate use of null hypothesis testing. *Psychological Methods, 1*, 379–90.

Friedman, H. (1968). Magnitude of experimental effect and a table for its rapid estimation. *Psychological Bulletin, 70*, 245–51.

Glass, G. V. (1976). Primary, secondary, and meta-analysis of research. *Educational Researcher, 5*, 3–8.

Goodman, L. A., & Kruskal, W. H. (1954). Measures of association for cross classification. *Journal of the American Statistical Association, 49*, 732–64.

Grant, D. A. (1962). Testing the null hypothesis and the strategy and tactics of investigating theoretical models. *Psychological Review, 69*, 54–61.

Grissom, R. J. (1994). Probability of the superior outcome of one treatment over another. *Journal of Applied Psychology, 79*, 314–16.

Grissom, R. J., & Kim, J. J. (2001). Review of assumptions and problems in the appropriate conceptualization of effect size. *Psychological Methods, 6*, 135–46.

Gulliksen, H. (1950). *Theory of mental tests*. New York: Wiley.

Haase, R. F., Waechter, D. M., & Solomon, G. S. (1982). How significant is a significant difference? Average effect size of research in counseling psychology. *Journal of Counseling Psychology, 29*, 58–65.

Harris, R. J. (1994). *ANOVA: An analysis of variance primer*. Itasca, IL: F. E. Peacock.

Harris, R. J. (1997). Reforming significance testing via three-valued logic. In L. L. Harlow, S. A. Mulaik, & J. H. Steiger (eds.), *What if there were no significance tests?* (pp. 145–74). Hillsdale, NJ: Erlbaum.

Hays, W. L. (1963). *Statistics for psychologists*. New York: Holt Rinehart and Winston.

Hedges, L. V. (1981). Distributional theory for Glass's estimator of effect size and related estimators. *Journal of Educational Statistics, 6*, 107–28.

Hedges, L. V., & Olkin, I. (1985). *Statistical methods for meta-analysis*. Orlando, FL: Academic Press.

Herzberg, P. A. (1969). The parameters of cross-validation. *Psychometrika Monograph Supplement, 16*, 1–67.

Howard, G. S., Maxwell, S. E., & Fleming, K. J. (2000). The proof of the pudding: An illustration of the relative strengths of null hypothesis, meta-analysis, and Bayesian analysis. *Psychological Methods, 5*, 315–32.

Huberty, C. J. (1994). *Applied discriminant analysis*. New York: Wiley.

Hunter, J. E. (1997). Needed: A ban on the significance test. *Psychological Science, 8*, 3–7.

Jones, L. V., & Tukey, J. W. (2000). A sensible formulation of the significance test. *Psychological Methods, 5*, 411–14.

Judd, C. M., McClelland, G. H., & Culhane, S. E. (1995). Data analysis: Continuing issues in the everyday analysis of psychological data. *Annual Reviews of Psychology, 46*, 433–65

Kaiser, H. F. (1960). Directional statistical decisions. *Psychological Review, 67*, 160–7.

Kelley, T. L. (1935). An unbiased correlation ratio measure. *Proceedings of the National Academy of Sciences, 21*, 554–9.

Kendall, M. G. (1963). *Rank correlation methods* (3rd edn.). London: Griffin.

Kendall, P. C., Marss-Garcia, A., Nath, S. R., & Sheldrick, R. C. (1999). Normative comparisons for the evaluation of clinical significance. *Journal of Consulting and Clinical Psychology, 67*, 285–99.

Kirk, R. E. (1995). *Experimental design: Procedures for the behavioral sciences* (3rd edn.). Monterey, CA: Brooks/Cole.

Kirk, R. E. (2001). Promoting good statistical practices: Some suggestions. *Educational and Psychological Measurement, 61*, 213–18.

Kraemer, H. C. (1983). Theory of estimation and testing of effect sizes: Use in meta-analysis. *Journal of Educational Statistics, 8*, 93–101.

Lax, D. A. (1985). Robust estimators of scale: Finite sample performance in long-tailed symmetric distributions. *Journal of the American Statistical Association, 80*, 736–41.

Lehmann, E. L. (1993). The Fisher, Neyman–Pearson theories of testing hypotheses: One theory or two. *Journal of the American Statistical Association, 88*, 1242–8.

Levin, J. R. (1967). Misinterpreting the significance of "explained variation." *American Psychologist, 22*, 675–6.

Lord, F. M. (1950). *Efficiency of prediction when a regression equation from one sample is used in a new sample*. Research Bulletin 50–110. Princeton, NJ: Educational Testing Service.

McGraw, K. O., & Wong, S. P. (1992). A common language effect size statistic. *Psychological Bulletin, 111*, 361–5.

Meehl, P. E. (1967). Theory testing in psychology and physics: A methodological paradox. *Philosophy of Science, 34*, 103–15.

Nickerson, R. S. (2000). Null hypothesis significance testing: A review of an old and continuing controversy. *Psychological Methods, 5*, 241–301.

Nosanchuk, T. A. (1978). Serendipity tails: A note on two-tailed hypothesis tests with asymmetric regions of rejection. *Acta Sociologica, 21*, 249–53.

O'Grady, K. E. (1982). Measures of explained variation: Cautions and limitations. *Psychological Bulletin, 92*, 766–77.

Olejnik, S., & Algina, J. (2000). Measures of effect size for comparative studies: Applications, interpretations, and limitations. *Contemporary Educational Psychology, 25*, 241–86.

Preece, P. F. W. (1983). A measure of experimental effect size based on success rates. *Educational and Psychological Measurement, 43*, 763–6.

Prentice, D. A., & Miller, D. T. (1992). When small effects are impressive. *Psychological Bulletin, 112*, 160–4.

Rindskopf, D. M. (1997). Testing "small," not null, hypotheses: Classical and Bayesian approaches. In L. L. Harlow, S. A. Mulaik, & J. H. Steiger (eds.), *What if there were no significance tests?* (pp. 319–32). Hillsdale, NJ: Erlbaum.

Rosenthal, R., & Gaito, J. (1963). The interpretation of levels of significance by psychological researchers. *Journal of Psychology, 55*, 33–8.

Rosenthal, R., & Gaito, J. (1964). Further evidence for the cliff effect in interpretation of levels of significance. *Psychological Reports, 15*, 570.

Rosenthal, R., & Rubin, D. B. (1982). A simple, general purpose display of magnitude of experimental effect. *Journal of Educational Psychology, 74*, 166–9.

Rosenthal, R., & Rubin, D. B. (1989). Effect size estimation for one-sample multiple-choice-type data: Design, analysis, and meta-analysis. *Psychological Bulletin, 106*, 332–7.

Rosenthal, R., & Rubin, D. B. (1994). The counternull value of an effect size: A new statistic. *Psychological Science, 5*, 329–34.

Rosnow, R., & Rosenthal, R. (1989). Statistical procedures and the justification of knowledge in psychological science. *American Psychologist, 44*, 1276–84.

Rosnow, R. L., Rosenthal, R., & Rubin, D. B. (2000). Contrasts and correlations in effect-size estimation. *Psychological Science, 11*, 446–53.

Rossi, J. S. (1997). A case study in the failure of psychology as cumulative science: The spontaneous recovery of verbal learning. In L. L. Harlow, S. A. Mulaik, & J. H. Steiger (eds.), *What if there were no significance tests?* (pp. 175–97). Hillsdale, NJ: Erlbaum.

Rozeboom, W. W. (1960). The fallacy of the null hypothesis significance test. *Psychological Bulletin, 57*, 416–28.

Särndal, C. E. (1974). A comparative study of association measures. *Psychometrika, 39*, 165–87.

Schmidt, F. L. (1996). Statistical significance testing and cumulative knowledge in psychology: Implications for the training of researchers. *Psychological Methods, 1*, 115–29.

Sedlmeier, P., & Gigerenzer, G. (1989). Do studies of statistical power have an effect on the power of studies? *Psychological Bulletin, 105*, 309–16.

Serlin, R. C. (1993). Confidence intervals and the scientific method: A case for Holm on the range. *Journal of Experimental Education, 61*, 350–60.

Serlin, R. C., & Lapsley, D. K. (1985). Rationality in psychological research: The good-enough principle. *American Psychologists, 40*, 73–83.

Serlin, R. C., & Lapsley, D. K. (1993). Rational appraisal of psychological research and the good-enough principle. In G. Keren & C. Lewis (eds.), *A handbook for data analysis in the behavioral sciences: Methodological issues* (pp. 199–228). Hillsdale, NJ: Erlbaum.

Shaver, J. P. (1993). What statistical significance testing is, and what it is not. *Journal of Experimental Education, 61*, 293–316.

Spencer, B. (1995). Correlations, sample size, and practical significance: A comparison of selected psychological and medical investigations. *Journal of Psychology, 129*, 469–75.

Tang, P. C. (1938). The power function of the analysis of variance tests with tables and illustrations of their use. *Statistics Research Memorandum, 2*, 126–49.

Tatsuoka, M. M. (1973). *An examination of the statistical properties of a multivariate measure of strength of association* (U.S. Office of Education, Bureau of Research, Contract No. OEG-5-72-0027). Urbana-Champaign, IL: Author.

Thompson, B. (1998). In praise of brilliance: Where that praise really belongs. *American Psychologist, 53*, 799–800.

Thompson, B. (2002). "Statistical," "practical," and "clinical": How many kinds of significance do counselors need to consider? *Journal of Counseling and Development, 80*, 64–71.

Tukey, J. W. (1991). The philosophy of multiple comparisons. *Statistical Science, 6*, 100–16.

Wherry, R. J. (1931). A new formula for predicting the shrinkage of the coefficient of multiple correlation. *Annals of Mathematical Statistics, 2*, 440–51.

Wickens, C. D. (1998). Commonsense statistics. *Ergonomics in Design, 6* (4), 18–22.

Wilcox, R. R. (1996). *Statistics for the social sciences.* San Diego, CA: Academic Press.

Wilcox, R. R. (1997). *Introduction to robust estimation and hypothesis testing.* San Diego, CA: Academic Press.

Wilcox, R. R., & Muska, J. (1999). Measuring effect size: A non-parametric analogue of $\omega^2$. *British Journal of Mathematical and Statistical Psychology, 52*, 93–110.

Yelton, W. H., & Sechrest, L. (1986). Use and misuse of no-difference findings in eliminating threats to validity. *Evaluation Review, 10*, 836–52.

## Further Reading

Gigerenzer, G. (1993). The Superego, the Ego, and the Id in statistical reasoning. In G. Keren & C. Lewis (eds.), *A handbook for data analysis in the behavioral sciences: Methodological issues* (pp. 311–39). Hillsdale, NJ: Erlbaum.

Harlow, L. L., Mulaik, S. A., & Steiger, J. H. (eds.) (1997). *What if there were no significance tests?* Hillsdale, NJ: Erlbaum.

Kirk, R. E. (1996). Practical significance: A concept whose time has come. *Educational and Psychological Measurement, 56,* 746–59.

McLean, J. E., & Kaufman, A. S. (eds.) (1998). Special issue: Statistical significance testing. *Research in the Schools, 5,* 1–65.

Wilkinson, L., & the Task Force on Statistical Inference (1999). Statistical methods in psychology journals. *American Psychologist, 54,* 594–604.

# CHAPTER SIX

# The Changing Face of Research Methods

## Randolph A. Smith and Stephen F. Davis

Stevens's (1951) *Handbook of Experimental Psychology* brought together chapters by the leading experimentalists of the day. In 1951, experimental psychology adhered tenaciously to an experimental model that stressed variable manipulation, control, and the determination of cause-and-effect relations. Significant changes have taken place in experimental psychology since the publication of the last major handbook in experimental psychology.

## Updating Brass Instruments, Questionnaires, Mental Testing, and Comparative Psychology

In Chapter 1 of this volume, Goodwin reflected on experimental psychology's foundations, listing four categories of research methodology that originated in the nineteenth century. In the first section of this chapter, we examine and update these four areas since Stevens's (1951) influential text.

### Brass instrument psychology

Although this title implies a focus on instrumentation, the topics studied with those instruments were the actual focal point. As Goodwin noted, researchers used this approach to study "such basic cognitive processes as sensation, perception, attention, and memory" (Goodwin, PSYCHOLOGY'S EXPERIMENTAL FOUNDATIONS, p. 4). In Stevens's (1951) text, all of these cognitive processes were covered. Sensation and perception were represented in the "Sensory Processes" section, which contained 11 chapters, almost a third of the text's chapters. The index also listed several references to various forms of attention in those chapters. On the other hand, cognition was barely present. There was one chapter, "Cognitive Processes," by Robert Leeper, within the "Learning and Adjustment" section of the text.

Today, these areas of research remain alive and well, but the balance seems to have shifted. For example, Perlman and McCann (1999), in a large-scale curriculum survey (400 college catalogs), found that only 26 percent of the schools listed a course in Sensation and Perception. On the other hand, cognition is alive, well, and flourishing. Perlman and McCann found that Cognition was the ninth most frequently listed course in psychology curricula for all colleges in 1997, after not being listed in the top 30 courses in 1975. Within doctoral universities, cognition was listed more often than Learning (88% to 78%) in 1997, after trailing substantially (45% to 100%) in 1975. Many journals focus on cognitive topics, but in even more broadly defined areas than ever before (e.g., "cognitive neuroscience"; Sarter, Berntson, & Cacioppo, 1996). A quick perusal of the journal database PRISM revealed well over 100 journals with "cognitive" or "cognition" in the title. Interestingly, the cognitive area has maintained a link to the era of brass instrumentation because it is still heavily identified with equipment. The equipment has shifted, of course, from brass instruments to computers. We address the topic of computers later in the chapter.

## Questionnaires and introspection

In Chapter 1, Goodwin noted the widespread use of questionnaires, thanks to pioneers such as Galton and Hall, and introspection, thanks to the work of Wundt and Titchener. By the time Stevens's (1951) handbook appeared, introspection was relegated to a few passing mentions in Leeper's chapter. Although Leeper said that introspection could be important in studying cognitive processes, he did list several shortcomings of the technique. The terms "questionnaire" and "survey" did not appear in Stevens's index. This absence is probably not surprising given the title of the volume (*Handbook of Experimental Psychology*) and the fact that the field was dominated by Woodworth's (1938; Woodworth & Schlosberg, 1954) view of experimental methodology (for an extended discussion, see the section below on Woodworth's influence).

Today, it is clear that surveys and questionnaires have survived (and thrived) whereas introspection has fallen on hard times. A convenience sample of 10 research methods texts showed that nine covered survey methodology and seven covered questionnaires, compared to only one that mentioned introspective data and one that listed introspection. The texts that covered introspection at all approached it as a method that researchers could use to generate ideas for experiments, but not as a legitimate research approach. Although Lieberman (1979) issued a call for a limited return to the use of introspection, there has been no groundswell of support. After one positive and one negative reply to his article and a reply of his, there has not been an article published in *American Psychologist* with "introspection" in the title since 1981. By contrast, Bornstein (2001) evaluated seven widely read psychology journals. He reported that a large number of studies in the *Journal of Personality and Social Psychology* (85%) and the *Journal of Applied Psychology* (63%) relied exclusively on questionnaires as an outcome measure.

Moreover, "when the data were collapsed across both years and journal, 40% of all published studies surveyed relied exclusively on questionnaire outcome measures" (Bornstein, 2001, p. 39). Is it any wonder that Bornstein wondered if psychology has become the science of questionnaires?

## Mental testing

As Goodwin noted in Chapter 1, Galton and Cattell had developed an approach to measuring individual differences that was generally considered as an experimental approach until Woodworth's (1938) distinction between experimental and correlational methods. In describing the experimental approach, Woodworth used familiar terms such as "independent variable," "dependent variable," "control," "rule of one variable" (p. 2), and "cause and effect" (p. 3). On the other hand, but equal in value to the experimental method, Woodworth described the "comparative and correlational method" (p. 3), which was based on individual differences. He described the correlational method as follows: "measuring two or more characteristics of the same individuals it computes the correlation of these characteristics and goes on to factor analysis" (p. 3). Finally, Woodworth noted that the correlational approach did not study cause and effect, but rather "the interrelation of different effects" (p. 3). Interestingly, Woodworth pointed out that the same psychologists had contributed to these two approaches and that close contact between them (the approaches) was desirable.

Unlike Woodworth, Stevens's (1951) opening chapter did not address methodology issues; instead, his chapter was titled "Mathematics, Measurement, and Psychophysics" (pp. 1–49). Here, Stevens introduced his notion of scales of measurement, one of his most famous contributions. References to specific experimental and correlational concepts were scant in Stevens. "Correlation" drew three mentions in the index, but all passages referred to statistical use of the term rather than a research approach. Searching Stevens's index for experimental terms is no more fruitful. There was one reference to "cause and effect," but again it was nothing more than a passing statement. However, a perusal of Stevens's chapters shows the clear influence of both approaches to gathering information. Although many of the chapters described experimental approaches to gathering data, many of the data presentations were in the form of charts and graphs, without clearly delineated statistical tests that psychologists expect to see in today's journals. Thus, during Stevens's era, the two approaches to gathering and dealing with data appeared to coexist relatively well.

Today, as Goodwin noted in Chapter 1, mental testing is an area that seems separate and distinct from experimental psychology. However, Perlman and McCann (1999) listed Tests and Measurement, Statistics, Experimental, and Research Methods within a larger category they labeled "Methodology/Experimental." Still, a search of the indexes of the previously mentioned sample of 10 research methods texts revealed no systematic coverage of psychological testing concepts. A few terms from testing did appear in the texts, but their coverage was in the context of experimental methods (e.g., "testing" as a threat to internal validity, "individual differences" as error). Today, it would seem that the areas overlap little, except for the possibilities that researchers may use tests to categorize participants into groups as an "independent variable" or that tests and surveys show up frequently as dependent measures in experiments (cf. Bornstein, 2001).

## Observing behavior (comparative psychology)

In Chapter 1 Goodwin noted that comparative psychology, rooted in Darwin's work, became a viable field of study in the late 1800s. This field of study led to the development of one of the most famous pieces of psychological laboratory equipment, the maze. As Goodwin pointed out, this development became such an important part of the discipline that Woodworth's (1938) text had a chapter on maze learning. Woodworth and Schlosberg's revised text (1954) retained this chapter.

Stevens (1951) did not include such a chapter, but the influence of comparative psychology is evident in the text. W. J. Brogden (University of Wisconsin) wrote a chapter on "Animal Studies of Learning" (pp. 568–612), which focused on several types of learning paradigms. A wide variety of chapters in Stevens's text contained research on animals, including chapters on the working of the neuron and synapse, sensory mechanisms, motor systems, homeostasis, neural maturation, ontogenetic development, behavior genetics, and phylogenetic comparison. However, information from animal research also appeared in chapters relating directly to behaviors, including reproductive activity, learnable drives and rewards, learning, and cognitive processes. Thus, comparative psychology was still vibrant in the 1950s.

Fifty years later, comparative psychology is certainly still alive, but is it well? Is it possible that the animal rights activists have made a dent in the breadth of this area of research? Some early studies were optimistic on this score, indicating an upsurge in submissions to the *Journal of Comparative Psychology* after a long decline (Hirsch, 1987) and growth in professional organizations for comparative psychology (Doré & Kirouac, 1987). Galef (1987) even declared that "the study of behavior of nonhuman organisms is today, as it has been for a century, a vital and active area within psychology. Comparative psychology is, therefore, by definition, alive and well" (p. 259). However, not all signs are positive. Viney, King, and Berndt (1990) examined research from 1967 to 1988 and found a decline in studies on animal species such as cats, dogs, and rabbits. Studies on many standard laboratory species did not show a comparable decline. Still, the storm clouds may be on the horizon; comparative psychologists should be vigilant in safeguarding their field of study.

## Woodworth's Influence and Challenges to the Status Quo

In 1938 Robert Woodworth irrevocably changed the face of modern experimental psychology. Although his highly influential book, *Experimental Psychology*, was essentially a compendium of research findings in the various areas of psychology (e.g., memory, retention, the conditioned response, maze learning, practice and skill, feeling, reaction time, association, the skin senses, hearing, thinking, etc.), Woodworth added a new emphasis.

In his introductory chapter, Woodworth indicated that:

> Today we are inclined to claim for experimental psychology a scope as wide as that of psychology itself, while admitting that we do not yet know exactly how to subject some of the biggest problems to a rigorous experiment. Until these problems are attacked experimentally, they probably will not be solved. (Woodworth, 1938, p. 1)

Woodworth's (1938) passionate argument for the experimental method included the following views:

> An experimenter is said to *control the conditions* in which an event occurs. He has several advantages over an observer who simply follows the course of events without exercising any control.
> 1. The experimenter makes the events happen at a certain time and place and so is fully *prepared* to make an accurate observation.
> 2. Controlled conditions being *known* conditions, the experimenter can set up his experiment and repeat the observation; and, what is very important in view of the social nature of scientific investigation, he can report his conditions so that another experimenter can duplicate them and check the data.
> 3. The experimenter can systematically *vary* the conditions and note the concomitant variation in the results. If he follows the old standard "rule of one variable" he holds all the conditions constant except for one factor which is his "experimental factor" or his "independent variable." The observed effect is the "dependent variable" which in a psychological experiment is some characteristic of behavior or reported experience. In an experiment on the effect of noise on mental work, noise is the independent variable controlled by the experimenter, and the dependent variable may be speed or accuracy of work or the subject's report of his feelings.
> As regards the rule of one variable, it applies only to the independent variable, for there is no objection to observing a variety of effects of the one experimental factor. With careful planning two or three independent variables can sometimes be handled in a single experiment with economy of effort and with some chance of discovering the interaction of the two or more factors. . . .
> Whether one or more independent variables are used, it remains essential that all other conditions be constant. Otherwise you cannot connect the effect observed with any definite cause. (Woodworth, 1938, pp. 2–3)

The now-familiar paradigm of studying cause-and-effect relations by manipulating independent variables (IVs) and recording changes in dependent variables (DVs), while controlling extraneous variables, was born. Woodworth's approach found favor among researchers and became the dominant methodology beginning in the 1940s. The influence of Woodworth's pronouncements (less than one page of text!) on experimental psychology has been, and continues to be, inestimable – just look at any beginning-level research methods or experimental psychology text. Is it any wonder that students believe this approach to research has existed for centuries and is the only "legitimate" way to gather data?

The pervasiveness of this approach notwithstanding, the status quo has received significant challenges in recent years. For example, we previously noted Bornstein's (2001) concern about the reliance on questionnaires. The widespread use of questionnaires is not the only challenge to the status quo. Murray Sidman (1960) fired an initial volley against the status quo nearly 45 years ago in his influential book, *Tactics of Scientific Research*. Here was a compelling rationale for the use of single subjects in scientifically valid research! The idiographic approach was truly coming of age. Despite minor squabbles, it came to exist peacefully alongside the firmly entrenched and dominant nomothetic approach; a different approach was introduced to experimentalists.

Campbell and Stanley (1966) fired a second volley against the status quo in 1966 with the publication of their influential *Experimental and Quasi-Experimental Designs for Research*. Some of the designs they presented allowed researchers to conduct projects when they were forced to use intact groups and could not randomly assign participants to the respective conditions – an obvious source of potential confounding. Campbell and Stanley's lucid presentation undoubtedly helped elevate these nonexperimental designs to a higher level of respectability. Another chink in the armor of the nomothetic IV→DV method was present.

As Woodworth's (1938) quotations indicate, the strength of the IV→DV method rests firmly on the assumption that this approach is the best and most scientific method for gathering research data. However, there are other ways to look at the world. Postmodernism provides one of the alternative views of reality that has challenged current research methodology. For example, the postmodernist view suggests that the type of research methodology used determines the *nature* of the reality that is described as much as it produces a description of that reality. In a more radical form postmodernism doubts the possibility of any grand or encompassing theory or explanation (Rosenau, 1992). Why? Because, according to Gubrium and Holstein (1997), "In postmodernism, with reality reduced to linguistic convention . . . , representation is relative and arbitrary – linguistically reflective rather than reality related" (p. 87).

## Qualitative Research: Overview and Strategies

Obviously, postmodernism's challenge cuts to the heart of traditional methodology in psychology and opens the door for the emergence of new methodologies. One of these "new" (actually it began in the late eighteenth century; Creswell, 1994) approaches is *qualitative research*.

The basic assumptions of qualitative research are similar to many of the tenets of postmodernism. For example, qualitative researchers believe that there is not a single, objective reality: there are multiple realities that are created by the participants in a study and their interactions with the researcher. Moreover, the values and biases of the researcher are an acknowledged component of qualitative research. Additionally, the written presentation of qualitative research differs considerably from the traditional APA-format paper. The qualitative research style is much less formal and impersonal and the reader can expect to find such additions as "definitions that evolved during a study" (Creswell, 1994, p. 7).

The observation that definitions might evolve during a study suggests that the vocabulary of the qualitative researcher may be quite different from the vocabulary of the traditional IV→DV researcher. It is. In fact, it is arguable that qualitative researchers have developed a whole new language (Gubrium & Holstein, 1997). Most qualitative descriptions feature substantially less scientific jargon, and the reader is likely to encounter more personal, even emotional, words. (The qualitative researcher believes that a full description of human behavior includes people's *feelings* in addition to what they are doing and how they are doing it.) If the participant is the final judge of what constitutes an accurate account or description of a situation, then personal terms will be the order of the day.

Reminiscent of the idiographic approach, the qualitative researcher is committed to studying *particular* people in *specific* settings. This commitment favors the reporting of details as opposed to generalizations. Concern for external validity is not an important issue. On the other hand, the concern for detail promotes a concern for the quality of life by the qualitative researcher.

Unlike the traditional laboratory scientist, qualitative researchers place a premium on naturalism. If the researcher wants to answer the *what* and *how* questions about the behavior and interactions of people in their typical environment, then what better place to study people than in their natural environment? According to Gubrium and Holstein (1997),

> The meaningful features of everyday life consist of participants' orientations to, and actions within, this world as they purposefully manage their realities. The naturalistic researcher strives to richly and accurately describe these realities without unduly disrupting – thus distorting – these worlds in the process. (Gubrium & Holstein, 1997, p. 19)

The type of reasoning and logic used by qualitative researchers differs significantly from the reasoning and logic used by the typical IV→DV researcher. For years the accepted mode of reasoning has involved deductive logic where hypotheses and theories spawn specific experiments designed to evaluate them. (However, Capaldi and Proctor noted that a growing number of professionals do not believe that theory-driven research is on solid ground. See Chapter 2.) Qualitative research prefers to use inductive logic where the data (information) provided by the participants is assimilated, and a pattern or theory to explain the phenomenon of interest emerges from this growing body of information.

The nature of the problem studied by qualitative research differs significantly from the typical IV→DV investigation. Unlike the IV→DV research problem, which likely will be associated with a significant amount of previously reported research, qualitative research deals with problems for which little or no information exists. It is the researcher's task to ferret out and delineate the relevant variables and determine how these variables are related to each other.

Unlike traditional hypothesis-testing research where the researcher develops a specific, rather narrowly focused experimental hypothesis, qualitative research begins with a more global question. These more global issues are frequently called grand tour questions (Werner & Schopfle, 1987) or guiding hypotheses (Marshall & Rossman, 1989). These grand tour questions or guiding hypotheses are often followed by several subquestions that reflect specific, more narrowed aspects of the research project. It is important that none of these research questions, whether they are global or subquestions, constrain the researcher.

Data analytic procedures also differ greatly between traditional quantitative approaches and the newer qualitative research strategies. For example, the time-honored procedure followed by generations of IV→DV researchers is to conduct the experiment (gather the research data), analyze the data, and then prepare a written report based on the results of the data analysis. To the contrary, qualitative researchers typically analyze their data "*simultaneously* with data collection, data interpretation, and narrative reporting writing" (Creswell, 1994, p. 153). This logic makes sense in view of the ever-developing nature of the qualitative research project: The categories of responses are forever emerging and changing and the nature of the explanation is forever being modified.

The general methodology employed by the qualitative research approach differs drastically from the typical IV→DV approach where the experimenter randomly assigns participants to treatment groups and implements other forms of extraneous variable control. Qualitative research draws its methodology from a diversity of sources that include psychology, anthropology, sociology, and consumer research. These methodologies include enthnographies, grounded theory, case studies, and phenomenological studies. We describe each of these approaches sequentially.

The purpose of this section is not to depict one approach to research as better than another approach; rather, our intent is to introduce our readers to research approaches with which they may not be familiar. The number of alternative research approaches is growing and likely will continue to expand in the future. Rather than condemn or praise a particular approach, we encourage researchers to become familiar with these new approaches and consider how they might be used to best advantage. For example, a rigorous qualitative study might precede and stimulate a more traditional, quantitative IV→DV study.

## Ethnography

Ethnography involves the prolonged study of an intact culture in its normal setting. The researcher gathers primarily observational data. It is important that the researcher begins the ethnographic study with an open mind. This open-mindedness allows a pattern or story to develop. As Creswell (1994) indicated, "This logic also suggests an emerging design, not a static design, wherein the categories [or themes described by the participants] develop during the study, rather than are predetermined before the study begins" (p. 44). *Critical ethnography*, a subcategory of ethnography, involves the investigation of social conditions with the intent of challenging previous research and policy and aiding actions that will result in social change (Thomas, 1993).


*Grounded theory*

In the grounded theory approach (Strauss & Corbin, 1990), "the researcher attempts to derive a theory by using multiple stages of data collection and the refinement and interrelationship of categories of information" (Creswell, 1994, p. 12). Although grounded theory is designed to be a precise and rigorous process, creativity is also an important part of the process in that the researcher needs to ask innovative questions and come up with unique formulations of the data – "to create new order out of the old" (Strauss & Corbin, 1990, p. 27).

  According to Smith and Davis,

> The heart of the grounded theory approach occurs in its use of coding, which is analogous to data analysis in quantitative approaches. There are three different types of coding used in a more-or-less sequential manner (Strauss & Corbin, 1990). *Open coding* is much like the description goal of science. During open coding the researcher labels and categorizes the phenomena being studied. *Axial coding* involves finding links between categories and subcategories from open coding. The final process, *selective coding*, entails identifying a core category and relating the subsidiary categories to this core. (Smith & Davis, 2001, p. 73)

  The final product of grounded theory is a "model of process and a transactional system which essentially tells the story of the research" (Smith & Davis, 2001, p. 73). "Process" refers to a linking of actions and interactions that result in some outcome. The transactional system allows researchers to examine the various interactions that have been observed. The grounded theory researcher frequently prepares a conditional matrix to visually display the transactional system.


*Case study*

Likely all researchers, as well as students in their first course on research methods, are familiar with the case study approach. According to Creswell (1994), the case study is an approach "in which the researcher explores a single entity or phenomenon ('the case') bounded by time and activity (a program, event, process, institution, or social group) and collects detailed information by using a variety of data collection procedures during a sustained period of time" (p. 12).

  As with the other qualitative research procedures, the conduct of case study research does not begin with a theory that the researcher seeks to prove. Rather, the theory or explanation develops during, and as a function of, the observations that are made. In fact, some qualitative researchers (e.g., Neuman, 1991) would prefer to call this explanation a "pattern theory" because it really represents a pattern in that "it contains an interconnected set of concepts and relationships, but does not require causal statements" (Neuman, 1991, p. 38). In turn, the researcher can compare these patterns with patterns reported by previous case studies or theory-derived patterns (Yin, 1989). According to Yin (1989), "explanation building," where the researcher searches for causal links in order to build an explanation, and "time-series analysis," where the researcher follows pattern changes over a period of time, are two additional main methods of data collection for the case study procedure.

*Phenomenological studies*

Based on the philosophic views of Husserl, Heidegger, and Sartre, the phenomenological method of qualitative research involves an examination of human experiences "through the detailed description of the people being studied. As a method the procedure involves studying a small number of subjects through extensive and prolonged engagement to develop patterns and relationships of meaning" (Creswell, 1994, p. 12). The phenomenological approach lends itself very well to a statement of the research question without reference to previous research or theory. Because it seeks to understand human experiences, this approach is likely to generate rather broad and general research questions. Given these parameters, it is not surprising that phenomenological researchers do not have any sort of pattern or framework to guide them as they analyze their data. Creswell (1994) suggested that "although the steps for data analysis are less structured and more open to alternate procedures, Dukes (1984) suggested that one look for 'structural invariants' of a particular type of experience – the patterns – and then submit these patterns to a different researcher for confirmation" (p. 157). This approach produces a descriptive, synthesized narrative of the phenomenon under study as the final product.

# Disciplinary Developments Impacting Experimental Research

In this section, we will document six developments that have had a major impact on research and research methods since the publication of Stevens's (1951) classic text on experimental psychology. Any such list, of course, is subject to debate, but we believe these developments truly have changed the landscape of research in psychology.

*Ethical guidelines*

Stevens's *Experimental Psychology* (1951) did not contain an index entry for "ethics"; neither did Woodworth (1938) nor Woodworth and Schlosberg (1954). This absence is not particularly surprising because the American Psychological Association (APA) did not have codified ethical guidelines at that time. Although work had begun on the ethical guidelines before the publication of Stevens's book (Hobbs, 1948), APA did not develop its first ethics code until 1953 (Ad hoc Committee on Ethical Standards, 1973). The ethical guidelines have been revised frequently (10 times from 1953 to 1992; Canter, Bennett, Jones, & Nagy, 1994). As far as experimental psychology is concerned, the important landmarks are the publication of *Ethical Principles in the Conduct of Research with Human Participants* (APA, 1973) and *Principles for the Care and Use of Animals* (APA, 1971). Both sets of guidelines have been revised more than once in the interim. APA was a pioneer in developing ethical guidelines for research with humans; it has collaborated with other professional societies (e.g., Society for Neuroscience, National Institutes for Health) in developing such guidelines for work with animals. In fact, the American Association for Accreditation of Laboratory Animal Care actually governs the treatment of laboratory animals in the USA (Nation, 1997). Richard Miller details ethical considerations in research with human participants in Chapter 7 of this volume.

Many textbook accounts of ethical concerns with humans cite the deception used by Milgram (1963) in his classic obedience study. The conclusion (either direct or implied) is that the ethical guidelines now in place would prevent the recurrence of such controversial research. West and Gunn (1978) worried that the ethical guidelines concerning deception "have been advanced in the absence of supportive data and that the possible consequences of a bowdlerized approach to experimentation may have a number of deleterious effects on the field of social psychology" (p. 36). However, Adair, Dushenko, and Lindsay (1985), in a survey of methodological and ethical practices reported in a year's publications in the *Journal of Personality and Social Psychology*, found that the articles had provided little information about ethical considerations. In addition, they reported that 58.5 percent of the empirical studies had used deception, a figure that had steadily increased since 1948 (14.3%). Ortmann and Hertwig (1997) took the radical stance that deception should not be an acceptable option at all. In response, three authors (Bröder, 1998; Kimmel, 1998; Korn, 1998) wrote rejoinders maintaining that deception, within ethical guidelines, should remain an option in the research process. Korn maintained that deception had decreased in more recent years. However, Ortmann and Hertwig (1998) did not back away from their position.

Psychologists of today may think of the animal rights movement as a recent threat to psychological research with animals. However, Dewsbury (1990) has documented early antivivisectionist and media attacks on G. Stanley Hall, John B. Watson, Ivan P. Pavlov, and Edward L. Thorndike for their research (or support thereof). Perhaps as a result of such controversy, APA established a Committee on Animal Research in early 1925; the Committee on Precautions in Animal Experimentation became a standing APA committee at the 1925 APA meeting. Dewsbury (1990) noted that the Committee served a dual purpose from its beginning: "both promulgating standards for animal use and working to ensure that humane animal research could be continued" (p. 324). The controversy over animal research, of course, did not disappear. Authors have repeatedly criticized animal research on ethical grounds (e.g., Bowd & Shapiro, 1993; Robinson, 1990; Ulrich, 1991). Two large polls showed support for animal research among APA members (Plous, 1996a) and psychology undergraduates (Plous, 1996b), but such findings did not decrease the calls for tighter regulation of animal research (e.g., Lau & Cheney, 1997; Shapiro, 1997; Vonk, 1997).

The critical question of concern, of course, is how the ethical guidelines have affected psychological research. There is no real evidence that ethical guidelines have reduced the amount of human research, but, according to Korn (1998), they may have changed the character of such research by reducing deception (for an opposing viewpoint, see Ortmann & Hertwig, 1998). On the other hand, there are indications that animal research may be in decline (e.g., Viney, King, & Berndt, 1990). Rowan and Loew (1995) estimated that the number of animals used in research declined 30–50 percent worldwide in the 20 previous years. Two surveys (Benedict & Stoloff, 1991; Gallup & Eddy, 1990) revealed that 15 percent or 21 percent of psychology departments had closed their animal laboratories and 19 percent or 18 percent of departments had held serious discussions about closing them.

The ethical principles added since Stevens's book have affected experimental research in one more important manner. Given that researchers in the United States must obtain Institutional Review Board (IRB) approval before conducting research, it is likely that researchers have self-censored proposals that they otherwise would have carried out. Certainly this outcome would be desirable in reducing unethical research. However, how many worthy ideas have been squelched because of a researcher's uncertainty about taking a proposal to an IRB? For example, Herrera (1997) maintained that "Milgram abided by APA guidelines, and probably could today . . . His work might not pass today's institutional review boards, which often enforce guidelines stricter than the psychologist's formal code, especially regarding debriefing" (p. 32).

## The "feminization" of psychology

Stevens's *Experimental Psychology* (1951) did not contain a chapter on either sex or gender; "gender" did not appear in the index, and there were only a few index references to "sex." Although Beach (1951) wrote a chapter in Stevens's text titled "Instinctive Behavior: Reproductive Activities," its focus was solely on animals. Woodworth's (1938) text contained one passing reference to heart rate during sexual behavior in humans; Woodworth and Schlosberg's (1954) update added only three brief mentions of sex, with two of those referring to rats. Thus, in the middle of the century, sex and gender research were not particularly important topics in experimental psychology.

Currently, matters are considerably different. A quick search of PsycINFO from 1998 to the present revealed 13 journals with either "sex" or "gender" in their titles (e.g., *Sex Roles; Gender and Society; Psychology, Evolution, and Gender*). Perlman and McCann (1999) reported that 32 percent of undergraduate psychology departments offered Human Sexuality in 1997 (22nd most listed course; up from 23% in 1975), and 29 percent offered Psychology of Women in 1997 (tied for 25th on course listing; did not make the list in 1975).

What has fueled this change? We highlight two factors, but it is impossible to at-tribute causality or degree of influence of these factors. First, psychology has become a discipline populated by women. Howard et al. (1986) reported that women earned only 14.8 percent of the psychology doctorates in 1950, 17.5 percent in 1960, 26.7 percent in 1972, but 50.1 percent in 1984. The figure had increased to 61.2 percent by 1991 (Pion et al., 1996). This trend in graduate education mirrored an earlier similar trend in undergraduate psychology majors: women comprised 36.8 percent of majors in 1950, 41 percent in 1960, 46.4 percent in 1972, 66.8 percent in 1982 (Howard et al., 1986), and 73 percent in 1991 (National Science Foundation, 1994). The second factor affecting psychology mirrored changes throughout society and science, as feminist thought and criticism made its way into traditionally male-dominated fields (e.g., see Gergen, 1988; Harding, 1986). Eagley (1995) has cited Maccoby and Jacklin's (1974) book, *The Psychology of Sex Differences*, as being particularly influential in bringing sex and gender issues to prominence within psychology.

Regardless of the genesis of the change, the change is real: psychology is much more gender conscious than it was 50 years ago. This change has clearly manifested itself in the area of experimental psychology. It is difficult to pick up a textbook that is research-based without finding at least a section, if not a chapter or chapters, that deal with research on the topic of sex or gender. It is likely that female students are interested in somewhat different issues than male students and thus ask different types of research questions. The field of experimental psychology is much richer for this change. (For information on a similar trend emphasizing diversity issues, see Chapter 9 in this volume.)

*Applied emphasis in psychology*

The primary emphasis and interest within psychology has also shifted over the past 50 years. Stevens's handbook (1951) was essentially an account of psychology laboratory research. There was one major section, however, devoted to the application of psychology research: Human Performance. This section was the forerunner of what we would call Industrial Psychology or Human Factors today, as it contained chapters on "Selection," "Training," "Engineering Psychology and Equipment Design," and "Work and Motor Performance." Stevens's text contained almost no references to the topics that students today believe to be the integral part of psychology: clinical, counseling, abnormal, educational, school, personality, and so on. The few references that did touch on those subjects were quite brief and often dealt with brain lesions or rats. Clearly, there has been a major shift within the discipline.

Traditionally, psychology was an experimental research discipline. Howard et al. (1986) noted that almost 70 percent of new PhDs prior to 1940 were in experimental psychology. However, Howard et al. provided a striking graph (p. 1313) depicting the rate of change in "health service provider" and "academic/research" PhDs in psychology between 1960 and 1984. The numbers for both groups were approximately equal between 1960 and 1972, showing growth rates of approximately 10 percent yearly. However, from 1972 to 1984, the health service area continued to grow at a healthy rate (and comprised 53.2% of new psychology PhDs in 1984), whereas the academic/research numbers leveled off and then fell dramatically. Pion et al. (1996) further documented this trend, showing that clinical PhDs had grown by 52 percent from 1971 to 1991, whereas experimental, physiological, and comparative PhDs had shrunk by 17 percent. In the same time period, overall psychology PhD production increased by 55 percent, with clinical psychology accounting for the lion's share of the increase.

Curriculum studies have shown a similar pattern. Keyes and Hogberg (1990) surveyed two cohorts of alumni (1967–76, 1977–86) from Albion College about the value of their undergraduate courses. The earlier cohort listed mostly "experimental/ theoretical" courses as valuable whereas the later cohort listed applied courses as most useful. An examination of Perlman and McCann's (1999) data contrasting the most frequently listed undergraduate courses for 1975 and 1997 (Table 2, p. 181) shows that most experimentally oriented courses have either remained fairly constant or have dropped in the number of offerings during that period. The only notable exceptions were two courses with recent origins (Cognitive and Biological) and Research Methods (21% to 42%). On the other hand, several applied courses showed gains of about 10 percent or more (Industrial/Organizational, Abnormal, Personality, Counseling). Thus, it is relatively clear that "professional psychology became preeminent" (Cummings, 1992, p. 846).

Although the focus within psychology may have shifted toward a more applied basis, that shift has not signaled an end to experimental research. Instead, the focus of the research questions many psychologists ask has simply shifted more toward applied topics. Although there were some tensions and uncertainties about psychologists turning to applied work and research, historical figures such as Walter Dill Scott and Hugo Münsterberg combined such interests in the early 1900s (Hilgard, 1987). So the interest in applied research is not new, but the degree of that interest has clearly changed over the past half century. Leibowitz (1996) summarized the current relation between basic research and its applications when he wrote "In thinking about basic science and its applications, I cannot recall a time when I considered them as separate. . . . I believe that an approach that views the search for fundamentals and the solution of societal problems to be interdependent is worthy of serious consideration" (p. 366).

## *Emphasis on undergraduate research*

Stevens's book was not meant to be a handbook for undergraduates: in describing the need for the text, Stevens (1951, p. vii) wrote: "Equally clear was the fact that the handbook should address itself directly to the advanced Scholar, to the graduate student who would use it as a textbook and the specialist who would use it as a reference source and as a guide to matters outside his own specialty." Although its addition was initially controversial, training in experimental psychology for undergraduates had been introduced before 1900, and a year of experimental work had become standard during the century's first decade (Benjamin, 2000). Certainly research training was an important component of the undergraduate curriculum in Stevens's day; Holder, Leavitt, and McKenna (1958) reported that 95 percent of a large sample of graduate department chairs recommended that undergraduates take a course in experimental psychology. Training in experimental psychology is crucial for today's students to be competitive for graduate school admissions (e.g., Lawson, 1995; Smith, 1985).

Taking a course in experimental psychology or research methods is one thing; actually completing a research study may be another. APA has conducted periodic surveys of the undergraduate psychology curriculum (e.g., Cooney & Griffith, 1994; Kulik, 1973; Scheirer & Rogers, 1985). Although the data from such surveys are not directly comparable, they seem to indicate the continuance of a trend that Kierniesky noted: "an increased involvement in independent data-collection research by upper-division psychology majors" (1984, p. 15).

Some related data indirectly support the conclusion that undergraduate psychology majors are more involved in actual research than in the past. Undergraduate research conferences for students to present their research findings began appearing on the scene in the late 1960s (Carsrud, 1975), although three such conferences are more than 25 years old (Society for the Teaching of Psychology, n.d.). The conferences rapidly spread around the country: Palladino, Carsrud, Hulicka, & Benjamin (1982) reported an increase in such conferences from four in 1970 to more than 25 by 1979 (with over 1,000 undergraduates presenting research). A similar trend has occurred with undergraduate research journals. Carsrud (1978) reported the founding of the *Journal of Undergraduate Psychological Research*; Smith and Davis (2001, p. 18) listed five journals that currently publish student research. Thus there are ample outlets for both student research presentation and publication; research is much less an activity that involves primarily graduate students or PhDs.

*Changing research trends*

Stevens's (1951) text contained a section labeled "Physiological Mechanisms," that contained chapters such as "Excitation and Conduction in the Neuron," "Synaptic Mechanisms," and "Sensory Mechanisms." The book also contained chapters on "Mechanisms of Neural Maturation" and several chapters on "Sensory Processes." All of this information was biological in nature and is the type of information that came to be known as physiological psychology, then biological psychology, biopsychology, or neuroscience.

Anyone who has taught introductory psychology courses for a number of years is aware of the ever broadening influence of neuroscientific information in that course. Although the specific chapter coverage of biological bases has shrunk since the introductory texts of the 1890s and 1910s (11% and 17%, respectively; Weiten & Wight, 1992), information with a biological slant now permeates perhaps half or more of the text chapters. A quick glance at one of the leading texts in the biological/physiological realm (e.g., Carlson, 2002, Kalat, 2001) helps strengthen this assertion. For example, the majority of Kalat's chapter titles sound like chapters or chapter sections from an introductory psychology text (e.g., "Vision," "Rhythms of Wakefulness and Sleep," "Emotional Behaviors"). Perlman and McCann (1999) documented a drop in physiological psychology courses from 1975 (57% of schools offered the course) to 1997 (46%), but showed biological psychology courses being taught at 29 percent of schools in 1997 (compared to no listing for 1975).

Thus it seems clear that neuroscience and biological psychology topics have made significant inroads into psychology. Interestingly, however, Robins, Gosling, and Craik (1999) had difficulty documenting this assertion when they studied research trends in psychology by analyzing data from flagship psychology journals, psychology dissertation subjects, and citation analyses. From their data, they were able to document only a small rise of the neuroscientific perspective within psychology. They did document a dramatic increase in neuroscience through membership numbers from the Society for Neuroscience and citations to neuroscience journals in *Science*. They concluded that it is possible "that neuroscience will continue to grow but not within mainstream psychology. At this point, neuroscience may be located more centrally in the biological sciences than in psychology and in some ways may already constitute its own independent scientific discipline" (pp. 125–6). The variety of names that subsume the research of this broad field certainly substantiate the notion that such research can be found in a variety of disciplines and types of journals. Regardless of where the research is published, it is a safe assumption that the field of neuropsychology has had a major impact on the research agenda within psychology.

Another major shift in research emphasis since Stevens's (1951) book is cognitive psychology. Although early psychologists were interested in the workings of the mind, Watson's behaviorism had a stifling impact on such research. However, Ellis and Hunt (1993) cited a variety of events in the 1950s that led to a renewed interest in cognitive psychology. In Stevens's (1951) text, there was no section labeled "Cognition," which is not surprising given the strong behavioristic influence in the first half of the century. Robert Leeper (University of Oregon) authored a "Cognitive Processes" chapter within the "Learning and Adjustment" section of Stevens (1951, pp. 730–57). However, this chapter is clearly somewhat historical and does not fit modern cognitive psychology well: Leeper wrote, in a section describing methods for studying cognitive processes, that "it still remains true that introspection has considerable value" (p. 736). The bulk of the chapter dealt with concept formation, focusing on inductive, deductive, and inventive approaches to the process. Leeper cited influential work by Adams and Tolman in the 1930s and Heidbreder and Hilgard in the 1940s; it appears clear that the study of cognition was in a state of flux. Although many readers may be surprised to discover that Stevens included such a chapter at the time, remember that Neisser's (1967) influential *Cognitive Psychology* was published only 16 years later.

Whether psychology was ready to move beyond behaviorism or there were many "closet cognitivists" awaiting change, the field has eagerly embraced the cognitive revolution and the face of experimental psychology has changed because of it. In 1975, cognitive psychology did not register in the top 31 undergraduate psychology courses (Perlman & McCann, 1999); by 1997, 48 percent of all schools offered such a course, making it tied with statistics as the ninth most-offered course. Robins, Gosling, & Craik (1999) found that cognitive psychology had grown tremendously as a research field in psychology. Flagship articles concerning cognitive psychology more than quintupled from 1950–2 to 1995–7, total psychology dissertations with cognitive keywords increased from about 5 percent to 9 percent from 1967 to 1973 and have remained at that level, and the number of citations to cognitive keywords in four flagship journals increased about fivefold from 1977 to 1996. Again, it seems abundantly clear that experimental psychology has experienced a significant shift in research emphasis toward cognitive psychology in the last 50 years.

*Computers in experimental psychology*

Despite the fact that we have saved computers as the last of the developments in experimental psychology in the past 50 years, it is by no means the least. In fact, computers are probably the most pervasive of these influences on the scientific enterprise of psychology. Paradoxically, although it is possible that computers have done more to revolutionize psychological research than any other single development, there is little evidence of that possibility in the psychological literature. Although the *American Psychologist* contained an article dealing with computers shortly after Stevens's (1951) text (Ward, 1955), and published a special issue on instrumentation in psychology with eight computer-related articles in March 1975, there is a dearth of overview or summary articles dealing with computers in recent years of the journal. Likewise, a PsycINFO search for books providing a review of computers' impact on the discipline resulted in no references. Thus, it seems that the use of computers is so pervasive today that the discipline has taken them for granted.

Still, it is clear that computers have been a boon to psychological research. A quick glance at any research journal will provide data to support this contention. Reviewing Methods sections will show a strong tendency for researchers to present stimuli and control experiments through the use of computers. Imagine how much more true Castellan's (1975, p. 211) statement is today: "It is possible to run experiments today on our PDP-11 system that are impossible to run without a computer." Looking at Results sections will show an even stronger tendency for computer use in data analyses. Examining the Author Notes reveals that researchers share e-mail addresses along with mailing addresses. A look around any psychology department will reinforce the ubiquitous nature of computers: try to find a faculty member who does not use a computer (or several computers!). It is virtually impossible to envision typing a manuscript for submission on a typewriter. It is not difficult to find undergraduate students using computers taking minutes for data analyses that entailed graduate students or even faculty submitting overnight punch-card jobs just a generation ago. It is indeed difficult to overestimate the impact computers have had on experimental psychology.

## Conclusion

It is interesting to see the dramatic changes that have taken place in research methodology over the past 50 years. These changes belie the notion that research methods is a static, unchanging field. Staying abreast of changes in methodology appears to be just as important as staying current in a content field of psychology. It will be interesting to see what the next 50 years hold.

# References

Ad hoc Committee on Ethical Standards in Psychological Research (1973). *Ethical principles in the conduct of research with human participants.* Washington, DC: American Psychological Association.

Adair, J. G., Dushenko, T. W., & Lindsay, R. C. L. (1985). Ethical regulations and their impact on research practice. *American Psychologist, 40,* 59–72.

American Psychological Association (1971). *Principles for the care and use of animals.* Washington, DC: American Psychological Association.

American Psychological Association (1973). *Ethical principles in the conduct of research with human participants.* Washington, DC: American Psychological Association.

Beach, F. A. (1951). Instinctive behavior: Reproductive activities. In S. S. Stevens (ed.), *Experimental psychology* (pp. 387–434). New York: John Wiley & Sons.

Benedict, J., & Stoloff, M. (1991). Animal laboratory facilities at "America's best" undergraduate colleges. *American Psychologist, 46,* 535–6.

Benjamin, L. T., Jr. (2000). The psychology laboratory at the turn of the 20th century. *American Psychologist, 55,* 318–21.

Bornstein, R. F. (2001). Has psychology become the science of questionnaires? *The General Psychologist, 36,* 36–40.

Bowd, A. D., & Shapiro, K. J. (1993). The case against laboratory animal research in psychology. *Journal of Social Issues, 49,* 133–42.

Bröder, A. (1998). Deception can be acceptable. *American Psychologist, 53,* 805–6.

Campbell, D. T., & Stanley, J. C. (1966). *Experimental and quasi-experimental designs for research.* Boston: Houghton Mifflin.

Canter, M. B., Bennett, B. E., Jones, S. E., & Nagy, T. F. (1994). *Ethics for psychologists: A commentary on the APA ethics code.* Washington, DC: American Psychological Association.

Carlson, N. R. (2002). *Foundations of physiological psychology* (5th edn.). Boston: Allyn & Bacon.

Carsrud, A. L. (1975). Undergraduate psychology conferences: Is good research nested under Ph.D.s? *Teaching of Psychology, 2,* 112–14.

Carsrud, A. L. (1978). Undergraduate research: Are we willing to support it? *Teaching of Psychology, 5,* 37–8.

Castellan, N. J., Jr. (1975). The modern minicomputer in laboratory automation. *American Psychologist, 30,* 205–11.

Cooney, B. R., & Griffith, D. M. (1994). *The 1992–1993 undergraduate department survey.* Washington, DC: American Psychological Association.

Creswell, J. W. (1994). *Research design: Qualitative & quantitative approaches.* Thousand Oaks, CA: Sage.

Cummings, N. A. (1992). Professional psychology's 50-year centennial. *American Psychologist, 47,* 845–6.

Dewsbury, D. A. (1990). Early interactions between animal psychologists and animal activists and the founding of the APA Committee on Precautions in Animal Experimentation. *American Psychologist, 45,* 315–27.

Doré, F. Y., & Kirouac, G. (1987). What comparative psychology is all about: Back to the future. *Journal of Comparative Psychology, 101,* 242–8.

Dukes, S. (1984). Phenomenological methodology in the human sciences. *Journal of Religion and Health, 23,* 197–203.

Eagley, A. H. (1995). The science and politics of comparing women and men. *American Psychologist, 50,* 145–58.

Ellis, H. C., & Hunt, R. R. (1993). *Fundamentals of cognitive psychology* (5th edn.). Madison, WI: Brown & Benchmark.

Galef, B. G. (1987). Comparative psychology is dead! Long live comparative psychology. *Journal of Comparative Psychology, 101,* 259–61.

Gallup, G. G., & Eddy, T. J. (1990). Animal facilities survey. *American Psychologist, 45,* 400–1.

Gergen, M. M. (ed.) (1988). *Feminist thought and the structure of knowledge.* New York: New York University Press.

Gubrium, J. F., & Holstein, J. A. (1997). *The new language of qualitative method.* New York: Oxford University Press.

Harding, S. (1986). *The science question in feminism.* Ithaca, NY: Cornell University Press.

Herrera, C. D. (1997). A historical interpretation of deceptive experiments in American psychology. *History of the Human Sciences, 10,* 23–36.

Hilgard, E. R. (1987). *Psychology in America: A historical survey.* San Diego, CA: Harcourt Brace Jovanovich.

Hirsch, J. (1987). Editor's introduction. *Journal of Comparative Psychology, 101,* 219–20.

Hobbs, N. (1948). The development of a code of ethical standards for psychology. *American Psychologist, 3,* 80–4.

Holder, W. B., Leavitt, G. S., & McKenna, F. S. (1958). Undergraduate training for psychologists. *American Psychologist, 13,* 585–8.

Howard, A., Pion, G., Gottfredson, G. D., et al. (1986). The changing face of American psychology: A report from the Committee on Employment and Human Resources. *American Psychologist, 41,* 1311–27.

Kalat, J. W. (2001). *Biological psychology* (7th edn.). Belmont, CA: Wadsworth.

Keyes, B. J., & Hogberg, D. K. (1990). Undergraduate psychology alumni: Gender and cohort differences in course usefulness, postbaccalaureate education, and career paths. *Teaching of Psychology, 17,* 101–5.

Kierniesky, N. C. (1984). Undergraduate research in small psychology departments. *Teaching of Psychology, 11,* 15–18.

Kimmel, A. J. (1998). In defense of deception. *American Psychologist, 53,* 803–5.

Korn, J. H. (1998). The reality of deception. *American Psychologist, 53,* 805.

Kulik, J. A. (1973). *Undergraduate education in psychology.* Washington, DC: American Psychological Association.

Lau, Y.-F., & Cheney, C. (1997). Respondent knowledge questioned. *American Psychologist, 52,* 1249.

Lawson, T. J. (1995). Gaining admission into graduate programs in psychology: An update. *Teaching of Psychology, 22,* 225–7.

Leibowitz, H. W. (1996). The symbiosis between basic and applied research. *American Psychologist, 51,* 366–70.

Lieberman, D. A. (1979). Behaviorism and the mind: A (limited) call for a return to introspection. *American Psychologist, 34,* 319–33.

Maccoby, E. E., & Jacklin, C. N. (1974). *The psychology of sex differences.* Stanford, CA: Stanford University Press.

Marshall, C., & Rossman, G. B. (1989). *Designing qualitative research.* Newbury Park, CA: Sage.

Milgram, S. (1963). Behavioral study of obedience. *Journal of Abnormal and Social Psychology, 67,* 371–8.

Nation, J. R. (1997). *Research methods.* Upper Saddle River, NJ: Prentice Hall.

National Science Foundation (1994). *Women, minorities, and persons with disabilities in science and engineering: 1994* (NSF 94-333). Arlington, VA: National Science Foundation.

Neisser, U. (1967). *Cognitive psychology.* New York: Appleton-Century-Crofts.

Neuman, W. L. (1991). *Social research methods: Qualitative and quantitative approaches.* Boston: Allyn & Bacon.

Ortmann, A., & Hertwig, R. (1997). Is deception acceptable? *American Psychologist, 52,* 746–7.

Ortmann, A., & Hertwig, R. (1998). The question remains: Is deception acceptable? *American Psychologist, 53,* 806–7.

Palladino, J. J., Carsrud, A. L., Hulicka, I. M., & Benjamin, L. T., Jr. (1982). Undergraduate research in psychology: Assessment and directions. *Teaching of Psychology, 9,* 71–4.

Perlman, B., & McCann, L. I. (1999). The most frequently listed courses in the undergraduate psychology curriculum. *Teaching of Psychology, 26,* 177–82.

Pion, G. M., Mednick, M. T., Astin, H. S., et al. (1996). The shifting gender composition of psychology: Trends and implications for the discipline. *American Psychologist, 51,* 509–28.

Plous, S. (1996a). Attitudes toward the use of animals in psychological research and education: Results from a national survey of psychologists. *American Psychologist, 51,* 1167–80.

Plous, S. (1996b). Attitudes toward the use of animals in psychological research and education: Results from a national survey of psychology majors. *Psychological Science, 7,* 352–8.

Robins, R. W., Gosling, S. D., & Craik, K. W. (1999). An empirical analysis of trends in psychology. *American Psychologist, 54,* 117–28.

Robinson, D. N. (1990). Comment on animal research labs. *American Psychologist, 45,* 1269.

Rosenau, P. M. (1992). *Post-modernism and the social sciences.* Princeton, NJ: Princeton University Press.

Rowan, A. N., & Loew, F. M. (1995). *The animal research controversy: Protest, process & public policy.* North Grafton, MA: Tufts University, Center for Animals & Public Policy.

Sarter, M., Berntson, G. G., & Cacioppo, J. T. (1996). Brain imaging and cognitive neuroscience: Toward strong inference in attributing function to structure. *American Psychologist, 51,* 13–21.

Scheirer, C. J., & Rogers, A. M. (1985). *The undergraduate psychology curriculum: 1984.* Washington, DC: American Psychological Association.

Shapiro, K. J. (1997). The separate world of animal research. *American Psychologist, 52,* 1250.

Sidman, M. (1960). *Tactics of scientific research: Evaluating experimental data in psychology.* New York: Basic Books.

Smith, R. A. (1985). Advising beginning psychology majors for graduate school. *Teaching of Psychology, 12,* 194–8.

Smith, R. A., & Davis, S. F. (2001). *The psychologist as detective: An introduction to conducting research in psychology* (2nd edn.). Upper Saddle River, NJ: Prentice Hall.

Society for the Teaching of Psychology (n.d.). *Undergraduate research conferences in psychology.* Retrieved October 18, 2001 from <http://teachpsych.lemoyne.edu/teachpsych/div/conferences-undergraduate.html>.

Stevens, S. S. (ed.) (1951). *Handbook of experimental psychology.* New York: John Wiley & Sons.

Strauss, A., & Corbin, J. (1990). *Basics of qualitative research: Grounded theory procedures and techniques.* Newbury Park, CA: Sage.

Thomas, J. (1993). *Doing critical ethnography.* Newbury Park, CA: Sage.

Ulrich, R. E. (1991). Animal rights, animal wrongs and the question of balance. *Psychological Science, 2,* 197–201.

Viney, W., King, D. B., & Berndt, J. (1990). Animal research in psychology: Declining or thriving? *Journal of Comparative Psychology, 104,* 322–5.

Vonk, R. (1997). Attitudes toward animal research. *American Psychologist, 52,* 1248–9.

Ward, J. H., Jr. (1955). Use of electronic computers in psychological research. *American Psychologist, 10,* 826–7.

Weiten, W., & Wight, R. D. (1992). Portraits of a discipline: An examination of introductory psychology textbooks in America. In A. E. Puente, J. R. Matthews, & C. L. Brewer (eds.),

*Teaching psychology in America: A history* (pp. 453–504). Washington, DC: American Psychological Association.

Werner, O., & Schopfle, G. (1987). *Systematic fieldwork: Vol. 1, Foundations of ethnography and interviewing*. Newbury Park, CA: Sage.

West, S. G., & Gunn, S. P. (1978). Some issues of ethics and social psychology. *American Psychologist, 33,* 30–8.

Woodworth, R. S. (1938). *Experimental psychology*. New York: Henry Holt and Company.

Woodworth, R. S., & Schlosberg, H. (1954). *Experimental psychology* (rev. edn.). New York: Holt, Rinehart and Winston.

Yin, R. K. (1989). *Case study research: Design and methods*. Newbury Park, CA: Sage.

# CHAPTER SEVEN

# Ethical Issues in Psychological Research with Human Participants

## Richard L. Miller

The pursuit of new knowledge is a valuable human endeavor that relies on systematic, empirical investigation as a key means for advancing that knowledge. Research helps people to make sense of the world in which they live and the events they experience. The knowledge gained through psychological research has provided many practical benefits as well as invaluable insights into the causes of human behavior. Despite the obvious advantages of the knowledge provided by research, the process of conducting scientific research can pose serious ethical dilemmas. Because research is a complex process, well-intentioned investigators can overlook the interests of research participants, thereby causing harm to the participants, scientists, science, and society.

## A Historical Review of Research Ethics

Concern about the ethical treatment of research participants came about partly as a result of the atrocities committed by Nazi investigators conducting concentration camp experiments. At the end of World War II, 23 Nazi researchers, mostly physicians, were tried before the Nuremberg Military Tribunal. At the trial, it was important for the prosecutors to distinguish between the procedures used in Nazi experiments and those used by US wartime investigators. To do this, the judges agreed on 10 basic principles for research using human participants. Interestingly, many of the key principles, for example, informed consent, echoed German regulations in place before and during the Nazi era, which also included provisions for nonexploitation of the needy, special consideration of cases involving minors, and prohibitions on the use of dying persons. The principles formulated by the Tribunal became known as the Nuremberg Code.

Many of the principles set forth in the Nuremberg Code continue to form the foundation for ethical practices used today, including voluntary consent of the human participant, the avoidance of unnecessary suffering or injury, limitations on the degree of risk allowed, and the opportunity for the research participant to withdraw. Although these principles were considered laudatory, many American investigators viewed them as relevant only to Nazi war crimes (Rothman, 1991).

In the United States, oversight has come about as a result of a history of ethical abuses and exploitation. In 1996, Beecher published an article in which he presented 22 examples of ethically questionable studies including the infamous study at the Willowbrook State School for the Retarded at which a mild strain of virus was injected into children. These and other abuses have often come at the expense of vulnerable participants (see Backlar, 2000), therefore undermining the trust needed by behavioral scientists to conduct research. Indeed, distrust of research is particularly common within certain segments of American society. For example, research projects such as the well-publicized Tuskegee Syphilis Study (Heller, 1972), have created reasonable doubt among African Americans as to the benevolence and value of research (Corbie-Smith, Thomas, Williams, & Moody-Ayers, 1999; Sugarman et al., 1998).

To address these ethical concerns, the National Commission for the Protection of Human Subjects of Biomedical and Behavior Research was created and is best known for the *Belmont Report*, which identifies three basic ethical principles and their application to research: respect for persons, beneficence, and justice (National Commission, 1978). These principles form the basis for provisions related to procedures insuring informed consent, assessment of risk and potential benefits, and selection of participants. In response to the *Belmont Report*, federal regulation of research became more systematic. While the primary responsibility for the ethical treatment of participants remains with the individual investigator, research in the USA conducted by individuals affiliated with universities, schools, hospitals, and many other institutions is now reviewed by a committee of individuals with a diverse background who examine the proposed research project for any breach of ethical procedures. These review committees, commonly called Institutional Review Boards (IRBs), were mandated by the National Research Act, Public Law 93–348, and require researchers to prepare an application or protocol describing various aspects of the research and to submit this protocol along with informed consent forms for approval prior to the implementation of a research project. The review of the proposed research by the IRB will include an examination of the procedure, the nature of the participants, and other relevant factors in the research design. The IRB will also identify the relevant ethical issues that may be of concern and will decide what is at stake for the participant, the researcher, and the institution with which the researcher is affiliated. If there are ethical concerns, the IRB will likely suggest alternatives to the proposed procedures. Finally, the IRB will provide the researcher with a formal statement of what must be changed in order to receive IRB approval of the research project.

The attempt by Institutional Review Boards to ensure ethical practices has caused some dissatisfaction among scientists. Because IRBs are not federal agencies but are instead created by local institutions, they have come under criticism for (a) a lack of standard procedures and requirements (Cohen, Dolan, & Eastman, 1996), (b) delays in completing the review process (Mitchell & Steingrub, 1988), and (c) creating the fear that IRBs will impose institutional sanctions on individual researchers (Brookhart, 2001). An additional criticism is that the rules, initially designed for medical studies, are poorly adapted to many behavioral science research projects (Brainard, 2001). To address these concerns, Rosnow and his colleagues (1993) suggest that IRBs should adopt more consistent guidelines for evaluating research protocols, place limits on the power given to the IRB (Prentice & Antonson, 1987), include an evaluation of the technical merit of a proposal as a means of determining risk/benefit ratios (Hershey, 1985), and develop a series of case studies to help sensitize members of an IRB to ethical dilemmas within the social sciences and ways they may be resolved. Rosnow et al. (1993) also point out that the decisions of IRBs reflect current norms within the scientific community and therefore are constantly changing. Moreno, Caplan, Wolpe, and the Members of the Project on Informed Consent, Human Research Ethics Group (1998) have made a number of specific recommendations for updating the current system used by IRBs. They recommend that IRBs adopt special provisions concerning cognitively impaired persons; encourage the recruitment of women, minorities, and children as research participants; adopt provisions that ensure students be given alternatives to participation in research when the research is a class requirement; and carefully review cases where a financial conflict of interest may occur. Recently, in response to a report by the American Association of Universities Task Force on Research Accountability (2000), federal agencies and individual Institutional Review Boards have taken steps to provide training for IRB staff and researchers involved in human participants research.

## Ethical Concerns in Recruiting Participants

One of the first ethical issues a researcher must address involves the recruitment of research participants. In the recruitment process, researchers must be guided by the principles of autonomy, respect for persons, and the principle of beneficence that requires that researchers minimize the possible harm to participants while maximizing the benefits from the research (Scott-Jones, 2000).

The first stage in the recruitment of participants is often an advertisement for the research project. The advertisement generally describes the basic nature of the research project and the qualifications that are needed to participate. The American Psychological Association (APA) and several scientists have described a variety of ethical issues in the selection and recruitment of participants in research including advertising, inducements and coercion, consent and alternatives to consent, institutional approval of access to participants, and rules related to using student subject pools (APA, 1982; Blanck, Bellack, Rosnow, Rotheram-Borus, & Schooler, 1992; Grisso et al., 1991; Kelman, 1967). An ethical lapse discussed by Rosenthal (1994) is "hyperclaiming," in which the researcher exaggerates the goals the research is likely to achieve in describing the project to prospective participants. Another ethical issue to be addressed in recruiting participants is whether or not the research design is of sufficient merit to warrant taking the participant's time. Pomerantz (1994) points out that many wasteful, inefficient, and incompetently designed studies are regularly approved by IRBs who may rationalize that there is no real harm because the procedures applied to the participant are relatively innocuous, incurring less than minimal risk.

Many studies provide some sort of monetary or other valued inducement to attract and compensate participants. It is important that researchers not exploit potential participants by offering inducements that are difficult to refuse. At the same time, researchers must weigh the costs to the participant and provide adequate compensation for the time they spend in the research process (Scott-Jones, 2000). It is especially important to consider carefully the coercive possibilities of the inducements offered when conducting research with vulnerable populations (Paradis, 2000; Regehr, Edwardh, & Bradford, 2000; Roberts, Solomon, Roberts, & Keith, 1998). Likewise, special provisions for research with prisoners are described in the Code of Federal Regulations (Title 45, Part 46; Office for Protection from Research Risks, 1991).

Most psychological research is conducted using students recruited from university subject pools, which raises ethical concerns related to coercion as the students' grades may be linked with participation (Jung, 1969; Higbee, Millard, & Folkman, 1982; Leak, 1981). Ethical practice requires that students be given a reasonable alternative to participation in order to obtain the same credit as those who choose to participate in research (APA's *Ethical Principles of Psychologists and Code of Conduct*, 1992, Principle 6.11d). The alternatives offered must not be seen by students as punitive or more stringent than research participation.

In the recruitment process, researchers should attempt to eliminate any potential participants who may be harmed by the research. Research protocols submitted to an IRB typically have a section in which the researcher describes this screening process and the criteria that will be used to include or exclude persons from the study. The screening process is of particular importance when using proxy decisions for incompetent persons (Lynn, 1998) and when conducting clinical research (Bersoff & Bersoff, 1999; Miller, 2000).

In the recruitment plan, it is important that the sample be representative of the population to which the research findings can be generalized. Blanck et al. (1992) have called for enhanced recruitment and the inclusion of more representative samples. Rosenthal and Rosnow have proposed a number of procedures to reduce volunteer bias in the recruitment of research participants so as to make the sample more representative (Rosenthal & Rosnow, 1991; Rosnow & Rosenthal, 1993). Sometimes portions of a population are excluded from participation because the researcher is unwilling to undertake procedures necessary for inclusion. For example, Bayer and Tadd (2000) have documented the unjustified exclusion of elderly people from research.

In summary, researchers should plan their recruitment of research participants in such a way as to be noncoercive, inclusionary to the extent possible, and representative of the larger population to which the research results may be applied.

## Informed Consent and Debriefing

Informed consent is the cornerstone of ethical research. Consent can be thought of as a contract in which the participant agrees to tolerate experimental procedures that may include boredom, deception, and discomfort for the good of science, while the researcher guarantees the safety and well-being of the participant. In all but minimal-risk research, informed consent is a formal process whereby the relevant aspects of the research are described along with the obligations and responsibilities of both the participant and the researcher. An important distinction is made between "at risk" and "minimal risk." Minimal risk refers to a level of harm or discomfort no greater than that which the participant might expect to experience in daily life. Research that poses minimal risk to the participant is allowed greater flexibility with regard to informed consent, the use of deception, and other ethically questionable procedures. However, in determining the risk : benefit ratio, even where minimal risk is involved, Rosenthal (1994) suggests that the likely quality of the results of the research is an important consideration. Even minor inconvenience to participants is perhaps too costly if the research is poorly designed and unlikely to be of any scientific value.

Informed consent presents difficulties when the potential participants are children (Edwards & Allred, 1999; Hall, 1991), the participants speak a different language than the experimenter (Berlin, 1995), the research is therapeutic but the participants are unable to provide informed consent (Wendler, 2000), and when the researcher holds multiple forms of personal bias that can influence the potential participants (Alver, 1995). Certain research methodologies make it difficult to obtain informed consent, as when the methodology includes disguised observation or other covert methods (Goode, 1996). Herrera (1999) defends the omission of informed consent in covert studies on the basis of the need to protect participants from nervousness, apprehension, and in some cases criminal prosecution. Studies that blur the distinction between consent for treatment or therapy and consent for research also pose ethical problems (Cannold, 1997). Mann (1994) found that many aspects of the research described in a consent form are not well understood, that participants may not understand the purpose and consequences of signing a consent form, and that longer consent forms that try to present a full and complete description of the research may be less well understood than shorter, more succinct consent forms. While most psychological research includes an informed consent process, it should be noted that federal guidelines permit informed consent to be waived if (a) the research involves no more than minimal risk to the participants, (b) the waiver will not adversely affect the rights and welfare of the particip-ants, and (c) the research could not be feasibly conducted if informed consent were required (Fischman, 2000).

Sieber (1992) suggests that the researcher should see informed consent as an on-going process in which good communication characterized by openness and honesty occur. The final stage of this on-going consent process is the debriefing, in which the particip-ant is given an opportunity to discuss the findings of the study. The need to adequately debrief participants in a research study has been addressed in several articles (Blanck et al., 1992; Holmes, 1976a; Stewart, 1992; West & Gunn, 1978), but, as McConnell and Krebs (1993) point out, is still the exception rather than the rule. Debriefing can serve four purposes. It can (a) remove fraudulent information about the participant given during the research process, (b) desensitize subjects who have been given poten-tially disturbing information about themselves, (c) remove the participants' negative arousal resulting from the research procedure (Holmes, 1976b; Schwartz & Gottlieb,

1980), and (d) provide therapeutic or educational value to the participant (Landrum & Chastain, 1995). With regard to the educational value of debriefing, it is worth noting that Miller (1981), in a study of top research universities, found little evidence that experimental participation was being used as a valuable educational tool, although the potential for providing educational value remains and is an important student expectation. Gurman (1994) has recommended that participants who are screened out of a study or voluntarily withdraw from a study should also be debriefed and that the information provided be informative as to why they might have been eliminated from the study. It has also been suggested that a description of the debriefing procedure be included in any scientific publication of the research (Korn & Bram, 1988; Perry & Abramson, 1980).

## The Use of Deception in Psychological Research

At one time deception was routinely practiced in behavioral science research, and by the 1960s research participants, usually college students, expected deception and as a result sometimes produced different results than those obtained from unsuspecting participants (Diener & Crandall, 1978). In general, psychologists use deception in order to prevent participants from learning the true purpose of the study, which might in turn affect their behavior. Many forms of deception exist, including the use of an experimental confederate posing as another participant, providing false feedback to participants, presenting two related studies as unrelated, and giving incorrect information regarding stimulus. The acceptability of deception remains controversial although the practice is common (Littlejohn, 1991). One of the earliest criticisms of deception was by Herbert Kelman (1967) who suggested that deception was often used as a preferred means of conducting research rather than as a last resort when other means would not provide a valid test of the hypothesis. Baumrind (1979) echoed Kelman's concerns and suggested that deception violates the fundamental moral principles of justice and reciprocity. More recently, Ortmann and Hertwig (1997), citing a dramatic increase in experiments utilizing deception, argued against using any deception of research participants because of the possible long-term negative consequences when using deception. Broder (1998) takes an opposing view, arguing that at times deception is needed and that most participants do not become jaded as a result of being deceived. Kimmel (1998) has called the suggestion that all forms of deception be eliminated "methodologically unsound and ethically misguided," because what is the most ethical is not always the most effective way of conducting research. Korn (1998) suggests that beginning in 1994 the number of studies that used deception has actually decreased. In a study with college students, Fisher and Fryberg (1994) found that researchers tend to be more concerned about the dangers of deception than do research participants. Students' evaluation of studies that used deception were directly related to the studies' scientific merit, value, methodological alternatives, discomfort experienced by the participants, and the efficacy of the debriefing procedures. Both participants and researchers tend to conduct a kind of cost–benefit analysis when assessing the ethics of deception, and participants view deception as a necessary aspect of certain types of research (Smith & Richardson, 1983) that is acceptable as long as the deception is for good reason (Christensen, 1988).

Several alternatives to using deception have been suggested. Geller (1982) suggests that role-playing can be used in lieu of deception and demonstrated results equivalent to those obtained by Milgram (1974) using a role-playing procedure. Simulation methods such as those employed by Zimbardo et al. (1973) in the well-known Stanford prison experiment have been suggested as an alternative to deception, although that study has also come under criticism for ethical insensitivity. In field research, many researchers have sought to develop reciprocal relationships with their participants (Wax, 1982) in order to promote acceptance of occasional deception. Such reciprocal relationships can provide direct benefits to the participants as a result of the research process. In cases where deception is unavoidable, the method of assumed consent can be used (Cozby, 1981; Berscheid, Baron, Dermer, & Libman, 1973). In this approach, a sample taken from the same pool as the potential participants is given a complete description of the proposed study, including all aspects of the deception, and asked whether they would be willing to participate in the study. A benchmark of 95 percent agreement allows the researcher to proceed with the deception manipulation.


## Avoiding Harm: Pain and Suffering


Participants' consent is typically somewhat uninformed in order to obtain valid information untainted by knowledge of the researcher's hypothesis and expectations. Because of this lack of full disclosure, it is important that the researcher ensure that no harm will come to the participant in the research process. Protection from harm is a foundational issue in research ethics. Types of harm that must be considered by the researcher include physical harm; psychological stress; feelings of having ones' dignity, self-esteem, or self-efficacy compromised; or becoming the subject of legal action (APA, 1982). Other types of potential harm include economic harm, including the imposition of financial costs to the participants, and social harms that involve negative affects on a person's interactions or relationships with others. In addition to considering the potential harm that may accrue to the research participant, the possibility of harm to the participant's family, friends, social group, and society must be considered (NBAC, 1999).

While conducting research, it is the researcher's responsibility to monitor actual or potential harm to the participant in case the level of harm changes during the course of the research. One way that the level of potential harm can change is as a result of a mistake made by the researcher. In the case of increased likelihood of harm, the researcher should inform the participant and remind him or her that voluntary withdrawal without penalty is available (Eyde, 2000).

A particular kind of harm addressed in the 1992 APA Code of Ethics is the harm caused by culturally incompetent researchers whose perceptions of gender and race are misinformed by the dominant group's view of social reality (Casas & San Miquel, 1993; Daniel, 1994; Mio & Iwamasa, 1993). Research designs constructed by researchers with uninformed views can reinforce negative stereotypes about the group studied (Fisher,

Jackson, & Villarruel, 1997). One way that has been suggested to avoid this ethical bias is to view research participants as partners as opposed to subjects in the research process (Fisher 1997; Fisher, Higgins, Rau, Kuther, & Belanger, 1996). The perception of partnership can be fostered by taking the participants into the researchers' confidence, providing a thorough debriefing and the opportunity for further involvement in a role other than "subject." Another type of harm that is not included in the usual lists is the harm that can result from disclosure of uncensored information (Akeroyd, 1991; Finnegan, 1992; Lee, 1993). This type of harm is of special concern to researchers engaged in field research (de Laine, 2000).

Although psychological research into certain processes, for example anxiety, depends on the arousal of some discomfort in the participant, it is the responsibility of the researcher to look for ways to minimize this discomfort. In many situations, discomfort is inherent in what is being studied. When nothing can be done to eliminate this type of discomfort, some ways that may minimize the psychological consequences of the discomfort include full and candid disclosure of the experimental procedures, providing opportunities for the participant to withdraw, and ensuring that there are no lingering ill effects of the discomfort. One particular type of lingering ill effect relates to the possibility of embarrassment that participants can experience as a result of their behavior during the research process. To protect participants from this type of harm, it is essential that researchers employ procedures to maintain confidentiality.

## Maintaining Confidentiality

Respecting the privacy of the research participant involves much more than just obtaining informed consent. Confidentiality is a complex, multifaceted issue. It involves an agreement, implicit as well as explicit, between the researcher and the participant regarding disclosure of information about the participant and how the participant's data will be handled and transmitted (Sieber, 1992). Diener and Crandall (1978) suggest three dimensions to consider when making a decision about privacy: sensitivity of the information, the research setting (public or private), and the dissemination of the information. The participant has the right to decide what information will be disclosed, to whom it will be disclosed, under what circumstances it will be disclosed, and when it will be disclosed (Singleton, Straits, Straits, & McAllister, 1988).

Participants must be informed about mandatory reporting requirements, for example, illegal activity, plans for sharing information about the participant with others, and the extent to which confidentiality can be legally protected (NBAC, 2001) It is the responsibility of review committees to ensure that the proposed research procedures will not unintentionally compromise confidentiality. Sieber (2000) points out that respect for participants' privacy is more difficult when the participant is different from the investigator in gender, age, ethnicity, locale, or socioeconomic status, and Folkman (2000) suggests that a breach of confidentiality can be particularly harmful in special populations.

There are exceptions to the rule regarding confidentiality. The 1992 APA Code of Ethics allows for a breach of confidentiality to protect third parties, and several states have embraced the Supreme Court ruling in Tarasoff v. Board of Regents of the University of California (1976) which requires the psychologist to take reasonable steps to protect potential victims. Researchers not trained in clinical diagnosis can find themselves in a difficult position interpreting the likelihood of harm from statements made by research participants.

At one time, removal of a person's name from the data associated with that person was considered sufficient to ensure confidentiality. New technologies (Libutti, 1999; Michalak, 1998), along with government statutes and access by third parties to data, can threaten confidentiality agreements although both state and federal courts have been willing to uphold promises of confidentiality made to research participants. Techniques to maintain confidentiality of data include data encryption and electronic security (Bongar, 1988; Fox & Tracy, 1986). Although most quantified data are presented in aggregate form, some types of data such as video recordings, photographs, and audio recordings require special care in order to protect participants' privacy. Distortion of the images and sounds can be done but the most important safeguard is to obtain permission from the participant to use the material (Folkman, 2000).

Similarly, qualitative research poses special difficulties for maintaining privacy and confidentiality (Turnbull, 2000; Wax, 1995). Techniques for maintaining confidentiality include the use of pseudonyms or fictitious biographies (LaRossa, Bennett, & Gelles, 1981) and the coding of tapes and other data recording methods in which participant identification cannot be disguised (Bussell, 1994). In qualitative research the most important ethical practice is to obtain informed consent throughout the research process, including the dissemination of the findings (Smythe & Murray, 2000). Also, it is the researchers' responsibility to take reasonable precautions to ensure that participants respect the privacy of other participants, particularly in research settings where others are able to observe the behavior of the participant (Bell-Dolan & Wessler, 1994). Lawson (1995) has proposed a contractualist conception of the research process that defines when certain types of ethically problematic research should be permissible, including the issue of confidentiality. Whatever procedures a researcher intends to use to maintain confidentiality should be discussed with the participant prior to the beginning of data collection. The participant should be satisfied that the procedures will be sufficient to ensure his or her privacy and typically the participant's satisfaction is formally recorded in an informed consent agreement.

## Assessing Risks and Benefits

One of the responsibilities of an IRB is to ask the question: will the knowledge gained from this research be worth the inconvenience and potential cost to the participant? Both the magnitude of the benefits to the participant and the potential scientific and social value of the research must be considered (Fisher & Fryberg, 1994). Some of the potential types of benefits of psychological research are (a) an increase in basic knowledge of psychological processes; (b) improved methodological and assessment procedures; (c) practical outcomes and benefits to others; (d) benefits for the researchers, including the educational functions of research in preparing students to think critically and creatively about their field; and (e) direct, sometimes therapeutic, benefits to the participants, for example in clinical research.

Some of the potential costs to the participant are social and physical discomfort, boredom, anxiety, stress, loss of self-esteem, legal risks, economic risks, social risks, and other aversive consequences. In general, the risks associated with the research should be considered from the perspective of the participant, the researcher, and society as a whole, and should include an awareness that the risks to the participant may come not only from the research process, but also from particular vulnerabilities of the participant or from the failure of the researcher to use appropriate strategies to reduce risk (Sieber, 2000).

The IRB's job of balancing these costs and benefits is difficult since the types of costs and benefits are so varied (Martin, Meslin, Kohut, & Singer, 1995). The deliberations of the IRB in arriving at a "favorable ratio" should be formed with respect to the guidelines provided in the *Belmont Report*, which encourages ethical review committees to examine all aspects of the research carefully and to consider, on behalf of the researcher, alternative procedures to reduce risks to the participants (National Commission, 1978). Meslin (1990) has proposed a model for improving risk judgments, which includes a quantification of the probability and magnitude of harm expected from different types of risks.

The careful deliberation of the cost : benefit ratio is of particular importance in research with those unable to provide informed consent, such as the cognitively impaired (Karlawish & Sachs, 1997); research where there is risk without direct benefit to the participant (Carpenter & Conley, 1999); research with such vulnerable populations as children and adolescents (Fisher & Wallace, 2000); and therapeutic research in which the participant in need of treatment is likely to overestimate the benefit and underestimate the risk, even when the researcher has provided a full and candid description of the likelihood of success and possible deleterious effects (Capron, 1972). It is also worth noting that when the benefits of the research to society are substantial, there is a tendency to want to extract information even from unwilling participants (Fox, 1974).

## Ethical Issues in Conducting Research with Vulnerable Populations

An important ethical concern considered by IRBs is the protection of those who are not able fully to protect themselves. Because determining vulnerability can be difficult (Candilis, 2001), several types of people can be considered vulnerable for research purposes, including people who lack resources or autonomy, people who have an abundance of resources, people who are stigmatized, people who are institutionalized, people who cannot speak for themselves, people who engage in illegal activities, and people who may be damaged by the information revealed about them as a result of the research (Sieber, 1992). One of the principal groups of research participants considered to be vulnerable is children and adolescents (Ackerman, 1995; Fisher & Wallace, 2000; Leikin, 1993; Mammel & Kaplan, 1995; Phillips, 1994; Porter, 1995; Rogers, D'Angelo, & Futterman, 1994; Scott-Jones, 1994; Sieber, 1994a; Theut & Kohrman, 1990). In addition to legal constraints on research with minors adopted by the United States Department of Health and Human Services (DHHS), ethical practices must address issues of risk and maturity, privacy and autonomy, parental permission, and the circumstances in which permission can be waived, and the assent of the institution (school, treatment facility) where the research is to be conducted (Hoagwood, Jensen, & Fisher, 1996).

Other vulnerable groups addressed in the literature include minorities (Harris, 1996; Scarr, 1988), prisoners (Megargee, 1995; Reilly, 1991), trauma victims (Thompson, 1995), the homeless (Hutz & Koller, 1999; Paradis, 2000), Alzheimers patients (High, 1993), gays and lesbians (Anonymous, 1995), individuals with AIDS and STDs (Ringheim, 1995), and juvenile offenders (Mulvey & Phelps, 1988).

Ethical issues involving research with the elderly have been examined (Strain & Chappell, 1982; Long, 1982), particularly issues regarding research with those confined to nursing homes where participants are often submissive to authority. Additional concerns include privacy and autonomy (Schuster, 1996), as well as the quality of reporting ethical practices when conducting nursing home research (Karlawish, Hougham, Stocking, & Sachs, 1999). On the other hand, Bayer and Tadd (2000) point out that some researchers place unjustifiable age limits on their participant population, excluding qualified elderly people from participating in research.

Several studies have examined ethical issues when conducting research with psychiatric patients (DeRenzo, 1994; Hyman, 1999; Miller & Rosenstein, 1997; Pinals, Malhotra, Breier, & Pickar, 1998; Roberts et al., 1998; Roberts & Roberts, 1999). Candilis (2001) reviews recent lapses in the practice of informed consent and suggests ways to determine individual vulnerability and protect research participants. A major ethical concern with clinical research is how to form a control group without unethically denying treatment to some participants, for example, those assigned to a placebo control group. Miller (2000) argues that an absolute ethical prohibition of placebo-controlled trials is unsound, and suggests that active-controlled trials could be an ethical alternative to placebo-controlled trials. In their article on research ethics with schizophrenics, Carpenter and Conley (1999) propose a means for viewing research proposals allowing autonomy and altruism regardless of diagnostic class. Their paper also discusses what should be done with proposals that include risk without direct benefit to the patient.

A number of ethical issues arise when studying families at risk (LaRossa, Bennett, & Gelles, 1981; Parker & Lidz, 1994). Among the ethical issues to be considered are the responsibility of the investigator in reporting abuse and neglect, conflict between research ethics and the investigator's personal ethics, identifying problems that cannot be solved, and balancing the demands made by family members and the benefits available to them (Demi & Warren, 1995).

Alcohol and substance abusers and forensic patients present particular problems for obtaining adequate informed consent. The researcher must take into account the participant's vulnerability to coercion and competence to give consent (Allebeck, 1997; Regehr, Edwardh, & Bradford, 2000; Tucker & Vuchinich, 2000). The experience of the investigator in dealing with alcoholics and drug abusers can be an important element in maintaining ethical standards related to coercion and competence to give consent (McCrady & Bux, 1999). A recent edition of the journal *Psychology of Addictive Behaviors* (vol. 14, No. 4) examines in detail ethical issues associated with research with alcoholics (Brandon & Lisman, 2000; Goldman, 2000; Wood & Sher, 2000; Tucker & Vuchinich, 2000).

Ethical issues in conducting research with abused women involve issues of safety for the participant and investigator, and the creation of an expectation on the part of the participant that action will be taken as a result of the investigation (Chatzifotiou, 2000; Jewkes, Watts, Abrahams, Penn-Xerkana, & Garcia-Moreno, 2000). Issues related to some of these conflicting ethical considerations are described by Campbell and Dienemann (2001).

One final vulnerable population addressed in the literature is the cognitively impaired (Karlawish & Sachs, 1997), with whom a major ethical concern involves adult guardianship laws (Tomossy & Weisstub, 1997) and the rules governing proxy decisions (Lynn, 1998). The question is: who speaks for the participant? Research with vulnerable participants requires the researcher to take particular care to avoid several ethical dilemmas including coercive recruiting practices, the lack of confidentiality often experienced by vulnerable participants, and the possibility of a conflict of interest between research ethics and personal ethics.

## Ethical Considerations Related to Research Methodology

### Ethical issues in conducting field research

Research conducted in the field confronts an additional ethical dilemma not usually encountered in laboratory studies. Often the participants are unaware that they are being studied, and therefore no contractual understanding can exist. In many field studies, especially those that involve observational techniques, informed consent may be impossible to obtain (Wax, 1995). This dilemma also exists when the distinction between participant and observer is blurred. Similarly, some laboratory experiments involving deception use procedures similar to field research in introducing the independent variable as unrelated to the experiment. Covert research that involves the observation of people in public places is not generally considered to constitute an invasion of privacy; however, it is sometimes difficult to determine when a reasonable expectation of privacy exists, for example, behavior in a public toilet (see Koocher, 1977; Warwick, 1973).

Because it is not usually possible to assess whether participants have been harmed in covert studies, opinions regarding the ethicality and legality of such methods vary markedly (Nash, 1975; Silverman, 1975; Wilson & Donnerstein, 1976). Four principles that must be considered in deciding on the ethicality of covert field research are (a) the availability of alternative means for studying the same question, (b) the merit of the research question, (c) the extent to which confidentiality or anonymity can be maintained, and (d) the level of risk to the uninformed participant.

One specific type of field research warrants special ethical consideration: socially sensitive research, which is defined as research where the findings can have practical consequences for the participants. Sieber and Stanley (1988) point out that ethical analysis of the research question, the research process, and the potential application of the research findings are particularly important in socially sensitive research. IRBs have been found to be very wary of socially sensitive research, more often finding fault with the research proposals (Ceci, Pewters, & Plotkin, 1985) and overestimating the extent of risk involved (Slovic, Fischoff, & Lichtenstein, 1981) as compared to their reviews of less sensitive research. Despite these difficulties, socially sensitive research has considerable potential for addressing many of society's social issues (Sieber & Stanley, 1988) and should be encouraged.

## Ethical issues in conducting archival research

Archival research can provide methodological advantages to the researcher in that unobtrusive measures are less likely to affect how participants behave (Kazdin, 1979). However, research involving archival data poses a problem for obtaining informed consent, since the research question may be very different from the one for which the data was originally collected (Fischman, 2000). In most cases, issues of privacy do not exist since an archive can be altered to remove identifying information. When the archival data involves patients' records, changes in the APA's Ethical Principles (1992) raise ethical and legal considerations related to confidentiality that must be addressed by the researcher (Taube & Burkhardt, 1997). One final ethical concern with archival research has to do with the possibility that those who create the archive may introduce systematic bias into the data set. This is of particular concern when the archive is written primarily from an official point of view that may not accurately represent the participants' attitudes, beliefs, or behavior (Rolph, 1998).

## Ethical issues in conducting Internet research

The Internet provides an international forum in which open and candid discussions of a variety of issues of interest to behavioral scientists take place. These discussions provide an opportunity for the behavioral scientist to "lurk" among Usenet discussion groups, Internet Relay Chat, and Multi-user dungeons (Miskevich, 1996). Cyberspace is typically thought of as public domain where privacy is not guaranteed and traditional ethical guidelines may be difficult to apply (Jones, 1994). A second ethical concern in Internet research is the possibility for online misrepresentation. For example, children or other vulnerable populations could be inadvertently included in research (Frankel & Siang, 1999). To address these concerns, a set of informal guidelines for acceptable behavior in the form of netiquette has developed (Smith & Leigh, 1997). In addition to these informal guidelines, APA (1997) has issued a brief statement on Internet-related ethics, and Michalak and Szabo (1998) have developed a lengthy set of rules consistent with general research guidelines and APA (1990) ethical practices to be applied to Internet research. Among other things, the guidelines suggest that researchers should identify themselves, ensure confidential treatment of personal information, obtain consent from those providing data whenever possible, and provide participants with information about the study.

Humphreys, Winzelberg, and Klaw (2000) describe the ethical responsibilities of psychologists participating in discussion groups both as professionals and peers. Bier,

Sherblom, and Gallo (1996) point out that researchers should be sensitive to possible unanticipated consequences to participants as a result of the research process, particularly in terms of potential harm to the participant in the form of stress, legal liabilities, and loss of self-esteem.

## Teaching Research Ethics as a Means of Promoting Ethical Practices

In her criticism of APA's (1992) code of ethics, Joan Sieber (1994b) pointed out that the code does not provide for education in research ethics or offer those facing an ethical dilemma a place to go for consultation. In the APA publication *Ethics in Research with Human Participants* edited by Bruce Sales and Susan Folkman, June Tangey (2000) has authored a chapter on training to help fill this void. In her chapter, Tangey suggests ways in which students can be trained in ethical practices and encourages context-based training as described by Whitbeck (1995, 1996). Tangey also describes procedures for ensuring that students and staff are competent, familiar with legal obligations, aware of safety regulations, sensitive to the need to avoid abusive or exploitative relationships, and clear about the nature of supervision and the need to honor agreements. The education of the research participant and the public is also addressed in the Tangey chapter. Several scientists have made contributions to ethics education. Bulger and Reiser (1993) provide a description of a course in research ethics. Sweet (1999) provides an educational exercise designed to teach professional ethical standards. Beins (1993) found that an exercise designed to generate the Barnum effect was effective in teaching students about the ethics of deception. Rosnow (1990) presents a classroom exercise involving role-play and discussion that can be used to sharpen critical thinking and an appreciation of research ethics. Strohmetz and Skleder (1992) provide evidence that the Rosnow role-playing exercise is effective. A process for integrating research ethics into the introductory psychology course curriculum is described by Fisher and Kuther (1997).

One of the most effective ways to teach research ethics is through the supervision of student research. Goodyear, Crego, and Johnston (1992) have identified several ethical problems that can hinder this teaching/learning experience, including incompetent or inadequate supervision, the abandonment of supervision, the intrusion of the supervisor's values, abusive and exploitive supervision, dual relationships, encouragement to fraud, and authorship issues. They suggest that one way to avoid many of these ethical difficulties is to incorporate a kind of informed consent agreement into the collaboration between faculty and students.

## Summary and Conclusion

Ethical issues must be considered when designing a research study with human participants. Specific issues to be addressed include the recruitment of participants, informed consent and debriefing procedures, the use of deception, potential psychological or physical harm to the participant, confidentiality, participant vulnerability, and privacy. Ethical practices require that the participant:

- be allowed the opportunity to decline to participate in the research and to withdraw from the research at any time without penalty;
- be informed of what will be asked of him or her as a function of participating in the research;
- be protected from psychological and physical harm;
- can assume that whatever information he or she has provided the researcher will be treated confidentially;
- has the opportunity to be debriefed in a manner which removes any misconceptions he or she has about the research.

Ethical dilemmas often arise from a conflict of interest between the needs of the researcher and the needs of the participant and/or the public at large. A conflict of interest can occur when the researcher occupies multiple roles, for example, clinician/researcher, or within a single role such as a program evaluation researcher who experiences sponsor pressures for results that may compromise scientific rigor.

In resolving ethical dilemmas, psychologists are guided in their research practices by APA guidelines as well as Federal regulations that mandate that research be approved by an Institutional Review Board. Sales and Lavin (2000) suggest a set of heuristics that can be used in finding solutions to the types of ethical conflicts that psychologists are likely to encounter. These heuristics include (a) using the ethical standards of the profession, (b) applying ethical and moral principles, (c) understanding the legal responsibilities placed upon the researcher, and (d) consulting with professional colleagues. In the final analysis, the researcher's conscience determines whether the research is conducted in an ethical manner. In general, serious ethical abuses such as mistreatment of participants are rare in psychological research, and few complaints about unethical practices are made. Research in psychology remains a rewarding activity for the researcher, the participants, and the general public and will continue to be so as long as scientists continue to respect the dignity of those who participate in their research.

## References

Ackerman, T. F. (1995). The ethics of phase I pediatric oncology trials. *IRB: A Review of Human Subjects Research, 17,* 1–5.

Akeroyd, A. V. (1991). Personal information and qualitative research data: Some practical and ethical problems arising from data protection legislation. In N. G. Fielding & R. M. Lee (eds.), *Using computers in qualitative research* (pp. 89–106). London: Sage.

Allebeck, P. (1997). Forensic psychiatric studies and research ethical considerations. *Nordic Journal of Psychiatry, 51,* 53–6, 73–95.

Alver, B. G. (1995). The uneasy borderline between ethical research ideals and practice. *Nord Nytt, 60,* 5–23.

American Association of Universities Task Force on Research Accountability (2000). Report on university protections of human beings who are the subjects of research. Washington, DC: American Association of Universities Task Force on Research Accountability.

American Psychological Association (1982). *Ethical principles in the conduct of research with human participants.* Washington, DC: American Psychological Association.

American Psychological Association (1990). Ethical principles of psychologists. *American Psychologist, 45,* 390–95.

American Psychological Association (1992). Ethical principles of psychologists and code of conduct. *American Psychologist, 42,* 1597–611.

American Psychological Association (1997). *Services by telephone, teleconferencing, and Internet: A statement by the Ethics Committee of the American Psychological Association.* Washington, DC: American Psychological Association. Retrieved September 5, 1999 from <www.apa.org/ethics/stmnt01.htm>.

Anonymous (1995). Recommendations for a research agenda in suicide and sexual orientation. *Suicide & Life-threatening Behavior, 25* (Suppl.), 82–8.

Backlar, P. (2000). Human subjects research, ethics, research on vulnerable populations. In T. Murray (ed.), *Encyclopedia of ethical, legal, and policy issues in biotechnology* (pp. 641–51). New York: Wiley-Interscience.

Baumrind, D. (1979). IRBs and social science research: The costs of deception. *IRB: A Review of Human Subjects Research, 1,* 8–10.

Bayer, A., & Tadd, W. (2000). Unjustified exclusion of elderly people from studies submitted to research ethics committee for approval: Descriptive study. *BMJ: British Medical Journal, 321,* 992–3.

Beecher, H. K. (1996). Ethics and clinical research. *The New England Journal of Medicine, 24,* 1354–60.

Beins, B. C. (1993). Using the Barnum effect to teach about ethics and deception in research. *Teaching of Psychology, 20,* 33–5.

Bell-Dolan, D., & Wessler, A. (1994). Ethical administration of sociometric measures procedures in use and suggestions for improvement. *Profession Psychology: Research and Practice, 25,* 23–32.

Berlin, M. (1995). Accessing organizations: Investigating attitudes towards technology in a South American country. *Technology Studies, 2,* 380–96.

Berscheid, E., Baron, R. S., Dermer, J., & Libman, M. (1973). Anticipating informed consent – an empirical approach. *American Psychologist, 28,* 913–25.

Bersoff, D. M., & Bersoff, D. N. (1999). Ethical perspectives in clinical research. In P. C. Kendall, J. N. Butcher, et al. (eds.), *Handbook of research methods* (2nd edn.) (pp. 31–53). New York: Wiley.

Bier, M. C., Sherblom, S. A., & Gallo, M. A. (1996). Ethical issues in a study of Internet use: Uncertainty, responsibility, and the spirit of research relationships. *Ethics & Behavior, 6,* 141–51.

Blanck, P. D., Bellack, A. S., Rosnow, R. L., Rotheram-Borus, M. J., & Schooler, N. R. (1992). Scientific rewards and conflicts of ethical choices in human subjects research. *American Psychologist, 47,* 959–65.

Bongar, B. (1988). Clinicians, microcomputers, and confidentiality. *Professional Psychology Research and Practice, 19,* 286–9.

Brainard, J. (2001). The wrong rules for social science? *Chronicle of Higher Education,* March 9, p. A21.

Brandon, T. H., & Lisman, S. A. (2000). Introduction to the special section on empirical underpinnings of the ethics of alcohol administration in research settings. *Psychology of Addictive Behaviors, 14,* 315–18.

Broder, A. (1998). Deception can be acceptable. *American Psychologist, 53,* 805–6.

Brookhart, S. (2001). IRBs and the review of psychological research. *American Psychological Society Observer, 14,* pp. 1, 7–8.

Bulger, R. E., & Reiser, S. J. (1993). Studying science in the context of ethics. *Academic Medicine, 68,* S5–9.

Bussell, D. (1994). Ethical issues in observational family research. *Family Process, 33,* 361–76.

Campbell, J. C., & Dienemann, J. D. (2001). Ethical issues in research on violence against women. In C. M. Renzetti, J. L. Edleson, et al. (eds.), *Sourcebook on violence against women* (pp. 57–72). Thousand Oaks, CA: Sage.

Candilis, P. J. (2001). Advancing the ethics of research. *Psychiatric Annals, 31,* 119–24.

Cannold, L. (1997). "There is no evidence to suggest . . .": Changing the way we judge information for disclosure in the informed consent process. *Hypatia, 12,* 165–84.

Capron, A. M. (1972). The law of genetic therapy. In M. Hamilton (ed.), *The new genetics and the future of man* (pp. 133–56). Grand Rapids, MI.: Eerdmans Publishing.

Carpenter, W. T., & Conley, R. R. (1999). Sense and nonsense: An essay on schizophrenia research ethics. *Schizophrenia Research, 35,* 219–25.

Casas, J. M., & San Miquel, S. (1993). Beyond questions and discussions, there is a need for action: A response to Mio and Iwamasa. *The Counseling Psychologist, 21,* 233–9.

Ceci, S. J., Pewters, D., & Plotkin, J. (1985). Human subjects review, personal values and the regulation of social science research. *American Psychologist, 40,* 994–1002.

Chatzifotiou, S. (2000). Conducting qualitative research on wife abuse: Dealing with the issue of anxiety. *Sociological Research* (August, on-line). Available at <www.socresonline.org.uk>.

Christensen, L. (1988). Deception in psychological research: When is its use justified? *Personality and Social Psychology Bulletin, 14,* 664–75.

Cohen, A., Dolan, B., & Eastman, N. (1996). Research on the supervision registers: Inconsistencies in local research ethics committee responses. *The Journal of Forensic Psychiatry, 7,* 413–19.

Corbie-Smith, G., Thomas, S. B., Williams, M. V., & Moody-Ayers, S. (1999). Attitudes and beliefs of African Americans toward participation in medical research. *Journal of General Internal Medicine, 14,* 537–46.

Cozby, P. C. (1981). *Methods in behavioral research.* Palo Alto, CA: Mayfield.

Daniel, J. H. (1994). Exclusion and emphasis reframed as a matter of ethics. *Ethics and Behavior, 4,* 229–35.

de Laine, M. (2000). *Ethnography: Theory and applications in health research.* Sydney: Macleannan and Petty.

Demi, A. S., & Warren, A. (1995). Issues in conducting research with vulnerable families. *Western Journal of Nursing Research, 17,* 188–202.

DeRenzo, E. G. (1994). The ethics in involving psychiatrically impaired persons in research. *IRB: A Review of Human Subjects Research, 16,* 7–9.

Diener, E., & Crandall, R. (1978). *Ethics in social and behavioral research.* Chicago: University of Chicago Press.

Edwards, R., & Allred, P. (1999). Children and young people's views of social research: The case of research on home–school relations. *Childhood, 6,* 261–81.

Eyde, L. D. (2000). Other responsibilities to participants. In B. D. Sales & S. Folkman (eds.), *Ethics in research with human participants* (pp. 61–74). Washington, DC: American Psychological Association.

Finnegan, R. (1992). *Oral traditions and the verbal arts: A guide to research practices.* London: Routledge.

Fischman, M. W. (2000). Informed consent. In B. D. Sales & S. Folkman (eds.), *Ethics in research with human participants* (pp. 35–48). Washington, DC: American Psychological Association.

Fisher, C. B. (1997). A relational perspective on ethics-in-science decision making for research with vulnerable populations. *IRB: A Review of Human Subjects Research, 19*, 1–4.

Fisher, C. B., & Fryberg, D. (1994). Participant partners: College students weigh the costs and benefits of deceptive research. *American Psychologist, 49*, 417–27.

Fisher, C. B., Higgins, A., Rau, J. B., Kuther, T. L., & Belanger, S. (1996). Referring and reporting research with participants at-risk: Views from urban adolescents. *Child Development, 67*, 2086–100.

Fisher, C. B., Jackson, J. F., & Villarruel, F. (1997). The study of ethnic minority children and youth in the United States. In W. Damon (series ed.) & R. M. Lerner (vol. ed.), *Handbook of child psychology: Vol. 1. Theoretical models of human development* (5th edn.) (pp. 1145–207). New York: Wiley.

Fisher, C. B., & Kuther, T. (1997). Integrating research ethics into the introductory psychology course curriculum. *Teaching of Psychology, 24*, 172, 175.

Fisher, C. B., & Wallace, S. A. (2000). Through the community looking glass: Reevaluating the ethical and policy implications of research on adolescent risk and psychopathology. *Ethics & Behavior, 10*, 99–118.

Folkman, S. (2000). Privacy and confidentiality. In B. D. Sales & S. Folkman (eds.), *Ethics in research with human participants* (pp. 49–58). Washington, DC: American Psychological Association.

Fox, J. A., & Tracy, P. E. (1986). *Randomized response: A method for sensitive surveys.* Beverly Hills, CA: Sage.

Fox, R. C. (1974). *The courage to fail.* Chicago: University of Chicago Press.

Frankel, M. S., & Siang, S. (1999). *Ethical and legal aspects of human subjects research on the Internet. Report of a workshop, June 10–11, 1999.* Washington, DC: American Association for the Advancement of Science.

Geller, D. M. (1982). Alternatives to deception: Why, what and how? In J. E. Sieber (ed.), *The ethics of social research: Surveys and experiments* (pp. 39–55). New York: Springer-Verlag.

Goldman, M. S. (2000). The culture of science and the ethics of alcohol administration in research. *Psychology of Addictive Behaviors, 14*, 335–41.

Goode, E. (1996). The ethics of deception in social research: A case study. *Qualitative Sociology, 19*, 11–33.

Goodyear, R. K., Crego, C. A., & Johnston, N. (1992). Ethical issues in the supervision of student research: A study of critical incidents. *Professional Psychology: Research and Practice, 23*, 203–310.

Grisso, T., Baldwin, E., Blanck, P. D., Rotheram-Borus, M. J., Schooler, N. R., & Thompson, T. (1991). Standards in research: APA's mechanism for monitoring the challenges. *American Psychologist, 46*, 758–66.

Gurman, E. B. (1994). Debriefing for all concerned: Ethical treatment of human subjects. *Psychological Science, 5*, 139.

Hall, D. (1991). The research imperative and bureaucratic control: The case of clinical research. *Social Science & Medicine, 32*, 333–42.

Harris, J. L. (1996). Issues in recruiting African American participants for research. In A. G. Kamhi, K. E. Pollock, et al. (eds.), *Communication development and disorders in African American children: Research, assessment, and intervention* (pp. 19–34). Baltimore: Brookes.

Heller, J. (1972). Syphilis victims in U.S. study went untreated for 40 years. *New York Times*, 26 July, p. A1.

Herrera, C. D. (1999). Two arguments for "covert methods" in social research. *British Journal of Sociology, 50*, 331–43.

Hershey, N. (1985). IRB jurisdiction and limits on IRB actions. *IRB: A Review of Human Subjects Research, 7* (2), 7–9.

Higbee, K. L., Millard, R. J., & Folkman, J. R. (1982). Social psychology research during the 1970's: Predominance of experimentation and college students. *Personality and Social Psychology Bulletin, 8,* 180–3.

High, D. M. (1993). Advancing research with Alzheimer disease subjects: Investigators' perceptions and ethical issues. *Alzheimer Disease and Associated Disorders, 7,* 165–78.

Hoagwood, K., Jensen, P., & Fisher, C. (1996). *Ethical issues in mental health research with children and adolescents.* Hillsdale, NJ: Erlbaum Associates.

Holmes, D. S. (1976a). Debriefing after psychological experiments: I. Effectiveness of post-experimental dehoaxing. *American Psychologist, 31,* 858–67.

Holmes, D. S. (1976b). Debriefing after psychological experiments: II. Effectiveness of post-experimental desensitizing. *American Psychologist, 31,* 868–75.

Humphreys, K., Winzelberg, A., & Klaw, E. (2000). Psychologists' ethical responsibilities in Internet-based groups: Issues, strategies, and a call for dialogue. *Professional Psychology, 31,* 493–6.

Hutz, C. S., & Koller, S. H. (1999). Methodological and ethical issues in research with street children. *New Directions for Child and Adolescent Development, 85,* 59–70.

Hyman, S. (1999). Protecting patients, preserving progress: Ethics in mental health illness research. *Academic Medicine, 74,* 258–9.

Jewkes, R., Watts, C., Abrahams, N., Penn-Xerkana, L., & Garcia-Moreno, C. (2000). Ethical and methodological issues in conducting research on gender-based violence in Southern Africa. *Reproductive Health Matters, 8,* 93–103.

Jones, R. A. (1994). The ethics of research in cyberspace. *Internet Research, 4,* 30–5.

Jung, J. (1969). Current practices and problems in the use of college students for psychological research. *Canadian Psychologist, 10,* 280–90.

Karlawish, J. H. T., Hougham, G. W., Stocking, C. B., & Sachs, G. A. (1999). What is the quality of the reporting of research ethics in publications of nursing home research? *Journal of the American Geriatrics Society, 47,* 76–81.

Karlawish, J. H. T., & Sachs, G. S. (1997). Research upon the cognitively impaired: Lessons and warnings from the emergency research controversy. *Journal of American Geriatric Society, 45,* 474–81.

Kazdin, A. (1979). Unobtrusive measures in behavioral assessment. *Journal of Applied Behavior Analysis, 12,* 713–24.

Kelman, H. C. (1967). Human use of human subjects: The problem of deception in social psychological experiments. *Psychological Bulletin, 67,* 1–11.

Kimmel, A. J. (1998). In defense of deception. *American Psychologist, 53,* 803–4.

Koocher, G. P. (1977). Bathroom behavior and human dignity. *Journal of Personality and Social Psychology, 35,* 120–1.

Korn, J. H. (1998). The reality of deception. *American Psychologist, 53,* 805.

Korn, J. H., & Bram, D. R. (1988). What is missing in the method section of APA journal articles? *American Psychologist, 43,* 1091–2.

Landrum, R. E., & Chastain, G. (1995). Experiment spot-checks: A method for assessing the educational value of undergraduate participation in research. *IRB: A Review of Human Subjects Research, 17,* 4–6.

LaRossa, R., Bennett, L., & Gelles, R. (1981). Ethical dilemmas in qualitative family research. *Journal of Marriage and the Family, 43,* 303–12.

Lawson, C. (1995). Research participation as a contract. *Ethics & Behavior, 5,* 205–15.

Leak, G. K. (1981). Student perception of coercion and value from participation in psychological research. *Teaching of Psychology, 8,* 146–9.

Lee, R. M. (1993). *Doing research on sensitive topics.* London: Sage.

Leikin, S. L. (1993). Minors' assent, consent, or dissent to medical research. *IRB: A Review of Human Subjects Research, 15,* 1–7.

Libutti, P. O. (1999). The Internet and qualitative research: Opportunities and constraints on analysis of cyberspace discourse. In M. Kopala & L. A. Suzuki (eds.), *Using qualitative methods in psychology* (pp. 77–88). Thousand Oaks, CA: Sage.

Littlejohn, S. W. (1991). Deception in communication research. *Communication Reports, 4,* 51–4.

Long, H. B. (1982). Analysis of research concerning free and reduced tuition programs for senior citizens. *Educational Gerontology, 8,* 575–84.

Lynn, J. (1998). Ethical concerns about research on incompetent persons. *Journal of the American Geriatrics Society, 46,* 660.

Mammel, K. A., & Kaplan, D. W. (1995). Research consent of adolescent minors and institutional review boards. *Journal of Adolescent Health, 17,* 323–30.

Mann, T. (1994). Informed consent for psychological research: Do subjects comprehend consent forms and understand their legal rights? *Psychological Science, 5,* 140–3.

Martin, D. K., Meslin, E. M., Kohut, N., & Singer, P. A. (1995). The incommensurability of research risks and benefits: Practical help for research ethics committees. *IRB: A Review of Human Subjects Research, 17,* 8–10.

McConnell, W. A., & Krebs, J. J. (1993). Providing feedback in research with human subjects. *Professional Psychology: Research and Practice, 24,* 266–70.

McCrady, B. S., & Bux, D. A. (1999). Ethical issues in informed consent with substance abusers. *Journal of Consulting and Clinical Psychology, 67,* 186–93.

Megargee, E. I. (1995). Assessment research in correctional settings: Methodological issues and practical problems. *Psychological Assessment, 7,* 359–66.

Meslin, E. M. (1990). Protecting human subjects from harm through improved risk judgements. *IRB: A Review of Human Subjects Research, 1,* 7–10.

Michalak, E. E. (1998). The use of the internet as a research tool: The nature and characteristics of seasonal affective disorder (SAD) amongst a population of users. *Interacting with Computers, 9,* 349–65.

Michalak, E. E., & Szabo, A. (1998). Guidelines for internet research. *European Psychologist, 3,* 70–5.

Milgram, S. (1974). *Obedience to authority.* New York: Harper & Row.

Miller, A. (1981). A survey of introductory psychology subject pool practices among leading universities. *Teaching of Psychology, 8,* 211–13.

Miller, F. G. (2000). Placebo-controlled trials in psychiatric research: An ethical perspective. *Biological Psychiatry, 47,* 707–16.

Miller, F. G., & Rosenstein, D. L. (1997). Psychiatric symptom-provoking studies: An ethical appraisal. *Biological Psychiatry, 42,* 403–9.

Mio, J. S., & Iwamasa, G. (1993). To do, or not to do: That is the questions for White cross-cultural researchers. *The Counseling Psychologist, 21,* 197–212.

Miskevich, S. L. (1996). Killing the goose that laid the golden eggs: Ethical issues in social science research on the Internet. *Science and Engineering Ethics, 2,* 241–2.

Mitchell, S. C., & Steingrub, J. (1988). The changing clinical trials scene: The role of the IRB. *IRB: A Review of Human Subjects Research, 10,* 1–5.

Moreno, J. D., Caplan, A. L., Wolpe, P. R., and the Members of the Project on Informed Consent, Human Research Ethics Group (1998). Updating protections for human subjects involved in research. *Journal of the American Medical Association, 280,* 1951–8.

Mulvey, E. P., & Phelps, P. (1988). Ethical balances in juvenile justice research and practice. *American Psychologist*, *43*, 65–9.

NBAC (National Bioethics Advisory Commission) (1999). *Research involving human biological materials: Ethical issues in policy guidance* (2 vols). Rockville, MD: U.S. Printing Office.

NBAC (National Bioethics Advisory Commission) (2001). *Ethical and policy issues in research involving human participants*. Bethesda, MD: U.S. Government Printing Office.

Nash, M. M. (1975). "Nonreactive methods and the law": Additional comments on legal liability in behavior research. *American Psychologist*, *30*, 777–80.

National Commission for the Protection of Human Subjects in Biomedical and Behavioral Research (1978). The Belmont Report; Ethical principles for the protection of human subjects of research. Washington, DC: US Government Printing Office, 1978. Dept. of Health, Education and Welfare (now Health and Human Services), publication # (OS) 78-00012. Appendix 1-0012, Appendix 2-004.

Office for Protection From Research Risks, Protection of Human Subjects, National Commission for the Protection of Human Subjects of Biomedical and Behavioral Research (1991). Protection of human subjects: Title 45, Code of Federal Regulations, Part 46 (GPO 1992 0-307-551). *OPRR Reports*, June 18, pp. 4–17.

Ortmann, A., & Hertwig, R. (1997). Is deception acceptable? *American Psychologist*, *52*, 746–7.

Paradis, E. K. (2000). Feminist and community psychology ethics in research with homeless women. *American Journal of Community Psychology*, *28*, 839–58.

Parker, L. S., & Lidz, C. W. (1994). Familial coercion to participate in genetic family studies: Is there cause for IRB intervention? *IRB: A Review of Human Subjects Research*, *16*, 6–12.

Perry, L. B., & Abramson, P. R. (1980). Debriefing: A gratuitous procedure? *American Psychologist*, *35*, 298–9.

Phillips, S. R. (1994). Asking the sensitive question: The ethics of survey research and teen sex. *IRB: A Review of Human Subjects Research*, *16*, 1–7.

Pinals, D. A., Malhotra, A. K., Breier, A., & Pickar, D. (1998). Informed consent in schizophrenia research. *Psychiatric Services*, *49*, 244.

Pomerantz, J. R. (1994). On criteria for ethics in science: Commentary on Rosenthal. *Psychological Science*, *5*, 135–6.

Porter, J. P. (1995). "Guidelines for adolescent participation in research: Current realities and possible resolutions": Reply. *IRB: A Review of Human Subjects Research*, *17*, 10.

Prentice, E. D., & Antonson, D. L. (1987). A protocol review guide to reduce IRB inconsistency. *IRB: A Review of Human Subjects Research*, *9*, 9–11.

Regehr, C., Edwardh, M., & Bradford, J. (2000). Research ethics and forensic patients. *The Canadian Journal of Psychiatry*, *45*, 892–8.

Reilly, P. R. (1991). Reviewing proposals to study biological correlates of criminality. *IRB: A Review of Human Subjects Research*, *13*, 8–9.

Ringheim, K. (1995). Ethical issues in social science research with special references to sexual behavior research. *Social Science and Medicine*, *40*, 1691–7.

Roberts, L. W., & Roberts, B. (1999). Psychiatric research ethics: An overview of evolving guidelines and current ethical dilemmas in the study of mental illness. *Biological Psychiatry*, *46*, 1025–38.

Roberts, L. W., Solomon, Z., Roberts, B. B., & Keith, S. J. (1998). Ethics in psychiatric research: Resources for faculty development and resident education. *Academic Psychiatry*, *22*, 1–20.

Rogers, A. S., D'Angelo, L., & Futterman, D. (1994). Guidelines for adolescent participation in research: Current realities and possible resolutions. *IRB: A Review of Human Subjects Research*, *16*, 1–6.

Rolph, S. (1998). Ethical dilemmas in historical research with people with learning difficulties. *British Journal of Learning Disabilities*, *26*, 135–9.

Rosenthal, R. (1994). Science and ethics in conducting, analyzing, and reporting psychological research. *Psychological Science*, *5*, 127–34.

Rosenthal, R., & Rosnow, R. L. (1991). *Essentials of behavioral research: Methods and data analysis* (2nd edn.). New York: McGraw-Hill.

Rosnow, R. L. (1990). Teaching research ethics through role-playing and discussion. *Teaching of Psychology*, *17*, 179–81.

Rosnow, R. L., & Rosenthal, R. (1993). *Beginning behavioral research: A conceptual primer*. New York: Macmillan.

Rosnow, R., Rotheram-Borus, M. J., Ceci, S. J., Blanck, P. D., & Koocher, G. P. (1993). The institutional review board as a mirror of scientific and ethical standards. *American Psychologist*, *48*, 821–6.

Rothman, D. J. (1991). *Strangers at the bedside: A history of how law and bioethics transformed medical decision making*. New York: Basic Books.

Sales, B., & Lavin, M. (2000). Identifying conflicts of interest and resolving ethical dilemmas. In B. D. Sales & S. Folkman (eds.), *Ethics in research with human participants* (pp. 109–28). Washington, DC: American Psychological Association.

Scarr, S. (1988). Race and gender as psychological variables: Social and ethical issues. *American Psychologist*, *43*, 56–9.

Schuster, E. (1996). Ethical considerations when conducting ethnographic research in a nursing home setting. *Journal of Aging Studies*, *10*, 57–67.

Schwartz, S. H., & Gottlieb, A. (1980). Participation in a bystander experiment and subsequent everyday helping: Ethical considerations. *Journal of Experimental Social Psychology*, *16*, 161–71.

Scott-Jones, D. (1994). Ethical issues in reporting and referring in research with low-income minority children. *Ethics & Behavior*, *4*, 97–108.

Scott-Jones, D. (2000). Recruitment of research participants. In B. D. Sales & S. Folkman (eds.), *Ethics in research with human participants* (pp. 27–34). Washington, DC: American Psychological Association.

Sieber, J. (1992). *Planning ethically responsible research: A guide for students and internal review boards*. Newbury Park, CA: Sage.

Sieber, J. E. (1994a). Issues presented by mandatory reporting requirements to researchers of child abuse and neglect. *Ethics & Behavior*, *4*, 1–22.

Sieber, J. E. (1994b). Will the new code help researchers to be more ethical? *Professional Psychology*, *25*, 369–75.

Sieber, J. E. (2000). Planning research: Basic ethical decision-making. In B. D. Sales & S. Folkman (eds.), *Ethics in research with human participants* (pp. 13–26). Washington, DC: American Psychological Association.

Sieber, J. E., & Stanley, B. (1988). Ethical and professional dimensions of socially sensitive research. *American Psychologist*, *43*, 49–55.

Silverman, I. (1975). Nonreactive methods and the law. *American Psychologist*, *30*, 764–9.

Singleton, R., Straits, B. C., Straits, M. M., & McAllister, R. J. (1988). *Approaches to social research*. New York: Oxford University Press.

Slovic, P., Fischoff, B., & Lichtenstein, S. (1981). Perceived risk: Psychological factors and social implications. In F. Warner & D. H. Slater (eds.), *The assessment and perception of risk* (pp. 17–34). London: The Royal Society.

Smith, M. A., & Leigh, B. (1997). Virtual subjects: Using the Internet as an alternative source of subjects and research environment. *Behavior Research Methods, Instruments, & Computers*, *29*, 496–505.

Smith, S. S., & Richardson, D. (1983). Amelioration of deception and harm in psychological research: The important role of debriefing. *Journal of Personality & Social Psychology, 44,* 1075–82.

Smythe, W., & Murray, M. (2000). Owning the story: Ethical considerations in narrative research. *Ethics & Behavior, 10,* 311–36.

Stewart, L. P. (1992). Ethical issues in postexperimental and postexperiential debriefing. *Simulation and Gaming, 23,* 196–211.

Strain, L. A., & Chappell, N. L. (1982). Problems and strategies: Ethical concerns in survey research with the elderly. *The Gerontologist, 22,* 526–31.

Strohmetz, D. B., & Skleder, A. A. (1992). The use of role-playing in teaching research ethics: A validation study. *Teaching of Psychology, 19,* 106–8.

Sugarman, J., Kass, N. E., Goodman, S. N., Perentesis, P., Fernandes, P., & Faden, R. R. (1998). What patients say about medical research. *IRB: A Review of Human Subjects Research, 20,* 1–7.

Sweet, S. (1999). Using a mock institutional review board to teach ethics in sociological research. *Teaching Sociology, 27,* 55–9.

Tangey, J. (2000). Training. In B. D. Sales & S. Folkman (eds.), *Ethics in research with human participants* (pp. 97–106). Washington, DC: American Psychological Association.

Tarasoff v. Board of Regents of the University of California (1976). 17 Cal. 3d 425, 551 P.2d 334.

Taube, D. O. & Burkhardt, S. (1997). Ethical and legal risks associated with archival research. *Ethics and Behavior, 7,* 59–67.

Theut, S. K., & Kohrman, A. F. (1990). Ethical issues in research in child psychiatry. In S. I. Deutsch, Wiezman, A., et al. (eds.), *Application of basic neuroscience to child psychiatry* (pp. 383–9). New York: Plenum Press.

Thompson, B. (1995). Ethical dimensions in trauma research. *The American Sociologist, 26,* 54–69.

Tomossy, G. F., & Weisstub, D. N. (1997). The reform of adult guardianship laws: The case of non-therapeutic experimentation. *International Journal of Law & Psychiatry, 20,* 113–39.

Tucker, J. A., & Vuchinich, R. E. (2000). Creating a research context for reducing risk and obtaining informed consent in human alcohol studies. *Psychology of Addictive Behaviors, 14,* 319–27.

Turnbull, A. (2000). Collaboration and censorship in the oral history interview. *International Journal of Social Research Methodology, 3,* 15–34.

Warwick, D. P. (1973). Tearoom trade: Means and ends in social research. *Hastings Center Studies, 1,* 27–38.

Wax, M. (1982). Research reciprocity rather than informed consent in fieldwork. In J. Sieber (ed.), *The ethics of social research: Fieldwork, regulation, and publication* (pp. 33–48). New York: Springer-Verlag.

Wax, M. (1995). Knowledge, power, and ethics in qualitative social research. *The American Sociologist, 25,* 22–34.

Wendler, D. (2000). Informed consent, exploitation and whether it is possible to conduct human subjects research without either one. *Bioethics, 14,* 310–39.

West, S. G., & Gunn, S. P. (1978). Some issues of ethics and social psychology. *American Psychologist, 33,* 30–8.

Whitbeck, C. (1995). Teaching ethics to scientists and engineers: Moral agents and moral problems. *Science and Engineering Ethics, 1,* 299–308.

Whitbeck, C. (1996). Ethics as design: Doing justice to moral problems. *Hastings Center Report,* May–June, 9–16.

Wilson, D. W., & Donnerstein, E. (1976). Legal and ethical aspects of nonreactive social psychological research: An excursion into the public mind. *American Psychologist, 31,* 765–73.
Wood, M. D., & Sher, K. J. (2000). Risks of alcohol consumption in laboratory studies involving human research participants. *Psychology of Addictive Behaviors, 14,* 328–34.
Zimbardo, P., Haney, C., Banks, W., & Jaffe, D. (1973). The mind is a formidable jailer: A Pirandellian prison. *New York Times Magazine,* April 8, 38–60.

## Further Reading

Adair, J. G. (2001). Ethics of psychological research: New policies; continuing issues; new concerns. *Canadian Psychology, 42,* 23–37. (Addresses a variety of ethical issues including the use of deception and undergraduate subject pools.)
Aronson, E., Ellsworth, P., Carlsmith, J. M., & Gonzalez, M. (1989). *Methods of research in social psychology* (2nd edn.). New York: McGraw Hill. (Provides a detailed description of how debriefing interviews should be conducted.)
Chastain, G., & Landrum, R. E. (1999). *Protecting human subjects: Departmental subject pools and institutional review boards.* Washington, DC: American Psychological Assocation. (Addresses practical issues related to the use of students in psychological research and the IRB process in approving research protocols.)
de Laine, M. (2000). *Fieldwork, participation and practice: Ethics and dilemmas in qualitative research.* Thousand Oaks, CA: Sage. (A timely and topical examination of the role of ethics in fieldwork.)
Kimmel, A. J. (1996). *Ethical issues in behavioral research.* Cambridge, MA: Blackwell. (An introduction to ethical issues suitable for upper-level students in all fields of the behavioral sciences.)
McMinn, M. R., Beins, B. C., Rosnow, R. L., et al. (1999). Teaching ethics. In M. E. Ware & C. L. Brewer (eds.), *Handbook for teaching statistics and research methods* (2nd edn.) (pp. 132–53). Mahwah, NJ: Erlbaum. (A compilation of articles designed to provide teachers of research methodology with some tools for raising student awareness of ethical issues.)
Sales, B., & Folkman, S. (2000). *Ethics in research with human participants.* Washington, DC: American Psychological Association. (Prepared by the APA Task Force charged with addressing newly emerging ethical issues and creating guidelines and practical solutions to ethical dilemmas.)
Stanley, B., Sieber, J. E., & Melton, G. B. (eds.) (1996). *Research ethics: A psychological approach.* Lincoln, NE: University of Nebraska Press. (Reviews research that contributes to the development of ethical principles.)
Wettstein, R. M. (1995). Research ethics and human subject issues. In H. A. Pincus. (ed.), *Research funding and resource manual: Mental health and addictive disorders* (pp. 423–7). Washington, DC: American Psychiatric Association. (Provides the mental health investigator with a summary of ethical issues in conducting research with patients.)

# CHAPTER EIGHT

# Research with Animals

## Jesse E. Purdy, Scott A. Bailey, and Steven J. Schapiro

## Introduction

It is a daunting task to contribute a chapter on research with nonhuman animals to the *Handbook of Research Methods in Experimental Psychology*. In this day of information explosion, how would one concisely portray all of the methods of science in psychology that involves the use of nonhuman animals? Indeed how would one go about identifying the various methods? Obviously, to be of value to the reader, the selection of methods must be restricted to those deemed to be of high quality by the scientific community. But how are these methods to be chosen?

To address these questions we relied on the words of Harry Harlow, a well-respected comparative psychologist whose methods of science taught us much about the cognitive capabilities of animals and about the importance of social interaction. In 1956 and 1957, Harlow published two papers in the *American Psychologist* (Harlow, 1956, 1957). In his 1957 paper, Harlow described and distinguished between two types of research: golden angel research and silver angel research. Harlow characterized golden angel research as research conducted by individuals who contributed groundbreaking papers that changed the way people thought about science. An example of golden angel research might be the paper by Garcia and Koelling (1966) that literally changed the way psychologists thought about learning and led to an exponential increase of studies on taste aversion and the biological constraints on learning. Silver angel research, on the other hand, occurs after golden angel research. Harlow characterized silver angel research as those publications that fine-tuned methodologies, provided proper control groups, and systematically conducted parametric research that led to real advances in knowledge. Whereas both types of research are critical to the advancement of science and knowledge, for the purposes of this chapter, it made sense to focus on silver angel research. Of course, a few publications will satisfy Harlow's criteria for both golden and silver angel research, but those papers are relatively rare.

Our next task was to choose those papers that represent silver angel research. Again, Harlow provided a clue. Harlow's 1956 paper was based on a presentation he made for the 1955 APA Day Symposium on the subject of "Recent Progress and Probable Break-Throughs in the Science of Psychology." In the opening paragraphs of his talk, Harlow argued that virtually all of the "giants" in the field of psychology were able to achieve their status because they enjoyed significant funding for their work. Harlow claimed that "it is no accident that this correlates almost perfectly with the temporal course of financial support from the Office of Naval Research, the Army Surgeon General, the Veterans Administration, the National Institutes of Health, and the National Science Foundation" (Harlow, 1956, p. 273). In his presentation Harlow asserted that "the most important current and future advance in these areas is comparatively adequate financial support" (p. 273). In the 1950s, psychologists working with animals enjoyed a high level of financial support from government funding agencies. This prosperity, Harlow felt, was critical to the advancement of science.

Given the connection between high levels of funding and high quality work, we focused on research with animals that was funded externally by highly competitive funding agencies. We felt that such work was subject to careful scrutiny by the top scientists in the field and would most likely be work of high quality. Most of the work in comparative psychology and behavioral neuroscience in the United States has been funded by two agencies, the National Science Foundation and the US Department of Public Health (Purdy & Domjan, 2001). Within the Department of Public Health, the National Institute of Mental Health has funded much of the work in psychology with nonhuman animals. Thus, our chapter focuses on research with animals that has been funded by either the National Science Foundation (NSF) or by the National Institute of Mental Health (NIMH). To counteract the potential for USA centrism inherent in this approach, we also examined the work of researchers who are not US citizens. These researchers, like US researchers, required evidence of competitive external funding to be included in our "analysis." In addition to focusing on funding, we felt that it was important to know that the funded individuals' work had impacted the work of others. To this end, we selected studies for analysis that had been conducted by individuals (1) who had recently published at least one article reflecting work with animal subjects in the field of psychology, (2) who held a current competitive research grant, and (3) whose work had received a large number of citations from other scientists. We used the database of the Institute of Scientific Information to determine the extent to which a researcher's work had been cited.

This chapter provides a partial survey of the methods of science in psychology in which nonhuman animals are the subjects of choice. We focus on the work of individuals who have demonstrated an ability to attract external funding and whose work has significantly impacted the field. To keep this chapter current, we chose to describe only empirical studies using animal subjects published between 1999 and 2001; theoretical or review papers were not included.

Table 8.1 provides a list of top (animal) investigators in three subareas of experimental psychology: animal learning/comparative psychology, behavioral neuroscience, and basic/applied animal behavior. Table 8.1 includes the investigator's name and affiliation, the total number of papers cited in 2000 and 2001, the total number of citations for

**Table 8.1**  Top investigators in animal research

## Top Investigators in Animal Learning/Comparative Psychology

| Name & affiliation | Total papers cited (2000–1) | Total citations (2000–1) | Funding source & grant number |
|---|---|---|---|
| 1. Robert A. Rescorla, U. of Pennsylvania | 144 | 8080 | NIMH; 1R01MH063845-01 |
| 2. N. J. Mackintosh, University of Cambridge | 86 | 4300 | BBSRC; Type R; S05789 |
| 3. Peter C. Holland, Duke University | 136 | 2940 | NIMH; 2R01MH053667-06 |
| 4. Russell M. Church, Brown University | 69 | 2830 | NIMH; 5R01MH044234-12 |
| 5. Allan R. Wagner, Yale University | 51 | 2740 | NSF; IBN-9904432 |
| 6. C. Randy Gallestel, Rutgers University | 62 | 2240 | NIMH; 1R21MH063866-01 |
| 7. Ralph R. Miller, SUNY, Binghamton | 106 | 2110 | NIMH; 5R01MH33881-20 |
| 8. John E. R. Staddon, Duke University | 70 | 2050 | NIMH; 5R01MH045856-10 |
| 9. Mark E. Bouton, University of Vermont | 109 | 2040 | NSF; IBN-9727992 |
| 10. Edward A. Wasserman, University of Iowa | 143 | 2030 | NSF; IBN-9904569 |
| 11. John M. Pearce, University of Wales | 73 | 2000 | BBSRC; Type R; S13755 |
| 12. Anthony A. Dickinson, Cambridge University | 100 | 1900 | UKMRC G-9805862 |
| 13. Geoffrey Hall, University of York, UK | 65 | 1890 | UKMRC G-9828709 |
| 14. M. E. Bitterman, University of Hawaii | 55 | 1670 | NSF; IBN-9982827 |
| 15. William A. Roberts, U. of Western Ontario | 58 | 1540 | NSERC |
| 16. Edmund J. Fantino, U. of California, San Diego | 58 | 1340 | NSF; IBN-9870900 |
| 17. Anthony A. Wright, U. of TX H S C, Houston | 91 | 1220 | NSF; IBN-9985670 |
| 18. Thomas R. Zentall, University of Kentucky | 71 | 1220 | NIMH; 5R01MH059194-03 |
| 19. Michael Domjan, University of Texas | 71 | 1180 | NIMH; 2R01MH039940-15 |
| 20. Donald S. Blough, Brown University | 35 | 1020 | NIMH; 5R01MH061782-02 |

**Table 8.1** (*continued*)

Top Investigators in Behavioral Neuroscience

| Name & affiliation | Total papers cited (2000–1) | Total citations (2000–1) | Funding source & grant number[a] |
|---|---|---|---|
| 1. Larry R. Squire, U. of California at San Diego | 314 | 20000 | NIMH; 5R01MH024600-29 |
| 2. Eric R. Kandel, Columbia University | 372 | 20000 | NIMH; 5R01MH050733-08 |
| 3. Gary Lynch, U. of California at Irvine | 249 | 13780 | NIMH; 1R01MH061007-01 |
| 4. James L. McGaugh, U. of California at Irvine | 226 | 3780 | NIMH; 5R01MH012526-34 |
| 5. Mortimer Mishkin, NIMH | 171 | 12180 | NIMH Section Chief, Cog Neuroscience |
| 6. Richard F. Thompson, U. of Southern California | 217 | 10800 | NSF; IBN-9215069 |
| 7. Daniel L. Alkon, Marine Bio Lab, Woods Hole | 158 | 6030 | NIMH; 1Z01NS002151-26 |
| 8. William T. Greenough, U. of Illinois, Champaign | 125 | 5300 | NIMH; 5R01AA009838-08 |
| 9. Michael S. Fanselow, UC at Los Angeles | 113 | 4660 | NIMH; 1R01MH048672-07 |
| 10. David Crews, University of Texas at Austin | 208 | 3940 | NIMH; 5R01MH041770-16 |
| 11. Thomas J. Carew, UC at Irvine | 85 | 3750 | NIMH; 5R01MH048672-07 |
| 12. Timothy Schallert, U. of Texas at Austin | 56 | 3410 | NIMH; 2P50NSo24707-15A29005 |
| 13. Karl H. Pribram, Radford University, VA | 80 | 3130 | Center for Brain Research and Info Sciences |
| 14. Shepard Siegel, McMaster University | 76 | 3050 | NIMH; 2R01DA011865-04 |
| 15. Norman E. Spear, SUNY Binghamton | 96 | 2570 | NIMH; 5R37MH035219-20 |
| 16. Michael Davis, Emory University | 45 | 2500 | NIMH; 5R01MH059906-03 |
| 17. Norman M. Weinberger, U. of California at Irvine | 67 | 2330 | NIMH; 5R01MH057235-05 |
| 18. William P. Smotherman, Cornell University | 102 | 2060 | NIMH; 6R37HD016102-20 |
| 19. Ilene L. Bernstein, University of Washington | 51 | 1500 | NIMH; 5R01DC000248-15 |
| 20. James W. Grau, Texas A & M University | 37 | 1020 | NIMH; 5R01MH060157-02 |

# Top Investigators in Basic/Applied Animal Behavior

| Name & affiliation | Total papers cited (2000–1) | Total citations (2000–1) | Funding source & grant number |
|---|---|---|---|
| 1. Robert Sapolsky, Stanford University | 242 | 11000 | NIMH; 5P01NS037520-049002 |
| 2. Bennett Galef, McMaster University | 132 | 2760 | NSERC |
| 3. Louis Herman, University of Hawaii | 122 | 1190 | NSF; IBN-0090744 |
| 4. Stephen Suomi, NICH & HD | 121 | 2390 | Intramural Investigator |
| 5. Robin I. M. Dunbar, U. of Liverpool, UK | 104 | 2320 | NERC |
| 6. Gordon Burghardt, University of Tennessee | 96 | 1840 | NSF; IBN-9411140 |
| 7. Frans de Waal, Emory University | 94 | 2060 | NSF; IBN-0077706 |
| 8. Charles Snowdon, University of Wisconsin | 89 | 1930 | NIMH; 2R01MH029775-22A1 |
| 9. Andrew Whiten, U. of St. Andrews, Scotland | 81 | 1170 | British Academy Research Readership |
| 10. Jeanne Altmann, Princeton University | 78 | 5200 | NSF; IBN-9985910 |
| 11. Judy Stamps, U. of California, Davis | 74 | 1740 | UC Davis Faculty Grant |
| 12. Paul Sherman, Cornell University | 71 | 3730 | NSF; DEB-9221504 |
| 13. Sara Shettleworth, University of Toronto | 70 | 1160 | NSERC |
| 14. Irwin S. Bernstein, University of Georgia | 61 | 2050 | Yerkes Primate Center |
| 15. Alan Kamil, Univ. of Nebraska, Lincoln | 61 | 1170 | NIMH; 5R01MH061810-02 |
| 16. Robert Seyfarth, University of Pennsylvania | 60 | 2520 | NIMH; 5R01MH62249-02 |
| 17. P.J.B. Slater, U. of St. Andrews, Scotland | 59 | 1170 | La Caixa/British Council |
| 18. Donald Owings, U. of California, Davis | 42 | 1020 | U. of California Faculty Research Grant |
| 19. John Hoogland, University of Maryland | 35 | 1350 | NSF; IBN-0113145 |
| 20. Stephen Glickman, U. of California, Berkeley | 30 | 1050 | NIMH; 5R01MH039917-17 |

[a] To access current grant information from top investigators go to the following websites and search for the name of the investigator:

BBSRC: http://www.bbsrc.ac.uk/tools/search/Welcome.html

La Caixa/British Council: http://www.britishcouncil.org

NERC: http://www.nerc.ac.uk

NIMH: http://www.fastlane.nsf.gov/a6/A6AwardSearch.htm

NSERC: http://www.nserc.ca/programs/results/2000/rg/12.htm

NSF: ntp://commons.cit.nih.gov/crisp3/crisp_query.generate_screen

UK MRC: http://www.mrc.ac.uk/index/search.htm?db=db&query=&cmd=

Yerkes Primate Center: http://www.cc.emory.edu/WHSC/YERKES/

these papers, funding source, and website URL for specific grant. As mentioned, researchers were included on this list on the basis of their science and their impact on the scientific endeavor. For each area, slightly different criteria for inclusion on the list were employed.

The remainder of this chapter is divided into three sections. The first section concerns behavioral research conducted in the laboratory that primarily pertains to issues of animal learning/comparative psychology. The second section also focuses on laboratory studies, but considers studies that relate to behavioral neuroscience. In the third section, we focus on both laboratory and field studies that address questions relevant to basic and applied animal behavior.

Each section is organized much like the method section of a manuscript. First, we discuss the characteristics of the subjects (species, demography, housing and maintenance, and potential sources). Second, we briefly describe various types of apparatus and potential sources for such equipment. Third, we discuss a procedure section from a top investigator from each of the three subareas. We focus on one published paper and note the control conditions utilized, data collection techniques, independent and dependent variables, and the means by which error variability was reduced.

The chapter concludes with a discussion of the limits of our approach for identifying the methods used in experimental psychology with animals, generalizations from our findings, and a brief discussion of the improvements in methodology since the early twentieth century.

## Laboratory Methods in Animal Learning and Comparative Psychology

### Subjects

Rats (*Rattus norvegicus*) and pigeons (*Columba livia*) dominate the laboratories of our top 20 investigators in animal learning/comparative psychology. Thirteen of these investigators use rats as their subjects and 10 investigators use pigeons. A majority of these researchers use more than one species; however, there is considerable variation in the choice of species. Five investigators use rats and pigeons and one investigator uses rats and rabbits (*Oryctolagus cuniculus*). Three investigators use pigeons significantly, but have also published recent papers using goldfish (*Carassius auratus*) and budgerigars (*Melopisittacus undulatus*), baboons (*Papio papio*), squirrel monkeys (*Saimiri sciureus*), rhesus monkeys (*Macaca mulatta*), capuchin monkeys (*Cebus apella*), and Japanese quail (*Coturnix japonica*). A few researchers have conducted multiple studies over many years on a single species other than rats or pigeons (e.g., Japanese quail or honeybees (*Apis mellifera*)).

*Rodents*  White rats and hooded rats, including the Listar, Long-Evans, Sprague-Dawley, and Wistar strains supplied by Charles River Laboratories and Harlan, Inc., remain the most commonly used animal subject in the animal learning/comparative psychology subarea. For investigations in which consumption of food (or water) is the reward for correct performance, food (or water) is typically restricted outside of the experimental test to enhance the subjects' motivation to perform the experimental task (Escobar, Matute, & Miller, 2001; Rescorla, 2001). In other investigations, access to a platform in a water maze is used as a reward (Redhead, Prados, & Pearce, 2001) and no deprivation is necessary. Typical housing conditions for laboratory rats include individual or pair housing in stainless steel cages or in plastic "shoebox" cages within colony rooms maintained at 21–3 °C on a 12 : 12 hr light : dark cycle. However, one laboratory (Escobar et al. 2001) routinely uses a 16 : 8 hr light : dark cycle and another (Redhead, Prados, & Pearce, 2001) uses a 14.5 : 9.5 hr light : dark cycle. Rats are typically handled prior to the onset of the experiment; in fact, one investigator reported that all rats in his laboratory were handled for 30 seconds three times a week from weaning to the onset of the experiment (Escobar et al., 2001). In most studies with rats, the rats are used in only one experiment.

*Birds* White Carneaux pigeons from various sources (e.g., on-site breeding colonies, feral, Palmetto Pigeon Plant, Abbotts Brothers) are the only strain of pigeon used by the top investigators in animal learning/comparative psychology. In a typical appetitive experiment, pigeons are food deprived anywhere from 80 to 85 percent of their free-feeding body weight (Rescorla, 2001). Pigeons are housed individually or in pairs in stainless steel cages with free access to grit and water within colony rooms maintained at constant temperature and humidity, with light cycles varying from 12 : 12 to 14.5 : 9.5 hrs. Unlike rats, pigeons are more likely to be used in more than one experiment. Japanese quail (*Coturnix japonica*) are obtained from local sources or a breeding colony is established on site. Birds are typically raised in mixed-sex groups until they reach 30 days of age, after which they are housed in a ventilated, temperature-controlled colony room with visual and auditory social stimulation and water available ad lib (Burns & Domjan, 2001; Dorrance & Zentall, 2001). Experimental and colony rooms are maintained on a 16 : 8 hr light : dark cycle in order to keep the quail in a state of reproductive readiness (Burns & Domjan, 2001). Female quail are group housed and are reproductively receptive; male quail are housed individually; and for some studies opportunities for males to copulate with receptive females provide the primary reinforcement. For other experiments, quail are deprived of food 22 to 23 hours per day prior to the experimental sessions and access to food provides primary reinforcement. Less frequently, budgerigars (*Melopisittacus undulatus*) have been used in experiments by the top researchers in animal learning/comparative psychology (Kazuchika, Staddon, & Cleaveland, 1997).

*Primates* The top researchers in animal learning/comparative psychology use a variety of primate species in their research. Landmark use has been studied in squirrel monkeys (Sutton, Olthof, & Roberts, 2000). The individually housed squirrel monkeys are allowed to interact with one another in an enriched play cage for three to four hours, six days a week. The light : dark cycle is 13 : 11 and subjects are fed Purina Monkey Chow, fruits, vegetables, and vitamins. Monkeys are not food deprived and are tested one hour prior to their daily feeding (Sutton et al., 2000). Rhesus and capuchin monkeys (Wright,

1997, 1998, 1999) and baboons (Fagot, Wasserman, & Young, 2001; Young, Peissig, Wasserman, & Biederman, 2001) are also used in studies of animal cognition. The work with baboons (*Papio papio*) usually involves two to six animals from a single social group. Subjects are not food deprived, but generally receive their daily food ration following completion of experimental trials. Similar to pigeons, primates are typically used in multiple experiments.

*Other species*  Honeybees are obtained locally and are typically maintained in university-owned hives. In one lab, subject bees are captured in a matchbox as they arrive at a 10–15 percent sucrose solution feeding station. Bees are then carried to the laboratory where they receive a 50 percent sucrose solution to increase their motivation to forage in the experimental setting and to prevent them from returning to the original feeding site. As the bees forage on the enriched sucrose solution in the experimental setting, they are marked with colored lacquer for identification purposes (Couvillon, Campos, Bass, & Bitterman, 2001). Rabbits (McNish, Betts, Brandon, & Wagner, 1997) and goldfish (*Carassius auratus*; Talton, Higa, & Staddon, 1999) complete the list of species used by top investigators in animal learning/comparative psychology.

*Apparatus*

Operant chambers for rats or pigeons dominate the apparatus used by the top researchers in animal learning/comparative psychology. Indeed, 75 percent of these researchers use operant conditioning chambers. These chambers can be obtained from a variety of sources (Med Associates, Campden Instruments, Ltd., Paul Fray, Coulbourn Instruments, BRS/LVE, Inc., and Lafayette Instrument Co.) and are similar in design and function. In the next subsections, we examine the various apparatuses used to study rats, pigeons, primates, and other species.

*Apparatuses for rats*  The top investigators who work with rats utilize a variety of apparatus. Such apparatuses include the operant conditioning chamber, radial arm mazes, Morris water mazes, reaction time apparatus, and adapted experimental chambers. Operant conditioning chambers are used to investigate questions in instrumental learning and classical conditioning. The description of the rat operant chamber that follows is taken primarily from the work of Bouton (Frohardt, Guarraci, & Bouton, 2000), but the information presented generalizes across many operant chambers. Typical operant chambers for rats measure 26 × 25 × 19 cm with the front, back, and one side constructed of aluminum. The remaining side and the ceiling are made of clear plastic. The floor of the chamber comprises tubular steel bars that are situated perpendicular to the front wall, commonly referred to as the intelligence panel. The intelligence panel typically consists of the food cup, sites for stimulus lights and tones, and operant manipulanda (usually response levers, sometimes retractable).

Retractable response levers provide the experimenter with the opportunity to use the apparatus in classical conditioning studies as well as in instrumental tasks. In some cases, a photocell and light source are recessed in the food cup to detect head movements into the food well. In many appetitive conditioning experiments food pellets (e.g., P. J. Noyes, Lancaster, NH) are the typical reward. Although food is a commonly used reward, liquid (e.g., Dickinson, Smith, & Mirenowicz, 2000), cocaine (e.g., Olmstead, Lafond, Everitt, & Dickinson, 2001), and electrical brain stimulation (e.g., Gallistel, Mark, King, & Latham, 2001) also have been used as positive reinforcers. Foot shock, when used, is provided through the bars in the floor of the chamber. Computers and appropriate interfacing equipment control stimulus presentations, time all events, operate the feeder, and store all response data. Operant chambers are routinely placed in sound and light attenuating chambers that enhance the salience of experimental stimuli. These attenuating chambers are equipped with fans that provide fresh air, masking noise and illumination. Occasionally, distinctive odors are placed in or near the box to allow for the manipulation of contextual stimuli (e.g., Frohardt et al., 2000).

Radial arm and Morris water mazes are used to investigate spatial learning and memory and landmark use (e.g., Hogarth, Roberts, Roberts, & Abroms, 2000). In a typical maze the arms are long (72.5 cm) and narrow (8.75 cm) and are equipped with a circular food cup located at the end (Hogarth et al. 2000). The octagonal center of the maze is 35.5 cm in diameter and the whole maze is positioned above the floor within a large room containing a number of extramaze landmarks. The typical Morris water maze is a large circular pool that is filled with water that is made opaque either by adding polystyrene latex, a nontoxic substance that does not spoil, or milk. The pool is kept at a constant temperature and is situated in a large room mounted on a wooden base. A transparent circular platform is mounted on a rod and base and is placed in the pool below the surface (Prados, Chamizo, & Mackintosh, 1999). Researchers have also used a second type of water maze, a rectangular gray fiberglass tank that is filled with water and is maintained at a constant temperature. A gray plastic partition located on the end wall separates the maze into two goal chambers. An escape platform, the top of which is below the surface of the water, is attached to the rear wall of each goal area. The platform is transparent plastic and has holes drilled to provide better footing for the rats. Stimuli are suspended above the surface of the water on the end wall of the goal box (George, Ward-Robinson, & Pearce, 2001).

Researchers also use reaction time apparatuses in their work with rats (Holland, Han, & Gallagher, 2000). The nine-hole reaction time chamber (Paul Fray, Cambridge, UK) has a curved stainless steel front wall that contains nine ports that are illuminated from behind. Opaque plastic inserts can be used to block access to the ports. An infrared phototransistor detects nose pokes. At the center of the rear wall, a recessed food cup that is covered by a hinged plastic door provides food. A house light and a speaker are mounted in the center of the top wall. In a reaction time trial, one of the holes randomly lights up. If the rat sticks its nose in the hole within a certain time period it receives food at the opposite end of the chamber.

Researchers in animal learning/comparative psychology also use different types of experimental chambers (Escobar et al. 2001) and simple plastic cages (Dwyer, Bennett, & Mackintosh, 2001). Miller's Plexiglas chambers are either rectangular (R) or V-shaped (V). The chamber floors are constructed of stainless-steel rods that allow for delivery of constant-current foot shock. The ceilings are clear Plexiglas and each chamber is equipped with a water-filled lick tube and is housed in a separate light and sound-attenuating environmental chamber. A dispenser system (Lafayette Instruments, Lafayette, IN) delivers variable amounts of liquid at specified intervals. To drink, rats insert their heads into the niche, thereby breaking the infrared photobeam. Conditioned stimuli (CS) consist of a variable brightness flashing light, high tone, low tone, click train, or buzzer.

*Apparatuses for pigeons*  The top investigators used only operant conditioning apparatus to investigate learning and memory in pigeons. A typical pigeon operant chamber (Rescorla, 2001; Young et al., 2001) is slightly larger (27 × 27 × 35 cm) than a rat operant chamber, with an opening in the intelligence panel that houses a food hopper for grain rather than a food cup.

   Unlike rat operant chambers, only the intelligence panel is aluminum in pigeon chambers. The remaining sides and the ceiling are clear plastic. Similar to a rat chamber, the floor of a pigeon chamber is made of tubular steel bars perpendicular to the intelligence panel. In some operant chambers, an 11.8 × 14.5 cm clear acrylic response key behind a rectangular opening in the chamber wall is centered above the food hopper. A set of relay contacts is mounted behind the response key to detect pigeon pecks. A computer generates and displays a variety of stimuli (differing in shape, size, and/or color) on a color television. In some pigeon chambers, an in-line projector projects different stimuli onto up to three circular response keys aligned horizontally on the intelligence panel. Stimulus color can be controlled by the use of Kodak Wratten Filters. Although stimuli are displayed on the vertical intelligence panel in most chambers, in Wright's laboratory, the touch screen is located on the floor and pigeons must peck on the horizontal plane. Wright argues that this procedure more closely simulates natural pigeon behavior (Wright, Cook, Rivera, Sands, & Delius, 1988). Like rat operant chambers, pigeon chambers are usually housed in sound and light-attenuating shells with fans for ventilation and noise masking.

   Wasserman (e.g., Young et al., 2001) uses a clear touch screen coated with mylar behind a brushed aluminum panel for stimulus presentation and response detection. Stimuli are presented through a central opening and pecks on the screen are processed by a serial controller board. Because the front of Wasserman's chamber is fairly crowded, he uses a rotary pellet dispenser that delivers pigeon pellets to the food hopper in the rear of the chamber. A house light provides constant illumination and is controlled by a digital input–output (I/O) interface board, as are the pellet dispenser, peripheral stimuli, and the recording of the pigeon's responses. In Wasserman's experiments (Young et al., 2001), the pigeon's monitor and an identical monitor located in an adjacent room are connected by a video splitter or by a distribution amplifier. Simple volumetric stimuli, or geons, (examples include brick or barrel shapes) are developed by the Ray Dream Studio at 300 dpi resolution. Using the icons provided by Macintosh computers, Wasserman and his colleagues are able to provide a large variety of additional stimuli.

*Apparatuses for primates*  The top investigators in animal learning typically use environmental chambers to study basic issues in associative learning and spatial learning and memory. These apparatuses may or may not have manipulanda. Roberts used a modified test chamber in a study of landmark use in squirrel monkeys (Sutton et al., 2000).

Monkeys foraged for food by digging through dry oatmeal for mealworms in any of 144 holes arranged in a 12 × 12 grid on the floor. Four wooden dowels served as landmarks and could be positioned in various arrangements in the holes across trials. In Wright's lab, rhesus and capuchin monkeys are tested in a custom aluminum test chamber with no holes or openings to visually distract the monkeys. Travel-slide pictures are presented on a 33 cm NEC video monitor (model JC-1401P3A Multisync color monitor with an 800 × 560 resolution). Touch responses to test pictures and the white rectangle are monitored by a Carroll Touch Infrared Smart-Frame (Model 50023801, Carroll Touch, Round Rock, TX). A Plexiglas template with cutouts matching the picture and response areas guides touch responses (Wright, 1998, 1999). In studies by Wasserman and Fagot, baboons are tested in an enclosure in which the baboon faces an analog joystick, a metal touch pad, and a 14 in color monitor that is driven by a Pentium-based computer. On the front of the enclosure there is a view port, a hand port, and a food dispenser that delivers 190 mg banana-flavored Noyes food pellets. Manipulation of the joystick causes isomorphic movement of a cursor on the monitor. The stimuli consist of highly discriminable computer-generated icons and appear as white pictures on a black background (Wasserman, Fagot, & Young, 2001; Wasserman, Young, & Fagot, 2001).

*Apparatuses for other species*  Eye blink conditioning in rabbits was used to study basic issues in animal learning by one of our top investigators. The rabbit's head protrudes from one end of the box. Conditioned stimuli include tones, flashing lights, and vibration and are followed by presentations of a mild electric shock that is delivered to the right paraorbital region of the eye. Stimulus presentations are under the control of the electronic pulse generators controlled by a laboratory computer. Closure of the rabbit's eye is monitored by an adaptation of the photoresistive transducer that is taped directly to the rabbit's head. The signal is adjusted so that a 0.5 mm eyelid closure produces a 1 mm deflection of a recording pen and is displayed on a polygraph. The eyeblink conditioning chamber is placed in an isolation chamber that measures 66 × 48 × 48 cm. Each chamber is lined with aluminum foil to provide a homogeneous visual surround. Ventilation fans provide a constant background masking noise (Myers, Vogel, Shin, & Wagner, 2001).

Simple plastic petri dishes with gray covers that are labeled with different colored plastic discs are used to study learning in honeybees (Couvillon, Ablan, Ferreira, & Bitterman, 2001). The colored plastic discs are 2.5 cm in diameter and are affixed to the gray covers. Olfactory stimuli are presented by drilling holes in the gray cover and filling them with cotton batting. Various scents (peppermint, geraniod, or other odors) are poured on the cotton. A strong anomaly in the geomagnetic field, produced by placing ceramic permanent magnets near the feeding dishes, can also serve as a CS. Drops of water containing varying concentrations of sucrose provide rewards.

To study the role of learning in reproductive behavior, Domjan uses experimental chambers that are made of plywood and painted white (Burns & Domjan, 2000). One side of the chamber is wire mesh to allow visual access to a smaller side cage that holds a receptive female quail. A wood panel door allows access to the female. A small moveable wooden block serves as the CS. In a typical experiment, every fifth trial is videotaped. In addition to abstract stimuli like wooden blocks and lights of differing colors, Domjan and his colleagues use natural stimuli, like the head and neck of a quail, as CS. The use of natural stimuli is not common among the top researchers in the field.

## Procedure

To determine causality using the scientific method, one attempts to maximize treatment variability and minimize error variability. To accomplish this task, Avery and Cross (1978) argued that the experimenter had to consider five items of critical importance. These five items were: (1) the manipulation of an independent variable or variables, (2) the adequate measurement or quantification of the dependent or response variable, (3) the control of other variables that could have an influence on the response being measured, (4) the reduction of intersubject differences, and (5) the presence of adequate control groups from which to evaluate the effect of the manipulation of the independent variable. If one considers these five items critically, one can reduce error variability and thereby increase the probability of demonstrating an effect of treatment.

We chose to do a content analysis of a recent paper by Rescorla (2001). This analysis considers each of the five items of critical importance and provides the reader with a sense of how the top investigators in the field reduce error variability.

One of the questions in animal learning that has plagued researchers for years is the relation between learning and performance. This problem is not easy to solve because learning per se is not observable and is often inferred from performance. Rescorla contends that it is a common assumption among learning theorists that performance and learning map right on top of one another. In addition, it is a common assumption among such theorists that learning follows a negatively accelerated function. Thus, in a learning situation, the gains in associative strength are greater at the beginning of acquisition and smaller later in acquisition. Certainly the early linear models of learning (Bush & Mosteller, 1951; Estes, 1950; Hull, 1943) argued that associative learning followed a negatively accelerated function and so did more contemporary models (Mackintosh, 1975; Rescorla & Wagner, 1972; Pearce, 1987). In spite of the success of these models, Rescorla argued that direct tests of the assumption that performance maps right on to learning are needed. His 2001 paper was such an attempt.

Rescorla (2001) conditioned rats using two stimuli, A and C. Two additional stimuli, B and D, were not used in conditioning trials. At the end of this phase, Rescorla reasoned that the compounds AB and CD supported similar levels of performance, since each compound consisted of a stimulus that had a high level of associative strength and a stimulus that had no associative strength. In the second phase of the experiment, he provided additional excitatory acquisition trials to stimuli A and B. In the final phase of the experiment Rescorla tested the compound pairs AD and BC. Rescorla hypothesized that if associative strength builds as a negatively accelerated function then the response to the AD compound should be lower than the response to the BC compound. This is true, because the additional training trials following Phase 1 should have added less associative strength to A than to B.

To test this hypothesis, Rescorla used 16 Sprague-Dawley rats that were approximately 150 days old and were housed individually and maintained at 80 percent of their free feeding body weight. Eight identical operant chambers were used and each was enclosed in a sound and light-attenuating chamber. Four types of conditioned stimuli were used, including presentation of white noise (N), a two second clicker (K), a light (L), and a flashing light (F). The primary means to reduce error is to make sure that each subject in a particular group receives the same experience. In Rescorla's study, relays and microprocessors controlled the presentation of the conditioned stimuli. This procedure insured that each conditioned stimulus was presented in exactly the same way to each subject for as many times as the experimental protocol required. The use of the sound and light-attenuating chamber also helps insure that each subject receives the same experience. This chamber reduces outside distraction and focuses the animal's atten-tion on the stimuli of importance. In addition, maintaining the rat at 80 percent of its free feeding body weight reduces motivational variables and tends to further limit distraction.

A good methodologist uses procedures to reduce subject and experimenter bias. Sub-ject bias is of less concern in animal research, but experimenter bias is a problem. By using computers and relays to present the various stimulus conditions, and by using the computer to record and analyze the data, the experimenter is able to reduce experi-menter bias considerably. Researchers who are not able to automate their data collection procedures reduce experimenter bias in other ways. Domjan (Burns & Domjan, 2000), for example, requires two observers to independently score a videotaped behavioral sequence and the degree of correlation between the two observers is assessed. Typically there is greater than 95 percent agreement between the two observers.

Automatic measurement of the dependent variable also reduces error. Rescorla meas-ured head entries into the food cup automatically. Each time the rat inserted its head into the food cup, it broke an infrared photobeam. The microprocessor detected and recorded the number of head entries into the food cup during the 30 second presenta-tion of the conditioned stimulus and during the 30 second period just prior to onset of the conditioned stimulus.

It is critical to control all other variables that could influence the response being measured. For example, certain stimuli may be more salient or animals might have individual preferences for one type of stimulus or reward. To control for these possible differences, researchers often use counterbalancing. Rescorla is no exception. Following one day of magazine training in which rats were presented with 20 noncontingent deliveries of food according to a variable time one minute schedule, he conducted conditioning trials. In these trials, rats received eight 30-second presentations of each of two stimuli followed by the delivery of a food pellet. Acquisition trials were held for 10 days. For one half of the rats, the N and K stimuli were presented independently and in a balanced order and for the other rats, the F and L stimuli were presented. The intertrial interval varied around 2.5 minutes.

Following a day in which all rats were preexposed to the two stimuli that they had not seen, F and L for one group and N and K for the other, all animals received condition-ing trials with two stimuli A and B. Thus, all animals received conditioning trials as before except one stimulus had been previously conditioned and the second stimulus had not. In this phase, one fourth of the animals received conditioning trials with N and L, one fourth were conditioned with N and F, one fourth conditioned with K and L, and one fourth received trials of K and F. During the test phase, animals received four additional reinforced trials of A and B and two nonreinforced test trials of AD and BC. Test trials were presented in counterbalanced order. The results showed that responding to the BC pair was significantly greater than responding to the AD pair. This meant that the amount of associative strength to B was greater than the additional amount of conditioning strength to A and supported the assumption that associative strength follows a negatively accelerated function.

Rescorla typically uses a within-subjects design in which all subjects receive all levels of treatment. This method is a great way to reduce intersubject differences as the comparison stays within a subject as opposed to between subjects. In addition, Rescorla used rats that were approximately the same age, from the same population, and were housed under identical conditions. These conditions served to reduce intersubject differences.

Rescorla's methodology in Experiment 1 reduced error to a minimum. But he did not stop there. In a second experiment, Rescorla replicated Experiment 1 with two important differences. He used pigeons as the subjects of choice and conducted the study using an autoshaping procedure. The same logic and research design from Experiment 1 was applied. The study provided important comparisons for animal learning theorists. Rescorla determined the generality of his findings across different species and across different methods of classical conditioning. Taken together, the two experiments made an important contribution to the literature on the learning vs. performance debate. But, again, Rescorla did not stop there. In Experiments and 3 and 4 he used rats and pigeons, respectively, to assess whether the negatively accelerated function in associative learning and performance applied to the process of extinction. It did.

Rescorla's paper (Rescorla, 2001) offers the reader valuable insight into the methods of science that a top investigator brings to the study of animal learning and comparative psychology. Each experiment stands alone and has high internal validity. Rescorla used a within-subjects design to reduce error and he used counterbalancing to rule out trivial explanations. In addition, his apparatus reduced distraction and enhanced the effects of treatment. A computer controlled all procedures and collected and recorded all data. An appropriate number of subjects insured reliability. In addition, Rescorla addressed the extent to which the data generalized to other species and procedures. Thus Rescorla also assessed external validity.

## Laboratory Methods in Behavioral Neuroscience

### Subjects

Rats and mice continue to be used by leading researchers in behavioral neuroscience. However, in contrast to the trend in animal learning to focus largely on a few species, behavioral neuroscientists employ many different animal models, including in vitro preparations involving only portions of the nervous systems of some species. It is common for individuals to have ongoing work in related areas with more than one species. The species employed varies as a function of the work being done. Thus while either

Long-Evans or Sprague-Dawley laboratory rats are commonly used, researchers who study a particular feature of behavior or the function of a particular part of neuroanatomy may elect to utilize other species.

*Lizards* In studies of aggression Crews and his colleagues (Yang, Phelps, Crews, & Wilczynski, 2001) selected lizards. The green anole lizard (*Abolis carolinensis*) makes an excellent subject for studies of aggressive behavior because its skin darkens and it develops eye spots as a function of increased hormonal activity resulting from aggression. Such obvious changes make for good dependent measures in experiments of this nature. Green anole lizards and others, including whiptail lizards (*Cnemidophorus uniparens*, a unisexual species, and *Cnemidophorus inornatus*, a sexual species), are housed in aquaria in rooms with 14 : 10 light : dark schedules and ambient room temperatures of approximately 32 °C during the day and 22 °C degrees at night. Spatial learning studies have been carried out in the home cage or simple arenas with heated rocks serving as environmental cues. In a study of the leopard gecko (*Eublepharis macularius*), Crews and his colleagues (Sakata, Coomber, Gonzalez-Lima, & Crews, 2000) manipulated housing conditions (in addition to egg incubation temperatures) to measure their effects on the functional connectivity of limbic brain areas.

*Rabbits* Rabbits are used in studies of the biological determinants of eyeblink conditioning. Thompson and his colleagues (Bao, Chen, & Thompson, 2000), for example, studied the role of cerebellar circuitry in acquiring a conditioned eyeblink response. Cavallaro, Schreurs, Zhao, D'Agata, & Alkon (2001) used the rabbit eyeblink conditioning paradigm to examine gene expression (see below for discussion of immunoreactivity as used to identify gene expression) during long-term memory consolidation.

*Primates and rodents* Rhesus monkeys and cynomolgus monkeys (*Macaca fascicularis*) are often used in experiments on recognition memory to determine the effects of physiological manipulations on visual matching and nonmatching to sample tasks (Málková, Bachevalier, Mishkin, & Saunders, 2001; Teng, Stefanacci, Squire, & Zola, 2000). However, recent work by Squire and his colleagues (Clark, Zola, & Squire, 2000) addressed visual recognition using rats with hippocampal lesions. Use of a rat model in such experiments offers methodological advantages. Visual recognition is necessary for matching and nonmatching to sample. Thus to study mechanisms involved in recognition in the rat will contribute to a broader understanding of the mechanisms necessary for matching and nonmatching tasks. Importantly, the use of rats to elucidate the degree of involvement of various brain nuclei in recognition experiments will reduce the number of similar projects with monkeys.

*Invertebrates* Because of its relatively simple nervous system, the invertebrate sea hare, *Aplysia californica*, has been a popular subject in experiments designed to investigate sensory and motor neuron connectivity and morphology (e.g., Fischer, Yuan, & Carew, 2000). In addition to using the intact animal, *Aplysia* (Antonov, Antonov, Kandel, & Hawkins, 2001), and also the marine snail, *Hermissenda crassicornis* (Tomsic & Alkon, 2000), are favorites to use when creating an in vitro preparation to examine synaptic plasticity and other molecular variables in the nervous system. These preparations simplify the nervous system to allow closer study of function. The tissue of interest is typically harvested from the subjects shortly after their arrival in the laboratory.

*Aplysia* (which may be obtained from Marinus of Long Beach, California) are maintained in an aquarium with artificial sea water (15 °C), and fed a diet of dried seaweed once every two to three days. The dissected tissue from *Aplysia*, for example the siphon tail and the central nervous system, is pinned to the floor of a recording chamber that is filled with circulating, aerated artificial sea water at room temperature (Antonov et al. 2001). The preparations rest for an hour before the beginning of the experiment and are no longer viable after a few hours of experimentation. *Hermissenda* (which may be purchased from Sea Life Supply Co., Sand City, CA) are maintained in 11–13 °C artificial sea water with fluorescent light filtered through yellow acetate to provide surface illumination on a 10 : 14 hr light : dark schedule. The animals are fed Hikari Gold fish every other day until their nervous systems are dissected. The dissected preparations are maintained under constant pH buffered artificial saltwater perfusion (Tomsic & Alkon, 2000). As with work using tissue from *Aplysia*, experiments involving the extracted nervous system of *Hermissenda* last only a few hours.

*Apparatuses and agents*

Research in behavioral neuroscience often involves the manipulation of neuronal tissue as an independent variable in order to determine the tissue's functional contribution to the animal's behavior. In addition, behavioral neuroscientists use the measurement of nervous tissue following experimentation to examine the effects of experimental manipulation on nervous system structure. Occasionally, sensory abilities are examined through the manipulation of the sensory environment rather than manipulation of neuronal tissue directly. For example, Smotherman and his colleagues (Petrov, Nizhnikov, & Smotherman, 2000) preloaded newborn rats' stomachs with either milk or water prior to exposing them to a surrogate nipple. The data suggested that newborns are capable of monitoring the caloric value of a solution that is delivered to the stomach via intubation and adjusting their subsequent consumption of milk from a surrogate nipple accordingly.

Behavioral neuroscience frequently involves the administration of pharmacological agents to subjects. These interventions range from drugs that have binding affinities for particular receptor types (e.g., the dopamine D1 receptor, see Woolley, Sakata, Gupta, & Crews, 2001; a glutamatergic acid receptor, see Goff et al. 2001) to those that have widespread effects on the body (e.g., the anxiolytic compound buspirone, see Paschall & Davis, 2002; alcohol, see Weise-Kelley & Siegel, 2001) or those that create excitotoxic lesions (Roozendaal, de Quervain, Ferry, Setlow, & McGaugh, 2001). Pharmacological agents may be self-administered orally, including during artificial rearing of early postnatal pups (Klinsova, Goodlett, & Greenough, 1999), or delivered by injection into bodily tissue (e.g., Sieve, King, Ferguson, Grau, & Meagher, 2001) or into specific regions of the brain (Tillerson et al., 2001). To study the relation between the nucleus accumbens and the basolateral nucleus of the amygdala, McGaugh and his colleagues administered the neurotransmitter NMDA to created excitoxic lesions of the nucleus accumbens (Roozendaal et al., 2001). Schallert and his colleagues (Tillerson et al., 2001) used a dopamine transmitter neurotoxin to impair functioning of rats' forelimbs. Following administration of the neurotoxin, they forced their subjects to use the impaired limbs by placing the other (unimpaired) forelimb in a cast. Both behavioral and neurochemical data from the study suggested that therapy is effective in sparing use of the affected limb and the striatal dopamine cells that give rise to such use.

Some drugs do not cross the blood–brain barrier and therefore must be delivered into the central nervous system directly. Thus these agents must be injected into the cerebrospinal fluid-containing ventricles or into more precise locations in the central nervous system. When the delivery of an agent to a precise location is necessary, this is facilitated by cannulae, which are permanently placed fine-gauge needles that are surgically implanted using a stereotaxic instrument (Kopf Instruments, Tujunga, CA). To make proper use of a stereotaxic instrument, one must employ three-dimensional brain coordinates derived from a stereotaxic atlas (e.g., Paxinos & Watson, 1997). Stereotaxic instruments and atlases are available for a host of species and are used for the precise placement of cannulae or electrodes into the central nervous system. Electrodes may be used to record, stimulate or lesion neuronal tissue. Further, the range of sizes of recording electrodes permits such work to be conducted at the single-cell level or macrocellular level (Huang, Martin, & Kandel, 2000). Weinberger and his colleagues (Miasnikov, McLin, & Weinberger, 2001) have performed several experiments on receptive field plasticity of individual cells in the auditory cortex. These projects involve inserting electrodes into individual cells in order to record responding to pure tones. King, Xie, Zheng, & Pribram (2000) used an array of 55 recording electrodes to map distributions of dendritic potentials while exposing rats to combinations of textural and temporal variations in fibrissa stimulation. The results indicated that the somatosensory (whisker barrel) cortex showed patterns that were asymmetric with respect to the spatial and temporal patterns of fibrissa stimulation.

Microscopes are used in surgery and dissection, the histological examination of tissue to verify cannula or electrode placement, and to determine whether and to what extent nervous tissue was influenced in an experiment. Dissection microscopes are used during surgery and to guide careful extraction of tissue for in vitro preparations or for histology. Light microscopes are used when examining stained cells or organelles within cells. Further, light microscopes, when combined with digital recording equipment, a computer, and proper software, are used in estimating the number of cells within specified regions that have expressed a particular gene, protein, or other markers of neuronal activity (see discussion of immunoreactivity below). Transmission electron microscopy continues to be important in studies of molecular changes in the nervous system.

Various chambers that are specially designed to house animals are routinely used to test the effects of physiological variables. These include cylinders for studying spatial learning (Rotenberg, Abel, Hawkins, Kandel, & Muller, 2000; Day, Crews, & Wilczynski, 2001), shock chambers for studying fear conditioning (Gale, Anagnostaras, & Fanselow, 2001), and chambers (Kim & Siegel, 2001) and restraint tubes (Meagher et al., 2001) for measuring pain tolerance. An obstacle course comprised of a variety of tasks was used in the therapeutic training of postnatal binge alcohol drinking rats in order to demonstrate ameliorated adverse effects of the drug on cerebellar tissue (Klinsova et al., 1999).

Adapted and conventional versions of the Wisconsin General Test Apparatus (WGTA) continue to be used in experiments involving tests of visual recognition and memory (Málková et al., 2001). The WGTA was developed by Harlow (1949) and is used to evaluate learning set ability across species.

Subjects receive a series of two-choice visual discrimination trials during which the organism typically adopts a win stay/lose shift strategy.

*Histology* Any time nervous system tissue is manipulated in an experiment it is important to verify the nature and extent of the manipulation. Additionally, histology may be used to examine the effects of experience or activity on intact nervous systems.

Histology is a process whereby scientists confirm the placement of electrodes or cannulae, or the nature and extent of ablated tissue, in order to correlate accurately the dependent measures from their experiments with the manipulations they perform. In addition, histological procedures are used to stain nervous system tissue with a contrast medium that permits closer examination of the tissue under a microscope. Some contrast media select for particular organelles within nerve cells, others stain whole nerve cells, and still others target the myelin cells that insulate nerve cell axons.

Immunoreactivity is a special form of histology that involves selectively staining immediate-early genes, genes that are expressed by nerve cells upon their having been activated (e.g., see Guzowski, Setlow, Wagner, & McGaugh, 2001). The technique is useful not only for identifying which brain regions were active at a particular time, but also for differentiating brain nucleus involvement that changes as a function of experience. Navarro, Spray, Cubero, Thiele, and Bernstein (2000), for example, identified significantly more Fos-like immunoreactivity (immunoreactivity that identifies cells that have expressed the immediate-early gene, cFos, as well as other similar genes) in the solitary tract nucleus in rats that underwent three rather than one paired taste aversion conditioning trials. The same technique may be used to identify the presence of proteins, such as the Fragile-X mental retardation protein that is synthesized upon neurotransmitter activation of a receptor site, the absence of which is thought to cause abnormal dendritic spine lengths and numbers (Irwin et al., 2000).

In essence, immunoreactivity involves creating sequential sections of tissue through the brain region of interest. The tissue sections are then bathed in solutions that identify whether the gene or protein of interest is present. This task is accomplished using antibodies with high binding affinities for the genes or proteins of interest. Once the antibodies have bound to the genes or proteins, a chemical tag, with known affinity for the antibody of choice, is exposed to the antibody-bound genes. The tag, which serves as a marker for sites of gene or protein activity, may be viewed under a light microscope.

When estimating the numbers of cells that are tagged in a given brain region, magnified images of the slide-mounted sections are captured by a digital camera that is attached to the microscope. The images are then fed into a computer, thereby permitting special software to generate cell-count estimates. These estimates, in turn, are used in statistical analyses in order to determine whether an independent variable had significant influence on gene or protein expression.

## Procedure

Among the behavioral neuroscientists who met the criteria for inclusion in this chapter, Larry R. Squire stands out clearly as a leader in terms of the number and nature of publications he has authored or coauthored, the number of times his work has been cited, and the degree to which his laboratory secures federal funding to support his research.

For many years, the work of Squire and his colleagues has focused on the functional anatomy of memory systems. Much of the work conducted in Squire's lab has involved the selective lesioning of hippocampal and related tissue to address questions concerning the organization and structure of memory. Although these researchers often employ monkeys as subjects, rats and amnesic humans have also been studied carefully in the effort to discern which anatomical and physiological features of the nervous system give rise to which memorial functions. In addition to using animal models to better understand the organization of human memory systems, Squire and his colleagues have noted the structural similarity in the memory systems of the different species.

In a recent paper (Teng et al., 2000), Squire and his colleagues reported findings from an experiment that utilized cynomolgus monkeys and involved different types of lesions to the hippocampal region (i.e., the hippocampus proper, the dentate gyrus, and the subiculum) or the hippocampal region plus lesions of the tail of the caudate nucleus. Lesions of the hippocampal region were made using either an ischemic procedure (carotid artery occlusion combined with pharmacologically induced hypotension), radio frequency, or ibotenic acid. The ischemic procedure is appropriate because it provides a useful model of one way in which humans experience brain injuries that result in amnesia. The ibotenic acid manipulation was used in order to minimize the effects of lesions on tissue that is adjacent to the hippocampal region (i.e., amygdala and entorhinal, perirhinal, and parahippocampal cortices). Radio frequency lesions were used to destroy tissue in both the hippocampal region and the tail of the caudate nucleus for those animals with caudate lesions. Unoperated control animals provide comparison data.

The focus of this project was to determine whether contrasting effects on memory would result from hippocampal or conjoint hippocampal-caudate lesions. Squire and his colleagues hypothesized that animals with different experimental lesions (i.e., with or without intact caudate nuclei) would perform differently on object discrimination tasks than on concurrent discrimination and pattern discrimination tasks. It is important to note that this reasoning reflects the challenges of these qualitatively different tasks. The object discrimination task involved training the animals on one object pair at a time; learning on this task occurs quickly within a single session in unoperated animals. By contrast, the concurrent discrimination and pattern discrimination tasks involve working with several pairs of objects at the same time; control animals typically learn to solve these tasks over hundreds of trials.

Squire and his colleagues reported two main findings: (1) the hippocampal region was required for normal learning and retention in a simple, two-choice object discrimination task, and (2) concurrent discriminative learning and pattern discrimination learning are dependent upon the integrity of the caudate nucleus. The data identified a distinction in the memorial roles served by the hippocampal region and the caudate memory system. The authors concluded that the hippocampus is a component of the medial temporal lobe memory system, a set of structures that is important for rapid learning. By contrast, the caudate nucleus is part of a corticostriatal system that is important for gradual learning and the development of habits and stimulus–reward associations.

Squire's work on the hippocampal system has contributed significantly to our understanding of the functional anatomy of the memory system. Creating lesions of hippocampal and associated tissue requires invasive, irreversible destruction of not only the target tissue, but, due to its subcortical location, other tissue as well. Nevertheless, his research team has systematically reported results that provide increasing insight into the complicated nature of memory.

## Methods in Basic/Applied Animal Behavior

Studies of basic/applied animal behavior do not lend themselves to the relatively straightforward compartmentalization strategies that have prevailed in the previous two sections of this chapter. Many studies of basic/applied animal behavior ask questions that fit within the general categorization of experimental psychology, but many address issues that ask additional questions that are harder to fit within the realm of traditional experimental psychology.

For example, these studies may utilize the methodologies of experimental psychology, but also may make use of the techniques of behavioral ecology, neuroscience, physiology, zoology, and anthropology as well. Whereas many of these investigations take place in the laboratory under controlled conditions that may lack naturalistic ecological relevance, many also occur in field settings, where ecological relevance is higher but tight control is difficult to achieve. Most of these field studies focus on natural populations of animals; therefore an extended discussion of housing conditions does not really make sense. Similarly, many field investigations address issues that do not require sophisticated experimental chambers or apparatuses, although well-controlled field experiments (such as playback experiments, Rendall, Cheney, & Seyfarth, 2000) can be performed. Finally, the identified investigators may not consider themselves experimental psychologists, but we are examining the techniques that have influenced significantly the methods used in animal research, where independent variables of psychological relevance are manipulated and behavior is measured as one of the dependent variables.

The "giants" to be discussed below work in the field of basic/applied animal behavior and met the requirements for inclusion in this chapter (recipient of a major grant and heavily cited in the recent literature). However, their research and publications are not necessarily considered as experimental psychology. Many of these investigators work within interdisciplinary teams, publishing papers in a variety of fields. For the purposes of this section, we will focus on (1) the one individual within the team that is most closely identified with experimental psychology, and (2) those recent publications that can be most easily considered relevant to experimental psychology. Investigators working primarily with nonhuman primates dominate the section that follows. However, an attempt was made to maximize the diversity of species represented by the research programs of those discussed.

## Subjects

Nonhuman primates are the most common subjects serving in the investigations of these 20 researchers in basic/applied animal behavior. Nine of the 20 investigators study primarily New World monkeys (cotton-top tamarins, *Saguinas oedipus oedipus*; common marmosets, *Callithrix jacchus*), Old World monkeys (baboons, *Papio spp.*; vervet monkeys, *Cercopithecus aethiops*; macaques, *Macaca spp.*), and/or Great Apes (chimpanzees, *Pan spp.*; gorillas, *Gorilla spp.*). The remaining 11 investigators work with a variety of different species including bottle-nosed dolphins (*Tursiops truncatus*), spotted hyenas (*Crocuta crocuta*), naked mole-rats (*Heterocephalus glaber*), prairie dogs (*Cynomus spp.*), ground squirrels (*Spermophilus beecheyi beecheyi*), Mongolian gerbils (*Meriones unguiculatus*), Clark's nutcrackers (*Nucifraga columbiana*), zebra finches (*Taeniopygia guttata*), black-capped chickadees (*Parus atricapillus*), garter snakes (*Thamnophis spp.*), and *Anolis* lizards (*Anolis aeneus*). A few investigators even work with rats (*R. norvegicus*; Galef & Whiskin, 2001) or pigeons (*C. livia*; Inman & Shettleworth, 1999). Whereas many of the investigators have focused their efforts on one "favorite" species, virtually all have also published studies on additional species to promote the comparative perspective.

*Primates* Four of the nine primate investigators specialize in the study of natural populations of wild nonhuman primates, with baboons being the most frequently studied species. In fact, all but one (Hill, Lycett, & Dunbar, 2000) of these investigators have made their major contributions to the methods of experimental psychology studying the wild baboons of Amboseli National Park in Kenya (Alberts & Altmann, 2001; Sapolsky & Share, 1998; Seyfarth, 1976). Robert Seyfarth has also studied the vervet monkeys of Amboseli (Cheney & Seyfarth, 1989) and his most recent projects involve baboons in Botswana (Rendall et al., 2000; Fischer, Metz, Cheney, & Seyfarth, 2001). Jeanne Altmann's work is well known (Alberts & Altmann, 2001) and her observational sampling methods paper from 1974 (Altmann, 1974) is one of the most heavily cited papers in the behavioral sciences. The work of Robert Sapolsky is well-regarded and may provide the single best example of how effectively research in animal behavior can be applied to other scientific investigations, particularly in the fields of neuroscience, immunology, and aging (Virgin & Sapolsky, 1997). Robin Dunbar (Hill et al., 2000) has studied another baboon species, the gelada baboons (*Theropithecus gelada*) living in Ethiopia.

   Of the five remaining primate researchers, two have made significant contributions from their studies of the behavior of captive chimpanzees (Preuschoft et al., 2002; Suddendorf & Whiten, 2001). Andrew Whiten has studied chimpanzees at a number of facilities throughout the world and in the wild. Focusing primarily on issues related to cognition, culture, and theory of mind in Great Apes, the techniques employed by Whiten in his work have helped shape a number of important research paradigms (Whiten, 1998). Whiten does not have a colony of chimpanzees at his institution, the

University of St Andrews in Scotland, but he has strategically made use of a number of large chimpanzee colonies, including the one at the Yerkes Regional Primate Research Center. Frans de Waal has concentrated much of his recent research on the social groups of chimpanzees living at the Yerkes Primate Center (Preuschoft et al., 2002). These animals are maintained in large groups (as many as 19 animals) in naturalistic 525–720 m² indoor–outdoor enclosures (Baker, Seres, Aurelli, & de Waal, 2000), an appropriate setting for the studies of cultural transmission, learning, and reconciliation conducted by de Waal (2000a).

Irwin Bernstein also studies the primates at Yerkes, but he has focused his research efforts on the macaque (*Macaca mulatta, M. arctoides, M. nigra*) and capuchin (*Cebus apella*) groups there (Cooper et al., 2001; Matheson & Bernstein, 2000). Like the chimpanzees, the macaques and capuchins at Yerkes are housed in large social groups (as many as 90 animals) in large (up to 19 × 38 m) indoor–outdoor enclosures. At the Wisconsin Regional Primate Research Center, Charles Snowdon has studied various aspects of the behavior and biology of the cotton-top tamarin (Roush & Snowdon, 2001). The cotton-tops are typically maintained in indoor enclosures in mated pairs (0.85 × 1.7 × 2.2 m) or family groups (2.1 × 1.7 × 2.2 m) that mimic group compositions of wild populations of this species. Stephen Suomi of the National Institutes of Health has been studying the biobehavioral development of rhesus monkeys for the last 30 years. His work – including early work in collaboration with his professor, Harry Harlow – has taught, and continues to teach, us a great deal about the biobehavioral development of primates (Champoux, Norcross, & Suomi, 2000; Champoux et al. 2002; Suomi, 2001). Suomi's carefully controlled experimental techniques have been employed with nursery-reared rhesus, rhesus that were mother-reared in the laboratory, and wild populations of rhesus macaques (Higley et al., 2000; Laudenslager et al., 1999).

*Nonprimate species* Lewis Herman has studied the cognitive abilities of bottlenosed dolphins for well over 25 years. His carefully crafted and controlled experimental studies provide a standard for all studies of aquatic mammals. In general, he works with small numbers of dolphins living socially in large (15.2 m diameter) pools in captivity (Herman, Matus, Herman, Ivancic, & Pack, 2001; Mercado, Killebrew, Pack, Macha, & Herman, 2000). Unlike the "experimental settings" of some of the primate researchers just discussed, Herman makes use of simple, yet precise, experimental apparatuses. Given the great cognitive capabilities of his cetacean subjects, there is need for specific control conditions in his work, including such accommodations as opaque goggles for the experimenters (to prevent inadvertent cueing of the dolphins) and typical "double-blind" procedures (Mercado et al., 2000).

Spotted hyenas (Glickman et al., 1997) have been studied in both the laboratory and the field. At the Field Station for Behavioral Research in Berkeley, CA, large social groups of hyenas are maintained in indoor–outdoor enclosures that range in size from 7.5 × 4.5 m to 8.7 × 4.5 m indoors and 18.6 × 6.9 m to 10.8 × 13.2 m outdoors. Glickman conducts his fieldwork in Amboseli National Park in Kenya where his work focuses on investigating the complex relation between hormones and dominance behavior (Glickman et al., 1997, 1998). Paul Sherman (Sherman, Braude, & Jarvis, 1999), John

Hoogland (Hoogland, 2001), and Donald Owings (Swaisgood, Owings, & Rowe, 1999) also study their species in both the laboratory and the field. For Sherman, the field is Kenya, the home of his species, the naked mole-rat, an important model for studies of altruism and kin selection, given their "eusocial" existence. In his laboratory, large social groups that simulate natural group compositions are maintained in quiet, warm (26–8 °C), humid (55–70%), and dim conditions that simulate their underground tunnel settings (Lacey & Sherman, 1991). Each social group is maintained in its own room. Hoogland (2001) observes several species of prairie dogs at various study sites on the Great Plains of the United States and focuses on questions related to reproductive behavior. Owings specializes in communication and antipredator behavior, specifically the antisnake behavior, of California ground squirrels living in the foothills of the Sierra Nevada Mountains of Northern California (Bursten, Berridge, & Owings, 2000; Swaisgood, Owings, & Rowe, 1999). He looks at both squirrels and snakes in his research program and maintains captive research colonies of both species in animal rooms at the University of California at Davis (Bursten et al., 2000).

Bennet Galef studies the fertility and parental behavior of Mongolian gerbils (Clark & Galef, 2001) in the laboratory. His animals are typically maintained in breeding pairs in polycarbonate cages on a 12 : 12 light : dark cycle. Specific social manipulations, such as the addition of foster sisters and foster fathers (Clark & Galef, 2001) are performed to explore their effects on pregnancy outcomes and infant survival.

Alan Kamil studies the cognitive abilities of a variety of bird species, primarily nutcrackers and jays (Bond & Kamil, 2002; Gibson & Kamil, 2001). His major research emphasis is on food selection, caching, and spatial memory in laboratory settings. Relatively little of his work has been conducted on wild Corvid populations. During nonexperimental time periods, his avian subjects live singly in colony rooms maintained at 22 °C on a 14 : 10 light : dark cycle at the University of Nebraska.

For over 25 years, P. J. B. Slater has been studying the vocal communication behavior of animals, focusing primarily, but not exclusively, on the singing behavior of zebra finches and other songbirds (Pearson, Mann, & Slater, 1999). Captive birds are typically maintained in a laboratory room with considerable exposure to natural lighting, a critical influence on singing behavior (Pearson et al., 1999). His recent publications examine the songs of wild populations of willow warblers (*Phylloscopus trochilus*) in the UK. In these well-crafted studies, he has analyzed specific song characteristics, in an effort to isolate specific social learning processes (Gil, Cobb, & Slater, 2001).

Sara Shettleworth has been studying many cognitive aspects of many species for many years. Publications within just the last four years from her lab have examined spatial learning in rats (Gibson, Shettleworth, & McDonald, 2001), mate choice in fish (Shettleworth, 1999), metamemory in pigeons (Inman & Shettleworth, 1999), and her most frequently researched topic, comparison of spatial memory in food-storing versus nonstoring birds (chickadees and juncos; Hampton, Shettleworth, & Westwood, 1998). With such a comparative approach to her work, it is difficult to discuss the subjects that she uses in detail. More useful to the reader, no doubt, will be the citation of the studies relevant to her methodological contributions to investigations of basic/applied animal behavior. Shettleworth, more than the others described above, utilizes the comparative approach in her studies of cognitive ecology (Shettleworth, 2001).

Gordon Burghardt's studies of garter snake foraging activities (Krause & Burghardt, 2001), both in the laboratory and along the lake shores of the Upper Midwestern United States have contributed numerous methodological advancements for the study of the behavior of small snakes. His work exemplifies the synergism that can result from addressing evolutionary questions with both tightly controlled laboratory techniques and more ecologically relevant field techniques. Snakes maintained in his greenhouse laboratory are generally housed in groups of five to seven in aquaria kept at 20–3 °C with a natural photoperiod (Terrick, Mumme, & Burghardt, 1995).

Finally, the studies by Judy Stamps of *Anolis* and other lizard species (Stamps & Krishnan, 1998) have elucidated a great deal about the territorial behavior of these species. Although her observations are primarily of behaviors and displays related to territorial interactions in naturalistic settings, her questions address the reproductive consequences of territorial behavior (or the lack of it) and sexual size dimorphism. Like some of those just mentioned, the primary manipulations in Stamps' studies involve changes to aspects of the social environment, specifically attempts to control the number of males available and the size of territories (Stamps & Krishnan, 1998).

## Apparatus

*Primates* The research programs of many of the investigators included in this section address questions in addition to those normally considered as experimental psychology. For the purpose of the apparatus section of this portion of the chapter, comments will be confined to those aspects of their research that relate most closely to experimental psychology.

For many of the field workers just discussed, the natural environment, both social and physical, serves as the apparatus for their studies. Altmann, Dunbar, Seyfarth, and Sapolsky are particularly well-known for their naturalistic observations of their respective species (Alberts & Altmann, 2001; Fischer, Cheney, & Seyfarth, 2000; Hill et al., 2000; Virgin & Sapolsky, 1997). In certain cases, the investigators may manipulate conditions (e.g., adding an individual, temporarily removing an individual, playing a recording of a sound, presenting a "model" of a predator). However, the prevailing philosophy for these scientists is to observe the animals as they respond to and adapt to changes in their natural physical and social environments (Alberts & Altmann, 2001; Virgin & Sapolsky, 1997).

Seyfarth (in collaboration with Cheney and others) in particular, is well-known for his field playback studies, employing strict experimental conditions and controls in the natural setting (Cheney & Seyfarth, 1989; Fischer, Cheney, & Seyfarth, 2000; Seyfarth, Cheney, & Marler, 1980). Briefly, their apparatus consists of high fidelity microphones, tape recorders/players, speakers, and video cameras. They record the vocalizations of members of the group in specific circumstances and then play back these vocalizations from hidden speakers to other members of the group. They then observe and record the behavioral responses of the subjects to the test stimuli (Seyfarth et al., 1980). Considerable understanding of vocal communication in vervet monkeys has resulted from this rigorous approach (Seyfarth et al., 1980). Seyfarth's work will be treated in more detail in the procedure subsection that follows.

De Waal (2000a), working with the social groups of chimpanzees at the Field Station of the Yerkes Primate Center, does not typically employ experimental apparatus, preferring instead to observe the unmanipulated behavior patterns of his study animals. From a methodological perspective, the observational techniques and operational definitions he has pioneered for studying reconciliation (de Waal & van Roosmalen, 1979; Preuschoft et al., 2002) in chimpanzees, bonobos, macaques, and capuchins represent a substantial contribution to the basic/applied animal behavior literature. Briefly, his technique for analyzing episodes of reconciliation involves observing animals after an aggressive incident (postaggression period) and during a similarly timed nonpostaggression period (the control observation). In this way, he can determine whether individuals are more likely to engage in affiliative/reconciliatory behaviors after an aggressive incident than they are during other periods (Preuschoft et al., 2002). De Waal will occasionally distribute various items (e.g., foraging items, toys) to the animals to stimulate the target behaviors. To study cooperation among capuchin monkeys (*Cebus apella*), de Waal (2000b) used a specially constructed cage in which neighboring subjects can reach into one another's cage to steal/share food.

Whiten, who also studies chimpanzee groups, employs a number of different "problems" in his studies of cultural learning (Suddendorf & Whiten, 2001). His comparative studies of cultural behavior require the animals (and children) to perform specific tasks in specified ways in order to receive reinforcement (reviewed in Whiten, 2000). His main interests are discovering (1) the learning processes that help subjects solve the problem, and (2) whether and how the techniques for solving the problem are communicated from chimpanzee to chimpanzee (or child to child). His apparatuses are simple, typically involving an "artificial fruit" that can only be opened in a limited number of ways (Whiten, 1998). He is interested in how the chimpanzees open the fruit after they have observed someone else open it.

Bernstein (Matheson & Bernstein, 2000) studies dominance interactions in large, captive (and wild) groups of macaques, and capuchins (Cooper et al., 2001). The emphasis is on observation of natural patterns of grooming, dominance, and affiliative behaviors. Occasionally, Bernstein and his colleagues manipulate group compositions, but they rarely make use of experimental apparatus, per se.

Snowdon's studies of reproductive and parenting behavior in marmosets and tamarins take place primarily in the species-typical social groups in which he maintains them at the Wisconsin Regional Primate Research Center (Roush & Snowdon, 2001). Snowdon's primary manipulation is to change the social or hormonal composition of the groups. To study vocalizations, Roush and Snowdon (1999) utilized recording, sound analysis, and playback equipment. A typical sound-attenuating chamber was often used for Snowden's early laboratory studies of vocalizations, but his recent studies have been conducted in more "open" settings (Roush & Snowdon, 1999, 2001).

A major component of the research performed by Stephen Suomi involves the repeated administration of an "assessment battery" during multiple stages of development in the lives of rhesus monkeys (Champoux et al., 2000). As one might expect, the specific tasks that comprise the assessment battery change as the monkeys age, but the underlying temperament variables that the tasks are designed to elucidate remain constant (Champoux et al., 2000). Suomi, like Sapolsky, is interested in the physiological correlates of the behavioral and temperamental variables that he measures, and much of his research focuses on the interplay among behavior, temperament, catecholamines, stress hormones, and immunological responses (Champoux et al., 2002).

*Nonprimate species*   The bottlenosed dolphins studied by Herman (Herman et al., 2001; Mercado et al., 2000) typically work in a large tank that essentially serves as an operant chamber. Stimuli are presented (by humans either above water or under water) and dolphins must respond by bumping the appropriate response paddle at water level. There are many parallels to the standard rat or pigeon Skinner box, but there is also one major difference. Because the questions being addressed relate primarily to dolphin intelligence, and because humans, rather than computers, are presenting the stimuli and administering the rewards, extreme precautions must be taken to eliminate the potential confound of the experimenters providing cues for the dolphins to use. Aside from the standard controls that are typically employed in operant learning procedures, Herman makes certain that those conducting the experiment can provide no useful information to the dolphins concerning the correct response. This includes making the experimenters wear opaque goggles (Mercado et al., 2000).

Glickman's studies of the development of behavior and of the reproductive endocrinology of the spotted hyena rely primarily on (1) naturalistic observations, and (2) surgical and/or hormonal manipulations of reproductive status (Glickman et al., 1997, 1998). Although captive hyenas may be manipulated (marked, videotaped, castrated, administered hormones, etc.), they are tested in experimental chambers.

Sherman's naked mole-rats are maintained in clear Plexiglas tubes that are designed to simulate the elaborate tunnel systems characteristic of this species in its natural habitat. Aside from providing the animals with living conditions that in many ways functionally simulate their natural setting, the use of Plexiglas tubes allows for the addition and removal of experimental chambers to test various components of the naked mole-rats' behavior (Judd & Sherman, 1996). In one study of foraging behavior that focused on the recruitment of colony mates to a food source, different Plexiglas rings accessible through closable shutters were attached to the burrow system to serve as food goals (Judd & Sherman, 1996). Numerous control manipulations had to be performed to study and isolate the recruitment behavior of colony members by scouts (Judd & Sherman, 1996), among the most important being the regular washing of the attached rings to eliminate residual olfactory cues.

Hoogland studies the reproductive parameters of natural populations of various species of prairie dogs at a number of study sites throughout the middle and western United States (Hoogland, 1998, 2001). Although he will observe, capture, weigh, and bleed his subjects in the field, he does not regularly employ any experimental manipulations.

Owings, on the other hand, makes use of recorded rattlesnake sounds and tethered rattlesnakes in his studies of California ground squirrel antipredator behavior. In one study (Swaisgood, Owings, & Rowe, 1999), recordings of different types of rattlesnake rattles (warm, cold, large, small, etc.) were played to squirrels as they approached a hidden speaker in their natural habitat. Behavioral responses were videotaped. Similarly, different stimuli were presented to the subjects in a well-controlled Latin square design. In another study (Swaisgood, Rowe, & Owings, 1999), rattlesnakes were tethered outside the burrows of ground squirrels and the squirrels' behavioral responses were measured. Again, different presentations of experimental stimuli were made using a counterbalanced design.

Galef maintains Mongolian gerbils and rats in his laboratory. His gerbil studies make use of primarily social manipulations, such as the removal of litters and/or the addition of specifically comprised foster litters (Clark & Galef, 2001). His studies of social learning in rats (Galef & Whiskin, 2001) make use of some of the more traditional methods in animal experimental psychology. Manipulating primarily characteristics of the subjects' diet and the exposure of the subjects to different diets, he has been able to examine critical issues in the area of social learning. Unlike most of the rat researchers discussed in the first section of this chapter (e.g., Frohardt et al., 2000), Galef does not routinely make use of experimental chambers.

Much of the work of Kamil and colleagues, focusing on food selection, caching, and spatial memory in birds (primarily jays and nutcrackers) has taken place in "arena" settings in laboratories (e.g., Gibson & Kamil, 2001). In most of these arenas, food is hidden and subject birds must find and remember the relation between the hidden or cached food and a variety of landmarks and other indicators of spatial location. The floors of the arenas are typically comprised of either bedding (e.g., wood shavings) or a grid of holes big enough to accommodate seeds and/or removable landmarks (dowels). In a recent and ingenious study (Bond & Kamil, 2002), blue jays were trained to peck moth icons on a computer screen in an attempt to determine whether crypticity and polymorphism affect prey selection. The apparatus created what Bond and Kamil called a "virtual ecology" that included not only the computer monitor that presented both the training and stimulus "moths," but also the software that generated the continuing evolution of the moth icons. It is likely that innovations that take advantage of similar computer-assisted technologies for presentation of stimuli will allow experimental psychologists to continue to refine their research techniques.

As one might expect in studies of vocal communications, the most important apparatus required is sophisticated audio recording equipment and effective analysis software. Slater makes use of such equipment and software (Gil et al., 2001, Pearson et al., 1999) in his studies of social learning processes in a variety of bird species. He has traditionally conducted most of his work in the natural setting.

Shettleworth's comparative investigations of cognition in the laboratory have made use of many of the apparatuses that have been discussed in earlier sections of this chapter. Recent studies of disorientation in rats have made use of both the Morris water maze and the radial arm maze (Gibson et al., 2001). Studies of metamemory in pigeons have used typical pigeon operant chambers (Inman & Shettleworth, 1999). These chambers also were used to compare the spatial memory of black-capped chickadees, a species that stores food, with dark-eyed juncos, a nonstoring species (Hampton et al., 1998).

Burghardt, like many of the field workers mentioned earlier in this section, does not make use of elaborate apparatus in his studies of wild garter snakes (Krause & Burghardt, 2001). His laboratory studies typically involve apparatuses that are quite simple, yet elegantly address the question at hand. For example, by using tape to create "wings" on the forceps used to offer prey to young snakes, Burghardt and colleagues were able to test the effects of aposematic coloration on prey recognition (Terrick et al., 1995).

Whereas no true apparatuses were utilized in the recent studies of territorial behavior of *Anolis* lizards conducted by Stamps and Krishnan (1998) on the island of Grenada, they did make use of some interesting methodological innovations in their fieldwork. Their basic technique involves constructing patches of habitat that are suitable for juvenile lizards and then releasing marked lizards into the patches in discrete trials. Across trials, the method of release is varied, with experimental conditions including simultaneous, sequential, low-density, and high-density trials. Dependent measures focus on aggressive interactions and their results. This is another example of an effective field "experiment," where ecological validity is maximized, yet considerable control over experimental variables is still maintained.

## Procedure

A recent published report from Robert Seyfarth's research group (Fischer et al., 2001) demonstrates outstanding methodology in applied behavioral research. Seyfarth's group was selected because their habituation-recovery method (Cheney & Seyfarth, 1988) clearly meets the criteria of Harlow's (1957) silver angel research. Additionally, their field experiments of vocal communication in nonhuman primates are particularly illustrative of the effective interaction between laboratory-type control and ecological relevance that can be obtained in the field.

In general, the work of Seyfarth's group revolves around measuring behavioral responses to recorded vocalizations. The critical factor in this type of research is to demonstrate that the target behavior (e.g., looking toward the source of the sound; Fischer et al., 2001) occurred because of the sound stimulus that was presented. To establish this relation between the sound and the behavior, it is necessary to control the variability in many aspects (1) of the stimuli and its presentation, and (2) of the setting and of the subject.

In this type of research, additional error variability can be eliminated by using observers who are blind to the experimental condition (when decoding videotapes). This study examined the behavioral responses of individuals in a large (n = 79–84) free-ranging group of baboons in Botswana to the presentation of different recorded "bark" vocalizations.

Baboon barks were recorded from the study troop in two separate circumstances; when the signaller was separated from the group (contact bark) and when the signaller spotted a crocodile or lion (alarm bark). The sophisticated acoustic analyses that characterize the work of Seyfarth's group were then performed, resulting in a "bark continuum" ranging from contact to alarm barks. For the purposes of this study, four distinct categories of bark vocalizations were established based on both their context and their acoustic characteristics.

These four categories of barks were (1) clear contact barks, (2) intermediate contact barks, (3) intermediate alarm barks, and (4) harsh alarm barks. In the habituation-recovery (Cheney & Seyfarth, 1988) technique applied in this study, subjects were presented with a series of five typical contact barks (habituation) followed by either a harsh or an intermediate alarm bark (test call). Each series of barks came from a single female and each bark was separated by a natural (7–9 sec.) silent period. The amplitude of the test call was adjusted to match the amplitude of the five habituation calls. In this technique, a behavioral response to the test stimulus suggests that it provides novel information to the recipient. The reverse design, in which a contact bark would follow five alarm barks, was not performed, since it seemed unlikely that subjects would remain stationary after five alarm barks. In a second experiment within this publication, subjects were presented with just a single exemplar of one of the four categories of barks.

Relatively few precautions have to be taken when presenting computer-controlled auditory stimuli to a single subject in an operant box within a sound-attenuating chamber. In the woodlands of Botswana, however, considerable attention must be paid to controlling potential setting-related and subject-related confounds to the research design. First of all, to make certain that the calls were presented in an ecologically relevant context, trials were only conducted when the group was peacefully scattered about the woodland portion of their habitat and no contact or alarm calls had been heard during the previous 30 minutes. Potential subjects could not be maternally related to the baboon that performed the stimulus calls and had to be sitting at least 3 m from another group member and in a position such that the loudspeaker could be hidden in the bush approximately 18 m away. The stimuli could not be played until the subject had spent at least 10 consecutive seconds looking in a direction other than at the loudspeaker. Behaviors were recorded on videotape for one minute prior to the playback and for 20 seconds after the playback. Trials were aborted if the subject did not respond to the first three habituation calls, if the subject moved away, or if another baboon approached the subject. In order to make sure that the baboons were not changing their behavior based on the behavior of the experimenters (hiding the speaker and setting up the video camera), 34 mock trials were performed in which the loudspeaker was hidden and the camera set up, but no calls were played.

The video clips of subjects' responses to the barks were analyzed without sound, so that the person scoring behavior did not know which experimental condition was being examined. Although the results of this study (Fischer et al., 2001) did not support the authors' initial hypotheses, the techniques utilized are highly illustrative of effective experimental field methodology. What is sacrificed in terms of control over independent variables in the woodlands of Botswana is more than compensated for by the ecological relevance of the natural physical and social setting. The playback techniques of Seyfarth and his group (Cheney & Seyfarth, 1988; Seyfarth et al., 1980) are among the strongest methodological contributions to experimental psychology from those studying basic/applied animal behavior.

## Conclusions

### *Limitations of this chapter*

This chapter portrayed the various methods of science in psychology used by individuals whose subjects are nonhuman animals and whose work in the three subareas of animal learning/comparative psychology, behavioral neuroscience, and applied and basic animal research is regarded highly. We examined the methods of science used by those individuals who currently hold competitive grants to fund their research and whose work has made an impact on the field and on their colleagues. The impact of one's work was measured by examining the total number of papers cited and the total number of citations the individual had received during the years 2000–1. We realize that this method of choosing the top investigators has limitations. Our selection system misses those individuals who are between grants, or whose work is funded by private or public sources other than those we examined. In addition, we may have missed those individuals who are at the beginning or end of their careers. This is necessarily so, because we required both current funding and because older papers have had more time to be cited than recent papers. Still, the investigators we chose are representative of the top investigators in the three subareas we considered and we are confident that the methods of science discussed in this chapter are representative of the science that Harlow (1957) would have recognized as silver angel research.

## Generalizations

There are several conclusions that one can draw from our analyses of the work by the top investigators. First, the top investigators in the fields of animal learning, behavioral neuroscience, and applied and basic animal behavior use a variety of species in their research. Even in animal learning, where investigators continue to use primarily rats and pigeons, investigators are branching out. One can now find rabbits, a number of different primates, quail and other birds being studied in the animal learning labs. Indeed, it is common to see investigators studying more than one species even within the same publication. In the fields of behavioral neuroscience and applied and basic animal behavior the level of diversity is even greater. It is significant to note that species are chosen with a view to providing an appropriate model for the question of interest. Second, the conduct of good science does not necessarily involve expensive equipment. The range of sophistication in the choice of apparatus is quite large. Some investigators in animal learning devote very few resources to equipment (Burns & Domjan, 2000) whereas others (Young et al., 2001) use much more sophisticated apparatuses. Certain investigators in animal behavior use little or no apparatus (Cooper et al., 2001). It does appear that expensive equipment and advanced technology is more prevalent in behavioral neuroscience research than in either animal learning or applied and basic animal behavior. Third, good science requires the use of appropriate control groups. It is not possible to decide if a treatment has had an effect if one cannot compare the results of treatment to a group that has not experienced that treatment. Each of the top investigators in this chapter uses appropriate control groups to rule out alternative explanations. The degree of sophistication in the use of controls has done much to advance our knowledge in the science of psychology.

## We've come a long way

Church (2001) argued that the twentieth century saw a substantial increase in the quality of animal research conducted by psychologists. He attributed this qualitative increase to improvements in animal husbandry, stimulus control, apparatus design, measurement techniques, procedural improvements, and greater sophistication in data analysis. Ironically, some of the improvements in the means by which animals are obtained and maintained can probably be attributed to reactions of the animal rights movements. It is now possible to obtain a sufficient quantity of a large variety of species that are healthy, genetically similar, of the same age, and who share a similar environmental history. These standardized procedures for raising and maintaining animal research subjects eliminate many of the confounds that confused earlier findings from the early twentieth century. Technological developments in the twentieth century led to the psychologist's ability to control precisely the presentation of a multitude of stimuli and to measure with great precision such variables as reaction time and response rates. Not only is it possible to measure with precision the quantitative aspects of various responses, it is now possible to measure qualitative differences. For example, in certain operant situations it is possible to measure the force with which a response is delivered which can provide motivational and emotional information about the organism making the response (Purdy & Eidson, 2002). In addition, the apparatuses used by today's animal researchers have the effect of enhancing the salience of stimuli, the reliability of response measures, and internal validity.

The improvement in animal research methodology can also be attributed to the use of methods that are repeatable. Church (2001) claimed that early work in animal psychology was characterized by a lack of replication. Often the researcher reported results from procedures that differed between and within animals. Today, psychologists routinely report the findings from 10–12 subjects who have all been treated exactly alike. This level of replication has improved dramatically the quality of the results and allowed for sophisticated statistical analyses including, among others, univariate and multivariate analyses of variance. Still, not all psychologists are able to conduct a large number of replications of a specific experiment. Psychologists working with more exotic subjects or subjects that are difficult to obtain and maintain, such as dolphins or primates, use fewer subjects. These psychologists tend to make up for the reduced number of subjects by testing the animal over multiple sessions and in more than one experiment. Indeed, the typical ABA design used by a number of operant conditioning researchers ensures that the experimental treatment is the causal factor.

Church (2001) argued that we can thank the overwhelming use of computers in the lab for many of the advances in animal research methodology. Computers are ubiquitous in the psychology laboratory and are used in all stages of experimentation from literature searches, to research design, data collection and analysis, and manuscript preparation. Computers control stimulus events with precision, determine random sequences of events with ease, and measure a number of dependent variables simultaneously or sequentially. In addition, computers allow for greater sophistication of statistical analyses of data and reduce considerably the time necessary to conduct such analyses. Computers have also increased the level and the scope of communication among scientists. Psychologists can now communicate with others around the world virtually instantaneously. Computers have allowed for collaborative efforts across laboratories around the world and the science of psychology has benefited from these interactions. In addition, computers have increased considerably the researcher's ability to access information. Literature searches can be done in a fraction of the time it used to take even 10 years ago. In short, computers have changed, in a positive direction, the way science is conducted and of course, allowed us to attempt a chapter such as this.

## References

Alberts, S. C., & Altmann, J. (2001). Immigration and hybridization patterns of yellow and anubis baboons in and around Amboseli, Kenya. *American Journal of Primatology, 53*, 139–54.

Altmann, J. (1974). Observational study of behavior: Sampling methods. *Behaviour, 49*, 227–67.

Antonov, I., Antonov, I., Kandel, E. R., & Hawkins, R. D. (2001). The contribution of activity-dependent synaptic plasticity to classical conditioning in *Aplysia*. *The Journal of Neuroscience, 21*, 6413–22.

Avery, D. D., & Cross, H. A., Jr. (1978). *Experimental methodology in psychology*. Monterey, CA: Brooks/Cole Publishing Company.

Baker, K. C., Seres, M., Aurelli, F., & de Waal, F. B. M. (2000). Injury risks among chimpanzees in three housing conditions. *American Journal of Primatology, 51*, 161–75.

Bao, S., Chen, L., & Thompson, R. F. (2000). Learning- and cerebellum-dependent neuronal activity in the lateral pontine nucleus. *Behavioral Neuroscience, 114*, 254–61.

Bond, A. B., & Kamil, A. C. (2002). Visual predators select for crypticity and polymorphism in virtual prey. *Nature, 415*, 609–13.

Burns, M., & Domjan, M. (2000). Sign tracking in domesticated quail with one trial a day: Generality across CS and US parameters. *Animal Learning and Behavior, 28*, 109–19.

Burns, M., & Domjan, M. (2001). Topography of spatially directed conditioned responding: Effects of context and trial duration. *Journal of Experimental Psychology: Animal Behavior Processes, 27*, 269–78.

Bursten, S. N., Berridge, K. C., & Owings, D. H. (2000). Do California ground squirrels (*Spermophilus beecheyi*) use ritualized syntactic cephalocaudal grooming as an agonistic signal? *Journal of Comparative Psychology, 114*, 281–90.

Bush, R. R., & Mosteller, F. (1951). A mathematical model for simple learning. *Psychological Review, 58*, 313–23.

Cavallaro, S., Schreurs, B. G., Zhao, W., D'Agata, V., & Alkon, D. L. (2001). Gene expression profiles during long-term memory consolidation. *European Journal of Neuroscience, 13*, 1809–15.

Champoux, M., Hibbeln, J. R., Shannon, C., Majchrzak, S., Suomi, S. J., Salem, N., & Higley, J. D. (2002). Fatty acid formula supplementation and neuromotor development in rhesus monkey neonates. *Pediatric Research, 51*, 273–81.

Champoux, M., Norcross, J., & Suomi, S. J. (2000). Rhesus monkeys with late-onset hydrocephalus differ from non-impaired animals during neonatal neurobehavioral assessments: Six-year retrospective analysis. *Comparative Medicine, 50*, 218–24.

Cheney, D. L., & Seyfarth, R. M. (1988). Assessment of meaning and the detection of unreliable signals by vervet monkeys. *Animal Behaviour, 36*, 477–86.

Cheney, D. L., & Seyfarth, R. M. (1989). Redirected aggression and reconciliation among vervet monkeys, *Cercopithecus aethiops*. *Behaviour, 110*, 258–75.

Church, R. M. (2001). Animal cognition: 1900–2000. *Behavioural Processes, 54*, 53–63.

Clark, M. M., & Galef, B. G. (2001). Socially induced infertility: Familial effects on reproductive development of female Mongolian gerbils. *Animal Behaviour, 62*, 897–903.

Clark, R. E., Zola, S. M., & Squire, L. R. (2000). Impaired recognition memory in rats after damage to the hippocampus. *The Journal of Neuroscience, 20*, 8853–60.

Cooper, M. A., Bernstein, I. S., Fragaszy, D. M., et al. (2001). Integration of new males into four social groups of tufted capuchins (*Cebus apella*). *International Journal of Primatology, 22*, 663–83.

Couvillon, P. A., Ablan, C. D., Ferreira, T. P., & Bitterman, M. E. (2001). The role of nonreinforcement in the learning of honeybees. *The Quarterly Journal of Experimental Psychology, 54B*, 127–44.

Couvillon, P. A., Campos, A. C., Bass, T. D., & Bitterman, M. E. (2001). Intermodal blocking in honeybees. *The Quarterly Journal of Experimental Psychology, 54B*, 369–81.

Day, L. B., Crews, D., & Wilczynski, W. (2001). Effects of medial and dorsal cortex lesions on spatial memory in lizards. *Behavioural Brain Research, 118*, 27–42.

de Waal, F. B. M. (2000a). Primates – A natural heritage of conflict resolution. *Science, 289*, 586–90.

de Waal, F. B. M. (2000b). Attitudinal reciprocity in food sharing among brown capuchin monkeys. *Animal Behaviour, 60*, 253–61.

de Waal, F. B. M., & van Roosmalen, A. (1979). Reconciliation and consolation among chimpanzees. *Behavioral Ecology and Sociobiology, 5*, 55–66.

Dickinson, A., Smith, J., & Mirenowicz, J. (2000). Dissociation of Pavlovian and instrumental incentive learning under dopamine antagonists. *Behavioral Neurocience, 114*, 468–83.

Dorrance, B. R., & Zentall, T. R. (2001). Imitative learning in Japanese quail (*Corturnix japonica*) depends on the motivational state of the observer quail at the time of observation. *Journal of Comparative Psychology, 115*, 62–7.

Dwyer, D. M., Bennett, C. H., & Mackintosh, N. J. (2001). Evidence for inhibitory associations between the unique elements of two compound flavours. *The Quarterly Journal of Experimental Psychology, 54B*, 97–107.

Escobar, M., Matute, H., & Miller, R. R. (2001). Cues trained apart compete for behavioral control in rats: Convergence with the associative interference literature. *Journal of Experimental Psychology: General, 130*, 97–115.

Estes, W. K. (1950). Toward a statistical theory of learning. *Psychological Review, 57*, 94–107.

Fagot, J., Wasserman, E. A., & Young, M. E. (2001). Discriminating the relation between relations: The role of entropy in abstract conceptualization by baboons (*Papio papio*) and humans (*Homo sapiens*). *Journal of Experimental Psychology: Animal Behavior Processes, 27*, 316–28.

Fischer, J., Cheney, D. L., & Seyfarth, R. M. (2000). Development of infant baboons' responses to graded bark variants. *Proceedings of the Royal Society of London B BIO, 267*, 2317–21.

Fischer, J., Metz, M., Cheney, D. L., & Seyfarth, R. M. (2001). Baboon responses to graded bark variants. *Animal Behaviour, 61*, 925–31.

Fischer, T. M., Yuan, J. W., & Carew, T. J. (2000). Dynamic regulation of the siphon withdrawal reflex of *Aplysia californica* in response to changes in the ambient tactile environment. *Behavioral Neuroscience, 114*, 1209–22.

Frohardt, R. J., Guarraci, F. A., & Bouton, M. E. (2000). The effects of neurotoxic hippocampal lesions on two effects of context after fear extinction. *Behavioral Neuroscience, 114*, 227–40.

Gale, G. D., Anagnostaras, S. G., & Fanselow, M. S. (2001). Cholinergic modulation of Pavlovian fear conditioning: Effects of intrahippocampal scopolamine infusion. *Hippocampus, 11*, 371–6.

Galef, B. G., & Whiskin, E. E. (2001). Interaction of social and individual learning in food preferences of Norway rats. *Animal Behaviour, 62*, 41–6.

Gallistel, C. R., Mark, T. A., King, A. P., & Latham, P. E. (2001). The rat approximates an ideal detector of changes in rates of reward: Implications for the law of effect. *Journal of Experimental Psychology: Animal Behavior Processes, 27*, 354–72.

Garcia, J., & Koelling, R. A. (1966). Relation of cue to consequence in avoidance learning. *Psychonomic Science, 4*, 123–4.

George, D. N., Ward-Robinson, J., & Pearce, J. M. (2001). Discrimination of structure: I. Implications for connectionist theories of discrimination learning. *Journal of Experimental Psychology: Animal Behavior Processes, 27*, 206–18.

Gibson, B. M., & Kamil, A. C. (2001). Tests for cognitive mapping in Clark's nutcrackers (*Nucifraga columbiana*). *Journal of Comparative Psychology, 115*, 403–17.

Gibson, B. M., Shettleworth, S. J., & McDonald, R. J. (2001). Finding a goal on dry land and in the water: Differential effects of disorientation on spatial learning. *Behavioural Brain Research, 123*, 103–11.

Gil, D., Cobb, J. L. S., & Slater, P. J. B. (2001). Song characteristics are age dependent in the willow warbler, *Phylloscopus trochilus*. *Animal Behaviour, 62*, 689–94.

Glickman, S. E., Coscia, E. M., Frank, L. G., Licht, P., Weldele, M. L., & Drea, C. M. (1998). Androgens and masculinization of genitalia in the spotted hyaena (*Crocuta crocuta*). 3. Effects of juvenile gonadectomy. *Journal of Reproduction and Fertility, 113*, 129–35.

Glickman, S. E., Zabel, C. J., Yoerg, S. I., Weldele, M. L., Drea, C. M., & Frank, L. G. (1997). Social facilitation, affiliation, and dominance in the social life of spotted hyenas. *Annals of the New York Academy of Sciences, 807*, 175–84.

Goff, D. C., Leahy, L., Berman, I., et al. (2001). A placebo-controlled pilot study of the ampakine CX516 added to clozapine in schizophrenia. *Journal of Clinical Psychopharmacology, 21*, 484–7.

Guzowski, J. F., Setlow, B., Wagner, E. K., & McGaugh, J. L. (2001). Experience-dependent gene expression in the rat hippocampus after spatial learning: A comparison of the immediate-early genes Arc, c-fos and zif268. *The Journal of Neuroscience, 21*, 5089–98.

Hampton, R. R., Shettleworth, S. J., & Westwood, R. P. (1998). Proactive interference, recency, and associative strength: Comparisons of black-capped chickadees and dark-eyed juncos. *Animal Learning & Behavior, 26*, 475–85.

Harlow, H. F. (1949). The formation of learning sets. *Psychological Review, 56*, 51–65.

Harlow, H. F. (1956). Current and future advances in physiological and comparative psychology. *American Psychologist, 11*, 273–7.

Harlow, H. F. (1957). Experimental analysis of behavior. *American Psychologist, 12*, 485–90.

Herman, L. M., Matus, D. S., Herman, E. Y. K., Ivancic, M., & Pack, A. A. (2001). The bottlenosed dolphin's (*Tursiops truncatus*) understanding of gestures as symbolic representations of its body parts. *Animal Learning & Behavior, 29*, 250–64.

Higley, J. D., Bennett, A. J., Heils, A., et al. (2000). Early rearing and genotypic influences on CNS serotonin and behavior in nonhuman primates. *Biological Psychiatry, 47*, 35 Suppl. S.

Hill, R. A., Lycett, J. E., & Dunbar, R. I. M. (2000). Ecological and social determinants of birth intervals in baboons. *Behavioral Ecology, 11*, 560–4.

Hogarth, L. A., Roberts, W. A., Roberts, S., & Abroms, B. (2000). Spatial localization of a goal: Beacon homing and landmark piloting by rats on a radial maze. *Animal Learning & Behavior, 28*, 43–58.

Holland, P. C., Han, J., & Gallagher, M. (2000). Lesions of the amygdala central nucleus alter performance on a selective attention task. *The Journal of Neuroscience, 20*, 6701–6.

Hoogland, J. L. (1998). Why do female Gunnison's prairie dogs copulate with more than one male? *Animal Behaviour, 55*, 351–9.

Hoogland, J. L. (2001). Black-tailed, Gunnison's, and Utah prairie dogs reproduce slowly. *Journal of Mammalogy, 82*, 917–27.

Huang, Y., Martin, K. C., & Kandel, E. R. (2000). Both protein kinase A and mitogen-activated protein kinase are required in the amygdala for the macromolecular synthesis-dependent late phase of long-term potentiation. *Journal of Neuroscience, 20*, 6317–25.

Hull, C. L. (1943). *Principles of behavior.* New York: Appleton-Century-Crofts.

Inman, A., & Shettleworth, S. J. (1999). Detecting metamemory in nonverbal subjects: A test with pigeons. *Journal of Experimental Psychology: Animal Behavior Processes, 25,* 389–95.

Irwin, S. A., Swain, R. A., Christmon, C. A., Chakravarti, A., Weiler, I. J., & Greenough, W. T. (2000). Evidence for altered Fragile-X mental retardation protein expression in response to behavioral stimulation. *Neurobiology of Learning and Memory, 73,* 87–93.

Judd, T. W., & Sherman, P. W. (1996). Naked mole-rats recruit colony mates to food sources. *Animal Behaviour, 52,* 957–69.

Kazuchika, M., Staddon, J. E. R., & Cleaveland, J. M. (1997). Control of vocal repertoire by reward in budgerigars (*Melopsittacus undulatus*). *Journal of Comparative Psychology, 111,* 50–62.

Kim, J. A., & Siegel, S. (2001). The role of cholecystokinin in conditional compensatory responding and morphine tolerance. *Behavioral Neuroscience, 115,* 704–9.

King, J. S., Xie, M., Zheng, B., & Pribram, K. H. (2000). Maps of surface distributions of electrical activity in spectrally deprived receptive fields of the rat's somato-sensory cortex. *Brain & Mind, 1,* 327–49.

Klinsova, A. Y., Goodlett, C. R., & Greenough, W. T. (1999). Therapeutic motor training ameliorates cerebellar effects of postnatal binge alcohol. *Neurotoxicology and Teratology, 22,* 125–32.

Krause, M. A., & Burghardt, G. M. (2001). Neonatal plasticity and adult foraging behavior in garter snakes (*Thamnophis sirtalis*) from two nearby, but ecologically dissimilar, habitats. *Herpetological Monographs, 15,* 100–23.

Lacey, E. A., & Sherman, P. W. (1991). Social organization of naked mole-rat communities: Evidence for divisions of labor. In P. W. Sherman, J. U. M. Jarvis, & R. D. Alexander (eds.), *The Biology of the Naked Mole-Rat* (pp. 275–336). Princeton, NJ: Princeton University Press.

Laudenslager, M. L., Rasmussen, K. L., Berman, C. M., et al. (1999). A preliminary description of responses of free-ranging rhesus monkeys to brief capture experiences: Behavior, endocrine, immune, and health relationships. *Brain, Behavior, and Immunity, 13,* 124–37.

Mackintosh, N. J. (1975). A theory of attention: Variations in the associability of stimuli with reinforcement. *Psychological Review, 82,* 276–98.

Málková, L., Bachevalier, J., Mishkin, M., & Saunders, R. C. (2001). Neurotoxic lesions of the perirhinal cortex impair visual recognition memory in rhesus monkeys. *Neuroreport: For Rapid Communication of Neuroscience Research, 12,* 1913–17.

Matheson, M. D., & Bernstein, I. S. (2000). Grooming, social bonding, and agonistic aiding in rhesus monkeys. *American Journal of Primatology, 51,* 177–86.

McNish, K. A., Betts, S. L., Brandon, S. E., & Wagner, A. R. (1997). Divergence of conditioned eyeblink and conditioned fear in backward Pavlovian training. *Animal Learning & Behavior, 25,* 43–52.

Meagher, M. W., Ferguson, A. R., Crown, E. D., et al. (2001). Shock-induced hyperalgesia: IV. Generality. *Journal of Experimental Psychology: Animal Behavior Processes, 27,* 218–38.

Mercado, E., Killebrew, D. A., Pack, A. A., Macha, I. V. B., & Herman, L. M. (2000). Generalization of "same–different" classification abilities in bottlenosed dolphins. *Behavioural Processes, 50,* 79–94.

Miasnikov, A. A., McLin, III, D., & Weinberger, N. M. (2001). Muscarinic dependence of nucleus basalis induced conditioned receptive field plasticity. *Neuroreport: For Rapid Communication of Neuroscience Research, 12,* 1537–42.

Myers, K. M., Vogel, E. H., Shin, J., & Wagner, A. R. (2001). A comparison of the Rescorla–Wagner and Pearce models in a negative patterning and a summation problem. *Animal Learning & Behavior, 29,* 36–45.

Navarro, M., Spray, K. J., Cubero, I., Thiele, T. E., & Bernstein, I. L. (2000). cFos induction during conditioned taste aversion varies with aversion strength. *Brain Research, 887,* 450–3.

Olmstead, M. C., Lafond, M. V., Everitt, B. J., & Dickinson, A. (2001). Cocaine seeking by rats is a goal-directed action. *Behavioral Neuroscience, 115*, 394–402.

Paschall, G. Y., & Davis, M. (2002). Olfactory-mediated fear-potentiated startle. *Behavioral Neuroscience, 116*, 4–12.

Paxinos, G., & Watson, C. (1997). *The rat brain in stereotaxic coordinates* (3rd edn.). San Diego, CA: Academic Press.

Pearce, J. M. (1987). A model of stimulus generalization for Pavlovian conditioning. *Psychological Review, 84*, 61–3.

Pearson, F. D., Mann, N. I., & Slater, P. J. B. (1999). Does leg-ring colour affect song tutor choice in zebra finches? *Animal Behaviour, 57*, 173–80.

Petrov, E. S., Nizhnikov, M. E., & Smotherman, W. P. (2000). Milk delivery schedules and stomach preloading alter patterns of suckling behavior by newborn rats on a surrogate nipple. *Behavioral Neuroscience, 114* (4), 783–96.

Prados, J., Chamizo, V. D., & Mackintosh, N. J. (1999). Latent inhibition and perceptual learning in a swimming-pool navigation task. *Journal of Experimental Psychology: Animal Behavior Processes, 25*, 37–44.

Preuschoft, S., Wang, X., Aureli, F., et al. (2002). Reconciliation in captive chimpanzees: A reevaluation with controlled methods. *International Journal of Primatology, 23*, 29–50.

Purdy, J. E., & Domjan, M. (2001). Comparative psychology and animal learning: Learning about animals and the animal in all of us. In S. Davis and J. Halonen (eds.), *The many faces of psychological research in the twenty-first century.* Web-based book published by Division 2 of the American Psychological Association, <http://teachpsych.lemoyne.edu/teachpsych/faces/script/Ch13.htm>.

Purdy, J. E., & Eidson, H. D. (2002). Fish aquatic studies. In M. Schwartz (ed.), *Encyclopedia of smart materials* (pp. 423–37). New York: Wiley.

Redhead, E. S., Prados, J., & Pearce, J. M. (2001). The effects of pre-exposure on escape from a Morris pool. *The Quarterly Journal of Experimental Psychology, 54B*, 353–67.

Rendall, D., Cheney, D. L., & Seyfarth, R. M. (2000). Proximate factors mediating "contact" calls in adult female baboons (*Papio cynocephalus ursinus*) and their infants. *Journal of Comparative Psychology, 114*, 36–46.

Rescorla, R. A. (2001). Are associative changes in acquisition and extinction negatively accelerated? *Journal of Experimental Psychology: Animal Behavior Processes, 27*, 307–15.

Rescorla, R. A., & Wagner, A. R. (1972). A theory of Pavlovian conditioning: Variations in the effectiveness of reinforcement and nonreinforcement. In A. Black & W. F. Prokasy (eds.), *Classical conditioning II* (pp. 64–99). New York: Appleton-Century-Crofts.

Roozendaal, B., de Quervain, D., Ferry, B., Setlow, B., & McGaugh, J. L. (2001). Basolateral amygdala-nucleus accumbens interactions in mediating glucocorticoid enhancement of memory consolidation. *Journal of Neuroscience, 21*, 2518–25.

Rotenberg, A., Abel, T., Hawkins, R. D., Kandel, E. R., & Muller, R. U. (2000). Parallel instabilities of long-term potentiation, place cells, and learning caused by decreased protein kinase A activity. *The Journal of Neuroscience, 20*, 8096–102.

Roush, R. S., & Snowdon, C. T. (1999). The effects of social status on food-associated calling behaviour in captive cotton-top tamarins. *Animal Behaviour, 58*, 1299–1305.

Roush, R. S., & Snowdon, C. T. (2001). Food transfer and development of feeding behavior and food-associated vocalizations in cotton-top tamarins. *Ethology, 107*, 415–29.

Sakata, J. T., Coomber, P., Gonzalez-Lima, F., & Crews, D. (2000). Functional connectivity among limbic brain areas: Differential effects of incubation temperature and gonadal sex in the leopard gecko, *Eublepharis macularius. Brain, Behavior & Evolution, 55*, 139–51.

Sapolsky, R. M., & Share, L. J. (1998). Darting terrestrial primates in the wild: A primer. *American Journal of Primatology, 44*, 155–67.

Seyfarth, R. M. (1976). Social relationships among adult female baboons. *Animal Behaviour, 24,* 917–38.

Seyfarth, R. M., Cheney, D. L., & Marler, P. (1980). Monkey responses to three different alarm calls: Evidence for predator classification and semantic communication. *Science, 210,* 801–3.

Sherman, P. W., Braude, S., & Jarvis, J. U. M. (1999). Litter sizes and mammary numbers of naked mole-rats: Breaking the one-half rule. *Journal of Mammalogy, 80,* 720–33.

Shettleworth, S. J. (1999). Female mate choice in swordtails and mollies: Symmetry assessment or Weber's law? *Animal Behaviour, 58,* 1139–42.

Shettleworth, S. J. (2001). Animal cognition and animal behaviour. *Animal Behaviour, 61,* 277–86.

Sieve, A. N., King, T. E., Ferguson, A. R., Grau, J. W., & Meagher, M. W. (2001). Pain and negative affect: Evidence the inverse benzodiazepine agonist DMCM inhibits pain and learning in rats. *Psychopharmacology, 153,* 180–90.

Stamps, J. A., & Krishnan, V. V. (1998). Territory acquisition in lizards. IV. Obtaining high status and exclusive home ranges. *Animal Behaviour, 55,* 461–72.

Suddendorf, T., & Whiten, A. (2001). Mental evolution and development: Evidence for secondary representation in children, great apes, and other animals. *Psychological Bulletin, 127,* 629–50.

Suomi, S. J. (2001). Uptight, laid-back, and jumpy monkeys: How genetic and environmental factors shape biobehavioral development. *Biological Psychiatry, 49,* 466 Suppl. S.

Sutton, J. E., Olthof, A., & Roberts, W. A. (2000). Landmark use by squirrel monkeys (*Saimiri sciureus*). *Animal Learning & Behavior, 28,* 28–42.

Swaisgood, R. R., Owings, D. H., & Rowe, M. P. (1999). Conflict and assessment in a predator–prey system: Ground squirrels versus rattlesnakes. *Animal Behaviour, 57,* 1033–44.

Swaisgood, R. R., Rowe, M. P., & Owings, D. H. (1999). Assessment of rattlesnake dangerousness by California ground squirrels: Exploitation of cues from rattling sounds. *Animal Behaviour, 57,* 1301–10.

Talton, L. E., Higa, J. J., & Staddon, J. E. R. (1999). Interval schedule performance in the goldfish (*Carassius auratus*). *Behavioural Processes, 45,* 193–206.

Teng, E., Stefanacci, L., Squire, L. R., & Zola, S. M. (2000). Contrasting effects on discrimination learning after hippocampal lesions and conjoint hippocampal-caudate lesions in monkeys. *The Journal of Neuroscience, 20,* 3853–63.

Terrick, T. C., Mumme, R. L., & Burghardt, G. M. (1995). Aposematic coloration enhances chemosensory recognition of noxious prey in the garter snake *Thamnophis radix. Animal Behaviour, 49,* 857–66.

Tillerson, J. L., Cohen, A. D., Philhower, J., Miller, G. W., Zigmond, M. J., & Schallert, T. (2001). Forced limb-use effects on the behavioral and neurochemical effects of 6-hydroxydopamine. *Journal of Neuroscience, 21,* 4427–35.

Tomsic, D., & Alkon, D. L. (2000). Background illumination effects upon in vitro conditioning in *Hermissenda. Neurobiology of Learning and Memory, 74,* 56–64.

Virgin, C. E., & Sapolsky, R. M. (1997). Styles of male social behavior and their endocrine correlates among low-ranking baboons. *American Journal of Primatology, 42,* 25–39.

Wasserman, E. A., Fagot, J., & Young, M. E. (2001). Same–different conceptualization by baboons (*Papio papio*): The role of entropy. *Journal of Comparative Psychology, 115,* 42–52.

Wasserman, E. A., Young, M. E., & Fagot, J. (2001). Effects of number of items on the baboon's discrimination of same from different visual displays. *Animal Cognition, 4,* 163–70.

Weise-Kelley, L. & Siegel, S. (2001). Self-administration cues as signals: Drug self-administration and tolerance. *Journal of Experimental Psychology: Animal Behavior Processes, 27,* 125–36.

Whiten, A. (1998). Imitation of the sequential structure of actions by chimpanzees (*Pan troglodytes*). *Journal of Comparative Psychology, 112,* 270–81.

Whiten, A. (2000). Primate culture and social learning. *Cognitive Science, 24,* 477–508.

Woolley, S. C., Sakata, J. T., Gupta, A., & Crews, D. (2001). Evolutionary changes in dopaminergic modulation of courtship behavior in *Cnemidophorus* whiptail lizards. *Hormones and Behavior, 40,* 483–489.

Wright, A. A. (1997). Concept learning and learning strategies. *Psychological Science, 8,* 119–23.

Wright, A. A. (1998). Auditory list memory in rhesus monkeys. *Psychological Science, 9,* 91–8.

Wright, A. A. (1999). Visual list memory in Capuchin monkeys (*Cebus apella*). *Journal of Comparative Psychology, 113,* 74–80.

Wright, A. A., Cook, R. G., Rivera, J. J., Sands, S. F., & Delius, J. D. (1988). Concept learning by pigeons: Matching-to-sample with trial-unique video picture stimuli. *Animal Learning & Behavior, 16,* 436–44.

Yang, E. J., Phelps, S. M., Crews, D., & Wilczynski, W. (2001). The effects of social experience on aggressive behavior in the green anole lizard (*Anolis carolinensis*). *Ethology, 107,* 777–93.

Young, M. E., Peissig, J. J., Wasserman, E. A., & Biederman, I. (2001). Discrimination of geons by pigeons: The effects of variations in surface depiction. *Animal Learning & Behavior, 29,* 97–106.

# CHAPTER NINE

# Cross-cultural Research

## David Matsumoto

Cross-cultural studies have become extremely common in recent years. Although they are the main type of study in flagship journals such as the *Journal of Cross-Cultural Psychology*, they are found in all academic research journals of psychology today. Their acceptance and their importance to the field are no longer debated, and cross-cultural research of all psychological processes is a serious endeavor with serious consequences.

Cross-cultural research helps to test the validity of many psychological truths and principles previously thought to be true for everyone. As the findings from cross-cultural research challenge those previously held beliefs, cross-cultural psychology helps to refine our psychological theories, and improve our conceptual understanding of the influence of culture on behavior.

Cross-cultural psychology also plays a large role in diversifying psychology. As workers in an applied field, psychologists should be concerned with whether the information that is derived from it is applicable to people from all walks of life, and all cultural backgrounds. In many respects, the increasing awareness and recognition of the importance of cross-cultural psychology in recent years has come about precisely because many psychologists have come to question whether mainstream psychological theories are applicable to the diverse and pluralistic world in which we live.

Issues concerning cross-cultural research are doubly important because they highlight many of the important issues that are pertinent to the conduct of monocultural studies as well. Indeed, as I mention below, all of the issues discussed here with regard to the conduct of cross-cultural research, with the exception of language issues, are applicable to general comparative experimentation; thus, becoming adept at cross-cultural research improves one's breadth and understanding of research in general.

In this chapter, I introduce readers to the conduct of cross-cultural research by first describing five different types of cross-cultural studies. Then I discuss in detail issues concerning the conduct of one of these types of research – cross-cultural comparisons – as these studies are the basic type of cross-cultural study to be found in the literature and conducted today. I go on to describe a newer type of cross-cultural study called unpackaging studies, which represent the field's evolution in thinking about cross-cultural research. I conclude the chapter by offering some thoughts concerning the impact of cross-cultural research on the culturalization of psychological theories.

## Types of Cross-cultural Research

There are many different types of cross-cultural studies, and it is important at the outset to elucidate them. The five typologies described below generally describe the range of approaches to cross-cultural research. Like all research approaches, however, studies are as varied as the individuals who design and conduct them. The descriptions provided here, therefore, are not intended as exhaustive categories of the breadth of cross-cultural approaches; rather they are general guidelines for the types of cross-cultural studies typically seen and conducted in the literature.

### Cross-cultural comparisons

The first type of study is the prototypical *cross-cultural comparison study*, which compares two or more cultures on some psychological variable of interest, often with the hypothesis that one culture will have significantly higher scores on the variable than the other(s). In a strict experimental sense, these studies are simply between-subject, between-group, quasi-experimental designs, in which specific cultures, typically operationalized by nationality, ethnicity, or race, serve as different levels of a culture factor. Thus all of the general considerations for the conduct of comparative studies of this sort apply to the conduct of cross-cultural comparisons as well.

The cross-cultural literature abounds with cross-cultural comparisons. Although this type of study merely shows the existence of differences among cultures, they have been important to the psychological literature because they have tested the limitations to knowledge generated in mainstream psychological research, and have helped to advance our theoretical and conceptual thinking in all areas of psychology. Thus cross-cultural comparisons have played a major role in cross-cultural psychology in the past.

### Unpackaging studies

Despite the importance of cross-cultural comparisons, recently there has been a call away from simple comparative research to studies that not only document the existence of cultural differences, but also examine why they occur. These studies not only look for differences among cultures on their target variables; they also include measurements of other variables that they believe will account for those differences. These studies are known as *unpackaging studies*, as they unpackage the contents of the global unspecific concept of culture into specific measurable psychological constructs, and examine their contribution to cultural differences. Poortinga and his colleagues likened these types of studies to the peeling of an onion – taking off layer after layer until nothing is left (Poortinga, van de Vijver, Joe, & van de Koppel, 1987). These researchers viewed culture in the following way:

> In our approach culture is a summary label, a catchword for all kinds of behavior differences between cultural groups, but within itself, virtually no explanatory value. Ascribing intergroup differences in behavior, e.g., in test performance, to culture does not shed much light on the nature of these differences. It is one of the main tasks of cross-cultural psychology to peel off cross-cultural differences, i.e., to explain these differences in terms of specific antecedent variables, until in the end they have disappeared and with them the variable culture. In our approach culture is taken as a concept without a core. From a methodological point of view, culture can be considered as an immense set of often loosely interrelated independent variables (cf. Segall, 1984; Strodtbeck, 1964). (Poortinga et al., 1987, p. 22)

These researchers suggest that culture as an unspecified variable should be replaced by more specific, measurable variables in order truly to explain cultural differences. These variables are called context variables, and should be measured in a study to examine the degree to which they statistically account for cultural differences. Inferences about the nature of cultural differences can then incorporate the degree of contribution by the context variables. If the context variables included in any study do not account for all of the differences between cultures, then other context variables should be incorporated in subsequent research to further account for more of the differences among cultures until the differences are gone. In a strict experimental sense, this approach is quite similar to that of identifying nuisance variables and using them as covariates to examine their contribution to between-group differences. In a theoretical sense, however, these studies play a large role in furthering knowledge of exactly what about cultures produces differences in behavior.

## Ecological level studies

Whereas most hypothesis-testing cross-cultural research involves persons as the units of analysis, a third type of hypothesis-testing study in cross-cultural psychology involves countries or cultures as the unit of analysis. These studies are called *ecological level studies*. Data may be obtained from individuals in those cultures, but they are often summarized or averaged for each culture, and those averages are used as data points for each culture, typically in a correlational analysis with means of other psychological variables of interest. Analyses based on this type of design are called ecological or cultural level analyses, and are different than traditional individual level analyses in psychological research. Examples of such ecological level analyses include Hofstede's studies of cultural values across more than 50 cultures (Hofstede, 1980, 1984), Triandis et al.'s (1988) study of the relationship between individualism and collectivism with incidence of heart attacks in eight cultures, Matsumoto's studies of the relationship between four cultural dimensions and incidence rates for six disease states (Matsumoto & Fletcher, 1996) and the relation between cultural dimensions and judgments of emotion in 15 cultures (Matsumoto, 1989).

There are important differences in the interpretations justified on the basis of ecological vs. individual level research. That is, a relation between a cultural and target variable on the ecological level does not necessarily mean that such a relation exists on the individual person level. For instance, demonstrating the existence of a correlation between ecological level individualism and the incidence of heart disease does not necessarily mean that such a correlation can predict individual level associations between the two variables. Even if such a relation exists on the ecological level, the relation may or may not exist on the individual level within the cultures studied, and may or may not be in the same direction even if it exists (also see Leung, 1989). A positive correlation between culture and a psychological variable on the ecological level can be associated with a positive, negative, or no correlation between the same two variables on the individual level. Regardless of this caveat, however, ecological level studies are important in elucidating the contribution of larger cultural systems to group level psychological phenomena.

## Cross-cultural validation studies

A fourth type of cross-cultural study is that which examines the validity of a psychological test or measure across cultures. These projects are known as *cross-cultural validation studies*. They examine whether a measure of a psychological construct that was originally generated in a single culture is applicable, meaningful, and thus equivalent in another culture. These studies do not test a specific hypothesis about cultural differences per se; rather, they test the equivalence of psychological measures and tests for use in other cross-cultural comparative research. Although these types of studies are not as common as hypothesis-testing cross-cultural research, they serve an important purpose in investigating the cross-cultural applicability of many of the methodological techniques used in research.

## Ethnographies

Finally, a fifth type of cross-cultural study, one that is more prevalent in psychological anthropology than in cross-cultural psychology per se, is that known as *ethnography*. These studies typically involve fieldwork, with the researchers visiting and often living together with the people they are interested in studying. Being immersed in a culture for an extended period of time, these researchers learn first hand the customs, rituals, traditions, beliefs, and ways of life of the culture to which they are exposed. Comparisons to other cultures are done on the basis of their own knowledge, experience, and education about their own and other cultures. This approach is not unlike the case study of individual lives, with cultures serving as the larger unit of analysis. As such, much of the advantages to that approach, including the richness and complexity of the data obtained, are applicable, as well as disadvantages to their generalizability. Nevertheless, these ethnographic approaches serve an important purpose in the field, complementing existing hypothesis testing research on specific psychological variables.

## Issues Concerning Cross-cultural Comparisons

There are only a few issues specific to the conduct of cross-cultural research that set it apart from general experimentation. This means that, in reality, the same problems and solutions that are typically used to describe issues concerning experimental methodology in general can and should be applied to most, if not all, cross-cultural comparisons, as well as to unpackaging studies. Most of the issues raised in this section, therefore, with the notable exception of language issues, are generally true of "good" experimentation in monocultural studies as well. Cross-cultural research, however, has been useful in highlighting them.

### Equivalence (and bias)

One concept that is of crucial importance in the conduct and evaluation of all aspects of cross-cultural comparison is that of equivalence, and its corresponding construct, bias. (Bias is generally viewed as nonequivalence; thus they are essentially one and the same. For this reason, I will generally refer to equivalence.) Equivalence in cross cultural research can be defined as a state or condition of similarity in conceptual meaning and empirical method between cultures that allows comparisons to be meaningful. In a strict sense, the greater the nonequivalence (thus bias) of any aspect of a cross-cultural study, in meaning or method, across the cultures being compared, then the less meaningful the comparison. Lack of equivalence in a cross-cultural study creates the proverbial situation of comparing apples and oranges. The results from a comparison are meaningful if, and only if, the theoretical framework and hypotheses have generally equivalent meaning in the cultures being compared, and the methods of data collection, management, and analysis have equivalent meanings.

Of course, this consideration is true in any between-group comparison study: the greater the nonequivalence among the groups in the comparison in any aspect of the study, the less meaningful the comparison becomes. Still, it is important to remember that the perfectly equivalent cross-cultural study is an impossibility; there will always be some aspect of the comparison that is not perfectly equivalent. Thus, it is probably more accurate to suggest that for cross-cultural comparisons to be valid and meaningful, they have to be "equivalent enough." The difficult part of this concept, however, that frustrates students and researchers alike, is that there is no direct method, no mathematical formula, no easy way, to determine what is "equivalent enough." Sometimes a study may have a lot of little nonequivalences, but still be meaningful. Sometimes a study may have one fatal nonequivalence, and thus be meaningless. These issues differ from study to study, and I cannot tell you here what the fatal flaw will always be. As usual, experience and conscientiousness are probably two of the largest teachers.

The issues described here, and in most descriptions of experimentation, therefore, are the ideals. The closer to the ideals the study is, the more valid the comparison (of course, this may also mean that it is farther from reality).

## Theoretical issues

People generate theories, and as such, they are bound and influenced by the cultural framework of the person who creates the theory. How we think about people, interpersonal relationships, basic human nature, fate, luck, supernatural forces, and the like are all influenced by our culture. Thus, when psychologists create theories about human behavior, it is important to remember that the cultural framework of the people who create them binds those theories themselves. If this is the case, then a question arises as to whether a theory created within that cultural framework is meaningful in the same ways to people who do not share that culture. If the theory is not meaningful in the same way, it may not be equivalent.

Similarly, research questions and specific hypotheses are generated from theories, and researchers who formulate research questions and hypotheses have their own cultural upbringing and backgrounds. These backgrounds produce biases on the part of researchers, regardless of whether these biases are good or bad, right or wrong, conscious or unconscious. These biases influence the types of questions we think are important and, thus, those questions we believe should be studied in cross-cultural research.

Questions also exist about whether a hypothesis that we believe is important for us to test may not be as important or meaningful in the same way to someone from a different cultural background. As every hypothesis-testing study examines hypotheses considered to be important to test that are generated from culture-bound theories, a major concern of cross-cultural research is the equivalence in meaning of the overall theoretical framework being tested, and the meaning and importance of the specific hypotheses being addressed. If the theories and hypotheses are not equivalent across the cultures participating in the study, then the data obtained from them may not be comparable, because they mean different things. If, however, the theoretical framework and hypotheses are equivalent across the participating cultures, the study may be meaningful and relevant.

This caveat is especially important for researchers who have been trained in European or American educational systems, because of the underlying sense of "logical determinism" and "rationality" that is characteristic of the educational systems and thinking of these cultures. People who live in cultures other than those in Europe or the USA may not think, feel, or behave in the same ways; they may have completely different worldviews that do not reduce to two-dimensional theories of behavior on paper that we often must rely on for our work. Because these possibilities exist, we must take care that the very theoretical framework and hypotheses being tested make sense in the cultures being tested.

Clearly, researchers simply cannot decide on their own which questions are important to study across cultures and then impose these questions on people of other cultures. More often than not, the questions a researcher creates are assumed to be equally important and have the same meaning in other cultures. This approach is an ethnocentric way of doing research that cannot be avoided if the researcher single-handedly conducts the study without ascertaining the validity of his or her biases first. Involving cultural informants, such as a collaborator, in each of the participating cultures is a step in the right direction (although it is not always a definitive step, as they, too, may be influenced in their thinking due to their own cultural or educational background).

A final point to remember in this section is that doing research itself is a cultural enterprise, and as such it may or may not be consonant with different cultures' worldviews. There are many cultures in the world that have quite different values and perspectives than the European–American one that underlies the very practice of conducting research. In these cultures, just conducting a study may be a concept that does not make sense, and may in fact influence the validity of data obtained.

## Methodological issues

*Definitions of culture*   Researchers need to insure that the comparisons they are making are indeed cross-cultural. Although this statement may appear to be extremely simple-minded, the issues are actually difficult and complex. In the past, as well as now, researchers typically operationalized culture according to self-reported nationality, race, or ethnicity. Group differences are then tested on the variable(s) of interest according to these predefined categories. To be sure, as mentioned earlier, cultural differences generated in this type of relatively simple design have been the staple of the cross-cultural diet for many years, and have played important roles in describing the boundaries of know ledge and theory in psychology. Yet the major limitation to this procedure, which has come to light in recent years, is that culture is generally assumed to underlie the differences. Because culture per se was never measured, however, that remains an assumption with little or no empirical justification. Moreover, the generic label of "culture" really provides little explanatory power to account for differences when they occur, as described above.

Thus, although cross-cultural comparison has been the leading type of cross-cultural study, the increasing recognition of its limitations has led to the call for unpackaging studies, which we introduced above and will describe in more detail below. For our purposes here, it is important for researchers to remember that culture, in its enormity, cannot be swallowed in a single gulp. Thus, any "measurement" of it, by nationality, race, ethnicity, or other means, really is at best only an approximation of culture within a single way of narrowly defining it, and as such will not be inclusive of culture in its entirety.

*Sampling adequacy*   Researchers need to insure that the participants in their study are adequate representatives of the cultures that they are supposed to represent. More often than not, researchers assume that people who happen to fit into the categorical label of culture as operationalized (e.g., by nationality) are "good" representatives of that particular culture. In doing so, there is an unacceptable assumption of homogeneity among the participants with regard to culture, which can, in its worse sense, only serve to perpetuate stereotypic impressions and interpretations based on the findings. That is, when differences are found, researchers assume that the differences are "cultural" because they assume that the samples are representatives of culture.

Although this issue is relatively straightforward and easy to understand, in practice it is extremely difficult to achieve. In its strictest sense, proper addressing of this issue would require the following steps: (1) the researcher would have to be able to define theoretically exactly what the cultures are that are being tested; (2) the researcher would have to be able to access a pool of individuals from the larger population that embodied those characteristics; (3) the researcher would have to randomly sample from that larger population; and (4) the researcher would have to measure those social, cultural, and psychological characteristics in their participants and empirically demonstrate that their culture manipulations occurred as intended.

Unfortunately, this is a tall order that is not, and perhaps cannot, be filled by current researchers, because of the limitations to our abilities to theorize about, and subsequently measure, culture on the individual level, and because of our inability to randomly access all members of any given cultural population. Given that we cannot currently achieve this ideal, the real issue facing researchers concerns the degree to which they understand how far from this ideal they are, and how much they use this information to temper their interpretations. In a practical sense, a sound cross-cultural comparison would entail the collection of data from multiple sites within the same cultural group, either in the same study or across studies, to demonstrate the replicability of a finding across different samples within the same culture.

*Noncultural, demographic equivalence* Researchers need to insure that the differences they obtain in a study are due to culture, and not to any other noncultural demographic variables on which the samples may differ. That is, researchers need to make sure the samples they compare are equivalent on variables such as sex, age, socioeconomic status (SES), educational level, religious orientation, geographic area (e.g., rural vs. urban), and such. If they are not equivalent on noncultural demographic variables, then those variables on which they are not equivalent may confound the comparison.

There are basically two ways of dealing with this problem, as it exists in monocultural studies. The first and best way to deal with this issue is to identify the major participant characteristics that need to be controlled, and to select individuals for participation by holding those variables constant in the selection. In doing so the experimenter can either hold those variables constant within and between groups (e.g., including only females of a certain age in the entire study in all cultures), or just between groups (e.g., including the same ratio of males and females in all cultures). Sex and age are relatively easy to hold constant, and certainly should be. They are not, however, the only variables that should be held constant by far.

The conceptual problem that arises in cross-cultural research, which is not as apparent in monocultural studies, is that some noncultural demographic characteristics are inextricably intertwined with culture such that researchers cannot hold them constant across samples in a comparison. Religion is a good example of such a variable. There are differences in the meaning and practice of religions across cultures that often make them inextricably bound to culture. Holding religion constant across cultures does not address the issue, because being Catholic in the USA just does not mean the same thing as being

Catholic in Japan or Malaysia. Randomly sampling without regard to religion will result in samples that are different not only on culture, but also on religion (to the extent that one can separate the influences of the two). Thus, presumed cultural differences often reflect religious differences across samples as well. The same is also true often for SES, as there are vast differences in SES across cultural samples from around the world.

The second way of dealing with this problem is to statistically assess and eliminate the possible effects of noncultural demographic variables. That is, researchers can find some solace in the fact that, if their samples differ on religious, SES, or other demographic variables, they can engage in specific analyses to examine their contribution to the group differences, depending on the nature of the distributions of these data across the samples. Of course, this procedure depends on the fact that the researchers will have measured these variables reliably in the first place, a step that many researchers fail to accomplish. Examining within-culture correlations between scalar demographic variables and the target dependents, for example, will assess the degree to which the demographics are related to the dependents; if they are related, covariance or regression analyses may be warranted in order to eliminate their effects in testing between-culture differences (assuming other assumptions of covariance and regression are met).

Still, if the cultures are confounded by noncultural demographics, after-the-fact analyses can only "take care" of noncultural demographic confounds to a certain degree. As with all methodologies, no amount of sophisticated analyses can "fix" real methodological problems, and researchers will often be left with such effects in their comparisons. The real issue, therefore, is not so much whether or not the cultural groups also differed on noncultural, demographic characteristics; rather, it is whether or not the researchers who conducted the study are aware of the existence of such differences, and whether they have done as much as can be reasonably expected of them to eliminate their effects in the between-culture comparisons. When differences are found, researchers who are not aware of the existence of noncultural demographic differences between their samples usually assume that the differences reflect cultural differences; this result may not necessarily be the case. Researchers who are well aware of these possibilities, however, will present data concerning their sample characteristics, engage in some formal statistical tests examining the contribution of these characteristics to their variables of interest, and temper their interpretations according to what they found (or did not find). A full demographic assessment and analysis is a must for most contemporary cross-cultural comparisons that are meaningful, so that rival hypotheses concerning the supposed between-culture differences are identified and eliminated.

*Measurement issues* Researchers need to insure that the psychological variables being measured in their studies are conceptually equivalent across the cultures being compared. Different cultures may conceptually define a construct differently, and/or may measure it differently regardless of similarities in conceptual definition. Common examples of constructs that have widely divergent meanings across cultures include such topics as intelligence, self-concept, personality, or emotion. Clearly, just because something has the same name in two or more cultures does not mean that it refers to the same thing in those cultures (Wittgenstein, 1953, cited in Poortinga, 1989). If a concept means different things to people of different cultures, then there is a lack of equivalence in the definition of the construct, and comparisons of cultures based on nonequivalent constructs will lack meaning. Researchers wishing to compare cultures on psychological constructs, therefore, have the onus of demonstrating, either empirically or conceptually, that the constructs themselves are equivalent across the cultures being compared.

In addition to construct equivalence, researchers also need to insure that the psychological variables being measured in their studies are empirically equivalent across the cultures being compared. Even if a construct is conceptually equivalent across cultures, reliable and valid measurement of it may take different forms across cultures. Concretely, this requires that researchers use measures that have been empirically demonstrated to reliably and validly measure the construct of interest in the cultures being studied. Clearly, simply taking an existing test developed in one culture and translating it for use in other cultures is not methodologically adequate, although this procedure has often been used previously. Cross-cultural validations often require extensive testing in the target cultures in order to establish a reasonable amount of reliability and validity parameters, especially with regard to convergent and predictive validity. Questionnaires that involve multiple scales and items will need to have been tested to establish the cross-cultural equivalence of item and scale meaning, especially concerning equivalence in factor structures and item loadings.

These are not easy issues to deal with, and cross-validation is not as easy as it seems. Some writers have suggested that tests of psychological abilities are inherently incomparable across cultures. Greenfield (1997), for example, argues that constructs such as intelligence and cognitive ability are inherently symbolic products of a culture. As such, the constructs and tests of it presuppose a certain cultural framework in the first place in order to be valid. As these frameworks are not usually universally shared, cross-cultural comparisons of ability and intelligence therefore becomes meaningless. Similar questions may exist concerning the equivalence in construct and operation of values. Peng and others, for example, have argued that common methods for assessing values, which include providing participants with a list of values and asking them either to rate them or rank them in order of importance, may not be valid across cultures (Peng, Nisbett, & Wong, 1997). They suggested that such methods may be invalid because of cultural differences in the meanings of specific value items, and because of the possibility that some value judgments are based on inherent social comparisons with others instead of making a direct inference about a private, personal value system. In order to investigate this possibility, these researchers examined four different value survey methods, comprising the traditional ranking, rating, and attitude scaling procedures, as well as a behavioral scenario rating method. The only method that yielded reasonable validity estimates was the behavioral scenario rating method, which is the most unorthodox of all measures tested.

Poortinga (1989) has suggested that when a measure has high content validity in all cultures being tested (i.e., it has been shown to mean the same thing in all cultures), and when the construct being measured is in a psychological domain that is similar or identical across cultures (e.g., color schemes, pitch scale for tones), valid comparisons are generally possible. When unobservable psychological traits and attributes of individuals are being measured, comparison may be possible as long as equivalence in the conceptual meaning of the psychological domain and its measurement in all participating cultures have been established. Other than these two situations, all other research situations, according to Poortinga, preclude valid comparison across cultures.

Earlier in this chapter, I mentioned that it is often difficult to find the single, fatal flaw of nonequivalence that renders a study meaningless. If there is one area in which such a fatal flaw is easier to occur, it would be in the conceptual or empirical nonequivalence of the psychological variables being measured. After all, regardless of how "perfect" all other aspects of the study may be, if the variables being measured are not equivalent across cultures, in a strict sense the comparison must be flawed. Thus, cross-cultural researchers have an obligation to demonstrate the cross-cultural validity of their measures in order to establish their equivalence for comparison. Researchers need to think critically about possible cultural differences in the conceptual definitions of different variables of interest in cross-cultural research; but researchers also have to examine *in detail* the exact methods they will use to measure those variables. Of all the issues concerning research reviewed and discussed in this chapter with regard to cross-cultural equivalence, issues concerning equivalence in the validity and reliability of the conceptual meaning and methodological operationalization of variables are arguably the most crucial to any cross-cultural study.

*Language and translation issues* Researchers need to insure that the research protocols used in their studies are linguistically equivalent across the cultures being compared. Although most other methodological issues described in this chapter pertain to all group difference research, monocultural or cross-cultural, this issue is one of the few that is specific to cross-cultural research.

Cross-cultural research often cannot be conducted solely in one language, because the samples being tested are frequently composed of two or more distinct language groups. There are generally two procedures used to establish linguistic equivalence. One is known as back translation (Brislin, 1970). Back translation involves taking the research protocol in one language, translating it to the other language(s), and having someone else translate it back to the original. If the back-translated version is the same as the original, they are generally considered equivalent. If it is not, the procedure is repeated until the back-translated version is the same as the original. The concept underlying this procedure is that the end product must be a semantic equivalent to the original English. The original language is decentered through this process (Brislin, 1970, 1993), with any culture-specific concepts of the original language eliminated or translated equivalently into the target language. That is, as the process of translation → back translation occurs, culture-specific meanings and connotations are gradually eliminated from the research protocols, so that what remains is something that is the closest semantic equivalents in both languages. Because they are linguistic equivalents, successfully back-translated protocols are comparable in cross-cultural hypothesis-testing research.

The second approach to establishing language equivalence in protocols is to utilize the committee approach, in which several bilingual informants collectively translate a research protocol into a target language. In doing so, they debate the various words and phrases in the target language that can be used, comparing them with their understanding of the language of the original protocol. The product of this process reflects a translation that is the shared consensus of a linguistically equivalent protocol across languages and cultures.

A third approach to translation is also available, which is a combination of the first two approaches. Here, a protocol may be initially translated and back-translated. Sometimes, however, this process never results in a perfectly back-translated protocol. Thus, the translation and back translation can be used as an initial platform by which a translation committee then works on the protocol, modifying the translation in ways they deem most appropriate, using the back-translation as a guideline.

Regardless of the approach, a major caveat for researchers here is that "closest semantic equivalent" does not mean "the same." Getting protocols that are "the same," in fact, is probably impossible. Even if the words being used in the two languages are the agreed-upon translations, there is no guarantee that those words have exactly the same meanings, with the same nuances, across cultures. There is also the additional problem to deal with concerning the difference between linguistic and cultural equivalence. That is, you can have a protocol that is linguistically equivalent to its original in another language, but that just does not make sense in the target language. In this case, the researcher needs to make a decision concerning whether to go with the literal translation, which may be awkward and difficult to interpret but is the closest semantic equivalent, or to go with the cultural translation, which will make sense but is not linguistically equivalent. There is no real answer about these issues, except that the astute researcher will take note of them and incorporate their subtle, and sometimes not so subtle (but unavoidable), influences in their interpretations of findings.

*The research environment, setting, and procedures* Researchers need to establish equivalence in all aspects of the data-collection procedures when conducting their study. For example, there can be major cultural differences in expectations about, and experience with, research participation that need to be dealt with in cross-cultural research. In many universities across the United States, for instance, students enrolled in introductory classes are required to participate in research in partial fulfillment of class requirements or complete an alternative activity. Because this is an established institution, there is a certain expectation of US students to participate in research as part of their academic experience. Indeed, many American students are "research-wise," knowing their rights as participants in experiments, expecting to participate in research, and so forth. Many other countries do not have this custom. In some countries, research is simply required of students because the professor of the class wants to collect the data. In some countries, students may be required to come to a research laboratory, and coming to a university laboratory for an experiment can have different meanings across cultures because of these expectations. In some countries, students may consider it a privilege rather than a chore or course requirement to participate in an international study.

Whether laboratory or field, day or night, questionnaire or behavior – all the decisions made by researchers to conduct their studies may have different meanings in different cultures. Cross-cultural researchers need to confront these differences in their work, and establish a basis by which these procedures, the environment, and the setting are equivalent across the cultures being compared in their study in order for cross-cultural comparisons to be valid.

## Data analysis issues

*Cultural response sets* Data analysis is part of the methodology of doing any study, and cross-cultural studies are no exception. When analyzing data, researchers need to be aware of the possible existence of cultural response sets, and if they do exist, they need to deal with them. Cultural response sets are tendencies for members of a culture to use certain parts of a scale when responding. For example, participants of culture A in a two-culture comparison may tend to use the entire scale, whereas participants of culture B may tend to use only a part of the scale (e.g., the middle). These tendencies to use various parts of a scale may exist for several reasons, including cultural differences in attitudes and values regarding self-expression of personal opinions. There have been numerous suggestions in the past that members of collectivistic cultures hesitate to use the extreme end points of a scale, in congruence with a cultural reluctance to "stick out," resulting in the use of the middle of a scale. There have also been some studies that have shown tendencies for members of some cultural groups to use the endpoints. Bachman and O'Malley, for example, found such evidence in extreme response styles among African Americans (Bachman & O'Malley, 1984), and Marin and colleagues found similar evidence for Hispanics (Marin, Gamba, & Marin, 1992).

If they exist, cultural response sets may confound between-culture differences. Thus it is difficult to know whether differences are occurring because of response sets, or because of "meaningful" differences in real scores on the target variables of interest. Moreover, it is difficult for the researcher to disentangle these possible influences on the data from the same data set. The best way to attempt to deal with the problem is to include additional data that may offer some insights into the possible operation of response sets. One type of additional data would be the inclusion of social desirability scales, to determine whether the cultures differ on social desirability (and thus response patterning). (The problem with this approach, however, is the reliance on the use of social desirability scales that may or may not be validated for use in the cultures in your study.) A second type of additional data comes from scalar data from other studies involving the same topic or construct. Examination of response patterning in these data may offer insights into the existence of possible cultural response sets in your data.

If the researcher does not have such additional data available to examine, then the only way possible to test for the existence of response sets would be to examine between-cultural differences at multiple levels of various factors within a multifactor design. Should the between-culture differences be so overwhelming and consistent regardless of how the data are analyzed, this result may be evidence of a response set. (In its strictest sense, however, the researcher can still never be sure that these differences do not also reflect just large and pervasive cultural differences.)

When researchers have determined that cultural response sets have been operating in their data, the typical way of eliminating their effects has been to standardize all the data of interest to the participant's respective culture mean and standard deviation, and to perform subsequent analyses on the standardized data. Cultural differences can still be found if the data have been standardized across different variables and/or factors in a factorial design. (If the study includes a single dependent variable in a single factor design, however, there is no way to standardize the data and test for mean differences, as the only available cell means will be transformed mathematically to zero.) If findings are generated on standardized data, it is important to remember that they reflect cultural differences relative to their own culture's means; they may or may not reflect differences in the absolute values of the original scales used to collect data. In reality, cultural differences generated from raw and standardized scores provide two different but important glimpses at how cultures operate, and in my opinion, both should be reported and interpreted whenever possible.

*Effect size analyses*   Cultural differences in mean values on any scale do not readily predict how individuals are different between cultures. Statistical significance does not mean "practical" significance in a realistic or pragmatic sense, especially because statistical significance is so dependent on sample size. One mistake that researchers and consumers of research alike make when interpreting group differences is that they assume that most people of those groups differ in ways corresponding to the mean values. Thus, if a statistically significant difference is found between Americans and Japanese, for instance, on emotional expressivity such that Americans had statistically significantly higher scores than the Japanese, people often conclude that all Americans are more expressive than all Japanese. This conclusion, of course, is a mistake in interpretation that is fueled by the field's fascination and single-minded concern with statistical significance.

In reality, there are statistical procedures available that help to determine the degree to which differences in mean values reflect meaningful differences among individuals. The general class of statistics that do this is called effect size statistics, and when used in a cross-cultural setting, Matsumoto and his colleagues called them cultural effect size statistics (Matsumoto, Grissom, & Dinnel, 2001). It is beyond the scope of this chapter to present them in detail; Matsumoto et al. (2001) present four such statistics that they deemed most relevant for cross-cultural analyses, with reanalyses from two previously published studies as examples. Whether cross-cultural researchers use these analyses or others, it is incumbent on them to include some kind of effect size analysis when comparing cultures so that informed readers can determine the degree to which the differences reported reflect meaningful differences among people.

### Interpretation issues

Several issues are especially pertinent to validly interpreting findings obtained in cross-cultural research. These issues include cause–effect vs. correlational types of interpretations, the role of researcher bias and value judgments, and dealing with nonequivalent data.

*Cause–effect vs. correlational interpretations*   In hypothesis-testing comparisons, cultural groups often are treated as independent variables in design and analyses of data. As such, they can be considered a form of quasi-experimental type of study. It is important to remember, however, that the data from such studies are basically correlational in nature, and the inferences drawn from such studies can only be correlational inferences. For example, if a researcher compared data from the USA and Japan on social judgments and found that Americans had significantly higher scores on a person perception task, one's interpretations of these data would be limited to the association between cultural membership (i.e., USA or Japan) and the ratings. Cause–effect inferences (e.g., being American causes one to have higher person perception scores) are unwarranted. Indeed, in order for such causal statements to be permitted, the researcher would have had to (1) create the conditions of the experiment (i.e., the cultural groups) and (2) randomly assign people to each of the conditions. These conditions are not possible because the grouping variable that is used in comparative cross-cultural research is a subject variable. It makes no more sense to assume a causal relation between cultural membership and a variable of interest than it does to assume such a relation on the basis of sex, hair color, height, or weight.

A related type of mistaken interpretation often made by cross-cultural researchers involves interpretations of specific reasons why cultural differences occurred even though those specific reasons were never measured in the study. For instance, in the example immediately above, a researcher may take the significant USA–Japan differences on the social judgment task and suggest that the differences occurred because of differences between individualism and collectivism in the cultures. Unless the researchers actually measured individualism and collectivism (IC) in their study, however, and showed that the two cultures differed on it and it accounted for the cultural group differences on social judgments, the interpretation that this construct (i.e., IC) is responsible for the group differences is unwarranted. In fact, this type of interpretation about why a cultural group difference has occurred is often made in cross-cultural research articles, and they should be taken merely as suggestions for possible context variables that could possibly account for the group differences. Problems occur when researchers and consumers assume that there is a relation between the cultures and the context variable, and that the context variable actually accounts for the cultural differences. In accordance with Poortinga et al.'s (1987) earlier suggestions, I believe that these types of context variables actually need to be measured in cross-cultural research for such interpretations to be warranted (see below for description of unpackaging studies), unless the researchers directly and explicitly specify that those interpretations are speculations that require measurement and testing.

*Researcher bias and value judgments* Just as culture can bias formulation of the research questions in a cross-cultural study, it can also bias the ways researchers interpret findings. Most researchers will inevitably interpret the data they obtain with their own cultural filters on. Of course, there are degrees to which this bias can affect the interpretation. Interpretation of group differences in means, for example, may simply indicate differences in degrees. If the mean response for Americans on a rating scale, for example, is 6.0, and the mean for Hong Kong Chinese is 4.0, one interpretation is that the Americans simply scored higher on the scale. Another interpretation may be that the Chinese are suppressing their responses.

This type of interpretation is common. But how do we know the Chinese are suppressing their responses? What if it is the Americans who are exaggerating their responses? What if the Chinese mean response of 4.0 is actually the more "correct" one, and the American one is the one that is off? What if we surveyed the rest of the world and found that the mean for the rest of the world is actually 3.0, and found that *both* the Chinese and the Americans inflated their ratings? When you consider this situation carefully, any interpretation that the Chinese are suppressing their responses really requires you to assume implicitly that the American data are the "correct" data. I myself have made this ethnocentric interpretation of research findings in a study involving American and Japanese judgments of the intensity of facial expressions of emotion without really giving much consideration to other possibilities (Matsumoto & Ekman, 1989). In fact, in later research, we were able to show that it indeed was the Americans who exaggerated their intensity ratings of faces, relative to inferences about subjective experience of the posers, not the Japanese who suppressed (Matsumoto, Kasri, & Kooken, 1999).

Examples such as this one are found throughout the cross-cultural literature. Any time researchers make a value judgment related to a finding, it is always possible that that interpretation is bound by a cultural bias. Interpretations of good or bad, right or wrong, suppressing or exaggerating, important or not important are all value interpretations that may be made in a cross-cultural study. These interpretations may reflect the value orientations of the researchers as much as they do the cultures of the samples included in the study. As researchers, we may make those interpretations without giving them a second thought – and without the slightest hint of malicious intent – only because we are so accustomed to seeing the world in a certain way. As consumers of research, we may agree with such interpretations when they agree with the ways we have learned to understand and view the world, and we will often do so unconsciously and automatically.

*Dealing with nonequivalent data* Despite the best attempts to establish equivalence in theory, hypothesis, method, and data management, cross-cultural comparisons are often inextricably, inherently, and inevitably nonequivalent. That is, it is impossible to create any cross-cultural study that means exactly the same thing to all participating cultures, both conceptually and empirically. What cross-cultural researchers often end up with are best approximations of the closest equivalents in terms of theory and method in a study.

Thus researchers are often faced with the question of how to deal with nonequivalent data. Poortinga (1989) outlined four different ways in which the problem of non-equivalence of cross-cultural data can be handled:

1. *Preclude comparison.* The most conservative thing a researcher could do is to not make the comparison in the first place, concluding that such a comparison would be meaningless.
2. *Reduce the nonequivalence in the data.* Many researchers engage in empirical steps to identify equivalent and nonequivalent parts of their methods, and then refocus their comparisons solely on the equivalent parts. For example, if a researcher used a 20-item scale to measure anxiety in two cultures and found evidence for nonequivalence on the entire scale, he or she may then examine each of the 20 items for equivalence, and rescore the test using only those items that are shown to be equivalent. Comparison would then occur on the newly rescored items.
3. *Interpret the nonequivalence.* A third strategy is for the researcher to interpret the nonequivalence as an important piece of information concerning cultural differences.

4. *Ignore the nonequivalence.* Although ignoring the nonequivalence is what most cross-cultural researchers should not do, it is in fact what many researchers end up doing. Poortinga (1989) suggests that this situation occurs because many researchers hold on to beliefs concerning scale invariance across cultures, despite the lack of evidence to support such beliefs.

Obviously, how researchers handle the interpretation of their data, given nonequivalence, is dependent on their experience and biases, and on the nature of the data and the findings. Because of the lack of equivalence in much cross-cultural research, researchers are often faced with many gray areas in interpreting findings from their cross-cultural studies. This situation is, of course, to be expected, because the study of culture is neither black nor white. Culture itself is a complex phenomenon that is replete with gray, and we see that in research every day and in the journals. It is the objective and experienced researcher who can deal with the gray area in creating sound, valid, and reliable interpretations that are justified on the basis of the data. It is the astute consumers of that research who can sit back and judge those interpretations relative to the data in their own minds and not be swayed by the arguments of the researchers.

## Issues Concerning Unpackaging Studies

The field has increasingly come to recognize the limitations of the traditional cross-cultural comparison in which two or more cultures, often operationalized by nationality, race, or ethnicity, are compared on one or more target dependent variables. As mentioned above, the problem with this approach is that "culture" is really only a label that summarizes many concrete and specific aspects of a group's way of life. As such, it is impossible for us to know, in a typical cross-cultural comparison, exactly what about cultures produced the differences we observed, and why.

To address this issue, researchers have begun to identify specific, concrete, and measurable psychological variables that they believe represent at least some of the contents of culture most pertinent to their variables of interest, and to include them in their cross-cultural comparisons. "Culture," then, as a global construct is replaced by these specific, measurable variables, which are called context variables. Analyses are then directed to examine the degree to which these context variables actually account for the cultural differences. In this sense, the context variables are akin to nuisance variables in traditional experimentation, and the approach is exactly that of studies of covariance, as the context (nuisance) variables are treated as covariates. These types of cross-cultural studies are called unpackaging studies.

There are several ways to analyze data in an unpackaging study, assuming the context covariates are scalar in nature. The two most common ways involve either hierarchical multiple regression or Analysis of Covariance (ANACOVA) (assuming, of course, that the data meet all the assumptions of these statistics). In regression, the context variables are entered into the regression on the target dependents, either as a block or individually, and then subsequently the categorical culture variable (e.g., nationality) is entered. This hierarchical approach addresses the degree to which the categorical culture variables add predictive variance to the target dependents above and beyond that already contributed by the context variables.

In the ANACOVA approach, the context variables are treated as covariates, and cultural differences on the categorical variable are tested after statistically eliminating the influence of the covariates. Cultural effect sizes can be computed, and compared to the effect size estimates of the group differences computed from simple ANOVA without the covariate. The differences in the effect sizes in this comparison, therefore, reflect the contribution of the covariates to the target dependents.

A number of examples of unpackaging studies can now be found in the literature. Bond and Tedeschi (2001), for example, give an excellent review of cross-cultural studies on aggression both with and without unpackaging. Singelis and his colleagues use the concept of self-construals to unpackage cultural influences on self-esteem and embarrassability (Singelis, Bond, Sharkey, & Lai, 1999). Matsumoto and his colleagues have used the concepts of individualism–collectivism and status differentiation to unpackage cultural differences in cultural display rules (Matsumoto et al., in press) and judgments of emotion (Matsumoto, Takeuchi, Andayani, Kouznetsova, & Krupp, 1998).

The beauty of an unpackaging study is that it first forces researchers to think about cultures in ways that they did not in the past, breaking them down to specific, measurable constructs in considering how they influence the target variables of interest. Thus unpackaging studies force theoretical developments in our understanding of culture. Secondly, unpackaging studies allow us to examine the specific degree to which the hypothesized context variables actually do account for between-culture differences. Inevitably, they do not account for 100 percent of the differences; thus, they force us to think about other ways in which culture influences our target constructs, helping us to refine our theoretical understanding of culture.

## Conclusion

Cross-cultural research has evolved to the point where its necessity and impact are no longer debated in academic psychology. It plays a pivotal role in providing valuable information about the validity of psychological theories across different cultural groups, thereby informing us about the nature of psychological processes in our ever-diversifying and pluralistic world.

Cross-cultural research itself has gone through its own evolution of sorts. For many years, cross-cultural comparisons were the main type of study that was conducted, and that could be found in the research literature. Once again, these studies were important because they highlighted how many of the truths and principles we thought were valid for everyone actually were not, causing the field to pause and reconsider whether its theories and methods actually reflected the diversity of the world accurately.

Yet, in recent years, cross-cultural psychologists themselves have come to realize the limitations of cross-cultural comparisons, and today the necessity for simple cross-cultural comparisons has dwindled considerably. Instead, today cross-cultural psychologists are calling for the full integration of unpackaging studies that can inform us on exactly what about cultures produce differences, and why. Unpackaging studies represent the next evolution in method within cross-cultural research, and in concept for cross-cultural theorizing, and thus will become a mainstay in the next decade or two.

Hopefully, unpackaging studies will eventually aid in the production of theories about psychological processes that incorporate culture as a factor, so that one day many of the theories to which we are witness in mainstream psychology will be culturalized to some extent. The routine incorporation of culture as a factor in psychology is a major goal of cross-cultural psychology and research, and unpackaging studies will help the field achieve that goal in the near future.

Still, in many senses, all psychologists who do research are concerned with culture, the only difference being whether their studies are monocultural or cross-cultural. Thus, many of the issues described here apply to the conduct of many different types of studies, whether explicitly cross-cultural or not.

As mentioned earlier, many of the issues we have discussed in this chapter represent the ideal, not the norm, in the conduct of research, whether cross-cultural or monocultural. Indeed, there is no such thing as the "perfect" cross-cultural study, and even "good" cross-cultural research is extremely difficult to design and conduct. In the end, one of the most important questions to me is whether or not researchers realize how far from the ideals their studies really are. After all, when you come right down to it, what we do in the field or laboratory is really only a very small approximation of life, with tiny glimpses of culture. If there is anything that is important to remember about cross-cultural research methods, it is that culture cannot be swallowed in a single gulp, no matter how large that gulp is.

## References

Bachman, J. G., & O'Malley, P. M. (1984). Black–white differences in self-esteem: Are they affected by response styles? *American Journal of Sociology*, *90* (3), 624–39.

Bond, M., & Tedeschi, J. (2001). Polishing the jade: A modest proposal for improving the study of social psychology across cultures. In D. Matsumoto (ed.), *The handbook of culture and psychology* (pp. 309–24). New York: Oxford University Press.

Brislin, R. (1970). Back translation for cross-cultural research. *Journal of Cross-Cultural Psychology*, *1*, 185–216.

Brislin, R. (1993). *Understanding culture's influence on behavior*. Fort Worth, TX: Harcourt Brace Jovanovich.

Greenfield, M. P. (1997). You can't take it with you. *American Psychologist*, *52*, 1115–24.

Hofstede, G. H. (1980). *Culture's consequences : International differences in work-related values*. Beverly Hills: Sage Publications.

Hofstede, G. H. (1984). *Culture's consequences : International differences in work-related values* (abridged edn.). Beverly Hills: Sage Publications.

Leung, K. (1989). Cross-cultural differences: Individual-level v. culture-level analysis. *International Journal of Psychology*, *24*, 703–19.

Marin, G., Gamba, R. J., & Marin, B. V. (1992). Extreme response style and acquiescence among Hispanics: The role of acculturation and education. *Journal of Cross-Cultural Psychology*, *23* (4), 498–509.

Matsumoto, D. (1989). Cultural influences on the perception of emotion. *Journal of Cross-Cultural Psychology, 20* (1), 92–105.

Matsumoto, D., Consolacion, T., Yamada, H., et al. (in press). American–Japanese cultural differences in judgments of emotional expressions of different intensities. *Cognition & Emotion.*

Matsumoto, D., & Ekman, P. (1989). American–Japanese cultural differences in intensity ratings of facial expressions of emotion. *Motivation & Emotion, 13* (2), 143–57.

Matsumoto, D., & Fletcher, D. (1996). Cultural influences on disease. *Journal of Gender, Culture, and Health, 1,* 71–82.

Matsumoto, D., Grissom, R., & Dinnel, D. (2001). Do between-culture differences really mean that people are different? A look at some measures of cultural effect size. *Journal of Cross-Cultural Psychology, 32* (4), 478–90.

Matsumoto, D., Kasri, F., & Kooken, K. (1999). American–Japanese cultural differences in judgments of expression intensity and subjective experience. *Cognition & Emotion, 13,* 201–18.

Matsumoto, D., Takeuchi, S., Andayani, S., Kouznetsova, N., & Krupp, D. (1998). The contribution of individualism–collectivism to cross-national differences in display rules. *Asian Journal of Social Psychology, 1,* 147–65.

Peng, K., Nisbett, R., & Wong, N. Y. C. (1997). Validity problems comparing values across cultures and possible solution. *Psychological Methods, 2,* 329–44.

Poortinga, Y. H. (1989). Equivalence of cross-cultural data: An overview of basic issues. *International Journal of Psychology, 24,* 737–56.

Poortinga, Y. H., van de Vijver, F. J. R., Joe, R. C., & van de Koppel, J. M. H. (1987). Peeling the onion called culture: A synopsis. In C. Kagitcibasi (ed.), *Growth and progress in cross-cultural psychology* (pp. 22–34). Berwyn, PA: Swets North America.

Segall, M. H. (1984). More than we need to know about culture, but are afraid to ask. *Journal of Cross-Cultural Psychology, 15* (2), 153–62.

Singelis, T., Bond, M., Sharkey, W. F., & Lai, C. S. Y. (1999). Unpackaging culture's influence on self-esteem and embarrassability. *Journal of Cross-Cultural Psychology, 30,* 315–41.

Strodtbeck, F. L. (1964). Considerations of meta-method in cross-cultural studies. *American Anthropologist, 66* (3), 223–29.

Triandis, H. C., Bontempo, R., Villareal, M. J., Asai, M., et al. (1988). Individualism and collectivism: Cross-cultural perspectives on self-ingroup relationships. *Journal of Personality & Social Psychology, 54* (2), 323–38.

Wittgenstein, L. (1953). *Philosophical investigations.* New York: Macmillan.

# PART III

*Selected Content Areas*

# CHAPTER TEN

# Comparative Psychology

## Mauricio R. Papini

## Introduction

### Defining comparative psychology

Psychologists who are interested in the evolutionary origin of psychological capacities, in the way in which those capacities contribute to the individual's reproductive success, in the development of animal models for understanding human behavior, and in the differences and commonalities in such capacities across animal species, call themselves comparative psychologists. As a field, comparative psychology is almost interdisciplinary by definition. Any serious attempt to accomplish the goals set in the opening sentence demands not only knowledge of psychological theories and techniques, but an understanding of behavioral neuroscience, comparative neurology, behavioral ecology, developmental biology, and evolutionary theory. In turn, comparative psychologists can provide a view of psychology based on an integrative perspective that effectively bridges the social and biological sciences. It is hoped that such an integration will contribute to a better understanding of the general principles governing behavior, as well as to the development of new ideas that will provide tools for behavioral interventions in all fields of application.

Comparative psychology could thus be defined as the branch of psychology concerned with the evolution (phylogenetic history and adaptive significance) and development (ontogenetic history and mechanism) of behavior. This definition adopts Tinbergen's (1963) view of behavioral studies, according to which any given instance of behavior may be approached from four different, but complementary, perspectives which may be phrased in terms of questions. Consider, for example, tool-use behavior, the ability of certain animals to use objects to have access to otherwise inaccessible food items. First, researchers may ask how widespread is tool use among animals and they may want to compare patterns of tool use across species. This problem relates to the *phylogenetic history* of tool-use behavior. Second, researchers may ask in what way tool use contributes to an efficient exploitation of resources, to the adjustment of individuals to their social group, and, ultimately, to the reproductive success of individuals. This issue concerns the *adaptive significance* of behavior. Together, these two levels of causal study provide a picture of the evolution of tool-use behavior or, in Tinbergen's terms, a theory of the ultimate causes of behavior. The key question could be "Why do animals use tools?" and a scientific answer to such a question would be framed in terms of phylogenetic patterns and adaptive significance.

However interesting this question and answer may be, they do not tell us much about how the skills involved in using any particular tool actually emerge in the behavioral repertoire of adult animals. Thus a third approach to the study of tool using looks for evidence of the behavioral skills involved in the behavior under study, the manner in which sensory experience (e.g., visual information) is related to motor outputs (e.g., manual dexterity), the role of brain processes (e.g., lateralization of function), and the environmental factors that trigger the behavior (e.g., culture). Any theory of tool-use behavior that emphasizes factors currently operating in invidual animals, their surrounding environment, their brain, their physiology, and the like, provides a view of the *mechanisms* that control such behavior. Finally, the researcher may ask the equally important question of the origin of the behavior under study in a particular individual. Each behavior has an individual history that relates to the influence of maturational processes, early experience, trial-and-error learning, observational learning, social interactions, and similar factors. Emphasis on these factors clarifies the *development* of behavior. Together, answers framed in terms of mechanisms and development are appropriate to questions posed in terms of "How do animals come to use tools?" Such factors were referred to by Tinbergen (1963) as the proximate causes of behavior.

*Historical roots*

Tinbergen's classification of causal levels was the result of intensive controversies between psychologists and biologists interested in animal behavior during the mid-portion of the twentieth century. However, interest in the origin and nature of animal behavior can be traced back to ancient times. This fact is hardly surprising for a species that has heavily relied on group hunting, domestication of animals, and agriculture, such as it is the case with modern humans. The domestication of dogs and other species has been achieved on the basis of artificial selection for a behavioral character that could be characterized as tamability (Morey, 1994; Trut, 1999). This outcome undoubtedly required extensive observations and a certain degree of "experimentation" with conditions that might affect an animal's behavior. Aristotle (fourth century BCE) left accurate descriptions of brood parasitism in European cuckoos and of the parental behavior of catfish, which indicate careful and meticulous observations given the peculiar difficulties of recording these two types of behavior (Aristotle, 1991). In his *Naturalis Historiae*, Pliny the Elder (first century CE) describes how seeds were protected from insects and rodents by soaking them in bitter solutions that deterred potential predators from consuming them before germination (Farrar, 1998). We also owe to ancient thinkers the first intellectual efforts to explain animal behavior (as well as other aspects of nature) in terms of natural processes. For example, Aristotle founded animal taxonomy and suggested that there was continuity among species. In his treatise on animal behavior, Aristotle concluded, like Tinbergen did much later, that behavior can be explained in terms of two independent sources of causation, namely, a mechanistic cause that refers to the physiological causes underlying behavior, and a functional cause (teleological explanation in Aristotle's terms) that refers to the goal-oriented nature of many behaviors (Nussbaum, 1978).

Whereas an interest in understanding animal behavior can be documented from ancient Greek and Roman thinkers, to the Arab scientists of the Middle Ages and the European Renaissance, the emergence of modern comparative psychology can be traced to the second half of the nineteenth century. It was the confluence of Darwin's theory of evolution by *natural selection* – with its corollary principle of *mental continuity* across species – and the new tools of experimental psychology that provided the impetus for the historical emergence of comparative psychology (Boakes, 1984). In the rest of this chapter I will review some of the major areas of research illustrating the various approaches to the understanding of behavior with specific research examples. Interested readers will find additional information in the list of references and suggested readings provided at the end.

## The Adaptive Significance of Behavior

### *Evolution and natural selection*

Following Darwin ([1859] 1993), but using modern terminology, I define *evolution* as an outcome resulting from the interplay of evolutionary processes (e.g., natural selection, correlation of traits, and genetic drift) and evolutionary patterns (e.g., phylogenetic constraints). Processes can be viewed as innovative forces that give rise to novelty and change, whereas patterns can be viewed as conservative forces that provide the raw material for change. For example, natural selection has modified the shape of the arm bones of terrestrial vertebrates (tetrapods) to produce a grasping hand (as in primates), a wing (as in birds), and a flipper (as in dolphins and penguins). However, natural selection was constrained by the basic plan of a tetrapod's arm involving a relatively fixed number of bones (e.g., humerus, ulna, radius, wrist bones, and phalanges). As a result, although hands, wings, and flippers are adapted for different functions, they have a common underlying bone structure. This section examines the evidence that suggests that behavior, like the shape of the vertebrate arm, is subject to the innovative forces of evolutionary processes.

It is widely believed that natural selection is a major evolutionary process leading to novelty and change in the organization of morphology and function. Natural selection requires three ingredients to occur: phenotypic variability in a given trait (e.g., the shape of the humerus varies across individuals in a population), differential reproductive success (individuals with a given humerus shape tend to leave more offspring than individuals with an alternative shape), and inheritance (humerus shape is in part determined by genes). Empirical evidence indicates that phenotypic variability is a ubiquitous characteristic of natural populations. Moreover, the relatively rapid response of laboratory animals to artificial selection for a wide variety of characters suggests that most traits have at least some genetic basis. However, the measurement of the third component of natural selection, namely, differential reproductive success, poses serious problems.

The ideal approach to collecting evidence that alternative traits confer differential reproductive success would be to measure the number of offspring reaching sexual maturity produced by individuals carrying alternative phenotypes over their entire lifetime. This is called *lifetime reproductive success* (*LRS*). It should be obvious to anybody with minimal knowledge of animal biology that such data are difficult to obtain. Progressively less ideal measurements are easier to obtain, but also more open to problems of interpretation. Number of offspring in a given breeding season, number of eggs, number of copulations, success in defending a territory, success in intraspecific aggressive encounters, and maximization in energy intake represent points in an imaginary scale of fitness progressively farther removed from the ideal LRS measure. In each case, the variable being measured is assumed to bear a positive correlation with the ideal variable, but this relation rarely can be demonstrated.

These limitations notwithstanding, available evidence provides support for the general hypothesis that alternative behavioral phenotypes can have differential reproductive success, thus supporting the more general notion that behavior has adaptive function. Consider, for example, the social behavior of lions (*Panthera leo*). Unlike most other large carnivores, lions tend to live in stable groups, a fact that prompts the question of whether social grouping has adaptive significance in this species. Packer et al. (1988) reported LRS data from a field study conducted in Tanzania, which demonstrates that lions that live in large groups accrue a greater individual reproductive success than lions that live in more isolated conditions. For males, for example, variation in the size of coalitions from one (isolated male) to six lions is correlated with increasing LRS. For females, LRS increases with pride size up to about four or five females and then declines. Large groups of females actually have a lower fitness because of a peculiar feature of population dynamics in lions. The larger the female pride, the higher the probability that a male coalition will take over the group; takeovers are usually followed by the killing of young animals. Infanticide speeds up the female's return to sexual receptivity, thus increasing the opportunities for copulation in males. These data demonstrate that grouping behavior confers greater fitness than an individualistic lifestyle, at least within some limits.

*Field and laboratory studies*

In any population in which alternative phenotypes with differential LRS coexist, the trait with higher success will (other things being equal) eventually displace the trait with lower success. What would happen if a variation were more successful under one set of ecological conditions and the alternative variation were more successful under different conditions? Field studies demonstrate that alternative morphological traits such as beak size in finches (Grant, 1986), hindlimb length in *Anolis* lizards (Losos, Warheit, & Schoener, 1997), and body size in guppies (Reznick, Shaw, Rodd, & Shaw, 1997) respond relatively rapidly to ecological changes (e.g., in a matter of years). Of course, similar conditions can be instrumented in the laboratory, where the process can be greatly accelerated by means of artificial selection techniques. *Artificial selection* involves the selective mating of individuals that display a specific phenotype. It is the process that led to the domestication of species and inspired Darwin to develop his notion of natural selection. As mentioned previously, many different traits can be used successfully as criteria for artificial selection, including such behavioral phenotypes as exploratory behavior, mating behavior, nest building, aggressive behavior, and courtship displays, as they occur in a wide variety of species.

In a long-term study (Ricker & Hirsch, 1985), fruit flies (*Drosophila melanogaster*) were tested for *geotaxis* (i.e., their tendency to move in relation to the ground) in a vertical maze. Fruit flies displaying positive geotaxis (i.e., a tendency to move in the direction of the ground) were paired with each other, thus establishing a low (L) population, whereas those displaying negative geotaxis (i.e., a tendency to move away from the ground) were also paired with each other, thus establishing a high (H) population. Fruit flies displaying no clear tendency were discarded. The offspring of L and H animals were in turn tested for geotaxis and again selectively paired according to their tendency to display positive or negative geotaxis, respectively. By allowing for breeding to be select-ive, the experimenter is effectively manipulating the animal's LRS much as natural selection does it in wild populations. For example, a fly exhibiting negative geotaxis would enjoy an elevated LRS if it develops in the L population, but its LRS would be drastically reduced if it develops in the H population (because this fly would be discarded for breeding purposes). When the selective breeding protocols are enforced for a substantial number of generations, the two populations may no longer be able to interbreed. Reproductive isolation is a major criterion to establish whether a given population has evolved into a new species. For example, in a follow-up experiment conducted after approximately 600 generations of selective breeding (Lofdahl, Hu, Ehrman, Hirsch, & Skoog, 1992), H and L flies displayed a strong tendency to mate with individuals of their own population (e.g., H males preferred H females), rather than mate with individuals of the opposite population (e.g., H males did not court L females). The implication is that sustained selective pressure for a behavioral phenotype may lead to sufficient genetic change in a population that the descendants may become reproductively isolated. New species may therefore evolve because of the reproductive advantages conferred by a behavioral phenotype.

Resources needed to survive and reproduce are generally limited. For example, the food available in a particular habitat may support a fraction of the total number of animals that a population may be able to produce. As the demand for a given food item increases, competition for that resource will tend to increase. Natural selection would thus tend to favor those animals bearing phenotypic traits that enhance their ability to compete. The evolutionary "conflict" between alternative phenotypes would tend to encourage specialization by means of a process known as *competitive exclusion*. Animals may evolve specialized structures to deal with resources that involve relatively less com-petition. For example, giraffes and antelopes may be considered the end points of a process of competitive exclusion that led to the evolution of alternative phenotypes (i.e., long vs. short neck), each phenotype efficient to deal with a particular resource (i.e., leaves located at various heights). However, the same process may lead to extinction of one of the competing populations in some cases. It is possible that the extinction of the South American fauna of carnivorous marsupials was prompted by the migration of carnivores from North America that started about three million years ago with the establishment of the Panama Ithsmus (Benton, 1990). Neanderthals, a species of archaic humans that lived in Europe until approximately 35,000 years ago, may have also been driven to extinction because of more efficient resource exploitation by migrating modern humans (Johanson & Edgar, 1996).

## Sexual selection

Competitive exclusion suggests that the evolutionary conflict should achieve its maximum strength among conspecifics. Indeed, competition for food, territories, display arenas, nesting areas, mates, shelter, and similar resources are pervasive features of animal behavior. As Darwin (1871) noted, competition is particularly exacerbated in the context of reproductive behavior. In many species, males are characterized by displaying a larger body size, colorful body features, and a higher propensity to aggressive behavior than females. This characterization is particularly true in species in which males compete with each other for accessing and defending reproductively active females – a mating system known as *polygyny*. These characters incur a heavy developmental cost (e.g., it takes time and energy to build a large body size) and entail a sizeable predatory risk (e.g., colorful males are also conspicuous preys). The fact that these features evolve despite the way in which they compromise the individual's existence clearly indicates that it is reproductive success, rather than survival per se, that matters in evolutionary terms. Darwin introduced the term *sexual selection* to refer to this evolutionary process. Interestingly, in many species in which females, rather than males, compete for access to males – a system known as *polyandry* – it is the females that show larger body size, colorful body features, and higher aggressive behavior. Moreover, in *monogamy*, a mating system characterized by reduced competition, males and females tend to be relatively inconspicuous and less distinct from each other. Different selective pressures occur both across mating systems and across sexes. For example, traits promoting success in intrasexual competition are selected for in polygynous males and polyandrous females. However, the opposite sex in each case can exert pressure by actively choosing among alternative phenotypes. For example, the colorful features in the peacock's tail and birds of paradise evolved as devices that attract females. Mate choice and intrasexual competition are the two essential components of sexual selection.

Why do female peacocks (*Pavo cristatus*) prefer males with numerous and colorful tail feathers? Researchers have long suspected that such features provide information about the male that is important from the female's point of view. Apparently, female peacocks concentrate their attention on the number of eye-like structures (ocelli) present in each feather of the male's tail (Petrie, Halliday, & Sanders, 1991). Their mating preference is directly correlated with the number of ocelli displayed by a male. Interestingly, if the researcher knows this number, the researcher can also estimate the age of a male, which implies that females are using the number of ocelli to estimate the male's longevity. Because longevity will depend at least to some extent on bearing certain genes, the female's choice ensures that her offspring will carry genes that tend to maximize LRS. Similar proxies of fitness appear to be used by humans in sexual situations. For example, women who have a waist-to-hip ratio around a value of 0.7 are rated as most attractive by men. Singh (1993) reported that the waist-to-hip ratio provides information about the woman's reproductive potential and general health state (e.g., the incidence of diabetes, cancer, mortality, and tendency to become pregnant correlate with this ratio). Obviously, animals are not designed to estimate directly the reproductive potential of their partners, but rather to use a proxy that generally correlates with such potential (much as sweetness is a proxy for the caloric content of a fluid).

A prominent feature of polygynous systems is that they introduce serious choice problems for the animals. Consider, for example, the case of a territorial species. A male that has established a territory for courtship and mating must determine whether incoming conspecifics are males (potential competitors) or females (potential sexual partners). An effective discrimination permits the selection of aggressive behavior in one case, but courtship behavior in the other. Experiments in which the incoming conspecific is signaled by an otherwise neutral stimulus demonstrate that a territorial male may profit significantly from such signaling. For example, male blue gourami fish (*Trichogaster trichopterus*) that are provided with a signal for an incoming female engage in courtship earlier and produce a greater number of offspring than males that do not have the benefit of a signal (Hollis, Pharr, Dumas, Britton, & Field, 1997). Similarly, male Japanese quail (*Coturnix japonica*), given the benefit of a signal for the incoming female, copulate faster and produce a larger volume of semen than males for which the female is unexpected (Domjan, Blesbois, & Williams, 1998). The process that leads to the acquisition of signal value, called *Pavlovian conditioning*, has been extensively studied by comparative psychologists from a mechanistic point of view (see below). However, studies demonstrating that the presence of a Pavlovian signal affects the reproductive success of individual animals provide compelling evidence of the adaptive significance of such learning mechanisms.

## Cooperation and reciprocity

Animals also interact in noncompetitive ways. For example, individuals may cooperate to obtain a resource that would be unobtainable if they acted in isolation. Unlike in the case of competition, *cooperation* is a win–win situation in which all participating individuals benefit. Juvenile ravens (*Corvus corax*) gather in groups to take over a carcass that may be defended by an adult. Usually, an adult can successfully displace an isolated juvenile, but it succumbs to a group of juveniles acting in a cooperative manner (Heinrich & Marzluff, 1995). The benefits of cooperation are accrued simultaneously to the co-operating individuals. However, sometimes the benefits are immediate for one animal but delayed for another, a type of interaction called *reciprocity*. After a successful foraging trip, a vampire bat (*Desmodus rutundus*) may be willing to share some of the blood by regurgitating it to a neighbour bat that has been unsuccessful. The roles may reverse on a future occasion depending on the foraging success of the individuals (Wilkinson, 1984). Reciprocity is obviously open to cheating if an individual is never willing to provide help, but always ready to receive it. The evolution of reciprocity presupposes the existence of mechanisms for detecting cheaters and depriving them of the benefits (Trivers, 1971).

An important feature of both cooperation and reciprocity is the fact that the animals engaged in these interactions are not particularly highly related. For example, DNA fingerprinting shows that the juvenile ravens that cooperate to obtain access to a carcass are not highly related (Heinrich & Marzluff, 1995). Other possibilities emerge in situations involving interacting animals that are also close relatives of each other. Particularly interesting are examples of animals that seem to postpone their ability to procreate directly by allocating their time and effort to helping others. In the cichlid fish *Lamprologus brichardi*, procreating parents receive help from close relatives that remain in the territory cleaning the eggs and providing defense against predators. These helpers significantly increase the reproductive success of the parents, as shown by the fact that clutch size is larger in nests with helpers than in nests without helpers (Taborsky, 1984). Helpers are sexually mature and would eventually become involved in reproduction directly, a fact that implies that they are delaying their ability to produce offspring. Hamilton (1964) pointed out that when such seemingly altruistic behavior is directed at highly related organisms, the cost of delayed direct reproduction may be offset by the benefit of increasing the reproductive success of relatives. Copies of genes underlying such altruistic behavior are likely to be present in the helper's relatives. Such basic ideas, known as *kinship theory*, suggest that traits may evolve by natural selection either when they confer a direct fitness advantage (as originally suggested by Darwin), or when they contribute to the success of a relative, over and above their deleterious effect on direct fitness. The sum of these two components, direct and indirect fitness, is referred to as *inclusive fitness*.

Kinship, reciprocity, and cooperation play a major role in the evolution of complex societies. Whereas the vast majority of animals live a rather solitary life punctuated by social interaction in the context of reproduction (e.g., territoriality, courtship, parental care, etc.), some species have evolved notoriously complex forms of social interaction and organization. A major example of such complexity is known as *subsociality*, that is, animal groups in which generations overlap and there is a substantial amount of care for the young. Many species of birds, mammals, and insects display subsocial behavior. True *sociality* emerges in species in which relatively large groups of individuals maintain a relatively stable structure over time, such as is observed in lions, baboons, and chimpanzees, among others. Chimpanzees (*Pan troglodytes*) are well known for their cultural differences in cooperative practices, such as group hunting (Boesch, 1994). A third category, known as *eusociality*, adds to the features already mentioned the presence of reproductively sterile individuals that provide specialized services for the community. For example, an ant colony could be characterized as a group in which only a few individuals reproduce and the vast majority provide such services as foraging, cultivating fungi, protecting the colony, and caring for larvae (Hölldobler & Wilson, 1990). Other species, including many bees, wasps, termites, sponge-dwelling shrimps, naked mole-rats, and aphids display eusocial behavior of great complexity that seems to depend upon various factors, including the degree of genetic relatedness among individuals, a relatively long life span that allows for generational overlap, complex patterns of care of the young, body specializations for colony defense, a tendency toward monogamy, and the establishment of colonies in locations that are relatively isolated and defensible (e.g., the hives of bees, the underground tunnels of naked mole-rats, and the colonies of termites in logs).

## Brain and Behavior in Phylogenetic Perspective

### Phylogenetic patterns

The definition of evolution given previously suggests that behavior should not only reflect the shaping action of evolutionary processes such as natural and sexual selection (as described in the previous section), but it should also exhibit historical properties. The phylogenetic basis of behavior is highlighted by a variety of findings suggesting that evolution is constrained taxonomically. A useful analogy may be found in certain morphological traits. Consider again the four-limbed body plan of tetrapods, which can be observed in all known amphibians, reptiles, birds, and mammals, independently of their adaptations to specific ecological conditions. Violations of such a plan are conceivable, as demonstrated by mythological creatures (e.g., the mammalian centaur and Pegasus, and the reptilian dragon, have six limbs, rather than four). The fact that real-life examples of analogous violations of the tetrapod body plan are not known suggests the presence of a constraint or limit. A tetrapod may transform its limbs (as in the wings of birds, bats, and pterodactyles) or even lose them completely (as in apodan amphibians, snakes, and whales), but the number of limbs cannot apparently be increased beyond four.

There are many examples of biological traits, including behaviors, that are restricted to specific taxa and exhibit little variation despite vast species differences in ecological adaptations. For example, all primates exhibit binocular vision and relatively large brain size, typically bear one or two offspring during pregnancy, and display complex patterns of parental care. Polygyny is the modal system among mammals, but monogamy predominates among birds. Mammals and birds have evolved adaptations to survive under a wider set of ecological conditions than is the case for any other vertebrate class; yet they all show endothermy, display a predominantly active way of life, and possess relatively larger brains. Among the insects, the *Hymenopthera* (bees, ants, and wasps) have a marked tendency to evolve complex eusocial systems; among the fishes, most of the 200 species from the order *Lophiiformes* have evolved specialized cryptic appearance, fishlike structures to attract prey, and sit-and-wait predatory behavior to obtain food; and among the primates, most species of the family *Callitrichidae* (marmoset and tamarin monkeys) are monogamous and regularly produce twins. Examples like these suggest that inheritance poses limits to the evolutionary process, determining which avenues are available for evolutionary change.

In some cases, the phylogenetic history of a particular species is reflected in its behavior. For example, whereas dolphins and whales are adapted to a continuous aquatic existence, their ancestors were terrestrial mammals. Such ancestry can be observed in the fact that their swimming behavior mirrors locomotion in terrestrial mammals. Unlike fish, which swim by moving their tail in the lateral plane, cetaceans swim by arching their spine in the vertical plane, much like quadruped mammals do when they run. Another example is provided by the parthenogenetic whiptail lizard (*Cnemidophorus uniparens*), a species consisting only of females that displays courtship behaviors similar to those behaviors observed in closely related species that reproduce sexually. Courtship behavior would seem to be superfluous in an animal capable of producing offspring from unfertilized eggs. However, the fact that such social interactions enhance female fertility (as well as the fact that they occur at all!) suggests that whiptail lizards evolved from sexually reproducing ancestors (Crews & Moore, 1986).

*Evolution of the vertebrate brain*

Phylogenetic patterns are also obviously present in the morphological and functional organization of the vertebrate brain. As the brain is the organ responsible for producing behavior, a comparative analysis of brain evolution is of paramount importance for comparative psychologists. Vertebrates are generally classified as a subphylum of the *Chordata*, which, together with some 35 or so additional phyla, constitute the kingdom *Animalia*. Among the animals, chordates (some 43,000 extant species) are characterized by possessing a dorsal nerve cord (dorsal with respect to the digestive system) that constitutes the *central nervous system* (*CNS*). Most chordates have an active way of life supported by an elongated body and a tail that permits free swimming. Unlike species of the other two chordate subphyla, the *Urochordata* (tunicates) and *Cephalochordata* (lancelets), the vertebrate CNS is characterized by an anterior enlargement called the brain, as well as highly developed sensory systems in the head and motor ganglia.

Chordate origins can be tracked as far back as the Cambrian fossil assemblage known as *Burgess Shale fauna*, first discovered in Canada and now recognized to be of worldwide distribution (Briggs, Erwin, & Collier, 1994). The Burgess Shale fauna, which existed about 520 million years ago (MYA), contains specimens that can be clearly assigned to the major animal phyla, including a small animal resembling extant lancelets known as *Pikaia gracilens*. As it is the case with lancelets, *Pikaia* fossils show a dorsal notochord and V-shaped muscles known as myotones that are responsible for the lateral movements of the body and tail during swimming. The fossil record of vertebrates begins in the late Cambrian and early Ordovician period, about 500 MYA, and continues uninterruptedly until the present. Living vertebrates are classified into seven classes which appear in fossil form in the following sequence: *Agnatha* or jawless fish, including lampreys and hagfish (about 500 MYA); *Osteichthyes* or bony fish, including salmon, tuna, and coelacanths, among many other species (about 400 MYA); *Amphibia*, including toads, frogs, and salamanders (about 380 MYA); *Chondrichthyes* or cartilaginous fish including sharks and rays (about 360 MYA); *Reptilia*, including turtles, lizards, snakes, and crocodiles (about 300 MYA); *Mammalia*, including the egg-laying, marsupial, and placental mammals (about 200 MYA); and *Aves* or birds (about 140 MYA). Despite enormous differences in body shape and size, lifestyle, and ecology, the same basic subdivisions of the CNS can be easily recognized in all living vertebrates. Additionally, because the brain is encased in a bony structure called the cranium, it is possible in some specimens to reconstruct the overall shape of the brain of extinct vertebrates from fossilized remains (Jerison, 1973).

The following are some of the most conservative aspects of the vertebrate CNS. The developing CNS may be thought of as a hollow cylinder. During embryogenesis, neuron precursors formed in the vicinity of the central canal migrate toward the periphery of the cylinder generating various swellings. The canal will eventually develop into the ventricular system, a highly conserved set of interconnected cavities filled with cerebrospinal fluid that provide a route for chemical communication as well as a cushion for attenuating the effects of sudden head movements on brain tissue. The main sections in which the CNS is divided include the spinal cord, rhombencephalon, mesencephalon, diencephalon, and telencephalon; these sections are perfectly recognizable in all vertebrates. The CNS communicates with peripheral targets (e.g., sensory receptors, muscles, organs, skin) by means of cranial nerves; the position of these nerves is so predictable across species that it is possible to identify some of them in the fossilized remains of cranial bones. Inside the CNS, neurons organize themselves into systems recognizable in terms of the neurotransmitter they release in chemical synapses. The cholinergic, dopaminergic, and serotoninergic systems, to name just a few, originate in mesencephalic nuclei and send projections both in the anterior and posterior directions. Many of these connections are notably stable across vertebrates and it seems likely that their behavioral function is also highly conserved.

Sensory and motor information is organized in terms of independent systems already differentiated at the *spinal cord* level. In all vertebrates, sensory information enters the spinal cord via the dorsal roots, whereas motor information leading to behavior exits via the ventral roots. The spinal cord contains circuits capable of organizing basic reflexes and of exhibiting cellular plasticity, as shown in experiments involving amphibians and mammals (Farel, Glanzman, & Thompson, 1973; Grau, Barstrow, & Joynes, 1998). Researchers have demonstrated phenomena such as habituation and conditioning by using a spinal preparation in which the spinal cord is isolated from the rest of the CNS by a surgical cut. In agnathans, bony fish, and some amphibians, the spinal cord contains giant neurons called Mauthner cells that trigger rapid escape responses in predatory encounters (Fetcho, 1991).

The *rhombencephalon* (pons, medulla, and cerebellum) and *mesencephalon* are located in an anterior position relative to the spinal cord. These areas contain the nuclei for most of the cranial nerves and a variety of areas of great behavioral importance, for example, the periaqueductal gray area, which modulates afferent pain signals at the spinal cord level; the locus coeruleus, the source of the noradrenergic system; the raphe nuclei, source of serotoninergic neurons; and the optic tectum, which processes visual information from the retina. The cerebellum is rudimentary in agnathans, but it is clearly present in all other vertebrates. Its cortex and subcortical nuclei receive multisensory inputs and participate in the control of movement. In mammals, the cerebellum has been implicated as a storage site for simple forms of motor learning, such as eyelid conditioning in rabbits (Thompson, 1986). The *diencephalon*, the next major division of the CNS, includes the thalamus, a massive group of nuclei involved in sensory processing; the epithalamus, a structure connected to the pineal gland which participates in the regulation of circadian rhythms; and the hypothalamus, another tightly packed set of very heterogeneous nuclei participating in the regulation of motivational states such as hunger, thirst, and pain. The hypothalamus is connected to another gland, the pituitary, which produces and releases a large variety of hormones that control other glands and regulate various aspects of reproductive behavior and physiology.

The most anterior portion of the CNS, called the *telencephalon*, is the part that exhibits the greatest degree of taxonomic diversity in its internal organization. However, despite that variability, the telencephalon of all vertebrates can be subdivided into two quite stable regions: the pallium, corresponding to the medial, dorsal, and lateral structures (including the mammalian neocortex and various structures of the limbic system), and the subpallium, which includes the striatum and septum among other structures. In the fishes and amphibians, the telencephalon can be characterized in general terms as exhibiting a more or less diffuse distribution of cells. Zones with a relatively low density of cell somas are used to demarcate the boundaries between telencephalic areas. It would be impossible to provide here a detailed summary of the functional anatomy of the telencephalon (see Nieuwenhuys, ten Donkelaar, & Nicholson, 1998). It suffices to say that relatively complex behaviors, including courtship displays, aggressive behavior, infant care behaviors, learning and memory, and complex perceptual and motor capacities have all been related to activity in various telencephalic areas. It seems likely that at least in some cases, telencephalic areas not only display homologous structures (recognized in terms of their location, afferent–efferent connections, and neurotransmitters), but also homologous functions. For example, the hippocampus (a pallial structure recognized in most vertebrates) is known to contribute to spatial learning in mammals, birds, and bony fish (Salas et al., 1996; Sherry, Jacobs, & Gaulin, 1992).

### Brain size and behavior

Although the general organization of the vertebrate CNS is rather conservative, the relative size and complexity of organization of the various structures can vary dramatically across species. When a species relies heavily on a particular type of sensory information, the nucleus that processes such information exhibits a relatively large size. Catfish, for example, obtain their food by filtering particles from the substratum; as a result, chemical senses play a particularly important role in feeding and the vagal nucleus of the rhombencephalon, which integrates gustatory and facial information, has evolved into a relatively large structure. Similar examples have been described in connection with cognitive functions. As noted previously, the hippocampus participates in spatial learning and it shows a relatively larger size in species that depend on such abilities to adjust to their environment. For example, birds that routinely store food and retrieve it after days or weeks on the basis of spatial cues display a hippocampal size that is larger than that of closely related species that do not store food (Sherry, Vaccarino, Buckenham, & Hertz, 1989). In insectivore mammals, fossorial species that live in burrows have a reduced visual cortex and enlarged somatosensory cortex, whereas semiaquatic species have enlarged striatal and cerebellar areas, both involved in motor control (Stephan, Baron, & Flahm, 1991).

These examples of correspondence between the relative size of a particular brain area (e.g., hippocampus) and the amount of information processed by that area (e.g., spatial learning in food-storing birds), illustrate a general principle of brain organization known as *proper mass*. However, just as specific brain areas increase in relative size according to the proper mass principle, researchers may raise the question of whether similar changes have occurred in terms of the overall size of the brain. There are advantages and disadvantages of considering a global measure such as the whole size of the brain. Among the advantages, brain size provides a basic measure of neural development that can be easily related to other organismic properties (e.g., foraging strategies, social behaviors, and antipredatory strategies), as well as to individual brain areas. For example, the conclusion that the hippocampal size of food-storing birds is larger than that of nonstorers was reached primarily by a comparison of hippocampal size relative to brain size. Similar studies involving a wider range of brain areas indicate their relative rate of change as a function of brain size (Finlay & Darlington, 1995). Additionally, because crania sometimes survive in fossilized remains it is possible to estimate the brain size of extinct species. This information provides a unique opportunity to study brain evolution in real time as these remains usually can be dated accurately (see Jerison, 1973 for information on brain size in Mesozoic mammals and birds). The main disadvantage of brain size as an organismic property is that its meaning is somewhat uncertain. Does brain size translate into some specific behavioral property?

Brain size varies across species most obviously as a function of body size. Animals with larger bodies (e.g., an elephant) must also have relatively larger organs (e.g., livers, hearts, and brains). The scaling of brain (E, encephalon) to body (S, soma) size is linear in double logarithmic axes and is described by the *allometric equation*: $E = aS^b$, where $a$ represents the point of origin of the regression line and $b$ its steepness or slope. Several extensive analyses of relative brain size for several vertebrate classes demonstrate two major points (Bauchot, Randall, Ridet, & Bauchot, 1989; Jerison, 1973; Martin, 1981; Northcutt, 1977, 1985; Platel, 1979). First, although there are variations across vertebrate classes in the size of the slope (from 0.47 in amphibians to 0.76 in mammals, depending on the study), the values are all below one. This finding implies that the size of the brain grows at a smaller rate than that of the body (i.e., larger animals have relatively smaller brains). This relation can be understood as passive growth in the sense that changes in brain size appear to be driven by evolutionary pressures on body size, just as is the case for other organs. Second, the distribution of data points shows at least three levels of relative brain size: lowest for agnathan fish; intermediate for bony fish, amphibians, and reptiles; and highest for birds and mammals. Cartilaginous fish exhibit a distribution that overlaps that of bony fish and mammals. The absence of overlap between reptiles on the one hand, and birds and mammals on the other, implies that, generally speaking, the brain of a bird or mammal is about 10 times bigger than that of a reptile of equal body size. Such differences are thought to represent examples of *encephalization*, that is, an active selective pressure on brain size (rather than body size) that operated in the early evolution of both birds and mammals from their reptilian ancestors (thecodonts and therapsids, respectively).

Jerison (1973) extended the principle of proper mass to the entire brain, arguing that brain size provides a rough approximation to the species' *biological intelligence*, defined as the ability to represent the properties of the external environment. For example, Jerison (1973) argued that the increase in brain size observed in birds resulted from an expansion of the visual system. This expansion was required by active movement (including flight) in forested habitats in which efficient depth perception and figure–background discrimination (e.g., between close and distant perching branches) were of great adaptive significance. By contrast, encephalization in mammals may have been the product of a higher reliance on olfactory and acoustic information in early mammals, relative to their reptilian ancestors, as a result of their shift to a nocturnal way of life. Similar trends in encephalization have occurred in a variety of groups, within each vertebrate class, by convergent evolution. For example, mormyrid fish have the largest relative brain size among bony fish; this is entirely attributable to their cerebellum, which plays a key function in electroreception.

Comparative psychologists have yet to understand what is the behavioral significance of encephalization. Research suggests that relative brain size may correlate with performance in some learning tasks. For example, there is some indication that encephalization (in this case, an index of relative neocortical size) correlates positively with performance in learning set situations (Riddel & Corl, 1977). The task known as *learning set* involves the acquisition of successive discriminations of the form A+/B– (one alternative is always correct, the other always incorrect) involving different pairs of stimuli (e.g., C+/D–, E+/F–, and so forth). Experiments with mammals suggest that as training progresses, new discriminations become easier to acquire. What is yet unclear is whether these correlations reflect a general learning capacity or a more restricted capacity to process visual information. Extensive research with primates, an order that shows encephalization relative to mammals as a whole, also indicates a positive correlation between brain size and *reversal discrimination learning* (Rumbaugh & Pate, 1984). Animals receive training in two discriminations, A+/B– and C+/D– until they reach a behavioral criterion. Then one of the discriminations is overtrained and, finally, both discriminations are reversed (e.g., A–/B+ and C–/D+). The question of interest is whether overtraining facilitates reversal (positive transfer) or interferes with it (negative transfer). The results from a range of species including prosimians, monkeys, and apes indicate that as relative brain size increases, there is a tendency for the effects of overtraining on reversal discrimination learning to shift from interference to facilitation, suggesting a connection between brain size and behavioral flexibility.

## Comparative Developmental Psychology

### Heterochrony

How do evolutionary processes modify the relative size of the brain? Developmental studies in mice selected for large and small relative brain size suggest that these phenotypes are achieved by regulating brain growth during embryonic development (Fuller

& Geils, 1972). Regulation of growth may be achieved by a variety of means, including hormonal action. Since hormones are directly under the control of genes, changes in the timing of operation of such genes can have important consequences for the adult pheno-type of the organism. Such changes in the relative timing of development of a particular trait (changes in the rate of development or in the moment at which a trait starts or stops developing) are generally referred to as *heterochrony* and they are supposed to be of major importance in the evolution of new species (McKinney & McNamara, 1991). There are two categories of heterochrony, paedomorphosis and peramorphosis, and they are best characterized in terms of the state of a specific trait in a descendant species relative to the state of that trait in the ancestor. In *paedomorphosis*, adult descendants express a trait that appears in the juvenile stages of ancestors. For example, the axolotl (*Ambystoma mexicanum*) is a salamander that becomes sexually mature (adult) while still a tadpole (juvenile morphology of the ancestor). In *peramorphosis*, adult descendants express traits that add to the stages of development in the ancestors. For example, the horns and antlers of some mammals evolve as additions in species selected for larger body size relative to their ancestors.

Experiments involving artificial selection techniques are particularly well suited to demonstrate how these concepts can be applied to behavioral development because the ancestral condition is known directly, rather than hypothesized as in most other approaches. Gariépy, Bauer, and Cairns (2001) selected lines of mice for high and low attack frequencies and measured the development of this behavior in the first (parental), fourth, and thirteenth generations. The developmental profile was particularly affected in the low line in which attack frequency decreased in adult descendant mice to levels typical of juvenile ancestors. Similarly, the low line also demonstrated a trend toward reduced levels of freezing behavior in early developmental stages; low freezing frequency was also characteristic of adult ancestors. Generational changes in levels of aggressive behavior were thus achieved by way of paedomorphosis, that is, by extending the pheno-type of juvenile ancestors into the adult stages of the descendants.

Gariépy et al. (2001) also found that repeated exposure to aggressive encounters in early development tended to reverse the effects of artificial selection for low attack frequency. The implication of this finding is that this particular phenotype, attack frequency, can be influenced by both maturational factors (as reflected in the pheno-type's response to artificial selection) and experience. This dependence of aggressive behavior on a complex interactive process involving genetic and nongenetic com-ponents, including experience, is typical of other behaviors. A simple-minded approach to behavioral development would posit that a behavior is either innate or acquired, giving rise to nativist and environmentalist views, respectively. These views were cham-pioned by classic ethologists and radical behaviorists, and they reached a certain the-oretical tension during the 1950s and 1960s, when the debate became known as the *nature–nurture controversy* (Lehrman, 1953). Upon reflection, however, it makes just as little sense to argue that a behavior is determined by genes (because genes can only produce proteins), as it does to imagine that experience can affect the organism's morphology and function without any genetic involvement (because gene transcrip-tion is needed for many such changes). The view that development is the result of complex interactions across levels of organization from genes, to cells, networks, and organism–environment interactions is known as the *epigenetic view* (Gottlieb, 1992). This epigenetic view has guided research in comparative developmental psychology over recent decades and has produced a wealth of empirical evidence that supports the basic notion that behavioral development is normally modulated by a multiplicity of factors. Two examples will be briefly examined in the rest of this section: imprinting in precocial birds and social behavior in primates.

## Imprinting

Young precocial birds, such as chickens, ducks, and quail, display a restricted capacity for attachment during an early period of development. The relevant information may be acquired anywhere between the last portion of incubation and the initial days after hatching, depending on the species. During this *sensitive period*, the chick learns to recognize its mother and develops an attachment that involves a strong preference to be close to its mother and a distress reaction that ensues on separation. A striking aspect of this phenomenon, known as *filial imprinting*, is the fact that young birds can develop an attachment to almost any object present during the sensitive period, no matter how seemingly arbitrary. Chicks rapidly learn to recognize such objects as a person, a stuffed version of a female, a rotating geometric form, a plastic bottle, and an intense light, among many other stimuli, as a "mother object" worthy of an attachment. No doubt these are not equally effective. As one might imagine, perceptually salient stimuli have an advantage, whether because of their movement (Eiserer & Swope, 1980) or their sheer intensity (Eiserer, 1980), and naturalistic stimuli including the head and neck region of an animal (not necessarily a conspecific) are also particularly effective (Johnson & Horn, 1988).

Although the definition of filial imprinting as a recognition process suggests the primacy of learning factors, the process works hand in hand with a strong motivation to approach and remain in close proximity to the object. In an early demonstration, Petterson (1960) trained ducklings (*Anas platyrhynchos*) to peck on a small key for an opportunity to set in motion a yellow cylinder to which the animals had become attached. Although the pecking response displayed properties familiar from studies involving food or water as the reinforcer, the ducklings did not exhibit any signs of satiety, that is, they continued to respond virtually indefinitely. The flexibility of the following response was uncovered in an experiment involving omission training (Hoffman, Stratton, & Newby, 1969). After imprinting to a moving bottle had occurred, approach to the stimulus ended its movement whereas withdrawal from the proximity of the stimulus made it resume its movement. Ducklings rapidly adjusted to this situation, remaining at the minimum distance required to keep the stimulus moving. Thus, the following response, like the pecking response in the previous experiment, is really an instrumental behavior aimed at bringing the animal in contact with a positive reinforcer. Similarly, distress calls emitted by young birds upon separation from their mother also have an instrumental component. Using a master–yoked design, Hoffman, Schiff, Adams, & Searle (1966) demonstrated that ducklings for which the presentation of the imprinting stimulus was contingent upon the emission of distress calls (master animals) displayed a higher frequency of vocalization than their yoked counterparts (exposed to the imprinting stimulus independently of their calls).

Although the word "imprinting" suggests a sort of instantaneous acquisition, the process is far more dynamic and gradual. Only some of the perceptual features of the imprinting stimulus are effective initially; however, as the young bird experiences the stimulus repeatedly, other perceptual elements develop control over the following response. Hoffman and Ratner (1973) suggested that such transfer of control to new elements of the configuration involves Pavlovian conditioning. According to this hypothesis, elements of the stimulus configuration that are particularly intense act in a manner analogous to unconditioned stimuli in typical conditioning situations (e.g., food or shock). For example, a large, moving object may have sufficient salience to induce attachment. Less salient stimuli that accompany the intense elements, such as the mother's call or plumage, acquire control over the imprinting process by virtue of their simultaneous pairing with the intense, unconditioned stimulus-like components. With sufficient experience, the chick may respond not just to the sight of the large moving mother, but to its call and appearance.

Experiments with artificial stimuli indicate that such associations between elements of the imprinting configuration are indeed acquired. For example, Bolhuis and Honey (1994) demonstrated that ducklings imprinted to a geometric shape (a visual element) exhibited significantly greater preference for this stimulus when it was accompanied by the species-typical maternal call. More relevant still, the preference for the visual element over a novel stimulus increased even when the auditory component was not present during the test. Interestingly, the control condition was one in which ducklings were exposed to the visual and auditory elements but in an unpaired fashion (i.e., stimuli were never presented in close temporal contiguity). Furthermore, presentation of the auditory element alone weakens the preference for the visual component; presumably, such presentations extinguished the association between the auditory and visual elements. It appears, therefore, that associative learning contributes to the development of the recognition process, as well as to the maintenance of responses such as distress calls that allow the young bird to communicate with its mother. Such experiential features blend with strong predispositions to produce an attachment of significant survival value to the relatively unprotected chick.

Another interesting aspect of filial imprinting is its involvement in a completely different area of the animal's behavior: sexual preferences in the adult. It has been known for a long time that young chicks imprinted to humans later tend to remain indifferent to conspecifics and, in fact, display sexual behavior toward humans. An early experience in the context of the mother–offspring bond may actually affect the choice of sexual partner in the adult bird. This effect is referred to as *sexual imprinting*. Importantly, the process is not completely determined by early experience, but only modulated by it. For example, birds imprinted to an arbitrary stimulus would prefer this stimulus to other arbitrary stimuli; but experience with a naturalistic model of a conspecific may reverse the preference for the imprinted stimulus (Vidal, 1980). Imprinting-like effects of early experience on adult social behavior have also been described in mammals. For example, dogs establish adult patterns of social behavior during a sensitive period ranging between 4 and 15 weeks after birth (Scott & Fuller, 1965). As in the case of sexual imprinting in birds, mammalian adult behavior is also the result of complex interactions of predispositions and experience.

## Primate social development

Primate mothers and infants can also form attachments with similar properties to those of precocial birds, namely, individual recognition, preference for the attached object, and separation distress. In squirrel monkeys (*Saimiri sciureus*), infants can recognize their mother and discriminate her from other females, and mothers can recognize their infants and discriminate them from others, including familiar infants (Cheney & Seyfarth, 1980; Kaplan & Russell, 1974). Upon separation, both mother and infant exhibit increased levels of cortisol, a hormone widely used as a marker of psychological stress (Coe, Mendoza, Smotherman, & Levine, 1978). The impact of mother–offspring separation on the infant's fitness is highlighted by studies that show impairment of immune function (Kling et al., 1992) and vulnerability to infections (Bailey & Coe, 1999) in infant monkeys.

It has been known since the classic studies of Harlow (1971) that tactile stimulation plays a fundamental role in the development of attachments in infant monkeys. Infants form strong attachments to mother models covered with cloth, even when they do not provide milk. Such attachments regulate the infant's emotional response to novelty, as well as its ability to interact with peers and its adult social behavior. For example, rhesus monkeys (*Macaca mulatta*) raised in laboratory confinement display abnormal and ineffective copulatory behavior as adults (Mason, 1960). Socially deprived females that become mothers provide deficient maternal care for the infant, often being aggressive toward them; such infants later exhibit higher levels of aggressive behavior compared to monkeys raised by normal mothers (Sackett, 1967). The strong predisposition for social behavior in primates can be used as a therapeutic tool to correct deficits induced by early experience. A deprived infant may also benefit from relatively brief exposure to other infants. In one study (Harlow & Suomi, 1971), six-month-old, socially isolated monkeys were permitted to join three-month-old, normally reared monkeys during periods of two hours per day. A three-month-old normal monkey provides clinging contact without becoming aggressive toward the socially deprived monkey, a combination that turned out to have some interesting properties. Such clinging contact provides a basis for the development of normal levels of social interaction in isolated monkeys. The interplay of social predispositions and experience during development extends even to allospecific companions. For example, socially deprived monkeys reared in the company of dogs show a greater complexity in their adult social interactions compared to those reared by artificial mothers (Capitanio, 1985). Although obviously dogs cannot provide the type of social exchange that is typical of primates, the dog's tendency to engage infant rhesus monkeys in a variety of interactions provides experience that allows adults to adjust to their species-typical social environment.

# Comparative Learning

## Generality of learning phenomena

As noted in the Introduction, comparative psychology originated historically as an attempt to provide empirical evidence for Darwin's notion of mental continuity. From the start, such research concentrated on psychological functions such as the ability of animals to learn, memorize, orient in the environment, solve problems, and the like. Darwin ([1881] 1982) himself opened the way with a set of studies on the "habits of earthworms" and their ability to represent objects. The study of learning has been, and continues to be, at the core of comparative psychology. During most of the twentieth century, the effort was centered on the study of basic processes of associative learning and cognition, on the broad assumption that such research would contribute to an understanding of complex behavior and of brain–behavior relationships. Comparative psychologists adopted a strategy common to other branches of science, including a focus on a small set of species intensely studied under the controlled conditions of the laboratory (e.g., rats, pigeons, and monkeys). Such strategy, much criticized and poorly understood by many, has led to success in other disciplines including genetics (for decades concentrated on fruit flies and mice) and developmental biology (sea urchins, amphibians, and chick embryos).

The task of understanding basic learning and cognitive processes proved more difficult than expected, but strong signs of interdisciplinary integration of behavioral theories and procedures with neurobiological and genetic research are emerging (e.g., Amsel, 1992; Blair, Schafe, Bauer, Rodrigues, & LeDoux, 2001; Dubnau & Tully, 1998; Gray & McNaughton, 2000; Rose & Rankin, 2001; Schmajuk, 1997). An understanding of learning and cognitive processes in a comparative framework is such a relevant and popular area of research that a specific chapter has been devoted to these issues in this book (see Chapter 11 by Barker & Katz). The rest of this section will thus concentrate on three issues of central importance in the study of comparative learning and cognition; the reader is referred to Barker and Katz's chapter for a more complete description of this field of research. These three issues are (1) the distinction between learning phenomena and mechanisms, (2) comparative methodology, and (3) the conceptual basis for a comparative-evolutionary theory of learning.

First, the main empirical goal in comparative research on learning and cognition is to identify similarities and differences in learning phenomena across species. *Learning phenomena* are behavioral regularities that can plausibly be attributed to the acquisition of information through experience. Most learning phenomena are induced by the use of one of two fundamental procedures: Pavlovian or classical conditioning and instrumental or operant conditioning. The basic *Pavlovian conditioning* procedure involves the temporal pairing of two stimuli, such that the one occurring initially (called the conditioned stimulus, CS) becomes a signal for the second stimulus (the unconditioned stimulus, US). As a result of such CS→US pairings, animals eventually respond to the CS either in terms of skeletal movements (e.g., pecking, freezing), glandular secretions (e.g., salivation, glucocorticoid release), autonomic responses (e.g., heart rate, galvanic skin response), sensory processing (e.g., pain thresholds), or some similar change. This basic theme has been greatly elaborated into a myriad of multiple paradigms (Papini, 1998), all sharing one basic procedural element: pairings occur independently of the animal's behavior. In contrast, *instrumental conditioning* procedures involve the pairing of a response (R) with a stimulus of significance to the animal, called the reinforcer ($S^R$). Such R→$S^R$ pairings usually lead to changes in the frequency, strength, or probability of the response. For example, the rate of occurrence of a particular response may be increased by pairing it with the presentation of an appetitive reinforcer (e.g., food) or with the removal of an aversive reinforcer (e.g., shock). In this case, therefore, pairings are dependent on the animal's behavior. Again, a variety of instrumental procedures has been devised to study learning and cognitive skills ranging from simple approach–avoidance tendencies to the most complex cognitive processes including concept formation, spatial mapping, and linguistic competence (Malott, 1998).

It could be argued that, for the most part, comparative research is still at this basic level of determining the nature of a basic set of learning phenomena across species. Such effects as acquisition, extinction, discrimination, and generalization as studied under both Pavlovian and instrumental procedures, are widely known properties of learning. In addition, much of the systematic research that characterized the field of learning during the twentieth century was aimed at describing other effects including some related to the processing of stimuli (e.g., latent inhibition, overshadowing), the distribution of practice (e.g., trial-spacing effect), the transfer of experience across situations (e.g., learned helplessness), the effects of various schedules of reinforcement on behavior (e.g., partial reinforcement effects), and a host of other phenomena. Together, these learning phenomena provide an inventory of the fundamental properties of associative learning that serve as a framework to understand similarities and differences across species (much as Mendel's research on garden peas provided a framework for subsequent research on genetics). What have we learned so far?

Except for the sponges (phylum *Porifera*), for which there is no evidence of the presence of neural cells, the most primitive neurons found in cnidarians (jellyfish, sea anemones, and coral) have properties that are surprisingly equivalent to those of neurons found in more derived species (Spencer, 1989). This commonality suggests that whatever aspects of learning depend on synaptic transmission and plasticity, for example, might be highly conserved across species. Whereas there is no evidence of basic associative processes in cnidarians and only controversial evidence in the simplest extant bilaterals, the planaria (Thompson & McConnell, 1955), the evidence is reasonably good for another group of relatively simple organisms: the nematodes (e.g., Wen et al., 1997). With its 302 neurons and a fully mapped genome, the nematode *Caenorhabditis elegans* is rapidly becoming a popular model system for the study of learning (Rose & Rankin, 2001). The presence of basic associative processes in relatively simple neural networks, such as those in *C. elegans* and in the mollusc *Aplysia californica* (Hawkins, Abrams, Carew, & Kandel, 1983), suggests that these psychological capacities should not necessarily be viewed as requiring a complex neural architecture, as it was thought previously. Indeed, the list of learning phenomena uncovered in research with insects in general, and honeybees in particular, is astonishingly similar to a description of learning phenomena in mammals (Bitterman, 1988, 1996).

In contrast, there are important differences in the macroanatomical organization of nervous systems across phyla. Cnidarians are characterized by a diffuse nerve net, whereas bilateral animals present a clear distinction between central and peripheral nervous systems. In turn, the CNS of many different types of animals (e.g., arthropods, molluscs, and vertebrates, to name those most commonly used in learning research), are characterized by a segmented organization that shows no clear homologies in terms of neuroanatomical organization (e.g., there is no clear correspondence between, e.g., the spinal cord of vertebrates and the ganglia in the nervous system of arthropods or molluscs). Thus, properties of learning that depend on the way neural networks are organized may vary substantially across widely divergent phyla (Bitterman, 1988).

## *Learning versus contextual factors*

The second main issue concerns the methodological problem of distinguishing between the contribution of learning mechanisms and that of *contextual factors* (e.g., perceptual, motor, and motivational processes) to the observed similarities and differences in learning phenomena. Learning, like many other central concepts in psychology, is referred to as an *intervening variable*, that is, an unobservable construct postulated to account for stimulus–response regularities. Species similarities and differences in learning phenomena must be inferred from behavioral data (much as Mendel inferred the genotype of garden peas from some key phenotypic characters, such as pea shape). Unfortunately, most acquired behaviors are characterized by a complex causality. With many factors other than learning processes contributing to behavior, the core of the research strategy consists of a careful experimental analysis aimed at disentangling the contributions to behavior of perceptual bias, motor skills, response strategies, motivation, and similar nonlearning factors that can account for species differences in learning phenomena without forcing the postulation of additional learning factors. Consider the following hypothetical example.

Imagine that a comparative psychologist is interested in comparing the learning abilities of rats and turtles in an experiment involving a runway, a single trial per day, and food reinforcement for moving from the start to the goal box. The speed of running is the main measure of acquisition and the species are chosen carefully, such that body size is about the same. All animals are equally deprived to 80 percent of their free-food weight, reinforced with five pellets of food (the same type of pellet), and given equal preexposure to the runway to familiarize them with the experimental apparatus. After 20 days of training, the animals in both groups are performing at a constant speed, with the rats' performance being significantly above that of the turtles. Can the experimenter conclude that rats are more efficient learners than turtles?

Despite the experimenter's attempt to carefully match all the conditions of the experiment (e.g., dependent measure, deprivation level, reinforcer magnitude, pretraining), the conclusion does not follow from the results for a multiplicity of reasons. First, there is the grossly evident species disparity in motor performance: rats are generally faster runners than turtles, so the difference may be attributed to motor factors, rather than learning processes. Less conspicuous are possible motivational differences that this experiment cannot help to resolve. For example, it is possible that the motivational impact of five pellets is different across species. What if rats were reinforced with one pellet and turtles with 10? Perhaps the turtles would outperform the rats under these conditions, thus forcing the opposite conclusion. The foraging styles of these two species may also get in the way of clean conclusions. For example, whereas rats actively look for patchily distributed food, many species of turtles are strictly herbivore and thus have evolved to deal with food resources that tend to be aggregated in a given area. Thus a task involving a less active strategy for food procurement might actually benefit the turtles over the rats. Because of reasons like these, the strategy of attempting to equate all possible variables across species, called *control by equation*, is utterly inadequate to draw conclusions about learning abilities in a comparative framework.

Bitterman (1975) suggested that a more productive research strategy is to concentrate on the issue of whether a particular learning phenomenon in different species is affected by the same variables. For example, instead of asking whether rats perform higher (or lower) than turtles, one may ask whether acquisition of a running task varies as a function of the same set of variables across species. Do magnitude of reinforcement (e.g., number of pellets), amount of training (e.g., number of trials), response effort (e.g., length of the runway), habituation to the apparatus (e.g., extent of preexposure to the runway), and similar such variables affect acquisition in the same manner in rats and turtles? If acquisition is similarly affected, then the most parsimonious conclusion is that the underlying learning processes are the same, even if the absolute speed scores are widely different across species. This is referred to as *control by systematic variation*.

## Evolution of learning mechanisms

The third main issue to discuss is highlighted by the conclusion just accepted on the grounds of parsimony. To stop the research process at the level of understanding illustrated in the rat–turtle example would be obviously inadequate from the evolutionary point of view. Imagine that a scientist was studying the flight behavior of bats and eagles and, upon discovering that the speed of the wind and the thermal currents affect flight in the same way in these two species, concluded that the behavior and the structures upon which it is supported (e.g., the wings) are based on the same underlying biological processes. In evolutionary terms, this conclusion would be equivalent to arguing for the homology of flight mechanisms in bats and eagles. *Homology* refers to the ascription of character similarity to inheritance from a common ancestor. In the bat–eagle example, an analysis of the neural control of flight and the bone structure of the wing (not to mention paleontological evidence), would clearly indicate that the similarites in flight are only superficial. *Homoplasy* is the term used to explain character similarity across species as a result of convergent evolution. In this case, similarity is driven by common ecological pressures (e.g., aerodynamic constraints on flight). Similarly, although rats and turtles may adjust to various environmental conditions in a similar manner, a deeper understanding of the processes underlying behavioral changes would be required before a hypothesis of homology is fully supported by empirical evidence. The simple manipulation of environmental (e.g., reinforcer magnitude) and organismic (e.g., deprivation level) factors is insufficient to demonstrate homology in learning processes. By the same token, if the behavior of rats and turtles were to be significantly different, further research would be required to show that this difference reflects evolutionary *divergence*, that is, the evolution of traits driven by adaptation to different ecological pressures.

Ultimately, a comparative theory of learning and cognition would have to be framed in terms of such concepts as homology, homoplasy, and divergence. However, it is not the learning phenomena that are evolving, because they are simply the outcome of experimentally arranged situations (rather than natural pieces of behavior), but the underlying *learning mechanisms* that are engaged by the experimental conditions of training. Traditionally, comparative psychologists have phrased such mechanisms in terms of S–S and S–R associations, attentional modulation, retrieval, rehearsal, controlability, and similar terms. It was generally assumed that the utility of these concepts would become fully apparent when researchers could incorporate manipulations aiming at lower levels of analysis. Again, the analogy with genetics is evident; concepts such as gene, homozygosity, and dominance, entirely derived from the study of phenotypes, were useful guides when genetic research moved into a more molecular level of analysis. Obviously, such behavioral capacities as acquisition of a food-reinforced running response in rats and turtles must be supported by activity in a set of somewhat specific brain sites, by the action of somewhat specific neurotransmitter systems, and by the engagement of somewhat specific cell-molecular processes supporting synaptic plasticity. So the concept of "mechanism" is really complex in the sense that it involves at least four levels of analysis; in a top-down direction, they are the psychological, neurobiological, neurochemical, and cell-molecular levels.

Each of these mechanistic levels can be approached by the use of methods and techniques that, for the most part, have been around for a long time. For example, researchers have used reinforcer-devaluation and inflation techniques as tools to assess the content of learning at the psychological level; brain lesion techniques to determine the neurobiological substrates of learning; pharmacological techniques to study the neuro-chemical level; and cell-molecular techniques to study the roles of second-messenger systems and gene transcription on learning. Thus this multilevel view of mechanisms does not imply a completely novel approach at the level of experimental practices. However, this view helps to integrate research aiming at different levels of analysis and, perhaps most importantly, to develop practical criteria for testing the evolutionary basis of learning mechanisms in a comparative context. As an example, an empirical criterion for homology of learning mechanisms in an instance of learning (e.g., fear conditioning) across two or more species (e.g., rats and humans) should require that the same mechanisms be operative at all four levels of analysis (e.g., that fear conditioning in these species is based on the same psychological, neurobiological, neurochemical, and cell-molecular mechanisms). Different mechanistic control of fear conditioning in these two species would support homoplasy (if the behavioral effect is similar), or divergence (if the behavioral effect is dissimilar).

An interesting possibility is suggested by recent research on the cell-molecular basis of learning. Researchers interested in the cellular basis of associative learning have noticed that the same second-messenger system (e.g., cyclic adenosine monophosphate, or cAMP) appears to be involved in conditioning in *Aplysia* (a mollusc), *Drosophila* fruit flies (an arthropod), and the mouse (a chordate). It seems unlikely that the cAMP pathway has become involved in conditioning by sheer chance, but this possibility cannot be fully discarded. However, as Kandel and Abel (1995) pointed out, the fact that the common ancestor of these three animal phyla lived in the deep past, more than 540 MYA (Knoll & Carroll, 1999), suggests that neural networks involved in behavioral plasticity operate according to highly conserved cell-molecular mechanisms. Another implication of these findings is, of course, that whereas learning effects may depend on divergent mechanisms at one level, they may be subserved by the same mechanism at another level. It is a fact that there are no neurobiological correspondences between the CNSs of molluscs, arthropods, and chordates; that is, there is nothing in molluscs and arthropods that can be considered homologous to the amygdala of mammals, for example. This decoupling of mechanistic levels suggests a modular arrangement according to which the same mechanism at one level could potentially be involved with more than one mechanism at an upper level in different species. This fact is why learning phenomena may be encapsulated at the neurobiological level, as suggested by research on fear conditioning (Ohman & Mineka, 2001), and yet be based on the same cell-molecular processes that operate in other types of conditioning (Blair et al., 2001). It seems possible that a better appreciation of the complexity of mechanistic processes may help resolve the long-standing controversy between researchers who support a general-process view of learning and researchers who believe learning mechanisms are adaptive specializations (see Papini, 2002).

## Concluding Comments: Complexity

The oldest evidence of bilaterally symmetrical animals is found in the fossilized traces of worm-like organisms in rocks from the Precambrian period (some may be as old as 1,000 million years). These old traces are characterized by being superficial (i.e., these animals were probably grazing for bacteria on the bottom surface of lakes or ponds) and by exhibiting numerous crossings. That is, the foraging behavior of these animals was apparently random in its trajectory (so-called irregular meanders). Similar fossil traces have been found in more recent deposit and an analysis of these foraging patterns has revealed an interesting trend (Crimes, 1992). In the transition from the Precambrian to the Cambrian periods (about 545 MYA), the irregular meanders of early traces are replaced by traces that lack the crossings. Traces without crossings are interpreted as representing a more efficient foraging pattern because the animal would have avoided an already visited location. The later appearance of deep, rather than superficial, tunnels also suggests the evolution of a coelon cavity with a muscular system capable of exerting sufficient pressure on the substratum to effectively burrow the animal in it.

These changes in the morphology of traces have been interpreted as reflecting an increase in complexity of sensory-motor capacities, neural organization, and body organization. I believe there can be little doubt that if animals could be organized along a scale of complexity, then the ones considered most complex would have to be necessarily of more recent evolution. A wealth of fossil evidence is consistent with the view that structurally complex organisms tend to be preceded by relatively simpler ones, rather than vice versa, as in the example of fossil traces. Unfortunately, complexity is one of those concepts that are extremely hard to define rigorously, but relatively easy to use, even in a scientific discussion (see McShea, 1996, for a rigorous treatment of this concept). In previous sections I made extensive use of this notion, as is typically done in discussions of any topic in comparative psychology. This use is less likely to be a concern when animal behavior is approached from the background provided by ecology, ethology, or any view that places a strong emphasis on adaptation. However, a balanced view of animal behavior requires a consideration of phylogenetic history and brain evolution, and it is in these areas where the notion of complexity acquires heuristic value. Similarly, it is impossible to deny the complexity of human behavior when considered in the context of natural science. Human language, culture, technology, social institutions, recreational behavior, music, art, and similar features have no counterpart in nonhuman animals. Obviously, it may be plausibly argued that these are differences of degree, rather than kind. However, even in this case, human behavior and sociality have produced some phenomena that are vastly more complex than those observed in other species (including the social insects). Therefore, from the perspective of psychology, the issue of complexity is unlikely to ever go away. What is needed is a basic understanding of how this concept could be fruitfully used in a scientific framework. The following four rules are suggested with this goal in mind.

First, the complexity exhibited by systems and functions is not an inevitable consequence of evolutionary (and developmental) processes. Sometimes structures actually lose complexity, becoming simpler. For example, an analysis of the vertebral column of mammals reveals as many trends toward increased complexity as toward increased simplification (McShea, 1993). Second, complexity should not be used to characterize an entire species, but only to characterize homologous traits across species. This consideration follows from the fact that evolutionary forces affect different traits at different rates, a phenomenon referred to as *mosaic evolution*. For example, whereas the human grasping hand has changed little compared to that of other primates, the human brain has increased in size significantly; thus applying the notion of complexity to humans as a whole would assume a kind of averaging of degrees of complexity that would make little sense. Third, complexity in structure and function arises directly from natural selection, but complexity and fitness are not necessarily scaled on the same dimension. Obviously, when a lineage exhibits a trend toward simplification, complexity must carry a fitness penalty. Thus the most complex system is not necessarily the one with the highest fitness. Finally, and in the spirit of Morgan's canon of parsimony, the existence of complex behavior does not necessarily imply that the underlying processes are complex. The challenge faced by comparative psychologists trying to account for complex learning and cognitive skills is to produce theories that explain such complexity on the basis of the simplest assumptions possible.

Comparative psychology is among the oldest fields within the general science of psychology, but its main contribution may not yet be fully realized. Animal behavior research during the twentieth century has made substantial contributions to our understanding of the evolution and development of behavior. However, there is still a substantial contribution that must be classified as "pending." At the scientific level, this second century of comparative research will surely bring a better understanding of brain–behavior–environment interactions and, with it, knowledge that will contribute significantly to a wide variety of applications. At the educational level, comparative psychologists have an important role to play in bridging the social and biological sciences. They are equipped with sophisticated knowledge of evolutionary principles and psychological theories, and bring with them a model of interdisciplinary research that will eventually lead to a more complete understanding of human psychology.

## References

Amsel, A. (1992). *Frustration theory*. Cambridge, UK: Cambridge University Press.

Aristotle (1991). *Historia animalium* (D. M. Balme, trans.). Cambridge, MA: Harvard University Press.

Bailey, M. T., & Coe, C. L. (1999). Maternal separation disrupts the integrity of the intestinal microflora in infant rhesus monkeys. *Developmental Psychobiology, 35,* 146–55.

Bauchot, R., Randall, J., Ridet, J.-M., & Bauchot, M.-L. (1989). Encephalization in tropical teleost fishes and comparison with their mode of life. *Journal für Hirnforschung, 30,* 645–69.

Benton, M. J. (1990). *Vertebrate paleontology*. London: Unwin Hyman.

Bitterman, M. E. (1975). The comparative analysis of learning. *Science, 188,* 699–709.

Bitterman, M. E. (1988). Vertebrate–invertebrate comparisons. In H. J. Jerison & I. Jerison (eds.), *Intelligence and evolutionary biology* (pp. 251–75). Berlin: Springer-Verlag.

Bitterman, M. E. (1996). Comparative analysis of learning in honeybees. *Animal Learning and Behavior, 24,* 123–41.

Blair, H. T., Schafe, G. E., Bauer, E. P., Rodrigues, S. M., & LeDoux, P. E. (2001). Synaptic plasticity in the lateral amygdala: A cellular hypothesis of fear conditioning. *Learning and Memory, 8,* 229–42.

Boakes, R. (1984). *From Darwin to behaviorism. Psychology and the minds of animals*. Cambridge, UK: Cambridge University Press.

Boesch, C. (1994). Cooperative hunting in wild chimpanzees. *Animal Behaviour, 48,* 653–67.

Bolhuis, J. J., & Honey, R. C. (1994). Within-event learning during filial imprinting. *Journal of Experimental Psychology: Animal Behavior Processes, 20,* 240–8.

Briggs, D. E. G., Erwin, D. H., & Collier, F. J. (1994). *The fossils of the Burgess Shale*. Washington, DC: Smithsonian Institution Press.

Capitanio, J. P. (1985). Early experience and social processes in rhesus macaques (*Macaca mulatta*): II. Complex social interaction. *Journal of Comparative Psychology, 99,* 133–44.

Cheney, D. L., & Seyfarth, R. M. (1980). Vocal recognition in free-ranging vervet monkeys. *Animal Behaviour, 28,* 362–7.

Coe, C. L., Mendoza, S. P., Smotherman, W. P., & Levine, S. (1978). Mother–infant attachment in the squirrel monkey: Adrenal response to separation. *Behavioral Biology, 22,* 256–63.

Crews, D., & Moore, M. C. (1986). Evolution of mechanisms controlling mating behavior. *Science, 231,* 121–5.

Crimes, T. P. (1992). The record of trace fossils across the Proterozoic-Cambrian boundary. In J. H. Lipps & P. W. Signor (eds.), *Origin and early evolution of the Metazoa* (pp. 177–202). New York: Plenum.

Darwin, C. ([1859] 1993). *The origin of species*. New York: Random House.

Darwin, C. (1871). *The descent of man, and selection in relation to sex*. London: Murray.

Darwin, C. ([1881] 1982). *The formation of vegetable mould, through the action of worms, with observations on their habits.* Chicago, IL: University of Chicago Press.

Domjan, M., Blesbois, E., & Williams, J. (1998). The adaptive significance of sexual conditioning: Pavlovian control of sperm release. *Psychological Science, 9*, 411–15.

Dubnau, J., & Tully, T. (1998). Gene discovery in Drosophila: New insights for learning and memory. *Annual Review of Neuroscience, 21*, 407–44.

Eiserer, L. A. (1980). Development of filial attachment to static visual features of an imprinting object. *Animal Learning and Behavior, 8*, 159–66.

Eiserer, L. A., & Swope, R. L. (1980). Acquisition of behavioral control by statis visual features of an imprinting object: Species generality. *Animal Learning and Behavior, 8*, 482–4.

Farel, P. B., Glanzman, D. L., & Thompson, R. F. (1973). Habituation of a monosynaptic response in the vertebrate central nervous system: Lateral column-motoneuron pathway in isolated frog spinal cord. *Journal of Neurophysiology, 36*, 1117–30.

Farrar, L. (1998). *Ancient Roman gardens.* Stroud, UK: Budding Books.

Fetcho, J. R. (1991). Spinal network of the Mauthner cell. *Brain, Behavior, and Evolution, 37*, 298–316.

Finlay, B. L., & Darlington, R. B. (1995). Lined regularities in the development and evolution of mammalian brains. *Science, 268*, 1578–84.

Fuller, J. L., & Geils, H. D. (1972). Brain growth in mice selected for high and low brain weight. *Developmental Psychobiology, 5*, 307–18.

Gariépy, J.-L., Bauer, D. J., & Cairns, R. B. (2001). Selective breeding for differential aggression in mice provides evidence for heterochrony in social behaviours. *Animal Behaviour, 61*, 933–47.

Gottlieb, G. (1992). *Individual development and evolution. The genesis of novel behavior.* New York: Oxford University Press.

Grant, P. R. (1986). *Ecology and evolution of Darwin's finches.* Princeton, NJ: Princeton University Press.

Grau, J. W., Barstrow, D. G., & Joynes, R. L. (1998). Instrumental learning within the spinal cord: I. Behavioral properties. *Behavioral Neuroscience, 112*, 1366–86.

Gray, J. A., & McNaughton, N. (2000). *The neuropsychology of anxiety. An enquiry into the functions of the septo-hippocampal system.* Oxford: Oxford University Press.

Hamilton, W. D. (1964). The genetical evolution of social behaviour. I, II. *Journal of Theoretical Biology, 7*, 1–52.

Harlow, H. F. (1971). *Learning to love.* San Francisco, CA: Albion Press.

Harlow, H. F., & Suomi, S. J. (1971). Social recovery by isolation-reared monkeys. *Proceedings of the National Academy of Sciences, USA, 68*, 1534–8.

Hawkins, R. D., Abrams, T. W., Carew, T. J., & Kandel, E. R. (1983). A cellular mechanism of classical conditioning in *Aplysia*: Activity-dependent amplification of presynaptic facilitation. *Science, 219*, 400–5.

Heinrich, B., & Marzluff, J. (1995). Why ravens share. *American Scientist, 83*, 342–55.

Hoffman, H. S., & Ratner, A. M. (1973). A reinforcement model of imprinting: Implications for socialization in monkeys and men. *Psychological Review, 80*, 527–44.

Hoffman, H. S., Schiff, D., Adams, J., & Searle, J. (1966). Enhanced distress vocalization through selective reinforcement. *Science, 151*, 352–4.

Hoffman, H. S., Stratton, J. W., & Newby, V. (1969). Punishment by response-contingent withdrawal of an imprinting stimulus. *Science, 163*, 702–4.

Hölldobler, B., & Wilson, E. O. (1990). *The ants.* Cambridge, MA: Harvard University Press.

Hollis, K. L., Pharr, V. L., Dumas, M. J., Britton, G. B., & Field, J. (1997). Classical conditioning provides paternity advantage for territorial male blue gouramis (*Trichogaster trichopterus*). *Journal of Comparative Psychology, 111*, 219–25.

Jerison, H. J. (1973). *Evolution of the brain and intelligence.* New York: Academic Press.

Johanson, D., & Edgar, B. (1996). *From Lucy to language.* New York: Simon & Shuster.

Johnson, M. H., & Horn, G. (1988). Development of filial preferences in dark-reared chicks. *Animal Behaviour, 36,* 675–83.

Kandel, E., & Abel, T. (1995). Neuropeptides, adenylyl cyclase, and memory storage. *Science, 268,* 825–6.

Kaplan, J., & Russell, M. (1974). Olfactory recognition in the infant squirrel monkey. *Developmental Psychobiology, 7,* 15–19.

Kling, A., Lloyd, R., Tachiki, K., Prince, H., Klimenko, V., & Korneva, E. (1992). Effects of social separation on immune function and brain neurotransmitters in cebus monkeys (*C. apella*). *Annals of the New York Academy of Sciences, 650,* 257–61.

Knoll, A. H., & Carroll, S. B. (1999). Early animal evolution: Emerging views from comparative biology and geology. *Science, 284,* 2129–37.

Lehrman, D. S. (1953). A critique of Konrad Lorenz's theory of instinctive behavior. *Quarterly Review of Biology, 28,* 337–63.

Lofdahl, K. L., Hu, D., Ehrman, L., Hirsch, J., & Skoog, L. (1992). Incipient reproductive isolation and evolution in laboratory *Drosophila melanogaster* selected for geotaxis. *Animal Behaviour, 44,* 783–6.

Losos, J. B., Warheit, K. I., & Schoener, T. W. (1997). Adaptive differentiation following experimental island colonization in *Anolis* lizards. *Nature, 387,* 70–3.

Malott, R. W. (1998). Operant conditioning. In G. Greenberg & M. M. Haraway (eds.), *Comparative psychology: A handbook* (pp. 576–85). New York: Garland.

Martin, R. D. (1981). Relative brain size and basal metabolic rate in terrestrial vertebrates. *Nature, 293,* 57–60.

Mason, W. A. (1960). The effects of social restriction on the behavior of rhesus monkeys: I. Free social behavior. *Journal of Comparative and Physiological Psychology, 53,* 582–9.

McKinney, M. L., & McNamara, K. J. (1991). *Heterochrony: The evolution of ontogeny.* New York: Plenum.

McShea, D. W. (1993). Evolutionary change in the morphological complexity of the mammalian vertebral column. *Evolution, 47,* 730–40.

McShea, D. W. (1996). Metazoan complexity and evolution: Is there a trend? *Evolution, 50,* 477–92.

Morey, D. F. (1994). The early evolution of the domestic dog. *American Scientist, 82,* 336–47.

Nieuwenhuys, R., ten Donkelaar, H. J., & Nicholson, C. (1998). *The central nervous system of vertebrates* (vols. 1–3). Berlin: Springer.

Northcutt, R. G. (1977). Elasmobranch central nervous system organization and its possible evolutionary significance. *American Zoologist, 17,* 411–29.

Northcutt, R. G. (1985). Brain phylogeny. Speculations on pattern and cause. In M. J. Cohen & F. S. Strumwasser (eds.), *Comparative neurobiology. Modes of communication in the nervous system* (pp. 351–78). New York: Wiley.

Nussbaum, M. C. (1978). *Aristotle's De Motu Animalium.* Princeton, NJ: Princeton University Press.

Ohman, A., & Mineka, S. (2001). Fears, phobias, and preparedness: Toward an evolved module of fear and fear learning. *Psychological Review, 108,* 483–522.

Packer, C., Herbst, L., Pusey, A. E., et al. (1988). Reproductive success of lions. In T. H. Clutton-Brock (ed.), *Reproductive success* (pp. 363–83). Chicago, IL: University of Chicago Press.

Papini, M. R. (1998). Classical conditioning. In G. Greenberg & M. M. Haraway (eds.), *Comparative psychology: A handbook* (pp. 523–30). New York: Garland.

Papini, M. R. (2002). Pattern and process in the evolution of learning. *Psychological Review, 109,* 186–201.

Petrie, M., Halliday, T., & Sanders, C. (1991). Peahens prefer peacocks with elaborate trains. *Animal Behaviour, 41,* 323–31.

Petterson, N. (1960). Control of behavior by presentation of an imprinted stimulus. *Science, 132,* 1395–6.

Platel, R. (1979). Brain weight–body weight relationships. In C. Gans, R. G. Northcutt, & P. Ulinski (eds.), *Biology of the reptilia* (vol. 9, pp. 147–71). London: Academic Press.

Reznick, D. N., Shaw, F. H., Rodd, F. H., & Shaw, R. G. (1997). Evaluation of the rate of evolution in natural populations of guppies (*Poecilia reticulata*). *Science, 275,* 1934–7.

Ricker, J. P., & Hirsch, J. (1985). Evolution of an instinct under long-term divergent selection for geotaxis in domesticated populations of *Drosophila melanogaster*. *Journal of Comparative Psychology, 99,* 380–90.

Riddel, W. I., & Corl, K. G. (1977). Comparative investigation of the relationship between cerebral indices and learning abilities. *Brain, Behavior, and Evolution, 14,* 385–98.

Rose, J. K., & Rankin, C. H. (2001). Analyses of habituation in *Caenorhabditis elegans*. *Learning and Memory, 8,* 63–9.

Rumbaugh, D. M., & Pate, J. L. (1984). The evolution of cognition in primates: A comparative perspective. In H. L. Roitblatt, T. G. Bever, & H. S. Terrace (eds.), *Animal cognition* (pp. 569–87). Hillsdale, NJ: Erlbaum.

Sackett, G. P. (1967). Some persistent effects of different rearing conditions on preadult social behavior of monkeys. *Journal of Comparative and Physiological Psychology, 64,* 363–5.

Salas, C., Broglio, C., Rodriguez, F., Lopez, J. C., Portavella, M., & Torres, B. (1996). Telencephalic ablation in goldfish impairs performance in a "spatial constancy" problem but not in a cued one. *Behavioural Brain Research, 79,* 193–200.

Schmajuk, N. A. (1997). *Animal learning and cognition. A neural-network approach.* Cambridge, UK: Cambridge University Press.

Scott, J. P., & Fuller, J. L. (1965). *Genetics and the social behavior of the dog.* Chicago, IL: University of Chicago Press.

Sherry, D. F., Jacobs, L. F., & Gaulin, S. J. C. (1992). Spatial memory and adaptive specialization of the hippocampus. *Trends in Neuroscience, 15,* 298–303.

Sherry, D. F., Vaccarino, A. L., Buckenham, K., & Hertz, R. S. (1989). The hippocampal complex of food-storing birds. *Brain, Behavior, and Evolution, 34,* 308–17.

Singh, D. (1993). Adaptive signficance of female physical attractiveness: Role of the waist-to-hip ratio. *Journal of Personality and Social Psychology, 65,* 293–307.

Spencer, A. N. (1989). Chemical and electrical synaptic transmission in the Cnidaria. In P. A. V. Anderson (ed.), *Evolution of the first nervous systems* (pp. 33–53). New York: Plenum.

Stephan, H., Baron, G., & Flahm, H. D. (1991). *Comparative brain research in mammals. Vol. 1. Insectivora.* New York: Springer-Verlag.

Taborsky, M. (1984). Broodcare helpers in the cichlid fish *Lamprologus brichardi*: Their costs and benefits. *Animal Behaviour, 32,* 1236–52.

Thompson, R. F. (1986). The neurobiology of learning and memory. *Science, 233,* 941–7.

Thompson, R., & McConnell, J. V. (1955). Classical conditioning in the planarian *Dugesia dorotocephala*. *Journal of Comparative and Physiological Psychology, 48,* 65–8.

Tinbergen, N. (1963). On aims and methods of ethology. *Zeitschrift für Tierpsychologie, 20,* 410–33.

Trivers, R. L. (1971). The evolution of reciprocal altruism. *Quarterly Review of Biology, 46,* 35–57.

Trut, L. N. (1999). Early canid domestication: The farm-fox experiment. *American Scientist*, *87*, 160–9.

Vidal, J.-M. (1980). The relations between filial and sexual imprinting in the domestic fowl: Effects of age and social experience. *Animal Behaviour*, *28*, 880–91.

Wen, J. Y. M., Kumar, N., Morrison, G., et al. (1997). Mutations that prevent learning in *C. elegans*. *Behavioral Neuroscience*, *111*, 354–68.

Wilkinson, G. (1984). Reciprocal food sharing in vampire bats. *Nature*, *308*, 182–4.

## Further Reading

Butler, A. B., & Hodos, W. (1996). *Comparative vertebrate neuroanatomy. Evolution and adaptation*. New York: Wiley.

Cartwright, J. (2000). *Evolution and human behavior*. Cambridge, MA: MIT Press.

Domjan, M. (1998). *The principles of learning and behavior* (4th edn.). Pacific Grove, CA: Brooks/Cole.

Greenberg, G., & Haraway, M. M. (eds.) (1998). *Comparative pychology: A handbook*. New York: Garland Press.

Greenberg, G., & Haraway, M. (2002). *Principles of comparative psychology*. Boston, MA: Allyn & Bacon.

Houck, L. D., & Drickamer, L. C. (eds.) (1996). *Foundations of animal behavior. Classic papers with commentaries*. Chicago: University of Chicago Press.

Macphail, E. M. (1982). *Brain and intelligence in vertebrates*. Oxford: Oxford University Press.

Papini, M. R. (2002). *Comparative psychology. Evolution and development of behavior*. Upper Saddle River, NJ: Prentice-Hall.

Roberts, W. (1997). *Principles of animal cognition*. Boston, MA: McGraw Hill.

Shettleworth, S. J. (1998). *Cognition, evolution, and behavior*. Oxford: Oxford University Press.

## Main Scientific Journals

*Animal Behaviour*: http://www.academicpress.com/anbehav

*Animal Cognition*: http://link.springer.de/link/service/journals/10071/

*Animal Learning and Behavior*: http://www.psychonomic.org/alb.htm

*Behavioural Processes*: http://www.elsevier.com/inca/publications/store/5/0/6/0/4/6/506046.pub.htt

*International Journal of Comparative Psychology*: http://rana.uqam.ca/ijcp

*Journal of Comparative Psychology*: http://www.ComparativePsychology.org

*Journal of the Experimental Analysis of Behavior*: http://www.envmed.rochester.edu/wwwrap/behavior/jeab/jeabhome.htm

*Journal of Experimental Psychology: Animal Behavior Processes*: http://www.apa.org/journals/xan.html

*Learning and Motivation*: http://www.academicpress.com/www/journal/lm.htm

*Quarterly Journal of Experimental Psychology: Comparative and Physiological Psychology*: http://www.tandf.co.uk/journals/pp/02724995.html

# CHAPTER ELEVEN

# Animal Learning and Animal Cognition

## Lewis Barker and Jeffrey S. Katz

## Introduction

Animal learning and animal cognition are separate but related fields of study within psychology, each with an identifiable history that often intertwines the other. Animal learning can be defined as a permanent change in behavior resulting from experiences in an environment. Most typically, however, animal learning is understandable as reinforced practice within a laboratory setting. Animal cognition refers to ". . . the mechanism by which animals acquire, process, store, and act on information from the environment" (Shettleworth, 1998, p. 5). In some ways Shettleworth's definition subsumes animal learning, because in most learning experiments an animal's responses are signaled (controlled) by stimulus information. Furthermore, nuances of language notwithstanding, the concept of learning presupposes a memory system in which response tendencies are stored. Animal learning and cognition can be conceptualized from within the general framework of Darwin's theory of evolution, in terms of brain mechanisms, and as systematic behavioral change in laboratory settings. The purpose of this chapter is to present an overview of animal learning and animal cognition, and to explore their similarities and differences in laboratory settings.

### Historical antecedents in animal learning

Arbitrary but defendable dates for the modern scientific interest in nonhuman animal behavior and animal mind are occasioned by three books published by Charles Darwin: *The Origin of Species* (1859), *Descent of Man* (1871), and *The Expression of Emotion in Man and Animals* (1872). In these books he simply pointed out the reasonableness of the proposition that humans share with other animals continuities of behavior and mind as well as body: "Psychology will be built on a new foundation, that of the necessary acquirement of each mental power and capacity by gradation" (Darwin, [1859] 1979, p. 458). Since that time diverse experiments and theory building in behavioral biology and, within psychology, in comparative psychology, animal learning, and animal cognition, have addressed how humans and other animals behave, perceive, learn, remember, and think.

Whereas comparative psychology and studies of animal behavior are concerned with cross-species differences in behavior (see Papini's chapter in this volume), animal learning is primarily concerned with the variability of behavior within a species. Given similar genes, how do members of the same species interact with specially constructed environments in laboratories in ways that provide insight into how they perceive, learn, remember, think, and behave differently from one another? Classical conditioning experiments over a century ago by Ivan Pavlov (summarized in Pavlov [1927] 1960), and instrumental learning experiments by Edward Thorndike (1898), supported the idea that species behave in a manner that reflects both their genetic endowment and their past learning experiences. Since that time, psychologists have become increasingly confident that their experiments also provide evidence about nonhuman animal thinking and other cognitive processes.

Contemporaneous with the growth of nonhuman animal learning, nonhuman animal cognition became an important part of experimental psychology around the turn of the twentieth century. In *Animal Intelligence* (1882), George J. Romanes supported Darwin's continuity hypothesis. Romanes, however, was criticized for relying on anecdotal evidence when making inferences concerning the cognitive abilities of animals (Morgan, [1894] 1977). Morgan espoused the importance of empirical investigation when reasoning about animal cognition (Morgan, [1894] 1977, p. 304). The methods were soon developed and experimenters began examining cognitive aspects of learning: in a puzzle box (Thorndike, 1911), in a delayed reaction procedure (Hunter, 1913; Tinklepaugh, 1932), in maze learning (Tolman & Honzik, 1930), and tool use (Kohler, 1925). Although the hegemony of behaviorism became strong in the 1930s and beyond, some studies continued to have a cognitive flavor (for a review see Dewsbury, 2000). But it was not until shortly after the cognitive revolution of the 1960s that nonhuman animal cognition had a renewed vigor. *Cognitive Processes in Animal Behavior* (Hulse, Fowler, & Honig, 1978) and *Animal Cognition* (Roitblat, Bever, & Terrace, 1984) signified this restored interest in animal learning and cognition. Since that time animal cognition has continued to mirror its analog, human cognition, in scope and focus while maintaining its roots in associative learning and ethology. A textbook comparison of cognitive psychology (e.g., Solso, 2001) and animal cognition (Roberts, 1998; Shettleworth, 1998) clearly emphasizes this point. The current status of animal cognition and its ambitious goal is a continued integration of animal learning, comparative psychology, cognitive science, neuroscience, and experimental ethology (Czeschlik, 1998; Roitblat, 1987; Wasserman, 1997).

## Animal Learning

Scientists study animal learning and cognition from several different perspectives, and often for very different reasons. In this section we will briefly review the main currents in contemporary animal learning. A later section will deal with experiments in animal cognition.

## Pavlovian conditioning

Ivan Pavlov's experiments and his resulting theory of associative conditioning continue to give direction to the study of animal learning. His early research focused on reflexes and anticipatory salivation in a dog about to be fed ("psychic secretions," caused by the dog's expectations). From the outset he framed these experiments within a modern biological context of both evolved adaptation and brain–behavior relations:

> It seems obvious that the whole activity of the organism should conform to definite laws. If the animal were not in exact correspondence with its environment, it would, sooner or later, cease to exist. To give a biological example: if, instead of being attracted to food, the animal were repelled by it, or if instead of running from fire the animal threw itself into the fire, then it would quickly perish. The animal must respond to changes in the environment in such a manner that its responsive activity is directed towards the preservation of its existence. (Pavlov, [1927] 1960, pp. 7–8)

Likewise, in a series of experiments on how new associations to the salivary reflex were learned (reported in Pavlov [1927] 1960) Pavlov and his collaborators investigated the role of the *visual analyzers* and *auditory analyzers* located in the dog's cerebral hemispheres. Although his understanding of physiology is now considered misguided, his strategy of studying brain–behavior relations provided a clear alternative to the black-box formulations of the behaviorists, as we see below.

Pavlov's genius was the simple recognition that reflexes could be modified. That is, he recognized that through the process of association formation, a new environmental signal (an arbitrary sight or sound) could take the place of the original eliciting stimulus of food in a salivation reflex. Likewise, other reflexes governed by other parts of the brain could also be conditioned by simply pairing the reflex with a unique signaling stimulus. Hence, Pavlov variously paired food (or a sour taste that also caused salivation) with an electric bell, a metronome, "bubbling water," tuning forks, pictures, stroking the skin, vibration, and other stimuli. What is important is that the bell or tuning fork is a *neutral stimulus* that by itself does not cause salivation. Pavlov referred to the food as the *unconditioned stimulus (US)* and the dog's salivation as the *unconditioned response (UR)*. For Pavlov's dog, a sour taste or the taste of food were USs that elicited the innate involuntary reflex of salivation, the UR. Conditioning is said to occur when, after repeated pairings, the neutral stimulus by itself (now called a *conditioned stimulus*, or *CS*) causes the animal to salivate (the *conditioned response*, or *CR*). This change in behavior as the result of experience, Pavlov recognized, was an example of learning.

Pavlov's interest in a dog's "visual analyzer" anticipated the growth of visual information-processing models in the mid-twentieth century, and yet more current interests in how vision is organized in avian and mammalian brains. Indeed, his early experiments in *animal psychophysics* anticipated research that has since provided a clearer understanding of the sensory and perceptual capacities of various animals. (Animal psychophysics clearly plays a role in the development of methodology in animal cognition experiments.) For example, Pavlov was interested in processes of stimulus generalization and discrimination.

In one series of experiments, he first conditioned a dog to salivate to a $CS^+$, a picture of a circle. Then, on alternate trials, he showed an ellipse to the dog, but never followed it with food. (By convention, a trial of "CS followed by food" is designated as a $CS^+$ *trial* and trials of "CS without food" are called $CS^-$ *trials.*) A *conditioned discrimination* developed when the dog reliably salivated to the $CS^+$ (circle) but not to the $CS^-$ (ellipse). This technique, applied to other visual stimuli, and to other sensory modalities, is a first example of how animal psychophysics, using animal learning techniques, provided information about what an animal perceives. Such techniques, then, are basic to the study of nonhuman animal cognition.

## Contemporary methods of classical conditioning

Few experimenters now study Pavlovian salivary conditioning, but many study association formation using methodologies such as a classical eyeblink conditioning procedure, fear conditioning, and taste aversion conditioning, using both human and nonhuman animals. We will briefly look at these three methods. In eyeblink conditioning, a puff of air to a human, rabbit, or rat's eye elicits a reflexive blinking response. When a tone (CS) is presented immediately prior to the air puff (US), animals can be conditioned to blink to the sound of the tone. A number of investigators have used this classical preparation for many years to study associative learning theory (Gormezano, Kehoe, & Marshall, 1983). More recently, human eyeblink conditioning has provided insight into the role of awareness in conditioning by demonstrating that humans aware of the CS–US contingency can be conditioned in fewer trials (Woodruff-Pak, 1999).

John B. Watson's classical experiment on "Little Albert," in which the sight of a rat (the CS) was paired with a loud noise (the US), was one of the first demonstrations of human fear conditioning in a laboratory setting (Watson & Rayner, 1920). The fear conditioning method used most frequently has been to sound a tone (CS) paired with electric shock (US) while a rat presses a lever to obtain food (Ferster & Skinner, 1957; Kamin, 1965). If the intensity of the shock is just strong enough to cause the rat to momentarily stop pressing the lever, after a number of tone–shock pairings, the rat will learn to associate the tone with shock. Then, when the tone is sounded alone, the rat will stop lever-pressing, presumably due to the tone's fear-inducing properties. This procedure is sometimes called *conditioned suppression*, because the tone suppresses the rat's lever-pressing. This method has proven to be most successful in building a theory of association formation (Rescorla, 1967, 1968; Rescorla & Wagner, 1972).

Association formation has also been intensively studied in conditioned taste aversion experiments in which laboratory rats are allowed to drink a novel-flavored drink (the CS) and then are made sick after being administered an illness-inducing drug or toxin (the US). Compared to a control group that has not experienced this pairing, the conditioned rats begin to avoid the flavored drink. They are said to have developed a *conditioned taste aversion* – disgust for a flavor that has been paired with illness (Barker, Best, & Domjan, 1977; Garcia, Ervin, & Koelling, 1966). We will discuss some relevant taste aversion experiments in a later section.

Classical conditioning has played an enormous role in the development of concepts in animal learning. By the early 1970s, one historian reported that over 7,000 conditioning experiments had been published in 29 languages, and that of the 59 most important terms and concepts that describe learning, 34 could be attributed to Pavlov (Razran, 1971). The similarities in outcome of these diverse classical conditioning procedures is evidenced by phenomena common to them all, beginning with predictable acquisition effects resulting from forward, backward, delay, and trace conditioning acquisition procedures. Likewise, rate and level of conditioning is predictably related to CS and US intensity. Such learning typically requires multiple trials and short intervals between the CS and the US. Other experimental manipulations produce response extinction, generalization and discrimination, blocking, higher-order conditioning, sensory precon-ditioning, conditioned inhibition, latent inhibition over a wide range of stimuli and reflexes of diverse animals (for relevant experiments and discussion of classical condition-ing as reflecting "general processes," see Barker, 2001; Domjan, 2003; Macintosh, 1983; Mazur, 2002).

## Instrumental learning

Edward Thorndike (Thorndike, 1911, 1932) also formulated general principles of learning following his observations of cats, chickens, and other animals attempting to escape confinement from an experimental chamber. Each of his puzzle boxes had a latching door that could be opened by animals trapped inside. With repeated trials they took less time to escape, and Thorndike proposed the *law of effect* to account for this. The law of effect simply states that across species, a response that is followed by a pleasant consequence (*satisfier*) will tend to be repeated, whereas a response that is followed by an unpleasant consequence (*annoyer*) will tend to decrease in frequency. In Thorndike's terms, the memory that formed when a hungry cat escaped from con-finement tended to be "stamped in," whereas unsuccessful movements were forgotten. Further, it can be argued that the law of effect is adaptive, necessarily guiding an animal's behavior to correct solutions (Dennett, 1975).

*Operant conditioning*   Most textbooks of animal learning that begin with classical condi-tioning, next describe Thorndike's famous "puzzle box" research, and then introduce *behaviorists*, and what has come to be known as the *experimental analysis of behavior*. Behaviorists also interpret their findings within a general process framework of associat-ive learning. In operant conditioning experiments, using (primarily) avian and mam-malian species, behaviorists investigated how an animal's behavior can be brought under stimulus control through the application of reinforcers and punishers. For several decades a relatively small number of behavioral learning theorists dominated the thinking of psychologists – even outside the area of animal learning (the writings of Clark Hull, 1943, 1952 and B. F. Skinner, 1938, 1963 are representative). Contemporary work with a few animal species continues to illustrate general learning processes in all animals (including humans), and is published in journals such as *Journal of the Experimental*

*Analysis of Behavior*, *The Journal of Experimental Psychology: Animal Behavior Processes*, *Animal Learning and Behavior*, and *Learning and Motivation*. Implicit in this philosophical framework is the notion that the study of a few species of birds and mammals can serve as models for how humans learn and behave.

What seems to be characteristic of human behavior, thought the Harvard behaviorist B. F. Skinner (1904–90), is how arbitrary so much of it is. Skinner thought that humans were unlike other animals in that our behavior was less predictable, more idiosyncratic. Individual differences characterize our species, and the human ecological niche seems to be whatever we want to make it. What was needed, Skinner reasoned, was a theory of learning that accounted for nonreflexive nonadaptive behavior. Skinner called his method of experimentally analyzing learned behavior *operant conditioning*. Starting in the 1930s and continuing for 50 years, he and his many students systematically studied how animals learn in an "operant chamber" (Skinner, 1938, 1963). For many years he focused his research strategy on how food reinforcers influence the rate and patterning of "arbitrary" operant responses such as lever pressing in rats and key pecking in pigeons. These methods continue to be used in laboratories around the world.

Skinner's operant conditioning is best thought of as a variant of Thorndike's instrumental learning. By removing animals from their natural environment, he intentionally sought to investigate behavior that was not heavily influenced by instinct (i.e., genetically organized). He selected the arbitrary responses of lever pressing and key pecking because they did *not* resemble the fixed action patterns ethologists studied, or other biologically prepared responses, such as how rats foraged in mazes. He called the lever-pressing response an *operant*, which he defined as a response that "operates" on the environment. Skinner showed that he could increase lever pressing in rats and key pecking in pigeons (both operant responses) by providing a *positive reinforcer* immediately following the desired response. Though he typically used food, Skinner defined a *positive reinforcer* as *any* stimulus following an operant response that had the effect of increasing the rate of responses. The process of *reinforcement* (or positive reinforcement) is effected by providing a hungry animal with food after it makes an operant response, such that the food *reinforces* the animal's performance of the operant. Skinner used the verb *to reinforce* in the way Pavlov used the verb *to condition*. In sum, what Skinner called *operant conditioning* involved selecting an improbable response, such as lever pressing, and, through the process of reinforcement, increasing the probability of its occurrence (Ferster & Skinner, 1957). Highly distinctive patterns of lever pressing are produced when reinforcement is delivered to animals following predetermined rules. The various ways in which responses are reinforced are called *schedules of reinforcement*. Schedules range from *continuous reinforcement*, in which each response is reinforced, to *partial reinforcement*, in which patterns of responses are reinforced.

One goal of the experimental analysis of behavior is to understand how an animal can be brought under the control of environmental stimuli. A stimulus that controls responding, by predicting that a response will produce a reinforcer, is called a *discriminative* stimulus (abbreviated $S^+$). A stimulus that signals that a response will not be reinforced is called a *negative discriminative stimulus* (abbreviated $S^-$). When trained animals respond reliably in the presence of an $S^+$, but do *not* respond in the presence of an $S^-$, they are said to be under *stimulus control*.

## *Evolutionary considerations in animal learning*

Together, operant conditioning and classical conditioning experiments define "animal learning." Contrast the forgoing Pavlovian and behaviorist approaches, which espouse a virtual interchangeability of behavior among species, with that of a comparative psychologist who either studies types of learning across a spectrum of species (Bitterman, 1975) or a particular species for the purpose of identifying the interaction of general learning processes with species-specific behaviors (Domjan, 1987; Galef, 1987; Papini, 2002).

The tension between general process learning approaches and behaviors specific to a species continues to the present (see Domjan, 1983; Timberlake, 1994; Shettleworth, 1998). Sara Shettleworth has proposed that all species show the general process of associative learning: "The generality of associative learning can be understood if it is seen as an adaptation for learning about physical causal relationships among all kinds of objects and events in the world" (Shettleworth, 1998, p. 43). Yet she also asserts that because each species occupies a particular niche, one that poses unique problems of survival, different species have evolved specific solutions to these problems – that is, species-specific behaviors. Next we look at several examples of the interaction of general processes with species-specific behaviors.

In their study of the role that conditioning plays in the sexual behavior of Japanese quail, Michael Domjan and his colleagues provide an example of how general learning processes interact with species-specific behaviors. They report that male quail make indiscriminate sexual approaches to either sex, and apparently learn to prefer females to males only after successful copulation with the former, a reinforcing event (Nash & Domjan, 1991). Further, they found that artificially colored feathers on birds associated with successful copulation were preferred to naturally colored feathers, as might be expected from a species-specific behavior perspective (Domjan, O'Vary, & Greene 1988).

Breland and Breland (1961) asserted that "general laws" of animal learning (cf. general processes) were not supported by some of their laboratory observations. They trained pigs, raccoons, chickens, and other animals to perform an instrumental response that resulted in an earned token. The animal would then pick up the token and drop it into a "bank," producing a food reinforcer. However, some animals "misbehaved": "Not only [would a raccoon] not let go of the coins, but he spent seconds, even minutes, rubbing them together . . . and dipping them into the [bank] . . . The rubbing behavior became worse as time went on, in spite of non-reinforcement" (Breland & Breland, 1961, p. 682). The Brelands interpreted such "misbehavior" as *instinctive drift*, innately determined, species-specific feeding behaviors that interfered with newly conditioned, arbitrary, operant responses.

Likewise, John Garcia proposed a biologically prepared form of learning that contradicted general process "laws," to wit, the necessity of multiple trials and short intervals between CSs and USs, and between responses and their consequences. In a series of experiments, he found that rats could learn taste aversions in one trial under conditions in which the CS (taste) was separated from the US (a sickness-inducing event) by several hours (Garcia et al., 1966). In other research, now known as the "bright, noisy, tasty water" experiment (Garcia & Koelling, 1966), rats learned specific associations better when cues matched their consequences. Rats licked a tube containing saccharin dissolved in water ("tasty" water), completing an electric circuit that briefly flashed a light ("bright water") that also produced a brief clicking noise – hence the conditioned stimulus of bright, noisy, tasty water. After drinking the bright, noisy, tasty water (the CS), half the rats were punished by being briefly shocked (a US); the other half were exposed to a sickening ionizing radiation experience (also a US). To assess the results of the conditioning, the researchers then separated the bright, noisy, tasty water into its component parts during extinction tests. They gave the rats a choice of drinking either bright, noisy water or tasty water. The rats easily learned to associate tastes with poisoning, and sights and sounds with electric shock, but not taste–shock associations or audiovisual–poison associations. Garcia reasoned that rats that rapidly learn that "if it tastes like this, it makes me sick" will live to reproduce another day. Likewise, Paul Rozin proposed that animals are evolutionarily prepared to learn certain things in certain ways: "What an organism learns in the laboratory or in his natural habitat is the result not only of the contingencies which he faces and has faced in his past but also of the contingencies which his species faced before him – its evolutionary history and genetic outcome" (Rozin & Kalat, 1971, p. 460).

Rozin's concept of preparedness, in turn, can be interpreted in terms of the distal (genetic) and proximal (learned) causes of behavior. The distal causes of a rat's feeding behavior include foraging strategies and other species-specific behavioral tendencies, such as neophobia when confronted with unfamiliar foods. Even hungry rats will approach new foods cautiously: they sniff, retreat, approach, sniff and nibble (taste), and retreat. The brain organization underlying this innate wariness toward new foods is likely to be the (distal) basis for the rat's ability to form flavor–illness associations in only one trial – the trial being a proximal cause of its feeding behavior.

From his research, John Garcia anticipated a model of learning that is now conceptualized in terms of evolved brain modules (Shettleworth, 1998). Specifically, he proposed that rats had evolved brain systems that processed gustatory-visceral information, and others, telereceptor-cutaneous information (Garcia & Ervin, 1968). Shettleworth's adaptively specialized modules are "like a Swiss Army knife, a general-purpose tool made of many specialized parts . . . encapsulated information-processing mechanisms" (Shettleworth, 1998, p. 567).

Despite Garcia's analysis, however, in most respects the results of taste aversion learning experiments support general process learning with respect to generalization and discrimination, extinction, higher-order conditioning, latent inhibition, conditioned inhibition, and other phenomena. That is, evolutionary preparedness and modules aside for the moment, taste aversion learning *is* similar to other forms of animal learning in a wide variety of species (Domjan, 1983). A typical one-trial learning taste-aversion experiment differs from other animal learning experiments in critical parametric ways that may account for the apparent differences. For example, a rat might drink a flavored solution (CS) for 10 minutes and then be administered a high dose of an emetic (US) causing 30 minutes or so of sickness. However, if the CS is 1 ml squirted on the rat's tongue (lasting a few seconds at most), and the rat is then administered a low dose emetic, the learning curve resembles more traditional conditioning experiments in that multiple trials and short CS–US intervals are required (Monroe & Barker, 1979). Other research has shown that tastes *can* be associated with electric shock, and sights and sounds with nausea.

## Animal Cognition

One of the central themes of animal learning and cognition has been how animals solve problems. In this section we briefly review several of the current topics representative of the field of animal cognition in regard to problem solving. Recall that Skinner rejected experiments on how rats solved mazes because he thought behavioral analyses of how reinforcers and punishers controlled simple responding would be more productive in building a science of behavior. Some animal learning researchers, working outside the tradition of classical and instrumental conditioning, asked more interesting questions of animals. What problems can an animal solve? Can problems be arranged that bear on whether or how animals "think"? What are the strategies that underlie such cognition? How do these strategies differ across species? The ultimate objective of animal cognition is determining the answer to these questions. For more in-depth discussion on these issues and others we recommend *Principles of Animal Cognition* by William Roberts (1998) and *Cognition, Evolution, and Behavior* by Sara Shettleworth (1998).

Research in animal cognition is reported in *Animal Cognition, Animal Learning & Behavior, Cognitive Science, Journal of Comparative Psychology, Journal of the Experimental Analysis of Behavior, Journal of Experimental Psychology: Animal Behavior Processes, Psychological Science, Psychonomic Bulletin & Review,* and others. A survey of journals and books devoted to animal cognition will find topics spanning perception and attention, memory, spatial cognition, timing, counting, serial learning, concept learning, problem solving, foraging, theory of mind, communication, and language. Instead of attempting to summarize each of these areas succinctly we will instead focus in greater detail on perception, attention, and concept learning. The overarching theme that binds this focus is one that involves the interaction between item-specific and relational strategies. Here a strategy describes a recurring pattern of behavior that depends on the presence or absence of certain cues. Animals may actively select strategically among such rules (cf. Krechevsky, 1932), but that is not what is intended by our use of the term. There is little compelling evidence that nonhuman animals actively select between strategies.

### Perception and attention

Research in animal perception and attention has been heavily influenced by theories in human perception and attention. Perception is often couched as involving an interaction between bottom-up and top-down processes. Bottom-up processes are stimulus-driven, preattentive, parallel, and automatic. Top-down processes are effortful, attentive, serial, and memory-based. The study of visual search reveals the interaction between these two processes. We selected visual search because it demonstrates the multidisciplinary approach of animal cognition better than other topics. Visual search (and texture segregation) has become a classic procedure in which to illustrate bottom-up and top-down processes in both human (e.g., Treisman & Gelade, 1980; Wolfe, 2000) and nonhuman species (Blough & Blough, 1997; Cook, Katz, & Cavoto, 1998; De Weerd, Vandenbussche, & Orban, 1992; Reid & Shettleworth, 1992). These experiments provide insight into the ways that animals search for objects.

Feature display

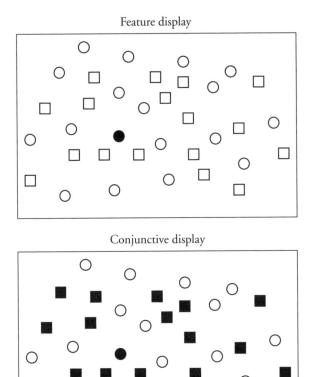

Conjunctive display

**Figure 11.1**   Representative examples of a feature display and a conjunctive display used in a typical visual search task. In the feature display the target (black circle) differs in the color dimension from the distractors, which allows for the target to pop out. In the conjunctive display the target (black circle) is defined by a combination of features shared in common with the distractors, which produces a slower more effortful search in comparison to the feature display.

*Visual search* In a visual search task, a subject searches for a target (e.g., an orange A) that is randomly embedded in a distractor surround (e.g., blue Us). The task is to indicate either where the target is located or whether a target is present or not. In visual search experiments involving nonhuman animals, birds in chambers, or chaired monkeys, view visual displays and receive reinforcement for accurate responses detected by panel contact or a touchscreen. To distinguish between parallel and serial searches participants are tested with *feature* and *conjunctive* displays. For feature displays (e.g., a black circle in a surround of white circles and squares), targets are rapidly found as they automatically "pop out" to the observer (see Figure 11.1). For conjunctive displays (e.g., a black circle in a surround of white circles and black squares), targets require more time to find than feature targets, as they require effortful serial search. The reason why search is more difficult for conjunctive targets is because all the features of the target are shared with the distractor features. By way of comparison with traditional animal learning experiments, the target features can be considered perceptually challenging *discriminative stimuli*, $S^+$s, and distractor features as *negative discriminative stimuli*, $S^-$s.

What else is known about effortful serial search? If the number of distractors surrounding the target is increased, reaction time is unaffected during feature searches. By contrast, during conjunctive searches, reaction time increases linearly with the number of distractors. Additionally, search time can be slowed if the similarity between the target and distractors is increased. All of these findings can be explained via the type of signal produced from bottom-up mechanisms (for further discussion see Treisman, 1986; Wolfe, 1994). These findings have been demonstrated in a number of species, including humans, pigeons, and blue jays (Blough & Blough, 1997; Bond, 1983; Cook, 2000; Cook, Cavoto, & Cavoto, 1996; Pietrewicz & Kamil, 1979; Reid & Shettleworth, 1992).

An interesting series of related experiments has focused on the mechanisms of search in avian species using a stimulus repetition procedure. Stimulus repetition effects on search involve a top-down process because search is directly influenced by the memory of a repeated item. Historically, Lucas Tinbergen (1960) inspired this research by proposing the concept of a search image. A search image is a (memorial) representation of the target item that is currently being searched for. Importantly, Tinbergen believed that by knowing the identity of the target item the searcher has an advantage in finding that item. A search image would be particularly useful when the target (e.g., bug, moth, grain) does not readily pop out; that is, when the target is cryptic. One way to test the search image hypothesis is through stimulus repetition. Typically, a repetition and a nonrepetition condition are conducted. In the repetition condition, a specific target item is repeated from trial to trial. In the nonrepetition condition the target item is pseudorandomly selected from a set of potential target items from trial to trial. Pietrewicz and Kamil (1979) found that blue jays were more accurate in their search for a cryptic moth on a bark substrate if the moth was repeated from trial to trial (i.e., repetition condition) in comparison to when the identity of the cryptic moth was not known from trial to trial (i.e., nonrepetition condition). This result is evidence for a search image effect because search is limited to one item, thereby allowing the bird to focus its attention and search for the features associated with the cryptic moth. Similar effects have also been found for repetition of cryptic grains and artificial computer-generated stimuli.

More recently, in a series of stimulus repetition experiments, Katz and Cook (2000, 2002) summarized five possible strategies in which animals may search for target items. Overall, pigeons are sensitive to two classes of strategies: relational and item-specific strategies. Relational strategies are derived from comparing different parts of visual displays and do not depend on learning the specific identity of the features of the targets and distractors. Item-specific strategies depend on the absolute identity of the features of the targets and distractors. The five strategies are as follows. First, an odd-item strategy is utilized when a target is highly dissimilar from the distractors (Blough, 1989; Bond & Riley, 1991; Cook, 1992; Katz & Cook, 2000; Reid & Shettleworth, 1992). When a target does not pop out, then other strategies are necessary. A relational distractor avoidance strategy is used when a target is cryptic and the target and distractor identity is unknown (Katz & Cook, 2000). Learning *within* a trial the identity of distractors, as defined by number and initial encounter, the searcher can find the target item by knowing what to avoid. Third, an item-specific distractor avoidance strategy can be used when a feature of the distractor item is known in advance, but target features are not known in advance (Katz & Cook, 2000). That is, learning *across* trials the identity of distractors, the searcher can find the target item by knowing specifically what to avoid. Fourth, a conditional expectancy strategy is used when a specific distractor predicts a specific target (Blough, 1993; Katz & Cook, 2002). Fifth, an item-specific target approach strategy (i.e., the search image hypothesis) is used when a feature of the target is known in advance (e.g., Blough & Blough, 1997; Bond, 1983; Katz & Cook, 2000; Langley, Riley, Bond, & Goel, 1996; Pietrewicz & Kamil, 1979).

In summary, birds are able to utilize virtually all the possible combinations of repeated stimulus information. We suspect the same is true for other highly visual animals. The current direction of this research is in further understanding when and why these strategies are utilized to solve different search problems. Factors for future research that are or may be important are experience, set size, frequency of repetitions (encounters), perceptual discriminability, and stimulus mapping to target and distractor sets.

## Strategies and concepts

In this section, we further look at some experiments that gave rise to contemporary interests in animal cognition related to rule learning and concept formation.

*Rule learning* Harry Harlow tested rhesus monkeys by showing them two small toys, a red block and a thimble, as exemplars. One of the two toys was designated "correct," and choosing the correct one was rewarded by allowing the monkey access to a raisin in a food cup beneath the toy. Harlow repeated this procedure, called a *learning set*, for six trials using the same two toys; then he introduced two new toys in a new learning set. A typical experiment involved hundreds of learning sets (Harlow, 1949). Harlow found that monkeys eventually learned a *win–stay, lose–shift strategy* that allowed them to make correct choices about 75 percent of the time. In this strategy, animals continue doing the same thing that produced reinforcement in the past (win–stay), and switch to something different when they are not reinforced (lose–shift).

Once the monkeys had mastered this concept, they no longer needed six trials to learn the correct response to each new set of paired objects. In Harlow's terms, they had learned how to learn, and began to apply the general strategy of win–stay, lose–shift on the second trial of each set. About 250 trials later, after *learning to learn*, Harlow's monkeys were about 98 percent accurate in their responses on the second trial of each newly introduced pair of stimuli. Further studies using the learning set procedure with other species (birds, cats, new world monkeys, rats, squirrels) demonstrated that these species could also demonstrate learning to learn (see Figure 11.2). Unfortunately, different rates in acquiring the learning strategies involved in learning to learn were used to rank species intelligence (see Shettleworth 1998 for arguments against such ranking). Such ranking of species intelligence became fashionable and other procedures were

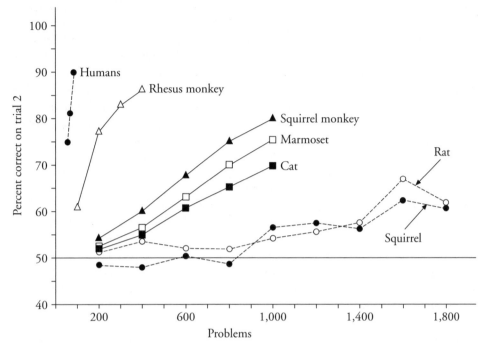

**Figure 11.2**   The percentage of correct responses on trial 2 of the learning set is plotted as a function of the number of problems encountered in training. On each learning set problem, the probability of making a correct response is 50 percent. Note that after a thousand trials, rats and squirrels finally begin to perform slightly better than chance. Rhesus monkeys clearly outperform cats and squirrel monkeys (from Warren, 1965). The data from children aged 2 to 5 years (Harlow, 1949) have been added to Warren's (1965) comparative data.

mistakenly used to assess such cognitive ability. One set of procedures used was aimed at exploring abstract concept learning.

*Abstract concepts*   Abstract concepts permit us to apply organized knowledge concerning specific situations to novel problems. There is debate over what constitutes an abstract concept (e.g., Delius, 1994; Herrnstein, 1990; Thompson, 1995). For clarity, when referred to in this chapter, concepts are abstract when their application transcends the examples (i.e., stimuli) used in their formation. One of the central themes of comparative research has been which species can or cannot attain abstract concepts. The motivation for this research was sparked by the challenges raised by some comparative psychologists and philosophers that nonhumans or nonlanguage-trained animals could not attain abstract concepts (Locke, [1690] 1975; Morgan, [1894] 1977; Premack, 1983b; for a review see Wasserman, 1993). The result of such beliefs has been theorists using concept learning ability to artificially rank species intelligence (D'Amato, Salmon, & Colombo, 1985; Premack, 1978, 1983a; Thomas, 1980). An important result from the challenge has been an impressive growing list of species that can attain abstract concepts, including human children, nonhuman primates, dolphins, sea lions, and birds (for reviews see

Barker, 2001; Carter & Werner, 1978; Roberts, 1998; Shettleworth, 1998; Thompson, 1995, Thompson & Oden, 2000; Tomasello & Call, 1997). Central to a growing list of species comparisons has been the discovery of strategies and mechanisms that produce abstract concept formation in a given species (Carter & Werner, 1978; Cook & Wixted, 1997; Katz, Wright, & Bachevalier, 2002; Killeen, 2001; Young & Wasserman, 1997; Wright 1992, 1997). How do these strategies differ within and across species?

Two categories of strategies or rules can be used to describe an animal's recurrent pattern of behavior to solve problems. As previously described regarding visual search, these strategies are item-specific or relational. We discuss these two classes of strategies in regard to concept learning (e.g., Carter & Werner, 1978; Farthing & Opuda, 1974; Wright, 1997). Item-specific strategies involve rote memorization of which responses to specific stimuli are reinforced, and which are not. Relational strategies (also known as abstract concepts) are not bound to the specific stimuli allowing them to be applied to novel stimuli and hence generalize to novel problems. A common procedure that can be used to distinguish between these two categories of strategies is matching-to-sample (MTS). In the MTS procedure, the participant is typically first presented with a sample item (e.g., red) and then presented with two choice items (e.g., red and blue). The subject is reinforced for selecting the choice item that matches the sample. If the sample is present at the time of choice the discrimination is called simultaneous MTS. If the sample is not present at the time of choice the discrimination is called delayed MTS. To determine whether item-specific or abstract learning occurs, transfer tests are conducted at the end of acquisition. Transfer tests consist of the presentation of novel stimuli. If the animal discriminates these novel items better than chance, then it is concluded that an abstract concept has been acquired. Such accurate performance on transfer tests is considered the hallmark of concept learning. If transfer performance is equal to chance then it is concluded that the animal is using an item-specific strategy. This item-specific strategy has been thought to involve learning a set of "if–then" rules (Carter & Werner, 1978), for example, "if red sample then select comparison red." However, another item-specific alternative is that the animal memorizes stimulus display configurations or patterns (Pearce, 1987; Wright, 1997). For example, if presented with the stimulus configuration "red–red–blue," where the sample is the middle item with its two choice items to the left and right, the animal learns to select the red left choice location based on the stimulus pattern.

In an ingenious experiment, Wright (1997) was able to distinguish between "if-then" and configural rule learning in a simultaneous MTS task by pigeons. He found that when pigeons do not learn the abstract concept they learn the stimulus display configurations. Training display configurations were constructed from three visual items (i.e., a duck, an apple, and grapes). In Wright's task with three elements there are 12 possible display configurations (see Figure 11.3). Importantly, only six of the display configurations were presented to the pigeons during acquisition (e.g., the top half of Figure 11.3). The other six untrained display configurations (e.g., the lower half of Figure 11.3) were presented as transfer tests after the pigeons had acquired the task. The training set of display configurations were selected such that if the pigeons learned the task by "if–then" rules (e.g., "if duck then select comparison duck"), they should successfully transfer these rules to "solve" the other six stimulus displays. However, if the pigeons solved the task by

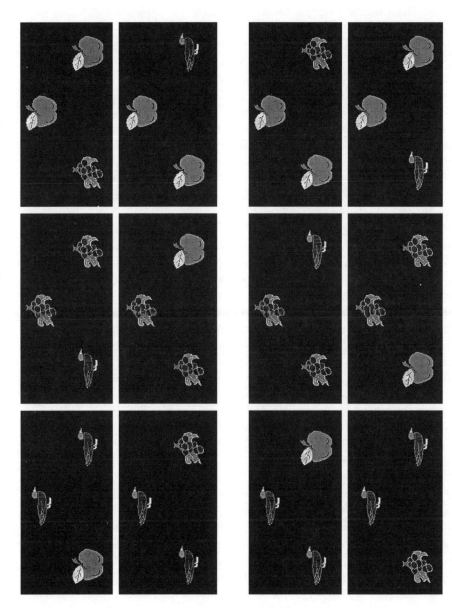

**Figure 11.3** The 12 display configurations that can be constructed from three visual items (duck, apple, grape) used in the matching to sample task from Wright (1997; stimuli reproduced with permission; NB Wright's stimuli were presented in color). Pigeons were trained with either the top or bottom six displays. Notice that each item in a training set is counterbalanced for sample frequency, correct comparison position, and incorrect comparison position.

memorization display configurations then the pigeons would fail this transfer test because each of the untrained display configurations has a different configuration than the trained display configurations. Pigeons failed the transfer test on the untrained displays configurations, indicating they had learned by memorizing the first six stimulus display configurations. These same pigeons also failed to accurately discriminate stimulus displays constructed from novel items (e.g., book, key, lobster).

Interestingly, when pigeons were trained to peck the sample 20 times (instead of once) they successfully transferred to the novel untrained display configurations and to novel items, indicating that they had learned the abstract concept. Why? The impact of increased pecking may have been to break up the display's configuration into its elemental components, thereby allowing the pigeons to learn the task relationally. Of note, this result combined with others suggest that pigeons, baboons, chimpanzees, and humans can selectively attend to and discriminate both configural and elemental information in a variety of tasks, including object recognition, visual search, and "Navon" discriminations (e.g., Cavoto & Cook, 2001; Fagot & Deruelle, 1997; Fagot & Tomonaga, 1999; Fremouw, Herbranson, & Shimp, 1998; Katz & Cook, 2002; Wasserman, Kirkpatrick-Steger, Van Hamme, & Biederman, 1993).

In part based on his collection of results, Wright (1997) hypothesized that item-specific learning may act as a "crutch" for relational learning. That is, before relational learning occurs, item-specific rule learning may be necessary. Pigeons are not the only species to use a combination of item-specific and abstract strategies. For example, such an interaction has been found with humans in MTS (e.g., Stromer & Stromer, 1989) and in other procedures with monkeys (e.g., Wright, Cook, & Kendrick, 1989) and humans (e.g., Hunt & McDaniel, 1993). Other theorists have also claimed that achieving concept learning involves an interaction between item-specific and abstract strategies (e.g., Premack, 1983b; Solso, 2001, p. 134). One way to think about these two processes is they are synergistic. That is, item-specific and abstract learning occur at the same time. Another way to think about these two learning processes is that they compete with each other. Item-specific processes lead the race (i.e., controlling performance) at the start of acquisition. Then abstract strategies emerge as the winner of the race with further experiences. This relation between item-specific and abstract strategies is an important part of the future of animal learning and cognition.

*Natural concepts* Abstract concepts are sometimes confused with "natural" concepts. An abstract concept is a rule that transcends the stimuli used to train the concept. Natural or object-based concepts are categories of items that are bound together based upon common properties (Bhatt, Wasserman, Reynolds, & Knauss, 1988; Cerella, 1979; Cook, Wright, & Kendrick, 1990; Hayes-Roth & Hayes-Roth, 1977; Herrnstein, Loveland, & Cable, 1976; Herrnstein & deVilliers, 1980; Roberts & Mazmanian, 1988; Smith & Medin, 1981; Thompson, 1995). Such object-based concepts (e.g., birds, cars, cats, mammals, people, trees) are bound to the absolute stimulus features of a specific category. This dependence on stimulus specifics does not mean that object-based concepts cannot be applied to novel items. But the successful categorization of a novel object is based on whether a novel object shares a feature in common with previously learned category exemplars. While it may be possible that the underlying mechanisms of abstract and natural concepts are similar, this is an empirical issue. That is, it would be a mistake to infer that a finding related to natural concepts applies to abstract concepts and vice versa.

*Analogical reasoning* Abstract and natural concepts are the basis for analogical reasoning. Analogical reasoning involves judging relations between relations (for a review of nonhuman primates see Thompson & Oden, 2000). In a task that involves judging relations between relations the goal is to indicate whether the relation between two items is the *same* or *different* as the relationship between two other items. For example, presented with two keys (*same*) and two bottles (*same*) the correct analogical judgment would be *same*; presented with a key and a bottle (*different*) and a hat and a cat (*different*) the correct analogical judgment would be *same*; presented with two keys (*same*) and a hat and a cat (*different*) the correct analogical judgment would be *different*. The ability to reason analogically has been regarded by some to be the hallmark of the human mind (e.g., Holyoak & Thagard, 1997).

Somewhat ironically, like learning to learn and abstract concept learning, analogical reasoning is implicitly being used to rank species intelligence. For example, at first, analogical reasoning was thought to be attainable only by humans and language-trained chimpanzees (Premack, 1983b). Then it was shown to be possible for language-naive chimpanzees (Thompson, Oden, & Boysen, 1997) but not for rhesus monkeys (Thompson & Oden, 2000). But now, new evidence suggests that baboons have the ability to analogically reason (Bovet & Vauclair, 2001; Fagot, Wasserman, & Young, 2001). Once again the ranking of species intelligence based on the attainment of solving problems that require abstract relations has started to crumble. It would seem only a matter of time before researchers figure out how to correctly measure analogical reasoning in other species in which conceptual thought has already been shown.

## Concluding Remarks

During the past century the study of animal learning and cognition exemplifies the progress that typifies a young science – diverse methodologies loosely testing too-general theories. The pursuit of general laws of learning allows some (albeit limited) cross-species prediction of experimental outcomes. That is, in laboratory environments, reinforcement works in predictable ways. In laboratory environments in which visual and auditory stimuli come to control responding, species are similar with respect to sensing such stimuli and acquiring response topographies (pressing levers, pecking keys, eating, and drinking) during acquisition and extinction, predictably showing generalization and learning discriminations, as well as other common phenomena. Even animals learning simple rules (here described as "a cognitive phenomenon") first acquire simpler responses via associative processes, often taking many hundreds of trials during acquisition. These processes are the basis for the aforementioned interaction between item-specific and relational learning. The understanding of these relationships, using the methods of experimental psychology, will allow us to understand the mechanisms that tie nonhuman cognition to that of humans.

## References

Barker, L. M. (2001). *Learning and behavior* (3rd edn.). Upper Saddle River, NJ: Prentice-Hall.

Barker, L. M., Best, M. R., & Domjan, M. (eds.) (1977). *Learning mechanisms in food selection.* Waco, TX: Baylor University Press.

Bhatt, R. S., Wasserman, E. A., Reynolds, W. F., & Knauss, K. S. (1988). Conceptual behavior in pigeons: Categorization of both familiar and novel examples from four classes of natural and artificial stimuli. *Journal of Experimental Psychology: Animal Behavior Processes, 14,* 219–34.

Bitterman, M. E. (1975). The comparative analysis of learning. *Science, 188,* 699–709.

Blough, D. S. (1989). Odd-item search in pigeons: Display size and transfer effects. *Journal of Experimental Psychology: Animal Behavior Processes, 15,* 14–22.

Blough, D. S. (1993). Effects on search speed of probability of target–distractor combinations. *Journal of Experimental Psychology: Animal Behavior Processes, 19,* 231–43.

Blough, D. S., & Blough, P. M. (1997). Form perception and attention in pigeons. *Animal Learning & Behavior, 25,* 1–20.

Bond, A. B. (1983). Visual search and selection of natural stimuli in the pigeon: The attention threshold hypothesis. *Journal of Experimental Psychology: Animal Behavior Processes, 9,* 292–306.

Bond, A. B., & Riley, D. (1991). Searching image in the pigeon: A test of three hypothetical mechanisms. *Ethology, 87,* 203–24.

Bovet, D., & Vauclair, J. (2001). Judgment of conceptual identity in monkeys. *Psychonomic Bulletin & Review, 8,* 470–5.

Breland, K., & Breland, M. (1961). The misbehavior of organisms. *American Psychologist, 16,* 681–4.

Carter, D. E., & Werner, J. T. (1978). Complex learning and information processing in pigeons: A critical analysis. *Journal of the Experimental Analysis of Behavior, 29,* 565–601.

Cavoto, K. K., & Cook, R. G. (2001). Cognitive precedence for local information in hierarchical stimulus processing by pigeons. *Journal of Experimental Psychology: Animal Behavior Processes, 27,* 3–16.

Cerella, J. (1979). Visual classes and natural categories in the pigeon. *Journal of Experimental Psychology: Human Perception and Performance, 5,* 68–77.

Cook, R. G. (1992). The acquisition and transfer of texture visual discriminations by pigeons. *Journal of Experimental Psychology: Animal Behavior Processes, 18,* 341–53.

Cook, R. G. (2000). The comparative psychology of avian visual cognition. *Current Directions in Psychological Science, 9,* 83–9.

Cook, R. G., Cavoto, K. K., & Cavoto, B. R. (1996). Mechanisms of multidimensional grouping, fusion, and search in avian texture discrimination. *Animal Learning & Behavior, 24,* 150–67.

Cook, R. G., Katz, J. S., & Cavoto, B. R. (1998). Processes of visual cognition in the pigeon. In S. Soraci & B. McIlvane (eds.), *Perspectives on Fundamental Processes in Intellectual Functioning, Volume 1: A survey of research approaches* (pp. 189–214). Greenwich, CT: Ablex.

Cook, R. G., & Wixted, J. T. (1997). Same–different discrimination in pigeons: Testing competing models of discrimination and stimulus integration. *Journal of Experimental Psychology: Animal Behavior Processes, 23,* 401–16.

Cook, R. G., Wright, A. A., & Kendrick, D. F. (1990). Visual categorization by pigeons. In M. L. Commons, R. J. Herrnstein, S. M. Kosslyn, & D. B. Mumford (eds.), *Quantitative Analyses of Behavior* (vol. VIII, pp. 187–214). Hillsdale, NJ: Erlbaum Associates.

Czeschlik, T. (1998). Animal cognition – the phylogeny and ontogeny of cognitive abilities. *Animal Cognition, 1,* 1–2.

D'Amato, M. R., Salmon, D. P., & Colombo, M. (1985). Extent and limits of the matching concept in monkeys (*Cebus apella*). *Journal of Experimental Psychology: Animal Behavior Processes*, *11*, 35–51.

Darwin, C. ([1859] 1979). *The origin of species.* New York: Random House.

Darwin, C. (1871). *The descent of man and selection in relation to sex.* London: John Murray.

Darwin, C. ([1872] 1965). *The expression of emotions in man and animals.* Chicago: University of Chicago Press.

Delius, J. D. (1994). Comparative cognition of identity. In P. Bertelson, P. Eelen, & G. d'Ydewalle (eds.), *International perspectives on psychological science* (pp. 25–40). Hilldale, NJ: Erlbaum.

Dennett, D. C. (1975). Why the law of effect will not go away. *Journal of the Theory of Social Behavior*, *5*, 169–87.

De Weerd, P., Vandenbussche, E., & Orban, G. A. (1992). Texture segregation in the cat: A parametric study. *Vision Research*, *32*, 305–22.

Dewsbury, D. A. (2000). Comparative cognition in the 1930s. *Psychonomic Bulletin & Review*, *7*, 267–83.

Domjan, M. (1983). Biological constraints on instrumental and classical conditioning: Implications for general process theory. In G. H. Bower (ed.), *The psychology of learning and motivation* (vol. 17, pp. 116–39). New York: Academic Press.

Domjan, M. (1987). Comparative psychology and the study of animal learning. *Journal of Comparative Psychology*, *101*, 237–41.

Domjan, M. (2003). The principles of learning and behavior (5th edn.). Belmont, CA: Wadsworth.

Domjan, M., O'Vary, D., & Greene, P. (1988). Conditioning of appetitive and consummatory behavior in male Japanese quail (*Coturnix coturnix japonica*). *Journal of Comparative Psychology*, *105*, 157–64.

Fagot, J., & Deruelle, C. (1997). Processing of global and local visual information and hemispherical specialization in human (*Homo sapiens*) and baboons (*Papio papio*). *Journal of Experimental Psychology: Human Perception and Performance*, *23*, 429–42.

Fagot, J., & Tomonaga, M. (1999). Global and local processing in humans (*Homo sapiens*) and chimpanzees (*Pan troglodytes*): Use of a visual search task with compound stimuli. *Journal of Comparative Psychology*, *113*, 3–12.

Fagot, J., Wasserman, E. A., & Young, M. E. (2001). Discriminating the relation between relations: The role of entropy in abstract conceptualization by baboons (*Papio papio*) and humans (*Homo sapiens*). *Journal of Experimental Psychology: Animal Behavior Processes*, *27*, 316–28.

Farthing, G. W., & Opuda, M. J. (1974). Transfer of matching-to-sample in pigeons. *Journal of the Experimental Analysis of Behavior*, *21*, 199–213.

Ferster, C. B., & Skinner, B. F. (1957). *Schedules of reinforcement.* New York: Appleton-Century-Crofts.

Fremouw, T., Herbranson, W. T., & Shimp, C. P. (1998). Priming of attention to local or global levels of visual analysis. *Journal of Experimental Psychology: Animal Behavior Processes*, *24*, 278–90.

Galef, B. G., Jr. (1987). Comparative psychology is dead! Long live comparative psychology. *Journal of Comparative Psychology*, *101*, 259–61.

Garcia, J., & Ervin, F. R. (1968). Gustatory-visceral and telereceptor-cutaneous conditioning – Adaptation in internal and external milieus. *Communications in Behavioral Biology, Part A*, *1*, 389–415.

Garcia, J., Ervin, F. R., & Koelling, R. A. (1966). Learning with prolonged delay of reinforcement. *Psychonomic Science*, *5*, 121–2.

Garcia, J., & Koelling, R. A. (1966). Relation of cue to consequence in avoidance learning. *Psychonomic Science*, *4*, 123–4.

Gormezano, I., Kehoe, E. J., & Marshall, B. S. (1983). Twenty years of classical conditioning research with the rabbit. In J. M. Prague & A. N. Epstein (eds.), *Progress in psychobiology and physiological psychology* (vol. 10, pp. 72–99). New York: Academic Press.

Harlow, H. F. (1949). The formation of learning sets. *Psychological Review, 56,* 51–65.

Hayes-Roth, B., & Hayes-Roth, F. (1977). Concept learning and the recognition and classification of exemplars. *Journal of Verbal Learning & Verbal Behavior, 16,* 321–38.

Herrnstein, R. J. (1990). Levels of stimulus control: A functional approach. *Cognition, 37,* 133–66.

Herrnstein, R. J., Loveland, D. H., & Cable, C. (1976). Natural concepts in pigeons. *Journal of Experimental Psychology: Animal Behavior Processes, 2,* 285–302.

Herrnstein, R. J., & deVilliers, P. A. (1980). Fish as a natural category for people and pigeons. In G. H. Bower (ed.), *The psychology of learning and motivation* (vol. 14, pp. 59–95). New York: Academic Press.

Holyoak, K. J., & Thagard, P. (1997). The analogical mind. *American Psychologist, 52,* 35–44.

Hull, C. L. (1943). *Principles of behavior.* New York: Appleton.

Hull, C. L. (1952). *A behavior system.* New Haven: Yale University Press.

Hulse, S. H., Fowler, J., & Honig, W. K. (1978). *Cognitive processes in animal behavior.* Hillsdale, NJ: Erlbaum.

Hunt, R. R., & McDaniel, M. A. (1993). Organization and distinctiveness as independent processes in memory. *Journal of Memory and Language, 32,* 421–45.

Hunter, W. S. (1913). The delayed reaction in animals. *Behavior Monographs, 2,* 21–30.

Kamin, L. J. (1965). Temporal and intensity characteristics of the conditioned stimulus. In W. F. Prodasy (ed.), *Classical conditioning* (pp. 118–47). New York: Appleton-Century-Crofts.

Katz, J. S., & Cook, R. G. (2000). Stimulus repetition effects on texture-based visual search by pigeons. *Journal of Experimental Psychology: Animal Behavior Processes, 26,* 220–36.

Katz, J. S., & Cook, R. G. (2002). The multiplicity of visual search strategies in pigeons. In S. Soraci, Jr. & K. Murata-Soraci (eds.), *Perspectives on fundamental processes in intellectual functioning: Visual information processing.* Westport, CT: Greenwood Publishing Group.

Katz, J. S., Wright, A. A., & Bachevalier, J. (2002). Mechanisms of *same/different* abstract-concept learning by rhesus monkeys (*Macaca mulatta*). *Journal of Experimental Psychology: Animal Behavior Processes, 28,* 358–68.

Killeen, P. R. (2001). Writing and overwriting short-term memory. *Psychonomic Bulletin & Review, 8,* 18–43.

Kohler, W. (1925). *The mentality of apes.* London: Routledge & Keegan Paul.

Krechevsky, I. (1932). "Hypotheses" in rats. *Psychological Review, 39,* 516–32.

Langley, C. M., Riley, D. A., Bond, A. B., & Goel, N. (1996). Visual search for natural grains in pigeons (*Columba livia*): Search images and selective attention. *Journal of Experimental Psychology: Animal Behavior Processes, 22,* 139–51.

Locke, J. ([1690] 1975). *An essay concerning human understanding.* Oxford: Clarendon Press.

Macintosh, N. J. (1983). *Conditioning and associative learning.* Oxford: Clarendon Press.

Mazur, J. E. (2002). *Learning and behavior* (5th edn.). Upper Saddle River, NJ: Prentice-Hall.

Monroe, B., & Barker, L. M. (1979). A contingency analysis of taste aversion conditioning. *Animal Learning and Behavior, 7,* 141–3.

Morgan, C. L. ([1894] 1977). *An introduction to comparative psychology.* London: Walter Scott.

Nash, S., & Domjan, M. (1991). Learning to discriminate the sex of conspecifics in male Japanese quail (*Coturnix coturnix japonica*): Tests of "biological constraints." *Journal of Experimental Psychology: Animal Behavior Processes, 17,* 342–53.

Papini, M. R. (2002). *Comparative psychology: Evolution and development of behavior.* Upper Saddle River, NJ: Prentice-Hall.

Pavlov, I. ([1927] 1960). *Conditioned reflexes*. New York: Dover.

Pearce, J. M. (1987). *An introduction to animal cognition*. Hillsdale, NJ: Lawrence Erlbaum Associates.

Pietrewicz, A. T., & Kamil, A. C. (1979). Search image formation in the blue jay (*Cyanocitta cristata*). *Science, 204*, 1332–3.

Premack, D. (1978). On the abstractness of human concepts: Why it would be difficult to talk to a pigeon. In S. H. Hulse, H. Fowler, & W. K. Honig (eds.), *Cognitive processes in animal behavior* (pp. 423–51). Hillsdale, NJ: Erlbaum.

Premack, D. (1983a). Animal cognition. *Annual Review of Psychology, 34*, 351–62.

Premack, D. (1983b). The codes of man and beasts. *The Behavioral and Brain Sciences, 6*, 125–67.

Razran, G. (1971). *Mind in evolution*. Boston: Houghton Mifflin.

Reid, P. J., & Shettleworth, S. J. (1992). Detection of cryptic prey: Search image or search rate? *Journal of Experimental Psychology: Animal Behavior Processes, 17*, 273–86.

Rescorla, R. A. (1967). Pavlovian conditioning and its proper control procedures. *Psychological Review, 74*, 71–80.

Rescorla, R. A. (1968). Probability of shock in the presence and absence of CS in fear conditioning. *Journal of Comparative and Physiological Psychology, 66*, 1–5.

Rescorla, R. A., & Wagner, A. R. (1972). A theory of Pavlovian conditioning: Variations in the effectiveness of reinforcement and nonreinforcement. In A. H. Black & W. F. Prokasy (eds.), *Classical conditioning II: Current research and theory* (pp. 64–99). New York: Appleton-Century-Crofts.

Roberts, W. A. (1998). *Principles of animal cognition*. Boston, MA: McGraw Hill.

Roberts, W. A., & Mazmanian, D. S. (1988). Concept learning at different levels of abstraction by pigeons, monkeys, and people. *Journal of Experimental Psychology: Animal Behavior Processes, 14*, 247–60.

Roitblat, H. L. (1987). *Introduction to comparative cognition*. New York: Freeman.

Roitblat, H. L., Bever, T. G., & Terrace, H. S. (1984). *Animal cognition*. Hillsdale, NJ: Erlbaum.

Romanes, G. J. (1882). *Animal intelligence*. London: Kegan Paul, Trench, & Co.

Rozin, P., & Kalat, J. W. (1971). Specific hungers and poison avoidance as adaptive specializations of learning. *Psychological Review, 78*, 459–86.

Shettleworth, S. J. (1998). *Cognition, evolution, and behavior*. New York: Oxford University Press.

Skinner, B. F. (1938). *The behavior of organisms*. Englewood Cliffs, N.J.: Prentice Hall.

Skinner, B. F. (1963). Behaviorism at fifty. *Science, 140*, 951–8.

Smith, E. E., & Medin, D. L. (1981). *Categories and concepts*. Cambridge, MA: Harvard University Press.

Solso, R. L. (2001). *Cognitive psychology* (6th edn.). Needham Heights, MA: Allyn & Bacon.

Stromer, R., & Stromer, J. B. (1989). Children's identity matching and oddity: Assessing control by specific and general sample-comparison relations. *Journal of the Experimental Analysis of Behavior, 51*, 47–64.

Thomas, R. K. (1980). Evolution of intelligence: An approach to its assessment. *Brain, Behavior, and Evolution, 17*, 454–72.

Thompson, R. K. R. (1995). Natural and relational concepts in animals. In Roitblat, H. L. & Meyer, J. A. (eds.), *Comparative approaches to cognitive science* (pp. 175–224). Cambridge, MA: MIT Press.

Thompson, R. K. R., & Oden, D. L. (2000). Categorical perception and conceptual judgments by nonhuman primates: The paleological monkey and the analogical ape. *Cognitive Science, 24*, 363–96.

Thompson, R. K. R., Oden, D. L., & Boysen, S. T. (1997). Language-naive chimpanzees (*Pan troglodytes*) judge relations between relations in a conceptual matching-to-sample task. *Journal of Experimental Psychology: Animal Behavior Processes, 23*, 31–43.

Thorndike, E. L. (1898). Animal intelligence: An experimental study of the associative processes in animals. *Psychological Review Monograph Supplement, 2*, 1–109.

Thorndike, E. L. (1911). *Animal intelligence: Experimental studies*. New York: Macmillan.

Thorndike, E. L. (1932). *Fundamentals of learning*. New York: Teachers College, Columbia University.

Timberlake, W. (1994). Behavior systems, associationism, and Pavlovian conditioning. *Psychonomic Bulletin and Review, 1*, 405–20.

Tinbergen, L. (1960). The natural control of insects in pinewoods: I. Factors influencing the intensity of predation by songbirds. *Archives Neelandaises de Zoologie, 13*, 265–343.

Tinklepaugh, O. L. (1932). Multiple delayed reactions with chimpanzees and monkeys. *Journal of Comparative Psychology, 13*, 207–43.

Tolman, E. C., & Honzik, C. H. (1930). "Insight" in rats. *University of California Publications in Psychology, 4*, 215–32.

Tomasello, M., & Call, J. (1997). *Primate cognition*. New York: Oxford University Press.

Treisman, A. M. (1986). Features and objects in visual processing. *Scientific American, 255*, 114–25.

Treisman, A. M., & Gelade, G. (1980). A feature-integration theory of attention. *Cognitive Psychology, 12*, 97–136.

Warren, J. M. (1965). Primate learning in comparative perspective. In A. M. Schrier, H. F. Harlow, & F. Stollnitz (eds.), *Behavior of non-human primates* (vol. 1, pp. 65–82). New York: Academic Press.

Wasserman, E. A. (1993). Comparative cognition: Beginning the second century of the study of animal intelligence. *Psychological Bulletin, 113*, 211–38.

Wasserman, E. A. (1997). The science of animal cognition: Past, present, and future. *Journal of Experimental Psychology: Animal Behavior Processes, 23*, 123–35.

Wasserman, E. A., Kirkpatrick-Steger, K., Van Hamme, L. J., & Biederman, I. (1993). Pigeons are sensitive to the spatial organization of complex visual stimuli. *Psychological Science, 4*, 336–41.

Watson, J. B., & Rayner, R. (1920). Conditioned emotional reactions. *Journal of Experimental Psychology, 3*, 1–14.

Wolfe, J. M. (1994). Guided search 2.0: A revised model of visual search. *Psychonomic Bulletin and Review, 1*, 202–38.

Wolfe, J. M. (2000). Visual attention. In K. K. De Valois (ed.), *Seeing* (pp. 335–86). San Diego, CA: Academic Press.

Woodruff-Pak, D. S. (1999). New directions for a classical paradigm: Human eyeblink conditioning. *Psychological Science, 10*, 1–3.

Wright, A. A. (1992). Learning mechanisms in matching to sample. *Journal of Experimental Psychology: Animal Behavior Processes, 18*, 67–79.

Wright, A. A. (1997). Concept learning and learning strategies. *Psychological Science, 8*, 119–23.

Wright, A. A., Cook, R. G., & Kendrick, D. F. (1989). Relational and absolute stimulus learning by monkeys in a memory task. *Journal of the Experimental Analysis of Behavior, 52*, 237–48.

Young, M. E., & Wasserman, E. A. (1997). Entropy detection by pigeons: Response to mixed visual displays after same-different discrimination training. *Journal of Experimental Psychology: Animal Behavior Processes, 23*, 157–70.

# CHAPTER TWELVE

# Sensation and Perception Research Methods

## Lauren Fruh VanSickle Scharff

Sensation and perception are two interrelated areas that have relied on many diverse research methods, including psychophysical, physiological, and computational techniques. Roughly speaking, sensation research investigates how the senses (the receptors and early neural processing stages) respond to stimuli. Perception research investigates stimulus-driven processes influencing behavior. The processes of identification of, and attention to, stimuli have traditionally been included within the more general domain of cognitive science. The distinctions between sensation, perception, and cognition have become increasingly fuzzy, especially with the strong evidence of top-down processes influencing both sensation and perception. Examples include attention modulating physiological activity in lower cortical visual areas and influencing psychophysical measures of basic visual sensitivities (e.g., Carrasco, Penpeci-Talgar, & Eckstein, 2000; Di Russo, Spinelli, & Morrone, 2001; Gandhi, Heeger, & Boynton, 1999).

As was mentioned in Chapter 1, some of the earliest research in perception, by Titchener and his students, relied on the highly subjective method of deep introspection. Because this method did not generate experimenter-independent conclusions about the relation between a stimulus and the perceptual response, it faded from popularity following Titchener's death. Research productivity in sensation and perception increased later in the 1800s, however, with the application of some standardized psychophysical methods developed by Fechner and Weber. Generally speaking, psychophysical methods allow researchers to systematically relate a stimulus input with a perceptual response. For example, a common response required by Fechner's methods to determine the absolute threshold was "I see the stimulus."

Although Fechner's methods were a major advancement from the descriptive, introspective methods used by Titchener and his students, they were subject to the criticism that they measured the subjective biases of the observers along with their sensitivity.

More specifically, the stimulus was always present at some level, and the participant's task was to report whether or not it was detected. Although this approach sounds reasonable on the surface, due to neural noise, there are no true absolute thresholds. Further, some participants tend to be very careful in their judgments, whereas others are more lenient in their decision making. Although their actual sensitivities may not differ by much, the more lenient participant would have a much lower threshold than the more careful participant. Thus, when using such a method, the response biases of participants cannot be separated from their sensitivities.

The popularization of the forced-choice and signal detection methodologies in the mid-1900s gave researchers more objective psychophysical techniques by which to study perception, and computational ways to assess response bias effects separately from participants' sensitivities. With the forced-choice method, a participant is forced to choose in which interval of a trial the stimulus appeared, or to simply identify which trials contained the stimulus. Usually, there are two intervals or choices (two-alternative forced-choice), although there may be many. This technique can be used either for detection tasks or modified slightly for identification tasks. The important concept is that there are right and wrong answers, and therefore researchers can interpret the data in a more objective manner. Threshold sensitivities acquired through this technique are generally lower and more consistent than thresholds acquired through Fechner's techniques, because all participants are forced to make a detection choice every trial, and thus the more careful participants will not have elevated thresholds.

With the signal detection method, the rates of hits, misses, false alarms, and correct rejections in a forced-choice (Yes–No) procedure are converted to sensitivity and bias measures. Both measures can be assessed as a function of the stimulus characteristics or the participant's motivation to say Yes or No (manipulated by changing the payoffs and costs for correct and incorrect responses, and/or by changing the a priori knowledge about the target likelihood). Trials that include the signal are considered to contain the signal plus noise (which can be internal or external), and trials that do not include the signal are considered to simply contain noise. The distributions of responses as the signal and the motivations are systematically manipulated are used to determine a participant's sensitivity to the stimulus.

A more recent advance based on signal detection is that of the ideal observer. This approach is useful when noise is added to the stimulus or the stimulus is inherently noisy; in such cases the ideal observer can provide a yardstick against which participant observers may be compared. Ideal observers are mathematical constructs that optimally use all available information in a stimulus in order to make a decision about the stimulus (detection or identification). Although they are an example of a computational technique, they are mentioned here because they are commonly used as a comparison to human psychophysical data (e.g., Knill, 1998; Scharff & Geisler, 1992). Such comparisons are enlightening with respect to what stimulus information a human observer actually uses for perceptual tasks; in many cases humans are not as efficient as an ideal observer, which means that there is meaningful information in the stimulus that we do not use. Comparisons with humans can also be made more interesting by incorporating into the ideal observer known human physiological characteristics at different levels of processing (e.g., light absorbed by the lens or missed by the receptors). The modified ideal observer's performance is then compared to a human's performance to see if additional human losses of efficiency occur in stages not yet incorporated into the ideal observer. For an excellent review of this approach, see Geisler (1989).

An even more recent modification of signal detection that is becoming increasingly popular is the use of classification images. As illustrated in the section on psychophysics below, classification images use the trial-by-trial variations in added noise to determine the features of a stimulus that a participant uses to perform stimulus discriminations.

Researchers studying sensation and perception have relied on more than just psychophysical techniques. Physiological methods have been particularly important in developing an understanding of the sensation processes and, more recently, the neurophysiology underlying perception. Many of the traditional physiological techniques are invasive (e.g., lesion work and intracellular recordings), so most previous work used animal participants rather than humans. The use of animals often restricts a researcher to the investigation of sensation. Changes in animal perceptions cannot be measured through verbal reports as they are in humans; instead they are studied through trained voluntary behavioral responses, but the range of possible responses is much more limited than with humans. Further, these invasive approaches have traditionally used anesthetized or dead animals, and, when performing electrical recordings, traditionally only one cell at a time has been recorded. Therefore, the resultant data should be interpreted with caution because the sensory processes of an awake animal may differ from those of an anesthetized animal, and groups of cells may interact in ways not apparent when recording from one cell at a time. More recently researchers have developed techniques to record simultaneously from multiple cells (e.g., Deadwyler, 2001) and from alert animals (e.g., McAdams & Maunsell, 2000; Shadlen & Newsome, 1996).

Except in special cases (e.g., an individual consenting to participate in an invasive physiological technique while already undergoing an invasive procedure such as brain surgery), physiological research using human participants has used noninvasive techniques. Examples that have been available for a few decades are the EEG (electroencephalogram) to measure brain waves in response to a stimulus and the EOG (electrooculogram) to measure eye movements. However, although they have been an asset to understanding many aspects of human processing, the EEG and EOG measure a very different set of responses than do the traditional invasive techniques used with animals. An additional point to consider is that animals and humans do not have identical brains or nervous systems. Thus, although a large amount of general knowledge about the neural bases of sensation and perception has been acquired through the use of physiological techniques, a major drawback has been determining to what extent the animal results are analogous with what happens in humans.

The fairly recent development of new, noninvasive physiological techniques has revolutionized the study of the neurophysiology of sensation and perception (and other areas), and has allowed better comparisons between human and animal data. These methods (e.g., PET scans, fMRI scans, SPECT) are called functional neuroimaging techniques because they measure fairly localized brain activity as specific functions/behaviors are performed. As seen through the research highlighted in the section on physiology below, functional neuroimaging has been used to investigate both clinical and pure research questions using human participants.

A third methodological approach that has seen major developments in the past decade is that of computational research, especially within the realm of visual perception. With this approach, researchers develop mathematical models or metrics of the visual system based on previously obtained psychophysical and physiological data. They then test their models or metrics by determining how well they are able to process stimuli or predict other psychophysical data. This approach has forced researchers to think more explicitly about the neural mechanisms of sensation that underlie perception. For example, current computational models include multiple stages of neural processing and many incorporate lateral and top-down interactions, all of which are more physiologically accurate than the early serial models. David Marr (1982), who developed a model of shape perception, is generally acknowledged as the forerunner in this field. Marr's major innovation was the strategy of describing a computational problem that the visual system faces (e.g., developing a representation of a 3-D world from two 2-D retinal images), and then trying to develop a computational solution to that problem rather than just depending on physiology or psychophysics to guide the model development. Advances in computer technology have allowed computational researchers to develop and test more complex models more easily. Further, this approach is now being used to address higher-level processes as well as the fundamental processes of sensation and perception. The section on computational research below highlights the development of a metric used to predict the readability of text displays.

Before addressing the specific recent examples of these general methodological approaches to studying sensation and perception, it is important to note that the different approaches are not used or developed in isolation from each other. For example, data from the development of multiple simultaneous recordings and the use of alert animals have benefited computational researchers as well as physiologists. Also, researchers using the new neuroimaging techniques often collect psychophysical data while collecting functional data (or they independently collect both and then compare them). Further, the neuroimaging techniques require complex mathematical computations, components of which are based on assumptions about neural processing, to create images from the raw data.

Finally, although the advances outlined above and the specific examples given below illustrate how much the sensation and perception methodologies have developed in the past decade, each technique has limitations as well as relative benefits when compared to the other techniques. The limitations will motivate further evolution of the methods, and the relative benefits mean that certain techniques are better than others to answer specific questions. Thus it is important for sensation and perception researchers to understand the fundamentals of all of the approaches rather than exclusively focusing on only one. The examples below support this contention because, although they are placed in separate methodology categories, they all incorporate multiple methodologies.

## Psychophysics: Classification Images

Traditionally in psychophysical research, the researcher makes a priori assumptions about the stimulus characteristics that influence perception. These stimulus characteristics are then systematically manipulated in order to determine the relationship between them and perception. Decades of research have shown this approach to be effective in increasing our understanding of perceptual processes. However, this approach has the drawback that researchers might miss important characteristics, simply because they were not apparent to the researchers and thus never studied. Also, when the stimulus characteristics are manipulated, the characteristics that are determining behavior may change also, making it difficult to ascribe a change in behavior to the use of a particular stimulus characteristic. In contrast, the classification images technique holds the stimulus variables constant and lets the variability of noise added on individual trials generate a picture of how the observer responses depend on the stimulus. Because the technique involves adding noise, the observer classification images can also be compared to those expected from an ideal observer.

The classification images approach was first used in auditory research, but in the mid-1990s it was adapted for use in vision research. The earliest research talk using this technique in vision was by Ahumada in 1996, while the first published classification images study in vision research was by Beard and Ahumada in 1998. Since then many researchers have begun using the technique for a variety of visual tasks (e.g., Abbey & Eckstein, 2000; Knoblauch, Thomas, & D'Zmura, 1999; Levi & Klein, 2002; Solomon, 2002).

## A classification images study used to examine vernier acuity

Beard and Ahumada (1998) describe the classification images approach and its application to a vernier acuity task. Vernier acuity refers to the smallest misalignment of two lines that is detectable by an observer. It is considered an example of a hyperacuity because the threshold misalignment (as small as one arcsec, see Appendix 12.1) is smaller than the spacing (about 30 arcsec) of the retinal cone array. Two main approaches to explaining how the task is performed are by simple cortical mechanisms performing (1) a local position measurement or (2) a local orientation discrimination. The orientation discrimination could be implemented by the single most discriminating cortical cell (here modeled by a single Gabor filter) or by the difference of a pair of such cells. The position discrimination mechanism is modeled as the difference between horizontal Gabors, whose output varies with the vertical position of a line. Figure 12.1 illustrates predicted classification images for each of these three models for both abutting and widely separated line stimuli. The images show why the psychophysical tests may have had difficulty distinguishing between the orientation theory and the position theory for abutting stimuli: the combination of two oriented Gabors is almost indistinguishable from the two horizontal Gabors.

The stimuli used by Beard and Ahumada (1998) were two short, dark, horizontal lines (5.0 by 0.93 arcmin) on a background with a constant mean luminance of 26.25 cd/m$^2$. The two lines were either abutting (gap = 0) or separated (gap = 10.2 arcmin). On each trial, the left vernier line was randomly either aligned with the right line or upwardly offset by 0.31 arcmin. Stimulus duration was 500 ms with an abrupt onset and offset.

Gabor filter             Oriented Gabor filter pair             Local position

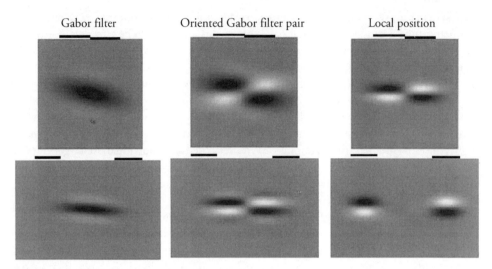

**Figure 12.1**  Predicted classification images for three theories (Gabor filter, a pair of oriented Gabor filters, and local position) that attempt to explain vernier acuity. The top set of panels shows the predictions for the abutting lines case, and the lower set shows the predictions for the separated lines case. Above each prediction image are example vernier lines for the case being predicted.

White noise was added to the vernier line stimuli (which were centered in the display area). In order to rapidly generate the computer stimulus images, the noise for all trials was actually the same noise pattern, with its phase shifted by a random amount in one dimension (with wrap-around). The noise contrast was adjusted so that the error rate was near 25 percent for each participant.

Three participants completed the abutting vernier task, and two of these observers also completed the separated vernier task. Trials were run in blocks of 100. The participants' task was to press one of two keyboard buttons to indicate whether or not the two lines were aligned (a two-interval forced-choice method). Tone feedback was given following each trial. Overall, participants completed between 3,000 and 4,900 trials for each condition (abutting or separated lines).

As is done when using signal detection, data were placed in one of four stimulus–response (S–R) categories: S 0–R 0, S 0–R 1, S 1–R 0, and S 1–R 1. For a simple detection task, the target is either present or not, while in this task the lines were either aligned (S1) or not (S0). Although they did not calculate a sensitivity $d'$ as is done in signal detection, they could have done so using the number of trials in each S–R category. Instead, they created classification images from the categorized noise images. These classification images reveal how the stimulus pixels contributed in an additive way to the observer responses; that is, a pixel-by-pixel average across all trials in an S–R category results in an image that portrays how variations in pixel luminance affected the response.

The classification images are computed from the S–R segregated noise images. First, four average noises are calculated using the noise images presented on trials from each of

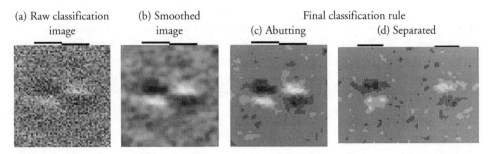

(a) Raw classification image    (b) Smoothed image    Final classification rule    (c) Abutting    (d) Separated

**Figure 12.2**   The classification images for the group data for the abutting vernier acuity task: (a) shows the raw classification image, (b) shows the smoothed image, and (c) and (d) show the final classification rule schematics for the abutting and separated cases, respectively.

the four S–R categories. Next, correlation images are calculated, which are the differences between the two response type averages for each stimulus type (S0R1–S0R0 and S1R1–S1R0). This subtraction reverses the image polarity of the R0 responses, and thus makes them compatible with the R1 responses. The raw classification image is the sum of the two correlation images (S0R1–S0R0 + S1R1–S1R0). An example of the group raw classification image for Beard and Ahumada's abutting vernier discrimination condition is shown in Figure 12.2a. In order to improve the visualization of the classification image, the raw image is then smoothed by computing a weighted averaged of adjacent pixels using a 5 × 5 kernel (see Figure 2b). Finally, the image is transformed so that any pixels that are not significantly different from zero ($p < 0.05$) are presented in a neutral gray, whereas other pixel gray values are presented in lighter or darker grays in one standard deviation steps. Figure 2c shows the final classification image, which Beard and Ahumada consider to be a schematic for the classification rule in detecting misalignment of abutting lines. Figure 2d shows the same for the separated lines.

The final classification images calculated by Beard and Ahumada (1998) were not consistent with the single Gabor filter theory for either the abutting or the separated cases. They were consistent with the oriented Gabor filter theory for the abutting case, but not the separated case. However, the classification images were consistent with the local position theory in both cases.

When compared with an ideal observer, the obtained classification images show that the observers did not follow the ideal approach to vernier acuity. The ideal observer classification image is the difference between the aligned and offset images: adjacent horizontal dark and light lines only shift on the left side of the stimulus (the ones on the right side subtract to zero since they do not shift). In contrast, the observer classification images show light and dark regions for both sides of the stimulus, indicating that observers used both the left and right lines to make their vernier decisions. In the spirit of Geisler's method, Beard and Ahumada (1998) suggest that much of the discrepancy between the predicted ideal observer classification image and the obtained classification image would be reduced by additionally assuming that the ideal observer is limited by both the image blur and the positional uncertainty that restrict the human observers.

In summary, Beard and Ahumada (1998) conclude that the classification image approach is a useful way by which to clarify theoretical questions regarding the receptive field properties of the underlying mechanisms for visual discriminations. The fact that many other researchers are also beginning to use this approach supports Beard and Ahumada's conclusion. Further, because this approach eliminates the need for a priori assumptions about the important stimulus characteristics, it is likely to result in some novel conclusions about visual processing.

## Physiology: Functional Neuroimaging Studies

Probably the most well-publicized psychology-related research in the past several years has been related to studies that use the recently developed functional neuroimaging techniques. This skewed dissemination of research is likely due to the facts that the participants are human, the questions asked are higher-level and thus of greater interest to the general population, and the public can see images of brains, which until recently were not easily accessible in living humans. For example, neuroimaging studies have been used to investigate brain-processing differences between males and females (e.g., Kimura, 2000), between normal individuals and murderers (e.g., Raine, 1999), and between normal individuals and dyslexics (e.g., Demb, Boynton, & Heeger, 1997, 1998). Although they may receive less media attention, studies using functional neuroimaging to investigate more fundamental research questions have captured the attention of researchers around the world, and have drawn many new students into the field.

Two often-highlighted functional neuroimaging techniques are positron emission tomography (PET) imaging and functional magnetic resonance imaging (fMRI). The electroencephalogram (EEG) is an additional functional measure that has been available for many decades, which may explain why it seems to have received less media attention in recent years. All of these techniques have undergone many modifications to improve them for specific uses, so they have multiple forms. Some of their basic characteristics and limitations are outlined below, but much more detailed descriptions can be found in texts and online (e.g., for a review of PET and fMRI see Seminowicz, 2001, and for a review of EEG methodological issues see Wieringa, 1993).

PET scans have been used for research since the 1970s. They require an injection of a radioactive substance, and thus are considered invasive (even though the brain itself is not exposed). This substance collects in neurons that are more active, and is able to highlight areas of the brain that are used for particular functions. One of the drawbacks to the PET technique is that the resultant images do not include anatomical information, so they must be combined with CAT (computerized axial tomography) or MRI (magnetic resonance imaging) scans to localize the activity to specific, identifiable brain areas. Alignment of the combination is difficult to do precisely.

Functional MRI was developed more recently as an evolution of the standard, anatomical MRI. FMRI works by measuring the amount of oxygenated blood in a given region of the brain, which is related to the amount of local brain activity. Although some specialized forms of the fMRI require the injection of contrast agents (e.g., perfusion MRI), the standard fMRI procedure is noninvasive. Functional MRI is much more accessible than PET because any standard MRI scanner (found in most hospitals as well as some research institutes) can be modified for functional use. Generally, PET scanners are only available in research settings. Further, when fMRI imaging is performed, an anatomical MRI image can be taken using the same equipment, so the problem of image alignment is not as severe as that experienced with the PET technique.

When evaluating functional neuroimaging data, it is important to consider issues of spatial and temporal resolution. PET and fMRI have spatial resolutions of 3 mm and 1–2 mm, respectively, which are much better than the standard EEG which has been used for decades; however, more recent variations of the EEG have many more electrode sites and are combined with MRI to achieve improved spatial resolution relative to the standard EEG. However, the spatial resolution of PET and fMRI is far poorer than that achieved using invasive intracellular recordings with animals. Also, the anatomical maps provided by CAT scans and MRIs are much poorer than those acquired through standard neuroanatomical techniques (although MRI is superior to CAT in this respect). Overall then, PET and fMRI are not precise enough to resolve activity in individual neural units. With respect to temporal resolution issues, the EEG is superior to both PET and fMRI because the EEG recordings can be up to 1000 herz per channel. When comparing the PET and fMRI, the superiority of the fMRI over PET is greater than it was for spatial issues. On average it takes about 60 to 120 seconds to acquire a single PET image. In contrast, it only takes one to six seconds to acquire an fMRI image. However, the blood flow and oxygenation measured with PET and fMRI are slow with respect to the rapid neural communication events that underlie the behaviors being studied. Intracellular recordings give essentially real-time measures, but as pointed out earlier, they cannot give a "picture" of the system as a whole, and they are generally not used with humans.

As mentioned above, functional neuroimaging has been used to study both pure research and clinical questions. An example of each is detailed below.

## A study of the neuronal basis of contrast discrimination

Boynton et al. (1999) explicitly compared psychophysical and functional imaging measures of contrast discrimination for two human participants. Contrast discrimination occurs when a participant indicates which of two (or more) stimuli has the most contrast (i.e., in which there is a larger difference between the light and dark areas of the stimulus). Boynton et al. used the blood oxygenation level-dependent (BOLD) fMRI technique (which is the most commonly used fMRI technique, especially for sensation, perception, and cognition studies). They sought to determine if the activity of groups of neurons in specific areas of the visual cortex (V1, V2v, V2d, V3v, V3d, V3A, and V4v) would correlate with psychophysical judgments. Contrast discrimination previously had been studied extensively using psychophysical techniques in humans and invasive physiological recording techniques in animals. Because they collected both

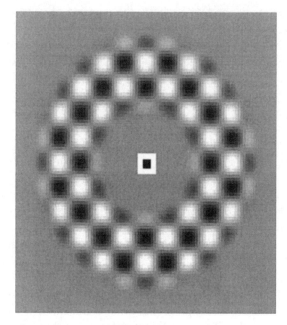

**Figure 12.3**   An example annulus stimulus plaid created using sine wave gratings. In the actual Boynton et al. (1999) experiment, the stimuli reversed contrast at a frequency of 8 Hz.
*Source*: Adapted with permission from Dr. Boynoton.

psychophysical and physiological data on humans, these researchers were better able to generalize between the two types of data.

The stimulus used by Boynton et al. was carefully chosen to maximize the fMRI abilities, while still being consistent with previous psychophysical work. More specifically, they limited the spatial extent of the annulus stimulus to an annulus two degrees in diameter (see Appendix 12.1 for an explanation of visual angle) and placed it in the periphery. It was important to limit the size of the stimulus because there are psychophysical and physiological changes as a function of eccentricity (i.e., where a stimulus is located on the retina relative to the fovea). A peripheral placement was chosen because it is difficult to identify (using neuroimaging) the boundaries between the different visual cortex areas for the foveal region.

The annulus stimuli consisted of contrast-reversing (8 Hz) plaids created from 0.5 or 2 cycle/degree sine wave gratings. (See Figure 12.3 for an example stimulus.) For each spatial frequency, responses were measured for six baseline contrasts. Psychophysical and fMRI data were collected during separate sessions, although the participants were placed in the same fMRI scanner for both types of data collection. As is standard for fMRI studies, stimuli were presented to the participants via an angled mirror placed above their faces (they lay on their backs in the scanner). The mirror reflected the stimuli from a rear-projected image on a screen placed near the opening of the bore of the magnet near the participant's knees. A central fixation mark was used to minimize eye movements and a bite bar was used to eliminate head movements.

The participants' task was to indicate in which of two trial intervals the plaid stimulus had the highest contrast (a two-alternative forced-choice procedure). The two stimulus intervals were temporally separated by a brief blank interval (a uniform gray field of the same average luminance as the plaid stimuli) and trials themselves were separated by a blank response interval. If the average luminance across the intervals had not been kept constant, then the neural responses would have also reflected luminance changes. Visual feedback was given after each trial, and used to help control for the attentional state of the participant.

The fMRI data analysis involved many steps (refer to the original paper for the details of this complex process). First, the boundaries of visual brain areas themselves were determined through a separate procedure that had been previously established by many other researchers (e.g., Engel, Glover, & Wandell, 1997; Schneider, Noll, & Cohen, 1993). In this procedure, a rotating wedge stimulus (moving like a radar sweep) was used to create a wave of activity in the retinotopically organized brain areas. (Retinotopic organization means that the spatial organization of the brain areas corresponds to the spatial organization of the retina.) The visual area boundaries are indicated by a reversal in the polar angle dimension of the retinotopic maps as the wave of activity moves through the different areas. Within each area, the radial component (which corresponds to the eccentricity of the neurons within an area) was determined using an expanding ring stimulus. Because a reference scan was completed at the beginning of each session, and a complete anatomical scan was performed on each participant, Boynton et al. feel that they were able (for this technique) to precisely localize the fMRI activity within each of the visual cortex areas.

Following the determination of the cortical visual area boundaries, the raw fMRI data for the contrast discrimination task were analyzed (using many more complex steps). Generally speaking, the average amplitudes and temporal phases of the fMRI time series for each condition were calculated for each brain area. In order to improve the signal-to-noise ratio, sample points that showed little response were removed from the calculations. Such points tend to be those that correspond to areas with high proportions of white matter or those that fall outside the stimulus area. The fMRI and psychophysical data were compared by creating neuronal contrast-response functions and psychophysical TvC (threshold versus contrast) curves, and performing simultaneous fits to the data. Simultaneous fits were plausible because, for both sets of data, the relative variability between the two types of data was used to "normalize" them.

Through the above process of analysis, Boynton, Demb, Glover, and Heeger (1999) found that a single criterion response value allowed the psychophysical data to be predicted from the physiological data for visual areas V1, V2d, V3d, and V3A. In other words, regardless of baseline contrast, two stimuli that produce fMRI responses that differ by at least 0.03 were distinguished by an observer 79 percent of the time. The other areas (V2v, V3v, and V4v) showed highly variable and nonmonotonic responses, so they were not analyzed further. The authors believed that the unreliable responses from the ventral areas (signified by the "v" after the area name) may have been due to the fact that these areas were further from the FMRI surface coil, and therefore they had reduced signal-to-noise ratios.

Boynton et al. (1999) concluded that psychophysical contrast discrimination judgments are constrained by neuronal signals in the early visual cortex areas. This relation holds even for the low contrast responses, which show facilitation, and the high contrast responses, which show masking effects.

## An fMRI study of the early visual pathways in dyslexia

With 3 to 9 percent of the population experiencing dyslexia (Shaywitz, Shaywitz, Fletcher, & Escobar, 1990), both the general population and researchers are motivated to understand the underlying neural deficits that are linked to the disorder. Although many theories have been proposed to explain dyslexia, one that has received recent support is that of a magnocellular (M) pathway deficit in the visual system. The M pathway begins in the retina and continues through several layers of the visual cortex. Cortical area MT in particular is associated with M-pathway input. This pathway is predominantly responsible for the processing of low-contrast, low-spatial frequency, and high-temporal frequency stimuli. Although most reading stimuli tend to be of relatively high contrast and spatial frequency, some researchers feel that, because reading involves rapid eye movements to successively fixate words, deficits in the M-pathway could interfere with optimal reading processes.

Demb et al. (1998) performed a study that compared five dyslexics and five normal readers on several reading performance measures, perceptual thresholds, and brain activity patterns in several visual cortex areas. Prior to their work, other researchers had suggested some M-pathway deficits in dyslexics, but the results had not consistently been supportive of the M-pathway (or transient deficit) hypothesis (e.g. Cornelissen, Hansen, Hutton, Evangelinou, & Stein, 1998; Keen & Lovegrove, 2000; Skottun, 2000). Five reading measures were used: Wide Range Achievement Test (WRAT) reading and spelling tests, the Word Attack subtest of the Woodcock–Johnson educational battery (which requires participants to sound out nonsense words), and the Nelson–Denny reading rate and comprehension measures.

The Demb et al. (1998) visual stimuli used to measure psychophysical speed discrimination thresholds were specifically designed to differentiate activity in the M pathway from other pathways. Their stimuli were fairly large (10 degree in width) moving (20.8 degree/sec) sine-wave gratings (0.4 cycles/degree) at a low mean luminance (5 cd/m²). The psychophysical procedure was adapted from that used by Merigan, Byrne, and Maunsell (1991) in their study of M-pathway-lesioned monkeys. Participants made a two-interval forced-choice decision about which trial interval contained the most rapidly moving stimulus. Stimulus contrast and duration were randomized across trials so participants had to make their decisions based on speed discrimination alone.

The fMRI measures used two sets of stimuli. The first was designed to optimally stimulate the M-pathway: slightly larger and dimmer (14 degree width at 2 cd/m²) but otherwise identical to that used in the threshold portion of the study. The second was a control stimulus designed to stimulate multiple visual cortical areas: a contrast-reversing (8.3 Hz) sinusoidal grating of the same frequency but at a higher mean luminance (36 cd/m²). In order to minimize neural adaptation, the orientation and direction of the moving (but not the control) gratings changed every 500 ms. The fMRI equipment set-up was as described above for the contrast discrimination study. The task for participants in this case was simply to observe the stimuli while keeping their heads as still as possible. The determination of the boundaries of the visual areas and the initial raw data analysis for each individual was performed as described above for the contrast discrimination study.

The results of the Demb et al. (1998) study lend support to the theory that there is at least a correlational relationship between M-pathway processing and dyslexia. More specifically they showed that, for the stimuli designed to optimally stimulate the M pathway, dyslexics had lower levels of brain activity in several visual cortical areas, but that there was no such difference when using the high-contrast stimuli designed to stimulate multiple areas. They concluded from this research that, in addition to supporting the theory of M-pathway differences, the decreased performance with the M-pathway stimuli was not due to general deficiencies in attention or motivation by the dyslexic participants. A second finding was that individuals with greater brain activity in areas V1 and MT+ (but not other areas) showed better motion discrimination performance. This finding was the first to show a link between individual differences in brain activity and human motion perception. A final major finding from this study was that brain activity correlated with measures of reading ability. More specifically, activity in all the areas they tested (V1, V2, V3, V3A, V4v, and MT+) correlated with the measure of reading rate, with stronger correlations for MT+ than for other areas. Reading comprehension showed a correlation with activity in V2, V3, and V3A. Activity in area V3 also correlated with nonword reading. No areas showed activity patterns that correlated with the measures of single-word reading or spelling. Demb et al. suggested that, even if the M-pathway deficit is not causal in the development of dyslexia, assessment of M-pathway abilities may serve as an early indicator of a predisposition for developing dyslexia.

## Computational Research: Models and Metrics

Computational research in perception uses the results from physiological and psychophysical research to develop algorithms that simulate what occurs in humans. Additional testing may be done to assess the accuracy of the algorithms, but often the human data used to assess their accuracy are from independent studies performed by other researchers.

The long-term benefit of computational research is the creation of models and metrics that allow accurate predictions of the process in question, without the need to actually test participants. Thus their use can save time and money in the design of perceptual interfaces, and also make it more likely that the design minimizes encounters with human perceptual system limitations.

Although "model" and "metric" are sometimes used interchangeably, in general a model of perception can be considered more complete or advanced than a metric of perception. A model should output a response similar to the process that it is modeling.

For example, the model of three-dimensional vision by Uttal, Liu, and Kalki (1996) produces as its final output a three-dimensional surface reconstruction of the input stimulus, similar to what the human visual system does when it views a stimulus surface.

In contrast, a metric may only produce an output that allows the researcher to relate aspects of the stimulus to human performance. The metric algorithms usually are based on theoretical models of the system, which themselves are based on physiological and psychophysical data. For example, as detailed below, Scharff, Hill, and Ahumada (2000) compared several discriminability metrics for their ability to predict previously acquired reading search times. The outputs of these calculations were not search times, but unitless numbers that were then correlated with the actual data.

Some computational research papers posit a fairly explicit, theoretical model of the visual system process of interest, but the actual computational procedure more strongly resembles the use of a metric. For example, Rovamo, Kankaanpaa, and Kukkonen (1999) propose a model that extends their detection model of achromatic spatial vision to include chromatic vision. Their model details several processing steps (based on physiological and psychophysical data) in which a stimulus is filtered by optical and neural mechanisms at various levels of the visual system. The final step is image interpretation in the brain. The purpose of their work was to explain the difference in the shapes of the luminance and chromatic contrast sensitivity functions, which they believed was mainly due to differences in the strength of the neural lateral inhibitions occurring for the two types of stimuli. In order to test their model, Rovamo et al. used algorithms to transform luminance and chromatic contrast sensitivity data from Mullen (1985). Removing the effects of lateral inhibition from the luminance data did not completely align the two data sets. Additional transformations (removal of quantal noise and redefining the chromatic contrast) were needed to superimpose the two data sets. Thus this study did not test the theoretical model by using it to create new contrast sensitivity functions based on the input of luminance and chromatic gratings. Instead, the model was evaluated through metric algorithms developed from the model.

This comparison of models and metrics is not meant to imply that one is better than the other, but to clarify the different approaches taken by computational researchers. In order to further highlight the usefulness of computational approaches, a more detailed example is given below.

## A study of discriminability measures for predicting the readability of text on textured backgrounds

Due to technology advances, the readability of text displays is important to an ever-increasing number of individuals. Further, although in many cases the text is legible, the design choices made for its display (e.g., color, font, contrast, size) render it likely to cause eye strain and fatigue in the reader. In turn, such displays will be more likely to slow reading and cause errors in reading. Vision scientists have investigated many aspects of legibility and readability, but often these findings do not make their way into design manuals. An area where this is especially true concerns the design of web pages for the Internet.

An element of web design often used to the detriment of readability is background texture. More crucially, background textures also influence the readability of displays such as head-up displays (HUDs) in planes and, more recently, in some automobiles. Although individual backgrounds could be psychophysically tested for their influence on readability, the endless possible number of text and background choice combinations make this solution to creating readable text displays unwieldy. (Further, most designers would have no idea how to perform reliable psychophysical tests.) So what might be most useful is a metric algorithm that could be used in design applications. Such a metric would output a relative rating of readability and help constrain a designer's choices of display characteristics.

Scharff et al. (2000) investigated how well several possible metrics would predict readability for three levels of text contrast and a range of backgrounds (plain, a periodic texture, and four spatial-frequency-filtered textures created from the periodic texture). Spatial-frequency-filtered backgrounds were incorporated because previous psychophysical research had suggested that specific ranges of frequencies might be more crucial for legibility (Legge, Pelli, Rubin, & Schleske, 1985; Parish & Sperling, 1991; Solomon & Pelli, 1994). Scharff, Ahumada, and Hill (1999) had previously developed the metrics used by Scharff et al. (2000), but had evaluated their effectiveness only with data collected using backgrounds that contained a full range of frequencies.

Notice that, although some visual system models are mentioned, the goal of this work was not to test the models (even indirectly as done by Rovamo et al., 1999). Rather, Scharff et al. (2000) attempted to find which of several metrics would best predict their readability data.

*Gathering the psychophysical data* Because no other researchers had previously collected the appropriate data using spatial-frequency-filtered backgrounds, Scharff et al. (2000) first designed a psychophysical experiment using stimuli and a procedure modified from their previous studies. More specifically, text displays were created by placing newspaper text excerpts on top of background textures that had an average background luminance of 62.5 cd/m$^2$. Three text contrasts were created (0.15, 0.35, and 0.95) by using three shades of text (light gray, medium gray, and black). The background texture used to make the spatial-frequency-selective textures was taken from a web site that offered free background textures to designers. It was originally chosen (Hill & Scharff, 1999) because it seemed to influence text readability without making the text unreadable. The four frequency-filtered textures were created using filters with a rectangular spatial-frequency response and a uniform orientation response. The resultant spatial frequency bands were as follows: Band 1 (0.1875–0.375 cycles per letter (cpl)), Band 2 (0.375–0.75 cpl), Band 3 (0.75–1.5 cpl) and Band 4 (1.5–3 cpl), with the upper limit being defined by the Nyquist limit for the monitor and viewing distance (475 mm).

The middle paragraph (99–101 words in length) of the text excerpts on each stimulus page contained one of three target words (square, circle, or triangle). Placement of the target word was counterbalanced, and each target word was used an equal number of times for each condition. At the bottom of each page (below the texture and text) were three corresponding shape symbols. The participants' task was to read the target paragraph

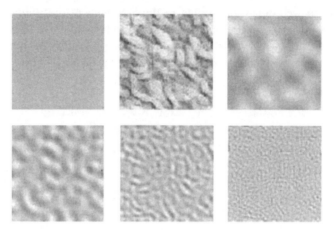

**Figure 12.4**   The texture samples show the plain texture, the unfiltered texture, and the filtered textures corresponding to bands 1–4.

and, as quickly and accurately as possible, find the target word and click (using the mouse) on the corresponding shape at the bottom of the page. The six background textures and an example stimulus are shown in Figures 12.4 and 12.5. The final design of the experiment ended up being incomplete because pilot testing revealed that, although the text was detectable on each of the six backgrounds, it was not readable for two of the low-text-contrast background conditions (those using the unfiltered periodic texture and the Band 3 filtered texture).

Results of the psychophysical experiment showed that the use of a textured background can influence readability (as measured by search times), especially when the background contains all frequencies or is limited to the frequencies in Band 3. Further, this effect was stronger for the low contrasts.

*Evaluation of the metrics*   Two image measures (text contrast and background RMS contrast) and two discriminability indices (metrics) were examined for their ability to predict the readability data (i.e., how well they correlated with the search times). Text contrast was calculated based on the text luminance and the average background luminance. Background RMS (root mean square) contrast describes the average contrast variability of the background texture itself. These two image measures led to Spearman rank correlation coefficients of −0.64 and 0.08, respectively.

The two discriminability indices were developed from image discrimination models, which are designed to predict the visibility of the difference between two similar images (where one image contains only noise and the other contains the signal plus noise). More specifically, such discrimination models take the two images as input, and output a prediction of just noticeable differences (JNDs) between them. Although their task was different from typical discrimination tasks, Scharff et al. (2000) hypothesized that text discriminability would affect readability, and thus should be predictive of reading search times. Therefore, even though the current stimuli always contained a target, the

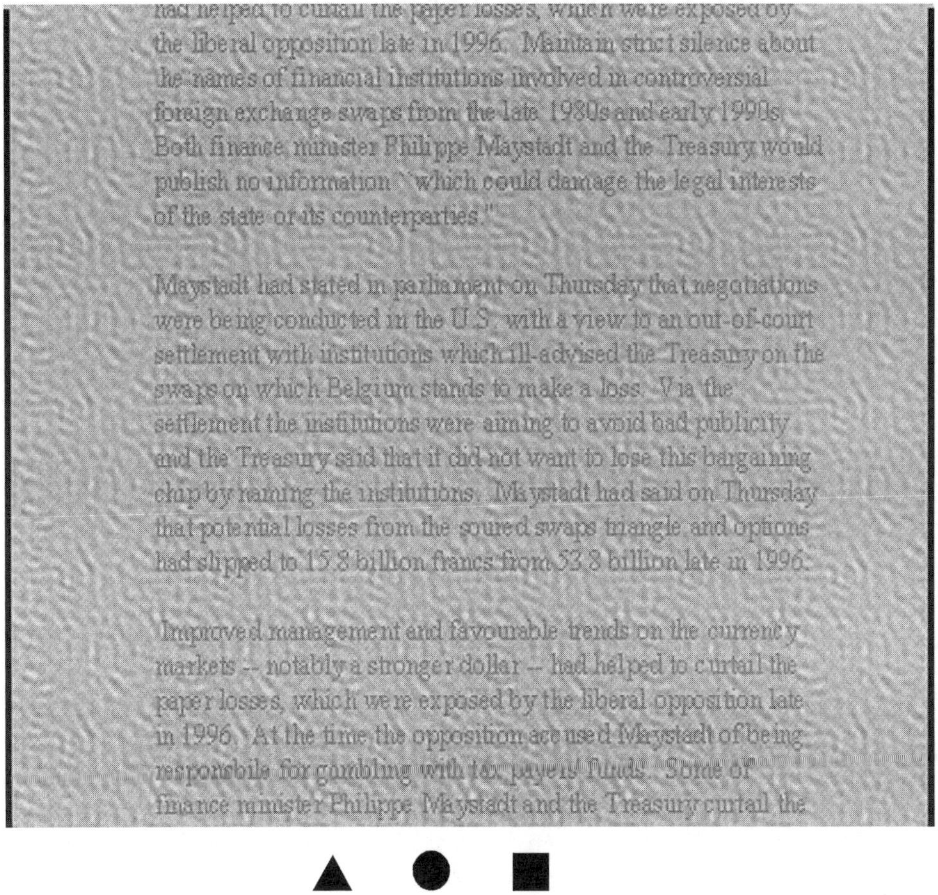

**Figure 12.5**   An example stimulus using a filtered texture (Band 3) and a text contrast of 0.35. The target word (triangle) is embedded in the middle paragraph. Once participants find the hidden word they click on the corresponding shape shown below the text and background area.

researchers considered the background alone to be a valid noise-only comparison image to use in the calculations. Mathematical derivations of these indices can be found in the original publications.

The first index was a global masking index. It combined text contrast and background RMS contrast using a single-filter image-discrimination model with global RMS contrast masking. This model assumes that the masking contrast energy is uniform over the target region and similar to the target in spatial frequency. Therefore, it was assumed that the output was independent of the size of the text target and the contrast sensitivity. For each text-plus-background condition, the final output of the global masking index was an equivalent text contrast: the text contrast that would give the same discriminability on a uniform background. These equivalent contrast numbers were then evaluated for their ability to predict the search times by using a Spearman rank correlation ($r = 0.84$).

The frequency-selective masking index was based on a model developed by Watson and Solomon (1997) that incorporates the known physiological existence of spatial-frequency and orientation-selective channels in the visual cortex. Such a model might better predict the effect of background masking when the spatial frequency content of the background varies or when the orientation of the pattern varies.

The Watson and Solomon (1997) model takes as input two images, which are then passed through a contrast sensitivity function (CSF) filter and an array of Gabor filters that vary in phase, spatial frequency, orientation, and spatial position. The filter array outputs then pass in parallel through both an excitatory and inhibitory nonlinearity. The inhibitory path passes through a linear pooling filter and then it divisively inhibits the excitatory signal. The resulting array representation from each of the two images is then subtracted and subjected to Minkowski pooling to obtain the prediction of the distance between the images in JND units ($d'$).

Scharff et al. (2000) modified Watson and Solomon's (1997) model to be consistent with the design of their experiment. Rather than using a large array of Gabor filters, an array was created that only included the four spatial frequency ranges of their stimuli. Four orientations were used (horizontal, vertical, and 45 degree diagonals to the left and right). Finally, rather than using a global CSF filter (as in the Global Masking Index), the gain of each spatial frequency channel was adjusted so that it matched the sensitivity curve for Gabor targets used by Watson and Solomon. The inhibitory pooling only summed over phase, unlike Watson and Solomon who also pooled over spatial frequency and orientation. When the $d'$ values obtained from this index were evaluated for their ability to predict the search times, the Spearman rank correlation was essentially the same as that obtained using the global masking index ($r = 0.81$).

Scharff et al. (2000) concluded that, for the background textures used in their experiment, the discriminability indices led to better predictability of readability (search times) than did the image measures alone. Because the Global Masking Index was much simpler computationally and it predicted readability as well as the Spatial Frequency Model index, Scharff et al. recommended its use when the background textures were fairly homogenous across the background region. However, because some background textures may show more spatial variation, an application to aid web designers may more strongly benefit from an implementation of the more complex Spatial Frequency Model index.

More recently, Scharff and Ahumada (2002) further improved the ability of the Global Masking Index to predict readability. This study used the same psychophysical procedure as Scharff et al. (2000), but examined the readability of transparent text (as seen with HUDs) on three textured backgrounds. In this case, the Global Masking Index again better predicted search times than did the image measures alone ($r = 0.83$, versus $r = -0.34$ for image contrast and $r = 0.77$ for background RMS contrast). However, as noted above, it was borrowed from models for signal detection, where the effect of the signal on masking and adaptation can be ignored. In this experiment, the text affected ~20 percent of the pixels. When both the text and the background were used to compute the text contrast and the masking RMS contrast, the adjusted index more accurately predicted readability ($r = 0.92$).

Although their adjusted Global Masking Index metric is relatively simple, and it does not take into account many of the known processing factors of the human visual system, it can account for a vast majority of the variation in search times for a reading task. Further, because it is simple, it may be more likely to be incorporated into other applications so that readability of text displays can be maximized without needing to test participants ahead of time.

## Summary

The above examples hopefully clarified three current approaches (classification images, functional neuroimaging, and metrics) used to study sensation and perception. As was mentioned above, the researchers using each of these approaches were also knowledgeable about the general methods of other approaches. Although much solid basic and applied research occurs using only isolated standard research methods, many of the recent, and most likely the upcoming, breakthroughs have and will require more integrated approaches. Advances in technology will continue and they will be modified and used by researchers who not only understand the fundamentals of the current sensation and perception research, but are also able to think beyond the limits of the current research environment.

## Appendix 12.1: The Calculation of Visual Angle

Visual angle is a way to indicate a stimulus size property without also having to describe the specific stimulus size or distance, although many researchers also redundantly give both the physical stimulus size and the viewing distance at some point in their methodology. The incorporation of visual angle is useful because as long as the visual angle is matched during replication, the stimulus size can be smaller (and placed closer to the eye) or larger (and be placed further from the eye). The use of the visual angle measure allows researchers to compare stimulus size and distance aspects more quickly and easily across different conditions and studies.

More specifically, visual angle predicts the amount of space on the retina (in degrees) that a stimulus image will cover. It can also be used to describe the relative locations of object images falling on the retina (how many degrees apart, etc.). Visual angle is also used to describe the frequency of gratings (e.g. 12 cycles per degree).

Visual angle subunits are minutes and seconds of arc. They are related as follows:

1 degree = 60 minutes of arc (or arcmin),

and

1 arcmin = 60 seconds of arc (or arcsec).

Visual angle ($\theta$) is calculated using simple geometry and the actual stimulus size and distance. Once the visual angle is known, the stimulus's image size on the retina can also be calculated using simple geometry (and the assumption of an average image distance from the lens of the eye). The geometrical relationships are illustrated below for an eye viewing the letter A of a specified

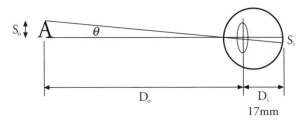

**Figure 12A.1**   Components used to calculate visual angle.

height $(S_o)$ and at a specified viewing distance $(D_o)$. The image size on the retina $(S_i)$ is based on an average image distance $(D_i)$ of 17mm (see Figure 12A.1).

The geometrical formulas for the relations between visual angle, size, and distance are as follows:

$$S_o/D_o = \tan \theta = S_i/D_i.$$

If the angle is not known, the geometry is easily manipulated to solve for it:

$$\theta = \arctan (S_o/D_o).$$

## References

Abbey, C., & Eckstein, M. (2000). Estimates of human-observer templates for simple detection tasks in correlated noise. In E. A. Krupinski (ed.) *Image Perception and Performance, SPIE Proceedings* (vol. 3981, pp. 70–7). Bellingham, WA: SPIE.

Ahumada, A. J. (1996). Perceptual classification images from vernier acuity masked by noise. *Perception, 26* (ECVP Suppl.), 18.

Beard, B. L., & Ahumada, A. J. (1998). A technique to extract relevant image features for visual tasks. In B. Rogowitz & T. Pappas (eds.), *Human Vision and Electronic Imaging III, SPIE Proceedings* (vol. 3299, pp. 79–85). Bellingham, WA: SPIE.

Boynton, G. M., Demb, J. B., Glover, G. H., & Heeger, D. J. (1999). Neuronal basis of contrast discrimination. *Vision Research, 39,* 257–69.

Carrasco, M., Penpeci-Talgar, C., & Eckstein, M. (2000). Spatial covert attention increases contrast senstivity across the CSF: Support for signal enhancement. *Vision Research, 40,* 1203–15.

Cornelissen, P., Hansen, P., Hutton, J., Evangelinou, V., & Stein, J. (1998). Magnocellular visual function and children's single word reading. *Vision Research, 38,* 471–82.

Deadwyler, S. (2001). *Neurobiological mechanisms of learning and memory and drug abuse.* Retrieved from <http://www.wfubmc.edu/physpharm/faculty/deadwyle.html>, November.

Demb, J. B., Boynton, G. M., & Heeger, D. J. (1997). Brain activity in visual cortex predicts individual differences in reading performance. *Proceedings of the National Academy of Science, 94,* 13363–6.

Demb, J. B., Boynton, G. M., & Heeger, D. J. (1998). Functional magnetic resonance imaging of early visual pathways in dyslexia. *The Journal of Neuroscience, 18* (17), 6939–51.

Di Russo, F., Spinelli, D., & Morrone, M. C. (2001). Automatic gain control contrast mechanisms are modulated by attention in humans: Evidence from visual evoked potentials. *Vision Research, 41,* 2435–47.

Engel, S. A., Glover, G. H., & Wandell, B. A. (1997). Retinotopic organization in human visual cortex and the spatial precision of functional MRI. *Cerebral Cortex, 7*, 181–92.

Gandhi, S. P., Heeger, D. J., & Boynton, G. M. (1999). Spatial attention affects brain activity in human primary visual cortex. *Proceedings of the National Academy of Science, 96*, 3314–19.

Geisler, W. S. (1989). Sequential ideal-observer analysis of visual discriminations. *Psychological Review, 96*, 267–314.

Hill, A., & Scharff, L. (1999). Readability of computer displays as a function of color, saturation, and background texture. In D. Harris (ed.), *Engineering Psychology and Cognitive Ergonomics*, vol. 4 (pp. 123–30). Aldershot, UK: Ashgate.

Keen, A., & Lovegrove, W. (2000). Transient deficit hypothesis and dyslexia: Examination of whole-parts relationship, retinal sensitivity, and spatial and temporal frequencies. *Vision Research, 40*, 705–15.

Kimura, D. (2000). A scientist dissents on sex and cognition. *Cerebrum, 2* (4), 68–84.

Knill, D. (1998). Discrimination of planar surface slant from texture: Human and ideal observers compared. *Vision Research, 38*, 1683–711.

Knoblauch, K., Thomas, J., & D'Zmura, M. (1999). Feedback, temporal frequency and stimulus classification. *Investigative Ophthalmology and Visual Science, 40*, S792.

Legge, G., Pelli, D., Rubin, G., & Schleske, M. (1985). Psychophysics of reading I. Normal vision. *Vision Research, 25*, 239–52.

Levi, D. M., & Klein, S. A. (2002). Classification images for detection and position discrimination in the fovea and parafovea. *Journal of Vision, 2* (1), 46–65, <http://journalofvision.org/2/1/7/, DOI 10.1167/2.1.7>.

Marr, D. (1982). *Vision*. San Francisco: W. H. Freeman.

McAdams, C., & Maunsell, J. (2000). Attention to both space and feature modulates neuronal responses in macaque area V4. *Journal of Neurophysiology, 83*, 1751–5.

Merigan, W. H., Byrne, C. E., & Maunsell, J. H. R. (1991). Does primate motion perception depend on the magnocellular pathway? *Journal of Neuroscience, 11*, 3422–9.

Mullen, K. T. (1985). The contrast sensitivity of human colour vision to red-green and blue-yellow chromatic gratings. *Journal of Physiology, 359*, 381–400.

Parish, D. H., & Sperling, G. (1991). Object spatial frequencies, retinal spatial frequencies, noise, and the efficiency of letter discrimination. *Vision Research, 31*, 1399–415.

Raine, A. (1999). Murderous minds: Can we see the mark of Cain? *Cerebrum, 1* (1), 15–29.

Rovamo, J. M., Kankaanpaa, M. I., & Kukkonen, H. (1999). Modelling spatial contrast sensitivity functions for chromatic and luminance-modulated gratings. *Vision Research, 39*, 2387–98.

Scharff, L. V., & Ahumada, A. J. (2002). Predicting the readability of transparent text. *Journal of Vision, 2* (9), 653–66, <http://journalofvision.org/2/9/7, DOI 10.1167/2.9.7>.

Scharff, L. V., Ahumada, A. J., & Hill, A. L. (1999). Discriminability measures for predicting readability. In B. Rogowitz & T. Pappas (eds.), *Human Vision and Electronic Imaging, IV, SPIE Proceedings* (vol. 3644, pp. 270–7). Bellingham, WA: SPIE.

Scharff, L. V., & Geisler, W. S. (1992). Stereopsis at isoluminance in the absence of chromatic aberrations. *Journal of the Optical Society of America, A 9*, 868–76.

Scharff, L. V., Hill, A. L., & Ahumada, A. J. (2000). Discriminability measures for predicting readability of text on textured backgrounds. *Optics Express, 6* (4), 81–91.

Schneider, W., Noll, D. C., & Cohen, J. D. (1993). Functional topographic mapping of the cortical ribbon in human vision with conventional MRI scanners. *Nature, 365*, 150–3.

Seminowicz, D. A. (2001). *PET and fMRI neuroimaging*. Retrieved from <http://www.uoguelph.ca/~dseminow/>, July.

Shadlen, M., & Newsome, W. (1996). Motion perception: Seeing and deciding. *Proceedings from the National Academy of Science, 93*, 628–33.

Shaywitz, S. E., Shaywitz, B. A., Fletcher, J. M., & Escobar, M. D. (1990). Prevalence of reading disability in boys and girls: Results of the Connecticut longitudinal study. *JAMA–Journal of the American Medical Association, 264*, 998–1002.

Skottun, B. (2000). The magnocellular deficit theory of dyslexia: The evidence from contrast sensitivity. *Vision Research, 40*, 111–27.

Solomon, J. A. (2002). Noise reveals visual mechanisms of detection and discrimination. *Journal of Vision, 2* (1), 105–20, <http://journalofvision.org/2/1/7/, DOI 10.1167/2.1.7>.

Solomon, J. A., & Pelli, D. G. (1994). The visual filter mediating letter identification. *Nature, 369*, 395–7.

Uttal, W. R., Liu, N., & Kalki, J. (1996). An integrated computational model of three-dimensional vision. *Spatial Vision, 9*, 393–422.

Watson, A. B., & Solomon, J. A. (1997). Model of visual contrast gain control and pattern masking. *Journal of the Optical Society of America A – Optics Image Science and Vision, 14*, 2379–91.

Wieringa, H. J. (1993). MEG, EEG and the integration with Magnetic Resonance Images. Ph.D. thesis, Enschede, The Netherlands. Retrieved from <http://www.neuro.com/megeeg/index2.htm>, September, 2001.

# CHAPTER THIRTEEN

# Taste

## Scott A. Bailey

Taste has been of interest to psychologists since psychology became a formal academic discipline. In 1900, Titchener recommended apparatuses and materials that a researcher might utilize when developing a basic psychological laboratory. Among these were materials to use when studying the various senses, including taste. Seashore (1909) published a paper concerning whether taste is a special sense. Notably, he employed a discrimination task involving the application of a drop of distilled water and a drop of the water plus a tastant on the tongues of humans. (A tastant is a stimulus – e.g., sucrose, salt, quinine – that is used to evoke a taste experience.) His participants successfully reported which drop contained the tastant even when the two drops were very near one another. He recommended adapting the use of this discrimination paradigm to the "lower senses" for the study of sensitivity thresholds and discrimination (Seashore, 1909).

Seashore's suggestion that taste may be a special sense was on the mark. The variety and nature of projects that researchers have conducted on taste and related phenomena since his time have been remarkable. Over the ensuing years the literature has developed with reports on taste research conducted on numerous species, as well as comparative work involving humans of different ages (Bartoshuk, 1989), sexes (Bartoshuk, Duffy, & Miller, 1995) and ethnic backgrounds (Soltan & Bracken, 1958; Steggerda, 1937), and humans and nonhuman animals (Murray, Wells, Kohn, & Miller, 1953; Richter & Campbell, 1940). The following is a partial listing of animals that have been involved in taste research over roughly 100 years: great tits (Warren & Vince, 1963), butterflies (Minnich, 1929), chimpanzees (Patton & Ruch, 1944), cockroaches (Frings, 1946), dogs (Kumazawa, Nakamura, & Kurihara, 1991), fish (Scharrer, Smith, & Palay, 1947), goats (Bell, 1963), guinea pigs (Warren & Pfaffmann, 1959), honey bees (Minnich, 1929), humans (Dallenbach & Dallenbach, 1943; Lashley, 1916; Meyer, 1952), kittens (Lashley, 1914), mice (Smith & Ross, 1960) monkeys (Boernstein, 1940), opossums (Pressman & Doolittle, 1966), pigs (Kare, Pond, & Campbell, 1965), pigeons (Duncan, 1964), quail (Brindley, 1965), rabbits (Pfaffman, 1955), rats (Benjamin, 1955; Garcia &

Koelling, 1966; Richter, Holt, & Barelare, 1937). Taste research with humans has addressed such issues as age-related changes in taste sensitivity (Byrd & Gertman, 1959; Cooper, Bilash, & Zubek, 1959) and the relation between ethnicity and the ability to taste phenylthiocarbamide (PTC) (Allison & Blumberg, 1959; Freire-Maia & Quelce-Salgado, 1960; Montenegro, 1964; Saldanha & Becak, 1959).

Psychologists have been interested in taste-related topics ranging from specific hungers resulting from dietary deficiencies (Richter et al., 1937; Young, 1941), to phylogenetic differences in taste perception and anatomy (Benjamin & Pfaffmann, 1955; Pfaffmann, 1955, 1959), to the role of taste in the eating behavior of humans, including those persons with eating disorders (Mitchell & Epstein, 1996; Polivy, Herman, & McFarlane, 1994) and other clinical syndromes (Graves, 1932; Henkin & Powell, 1962). The potential scope of a paper on the topic of taste is enormous. The present chapter is narrower in focus, giving attention to the function of taste across species; universal issues in taste; taste-related phenomena; the physiology of taste, including sensory transduction and neuronal projection to gustatory cortex; taste learning; and current issues in taste research.

## Function of Taste

The chemical senses, taste and smell, facilitate the consumption of foods and fluids that contribute to the satisfaction of an organism's metabolic and hydration needs. Given their relation to the oral cavity, the chemical senses also serve to protect an organism from ingesting potentially harmful substances. Aquatic species experience taste and smell together as the nature of their environment and means of extracting oxygen cause them to undergo chemical stimulation upon contacting both desirable and harmful water-borne chemistry (Marcstroem & Steinholtz, 1982). It is interesting to note that taste sensation in aquatic species commonly occurs via receptors located on the body in addition to those in the oral cavity. This situation is also true, for example, of insects that experience taste upon landing on potentially valuable food sources (Stocker, 1994).

Taste and smell occur as separate senses for animals that dwell outside the water. In land-dwelling mammals, smell facilitates recognition of food sources and water at a distance, and is employed when determining whether to approach or avoid a given substance. Taste, generally in combination with smell (Miller & Erickson, 1966), provides the final analysis of the potential value of a substance. The oral cavity, with its myriad taste receptor cells, membrane receptors, and receptor subunits, is the final gate through which potential food sources must pass in order to be admitted into the digestive system. Once in the digestive system, the constituent components of the ingested material, whether harmful or nutritious, are delivered into the organism's circulatory system. If the material produces a rapid change in blood chemistry, this change will be detected in the brainstem's medulla oblongata, which is not protected by the blood–brain barrier. In such a circumstance, a protective reflex may occur in which the medulla signals the gut to regurgitate its contents, thereby sparing the brain and body from prolonged exposure to potentially harmful substances. Normally, however, material that is ingested and delivered to the gut is processed by the intestines and delivered to target organs and bodily tissue via the circulatory system.

## Universals in Taste

Humans and many nonhuman animals experience four basic tastes: sweet, salty, sour, and bitter. Common stimuli used to study these tastes are sucrose, table salt (NaCl), hydro-chloric and other acids, and quinine, respectively. A potential fifth taste category, umami, has been of interest to researchers for some time. Umami is stimulated when tasting foods that are rich in glutamate (Mosel & Kantrowitz, 1954).

Sweet and salty tasting foods and fluids are characteristically ingested, though often with caution, even upon novel exposures. Such ingestion likely occurs because sweet tastes are usually associated with caloric value, and because sodium is vital to the func-tioning of biological systems. Sour and bitter, on the other hand, are characteristically rejected upon novel exposure, although humans and nonhuman animals frequently learn to acquire taste preferences for some sour and bitter substances. The tendencies to avoid sour and bitter are adaptive given that sour results when the acidity of food is increased as a function of the presence of bacteria that will likely cause gastric disturbance or worse. Bitter is characteristically associated with poison.

The taste sensation of umami is created when taste cell membrane receptors are stimulated by particles of glutamate, which is found in most protein-containing foods and in the food additive monosodium glutamate (MSG). Recent data suggest that umami is a separate taste category, but that it is experienced as a result of stimulating membrane receptors that are shared partially by sweet receptors (Li et al., 2002). Having evolved a taste mechanism that is maximally sensitive to protein-rich foods would certainly be adaptive, and it is perhaps of no surprise that the sensation of umami shares receptor complex subunits that facilitate sensation by calorie-rich sweets.

It is often said that the exception makes the rule. Although the four, or five, basic tastes are apparently experienced by nearly all humans, there is an interesting exception. Researchers have given a tremendous amount of effort to studying another bitter substance, phenylthiocarbamide (PTC), and its synthetic counterpart, propylthiouracil (PROP). Curiously, not everyone can taste these compounds. The capacity to taste PTC and PROP is genetically based. Approximately 25 percent of humans are very sensitive to the compounds (Bartoshuk, 2000), and interestingly are also sensitive to tastes such as those associated with coffee, grapefruit juice, and green tea. These super tasters experience saccharin and sucrose as sweeter than other people do and are more sensitive to capsaicin, the spicy "hot" ingredient in chili peppers (Bartoshuk et al., 1995). Roughly 50 percent of the population tastes PTC and PROP at levels below the extreme sensitivity shown by those persons just mentioned. Those persons who do not detect the substances exhibit a recessive genetic trait (Blakeslee & Fox, 1932).

Elements from each of the basic taste categories, alone or in combination, give rise to the more complex tastes that are associated with most foods. The sense of taste (gusta-tion) and the sense of smell (olfaction; see Chapter 14 by Batsell in this volume) work in combination to give rise to the experience of flavor. As a result of associative experience with palatable tastes and pleasant, food-related smells, naturally aversive tastes such as sour and bitter can come to be experienced as palatable. Among humans, there is one universally disgusting taste–smell combination: that of feces. Paul Rozin (e.g., Rozin & Fallon, 1987), whose research on taste has led him to study humans in a host of cultures has gathered data to support the claim of feces as universally disgusting.

Rozin's research has also addressed how humans come to acquire taste preferences for piquant foods, notably the capsicums (peppers). One might intuit that, among cultures that dwell in places where soil and climate conditions make growing vitamin-rich foods difficult, there would be a natural tendency to prefer regional vegetables even if they are piquant. This scenario, however, does not appear to be the case. Rather, Rozin and his colleagues (e.g., Rozin & Schiller, 1980) noted that among those people who live in the mountains of Mexico, it is customary to spare the very young from ingesting hot peppers. When children in the culture ask for permission to eat peppers, usually after having watched adults do so for at least a few years, they are allowed to do so, but with limited quantities. It is interesting to note that, as in most cultures, there are many adults who avoid consuming piquant foods; such people are not ostracized by their peers.

## Neuroanatomy of Taste System

### Tongue

Taste stimulation results when a molecule of food- or fluid-borne tastant fits the receptors on the microvilli at the tops of taste sensory cells. The protrusions of the microvilli, which effectively increase the sensitive surface area of the cell, extend into the taste pore, a microscopic balloon-like structure with an opening near the surface of the tongue. Together, these cells comprise the taste bud. Each taste bud may contain dozens of taste receptor cells, each of which has receptors for each of the taste categories (Smith & Travers, 1979). Many taste buds cover the surfaces of the macroscopic papillae (folds of skin), structures that may be seen on the tongue without magnification. There are two kinds of papillae that are well developed in humans. Fungiform papillae are innervated by cranial nerve VII (the facial nerve), and may be found in the anterior two thirds of the tongue. Circumvallate papillae are innervated by cranial nerve IX (the glossopharyngeal nerve), and may be found in the posterior one third of the tongue.

Stimulation of the microvilli occurs differently, as a function of the basic properties of a given tastant. Researchers once thought that the human tongue was mapped such that discrete populations of cells, each of which specialized in sensitivity to the four basic tastes, were distributed in a stereotypical pattern on the surface of the tongue. The conception of the tongue as being highly organized, as represented in the tongue maps in many textbooks, is wrong (Bartoshuk, 1993). Presently, it is thought that taste buds throughout the tongue are capable of responding to each category of taste (Smith & Margolskee, 2001), although maximal sensitivity may vary as a function of location on the tongue's surface.

Sweet taste sensation results when a substance such as sugar contacts microvilli and binds to G-protein-coupled receptors. Each receptor is coupled to G-proteins inside the cell. The G-protein complex is called gustducin, and is structurally and functionally similar to the transducin that is essential in rod-initiated vision. Activation of gustducin triggers a cascade of intracellular activity that causes potassium channels to close, which in turn leads to depolarization of the cell, ultimately resulting in sweet sensation.

Salty tastes stimulate receptors that gate sodium ion channels directly. Upon entering the cell, sodium ions cause depolarization of the cell until its firing threshold is reached and an action potential is generated. It is interesting to note that the number of salt receptors is regulated by aldosterone (Lin, Finger, Rossier, & Kinnamon, 1999), a hormone that serves to regulate sodium levels in the body.

Sour results when hydrogen ions block taste cell membrane potassium channels, causing the cells to depolarize until they fire. Due to their acidic nature, sour substances are often sensed via olfaction before they are consumed and able to contact taste cells. Given the natural tendency to avoid sour, and owing to the capacity to identify sour substances via the olfactory sense, physical proximity to a sour substance commonly results in the rejection of the food or fluid in question.

Bitter sensation has been of particular interest to psychologists. Bitter taste is experienced when a substance binds to a transmembrane receptor that is coupled to gustducin, similar to the process involved in sweet sensation. Interestingly, humans have at least two dozen variants on the G-protein subunit, each of which is involved in qualitatively different bitter reception. Individual taste cells seem to prefer to respond to some bitter-tasting molecules over others.

As is true elsewhere in the nervous system, receptor sensitivity in the taste system is dynamic. The up- and down-regulation of salt receptors by aldosterone, mentioned earlier, is an example of changing taste sensitivity. Other interesting taste sensitivity shifts that have been reported by humans include the experiencing of sour substances as sweet following ingestion of miracle fruit (*synsepalum dulciferum*) (Bartoshuk, Gentile, Molkowitz, & Meiselman, 1974). Ziziphins, the plant family from which jujube berries come, temporarily block sweet taste perception (Smith & Halpern, 1983).

## Neuronal projections from the tongue to the gustatory cortex

Taste receptor cells do not project to the central nervous system directly, but rather stimulate one of two cranial nerves. The chorda tympani branch of the facial nerve (cranial nerve number VII) is stimulated by taste cells on the lateral aspects of the tongue. The glossopharyngeal nerve (cranial nerve number IX) carries fibers from the rostral tongue.

The two taste nerves project to the solitary tract nucleus (NTS) of the medulla (Torvik, 1956). The NTS also receives input via the vagus nerve (cranial nerve X), from the gut, thereby making it an important site for integrating taste and postingestive feedback information. The NTS projects to the thalamus (Saper & Loewy, 1980). The ventral posteriomedial nucleus of the thalamus (VPM) projects to the gustatory cortex. In addition to the NTS–VPM pathway, the NTS also projects to the parabrachial nucleus of the pons (PBN) (Norgren, 1978), which in turn projects to the lateral hypothalamus and to the central nucleus of the amygdala (CN). The CN projects to the gustatory cortex, and is known to be involved in emotional responding as well. The gustatory cortex receives input, then, from both projection paths originating in the NTS. Projections to the hypothalamus may play a role in the reinforcing effects of sweet and salty tastes when one is hungry.

## Gustatory cortex

The functional role and neuroanatomical location of the gustatory cortex (GC) have received considerable research attention. For many years, the function of the GC was studied by experimentally ablating it and then measuring the resulting behavioral changes and deficiencies. More recently, intact animals have undergone associative training, with subjects being subsequently sacrificed and their brains labeled and stained using modern immunohistochemical techniques to look for activity markers that correlate with the behavioral experiences of the subjects prior to their being sacrificed (Lamprecht & Dudai, 1995). Recent experiments suggest that c-Fos, a protein that is expressed by cells during activity, may play an important role in the GC during taste learning (Navarro, Spray, Cubero, Thiele, & Bernstein, 2000) (see next section for discussion of taste learning). These experiments have used c-Fos immunohistochemistry to identify nuclei involved in the recognition of the conditional stimuli (CS), unconditional stimuli (US), and the CS–US association (Yamamoto, Shimura, Sako, Yasoshima, & Sakai, 1994).

Of the species used in experimental examinations of the GC, the rat has been the most common. The GC of the rat has been examined generally in the context of taste–illness training and testing. This brain region is a bilateral structure, located dorsal to the rhinal fissure and just anterior to the middle cerebral artery (Ables & Benjamin, 1960; Kosar, Grill, & Norgren, 1986a, 1986b; Wolf, 1968). Given that this brain region receives afferent taste fibers (Yamamoto & Kawamura, 1972) and fibers involved in feedback from the gut (Cechetto & Saper, 1990), the GC is particularly well-positioned to integrate stimulus inputs and facilitate adaptive behavioral responding to potential food sources.

A number of experiments have indicated that the GC mediates partially the associative salience necessary for appropriate formation of conditioned taste aversions (Bermudez-Rattoni & McGaugh, 1991; Braun, Slick, & Lorden, 1972; Kiefer & Braun, 1979; Yamamoto, Matsuo, & Kawamura, 1980). The learning deficit that results from ablation of the GC has been termed taste agnosia (Kiefer, Leach, & Braun, 1984). The deficit does not appear to reflect ageusia (an inability to detect tastes), as GC rats show characteristically normal responses to inherently aversive and appetitive tastes (Braun, Lasiter, & Kiefer, 1982).

Rats lacking GC are deficient specifically in the capacity to associate tastes with outcomes; they form appropriate aversions to odor stimuli and form taste-potentiated odor aversions (Braun, 1990; Kiefer et al., 1984; Kiefer & Morrow, 1991). Further, the behavioral changes exhibited by rats lacking GC occur independently of abilities to react to taste cues, or to respond to visceral inputs, as these functions remain intact in animals with lesions (Yaxley, Rolls, & Sienkiewicz, 1988). When other cues are available (e.g., odors, environment, postingestional effects, orofacial response feedback, temperature), GC rats are capable of learning to avoid conditional stimuli (Braun & Nowlis, 1989). A shift in attention to nontaste cues may explain the relative deficiencies in taste–illness association learning by GC rats. The deficiencies resulting from utilization of nontaste cues are consistent with Seligman's (1970) concept of preparedness for specific categories of learning (see also Garcia & Koelling, 1966); gastrointestinal feedback is associated more easily with taste than with auditory or visual cues.

Whereas the majority of research on the GC has involved the study of deficiencies exhibited by animals lacking GC, the immunohistochemical techniques mentioned above have permitted researchers to study normal functioning of the GC by intact animals. The work of Bernstein and her colleagues (e.g., Navarro et al., 2000) and Dudai and his colleagues (e.g., Lamprecht & Dudai, 1995) provide examples of c-Fos labeling of GC tissue during taste aversion acquisition. Beyond aversive associative conditioning, c-Fos immunochemistry may be used to examine the neuroanatomy of CTA extinction. Mickley and his colleagues have identified cells in the GC that were active while recognizing a familiar taste (Kenmuir, McMullen, Dengler, Remmers-Roeber, & Mickley, 2001b) and while the animals were extinguishing conditioned taste aversions (Kenmuir, McMullen, Dengler, Remmers-Roeber, & Mickley, 2001a). It is interesting to note that the numbers of marked cells that Mickley and his colleagues identify are significantly lower than those generated in laboratories by others performing similar experiments. This difference is likely the result of differences in criteria for counting a marked cell. As the techniques for using c-Fos become more standardized, it is expected that such inconsistencies will disappear.

## Taste Learning

Animals can learn to approach or avoid a given tastant, though studies in which a novel taste CS is paired with a noxious stimulus US on one or more occasions have predominated associative taste research. Typically this conditioning is done with animals that are maintained on restricted water access schedules. On acquisition trials, the CS is presented in lieu of water, and the US is presented afterward. Comparison groups in such experiments include those in which the CS is paired with an inert US, such as an injection of physiological saline, and those in which animals receive both the CS and the noxious US, but in an explicitly unpaired fashion (e.g., the US is presented in advance of the CS, or 24 hours later). Upon subsequent exposure to the CS, the experimental animals avoid consumption. The consumption avoidance that is exhibited by animals in nausea-paired conditions has been termed a conditioned taste aversion (CTA). Work from the last 20 years suggests that the term avoidance may be more appropriate than aversion as animals sometimes learn to avoid consuming tastes that they find palatable.

Domjan (1977) suggested that rats make good subjects in taste aversion experiments because they are omnivorous, but are unable to reject dangerous materials by vomiting. This combination of characteristics means that a rat must select carefully the potential nutrient sources that it consumes. Rats are well equipped to be selective and cautious in approaching food and fluid as their olfactory bulbs are proportionately large, thereby facilitating the capacity to identify both potentially harmful and desirable food sources at a distance.

Traditionally, researchers have relied on patterns of consumption to determine whether a rat "likes" or "does not like" a given taste stimulus. Moreover, researchers frequently study tastes that are presented in fluid media, as they are convenient to mix and fluid consumption is easy to measure. Some tastes, such as sweet and salty, are innately preferred by rats. That is, rats consume these tastes fairly freely during their first prolonged exposures to them. Bitter and sour tastes, on the other hand, are commonly avoided. Bitter or sour tastes are approached only with great trepidation, and only when "safe" tastes are not available as alternatives.

A common paradigm for studying taste learning, then, involves presenting a rat with a novel taste stimulus in a bottle on its cage. After the rat consumes some of the fluid, it is exposed to a noxious stimulus such as radiation or an injection of lithium chloride. After a single acquisition trial, a rat will avoid consumption of the conditional taste stimulus upon subsequent exposure to it. This phenomenon is labeled taste aversion learning, and is reliable and robust.

For many years it was common to demonstrate consumption avoidance using a timed two-bottle test. In such a test, the rat has access to both the illness-paired taste and to water. Following the two-bottle exposure, a consumption ratio may be calculated in which the amount of the tastant consumed is divided by the total quantity of fluid consumed. When the quotient exceeds 0.5 this is interpreted as an indication of preference for the taste. When the ratio is below 0.5, it is said to reflect an aversion. Under normal circumstances, trained rats will consume virtually none of the experimental fluid.

An alternative to the two-bottle test involves exposing rats to a single bottle that contains the fluid that was associated with illness. Batsell and Best (1993) argued that the one-bottle consumption test is a more appropriate test to use in taste aversion experiments. With the one-bottle approach, consumption patterns are viewed in relative terms – for example, experimental rats consume less than their control rat counterparts.

Garcia proposed that in order for a subject to develop a conditioned taste aversion, it must undergo a hedonic shift for the taste in question (Garcia, Hankins, & Rusiniak, 1974). That is, although a taste may have been highly palatable when it was first experienced, it actually comes to taste bad as a function of its association with resulting malaise. For example, if an unfamiliar sweet taste becomes associated with illness, it will be avoided upon subsequent exposure because the taste has become unpleasant. When researchers study diminished consumption patterns as indexes of taste learning, it is assumed that the reduction in consumption indicates that the fluid tastes "bad." Some researchers have argued that this pattern is more appropriately labeled consumption avoidance as it does not provide any indication of the quality of the taste (Grill, 1985; Kiefer & Orr, 1992).

The term consumption avoidance may be more appropriate as other variables such as associations with postingestive effects may play significant roles in the organization of behavior. For instance, a human might avoid consuming a highly palatable food because its consumption has become associated with gastric upset. On the other hand, some people consume alcohol, even though it tastes bad to them, because it has desirable postingestive effects. In short, an organism's willingness to consume a particular stimulus may not reflect whether it tastes good or bad.

Grill and his colleagues (Berridge & Grill, 1983; Grill & Norgren, 1978; Pelchat, Grill, Rozin, & Jacobs, 1983) have developed a technique – the taste reactivity procedure – for assessing the palatability of taste stimuli for rats. The taste reactivity procedure involves infusing a small amount of fluid, typically one milliliter, into a rat's oral cavity via a surgically implanted fistula, and then noting stereotyped orofacial responding. The responses that rats make to fluids presented this way may be categorized as being one of two types of behaviors: ingestive or aversive. Ingestive responding includes activity that serves to move the fluid back into the rat's oral cavity as though it is being consumed. Aversive responding involves activity that indicates rejection of the fluid.

The prototypical ingestive response is called a tongue protrusion, and resembles the licking behavior rats exhibit when they consume fluid from a sipper tube. The prototypical aversive response is called a gape. A gape involves a high-amplitude opening of the mouth, associated with retraction of the cheeks and extension of the tongue so as to expel the fluid.

The taste reactivity procedure has been considered an effective means for assessing the palatability of taste solutions. As such, researchers have used it to assess the acquisition of conditioned taste aversions in rats. Its advantages for estimating palatability are that the taste stimuli are presented in small quantities, and that resulting responses may be videotaped for future scoring by someone who is blind to the rats' group affiliations. Because responses are taped concurrently with brief exposures to the fluid, it is reasonable to assume that the responses do not occur as a function of postingestive feedback.

In addition to studying aversive taste learning, researchers also study the acquisition of taste preferences. Learned taste preferences may result from two kinds of experiences: the positive association of a CS with a physiological outcome (Lett & Grant, 1989) or as an artifact of a neophilic response (Davis, Bailey, & Thompson, 1993). The neophilic response is demonstrated when an animal that has received a deficient diet for an extended time readily consumes a novel food or fluid, the taste of which, if it becomes associated with recovery from the deficiency, comes to be preferred. The neophilic response has also been called the conditioned medicine effect, a reflection of the animal's association of taste and return to wellness.

## Current Trends and New Directions in Taste Research

Researchers still have much to learn about the ways in which human and nonhuman animals experience taste and develop taste associations. It is predictable that research in these areas of research will involve increasingly molecular techniques for studying the nervous system in general and the taste system specifically. The immunohistochemical labeling research on the taste system represents only a beginning in the process of developing a comprehensive understanding of how the taste system works, from the taste receptor cells to the host of brain nuclei and regions that are necessary for normal acquisition and extinction of taste-related associations. Although researchers have reliably measured the expression of c-Fos-related proteins, for example, the functions of these proteins are as yet unknown. Are these proteins necessary for taste learning? Would blocking their expression result in compromised learning, or are they merely markers of activity? Antisense technology may give some insight into these questions. Antisense technology involves using a pharmacological agent to block the expression of gene proteins such as c-Fos. Not until the binding affinity of antisense is both reliably strong and highly selective, however, will researchers be able to understand more clearly the function(s) of c-Fos (and other similar gene proteins).

In addition to developing clearer pictures of how taste is sensed in the tongue (and elsewhere as with insects and fishes), it will be important to elucidate the roles of each of the brain nuclei in the taste learning pathway. This importance is true for both the nuclei involved in both the initial acquisition of taste associations and for extinction of such associations. Karl Lashley, the father of physiological psychology, was extremely important in popularizing the concept of the engram, the precise address or location of a memory (trace). Richard Thompson has discovered that, at least for the nictitating membrane response in rabbits, the engram migrates from limbic and cortical structures to the cerebellum. It is fascinating to consider that the engram for associative taste memories may be different for acquisition than for extinction. Developing the methodologies and associated technologies for addressing these issues will surely be valuable for understanding more clearly the associative processes involved in other kinds of learning.

Taste learning is very robust, and thus provides an excellent model for addressing the mechanisms by which areas throughout the nervous system are modified as a function of experience. Given that taste learning occurs in both appetitive and aversive dimensions, the future of taste learning research will surely provide meaningful insight into a host of issues and problems of interest to psychologists.

## References

Ables, M. F., & Benjamin, R. M. (1960). Thalamic relay nucleus for taste in albino rat. *Journal of Neurophysiology*, 23, 376–82.

Allison, A. C., & Blumberg, B. S. (1959). Ability to taste phenylthiocarbamide among Alaskan Eskimos and other populations. *Human Biology*, 31, 352–9.

Bartoshuk, L. M. (1989). Taste: Robust across the age span? *Annals of the New York Academy of Sciences*, 561, 65–75.

Bartoshuk, L. M. (1993). The biological basis for food perception and acceptance. *Food Quality and Preference*, 4, 21–32.

Bartoshuk, L. M. (2000). Comparing sensory experiences across individuals: Recent psychophysical advances illuminate genetic variation in taste perception. *Chemical Senses*, 25, 447–60.

Bartoshuk, L. M., Duffy, V. B., & Miller, I. J. (1995). PTC/PROP taste: Anatomy, psychophysics, and sex effects: Erratum. *Physiology and Behavior*, 58, 203.

Bartoshuk, L. M., Gentile, R. L., Molkowitz, H. R., & Meiselman, H. L. (1974). Sweet taste induced by miracle fruit (*synsepalum dulcificum*). *Physiology and Behavior*, 12, 449–56.

Batsell, W. R., & Best, M. R. (1993). One bottle too many? Method of testing determines the detection of overshadowing and retention of taste aversions. *Animal Learning & Behavior, 21,* 154–8.

Bell, F. R. (1963). Alkaline taste in goats assessed by the preference test technique. *Journal of Comparative and Physiological Psychology, 56,* 174–8.

Benjamin, R. M. (1955). Cortical taste mechanisms studied by two different test procedures. *Journal of Comparative and Physiological Psychology, 48,* 119–22.

Benjamin, R. M., & Pfaffmann, C. (1955). Cortical localization of taste in albino rat. *Journal of Neurophysiology, 18,* 56–63.

Bermudez-Rattoni, F., & McGaugh, J. L. (1991). Insular cortex and amygdala lesions differently affect acquisition of inhibitory avoidance and conditioned taste aversion. *Brain Research, 549,* 165–70.

Berridge, K. C., & Grill, H. J. (1983). Alternating ingestive and aversive consummatory responses suggest a two-dimensional analysis of palatability in rats. *Behavioral Neuroscience, 97,* 563–73.

Blakeslee, A. F., & Fox, A. L. (1932). Our different taste worlds. *Journal of Heredity, 23,* 97–110.

Boernstein, W. S. (1940). Cortical representation of taste in man and monkey. I. Functional and anatomical relations of taste, olfaction and somatic sensibility. *Yale Journal of Biology and Medicine, 12,* 719–36.

Braun, J. J. (1990). Gustatory cortex: Definition and function. In B. Kolb and R. C. Tees (eds.), *The cerebral cortex of the rat* (pp. 407–30) Cambridge, MA: MIT Press.

Braun, J. J., Lasiter, P. S., & Kiefer, S. W. (1982). Gustatory neocortex of the rat. *Physiological Psychology, 10,* 13–45.

Braun, J. J., & Nowlis, G. G. (1989). Neurological foundations of learned appetitive aversions. *Nutrition 5,* 121–7.

Braun, J. J., Slick, T. B., & Lorden, J. F. (1972). Involvement of gustatory neocortex in the learning of taste aversions. *Physiology and Behavior, 9,* 637–41.

Brindley, L. D. (1965). Taste discrimination in Bob-white and Japanese quail. *Animal Behaviour, 13,* 507–12.

Byrd, E., & Gertman, S. (1959). Taste sensitivity in aging persons. *Geriatrics, 14,* 381–4.

Cechetto, D. F., & Saper, C. B. (1990). Role of the cerebral cortex in autonomic function. In A. D. Loey and K. M. Spyer (eds.), *Central regulation of autonomic function* (pp. 208–23) New York: Oxford University Press.

Cooper, R. M., Bilash, I., & Zubek, J. P. (1959). The effect of age on taste sensitivity. *Journal of Gerontology, 14,* 56–8.

Dallenbach, J. W., & Dallenbach, K. M. (1943). The effects of bitter-adaptation on sensitivity to the other taste-qualities. *American Journal of Psychology, 56,* 21–31.

Davis, S. F., Bailey, S. A., & Thompson, A. M. (1993). Exposure to a protein- and tryptophan-deficient diet results in neophilia. *Bulletin of the Psychonomic Society, 31,* 213–16.

Domjan, M. (1977). Selective suppression of drinking during a limited period following aversive drug treatments in rats. *Journal of Experimental Psychology: Animal Behavior Process, 3,* 66–76.

Duncan, C. J. (1964). The sense of taste in the feral pigeon. The response to acids. *Animal Behaviour, 12,* 77–83.

Freire-Maia, A., & Quelce-Salgado, A. (1960). Taste sensitivity to P.T.C. in samples from three Brazilian populations. *Annals of Human Genetics, 24,* 97–102.

Frings, H. (1946). Gustatory thresholds for sucrose and electrolytes for the cockroach, *Periplaneta americana* (Linn.). *Journal of Experimental Zoology, 102,* 23–50.

Garcia, J., Hankins, W. G., & Rusiniak, K. W. (1974). Behavioral regulation of the milieu interne in man and rat: Food preferences set by delayed visceral effects facilitate memory research and predator control. *Science, 185,* 824–31.

Garcia, J., & Koelling, R. A. (1966). Relation of cue to consequence in avoidance learning. *Psychonomic Science, 4*, 123–4.

Graves, T. C. (1932). Non-specific therapy in mental disorder. *Lancet, 223*, 115–21.

Grill, H. J. (1985). Physiological mechanisms in conditioned taste aversions. *Annals of the New York Academy of Science, 443*, 67–88.

Grill, H. J., & Norgren, R. (1978). The taste reactivity test: I. Mimetic responses to gustatory stimuli in neurologically normal rats. *Brain Research, 143*, 263–79.

Henkin, R. I., & Powell, G. F. (1962). Increased sensitivity of taste and smell in cystic fibrosis. *Science, 138*, 1107–8.

Kare, M. R., Pond, W. C., & Campbell, J. (1965). Observations on the taste reactions in pigs. *Animal Behaviour, 13*, 265–9.

Kenmuir, C. L., McMullen, C. A., Dengler, C. M., Remmers-Roeber, D. R., & Mickley, G. A. (2001a). Changes in brain c-fos expression during extinction of a conditioned taste aversion (CTA). (Abstract) Poster presented at the annual meeting of the International Behavioral Neuroscience Society, April 25–9, Cancun, Mexico.

Kenmuir, C. L., McMullen, C. A., Dengler, C. M., Remmers-Roeber, D. R., & Mickley, G. A. (2001b). A role for gustatory neocortex (GNC) in the detection of a familiar taste and the extinction of a conditioned taste aversion (CTA). (Abstract) Poster presented at the annual meeting of the Society for Neuroscience, November 10–15, San Diego, CA.

Kiefer, S. W., & Braun, J. J. (1979). Acquisition of taste avoidance habits in rats lacking gustatory neocortex. *Physiological Psychology, 7*, 245–50.

Kiefer, S. W., Leach, L. R., & Braun, J. J. (1984). Taste agnosia following gustatory neocortex ablation: Dissociation from odor and generality across taste qualities. *Behavioral Neuroscience, 98*, 590–608.

Kiefer, S. W., & Morrow, N. S. (1991). Odor cue mediation of alcohol aversion learning in rats lacking gustatory neocortex. *Behavioral Neuroscience, 105*, 25–32.

Kiefer, S. W., & Orr, M. R. (1992). Taste avoidance, but not aversion, learning in rats lacking gustatory cortex. *Behavioral Neuroscience, 106*, 140–6.

Kosar, E., Grill, H. J., & Norgren, R. (1986a). Gustatory cortex in the rat. I. Physiological properties and cytoarchitecture. *Brain Research, 379*, 329–41.

Kosar, E., Grill, H. J., & Norgren, R. (1986b). Gustatory cortex in the rat. II. Thalamocortical projections. *Brain Research, 379*, 342–52.

Kumazawa, T., Nakamura, M., & Kurihara, K. (1991). Canine taste nerve responses to umami substances. *Physiology and Behavior, 49*, 875–81.

Lamprecht, R., & Dudai, Y. (1995). Differential modulation of brain immediate early genes by intraperitoneal LiCl. *Neuroreport: An International Journal for the Rapid Communication of Research in Neuroscience, 7*, 289–93.

Lashley, K. S. (1914). A note on the persistence of an instinct. *Journal of Animal Behavior, 4*, 293–4.

Lashley, K. S. (1916). The human salivary reflex and its use in psychology. *Psychological Review, 23*, 446–64.

Lett, B. T., & Grant, V. L. (1989). Conditioned taste preference produced by pairing a taste with a low dose of morphine or sufentanil. *Psychopharmacology, 98*, 236–9.

Li, X., Staszewski, L., Xu, H., Durick, K., Zoller, M., & Adler, E. (2002). Human receptors for sweet and umami taste. *Proceedings of the National Academy of Sciences, 99*, 4692–6.

Lin, W., Finger, T. E., Rossier, B. C., & Kinnamon, S. C. (1999). Epithelial Na+ channel subunits in rat taste cells: Localization and regulation by aldosterone. *Journal of Comparative Neurology, 405*, 406–20.

Marcstroem, A., & Steinholtz, G. (1982). A new method for measuring the ability of fish to orient in chemical gradients. *Physiology and Behavior, 29,* 1183–4.

Meyer, D. R. (1952). The stability of human gustatory sensitivity during changes in time of food deprivation. *Journal of Comparative and Physiological Psychology, 45,* 373–6.

Miller, S. D., & Erickson, R. P. (1966). The odor of taste solutions. *Physiology and Behavior, 1,* 145–6.

Minnich, D. E. (1929). The chemical senses of insects. *Quarterly Review of Biology, 1,* 100–12.

Mitchell, S. L., & Epstein, L. H. (1996). Changes in taste and satiety in dietary-restrained women following stress. *Physiology and Behavior, 60,* 495–9.

Montenegro, L. (1964). P. T. C. tasting among Tucano Indians. *Annals of Human Genetics, 28,* 185–7.

Mosel, J. N., & Kantrowitz, G. (1954). Absolute sensitivity to the glutamic taste. *Journal of General Psychology, 51,* 11–18.

Murray, E. J., Wells, H., Kohn, M., & Miller, N. E. (1953). Sodium sucaryl: A substance which tastes sweet to human subjects but is avoided by rats. *Journal of Comparative and Physiological Psychology, 46,* 134–7.

Navarro, M., Spray, K. J., Cubero, I., Thiele, T. E., & Bernstein, I. L. (2000). cFos induction during conditioned taste aversion expression varies with aversion strength. *Brain Research, 887,* 450–3.

Norgren, R. (1978). Projections from the nucleus of the solitary tract in the rat. *Neuroscience, 3,* 207–18.

Patton, H. D., & Ruch, T. C. (1944). Preference thresholds for quinine hydrochloride in chimpanzee, monkey and rat. *Journal of Comparative Psychology, 37,* 35–49.

Pelchat, M. L., Grill, H. J., Rozin, P., & Jacobs, J. (1983). Quality of acquired responses to tastes by *Rattus norvegicus* depends on type of associated discomfort. *Journal of Comparative Psychology, 97,* 140–53.

Pfaffmann, C. (1955). Gustatory nerve impulses in rat, cat and rabbit. *Journal of Neurophysiology, 18,* 429–40.

Pfaffmann, C. (1959). The afferent code for sensory quality. *American Psychologist, 14,* 226–32.

Polivy, J., Herman, C. P., & McFarlane, T. (1994). Effects of anxiety on eating: Does palatability moderate distress-induced overeating in dieters? *Journal of Abnormal Psychology, 103,* 505–10.

Pressman, T. G., & Doolittle, J. H. (1966). Taste preferences in the Virginia opossum. *Psychological Reports, 18,* 875–8.

Richter, C. P., & Campbell, K. H. (1940). Sucrose taste thresholds of rats and humans. *American Journal of Physiology, 128,* 291–7.

Richter, C. P., Holt, L. E., Jr., & Barelare, B., Jr. (1937). Vitamin B-sub(1) craving in rats. *Science, 86,* 354–5.

Rozin, P., & Fallon, A. E. (1987). A perspective on disgust. *Psychological Review, 94,* 23–41.

Rozin, P., & Schiller, D. (1980). The nature and acquisition of a preference for chili pepper by humans. *Motivation and Emotion, 4,* 77–101.

Saldanha, P. H., & Becak, W. (1959). Taste thresholds for phenylthiourea among Ashkenazic Jews. *Science, 129,* 150–1.

Saper, C. B., & Loewy, A. D. (1980). Efferent connections of the parabrachial nucleus in the rat. *Brain Research, 197,* 291–317.

Scharrer, E, Smith, S. W., & Palay, S. L. (1947). Chemical sense and taste in the fishes, *Prionotus* and *Trichogaster*. *Journal of Comparative Neurology and Psychology, 86,* 183–98.

Seashore, C. E. (1909). Discussion. Is taste a spatial sense? *Psychological Bulletin, 6,* 151.

Seligman, M. E. (1970). On the generality of the laws of learning. *Psychological Review, 77* (5), 406–18.

Smith, D. V., & Margolskee, R. F. (2001). Making sense of taste. *Scientific American* (Online), March 2001. <http://www.sciam.com/article.cfm?articleID=000641D5-F855-1C70-84A9809EC588EF21&catID=2>.

Smith, D. V., & Travers, J. B. (1979). A metric for the breadth of tuning of gustatory neurons. *Chemical Senses and Flavor, 4,* 215–29.

Smith, M. P., & Ross, S. (1960). Acceptance of sodium sucaryl by C57 black mice. *Journal of Genetic Psychology, 96,* 101–4.

Smith, V. V., & Halpern, B. P. (1983). Selective suppression of judged sweetness by ziziphins. *Physiology and Behavior, 30,* 867–74.

Soltan, H. C., & Bracken, S. E. (1958). The relation of sex to taste reactions for P.T.C., sodium benzoate and four "standards." *Journal of Heredity, 49,* 280–4.

Steggerda, M. (1937). Testing races for the threshold of taste, with PTC. *Journal of Heredity, 28,* 309–10.

Stocker, R. F. (1994). The organization of the chemosensory system in *Drosophila melanogaster*: A review. *Cell and Tissue Research, 275,* 3–26.

Titchener, E. B. (1900). The equipment of a psychological laboratory. *American Journal of Psychology, 11,* 251–65.

Torvik, A. (1956). Afferent connections to the sensory trigeminal nuclei, the nucleus of the solitary tract and adjacent structures. *Journal of Comparative Neurology, 106,* 51–132.

Warren, R. P., & Pfaffmann, C. (1959). Early experience and taste aversion. *Journal of Comparative and Physiological Psychology, 52,* 263–6.

Warren, R. P., & Vince, M. A. (1963). Taste discrimination in the great tit (*Parus major*). *Journal of Comparative and Physiological Psychology, 56,* 910–13.

Wolf, G. (1968). Projections of thalamic and cortical gustatory areas in the rat. *Journal of Comparative Neurology, 44,* 440–54.

Yamamoto, T., & Kawamura, Y. (1972). Summated cerebral responses to taste stimuli in the rat. *Physiology and Behavior, 9,* 789–93.

Yamamoto, T., Matsuo, R., & Kawamura, Y. (1980). Localization of cortical gustatory area in rats and its role in taste discrimination. *Journal of Neurophysiology, 44,* 440–54.

Yamamoto, T., Shimura, T., Sako, N., Yasoshima, Y., & Sakai, N. (1994). Neural substrates for conditioned taste aversion in the rat. *Behavioral Brain Research, 65,* 123–37.

Yaxley, S., Rolls, E. T., & Sienkiewicz, Z. J. (1988). The responsiveness of neurons in the insular gustatory cortex of the macaque monkey is independent of hunger. *Physiology and Behavior, 42,* 223–9.

Young, P. T. (1941). The experimental analysis of appetite. *Psychological Bulletin, 38,* 129–64.

# CHAPTER FOURTEEN

# Olfaction: Recent Advances in Learning about Odors

## W. Robert Batsell, Jr.

The empirical analysis of olfaction and odors covers a wide range of possible topics in experimental psychology. At one extreme are studies of physiology and perception that advance our understanding of how odors are transduced into neuronal information and how this information is interpreted by specific brain regions. On the other hand, other studies may examine how odors serve as signals for important biological events such as the presence of food sources or the presence of predators. To provide a more coherent summary of recent studies using odors as signals, this chapter will eschew advances in studies of olfaction (for a current review of these topics see Doty, 2001); instead, the focus of this chapter will be on recent empirical advances in learning about odors. Most experiments that examine learning about odors occur in one of two types. Some studies use odors because they are the medium by which this signal is produced or conveyed, whereas other studies involve an odor cue because it is a more effective stimulus for rodents than visual or auditory stimuli. The present chapter will focus on recent advances or new techniques in three broad areas: the unique interactions of odors and tastes in feeding situations, odor learning in human evaluative conditioning and perception studies, and odors as signals of anxiety/fear-producing events. There are many other examples of odor research that would be appropriate for this chapter, such as learning about odors as signals of goal events (e.g., Ludvigson, 1999), learning about the food substances consumed by conspecifics (e.g., Galef, 1996), and recent examinations of transitive inference in rodents with odors (Eichenbaum, 1999), but space limitations dictate that some areas will not be represented.

## Odors as Signals of Food

One area in which olfaction plays a vital role in the survival of the organism is in the detection of edible and poisonous foods. The organism that can identify safe and unsafe foods via olfactory cues will have an advantage over other organisms that must consume the food – possibly with fatal consequences. Thus two areas in which learning about odors has been the primary research focus are flavor-aversion and flavor-preference learning. In particular, some of the most interesting research done in this area has focused on the unique patterns of learning that occur when tastes and odors are conditioned in compound.

### *Flavor-aversion studies*

In the flavor-aversion learning paradigm, an organism consumes a food or liquid prior to induction of an illness episode (typically by the administration of a mild toxin such as lithium chloride). Flavor-aversion learning is a type of classical conditioning in which the taste or odor is the conditioned stimulus (CS), the illness-inducing agent is the unconditioned stimulus (US), illness is the unconditioned response (UCR), and subsequent refusal to reconsume the taste is the conditioned response (CR). John Garcia and his colleagues conducted many of the initial studies in taste-aversion learning. They demonstrated that taste-aversion learning could be acquired very rapidly, within one or two pairings of taste with illness, and that it differed from other forms of classical conditioning in certain regards. Garcia and his colleagues used the results from three different phenomena to conclude that flavor-aversion learning principles had evolved to preferentially associate tastes, and not odors, with illness. These three phenomena are cue-to-consequence learning, long-delay learning, and taste-mediated potentiation.

*Cue-to-consequence learning* Garcia and Koelling (1966) introduced the concept of *cue-to-consequence learning* in their classic "bright, noisy, tasty water" experiment. In this experiment, rats had the opportunity to drink a flavored substance from an apparatus that produced flashing lights and clicking noises with each tongue contact. Then half of the rats received an illness-inducing US whereas the other half received a shock US. During testing, all rats had a choice of drinking the flavored substance or water in the presence of the light and noise cues. It was observed that rats that experienced the illness US showed a stronger aversion to the taste CS whereas rats that experienced the shock US showed a stronger aversion to the audiovisual CSs. These findings demonstrated that certain cues (CSs) are better associated with certain consequences (USs), and taste cues are the best cue for illness.

*Long-delay learning* The principle of long-delay learning can be demonstrated by varying the CS–US interval (i.e., the period of time between offset of the CS and onset of the US). In most classical conditioning preparations (fear conditioning, salivation conditioning), the optimal CS–US interval is less than one second, and reliable conditioning will not occur with CS–US intervals that are greater than 10 seconds (e.g., Barker, 2001). In flavor-aversion learning, however, not only can reliable aversions be conditioned with very long CS–US intervals, but conditioning at short CS–US intervals is often weak. For example, Kalat and Rozin (1971) allowed rats to drink sucrose, and then illness was induced via lithium chloride after CS–US intervals of 0.5, 1, 1.5, 3, 6, and 24 hours. Experimental rats with CS–US intervals up to three hours showed significantly stronger taste aversions than controls that never received taste plus illness pairings. Rats with the six-hour and the 24-hour CS–US interval did not show reliable taste aversions.

More recently, Schafe, Sollars, and Bernstein (1995) compared conditioning with either a very short CS–US interval (10 seconds) or a moderate CS–US interval (15 minutes). They used a procedure that allowed for direct delivery of the saccharin CS into the rat's mouth and the lithium chloride US into the rat's gut. They determined that rats conditioned with the 15-minutes CS–US interval had significantly stronger taste aversions than rats conditioned with the 10-second CS–US interval. In sum, taste-aversion learning appears to be unique because it can occur following rather long CS–US intervals, and appears to be more effective after moderate CS–US intervals. In contrast, odor-aversion conditioning has been characterized as being weaker than taste-aversion conditioning. For example, many researchers have noted that reliable odor aversions are not established if the CS–US interval extends beyond 15 minutes (e.g., Bouton, Jones, McPhillips, & Swartzentruber, 1986; Rusiniak, Hankins, Garcia, & Brett, 1979).

*Taste-mediated odor potentiation* In 1979, Rusiniak et al. introduced the concept of taste-mediated odor potentiation. They paired a taste, a weak odor, or the taste plus odor compound, with illness. They found little to no conditioning to the odor cue alone – a finding that is relatively consistent with prior work with odor-aversion learning. Interestingly, the rats that received aversion conditioning with the odor plus taste compound demonstrated a significantly stronger odor aversion. Rusiniak et al. argued that the presence of the salient taste cue served to enhance or *potentiate* odor conditioning. Furthermore, when the compound conditioning groups were tested with the taste element of the compound, they showed a weak or *overshadowed* taste aversion relative to rats that received taste alone conditioning. This outcome is of theoretical interest because compound conditioning normally produces weak conditioning to both elements of the compound, or the more salient element overshadows conditioning to the weaker element (e.g., Pavlov, 1927). Thus the results from taste plus odor compound conditioning differ from other classical conditioning paradigms in that conditioning is potentiated to the weak element of the compound (the odor) and overshadowed to the strong element of the compound (the taste).

On the basis of these three phenomena, Garcia and his colleagues proposed the sensory and gate channeling model (Garcia, Lasiter, Bermudez-Rattoni, & Deems, 1985). In this model, taste cues are processed exclusively within the internal or gut defense system, where tastes are preferentially associated with illness sensations. This gut defense system allows for associations to be formed even following very long CS–US periods. Auditory and visual cues are processed within the external defense system, apparently because most threats to the periphery would be signaled by audiovisual cues. Olfactory cues are unique because they may be processed within either defense system. For example, an odor such as smoke that signals external threat would be processed within the external defense system, whereas an odor arising from a food source would be processed by the internal defense system. Furthermore, it is the ability of the taste cue to "gate" the odor cue into the internal defense system that produces taste-mediated odor potentiation. Because presentation of the taste plus odor compound allows the odor to enter the internal defense system, it is processed similarly to the salient taste, and thus a stronger odor aversion is observed. Thus, within this framework, odors are weakly associated with illness unless they are accompanied by a taste (for a discussion of theoretical accounts of potentiation, see LoLordo & Droungas, 1989).

*Recent research in odor-aversion conditioning*  Two recent lines of research investigating odor-aversion conditioning have revealed new insight into odor's associability across long CS–US intervals, and the interaction of tastes and odors in compound. First, in 1997, Slotnick, Westbrook, and Darling reported the results from a series of experiments that were designed specifically to test some of the claims of the sensory and gate channeling model. In particular, the basis for their experiments was the idea that tastes are not more readily associated with illness than are odors, but that tastes are a more salient aspect of ingested food than are odors. If this hypothesis is correct, a highly salient odor should have many of the properties of a salient taste, including the ability to show long-delay learning and to potentiate conditioning to weaker stimuli. With the use of an olfactory discrimination task, Slotnick et al. established that 0.1 percent and 0.01 percent aqueous isoamyl acetate solutions were olfactory stimuli with little to no stimulus control by the gustatory properties of the solution. In Experiment 3, rats were given either a taste solution (0.1% or 0.25% saccharin) or an odor solution (0.15% aqueous isoamyl acetate solution), and injected with lithium chloride after a one-hour, four-hour, or 12-hour interval. As expected, testing of either stimulus revealed that aversion strength decreased as the CS–US interval increased. However, of particular note, rats that had the odor solution paired with illness at one-hour and four-hour intervals showed a significantly stronger odor aversion than the saccharin aversions of rats conditioned with taste at comparable intervals. Thus this outcome demonstrated that a salient odor cue can be associated with illness even when long intervals separate the presentation of the CS and the US.

In Experiments 4 and 5, Slotnick et al. examined aversion conditioning of an isoamyl acetate odor plus saccharin compound. They found that mixing the strong taste with the weak odor potentiated the odor aversion relative to controls that only experienced odor conditioning; this replicates the previously described work in taste-mediated odor potentiation (e.g., Rusiniak et al., 1979). Moreover, they also found that the strong odor potentiated the aversion to the weak taste relative to controls that only experienced taste-alone conditioning. This outcome is theoretically important because it confirms that potentiation can be produced by a stimulus modality other than taste. In addition, it suggests that potentiation is produced by the relative salience of the two elements of the compound: a highly salient stimulus can potentiate responding to a much less salient stimulus. Further support for this interpretation of potentiation arises from the observation that when tastes and odors of equivalent salience were conditioned in compound, potentiation was not observed with either stimulus (see Experiment 5, Slotnick et al., 1997).

The second major finding that suggests that odors play a more pronounced role in aversion learning comes from another cue competition design, the A+/AX+ or blocking design (Batsell & Batson, 1999; Batson & Batsell, 2000). The blocking design was introduced by Kamin (1969) when he demonstrated that preconditioning of one cue (A), prior to compound conditioning of Stimulus A along with a novel Stimulus X, prevented any learning to Stimulus X. Thus, learning to A blocked learning to X. Batson and Batsell (2000) preconditioned a weak almond odor solution (A) on Day 1, and conducted compound conditioning of this almond odor mixed in solution with the highly salient taste denatonium saccharide (X) on Day 3. Subsequent taste testing revealed a significantly stronger denatonium aversion compared to controls that received only odor plus taste conditioning on Day 3. This demonstration of enhanced conditioning within the blocking design has been termed *augmentation*. It is noteworthy in this case that a weak odor cue, which typically produces overshadowing of the taste cue during compound conditioning, can enhance conditioning to the taste following preconditioning of the odor. It is important to note that the symmetrical effect has also been demonstrated: preconditioning of the taste cue augments conditioning to an odor cue in the A+/AX+ design (Batsell, Paschall, Gleason, & Batson, 2001). Although the mechanism of the augmentation effect is still under investigation, the ability of an odor to increase conditioning to a taste is incompatible with predictions based on the sensory and gate channeling model. Instead, the present data are most consistent with interpretations based on the formation of within-compound associations between the taste and odor with the illness US (e.g., Durlach & Rescorla, 1980) or the formation of a configural taste plus odor stimulus.

In sum, for the past 20 years, the prevailing viewpoint in flavor-aversion learning research has been that taste cues have privileged status as signals of illness events. This conclusion was based on research from cue-to-consequence experiments, long-delay learning studies, and studies of taste-mediated odor potentiation. In the past decade, studies have shown that odor-aversion learning can also occur following long-delay learning, and that strong odor cues (Slotnick et al., 1997) or preconditioned odors (Batsell & Batson, 1999; Batson & Batsell, 2000) can enhance conditioning to salient tastes. Thus, these studies challenge the assumption that taste cues have privileged status in flavor-aversion learning.

## Flavor-preference studies

Just as organisms can learn about odors, tastes, and odor plus taste compounds as signals of illness, these same cues can signal liked and nutritious foods (i.e., food preferences). Elizabeth Capaldi (1996) described four different mechanisms that contribute to flavor preferences: mere exposure, the medicine effect, flavor–flavor learning, and flavor–nutrient learning. The two most common experimental procedures are the flavor–flavor and flavor–nutrient paradigms. In the flavor–flavor paradigm, the target CS (e.g., tea flavoring) is paired with a preferred or sweet-tasting substance, such as saccharin. In the flavor–nutrient paradigm, the target CS is paired with a substance that provides nutrients or calories (e.g., starch, polycose). Following pairings with a liked substance or a nutrient-rich substance, the target CS will be consumed in greater quantities.

*Odor preference conditioning*   The number of preference learning experiments is considerably less than the number of aversion learning studies, but enough experiments have been conducted to draw reliable conclusions. In fact, many of the flavor-preference experiments conducted over the past 20 years mirror the issues in flavor-aversion learning: the role of the CS–US interval and the interactions of tastes and odors in compound. Of theoretical interest is whether the pattern of results of a taste plus odor compound is the same when the US is aversive (lithium chloride) or appetitive (nutrient-rich solution).

In both the flavor–flavor and flavor–nutrient paradigms, the target CS may be a taste, an odor, or a taste plus odor compound stimulus. Holman (1975) provided the first report of an odor in a flavor-preference experiment. During a 20-day training regimen, rats were presented with an alternating schedule of a concentrated saccharin solution (0.32%) and a dilute saccharin solution (0.065%). A distinctive odor (almond or banana) was mixed into each of the solutions. During testing, the rats were given a choice test between the almond odor solution and the banana odor solution. During both tests, the rats preferred to consume the odor solution that had been paired with the concentrated saccharin during training. This outcome provides evidence that the odor was involved in flavor preference conditioning. Holman also investigated whether the flavor preference could be learned with a forward pairing (odor solution followed by saccharin solution) instead of the simultaneous pairing used in earlier experiments. The results showed the rats preferred the target solution (CS+) that was followed immediately by the concentrated saccharin solution significantly to the nonreinforced flavor (CS–).

In a subsequent experiment, Holman investigated whether flavor preference conditioning could be supported when the CS–US interval between the CS+ solution and the reinforcing saccharin solution was extended to 30 minutes. There were no significant differences in preference for the CS+ and CS– flavors during testing. Thus, flavor–flavor conditioning cannot be produced with a 30-minute CS–US interval. However, when Holman used a nutrient-based reinforcer (20% dextrose solution mixed with quinine, to dilute any sweet taste) instead of the hedonic-based reinforcer (saccharin), significant flavor preferences were observed even after the 30-minute CS–US interval. In sum, Holman's studies introduced two major contributions to the flavor-preference literature: (1) the results demonstrated that an odor cue mixed in solution was a reliable CS for studying preference learning, and (2) flavor–nutrient learning extends over much longer CS–US intervals than does flavor–flavor learning.

Although Holman's technique would often be replicated, this technique does not provide unequivocal evidence of a learned odor preference because the odor extract is mixed in solution with a taste. Thus, the more accurate description is that these experiments demonstrate *flavor* preferences instead of *odor* preferences. One advance in obtaining an odor preference was shown by Holder (1991), who reported the first demonstration of a conditioned odor preference where the odor extract was not mixed in solution, but presented on a disk below the water drinking spout. In this manner, the odor and the reinforcing solution were at least spatially removed, but the possibility still allowed for the odor to be experienced while the food was tasted.

To address the confounding of having rats taste the odor mixed with the reinforcing solution, Lucas and Sclafani (1995) employed two procedural variations. First, the odor container was mounted above the drinking container so the odor only had olfactory properties (this was Holder's 1991 modification). Second, to eliminate the taste component of the reinforcing solution, they used an intragastric (IG) infusion technique in which the nutritive solution could be delivered directly into the rat's esophagus. With the use of these procedural variations, Lucas and Sclafani used a differential conditioning procedure in which one odor (e.g., almond) was paired with IG infusion of a nutritive substance (32% of polycose) and the second odor (e.g., anise) was paired with IG infusion of water. Interestingly, the initial use of this technique, in which the odor was presented either with water or with a flavored solution, failed to produce an odor preference in either case (see Experiment 1, Lucas & Sclafani, 1995). In contrast to Experiment 1, successful odor preferences were shown in Experiment 3 when the CS+ and CS− odors were differentially presented with a sour taste or a bitter taste. During a two-bottle choice test, the rats consumed significantly more water in the presence of the CS+ odor. Furthermore, in agreement with previous flavor studies, once the CS+ odor preference was established, it was very resistant to extinction. Thus it is now clear that a "pure" odor preference can be learned, but this effect may be dependent on interactions between specific odors and a specific type of taste (e.g., bitter vs. sweet).

*Odor plus taste compound preference conditioning* Once it was established that odor preferences could be conditioned, researchers sought to determine if odor plus taste interactions in flavor-preference learning are similar to those observed in flavor-aversion conditioning. Holder (1991) conducted additional flavor-preference learning experiments to ascertain whether taste plus odor interactions in this paradigm were similar to those observed in flavor-aversion learning experiments. For example, in one experiment, rats were exposed to two different compound stimuli. Stimulus 1 included a distinct taste and a distinct odor (although the odor was not mixed in solution with the taste), which were mixed with a sweet and nutritive sucrose solution. Stimulus 2 also included distinct taste and odor components, but they were mixed with a sweet saccharin solution. Testing involved separate presentations of the taste cues and the odor cues, in the absence of sucrose or saccharin. The results of odor-alone testing and taste-alone testing showed that both stimuli paired with sucrose were consistently preferred to those paired with saccharin. These results are of interest because they indicate odors may be as effective as tastes as CSs in flavor-preference conditioning.

Holder conducted a subsequent experiment to determine if conditioning a taste or odor preference in compound produces a stronger (potentiated) or weaker (overshadowed) preference compared to a group that receives single-element conditioning. In this experiment, rats either had an odor paired with sucrose, a taste paired with sucrose, or the odor plus taste compound paired with sucrose. Subsequent testing revealed no differences in odor preference or taste preference in regard to whether the stimulus had been conditioned alone or in the compound. Again, the absence of any overshadowing or potentiation of the preference differs from typical findings in flavor-aversion learning.

Following the failure to see any stimulus competition during compound conditioning, Holder (1991) turned to the A+/AX+ design to determine if prior conditioning of a preference (A) would later block the preference to a second cue (X). Phase 1 occurred over four days of training when rats received odor plus sucrose, taste plus sucrose, or sucrose-alone conditioning trials. Phase 2 conditioning occurred over the next five days, and it involved pairing the taste plus odor compound with sucrose. In contrast to the first two experiments, in which no evidence of cue competition was observed, the results of Experiment 3 provided evidence of blocking. Rats that had odor preconditioning prior to odor plus taste preference conditioning showed a decreased or blocked taste preference. Similarly, rats that had taste preconditioning prior to odor plus taste preference conditioning, showed a blocked odor preference. Similar results of blocking were observed in Experiment 4. Thus Holder's results are somewhat paradoxical because neither cue competition nor synergistic conditioning was seen with a compound conditioning design, but cue competition was seen with the A+/AX+ (blocking) design.

Capaldi and Hunter (1994) also examined preference conditioning to the elements of an odor plus taste compound. In their first experiment, rats experienced one odor (CS+) with sucrose and a second odor (CS−) with saccharin. Other rats had one taste (CS+) paired with sucrose and a second taste (CS−) paired with saccharin. A third group of rats had an odor plus taste compound (CS+) with sucrose while a second odor plus taste compound (CS−) was paired with saccharin. It is important to note that in contrast to the method used by Holder (1991), Capaldi and Hunter mixed the odor extract in solution along with the CS+/CS− flavor and the reinforcing solution (sucrose or saccharin). There were 10 days of training followed by two days of testing. During testing, the odor groups had a choice test that paired the two odors without taste; the taste groups were given a two-taste choice test in the absence of odor; half of the compound group was given the two-odor choice test while the other half was given the two-taste choice test. The results showed that there were not pronounced differences in the odor preference between the groups that had odor-alone conditioning or odor plus taste conditioning. However, differences did occur with taste testing: the taste preference was significantly weaker in the group that had compound conditioning relative to the group that had taste-alone conditioning. This result suggests that the odor element of the compound overshadowed conditioning to the taste, but the taste did not overshadow or potentiate the odor preference.

In Experiment 2, Capaldi and Hunter conducted taste preconditioning prior to odor plus taste compound conditioning, using the conditioning procedures developed by Holder (1991). Both the preconditioning phase and the compound conditioning phase lasted for 10 days. During testing, rats were given both an odor-choice test and a taste-choice test. In contrast to the findings of Holder, odor testing revealed no evidence of blocking. The groups showed similar preferences for odor, even when it had been paired with a preconditioned taste. Experiment 3 used the same design as Experiment 2, but the effect of odor preconditioning on the taste element of the compound was explored. The results of Experiment 3 showed no differential group effects: all groups showed relatively similar preferences for the taste. Thus there was no evidence of blocking or augmentation of the taste due to odor preconditioning.

Although numerous experiments have examined taste plus odor interactions in the flavor-aversion paradigm, to date, the previously described research by Holder (1991) and Capaldi and Hunter (1994) are the only flavor-preference experiments that have systematically compared odor plus taste preference conditioning to the appropriate taste-alone or odor-alone controls. A comparison of these studies is of interest because Holder found no evidence of overshadowing, but he did report evidence of blocking. In contrast, Capaldi and Hunter observed overshadowing, but not blocking. The primary procedural difference between the Holder experiments and the Capaldi and Hunter experiments was the manner in which the taste plus odor compound was presented. As described previously, in the Holder experiments the taste and the odor were spatially separated. Although this procedure still allowed for both stimuli to be experienced contiguously, the spatial separation of the stimuli may have prevented the formation of within-compound associations between the taste and the odor or the formation of a taste plus odor configural cue. In the Capaldi and Hunter experiment, the taste and odor were mixed together and presented as a single solution, thus providing the opportunity for within-compound associations or configural learning.

In fact, Capaldi and Hunter (1994) explained their results in terms of configural learning. They argued that the taste plus odor compound is discriminably different from the odor alone or the taste alone, but it has greater generalizability to the odor alone than the taste alone. Therefore, significant odor preferences are observed following odor plus taste compound conditioning, but significant taste preferences are not. Furthermore, the relative difference between the elements alone and the configural compound stimulus can be used to explain the absence of blocking. Following odor (or taste) preconditioning, the odor plus taste are conditioned in compound. Because the compound is perceived as different from each element, the typical blocking sequence (A+ followed by AX+) does not occur. Instead, Capaldi and Hunter might argue that the experience is similar to A+ followed by X+.

## Comparison of flavor-preference and flavor-aversion outcomes

Because of the few studies that have examined compound conditioning in the flavor-preference design, it is difficult to draw broad comparisons between the flavor-preference and flavor-aversion paradigms, but there are some relevant issues for future study. First, in both paradigms, a compound taste plus odor cue is paired with an outcome, but the pattern of results appears to be different. As described earlier, taste plus odor aversion conditioning can result in synergistic conditioning (potentiation or augmentation), in which conditioning to one of the stimuli is stronger than if that stimulus had been conditioned alone. Although overshadowing and blocking were not observed in all cases of flavor-preference learning, there was no evidence of synergistic conditioning in either flavor-preference experiment. It is worth noting that the absence of synergistic conditioning in the flavor-preference design does not indicate that it is impossible, but it may be that the proper procedures for producing synergistic conditioning have not been employed. For example, many flavor-aversion experiments used the A+/AX+ design and obtained blocking, not augmentation, of Stimulus X (e.g., Gillan & Domjan,

1977; Revusky, 1971). The primary procedural difference that produces augmentation or blocking appears to be whether the A and X stimuli are presented simultaneously or sequentially during Phase 2 conditioning. If the taste and odor were presented sequentially, blocking was observed; but if the stimuli were presented simultaneously, augmentation was recorded (Batsell & Batson, 1999; Batsell et al., 2001). Considering that the taste and odor were presented together in solution in the studies of Capaldi and Hunter (1994), this technique may facilitate detection of synergistic conditioning in the flavor-preference paradigm.

Second, although the flavor-aversion and flavor-preference designs appear to be similar, the described experiments differ in terms of the stimulus compound. In the flavor-aversion experiments, rats experience a taste and an odor followed by the illness-inducing agent. In this design, the rat may experience taste and odor as separate elements or it may combine them into a configural cue; however, these are the only stimuli that are perceived through the gustatory and olfactory senses because illness is typically induced via an injection of lithium chloride directly into the stomach cavity. In contrast, the procedure used in the Holder (1991) and Capaldi and Hunter (1994) studies involved a presentation of the target taste, the target odor, and sucrose. Thus the rat experienced two taste cues along with the odor. It is entirely possible that the within-compound associations or configuring necessary to link three elements is different from the processes used with two stimuli. One means to examine taste plus odor learning in the absence of the confounding taste US is to present the reinforcing US via intragastric infusion similar to the procedure used by Lucas and Sclafani (1995).

Third, an additional problem in interpreting the results from the Holder (1991) experiments and the Capaldi and Hunter (1994) experiments is that sucrose was the crucial US in these experiments. Sucrose has both a sweet taste and nutritive properties, thus it can produce both flavor–flavor learning and flavor–nutrient learning. For example, Harris, Gorissen, Bailey, & Westbrook (2000) manipulated the rat's motivational state (food-deprived or not food-deprived) during the learning of an odor preference to determine whether the nutrient component of sucrose and the hedonic component of sucrose made separate contributions to the learning of a flavor preference. Their results showed that when rats were food-deprived, the association between odor and the nutritive properties of sucrose was the primary association. In contrast, when the rats were sated, the association between odor and the hedonic properties of sucrose was the primary association. These outcomes support the hypothesis that the organism's motivational state is crucial in determining whether flavor–flavor or flavor–nutrient associations form between odor and sucrose during preference conditioning. Thus interpretation of compound conditioning effects in flavor-preference studies may be facilitated if taste stimuli that only have hedonic properties or nutritive properties are used.

In sum, the flavor-aversion and flavor-preference paradigms are well-established classical conditioning procedures that produce reliable results. Interestingly, the inclusion of an odor along with a taste in these designs produces an outcome that differs from that seen with other classical conditioning designs. At the present time, the two best candidate mechanisms for taste plus odor compound conditioning are the within-compound association approach and the configural cue approach. It remains to be seen if these mechanisms mediate taste plus odor learning in both flavor-preference and flavor-aversion learning.

## Odors as Signals for Humans

The aforementioned flavor–flavor experiments involve an organism consuming a neutral flavor cue along with a preferred flavor. Later testing of the neutral flavor alone shows that the organism will consume more of that substance compared to pretest consumption levels. The use of this procedure with human participants not only provides evidence of flavor-preference learning, but because of humans' ability to self-report on their emotional experience and perceptions, it provides new insight into learning about odors. Over the past decade, a number of evaluative conditioning and perception studies have successfully used odors in a modification of the flavor-preference design.

### *Odor plus taste pairings in humans*

*Evaluative conditioning experiments* Evaluative conditioning is a form of classical conditioning in which a neutral CS is paired with a stimulus that evokes either a positive or negative emotional response (e.g., Baeyens, Crombez, Hendrickz, & Eelen, 1995). In this manner, an individual can learn likes and dislikes to the neutral stimulus. One common procedure for studying evaluative conditioning comes from the flavor-preference literature (Zellner, Rozin, Aron, & Kulish, 1983). Rozin and his colleagues have argued that the learning of food likes and dislikes are a common means by which people acquire dietary patterns. In an experimental setting, human participants consumed a neutral flavor prior to the consumption of a sweetened solution. Following a number of training trials, the neutral flavor elicits the same evaluative response as the reinforcing flavor.

Baeyens, Eelen, Van den Bergh, & Crombez (1990), using an adaptation of the flavor-preference design developed by Zellner et al. (1983), demonstrated that the liking of a flavor substance could change following evaluative conditioning. Baeyens et al. used either the flavor (taste plus odor) or the color of a solution as the CS cue. In their experiment, Baeyens et al. first obtained affective ratings for the colors and the flavors; these ratings were marked on a 200-mm scale with "very disliked" as one anchor and "very liked" as the other anchor. Following the pretest ratings, participants sampled a number of the colored or flavored solutions that contained the US. There were three US conditions: a sweet US condition (sugar solution), a bitter US condition (Tween 20 solution), and a neutral US condition (no US). Following conditioning, the participants sampled and rated the color CSs and the flavor CSs. The flavors that were paired with the bitter Tween 20 solution were now rated as significantly more disliked compared to the pretest rating. Conversely, the increase in liking for the flavors paired with the sweet sugar solution did not surpass statistical significance. Thus these results do show that evaluative conditioning can occur with flavor cues, but the effects are more pronounced with the negative US. Interestingly, no evaluative change was observed to the color cues, regardless of the US type. This outcome may be similar to the cue-to-consequence idea discussed in regard to flavor-aversion learning. Over the past decade, Baeyens and his colleagues have conducted many experiments with this technique, and they established that it has a number of unique characteristics, including being very resistant to extinction (e.g., Baeyens et al.,1990).

*Odor perception experiments*   The basic odor plus flavor preference procedure used in the evaluative conditioning studies can also be used to study changes in odor perception. In a series of experiments, Stevenson, Boakes, and their colleagues have examined odor perception (sweetness, sourness) when odors are combined with tastes. Their research has expanded on a number of novel nuances of odor perception including the tasty-smell effect and its resistance to extinction, the sweetness enhancement effect, the sweetness suppression effect, and mechanisms of odor plus taste learning in humans.

In their initial studies, Stevenson, Prescott, and Boakes (1995) investigated the *tasty-smell effect*. Their basic procedure involved five training sessions spread across five days. Session 1 was a pretest to establish sweetness, sourness, intensity, and liking scores for the odors, tastes, and odor–taste mixtures. Sessions 2 through 4 were conditioning trials in which participants sampled various solutions including flavor plus sucrose pairings and flavor plus citric acid pairings. Session 5 was the posttest when participants smelled and rated the odors, tastes, and compound solutions. The main results showed that the sweetness rating of the odor paired with sucrose increased significantly whereas the sweetness ratings of the odor paired with citric acid decreased significantly. Also, sourness ratings of the odor paired with citric acid increased significantly. This outcome was replicated in a second experiment and, collectively, these results show that odor perception can change following odor plus taste experiences. Specifically, the tasty-smell effect occurs when an odor is experienced in combination with a taste, and later perception of that odor alone includes associated taste attributes (e.g., increased sweetness following pairings with a sucrose solution). Although significant changes in odor perception were recorded, no changes in liking/disliking were observed. Thus, in contrast to the studies of evaluative conditioning, the experiments of Stevenson et al. (1995) found no evidence of a hedonic shift. It should be noted that the two solutions used in this experiment were sweet and sour; Baeyens et al.'s (1990) research has only shown consistent hedonic changes with a bitter solution.

The perception ratings of these odor-perception experiments resemble the liking ratings recorded in the flavor evaluative conditioning studies (c.f., Baeyens et al., 1990). Specifically, both measures appear to be resistant to extinction. To confirm that changes in odor perception are indeed resistant to extinction, Stevenson, Boakes, and Wilson (2000a) adapted their procedure of testing odor perception and the tasty-smell effect to examine both odor–taste compounds and color–taste compounds. Human participants smelled and tasted a number of different solutions, with at least four key pairings: one odor paired with a sweet taste (sucrose), one odor paired with a sour taste (citric acid), one color paired with a sweet taste (sucrose), and one color paired with a sour taste (citric acid). In the key experiments, an extinction phase that altered the odor or the color paired with the sour citric was inserted between training and testing. During subsequent tests of the odor alone or the color alone, participants showed extinguished (weakened) sour ratings of the color, but no change was observed to the odor.

In a follow-up experiment, Stevenson, Boakes, and Wilson (2000b) explored whether the resistance to extinction of an odor–sour taste association could be reversed via counterconditioning. In this within-subjects experiment, odors were first paired with a sour-tasting citric acid solution, thus imbuing these odors with sour properties (as demonstrated via increased sourness ratings). In a subsequent phase, human participants experienced one of these odors mixed in solution along with a sweet-tasting sucrose solution; a manipulation Stevenson et al. (1995) had shown to increase sweetness ratings to an odor. The other odor–sour taste association was left intact. In spite of this training regimen, the counterconditioning procedure did not increase the sweetness ratings of the counterconditioned odor relative to the control odor. In contrast, a similar training procedure was conducted with a color stimulus; yet in this case, the counterconditioning procedure did reverse the sourness ratings learned to the color. Thus the results of the extinction and counterconditioning experiments provide converging evidence that once established, the tasty-smell effect is immutable.

In other experiments, these authors have examined the *sweetness enhancement effect*, which occurs when a sweet-smelling odor is added to sucrose, making the solution taste sweeter than sucrose alone. This result is paradoxical because the nose contains no receptors for sweetness. Stevenson, Boakes, and Prescott (1998) investigated whether the sweetness enhancement effect was due to associative learning. To determine how this odor plus taste learning occurred, Stevenson et al. adopted a procedure in which participants sampled one solution through a straw and tasted the other solution directly though the mouth. The logic of this manipulation is that the straw technique would only activate odor receptors in the mouth (retronasal) whereas the mouth technique could activate odor receptors in the nose (orthonasal) prior to the taste experience. If equivalent changes in odor sweetness were seen with both techniques, it would suggest that retronasal experience was sufficient to produce the sweetness enhancement effect. In fact, the results demonstrated similar patterns of sweetness learning with both the straw and mouth techniques. Stevenson et al. (1998) concluded that the evidence of retronasal processing suggests that the taste and odor cue may be perceived as a unitary or configural cue and that the sweetness enhancement effect may reflect a case of learned synesthesia (or mixing of different sense modalities). Furthermore, odorants rated as low in sweetness were able to decrease the sweetness ratings of sucrose solution when they were mixed in solution (the *sweetness suppression effect*) (Stevenson, Prescott, & Boakes, 1999).

Stevenson and his associates (1998) account for the results of their various experiments in terms of "the formation of a within-compound association which is experienced as a configural stimulus and which can be viewed as an example of learned synesthesia" (pp. 128–9). In other words, the sweet taste is processed along with the retronasal perception of the odor to produce a unitary sensation in the participant. Because the taste and odor were associated across conditioning trials, later odor testing will elicit an experience of taste, producing the synesthesia experience. Finally, it is important to note that the mechanisms invoked by Stevenson et al. (1998) to account for taste plus odor learning in their experiments with humans are the same mechanisms applied to taste plus odor learning in nonhumans (see previous section).

## *Evaluative odor conditioning*

Although interest in evaluative conditioning increased during the 1990s, the initial demonstration of evaluative conditioning occurred in the 1970s. Levey and Martin (1975) described a technique in which human participants viewed neutral faces paired with either attractive (liked) faces or disgusting (disliked) faces. Following a number of pairings, the neutral faces elicited an evaluative response that was congruent with their training history (negative evaluation from pairing with disliked faces and positive evaluation from pairings with liked faces). Within this paradigm for examining evaluative conditioning, odors may be a particularly effective stimulus for a number of reasons. First, on the basis of few odor rejections from infants, it has been argued that nearly all odor preferences or rejections are not innate, but are learned (Engen, as cited by Baeyens, Wrzesniewski, De Houwer, & Eelen, 1996). Second, both anecdotal and experimental reports indicate that odor-evoked memories or associations are more emotional than those memories/associations elicited by other stimuli (Herz & Cupchik, 1992, 1995). Thus various researchers have used odors as either the CS or the US in evaluative conditioning experiments other than the flavor preference design, but these studies have produced mixed results.

Todrank, Byrnes, Wrzesniewski, & Rozin (1995), who sought to determine if affective valenced odors could serve as a US in an evaluative conditioning design, reported significant results. After the experimenters obtained a number of neutral face photographs, participants experienced eight pairings of specific faces either with a liked odor, a neutral odor, or a disliked odor. While viewing the picture–odor combinations, participants made a personality sketch of the individual (Experiment 1) or they simply labeled the odor and matched it to the picture's characteristics (Experiments 2 and 3). The dependent measure was the change from pretest face rating to posttest face rating. Their results showed changes in affective rating in accordance with the valenced odors (more dislike after a pairing with a disliked odor and more liking after a pairing with a liked odor) when the odors were "plausibly" human, but no change to "nonplausibly" human odors. Todrank et al. described a plausibly human odor as

> one that is either naturally produced by people or is typically applied to people through the use of scented products such as cosmetics and perfumes; a "nonplausibly human" odor is one that is more typically associated with objects other than people or scented products used by people, even though people may under certain circumstances take on the odor of these objects through contact with them. (Todrank et al., 1995, pp. 131–2)

Thus the mere presence of a disliked odor or a liked odor was not sufficient to produce evaluative conditioning. This outcome suggests that certain combinations of odors and photograph CSs are necessary for conditioning to occur.

In light of the fact that evaluative conditioning has been argued to be a mechanism of learned likes and dislikes in the real world (e.g., Todrank et al., 1995), evidence from naturalistic studies should provide particularly compelling evidence. Baeyens et al. (1996) reported such evidence for evaluative odor conditioning in two naturalistic experiments. First, they manipulated the odor that was present in a toilet room. In their experiment, they presented the odor (either pine odor or lavender odor) in one of two toilet rooms within a large office building. The two toilet rooms were on opposite sides of the building, and office workers tended to use exclusively one set of toilet rooms. The odors were presented in each toilet room for a period of 2.5 weeks, and then one week later, office workers were contacted to help with an odor perception study. At this time, each office worker was asked to smell and rate each odor. For each individual, one odor would have been paired with the toilet room experience (CS+) and the other would serve as the control odor (CS−). Baeyens et al. were cognizant of the fact that not all individuals would enjoy toilet visits. Therefore, each participant provided "liking to go" ratings in which they reported whether they found a visit to the toilet to be "a necessary evil" (−10) or to be an "agreeable break from work" (+10). The results showed a significant interaction related to the participant's liking to go to the toilet room. Participants who rated the toilet room experience as positive preferred the CS+ odor significantly more than the control CS− odor. In contrast, those individuals who rated the toilet room experience as negative showed negative evaluative odor conditioning as evidenced by a lower rating of the CS+ odor compared to their CS− odor rating.

In a second naturalistic study, Baeyens et al. (1996) examined odor evaluative conditioning with the help of a trained massage therapist. On the basis of an individual's medical diagnosis, they were given either a positive/relaxing massage with an odor scented massage oil or a negative/painful massage with an odor-scented massage oil. To show conditioning effects, two neutral odors were counterbalanced across conditions. Participants received an average of 10 30-minute massages. After the final massage session, the physiotherapist asked each participant to rate odors for potential massage oils. The results of the massage rating showed that the participants who received a relaxing massage experienced it as positive, but those who received the painful massage did not rate the experience as negative; therefore, the negative/painful group did not satisfy the experimental criterion. Thus a significant conditioning effect was seen in the positive massage group (CS+ odor rated significantly higher than CS−), but no differences were seen in the negative massage group.

Collectively, the results of the Todrank et al. (1995) and Baeyens et al. (1996) experiments demonstrate that evaluative odor conditioning can occur in both laboratory and naturalistic conditions. Unfortunately, there have also been a number of studies that used odor cues as CSs in the evaluative conditioning design that produced no evidence of evaluative conditioning. Rozin, Wrzesniewski, and Byrnes (1998) described four such experiments. In the first two experiments, Rozin et al. attempted to obtain evaluative conditioning in real-world situations, similar to the results reported by Baeyens et al. (1996). Human participants were selected based on self-report of whether they liked hair washing or they were neutral about hair washing. Once in the lab, participants rated seven different shampoos on the quality of their odor. Participants were assigned the shampoo that they had rated as closest to neutral. The participants then used the shampoo over the next two weeks, and provided final evaluative ratings of the shampoo. There was no difference in shampoo ratings between the two groups (hair wash likers vs. hair wash neutral). In a second study investigating evaluative conditioning of odor in a real-world setting, Rozin et al. (1998) had participants pair an odor with a neutral, positive, or negative activity. For example, participants would pair a neutral odor (based on participants' ratings) with a specific event. No significant changes in odor rating were observed from the pretest to the posttest ratings.

On the basis of the failures to observe any evaluative conditioning in the uncontrolled real-world situations, Rozin et al. (1998) adopted the procedure of Levey and Martin (1975) in two lab experiments to observe evaluative odor conditioning. Participants were first pretested to obtain ratings of the odor CSs and the picture USs. During training, a given participant would receive an opened box that contained the odor cue (e.g., lavender) along with a neutral picture (e.g., pencil sharpener), a positive picture (e.g., American flag), or a negative picture (e.g., cockroach). Each participant experienced eight odor–picture pairings. In almost all cases, there was little evidence that an odor paired with an affective picture produced any change in odor ratings. The one notable exception was a decrease in the rating of the odor paired with the negative cockroach.

*Interim summary*  The results of human odor conditioning experiments provide a unique window into the processing of odors that cannot occur in nonhuman experiments. Because humans can self-report on their perception of a stimulus and their affective response to that stimulus, different measures can be employed. As described above, human experiments that have combined odor plus taste cues have shown that these stimuli are perceived as a unitary sensation, and that learned associations can form between these stimuli. Later tests of the odor show that the odor acquires taste-like properties and is more liked than before the odor plus taste pairings. Although odors can be effective in other lab and naturalistic evaluative conditioning experiments, the results of these latter experiments do not appear to be as reliable or as robust as those produced in taste plus odor designs.

## Odors as Signals of Anxiety and Fear

Recently, experts in the study of anxiety have argued that animal models of anxiety should use stimuli with ethological significance, such as predator odors, rather than artificial lab stimuli such as flashing lights (e.g., Rogers, as cited in Dielenberg, Hunt, & McGregor, 2001). Similar claims have been made by researchers in the field of fears and phobias (Ohman & Mineka, 2001); specifically, the use of fear-irrelevant stimuli may not be as effective as using fear-relevant stimuli. Instead, animal models of fear and anxiety may be most useful if these models employed stimuli that the organism might encounter in the natural world. Because mice and rats are the most commonly used species in anxiety/fear research, odors may be ideal signals for anxiety- and fear-producing events.

*Predator odor*

Organisms use a variety of stimuli (visual, auditory, olfactory) to detect predators or other aversive events. The ability to recognize odors as signals of danger may come from both unconditioned and conditioned sources. Because many nonhumans use odors to aid in predator detection, they may be particularly good cues for studying fear and anxiety. Since the 1990s, much research has focused on the rat's unconditioned responses to the odors of their natural predators (e.g., cat odor, fox urine odor). McGregor, Dielenberg, and their colleagues have devised a novel technique for studying the effects of predator odor on rats, and thus for studying anxiety in nonhumans (e.g., Dielenberg & McGregor, 1999). They examined the effects of cat odor on a rat in a two-chamber apparatus. In their apparatus, a main chamber (45 cm long × 26 cm wide × 36 cm high) connects through an opening to an enclosed "hide" box (15 cm long × 24 cm wide × 22 cm high) in which the rat could escape. On the wall of the main chamber, opposite the hide box, is a clip for holding a strip of cat collar. The placement of photobeams allow for determination of the rat's approach time (time spent within 7 cm or less of the cat collar) and the rat's hide time (time spent within the hide box). Following familiarization within the odor-free apparatus, the exposure trials are conducted. During exposure trials, the experimental rat is placed in the main chamber along with a strip of fabric cat collar, which has been worn by a cat for a period of three weeks; the control rat is exposed to an unworn (control) collar. On the initial exposures, naive rats exposed to the cat collar spend significantly more time in the hide box and significantly less time in the approach area compared to rats exposed to the control collar. From these data, it was inferred that a cat odor emanated from the worn cat collar, and this odor triggered a number of the rats' defensive/escape behaviors. If this cat odor technique represents an improvement in animal models of unconditioned anxiety, anxiolytic drugs should ameliorate the anxiety produced by cat odor, and the defense reactions induced by cat odor should be more pronounced than those produced by other odor models of anxiety.

To determine whether the cat odor procedure is a viable animal model of anxiety, McGregor and Dielenberg (1999) sought to determine whether anxiolytic agents could decrease the rat's defensive behaviors in response to cat odor. The use of the benzodiazepene midazolam revealed an interesting dissociation in the rat's response to cat odor. Their procedure used two cat odor exposures in which drug administration could occur during either phase, both phases, or neither phase. Not surprisingly, rats who never received midazolam showed the characteristic pattern of greater hide times and lesser approach times. Also, in support of the anxiety-producing nature of this technique, rats given midazolam on both trials showed no fear on either trial. Interestingly, the use of midazolam was only effective if the drug was administered on the first trial; if the organism had previous experience with the odor cue on Trial 1, later administration of midazolam during odor exposure on Trial 2 had no effect on defensive behaviors. In contrast, rats given midazolam on Trial 1, but not on Trial 2, showed no fear response to cat odor during Trial 2. The demonstration of the inadequacy of midazolam to affect fear on Trial 2 has also been observed in other anxiety measures (e.g., elevated maze; File, Zangrossi, Viana, & Graeff, 1993), but the exact mechanism of this effect remains to be determined.

Recent experiments have compared the cat odor technique to other animal models of anxiety. Specifically, a similar animal model of anxiety uses an odorous extract containing an extract of fox feces, a solution that contains the active ingredient TMT (2, 4, 5 Trimethylthiazoline) (e.g., Wallace & Rosen, 2000). McGregor, Schrama, Ambermoon, & Dielenberg (2001) compared cat odor to TMT odor and other noxious odors on a number of measures, including the hide box technique (cf., Dielenberg & McGregor, 1999), the elevated maze task (cf., File et al., 1993), and responsiveness to benzodiazepenes (McGregor & Dielenberg, 1999). With the use of the hide box technique, McGregor et al. (2001) found that both cat odor and TMT odor produced a retreat to the hide box. In comparison to TMT odor, however, cat odor yielded more hide time, more immobility, and more "head out" behavior (head out is a distinctive behavior in which the rat retains its body within the hide box, but peeks its head through the opening, as if searching the environment). Following this exposure to cat odor or TMT odor, rats were placed immediately in the elevated maze. If the odor exposure produces anxiety, locomotion on the elevated maze should be greatly reduced. The rats exposed to cat odor spent significantly less time in the open arms of the maze than the TMT odor rats, suggesting the cat odor rats had greater anxiety. Finally, in Experiment 1, all rats were returned to the training environment one day after odor exposure. Even though no odor cues were present, the rats previously exposed to cat odor retreated to the hide box while the other rats did not. Thus only cat odor was sufficient to produce context fear that persisted for at least 24 hours. Collectively, cat odor produced stronger defensive reactions than TMT odor on three different measures (hide box escape, elevated maze, and conditioned fear).

As stated earlier, in determining the efficacy of the cat odor technique as an animal model of anxiety, it is important to show that this anxiety can be reduced by the administration of anxiolytics. In Experiment 2, McGregor et al. (2001) compared the effects of midazolam in decreasing the rats' defensive responses to cat odor or TMT. For the rats treated with midazolam, only those exposed to cat odor showed significant increases in approach/activity and significant decreases in hide time. The presence of midazolam did not alter the behavior of the rats exposed to TMT odor. In fact, the responses of the TMT–midazolam rats were similar to rats exposed to the noxious odor formaldehyde. These results suggest that the behavioral effects induced by TMT may be produced by its aversive and acrid qualities more than to any anxiety-producing properties. In sum, the results of Experiments 1 and 2 suggest that the cat odor technique is superior to the TMT technique as an animal model of anxiety.

In sum, the cat odor technique developed by Dielenberg, McGregor, and their associates is an ethologically relevant animal model of unconditioned anxiety. This technique appears to be sensitive to the effects of anxiolytic drugs and it is superior to other animal models that use odor cues (cf., McGregor et al., 2001). In addition, this technique has already been useful in identifying brain regions that are most active after exposure to cat odor (Dielenberg, Hunt, & McGregor, 2001). Thus this technique has the potential both to serve as an animal model of anxiety and to promote understanding of the brain regions that process predator odors and activate defense systems.

*Odor-potentiated startle*

The previously described cat odor studies demonstrate how an odor cue can be used as a US to produce anxiety, but odor cues may also be very effective CSs in a fear-conditioning design. Over the past decade, Davis and colleagues have developed the fear-potentiated startle technique to study learned fear responses. The fear-potentiated startle technique amplifies an organism's natural startle response. For example, when a rat hears a sudden loud noise its muscles suddenly contract and, if startled enough, the rat may jump into the air. The higher the jump, the greater the startle magnitude. The fear-potentiated startle technique involves three stages. First, in Phase 1, the rat learns conditioned fear to the house light when the overhead house light is followed by shock across multiple trials. Then, in Phase 2, the rat is returned to the darkened chamber, and a loud noise is presented to measure the startle magnitude. No shocks are given during Phases 2 or 3. During Phase 3, the rat's startle response to the loud noise is tested when the chamber is dark and when the house lights are illuminated. The rat's startle response to the noise is significantly higher when the light is on than when it is not on. In other words, conditioned fear to the light potentiated the startle response to the noise. One reason that the fear-potentiated startle paradigm is a valuable technique for studying learned fear is that it is a behavioral analog for studying post-traumatic stress disorder (PTSD), because exaggerated startle is a primary clinical symptom of PTSD. In fact, fear-potentiated startle has been demonstrated in various human populations diagnosed with PTSD, such as Vietnam veterans (Morgan, Grillon, Southwick, Davis, & Charney, 1995).

The fear-potentiated startle paradigm has been used with a number of different stimuli that might represent threats in the organism's environment. Falls and Davis (1994) reported one such experiment that compared three different stimulus modalities (visual, auditory, and tactile stimuli) in their ability to potentiate the startle response. This study employed three groups that differed in their CS+: Group Light had the light from an 8 W fluorescent bulb, Group Noise had a 2 kHz noise, and Group Fan experienced air from a fan for a 3.7 s interval. All groups received 10 pairings of their CS+ along with a 500 msec, 0.6 mA footshock. During testing, each rat was replaced in the chamber where it received 15 trials with the fan, the light, the noise, and no CS. The results showed that the startle response was significantly greater (i.e., potentiated) when a group was tested with their CS+ (e.g., Group Fan showed the greatest startle response to the fan CS plus noise burst) than when they were tested in the no CS condition or in the untrained CS conditions. In sum, this experiment demonstrated that auditory, visual, and tactile stimuli can all be useful CSs in the fear-potentiated startle design. Considering the importance of olfactory cues to the animals' navigation of its environment, it is a little surprising that odors have not been examined more extensively within the fear-potentiated startle paradigm. Nonetheless, a handful of recent studies have studied odor cues in this design, and they are finding some rather interesting results (e.g., Paschall & Davis, 2002; Richardson, Vishney, & Lee, 1999).

Richardson and his associates were the first to demonstrate that odor stimuli could be effective CSs in the fear-potentiated startle design (Richardson, Paxinos, & Lee, 2000; Richardson et al., 1999; Vishney & Richardson, 2000). In their initial study, Richardson et al. (1999) used a paired group and an unpaired group during training. In these experiments, the odor stimulus was presented by placement of 0.1 ml of grape odor solution on a piece of paper towel that was inserted 10 cm below the chamber floor. The paired group received 15 exposures of the odor with a mild footshock, whereas the unpaired group received 15 exposures to each stimulus, but in an unpaired fashion. During testing, the paired group showed a significantly stronger startle response than the unpaired group on trials when the odor and the startle noise were both present. Interestingly, extinction of startle responding in the presence of the odor was quite resistant to extinction. In subsequent experiments, Richardson's lab has demonstrated that responding in the presence of the conditioned odor is specific to the odor used during training (Experiment 5, Richardson et al., 1999), fear-potentiated startle to an odor emerges 23 days after birth (Richardson et al., 2000), and odor potentiation of startle is similar to other types of startle because it can be attenuated by the presentation of an anxiolytic (diazepam) prior to testing (Vishney & Richardson, 2000).

More recently, Paschall and Davis (2002) have refined the technique for producing odor-potentiated startle (OPS), and they have extended the findings in this area. The major procedural variation introduced by Paschall and Davis was the technology for discrete presentation of the odor. With the use of an olfactometer, a constant airflow was directed throughout the startle chamber. In all experiments, odor presentations occurred for a four-second interval and the odor flow was accompanied by a decrease in clean air flow so there was no change in air flow. The odor CS was amyl acetate diluted in propylene glycol and the US was a 0.5 sec presentation of footshock (0.4 or 0.6 mA).

These experiments advanced the knowledge of OPS in a number of significant ways. First, they showed that there was no unconditioned effect of presenting amyl acetate odor when rats had not received explicit odor plus shock pairings. Second, they demonstrated that even though OPS effects dissipated across time, significant OPS effects were still recorded after a 40-day retention interval, which is similar to the retention interval for other stimulus modalities in this design (e.g., Lee, Walker, & Davis, 1996). Third, significant OPS was obtained after one pairing of odor with footshock (see Experiment 2). It is notable that in this experiment, the odor was only presented for four seconds. The only other demonstration of one-trial potentiated startle used a visual CS with a duration of 51.2 seconds (Davis, Schlesinger, & Sorenson, 1989). Although direct comparisons across sense modality were not conducted in the same experiment, the data suggest that odors may be much more effective cues for potentiated startle than are visual cues.

*Interim summary* In sum, it is clear that odor cues can be very effective stimuli for signals of fear-producing events. At the present time, although the unconditioned effects of odor on startle have been investigated in both human and nonhuman populations, the effects of a conditioned odor on potentiated startle in humans has not yet been investigated.

# Conclusions

In sum, the past decade has shown the development of a number of new lines of research to investigate the role of odors in learning. For example, examinations of odors in flavor-preference conditioning studies, evaluative odor experiments, and animal models of fear and anxiety with odors are all relatively new experimental techniques. In addition, other paradigms, such as the flavor-aversion paradigm, are revealing new complexities to odor conditioning that were not evident in previous research. Collectively, these different experimental techniques are showing that odors are effective stimuli in learning preparations, and their ability to interact in a unique fashion with taste cues may provide information about how the brain integrates information from two sense modalities.

## References

Baeyens, F., Crombez, G., Hendrickz, H., & Eelen, P. (1995). Parameters of human evaluative flavor–flavor conditioning. *Learning and Motivation, 26*, 141–60.

Baeyens, F., Eelen, P., Van den Bergh, O., & Crombez, G. (1990). Flavor–flavor and color–flavor conditioning in humans. *Learning and Motivation, 21*, 434–55.

Baeyens, F., Wrzesniewski, A., De Houwer, J., & Eelen, P. (1996). Toilet rooms, body massages, and smells: Two field studies on human evaluative odor conditioning. *Current Psychology, 15*, 77–96.

Barker, L. M. (2001). *Learning and behavior: Biological, psychological, and sociocultural perspectives* (3rd edn.). Upper Saddle River, NJ: Prentice Hall.

Batsell, W. R., Jr., & Batson, J. D. (1999). Augmentation of taste conditioning by a preconditioned odor. *Journal of Experimental Psychology: Animal Behavior Processes, 25*, 374–88.

Batsell, W. R., Jr., Paschall, G. Y., Gleason, D. I., & Batson, J. D. (2001). Taste preconditioning augments odor-aversion learning. *Journal of Experimental Psychology: Animal Behavior Processes, 27*, 30–47.

Batson, J. D., & Batsell, W. R. Jr. (2000). Augmentation, not blocking, in an A+/AX+ flavor-conditioning procedure. *Psychonomic Bulletin & Review, 7*, 466–71.

Bouton, M. E., Jones, D. L., McPhillips, S. A., & Swartzentruber, D. (1986). Potentiation and overshadowing in odor-aversion learning: Role of method of odor presentation, the distal-proximal cue distinction, and the conditionability of odor. *Learning and Motivation, 17*, 115–38.

Capaldi, E. D. (1996). Conditioned food preferences. In E. D. Capaldi (ed.), *Why we eat what we eat: The psychology of eating* (pp. 53–80). Washington, DC: American Psychological Association.

Capaldi, E. D., & Hunter, M. J. (1994). Taste and odor in conditioned flavor preference learning. *Animal Learning & Behavior, 22*, 355–65.

Davis, M., Schlesinger, L., & Sorenson, C. (1989). Temporal-specificity of fear conditioning: Effects of different conditioned stimulus-unconditioned stimulus intervals on the fear-potentiated startle effect. *Journal of Experimental Psychology: Animal Behavior Processes, 15*, 295–310.

Dielenberg, R. A., Hunt, G. E., & McGregor, I. S. (2001). "When a rat smells a cat": The distribution of fos immunoreactivity in rat brain following exposure to a predatory odor. *Neuroscience, 104*, 1085–97.

Dielenberg, R. A., & McGregor, I. S. (1999). Habituation of the hiding response to cat odor in rats (*Rattus norvegicus*). *Journal of Comparative Psychology, 113*, 376–87.

Doty, R. L. (2001). Olfaction. *Annual Review of Psychology, 52*, 423–52.

Durlach, P. J., & Rescorla, R. A. (1980). Potentiation rather than overshadowing in flavor-aversion learning: An analysis in terms of within-compound associations. *Journal of Experimental Psychology: Animal Behavior Processes, 6*, 175–87.

Eichenbaum, H. (1999). The hippocampus and mechanisms of declarative memory. *Behavioural Brain Research, 103*, 123–33.

Falls, W. A., & Davis, M. (1994). Fear-potentiated startle using three conditioned stimulus modalities. *Animal Learning & Behavior, 22*, 379–83.

File, S. E., Zangrossi, H., Viana, M., & Graeff, F. G. (1993). Trial 2 in the elevated plus-maze – a different form of fear. *Psychopharmacology, 111*, 491–4.

Galef, B. G., Jr. (1996). Social influences on the food preferences and feeding behaviors of vertebrates. In E. D. Capaldi (ed.), *Why we eat what we eat: The psychology of eating* (pp. 207–30). Washington, DC: American Psychological Association.

Garcia, J. & Koelling, R. A. (1966). Relation of cue to consequence in avoidance learning. *Psychonomic Science, 4*, 123–4.

Garcia, J., Lasiter, P. S., Bermudez-Rattoni, F., & Deems, D. A. (1985). A general theory of aversion learning. In N. S. Braveman & P. Bronstein (eds.), *Experimental assessments and clinical applications of conditioned food aversions* (Annals of the New York Academy of Sciences, vol. 443, pp. 8–21). New York: New York Academy of Sciences.

Gillan, D. J., & Domjan, M. (1977). Taste-aversion conditioning with expected versus unexpected drug treatment. *Journal of Experimental Psychology: Animal Behavior Processes, 3*, 297–309.

Harris, J. A., Gorissen, M. C., Bailey, G. K., & Westbrook, R. F. (2000). Motivational state regulates the content of learned flavor preferences. *Journal of Experimental Psychology: Animal Behavior Processes, 26*, 15–30.

Herz, R. S., & Cupchik, G. C. (1992). An experimental characterization of odor-evoked memories in humans. *Chemical Senses, 17*, 519–28.

Herz, R. S., & Cupchik, G. C. (1995). The emotional distinctiveness of odor-evoked memories. *Chemical Senses, 20*, 517–28

Holder, M. D. (1991). Conditioned preferences for taste and odor components of flavors: Blocking but not overshadowing. *Appetite, 17*, 29–45.

Holman, E. W. (1975). Immediate and delayed reinforcers for flavor preferences in rats. *Learning and Motivation, 6*, 91–100.

Kalat, J. W., & Rozin, P. (1971). Role of interference in taste-aversion learning. *Journal of Comparative and Physiological Psychology, 77*, 53–8.

Kamin, L. J. (1969). Predictability, surprise, attention, and conditioning. In B. A. Campbell & R. M. Church (eds.), *Punishment and aversive behavior* (pp. 279–96). New York: Appleton-Century-Crofts.

Lee, Y., Walker, D., & Davis, M. (1996). Lack of a temporal gradient of retrograde amnesia following NMDA-induced lesions of the basolateral amygdala assessed with the fear-potentiated startle paradigm. *Behavioral Neuroscience, 110*, 836–9.

Levey, A. B., & Martin, I. (1975). Classical conditioning of human "evaluation" responses. *Behavior Research & Therapy, 13*, 221–6.

LoLordo, V. M., & Droungas, A. (1989). Selective associations and adaptive specializations: Taste aversions and phobias. In S. B. Klein & R. Mowrer (eds.), *Contemporary learning theories: Instrumental conditioning theory and the impact of biological constraints on learning* (pp. 145–79). Hillsdale, NJ: Erlbaum.

Lucas, F., & Sclafani, A. (1995). Carbohydrate-conditioned odor preferences in rats. *Behavioral Neuroscience, 109,* 446–54.

Ludvigson, H. W. (ed.) (1999). Odorous, behavioral, and physiological reactions of rats to episodes of reward, frustration, illness, attack, and threat (Special issue). *The Psychological Record, 49.*

McGregor, I. S., & Dielenberg, R. A. (1999). Differential anxiolytic efficacy of a benzodiazepene on first versus second exposure to a predatory odor in rats. *Psychopharmacology, 147,* 174–81.

McGregor, I. S., Schrama, L., Ambermoon, P., & Dielenberg, R. A. (2001). Not all "predator odours" are equal: Cat odour but not 2, 4, 5 trimethylthiazoline (TMT; fox odour) elicits defensive behaviours in rats. *Behavioural Brain Research, 129* (1–2), 1–16.

Morgan, C. A. III, Grillon, C., Southwick, S. M., Davis, M., & Charney, D. S. (1995). Fear-potentiated startle in posttraumatic stress disorder. *Biological Psychiatry, 38,* 378–85.

Ohman, A., & Mineka, S. (2001). Fears, phobias, and preparedness: Toward an evolved module to fear and fear learning. *Psychological Review, 108,* 483–522.

Paschall, G. Y., & Davis, M. (2002). Olfactory-mediated fear-potentiated startle. *Behavioral Neuroscience, 116,* 4–12.

Pavlov, I. P. (1927). *Conditioned reflexes.* London: Oxford University Press.

Revusky, S. (1971). The role of interference in associations over a delay. In W. K. Honig & P. H. R. James (eds.), *Animal memory* (pp. 155–213). New York: Academic Press.

Richardson, R., Paxinos, G., & Lee, J. (2000). The ontogeny of conditioned odor potentiation of startle. *Behavioral Neuroscience, 114,* 1167–73.

Richardson, R., Vishney, A., & Lee, J. (1999). Conditioned odor potentiation of startle in rats. *Behavioral Neuroscience, 113,* 787–94.

Rozin, P., Wrzesniewski, A., & Byrnes, D. (1998). The elusiveness of evaluative conditioning. *Learning and Motivation, 29,* 397–415.

Rusiniak, K. W., Hankins, W. G., Garcia, J., & Brett, L. P. (1979). Flavor–illness aversions: Potentiation of odor by taste in rats. *Behavioral and Neural Biology, 25,* 1–17.

Schafe, G. E., Sollars, S. I., & Bernstein, I. L. (1995). The CS–US interval and taste aversion learning: A brief look. *Behavioral Neuroscience, 109,* 799–802.

Slotnick, B. M., Westbrook, F., & Darling, F. M. C. (1997). What the rat's nose tells the rat's mouth: Long delay aversion conditioning with aqueous odors and potentiation of taste by odors. *Animal Learning & Behavior, 25,* 357–69.

Stevenson, R. J., Boakes, R. A., & Prescott, J. (1998). Changes in odor sweetness resulting from implicit learning of a simultaneous odor–sweetness association: An example of learned synesthesia. *Learning and Motivation, 29,* 113–32.

Stevenson, R. J., Boakes, R. A., & Wilson, J. P. (2000a). Resistance to extinction of conditioned odor perceptions: Evaluative conditioning is not unique. *Journal of Experimental Psychology: Learning, Memory, and Cognition, 26,* 423–40.

Stevenson, R. J., Boakes, R. A., & Wilson, J. P. (2000b). Counter-conditioning following human odor–taste and color–taste learning. *Learning and Motivation, 31,* 114–27.

Stevenson, R. J., Prescott, J., & Boakes, R. A. (1995). The acquisition of taste properties by odors. *Learning and Motivation, 26,* 433–55.

Stevenson, R. J., Prescott, J., & Boakes, R. A. (1999). Confusing tastes and smells: How odours can influence the perception of sweet and sour tastes. *Chemical Senses, 24,* 627–35.

Todrank, J., Byrnes, D., Wrzesniewski, A., & Rozin, P. (1995). Odors can change preferences for people in photographs: A cross-modal evaluative conditioning study with olfactory USs and visual CSs. *Learning and Motivation, 26,* 116–40.

Vishney, A., & Richardson, R. (2000). Diazepam attenuates conditioned odor potentiation of startle in rats. *Psychobiology, 28,* 515–19.

Wallace, K. J., & Rosen, J. B. (2000). Predator odour as an unconditioned fear stimulus in rats: Elicitation of freezing by trimethylthiazoline, a component of fox faeces. *Behavioral Neuroscience, 114,* 912–22.

Zellner, D. A., Rozin, P., Aron, M., & Kulish, C. (1983). Conditioned enhancement of liking for flavors by pairing with sweetness. *Learning and Motivation, 14,* 338–50.

# CHAPTER FIFTEEN

# Physiological Psychology: Biological and Behavioral Outcomes of Exercise

**Brenda J. Anderson, Daniel P. McCloskey, Despina A. Tata, and Heather E. Gorby**

Physiological psychology is the area of psychology concerned with the machinery behind the mind. This area of psychology focuses on the mind and behavior as products of a biological machine – the brain. These beliefs began with Galileo and Newton's interpretation of the world being mechanical in nature. Once Newton established that the laws of nature extended to the stars and planets, philosophers began to question why the body and mind should be excluded from these laws. Ultimately, the Empiricists began to believe that the mind could be studied like the natural world, and that it is a product of the natural world. They believed that thoughts are based solely on sensory experiences and associations between those experiences. Eventually they reasoned that sensory impressions and associations are formed within the brain. These philosophical ideas form the basis of our current belief that the mind and its output, behavior, are a product of the brain. Since the development of these beliefs, methodological advances have provided empirical support for these ideas. It is the intrinsic link between the mind and brain that leads physiological psychologists to believe that a full understanding of the brain is necessary for a complete understanding of behavior.

Many psychologists adhere to the belief that behavior can be studied sufficiently by studying the relations between sensory input and behavioral output. This belief disregards any constraints placed on behavior by intermediate neural processes. These constraints, however, have been highlighted in a number of instances. Behaviorists were confronted with fixed action patterns, which are species-typical responses to specific stimuli. The inability to modify these fixed behaviors forced the recognition that even

We would like to thank Michael Hadjiargyrou for help with the manuscript. This chapter was prepared with support from MH 62075.

some normal behaviors are "hard-wired." Similarly, Noam Chomsky, a linguist, put forward the argument that there are common features across languages, and that these commonalities must reflect the influence of the organization of brain structures responsible for language processing. Brain development and aging also influence response tendencies. Therefore we see that knowledge of brain function and organization will be necessary for a complete understanding of behavior. Toward this end, psychologists, with their expertise in behavioral analysis, have borrowed methods from other disciplines to relate brain function to behavior. Physiological psychology, then, is the study of brain and behavior relations through the combined use of behavioral and biological approaches.

Many students are confused by the numerous terms used to describe scientists investigating the relation between the brain and behavior. The present chapter focuses on research within the field of "physiological psychology," which is also known as "biological psychology" or "behavioral neuroscience." Any of these terms can be used to describe the study of the relation between the brain and behavior. Although physiological and biological psychologists would be found in psychology departments, behavioral neuroscientists might also be found in the schools of life science and medicine. Quite often the subjects of their studies are animals. The term "neuropsychologist," in contrast, is reserved as a description for investigators interested in correlating brain damage in humans with behavioral deficits. Clinicians also use "neuropsychological" tests to diagnose brain damage. Thus neuropsychologists can have a basic or clinical research focus. More recently the term "cognitive neuroscientist" has emerged. This term is beginning to selectively refer to investigators who use imaging and electrophysiological recording methods in human subjects to answer basic research questions. Having made this distinction, the present chapter will focus on emerging areas of interest for physiological psychology, or the study of brain–behavior interactions in animals.

Earlier we noted that the Empiricists believed that complex thoughts were the outcome of associations between sensory experiences. Continuing from these early thoughts, experimental psychologists are still very interested in how we learn, and believe that associations form the basis for learning. We know that learning is a change in the potential for future behavior that is brought about by experience. If, as the Empiricists believed, the brain controls behavior, then any change in the potential for future behavior must occur through a change in the brain. As a result, experience must alter the brain. Cajal in 1911 (1988) might have been the first person to express hypotheses about how the brain could be modified by behavior and experience. This general idea gained empirical support in the 1960s, when it was discovered that housing young rats in large toy-filled cages increases brain weight, visual cortical thickness (Renner & Rosenzweig, 1987), and synapses per neuron (Greenough, 1984). These were clear indications that the brain can be modified by experience. Subsequent work demonstrated that these effects generalize across species and life stages (Greenough, 1984). Similarly, subsequent investigators have tested whether the *activity* of the neurons sensing and responding to the environment accounts for the neuronal modifications (plasticity), or whether altered patterns of activation that make up learning accounts for the plasticity. These studies have focused on the cerebellum and motor cortex.

Here we will discuss brain modifiability – plasticity – in response to changing the level of physical activity. There is emerging evidence that behavior as simple as movement can have a long-term influence on brain function. The ability of exercise to influence brain function is an important area of study because of the increasingly sedentary nature of our society. As we reduce our levels of physical activity, we are affecting our health, and we may be affecting the health of our brain. We first review behavioral evidence that exercise affects human cognition. This evidence motivates the search for effects of exercise in the brain. Then we discuss the strategy of using animal models to test the effects of exercise on the brain. Next, we see that exercise influences rodent learning and memory. Following that consideration we review how to identify brain structures that are activated during exericise. Then we discuss exercise-related long-term alterations in a number of variables in four brain structures, the cerebellum, motor cortex, striatum, and hippocampus. Last, we discuss the importance of methodological advancements to physiological psychology, and the emerging methods for the analysis of gene and protein expression.

## Exercise Affects Human Cognition

Exercise is a lifestyle factor that is well known for influencing health, well-being, risk for disease, muscles, heart, and the vascular system. These effects accumulate to provide positive benefits for health that lead to longer survival (Holloszy, 1988) and reduce all-cause mortality (Paffenbarger, Hyde, Wing, & Hsieh, 1986; Blair et al., 1989). Less well known are reports that indicate a relation between exercise and cognitive performance. Retirement-aged adults who continued working or remained active, maintained cerebral blood flow and cognitive function over three years relative to the decline seen in adults who became physically inactive (Rogers, Meyer, & Mortel, 1990). More recently, a prospective study of women showed that those self-reporting higher levels of physical activity were less likely to have cognitive decline over a six to eight year period (Yaffe, Barnes, Nevitt, Lui, & Covinsky, 2001). The relation between physical activity and cognitive decline remained after adjusting for age, educational level, health status, smoking, and the use of estrogen. In another study, exercise influenced fluid intelligence. Adult men categorized as high fit-young and high fit-old had higher fluid intelligence, but not crystallized intelligence scores, than subjects categorized as low fit-young and low fit-old (Elsayed, Ismail, & Young, 1980). The observational nature of the data from these studies raises the following questions. Do active lifestyles influence cognitive function and cerebral blood flow? Or are individuals with declining cognitive function and blood flow more likely to become sedentary?

Several investigators have recruited subjects for participation in exercise or control conditions. The results from these studies suggest that exercise can alter cognitive ability. Elderly adults who walked fast or jogged slowly at 70–80 percent of their heart rate reserve for one hour a session, three times a week for four months improved performance on cognitive tasks relative to elderly adults who took part in strength and flexibility exercises with heart rate kept low, and relative to elderly subjects who did not exercise (Dustman et al., 1984). Some evidence exists that exercise can improve cognitive function in younger adults as well. Adult women who jogged 25 minutes and performed calisthenics for 35 minutes three times a week for eight months exhibited significant improvements in physical fitness and performed significantly better on a hypothesis-testing task than control subjects (Suominen-Troyer, Davis, Ismail, & Salvendy, 1986). Exercise did not affect risk-taking behavior, personality measures, or psychomotor performance. In a study of 60–75-year-old adults, subjects in the aerobic (walking) condition, but not those subjects in the anaerobic condition (stretching and toning), increased their maximum rate of oxygen consumption and improved performance on tests of prefrontal and frontal cortical function (Kramer et al., 1999). The aerobic condition did not influence measures from the same tasks (e.g., simple reaction time) that were not dependent upon the prefrontal and frontal cortex. The authors argue that the selectivity of the effects to the prefrontal and frontal cortex is related to the greater amount of aging in these structures relative to other areas of the brain. As a result, they argue that exercise is capable of reversing some of the age-related decline in the frontal cortex.

Although Suominen-Troyer et al. (1986) and Kramer et al. (1999) reported no effect of exercise on psychomotor performance, Spirduso, MacRae, MacRae, Prewitt, and Osborne (1988) reported that active women between the ages of 20 and 59 had shorter simple reaction times than same-age sedentary women. Older active and sedentary women did not differ on this measure. As much as 28–30 percent of the difference in simple reaction time can be accounted for by differences in muscle contraction mechanisms between active and sedentary individuals. In contrast, active women in all age groups (range 20–79 years) had faster discrimination reaction times than sedentary women. When simple reaction times were subtracted from discrimination reaction time to yield a measure of discrimination time, active women at all ages except between 70 and 79 years were still faster than sedentary women. This latter measure should reflect differences that are localized to the central nervous system. Perhaps the different outcomes on psychomotor performance reflect the need for more experimental studies that incorporate longer treatment conditions and greater aerobic conditioning. Alternatively, differences in reaction time reflect inherent differences in the level of activity, but are not influenced by changing the levels of activity. Future studies will be needed to clarify the differences between these three studies.

Although some of these studies were designed to test exercise effects on cognition, drop-out rates are often high in the exercise groups. The greater number of individuals dropping out of the exercise training condition may leave a select group of more fit individuals in the exercise condition. In contrast, the control group may be more representative of the general population. Such an outcome violates statistical tests that assume that both samples are drawn from the same population. The data then reveal a relation, but not one that is necessarily cause–effect in nature.

All of these studies cause us to ask a number of questions about the nature of the relation between exercise and neural function. Do cognitive ability and neural health influence the amount of physical activity in a person's life? Or does physical activity directly or indirectly influence cognitive function and neural health? Alternatively, are these factors the outcome of a separate factor that affects cognitive ability, neural health, and the level of physical activity? Teasing apart these cause–effect relations will be greatly dependent upon animal models, because animal models of exercise provide the opportunity to examine the effects of exercise on behavior while controlling many of the confounding variables that are present when using human subjects. Animal models offer the opportunity to control drop-out rates, and they are less expensive than human studies. These models also offer the opportunity to investigate the effects of exercise on brain structure, electrophysiology, and metabolism.

## Using Animal Models to Test the Effects of Exercise on the Brain and Behavior

Models of aerobic exercise in the rat take two forms, voluntary exercise in running wheels attached to the home cage, or forced walking or running in a treadmill. Some investigators use swimming, but at the same time other investigators consider forced swimming to be a model of stress. For that reason, the following review does not include studies on the effects of swimming. For voluntary exercise and treadmill running there is no standard model. In the voluntary exercise condition, rats, mice, or gerbils usually have access to a running wheel 24 hours per day, seven days a week. The duration of the study can be short (e.g., two days; Neeper, Gomez-Pinilla, Choi, & Cotman, 1996) or long (e.g., six months; McCloskey, Adamo, & Anderson, 2001). In the alternative model, rats are forced to run in a treadmill, usually for a maximum of one hour per day for five to seven days per week. Running speed varies. Some studies have reported effects of a rapid walk (10 m/min; Isaacs, Anderson, Alcantara, Black, & Greenough, 1992). Others pace rats relative to 70–90 percent of the maximum oxygen consumption ($VO_2$ max; e.g., Spirduso & Farrar, 1981; Gilliam et al., 1984), which can be twice the speed of a rapid walk (18–27 m/min). Studies using forced running in the treadmill range in duration from one month (Isaacs et al., 1992) to six months (MacRae, Spirduso, Walters, Farrar, & Wilcox, 1987). Few studies have utilized conditions comparable to the human studies, where subjects are typically asked to exercise three times per week.

Like swimming, running in a treadmill is forced, not voluntary. As a result, it may be stressful to the subjects. Typically, two strategies are employed to reduce the stress. First, all animals for the study are placed on a treadmill and forced to run before initiating the study. The animals that refuse to run are thrown out of the study and the remaining animals are divided into the running and control conditions (Spirduso & Farrar, 1981). A second strategy involves slowly increasing the speed and duration of running over several weeks until the animals are trained to run the desired speed and duration. In studies using high speeds of running, shock is often used to reinforce running. Unfortunately, investigators do not report the number of shocks required so it is unclear how shock influences the nature of the treatment.

There remains concern that forced running can cause emotional stress. Differentiating the potential psychological stress from the physical stress from running is difficult. For example, glucocorticoids are elevated during both states. Adrenal gland growth can result from both repeated psychological stress and repeated running (even voluntary running). Although emotional stress and exercise share outcomes on some biological factors, they differ in their outcomes on other factors. For example, in the hippocampus, they cause opposing effects on numerous variables. It is possible that emotional stress concurrent with physical activity is less damaging than emotional stress alone. For that reason the following review will include studies that used forced treadmill running.

Similar to the studies of exercise in humans, most studies of exercise in animals include measurements of one or two variables that can be used to confirm improvements in fitness. Ideally, an investigator would show that the maximum oxygen consumption has increased after training (e.g., Spirduso & Farrar, 1981), but the equipment needed for these measures is expensive. The procedure is also stressful and could compromise other aspects of the study. Other investigators have measured the capacity for energy production in muscles by measuring metabolic enzymes (e.g., cytochrome oxidase activity; Gilliam et al., 1984). Unfortunately, these latter measures are not available to all labs, and more often are not compatible with specialized fixation methods required for the preservation of brain tissue. Fortunately, weighing muscle, adrenal gland and heart (Isaacs et al., 1992) is a simple third alternative for the measure of fitness. These measures are economical and compatible with most experimental methods.

## Can exercise influence rodent learning and memory?

We next must ask whether these models of exercise can influence cognitive function in animals. Following is a review of many of the studies that have been performed so far. A great challenge, of course, is the assessment of cognitive function in animals. In rodents, the behavior closest to requiring "cognition" is spatial learning. Spatial learning is dependent upon the hippocampus, a structure that is believed to be involved in declarative forms of memory in humans, and that is believed to associate items that are discontiguous over space and time (Wallenstein, Eichenbaum, & Hasselmo, 1998).

Fordyce and Farrar (1991) first tested the effects of treadmill training on spatial working memory using the Morris water maze. Typically rats in this maze must remember over daily trials the position of an escape platform submerged in a pool of water. Rats naturally use spatial cues outside of the water maze to find the location of the platform. The standard version of this maze assesses spatial *reference* memory because platform location becomes a "rule" of the task Fordyce and Farrar utilized a slightly different procedure in this maze. In their procedure, the place-learning set version, rats have pairs of trials with the same goal position. On trial 1 of each pair, a new goal position is introduced. On trial 2, memory for the position on trial 1 is tested. This version tests spatial *working* rather than *reference* memory. Working memory is a transient memory that is operationally defined in animal research as memory for events dependent upon the previous trial. In this study, forced treadmill training at a speed of 20 m/min (0% grade) for 14 weeks (five days per week) was reported to improve the rats' ability to find the submerged platform by as much as 2–12 fold relative to the performance of sedentary rats. Similar results have been reported for forced exercise (12 m/min, 0% grade, 60 min per day for five days per week) for eight weeks in mice (Fordyce & Wehner, 1993). Both reports of improvements in spatial learning in rodents after chronic exercise have used the place-learning set version of the Morris water maze. In both studies the groups did not differ in their speed of swimming, so the authors argue that the differences in physical fitness could not account for the improved performance. More recently, van Praag, Christie, Sejnowski, and Gage (1999) found similar results in mice that voluntarily exercised in running wheels. As with the previous studies, the swim speed did not differ between the two groups. These studies, however, tested spatial reference memory.

Group differences in the response to the aversive aspect of the Morris water maze might have contributed to the differences reported by the previous investigators. Because the rats are forced to swim in water to search for a submerged platform, this test is aversive and stressful. Exercise is a physical stress hypothesized to enhance an organism's response to other stressors. If exercise altered how the animals respond to the aversive nature of the water maze, this alteration rather than improved memory might account for the improved performance.

To avoid the potential confound from differences in the response to stress, an appetitive spatial learning task was utilized to further test for exercise-related improvements in spatial learning. We have used the eight-arm radial maze, an appetitive spatial learning task that is dependent upon the hippocampus (Becker, Walker, & Olton, 1980). In this task, rats simply walk down one of eight arms at their desired speed to obtain drops of water. Differences in physical ability are less likely to influence performance and attention in the eight-arm maze than in the water maze. With this paradigm we found that female rats that voluntarily ran in wheels attached to their home cage for seven weeks had greater heart weights and acquired criterion level performance on the eight-arm maze in significantly fewer days than littermate controls (Anderson et al., 2000). Rats in both groups took the same average time to travel down each arm of the maze. Our data support the earlier conclusions that exercise improves spatial memory. We have repeated this study to include a group of rats that received locked wheels to control for differences in spatial experience in the home cage. In this study, rats with locked wheels required a similar number of trials to reach criterion as control rats, and significantly more than exercise rats (unpublished observations). In the first study we gave exercise rats additional water in an attempt to control for differences in motivation. In the second study we gave both groups access to water bottles for the same amount of time. In both studies the exercise group required fewer trials to reach criterion. Once rats reached criterion performance in both studies, the performance of the two groups no longer differed. In other words, practice made perfect whether the rats exercised or not, but exercise gave the voluntary running group an early advantage.

One study has failed to report an effect of exercise. Using young (six-month-old) and old (27 months) rats, Barnes et al. (1991) tested the influence of exercise on spatial learning ability. Rats in the exercise condition were trained to run for one hour per day for five days per week over 10 weeks. Rats were trained to a speed that was equal to 75 percent of their maximal oxygen consumption. This training regimen was shown to increase the heart-to-body weight ratio. After training, the animals were able to run faster at maximal capacity than prior to exercise training. In this study, the Barnes maze was used to test for spatial learning ability. The Barnes maze is a circular platform with holes around the periphery. Rodents must find the one hole that lies over a darkened goal box. The task is somewhat analogous to the standard version of the Morris water maze, because rats are required to find a single goal position using reference memory. Unlike the water maze, the Barnes maze uses only mildly aversive stimuli, a well-lit room and white platform, to entice the animal into a dark, safe, goal box. In this study, the investigators kept the same goal location for the first 13 trials, and a new goal position for trials 14–17. They report only the number of errors averaged over days 11–13, and on trial 17. All of these trials reflect well-learned responses. The authors found no effect of exercise in this study. These results are in agreement with the failure to find effects of exercise after animals achieved criterion-level performance in the eight-arm radial maze study (Anderson et al., 2000). It would be interesting to know whether exercise can influence the number of trials required to reach criterion performance in this task.

Several studies have tested whether exercise influences more fundamental behaviors. One study reported that exercise improves reactive avoidance. Treadmill training consisted of having rats run up to 30 meters per minute for 60 minutes a day over a period of eight weeks. Oxygen utilization in muscle increased in both the young and old trained rats relative to controls. Treadmill training reduced both the latency to release a lever after shock and the latency to release a lever to avoid shock (Spirduso & Farrar, 1981). Old controls had a lower percentage of correct avoidances relative to their percentage in a pretest taken at a younger age. In contrast, old trained rats maintained their percentage of correct avoidances relative to their younger-age response levels.

In another study, age-related changes in behavior were reduced by exercise. Treadmill training from 5–23 months influenced age-related declines in spontaneous activity (Skalicky, Bubna-Littitz, & Viidik, 1996). Differences in spontaneous activity began to develop after the age of 10 months, and continue to grow over the following months. These same investigators found that continuous training (at 3 km per week) from 12–24 months was effective at attenuating these age-related changes. It is interesting to note that doubling the distance covered per week (6 km per week) while dividing training into weeks of exercise and rest was less effective at reducing the age-related reduction in activity. These results suggest that lower intensity, continuous exercise is better than intermittent high intensity exercise (Skalicky & Viidik, 1999).

In summary, studies of both animals and humans indicate that exercise can influence subsequent task performance. More work with animals is needed to test whether the differences in spatial learning after exercise reflect differences in motivation or the response to stress. Likewise, more studies are needed to test the possibility that the altered performance after exercise might be the result of more fundamental behavioral changes, such as changes in attention and vigilance. Until all of these possibilities are ruled out, we will not know for sure how exercise is influencing spatial learning and reactive capacity in rodents. The evidence, however, is substantial enough to suggest that exercise is changing the brain.

## Identifying Brain Structures that are Modified by Exercise

Initially, we can hypothesize that exercise will influence the brain through neural activity selectively related to the production of movement, or reception of sensory feedback during movement. To explore the effects of exercise on the brain then, we will want to start by investigating movement or sensory related structures. The first structures of interest are those that play a role in movement. Electrophysiological recording and measures of metabolism can be used to confirm neural activity in motor structures during exercise. Structures that control behaviors that are influenced by exercise are also of interest. These latter structures do not need to be movement-related brain structures. For example, spatial learning was influenced by exercise, and is believed to be dependent upon the hippocampus. For these reasons the following review will cover exercise-related plasticity in the cerebellum, motor cortex, and striatum, three motor structures, as well as the hippocampus, which is necessary for spatial learning.

Consistent with our hypothesis that exercise will influence brain structures active during exercise, we want to know whether or not a brain area has neural activity that is increased during exercise. Electrical recording provides a direct answer, but limits the number of structures that can be investigated at any one time, and provides data from only restricted regions within any single structure. There are other methods that can provide indirect measures of neuronal activity. These measures are based on the close relation between metabolic activity and neuronal activity. Because many of these measures have been used to identify regions that are active during exercise, we will briefly discuss their basis.

The brain requires proportionally more energy than any other part of the body. It uses 15–20 percent of the oxygen consumed despite making up only 2 percent of the body weight. Even though it has a high demand for energy, it stores very little ATP (adenosine triphosphate), which is the source of free energy. Instead, the brain makes ATP as it is needed. The online production of ATP requires that products of neural activity serve as signals to accelerate multiple stages of metabolism. For example, as neuronal activity increases, it produces signals that increase local blood flow, thereby increasing the availability of oxygen and glucose. It is the close coupling between neural activity and blood flow that allows functional magnetic resonance imaging (fMRI) to be used to localize brain areas activated during behavioral tasks. During neural activity, oxygen and glucose are transported as needed from the blood capillaries into brain tissue. Glucose is used for glycolysis, which produces pyruvate, lactate, and ATP. Although glycolysis produces ATP, it does not produce as much as a later stage of metabolism, oxidative phosphorylation. Two of the products of glycolysis, pyruvate or lactate (the latter can be converted to pyruvate) are used in the Krebs (tricarboxylic acid – TCA) cycle, or the second stage of metabolism. The Krebs cycle ultimately produces compounds needed for oxidative phosphorylation. When neural activity increases, more ATP is broken down to produce energy. The products of this chemical reaction, in turn, signal the acceleration of many stages of metabolism so that the production of ATP can be elevated. Thus there is a tight coupling between neuronal activity and almost all stages of metabolism. Because of this tight coupling, the activity of multiple stages of metabolism can be used as indirect indicators of the rate of neuronal activity.

The close relation between neural activity and metabolic rate forms the basis of our ability to map brain activation across multiple sites during the performance of a task. This relation forms the basis of the imaging methods (fMRI and positron emission tomography – PET) that are used by cognitive neuroscientists. In animals 2-DG and cytochrome oxidase histochemistry provide measures from many neural areas at once. The price paid for the broader picture of brain activity obtained by these metabolic mapping methods, however, is a loss of temporal resolution. These indirect measures of neural activity are measured over seconds to minutes or hours, whereas electrophysiological recordings are measured in milliseconds.

It is possible that exercise does not influence the brain through increased neural activity in specifically activated brain regions. Exercise has well-known effects on the cardiovascular system and hormones (Kjaer, 1998; Samorajski, Rolsten, Przykorska, & Davis, 1987), two factors that could provide broad, distributed effects on the nervous system. In the following discussion of plasticity in brain structures that are active during exercise, there will be evidence to suggest that the changes are not broadly distributed, but instead are likely to be directly related to the neural activity associated with exercise.

## Cerebellum

The cerebellum, a motor structure in the central nervous system, controls posture and coordination, and plays a role in involuntary movements. Although the cerebellum is considered a motor area of the brain, it receives somatosensory and vestibular input. It may be fairer to say that it integrates sensory information to influence movement. It is no surprise then that treadmill running in dogs increases regional cerebral blood flow in the cerebellum (Gross, Marcus, & Heistad, 1980).

The cerebellum, like the visual cortex, undergoes structural alterations in response to enriched housing (Greenough, 1984). Because the enriched environment increases the opportunity for physical activity, subsequent studies have tested whether exercise and skill learning separately influence the cerebellum. To differentiate the effects of learning from those of the additional physical activity in the environment, Black, Isaacs, Anderson, Alcantara, and Greenough (1990) studied the effects of motor skill learning and exercise on the anatomical structure of the cerebellum. To get rats to learn new motor skills, rats were allowed to traverse an obstacle course that required them to learn new spatiotemporal muscle activation patterns and to develop their balance and coordination. Two exercise conditions were used to control for the physical activity required to traverse the maze. Rats in the voluntary exercise condition had wheels attached to their home cages. Rats in the forced exercise condition were trained to walk rapidly in a treadmill for up to one hour per day. The strategy was to create very robust training on two different dimensions. If skill learning, but not exercise, influenced a variable such as synapse number, it would be difficult for skeptics to argue that the skill learning condition required more physical activity than the exercise conditions. Likewise, if exercise, a simple repetitive task with relatively little skill learning, influenced a variable, it would be difficult to argue that exercising rats could have *learned* more than rats in the skill learning condition. Following training, the number of synapses per neuron was measured in the paramedian lobule (PML), a cerebellar lobule that receives somatosensory input from forelimbs and hindlimbs. In this region, the skill learning group that traversed an obstacle course requiring balance and coordination had a greater number of synapses per neuron in the molecular layer than the control, voluntary exercise, and forced exercise groups (Black et al., 1990). Taken in contrast to enriched conditions where rats are housed in the environment for 24 hours a day, these findings were particularly dramatic in light of the little time spent on the obstacle course, 15 minutes per day. The selective association between learning and greater synapse numbers suggests that altering the number of synapses may be a mechanism for learning in the cerebellum.

Exercise, like skill learning, produced structural alterations, but they took a different form than those observed after skill learning. Both the voluntary and forced exercise conditions caused an increase in the density of capillaries in the paramedian lobule of the cerebellum (Isaacs et al., 1992). These data suggest that the additional neural activity associated with running created a greater need for oxygen and glucose, which was met by increasing capillary density.

The dissociation between additional synaptic numbers following skill learning, and the greater capillary density following exercise, provided the opportunity to test whether glial cells, which are support cells that have a role in both metabolism and synaptic transmission, grow in relation to synapses or capillaries. We found that glial volume in the cerebellum changed in the skill learning condition, but not in the exercise condition (Anderson et al., 1994). The results suggest that glial volume is more closely associated with synaptic numbers than with capillary density.

Exercise also protects the cerebellum from aging. Rats that ran on a horizontal tread-mill at 20 meters per minute from 5 to 23 months of age had 11 percent more Purkinje cells than sedentary controls (Larsen, Skalicky, & Viidik, 2000). No difference in the number of Purkinje cells was found between the exercising aged rats and young rats. These findings support the hypothesis that exercise can prevent or delay cell loss related to aging.

Taken together, these studies indicate that exercise increases the availability of oxygen and glucose in the PML of the cerebellum. Perhaps neurons in this region are capable of sustaining increased activity associated with running. Whereas skill learning increased the number of synaptic connection to the region, exercise had no such effect. Last, exercise retards age-related cell loss in this region.

*Motor cortex*

The superficial layers of the motor cortex, layers II/III, receive input from other cortical regions, process that input, and then relay it to the lower lying neurons that project directly, over a long distance, to the motor neurons in the spinal cord. In the rat, unlike the human, much of the motor cortex overlaps with the somatosensory cortex. The anatomical connections of these neurons place them in a unique position to influence reaction time.

Metabolic mapping studies have shown that movement is associated with increases in regional cerebral blood flow in the motor cortex in humans (Roland, Meyer, Shibasaki, Yamamoto, & Thompson, 1982). Likewise, treadmill running increases regional cerebral blood flow in the sensorimotor cortex in dogs (Gross et al., 1980). Consistent with these findings, transient increases in local cerebral glucose utilization occur in the motor cortex during exercise in rats (Vissing, Andersen, & Diemer, 1996). Because of the tight coupling between neural activity, blood flow, and glucose utilization, these results indicate that running increases neural activity in this region.

The motor skill learning condition that influenced the cerebellum also influences the motor cortex. In the motor cortex, motor-skill learning increases the number of synapses per neuron compared to that seen in control and yoked activity groups (Kleim, Lussnig, Schwarz, Comery, & Greenough, 1996). In another study, we tried to assess the distribution of the effects of exercise and skill learning by measuring cortical thickness. In this study, the younger exercising rats ran seven times the number of wheel rotations as voluntarily running animals from the cerebellar study by Black et al. (1990). Like the voluntary exercise condition from the Black et al. (1990) study, these rats had greater heart weight. The effectiveness of the exercise condition was also reflected by an increase in adrenal gland weight. Unlike the pattern of results in the cerebellum, this study indicated that both exercise and skill learning could increase tissue volume (Anderson, Eckburg, & Relucio, 2002). The exercise-related increase in thickness is also likely to be related to an increase in the number of synapses per neuron in the motor cortex. Such a finding would be consistent with findings that the enriched environment can increase cortical thickness, and that changes in thickness correspond to increases in the number of synapses per neuron in the visual cortex (Greenough, 1984). Similarly, in the cerebellum, increases in the molecular layer volume corresponded to increases in the number of synapses per neuron (Black et al., 1990). If exercise increases the number of synapses per neuron in the motor cortex, the findings would be consistent with the findings of several related studies. In these studies, increased electrical activity, rather than altered patterns of neural activity, was able to induce anatomical change (Rutledge, Wright, & Duncan, 1974; Keller, Arissian, & Asanuma, 1992).

We have also questioned whether exercise alters metabolic capacity in the motor cortex. First, we asked whether or not it increases capillary density in the motor cortex as it does in the cerebellum. We matched our treatment condition to the forced exercise condition used by Isaacs et al. (1992), which increased capillary density in the cerebellum. The rats were forced to exercise for one month. Each day they walked for one hour at 11 m/min with a 10 minute break after the first 30 minutes. To ensure that we did not create a stressful condition, the animals in this study, unlike the earlier study, were given the opportunity for a two minute rest every 10 minutes. We have failed to find an effect of forced exercise on capillary density, although we have limited our investigations to the posterior portion of the primary motor cortex, which does not represent forelimbs, but does represent hindlimbs (unpublished observations).

We have also tested the capacity for oxidative metabolism after voluntary exercise by measuring cytochrome oxidase reactivity. Activity of the cytochrome oxidase enzyme is coupled to the production of ATP. Rats that had access to exercise wheels attached to their home cage for six months (from 5–11 months of age) had greater metabolic capacity in the motor cortex (McCloskey et al., 2001), but no greater activity in control regions of the striatum (i.e., regions that process facial information).

Like the cerebellum, the motor cortex is influenced by exercise and motor skill learning. In both structures, exercise alters variables related to metabolism. Unlike the cerebellum, however, the motor cortex appears to increase in volume in response to exercise. Perhaps plasticity in the motor cortex after exercise is related to greater endurance and improved reactive capacity. Further work will be necessary to test such a hypothesis.

*Striatum*

The striatum includes the caudate and putamen, two of the three nuclei that make up the basal ganglia (the caudate, putamen, and globus pallidus). The striatum receives input from the motor cortex and other cortical regions. These nuclei work together and indirectly send their output to the motor areas of the cortex. The striatum is considered a motor region that has a role in planning and the initiation of voluntary movements. Activity in this structure is disrupted in Parkinson's disease, a disease associated with the presence of resting tremors, a slow shuffling gait, and difficulty initiating voluntary movement.

As predicted by its known role in movement, the striatum is active during exercise. Movement is associated with increases in regional cerebral blood flow in the striatum in humans (Roland et al., 1982). In rats running on a treadmill at 85 percent of their maximal oxygen consumption, local cerebral glucose uptake increases in the striatum (Vissing et al., 1996). As noted earlier, these data are indirect indicators that exercise increases neural activity in the striatum.

No studies have yet tested whether or not exercise can alter the structure of the striatal neurons, but studies testing the effects of the enriched environment suggest that neural structure in this region is modifiable. Enriched housing increases the number of spines, sites of excitatory synaptic contact, on medium spiny neurons in the dorsolateral striatum (Comery, Shah, & Greenough, 1995). The neurons that have this morphological altera-tion are the neurons that are known to express dopamine receptors. Two-year-old rats exposed to an enriched environment have a greater ratio of dopamine type 1 receptors to muscarinic ACh receptors, but no change in dopamine type 2 receptors (Anderson, Gatley, Rapp, Coburn-Litvak, & Volkow, 2000). Taken together these studies suggest that behavioral conditions can alter neuronal structure and receptor expression in the striatum.

In contrast to the enriched environment, treadmill running (27 m/min at 0% grade for approximately 80 percent of the subject's maximum oxygen consumption for one hour per day over a period of six months) has been reported to increase the density of dopamine type 2 receptors in the striatum of adult rats (MacRae, Spirduso, Cartee, Farrar, & Wilcox, 1987). Training significantly increased the maximal oxygen consump-tion relative to control rats. In a similar study D2 receptor binding was studied in aged rats (MacRae et al., 1987). The rats were trained to run on a treadmill up to 20 meters per minute for 60 minutes per day for five days per week over 12 weeks. The metabolic capacity of the gastrocnemius-plantaris was increased by 27 percent in the old (21-month-old) treadmill trained group relative to the young (six-month-old) untrained group. From 6 to 12 months, D2 receptor binding sites decreased in controls, but treadmill training reduced this age-related decrease. Exercise also influenced a dopamine metabolite, DOPAC. Although age increased DOPAC, treadmill training prevented this age-related effect. These studies indicate that forced exercise can alter the expression of neurotransmitter receptors in adult animals, and that exercise can attenuate age-related changes in the expression of neurotransmitter receptors.

Dopamine is not the only neurotransmitter system in the striatum that is influenced by exercise. In young rats, treadmill training (25–30 m/min at 0% grade for 60 minutes each of six days per week for eight weeks) and voluntary exercise elevated striatal GABA relative to controls (Dishman et al., 1996). Activity wheel running reduced $GABA_A$ receptor binding, whereas the treadmill training did not. These results are particularly interesting because activity wheel running, but not treadmill training, increased open field activity. A relation between open field activity and $GABA_A$ density is supported by earlier findings that blocking $GABA_A$ receptors increases open field locomotion (Plaznik, Stefanski, & Kostowski, 1990). These results are consistent with the hypothesis that there is a direct link between the effects of exercise on this transmitter system, and alterations in open field behavior.

We have investigated the possibility that exercise causes a long-term up-regulation of metabolic capacity in the striatum. A simple histochemical reaction allows us to measure the capacity to produce ATP. We investigated structures within the striatum that should be active during limb movements, as well as structures that should not be active during limb movements. We found that rats that exercised for six months had relatively greater metabolic capacity in the presumed limb movement representations of the striatum (McCloskey et al., 2001). In contrast, metabolic capacity was not changed in regions of the striatum that are believed to process face information. Not only do these results suggest that neurons in the limb regions of the striatum have a greater metabolic capacity after six months of exercise, but the data also indicate that the effects are restricted within the striatum to regions that are likely to have elevated neural activity during running.

We noted earlier that neural cells have a relatively high metabolic demand, but store very little ATP. This feature of neural cells leaves them very vulnerable to episodes of low oxygen and/or glucose. Ischemia refers to a disruption in the blood supply, which can occur during obstructive and hemorrhagic stroke. We have already seen that exercise alters the capacity for the metabolism of neurons in select regions of the striatum. Perhaps these alterations protect neurons during damaging events like ischemia. Although this has not been tested directly, or in rats, there is some evidence from gerbils that exercise protects neurons in the striatum from ischemia. Gerbils had access to standard cages or running wheels for two weeks before they had blood flow in the carotid artery blocked for 15 or 20 minutes. Two weeks after this procedure only 21 percent of the nonrunners survived, whereas all of the runners survived (Stummer, Weber, Tranmer, Baethmann, & Kempski, 1994). More relevant to the striatum, 15 minutes of ischemia caused a loss of 90 percent of the neurons in the limb-related region of control gerbils, whereas only 50 percent of neurons were lost in the same region in gerbils that ran for two weeks before the ischemic episode. More work is needed to determine which effects of exercise bring about these protective effects, and whether they generalize across species.

Here we have seen that the striatum is active during exercise. Exercise influences the density of some types of transmitter receptors, and the concentration of some transmitters and their metabolites. Exercise influences striatal metabolic capacity in limb-related subregions, but not face-related subregions. Last, exercise-related modifications protected neurons from ischemia. Although measures from many studies were taken from the whole striatum, one study showed that exercise-related effects were restricted to subregions that process limb-related information. Thus exercise influences both striatal physiology and vulnerability, and may do so in a regionally selective manner.

## *Hippocampus*

Earlier we reviewed several studies that indicated that exercise improves spatial learning in rats and mice. The effects of exercise on spatial learning most likely occur in the hippocampus, which is responsible for associating discontiguous events and places (Wallenstein et al., 1998). Cells in the hippocampus are activated by positions in space (Czurko, Hirase, Csicsvari, & Buzsaki, 1999). It appears that these "place" cells work together to form memories for places in space and their relationships to spatial cues in the environment. Although the hippocampus is not considered a motor structure, movement-related information is evident in place cell activity. The velocity of movement is reflected in the frequency of a neuron's activity when the head is in the cell's preferred position in space (Czurko et al., 1999). This finding has been shown more clearly by holding rats in a stationary position by putting them in a running wheel. When recordings are made from cells that represent the position in the running wheel space, the discharge rate of the cell is related to the speed of running (Czurko et al., 1999). Other researchers have found that jumping, running, and walking increase hippocampal electrophysiological activity (Bland & Vanderwolf, 1972; Vanderwolf, 1988).

Metabolic methods provide further evidence that hippocampal neural activity is related to locomotion. Glucose utilization increases in the CA1 subregion of the hippocampus during exercise (Vissing et al., 1996). Extracellular lactate, a product of glycolysis, increases in the rat hippocampus during physical movement by as much as 15 percent (De Bruin, Schasfoort, Steffens, & Korf, 1990). Taken together these data indirectly indicate that neural activity increases in the hippocampus during exercise. Similarly, measures of transmitter activity also suggest that hippocampal activity is related to movement. Treadmill running causes an increase in acetylcholine release in the hippocampus (Dudar, Whishaw, & Szerb, 1979). Conversely, when acetylcholine is injected into the hippocampus, rats begin to locomote (Mogenson & Nielsen, 1984). These investigators have suggested that the hippocampus plays a role in initiating locomotor activity. There is also evidence that the hippocampus uses internal movement information as one method of coding the distance traveled in an environment (Wallace, Hines, & Whishaw, 2002), and that this information is integrated with other spatial information.

Next, we will review evidence that exercise brings about long-term plasticity in the hippocampus. The long-term effects of exercise on the hippocampus have been studied on five general variables, (1) receptor density, (2) growth factors, (3) metabolism, (4) rates of cell division, and (5) cell survival after damaging events.

Chronic exercise, like acute exercise, influences hippocampal neurochemistry. Acute treadmill running at 20 m/min for 60 minutes elevated high affinity choline uptake in the hippocampus. In contrast, repeated running for five days per week for 14 months caused choline uptake to decrease (Fordyce & Farrar, 1991). This reduction suggests that after repeated running there is a reduction in amount of septal input, the source of ACh to the hippocampus. When chronic running was combined with spatial memory testing, high affinity choline uptake was increased. Long-term training alone or combined with spatial memory testing increased ACh receptor binding in the hippocampus

(Fordyce & Farrar, 1991). These authors have also shown that ACh receptor density decreases with age, but the decrease can be attenuated by chronic exercise in aging animals (Fordyce, Starnes, & Farrar, 1991). The latter finding is consistent with the general belief that exercise can retard, and possibly even reverse, some forms of aging.

Growth factors have also been investigated after exercise. One family of growth factors, the neurotrophins, support growth of processes, and protect the brain from aging and damage. These properties make neurotrophins of interest in studies of the effects of exercise on the hippocampus. The effects of exercise on the regulation of the gene expression for two neurotrophins, the brain-derived neurotrophic factor (BDNF) and nerve growth factor (NGF) have been tested in the cerebellum, hippocampus, and frontal, middle, and caudal cortex (Neeper, Gomez-Pinilla, Choi, & Cotman, 1995, 1996). Free access to running wheels for two, four, or seven days rapidly increased the amount of mRNA for BDNF and NGF in the hippocampus and caudal cerebral cortex relative to control rats. Smaller but still significant increases in BDNF occurred in the cerebellum and frontal cortex.

Earlier we reviewed evidence that exercise improves spatial learning, a hippocampus-dependent behavior. With that in mind, it is interesting to note that infusing NGF into the hippocampus improves spatial leaning (Fischer et al., 1987; Markowska, Price, & Koliatsos, 1996). In a similar study, infusion of NGF improved spatial learning in cognitively impaired aged rats, whereas infusion of BDNF did not (Pelleymounter, Cullen, Baker, Gollub, & Wellman, 1996). If the extra NGF mRNA associated with exercise leads to an overall increase in NGF, the excess may play a role in the exercise-related improvements in spatial learning.

Exercise in humans is an effective antidepressant. In contrast, stress increases the susceptibility to depression. Exercise and stress have many opposing effects in the brain, and their effects on BDNF are no exception. Both exercise and antidepressant treatment in rats increases BDNF mRNA in the hippocampus (Neeper et al., 1995, 1996). In contrast, stress reduces BNDF mRNA (Smith, Makino, Kvetnansky, & Post, 1995). Exercise and antidepressants can block stress-related suppression of BDNF (Russo-Neustadt, Beard, Huang, & Cotman, 2000). Although it is difficult to directly test a cause–effect relation between BDNF levels and depression, the results across these studies and conditions are consistent with that hypothesis.

Exercise has other surprising effects in the hippocampus. It has long been believed that the adult brain does not have the potential for the addition of new neural cells, and consequently the number of neurons is determined during development. Over time, exceptions to this rule have been found. For example, the subgranular zone of the dentate gyrus in the hippocampus contains cells that can divide even into adulthood to form new neurons and glial cells. This area is one of only two zones within the brain that contain cells capable of dividing into neurons (i.e., progenitor cells). The presence of progenitor cells in the subgranular zone has been confirmed in rodents, primates, and humans. Quite amazingly, the rate of cell division and the survival of the new neurons (i.e., neurogenesis) can be increased by behavioral experiences, including enriched housing (Kempermann, Kuhn, & Gage, 1997), and voluntary running (van Praag et al., 1999). In the latter study, exercise was shown to enhance spatial learning, long-term potentiation of synapses, and neural cell division and survival in the same animals. In support of a relation between the neurogenesis and the enhanced learning, Shors, Beylin, Wood, and Gould (2000) have shown that a hippocampal-dependent form of Pavlovian conditioning was impaired when cell division in this region was blocked. These data, taken together, suggest that neural cell division is not only influenced by exercise, but may be one mechanism by which exercise influences learning.

Given the number of variables in the hippocampus that are modified by exercise, we began to question whether exercise might also influence hippocampal metabolism. We have tested the effects of exercise on a number of variables related to metabolism. Although we found that six months of wheel running increased metabolic capacity in the motor cortex and limb regions of the striatum, we failed to find any effect of exercise on metabolic capacity (cytochrome oxidase reactivity) in the hippocampus (McCloskey et al., 2001). We have also used treadmill training to test for an effect of exercise on hippocampal capillary density. In this study we used the same parameters used by Isaacs et al. (1992) who showed that exercise increased cerebellar capillary density. This same treatment, fast walking for one hour a day for 30 days, did not influence capillary density in the hippocampus. Within-group variance was low enough to have detected differences if they had existed. So far we have not been able to detect exercise-related plasticity of metabolic variables in the hippocampus. There are more variables and parameters that will need to be tested before we can conclude that the exercise-related alterations in hippocampal neurochemistry and neuron number do not alter hippocampal metabolic capacity as well.

Although we have not found changes in metabolism, there is evidence to suggest that exercise can protect the hippocampus from damaging events. Previously we mentioned that exercise spared neurons in the striatum from death caused by ischemia. In that same study (Stummer et al., 1994), 50 percent of neurons in the CA3 subregion of the hippocampus of exercising gerbils survived after 15 minutes of ischemia, whereas only 10 percent of neurons survived in the control gerbils. The sparing was restricted to CA3, and was not seen in CA1, a subregion of the hippocampus particularly vulnerable to ischemia.

The findings that exercise influences spatial learning have led a number of investigators to test the effects of exercise on many different variables in the hippocampus. We have seen that the effects vary, and include effects on transmitter receptors, the potential for growth factor expression, cell proliferation and survival, and neuron survival after ischemia. Our initial efforts have failed to identify exercise effects on metabolic capacity or capillary density. Clearly, behaviors like exercise, which are known to activate the hippocampus, can influence hippocampal physiology. Some or all of these effects may contribute to the improved spatial learning after exercise, but the relations have yet to be demonstrated as cause–effect in nature.

## Methodological Advances

Physiological psychology, more than any other area of psychology, is driven by methodological advances. Some of the advances that lie ahead are certain to be related to the current explosion of new methods to investigate the expression of genes and proteins. The basic tenet of molecular biology states that genes, transcribed into mRNA, ultimately lead to proteins, which provide feedback to influence gene expression. We have seen that behaviors like exercise can alter mRNA and protein expression (e.g., receptor density). Similarly exercise alters hormones that can influence gene expression. It is clear then that the bidirectional pathway between the brain and behavior interacts with the bidirectional communication between genes and proteins. As a result the new methods in molecular biology are relevant for the study of exercise.

All cells have the same genes. What determines an individual cell's function is the gene expression in that cell. Genes can be expressed in multiple forms of mRNA through alternative splicing. As a result, the workload required to describe the genome is multiplied when we move to the study of gene products, or mRNA. Each mRNA translates a single protein, but the amount of mRNA does not necessarily relate to the amount of protein produced. Because the proteins are biologically active, it is the protein complement of a cell that directly dictates the cell's function. Thus ultimately we want to know how exercise changes gene and protein expression in cells of interest. New methods exist at each of these levels of study. Microarrays, SAGE (serial analysis of gene expression), and subtractive hybridization allow the study of thousands of gene products simultaneously (Datson, van Der Perk, de Kloet, & Vreugdenhil, 2001; Tong, Shen, Perreau, Balazs, & Cotman, 2001). Out of thousands of gene products, hundreds change in response to experimental treatments, exercise being no exception (e.g., Tong et al., 2001). As with any study using these techniques, the investigators face the challenge of choosing one or two of the many genes with altered expression for further research. There are a number of reasons to view these amazing results with caution. Current analyses require a two-fold change in gene expression for the effect to be considered significant. Thus any subtle change in expression will be overlooked. The prohibitive cost of these methods reduces the number of animals per group and the number of groups investigators choose to study. Because some genes are influenced by subtle behavioral manipulations, careful behavioral controls will need to be included in these studies. Ultimately, altered gene expression identified through these techniques should be verified with more traditional approaches.

To study the protein content of tissue, 2-D gel electrophoresis and protein chips can be used to survey hundreds of proteins at once. Here, as before, investigators face the challenge of choosing which proteins of many with altered content should be targeted for further research. Currently these methods have limitations, but they will continue to develop. All of these methods provide a seemingly unlimited opportunity to develop a greater understanding of the influence behavior has on gene and protein expression, and in turn, the influence gene and protein expression have on behavior.

## Final Thoughts

Many investigators question whether the control conditions used in the studies discussed might be better thought of as the treatment conditions. After all, the laboratory cage does not emulate the typical life of a feral rat, which is free to roam, face danger, forage for food, and, being a gregarious species, cluster in groups. Many of the feral rat's behaviors include physical activity. In contrast, the control rodent lives in a large clear tub with no opportunities for exercise or learning. Either way you choose to interpret the conditions, the data suggest that the brain is responsive in general to the level of physical activity, whether it is less activity or activity above normal levels.

Earlier we stated the overall hypothesis that exercise would exert influence on the brain through increases in neural activity associated with walking and running. This hypothesis assumes that the plasticity in response to exercise will be localized to structures that are active during running. Alternatively, we noted that the multiple effects of exercise on the brain could arise from general hormonal or cardiovascular effects. These effects, in contrast, should be distributed throughout the brain. A number of the studies reviewed support the former hypothesis with findings that effects are regionally specific. For example, exercise spared neurons from damage in the striatum, and CA3 region of the hippocampus, but not in the CA1 region (Stummer et al., 1994). Similarly, exercise increased metabolic capacity in the motor cortex and striatum, but not in the hippocampus (McCloskey et al., 2001). Chennaoui et al. (2001) have also found that intense exercise decreases a selective type of serotonin receptor in the cerebellum, but not in the striatum or hippocampus. Although exercise does appear to have widespread effects, these studies illustrate that the effects tend to be regionally selective when multiple regions have been studied. As a result, the data are consistent with the hypothesis that exercise-induced plasticity is a direct consequence of increased neural activity in individual brain structures rather than an indirect consequence of exercise effects on the cardiovascular and hormonal systems in the periphery.

The physiological psychologist is ultimately interested in the relation between these forms of biological plasticity and their functional consequences. In other words, which forms of plasticity influence behavior? We have spoken about the effects of exercise on transmitter systems, growth factors, neuronal cell division, vasculature, and even cell survival from challenging events. Within the same animals or animals treated similarly, it is possible to *correlate* exercise-related neural plasticity with exercise-related effects on behavior. It is much more difficult, however, to establish that one form of plasticity alters behavior. To do this, several strategies are theoretically possible. We might block plasticity to show that learning is no longer improved. Unfortunately, we rarely know how to block plasticity. When it is possible, careful analysis will be needed to test whether the treatment impairs fundamental cellular functions in addition to plasticity. An alternative strategy is to increase the capacity for plasticity and show that learning is facilitated. This strategy is difficult as well, because we often do not know how to increase the potential for plasticity. In a similar vein, some investigators have used the strategy of inducing plasticity in order to exhaust the capacity for it. Afterwards, they demonstrated that learning was impaired (Moser & Moser, 1999). Again, this strategy requires the knowledge of how to exhaust the capacity for plasticity prior to the behavioral manipulation. Clearly, identifying the exact relationship between neural plasticity and behavioral alterations is a difficult challenge for physiological psychologists. As neuroscientists continue to develop knowledge about the complex biochemical cascades that make up forms of plasticity, this knowledge will increase the opportunities to use these strategies. With time and patience, we will have the opportunity to better understand the nature of the relation between the forms of brain plasticity described here and their behavioral consequences.

# References

Anderson, B. J., Eckburg, P. B., & Relucio, K. I. (2002). Alterations in the thickness of motor cortical subregions after motor-skill learning and exercise. *Learning and Memory, 9,* 1–19.

Anderson, B. J., Gatley, S. J., Rapp, D. N., Coburn-Litvak, P. S., & Volkow, N. D. (2000). The ratio of striatal D1 to muscarinic receptors changes in aging rats housed in an enriched environment. *Brain Research, 872* (1–2), 262–5.

Anderson, B. J., Li, X., Alcantara, A. A., Isaacs, K. R., Black, J. E., & Greenough, W. T. (1994). Glial hypertrophy is associated with synaptogenesis following motor-skill learning, but not with angiogenesis following exercise. *Glia, 11* (1), 73–80.

Anderson, B. J., Rapp, D. N., Baek, D. H., McCloskey, D. P., Coburn-Litvak, P. S., & Robinson, J. K. (2000). Exercise influences spatial learning in the radial arm maze. *Physiology and Behavior, 70* (5), 425–9.

Barnes, C. A., Forster, M. J., Fleshner, M., et al. (1991). Exercise does not modify spatial memory, brain autoimmunity, or antibody response in aged F–344 rats. *Neurobiology of Aging, 12* (1), 47–53.

Becker, J. T., Walker, J. A., & Olton, D. S. (1980). Neuroanatomical bases of spatial memory. *Brain Research, 200* (2), 307–20.

Black, J. E., Isaacs, K. R., Anderson, B. J., Alcantara, A. A., & Greenough, W. T. (1990). Learning causes synaptogenesis, whereas motor activity causes angiogenesis, in cerebellar cortex of adult rats. *Proceedings of the National Academy of Science of the United States of America, 87* (14), 5568–72.

Blair, S. N., Kohl, H. W. 3rd, Paffenbarger, R. S., Jr., Clark, D. G., Cooper, K. H., & Gibbons, L. W. (1989). Physical fitness and all-cause mortality. A prospective study of healthy men and women. *JAMA–Journal of the American Medical Association, 262* (17), 2395–401.

Bland, B. H., & Vanderwolf, C. H. (1972). Electrical stimulation of the hippocampal formation: Behavioral and bioelectrical effects. *Brain Research, 43* (1), 89–106.

Cajal, R. (1988). Anatomicophysiological considerations on the cerebrum (1911). In J. DeFelipe & E. G. Jones (eds.), *Cajal on the cerebral cortex: An annotated translation of the complete writings* (pp. 484–5). New York: Oxford University Press.

Chennaoui, M., Drogou, C., Gomez-Merino, D., Grimaldi, B., Fillion, G., & Guezennec, C. Y. (2001). Endurance training effects on 5-HT(1B) receptors mRNA expression in cerebellum, striatum, frontal cortex and hippocampus of rats. *Neuroscience Letters, 307* (1), 33–6.

Comery, T. A., Shah, R., & Greenough, W. T. (1995). Differential rearing alters spine density on medium-sized spiny neurons in the rat corpus striatum: Evidence for association of morphological plasticity with early response gene expression. *Neurobiology of Learning and Memory, 63* (3), 217–9.

Czurko, A., Hirase, H., Csicsvari, J., & Buzsaki, G. (1999). Sustained activation of hippocampal pyramidal cells by "space clamping" in a running wheel. *European Journal of Neuroscience, 11* (1), 344–52.

Datson, N. A., van Der Perk, J., de Kloet, E. R., & Vreugdenhil, E. (2001). Identification of corticosteroid-responsive genes in rat hippocampus using serial analysis of gene expression. *European Journal of Neuroscience, 14* (4), 675–89.

De Bruin, L. A., Schasfoort, E. M., Steffens, A. B., & Korf, J. (1990). Effects of stress and exercise on rat hippocampus and striatum extracellular lactate. *American Journal of Physiology*, *259* (4,2), R773–9.

Dishman, R. K., Dunn, A. L., Youngstedt, S. D., et al. (1996). Increased open field locomotion and decreased striatal GABA$_A$ binding after activity wheel running. *Physiology and Behavior*, *60* (3), 699–705.

Dudar, J. D., Whishaw, I. Q., & Szerb, J. C. (1979). Release of acetylcholine from the hippocampus of freely moving rats during sensory stimulation and running. *Neuropharmacology*, *18* (8–9) 673–8.

Dustman, R. E., Ruhling, R. O., Russell, E. M., et al. (1984). Aerobic exercise training and improved neuropsychological function of older individuals. *Neurobiology of Aging*, *5* (1), 35–42.

Elsayed, M., Ismail, A. H., & Young, R. J. (1980). Intellectual differences of adult men related to age and physical fitness before and after an exercise program. *Journal of Gerontology*, *35* (3), 383–7.

Fischer, W., Wictorin, K., Bjorklund, A., Williams, L. R., Varon, S., & Gage, F. H. (1987). Amelioration of cholinergic neuron atrophy and spatial memory impairment in aged rats by nerve growth factor. *Nature*, *329* (6134), 65–8.

Fordyce, D. E., & Farrar, R. P. (1991). Physical activity effects on hippocampal and parietal cortical cholinergic function and spatial learning in F344 rats. *Behavioural Brain Research*, *43* (2), 115–23.

Fordyce, D. E., Starnes, J. W., & Farrar, R. P. (1991). Compensation of the age-related decline in hippocampal muscarinic receptor density through daily exercise or underfeeding. *Journal of Gerontology*, *46* (6), B245–8.

Fordyce, D. E., & Wehner, J. M. (1993). Physical activity enhances spatial learning performance with an associated alteration in hippocampal protein kinase C activity in C57BL/6 and DBA/ 2 mice. *Brain Research*, *619* (1–2), 111–19.

Gilliam, P. E., Spirduso, W. W., Martin, T. P., Walters, T. J., Wilcox, R. E., & Farrar, R. P. (1984). The effects of exercise training on [3H]-spiperone binding in rat striatum. *Pharmacology Biochemistry and Behavior*, *20* (6), 863–7.

Greenough, W. T. (1984). Structural correlates of information storage in the mammalian brain: A review and hypothesis. *Trends in Neurosciences*, *7* (7), 229–33.

Gross, P. M., Marcus, M. L., & Heistad, D. D. (1980). Regional distribution of cerebral blood flow during exercise in dogs. *Journal of Applied Physiology*, *48* (2), 213–17.

Holloszy, J. O. (1988). Exercise and longevity: Studies on rats. *Journal of Gerontology*, *43* (6), B149–51.

Isaacs, K. R., Anderson, B. J., Alcantara, A. A., Black, J. E., & Greenough, W. T. (1992). Exercise and the brain: Angiogenesis in the adult rat cerebellum after vigorous physical activity and motor skill learning. *Journal of Cerebral Blood Flow and Metabolism*, *12* (1): 110–19.

Keller, A., Arissian, K., & Asanuma, H. (1992). Synaptic proliferation in the motor cortex of adult cats after long-term thalamic stimulation. *Journal of Neurophysiology*, *68* (1), 295–308.

Kempermann, G., Kuhn, H. G., & Gage, F. H. (1997). More hippocampal neurons in adult mice living in an enriched environment. *Nature*, *386* (6624), 493–5.

Kjaer, M. (1998). Adrenal medulla and exercise training. *European Journal of Applied Physiology and Occupational Physiology*, *77* (3), 195–9.

Kleim, J. A., Lussnig, E., Schwarz, E. R., Comery, T. A., & Greenough, W. T. (1996). Synaptogenesis and Fos expression in the motor cortex of the adult rat after motor skill learning. *Journal of Neuroscience*, *16* (14), 4529–35.

Kramer, A. F., Hahn, S., Cohen, N. J., et al. (1999). Ageing, fitness and neurocognitive function. *Nature*, *400* (6743), 418–19.

Larsen, J. O., Skalicky, M., & Viidik, A. (2000). Does long-term physical exercise counteract age-related Purkinje cell loss? A stereological study of rat cerebellum. *Journal of Comparative Neurology, 428* (2), 213–22.

MacRae, P. G., Spirduso, W. W., Cartee, G. D., Farrar, R. P., & Wilcox, R. E. (1987). Endurance training effects on striatal D2 dopamine receptor binding and striatal dopamine metabolite levels. *Neuroscience Letters, 79* (1–2), 138–44.

MacRae, P. G., Spirduso, W. W., Walters, T. J., Farrar, R. P., & Wilcox, R. E. (1987). Endurance training effects on striatal D2 dopamine receptor binding and striatal dopamine metabolites in presenescent older rats. *Psychopharmacology, 92* (2), 236–40.

Markowska, A. L., Price, D., & Koliatsos, V. E. (1996). Selective effects of nerve growth factor on spatial recent memory as assessed by a delayed nonmatching-to-position task in the water maze. *Journal of Neuroscience, 16* (10), 3541–8.

McCloskey, D. P., Adamo, D. S., & Anderson, B. J. (2001). Exercise increases metabolic capacity in the motor cortex and striatum, but not in the hippocampus. *Brain Research, 891* (1–2), 168–75.

Mogenson, G. J., & Nielsen, M. (1984). A study of the contribution of hippocampal-accumbens-subpallidal projections to locomotor activity. *Behavioral and Neural Biology, 42* (1), 38–51.

Moser, E. I., & Moser, M. B. (1999). Is learning blocked by saturation of synaptic weights in the hippocampus? *Neuroscience and Biobehavioral Reviews, 23* (5), 661–72.

Neeper, S. A., Gomez-Pinilla, F., Choi, J., & Cotman, C. (1995). Exercise and brain neurotrophins. *Nature, 373* (6510), 109.

Neeper, S. A., Gomez-Pinilla, F., Choi, J., & Cotman, C. (1996). Physical activity increases mRNA for brain-derived neurotrophic factor and nerve growth factor in rat brain. *Brain Research, 726* (1–2), 49–56.

Paffenbarger, R. S., Jr., Hyde, R. T., Wing, A. L., & Hsieh, C. C. (1986). Physical activity, all-cause mortality, and longevity of college alumni. *New England Journal of Medicine, 314* (10), 605–13.

Pelleymounter, M. A., Cullen, M. J., Baker, M. B., Gollub, M., & Wellman, C. (1996). The effects of intrahippocampal BDNF and NGF on spatial learning in aged Long Evans rats. *Molecular and Chemical Neuropathology, 29* (2–3), 211–26.

Plaznik, A., Stefanski, R., & Kostowski, W. (1990). GABAergic mechanisms in the nucleus accumbens septi regulating rat motor activity: the effect of chronic treatment with desipramine. *Pharmacology Biochemistry and Behavior, 36* (3): 501–6.

Renner, M. J., & Rosenzweig, M. R. (1987). *Enriched and impoverished environments: Effects on brain and behavior.* New York: Springer-Verlag.

Rogers, R. L., Meyer, J. S., & Mortel, K. F. (1990). After reaching retirement age physical activity sustains cerebral perfusion and cognition. *Journal of the American Geriatrics Society, 38* (2), 123–8.

Roland, P. E., Meyer, E., Shibasaki, T., Yamamoto, Y. L., & Thompson, C. J. (1982). Regional cerebral blood flow changes in cortex and basal ganglia during voluntary movements in normal human volunteers. *Journal of Neurophysiology, 48* (2), 467–80.

Russo-Neustadt, A. A., Beard, R. C., Huang, Y. M., & Cotman, C. W. (2000). Physical activity and antidepressant treatment potentiate the expression of specific brain-derived neurotrophic factor transcripts in the rat hippocampus. *Neuroscience, 101* (2), 305–12.

Rutledge, L. T., Wright, C., & Duncan, J. (1974). Morphological changes in pyramidal cells of mammalian neocortex associated with increased use. *Experimental Neurology, 44* (2), 209–28.

Samorajski, T., Rolsten, C., Przykorska, A., & Davis, C. M. (1987). Voluntary wheel running exercise and monoamine levels in brain, heart and adrenal glands of aging mice. *Experimental Gerontology, 22* (6), 421–31.

Shors, T. J., Beylin, A. V., Wood, G. E., & Gould, E. (2000). The modulation of Pavlovian memory. *Behavioural Brain Research, 110* (1–2), 39–52.

Skalicky, M., Bubna-Littitz, H., & Viidik, A. (1996). Influence of physical exercise on aging rats: I. Life-long exercise preserves patterns of spontaneous activity. *Mechanisms of Ageing and Development, 87* (2), 127–39.

Skalicky, M., & Viidik, A. (1999). Comparison between continuous and intermittent physical exercise on aging rats: Changes in patterns of spontaneous activity and connective tissue stability. *Aging (Milano), 11* (4), 227–34.

Smith, M. A., Makino, S., Kvetnansky, R., & Post, R. M. (1995). Stress and glucocorticoids affect the expression of brain-derived neurotrophic factor and neurotrophin-3 mRNAs in the hippocampus. *Journal of Neuroscience, 15* (3,1), 1768–77.

Spirduso, W. W., & Farrar, R. P. (1981). Effects of aerobic training on reactive capacity: An animal model. *Journal of Gerontology, 36* (6), 654–62.

Spirduso, W. W., MacRae, H. H., MacRae, P. G., Prewitt, J., & Osborne, L. (1988). Exercise effects on aged motor function. *Annals of the New York Academy of Science, 515*, 363–75.

Stummer, W., Weber, K., Tranmer, B., Baethmann, A., & Kempski, O. (1994). Reduced mortality and brain damage after locomotor activity in gerbil forebrain ischemia. *Stroke, 25* (9), 1862–9.

Suominen-Troyer, S., Davis, K. J., Ismail, A. H., & Salvendy, G. (1986). Impact of physical fitness on strategy development in decision-making tasks. *Perceptual and Motor Skills, 62* (1), 71–7.

Tong, L., Shen, H., Perreau, V. M., Balazs, R., & Cotman, C. W. (2001). Effects of exercise on gene-expression profile in the rat hippocampus. *Neurobioliogy of Disease, 8* (6), 1046–56.

van Praag, H., Christie, B. R., Sejnowski, T. J., & Gage, F. H. (1999). Running enhances neurogenesis, learning, and long-term potentiation in mice. *Proceedings of the National Academy of Science of the United States of America, 96* (23), 13427–31.

Vanderwolf, C. H. (1988). Cerebral activity and behavior: control by central cholinergic and serotonergic systems. *International Review of Neurobiology, 30*, 225–340.

Vissing, J., Andersen, M., & Diemer, N. H. (1996). Exercise-induced changes in local cerebral glucose utilization in the rat. *Journal of Cerebral Blood Flow and Metabolism, 16* (4), 729–36.

Wallace, D. G., Hines, D. J., & Whishaw, I. Q. (2002). Quantification of a single exploratory trip reveals hippocampal formation mediated dead reckoning. *Journal of Neuroscience Methods, 113* (2), 131–45.

Wallenstein, G. V., Eichenbaum, H., & Hasselmo, M. E. (1998). The hippocampus as an associator of discontiguous events. *Trends in Neurosciences, 21* (8), 317–23.

Yaffe, K., Barnes, D., Nevitt, M., Lui, L. Y. & Covinsky, K. (2001). A prospective study of physical activity and cognitive decline in elderly women: Women who walk. *Archives of Internal Medicine, 161* (14), 1703–8.

## Further Reading

Kandel, E. R., Schwartz, J. H., & Jessel, T. M. (2000). *Principles of neural science*. New York: McGraw-Hill.

Roland, P. E. (1993). *Brain Activation*. New York: Wiley-Liss.

Zigmond, M. J. (1999). *Fundamental neuroscience*. New York: Academic Press.

# CHAPTER SIXTEEN

# Research Methods in Human Memory

## Deanne L. Westerman and David G. Payne

There are many levels at which researchers can study human memory. The diversity of the methods used to study memory underscores both the complexity of human memory processes and the wide range of perspectives that different researchers bring to the field. The present chapter attempts to review some of the methods that are commonly used to study human memory from a cognitive perspective. The experimental study of human memory began approximately 120 years ago with the publication of Ebbinghaus's ([1885] 1964) seminal work on the subject.[1] Obviously, there is not space for a thorough description of the methods that have been used since that time. However, this chapter will review some of the predominant strategies and the most common techniques used by cognitive psychologists to develop and test theories of human memory.

## Methodological Contributions of Ebbinghaus

Many of the conventions that are adopted by contemporary memory researchers can be attributed to the insights of Ebbinghaus ([1885] 1964). Although Ebbinghaus made a great empirical contribution, he is perhaps best known for developing a methodology to study human memory experimentally (see Slamecka, 1985). Ebbinghaus's influence on the field is still evident in contemporary research on human memory. For example, in Ebbinghaus's experiments – and in the majority of contemporary experiments on human memory – the event or information that is to be remembered is presented during the experiment. This convention allows the experimenter a measure of control over the information that is learned and the way in which the information is initially processed. Although there have been many fascinating studies of memory for events that occurred outside of the experimental context (e.g., Bahrick, Hall, & Berger, 1996;

Brown & Kulik, 1977; Neisser, 1981; Rubin, 2000; Sheen, Kemp, & Rubin, 2001), most researchers study memory for events that occurred during the experimental session.

The methods that are used to measure memory differ greatly in their sensitivity. For instance, there are times when a person may not be able to recall a piece of information but may be able to recognize the information if it were presented. Ebbinghaus ([1885] 1964) was alert to the differential sensitivity of different memory measures and used a very sensitive index of relearning speed (termed *savings*) as the dependent variable in his studies. Ebbinghaus's use of savings over more straightforward memory measures, such as recall, reflected his theory that prior experiences will often alter behavior, even when the event is not accessible to conscious awareness. This perspective predated by nearly 100 years the enormous amount of interest that would later be devoted to indirect measures of memory retrieval, which are memory tasks that do not require participants to attempt deliberately to recollect an event from the past.

## The Three Phases of Memory Experiments

For the most part, current experimental work on episodic memory conforms to the same three-phase structure developed by Ebbinghaus ([1885] 1964). The exception to this rule is research on autobiographical memory. For example, research on flashbulb memories investigates participants' memories for highly surprising and emotionally laden events that occurred prior to their participation in the study (e.g., Neisser & Harsch, 1993). The encoding phase of memory experiments is followed by a retention interval, which could range from a few milliseconds (e.g., Sperling, 1960) to a half century (e.g., Bahrick & Hall, 1991) depending on the questions addressed by the experiment. The third stage is a retrieval phase, which is an opportunity for the previously encoded information to be revived. A key strategy among memory researchers is to manipulate the conditions of one or more of the three phases to try to understand the functional aspects of memory.

The view that memory can be studied as three distinct stages is a simplified description of memory processes, as there is ample evidence of overlap in the stages. For example, there are numerous situations in which the encoding of an event is influenced greatly by the retrieval of previously stored information (e.g., Bransford & Johnson, 1972). Similarly, the retrieval of an event can also be viewed as an additional encoding opportunity (e.g., Whitten & Bjork, 1977). Still, the convention of describing memory as involving three separate stages provides a useful system to describe the various research paradigms upon which contemporary memory theories have been developed.

### Methods of manipulating encoding

It has been well established that the way in which a stimulus is encoded affects the likelihood that it will be remembered. One method that has been used to investigate the influence of encoding conditions on memory is to increase participants' involvement in the encoding process by presenting the to-be-remembered stimuli in an incomplete or perceptually impoverished form during the encoding phase. For example, Slamecka and Graf (1978) initiated research on what has been termed the *generation effect* in memory. In generation effect studies, information is first presented in an incomplete form, and the participant generates the complete version of the stimulus. Many different methods of stimulus generation have been used; for instance, the generation task may involve solving a word fragment, or generating a synonym or an antonym from a word that is provided as a cue (e.g., generating the word "cold" when presented with the cue "hot– c____"). In these experiments, memory for the generated items is compared to memory for items that were simply read by the participant during the encoding phase, with the canonical finding being superior memory performance for words that were generated by the participant during the encoding phase (e.g., Greene, 1988; Nairne, Pusen & Widner, 1985; Nairne & Widner, 1988).

Researchers have used several other methods to test the effects of incomplete or perceptually impoverished study conditions on memory. Kolers and Ostry (1974) had participants read text that was inverted during the encoding phase; they later found that the text that had been inverted during encoding was remembered better than text that appeared normally. Similarly, when words are presented very rapidly and are partially masked by visual noise, memory for the masked words is superior compared to words that are presented for a much longer duration and are easily perceived (e.g., Mulligan, 2000; Nairne, 1988; Westerman & Greene, 1997).

A classic study by Craik and Tulving (1975) illustrates another method of demonstrating the important role of encoding conditions in memory. Craik and Tulving's experiment used an *incidental encoding* procedure; participants were exposed to a word list during the first phase of the experiment, but were not told to expect a later memory task. Instead, participants answered questions about the words as they were presented. Each question required a yes or no response, and addressed different aspects of the words. The questions were one of three types: they pertained to the structural aspects of the word (e.g., Is the word in capital letters?), the sound of the word (e.g., Does the word rhyme with mouse?) or the meaning of the word (e.g., Would the word fit into the sentence: "They moved into a new _____.") After answering one question for many different target words, the researchers gave the participants a surprise recognition test for the target words. The results of the recognition test showed that memory for the test word depended greatly upon the type of question that was answered during the encoding phase. When the question focused on the meaning of the target word, memory performance was highest, and when the question focused on the structural aspects of the target word, memory performance was lowest. When the question focused on the sound of the target word, memory performance fell between the meaning and the structural conditions. These results, which have been replicated many times and have been found in both recall and recognition tests (see Lockhart & Craik, 1990, for a review) were viewed as support for the levels of processing framework that had been proposed by Craik and Lockhart (1972). The levels of processing framework proposes that memory depends on the depth to which a stimulus is processed. According to this framework, stimuli that are processed in a way that highlights structural characteristics will be remembered poorly compared to stimuli that are processed in a manner that emphasizes meaning.

Although the levels of processing framework highlighted the importance of encoding processes in memory and had a tremendous influence on the field of memory research (see Lockhart & Craik, 1990), some aspects of the account were found to be inaccurate. For example, the levels of processing framework predicts that semantic processing will result in better memory performance compared to phonological and structural processing. Although it is generally true that semantic processing during encoding leads to the highest level of recall and recognition, many exceptions to this rule have been reported, as semantic processing does not always lead to superior memory performance compared to processing that is at a more "shallow" level. Rather, the type of processing that is most beneficial for later memory performance depends on the type of memory task that will be performed. For example, Fisher and Craik (1977) found that phonological processing during the study phase led to better performance than semantic processing on a memory test that included phonological information (rhymes) as a retrieval cue. Alternately, semantic processing led to better memory performance when participants used semantic information (a category name or a sentence) as the retrieval cue. The findings of Fisher and Craik, as well as similar finding (e.g., Morris, Bransford, & Franks, 1977), led to the view that memory performance is not predominately a function of the encoding processes; rather, it is determined by the match between the encoding and retrieval phases. This view has been formalized by the terms *the transfer-appropriate processing principle* (Morris, Bransford, & Franks, 1977) and *the encoding specificity principle* (Tulving & Osler, 1968); both terms refer to the now well-established finding that memory performance is determined by the extent to which the cues that were present during encoding (i.e., the encoding context, as well as the cognitive operations performed during encoding) are also present at the time of retrieval.

The point of going into such detail about the different perspectives on encoding processes and the extent to which they determine later memory performance is that the numerous experimental results that support a transfer-appropriate processing approach to memory have all used a similar research design. This design, which has been termed the *encoding/retrieval paradigm* (Tulving, 1983), generally includes two encoding conditions and two retrieval conditions. The encoding and retrieval conditions are designed such that each retrieval condition reinstates some aspect of one of the encoding conditions. For example, a memorable experiment conducted by Godden and Baddeley (1975) used a encoding/retrieval paradigm to test the influence of contextual cues on memory. Godden and Baddeley asked scuba divers to encode a list of words either on land or underwater. Later, the scuba divers recalled the word list either on land or underwater. The results showed that memory performance was better when there was a match between the encoding and retrieval contexts. Participants who encoded the word list while on land performed better when the recall test was also on land; participants who encoded the list while underwater performed better when the recall test was also underwater. There are numerous other examples of experiments that have used an encoding/retrieval paradigm to study the interaction between encoding and retrieval conditions. The memory effects of drug state (Eich, Weingartner, Stillman, & Gillin, 1975), mood (Bower, 1981; Eich & Metcalfe, 1989), and many different aspects of physical context

(Eich, 1985; Schab, 1990; Smith, Glenberg, & Bjork, 1978) have been studied using the encoding/retrieval paradigm.

The encoding manipulations that are described above have been used extensively to study human memory. Although each phenomenon has been studied using different methods, and has been explained through somewhat different mechanisms, there are similarities among the phenomena that allow some general principles to be extracted. One principle that can be extracted is that memory performance is a function of the amount of cognitive resources that are devoted to an event at the time of encoding. Evidence of this effect can be found in the research on the effect of stimulus generation (Slamecka & Graf, 1978), perceptual interference (Nairne, 1988) and reading inverted text (Kolers & Ostry, 1974). In these cases, the encoding of the stimuli was made more difficult: it was incomplete, inverted, or perceptually distorted. In all of these cases, memory was improved relative to a condition in which encoding was very easy. As further evidence that more "work" during encoding leads to better memory, research on the effect of text inversion has found that the memorial benefit that is found when text is inverted during encoding disappears once the reader becomes proficient at reading upside down (Kolers, 1975).

The aforementioned studies also demonstrate that the likelihood of a memory being retrieved depends critically on the qualities of the stimulus that are emphasized during encoding. For most memory tasks, performance is best when the semantic properties of a stimulus are emphasized during encoding. However, if a particular memory task relies on phonological or structural cues rather than meaning, the encoding processes that are most similar to the memory task will produce the highest level of memory retrieval (e.g., Fisher & Craik, 1977). The finding that a semantic orienting task typically leads to superior memory performance suggests that the meaning of a stimulus is more likely to be used as a retrieval cue compared to other types of information.

*Methods of studying retrieval*

The retrieval of previously stored information is extremely flexible, and there is a rich collection of methods that are commonly used to measure memory retrieval. The most straightforward measures of memory are those measures that ask a person to recall or recognize information that was presented earlier. However, memory retrieval can also be tested more indirectly. For example, researchers have used affective judgments, fame judgments, and validity judgments to demonstrate the retrieval of information from memory. Because there is such a wide range of different memory measures, several different systems have been proposed to try to classify them (e.g., Richardson-Klavehn & Bjork, 1988; Schacter & Tulving, 1994; Squire, 1992). Johnson and Hasher (1987) suggested one simple (and theoretically neutral) classification scheme that distinguishes between *direct measures*, such as recall and recognition, and *indirect measures*, such as the various judgment tasks that were mentioned above. Direct measures of memory are those measures that instruct participants to retrieve an event and respond in a manner that is consistent with their memory. On the other hand, indirect measures of memory make no reference to the previously experienced event. Rather, participants complete a task that is ostensibly unrelated to the previous event. The experimenter records the performance on the task and measures the degree to which participants' behavior is influenced by the previously experienced event.

*Direct memory tasks* On tests of recall, participants reproduce information that was presented earlier. In *free recall*, they can reproduce the material in any order, whereas in *serial recall*, they are to reproduce the material in the order in which it was presented during the encoding phase. The administration of recall tests is very straightforward; the researcher provides a retrieval cue ranging from very general (write down all of the words from the list that you just saw) to very specific (write down a word from the list that rhymes with "lake"), and participants try to produce the material verbally or in writing. Retrieval cues can be based on a prior association with the target word (e.g., "envious" may be used as a retrieval cue for the word "jealous") or an association that was formed during the study phase of the experiment. For instance, if the study list contained a pair of words such as "ice – jealous," the word "ice" may be presented as a retrieval cue to recall the word "jealous."

Thomson and Tulving (1970) addressed the effectiveness of different types of retrieval cues in a classic study. In their study, participants studied target words that were either presented alone or presented with another word that had either a strong or a weak semantic relationship with the target. For example, participants studied the target word "black" with the word "white" (strong associate), the word "train" (weak associate), or the target presented alone. Later, participants took a recall test that presented either the weak associate or the strong associate as a retrieval cue. Compared to a condition in which there was no cue presented, the presence of the strong associate facilitated recall regardless of whether the target had been presented alone, with a weak associate, or with a strong associate during encoding. In other words, "white" was an effective retrieval cue for "black" regardless of the cue that had been presented during encoding. However, the recall benefit was especially pronounced when "white" had been presented with the target at the time of encoding. The effectiveness of the weak associate ("train") as a retrieval cue depended entirely on whether it had appeared with the target during the encoding phase. Recall was facilitated when the weak associate had appeared with the target during the encoding phase; however, the presence of the weak associate during the recall test impaired performance when the strong associate or no associate had appeared with the target during the encoding phase. In other words, "train" was an effective retrieval cue for "black" only when "train – black" had appeared together on the study list. These results were interpreted as further evidence in support of the principle of encoding specificity. Although semantic associates can be a useful retrieval cue, the effectiveness of any retrieval cue is moderated by the degree to which the cue reinstates the original encoding context.

The analysis of recall data is not as simple as the administration of the test. A key assumption that underlies the analysis of data from free recall tasks is that the material that is recalled is not random. Rather, the type of information that is recalled, the serial position that the item held when it appeared in the study phase, and the order and organization of the material that is recalled can offer important insights into the nature of memory processes and the representation of information in memory. One of the first issues to consider when interpreting recall data is the accuracy of recall. There are two types of possible errors on recall tests: double recalls (recalling the same item more than once) and intrusions (recalling an item that was not presented on the study list). A common approach to the issue of errors on recall tests is to simply ignore them (Murphy & Puff, 1982). However, systematic errors on recall tests may be quite informative. In recent years there has been tremendous interest devoted to trying to understand why people will recall information that they had not actually experienced. Roediger and McDermott (1995) revived interest in a study originally conducted by Deese (1959) that demonstrated high levels of false recall for words that are semantically related to several of the words that were presented on the study list. For example, if participants study a list of words such as "mad, rage, hate, fury, temper" there is a very high probability that participants will falsely recall the word "anger." High rates of false recall have also been found for words that are phonologically similar to words that were studied (Sommers & Lewis, 1999).

Another factor that is often taken into consideration when interpreting the data from a free recall task is the order and organization of the output. A seminal study by Bousfield (1953) demonstrated that when items from several different semantic categories (e.g., furniture, animals, occupations) are presented during the study phase, items that belong to the same category will be recalled close together even when they had been presented separately on the study list. Bousfield termed this phenomenon *clustering* (see Pellegrino & Hubert, 1982 and Roenker, Thompson, & Brown, 1971 for comparisons of the many different indices of clustering). The tendency for clusters of related material to be recalled is very robust and occurs when both natural categories and artificial categories are studied (Casey & Heath, 1983; Galizio, Stewart, & Pilgrim, 2001).

Other direct measures of memory involve presenting items to participants and asking them for some sort of judgment that is related to their memories for the items. The most common judgments that participants are asked to make are *recognition* judgments. On tests of recognition memory, participants are asked to discriminate between items that were previously experienced and items that are new. There are several different ways to test recognition memory. One way is with a *study–test method*. With this method, participants first study a list of items. Later, they take a recognition test for the items that were presented in the study phase. On a free choice recognition test, items that were presented on the study list are represented intermixed with an equal number of new items. The participant's task is to classify each item as being "old" (presented in the study phase) or "new" (not presented in the study phase). Recognition memory can also be tested with a *forced choice recognition task*, which is essentially a multiple choice test in which two or more items are presented for each recognition trial, with one of the items having appeared during the earlier study phase. The participant's task is to select the item that was previously presented in the study phase. Another technique for testing recognition is a *continuous recognition task* (Shepard & Teghtsoonian, 1961). With this method, there is not a sharp divide between the study and the test phases; rather, stimuli are presented to the participant sequentially. Sometimes, a stimulus is presented that had already been presented at an earlier point on the list. The participant's task is to respond to each item by indicating whether or not it had already appeared on the list.

Participants' responses to recognition test items can be either self-paced (i.e., the participants work through the recognition test trial by trial, responding whenever they are ready) or experimenter paced (i.e., participants have to respond within a time frame determined by the experimenter).

One method that is used to impose a pace on a recognition test is the *response–signal technique* (e.g., Gronlund & Ratcliff, 1989; Hintzman & Curran, 1994; Rotello, Macmillan, & Van Tassel, 2000). With this method, a signal, such as a tone, is presented at different intervals (ranging, e.g., from 100 ms to 2000 ms) after the recognition test item appears, and the participant gives a recognition response as soon as the tone is heard. An advantage of using an experimenter-paced recognition test, such as the response signal technique is that it provides a window into the processes that underlie recognition memory. For example, a topic currently of great interest to memory researchers is whether recognition memory involves a single familiarity-assessment process (e.g., Gillund & Shiffrin, 1984; Hintzman, 1988; Shiffrin & Steyvers, 1997; for a review, see Clark & Gronlund, 1996) or whether there is also a second, recall-like process that contributes to recognition memory decisions (e.g., Jacoby, 1991; Mandler, 1980). It has been proposed that familiarity assessment is a very fast and automatic process, whereas recollection is generally thought to be a slower and a more effortful process (e.g., Atkinson & Juola, 1973; Hintzman & Curran, 1994; Jacoby, 1991; Yonelinas, 1997). The response–signal technique and other experimenter-paced recognition tests (Lewis & Ellis, 2000; Westerman, 2001) allows for an examination of questions related to this debate. For example, the influence of certain variables on recognition memory have been found to depend upon the speed with which the recognition decision is made; when responses are made quickly, variables that enhance the familiarity of a stimulus seem to have a greater effect on recognition responses compared to when responses are made more slowly (e.g., Hintzman & Curran, 1994; Westerman, 2001).

On a free choice recognition test, each response will fall into one of four categories: *hits* (an old item that is called old), *misses* (an old item that is called new), *false alarms* (a new item that is called old), and *correct rejections* (a new item that is called new). A response on a free choice recognition test can be thought of as being determined by two factors: retrieval (which may result in a sense of familiarity for an item or the recollection of information about the item) and the decision criterion used to classify a test item as "old." Because recognition judgments involve a decision criterion, a researcher cannot think about accuracy without considering both the hit rate and the false alarm rate of a participant, as two participants with very different hit rates may actually be equivalent in terms of accuracy depending on their false alarm rates. To assess both accuracy and the decision criterion, the principles of signal detection theory are frequently used to analyze data from recognition memory tasks (see Green & Swets, 1966 for more on the application of signal detection theory to recognition memory and Snodgrass & Corwin, 1988 for a review of different signal detection measures). Unlike free-choice recognition tests, forced choice recognition tasks are assumed to be criterion-free. That is, judgments on forced choice recognition tasks do not involve criterion setting on the part of the participant; rather it is assumed that when given two choices the participant responds positively to the stimulus that is more familiar (Green & Swets, 1966; Macmillan & Creelman, 1991).

Although recognition memory is the most common type of direct memory judgment, there are many others. For example, participants can be asked to judge the frequency with which an item occurred on a study list (e.g., Greene, 1984; Hintzman 2001a; Hintzman & Block, 1971), or be asked to judge how recently the item occurred (Guttentag & Carroll, 1997; Hintzman, 2001b), or judge the context of its occurrence (Johnson, Hashtroudi, & Lindsay, 1993). Judging the context in which an item occurred, which is termed *source monitoring*, requires much more of the participant than a standard recognition task. Instead of simply indicating whether an item was previously experienced or not, participants must indicate the specific context in which it occurred. For example, participants might be given two different lists of words and then be asked to judge whether a word came from list 1 or 2 (e.g., Cleary & Greene, 2001; Hintzman, Caulton, & Levitin, 1998). Alternately, participants may hear words read by different speakers and later be asked to judge whether a word was read by speaker 1 or speaker 2 (Schacter, Harbluk, & MaLachlan, 1984).

*Indirect measures of memory*   Memory research prior to the mid-1980s was conducted predominately with direct measures of memory retrieval. That is, the memory test given by the experimenter asked the participant to retrieve a previous experience. In the early 1980s (e.g., Jacoby & Dallas, 1981) there was a shift in interest toward understanding how a previously experienced event can influence behavior even when there is not a deliberate attempt to retrieve information, and there is a lack of awareness of any connection between the previous event and a current task. The tasks that are used to investigate memory from this perspective are termed indirect memory tasks. Jacoby and colleagues (Jacoby, 1983; Jacoby & Dallas, 1981) popularized one such task. In a *perceptual identification* task, participants are first exposed to stimuli, such as a list of words, with each word being presented individually. Later, they are shown words that were presented during the encoding phase again along with some words that were not presented in the encoding phase. However, this time the words are presented so briefly (e.g., 35 ms) that they cannot be fully identified by the participants. Nevertheless, participants are instructed to try to identify the words as they appear. The typical finding in such a situation is that words that were presented in the earlier study phase are much more likely to be identified when presented for 35 ms compared to words that had not been presented in the earlier study phase. For example, in Experiment 1 reported by Jacoby and Dallas (1981) the identification rates were 81 percent for the previously presented words and 65 percent for the words that had not been previously presented. The critical feature of this work is that this task did not rely on participants' efforts to retrieve the words that were previously encoded; participants were simply asked to identify the words, and no reference was made to the earlier encoding phase.

There are many other methods that are used to test memory indirectly. Another common way to measure memory indirectly is in the form of a completion task. In completion tasks, participants are presented with materials under incidental encoding instructions. Later, they are given a test that asks them to complete a word from a fragment (e.g., RA__D_OP) or to complete a word stem (e.g., RAIN____) with the first word that comes to mind. Some of the fragments can be completed with words that were presented during the earlier encoding phase; however, this information is not revealed to participants. The results of this type of experiment consistently show that a word (e.g., RAINDROP) is more likely to be offered as a solution to the word fragment or the word stem if it had appeared during the earlier study phase (e.g., Graf & Mandler, 1984; Tulving, Schacter, & Stark, 1982). This finding is true even when participants claim not to be aware of the connection of the test to the earlier encoding phase.

Some indirect memory tasks are similar to recognition tests, insofar as they require a participant to make a judgment about an item that may or may not have been previously presented; however, the judgments used to measure memory indirectly do not refer to an earlier encoding phase. For example, the method used to demonstrate the *mere exposure effect* (Whittlesea & Price, 2001; Zajonc, 1968) is an indirect measure of memory, as there is no reference to an earlier episode. Other types of judgments are influenced by previous exposure to a stimulus. For instance, validity judgments (Hasher, Goldstein, & Toppino, 1977), fame judgments (Jacoby, Kelley, Brown, & Jasechko, 1989), and judgments about the brightness and darkness of a stimulus (Mandler, Nakamura, & Van Zandt, 1987) are all affected by recent exposure to the stimulus.

Researchers have conducted a significant number of studies to try to understand the relation between direct and indirect measures of memory. One of the most intriguing findings from this research is the striking dissociations that occur between direct and indirect memory measures. That is, variables that have a robust effect on direct measures of memory sometimes have little or no effect (or the opposite effect) on indirect measures of memory. For example, encoding manipulations such as depth of processing and stimulus generation – which exert a strong influence on tests of recall and recognition – do not affect indirect measures, such as perceptual identification (Jacoby & Dallas, 1981). In fact, Jacoby and Dallas (1981) found a slight reversal of the generation effect on a test of perceptual identification. Another type of dissociation that has been of great interest to memory researchers is the effect of certain types of brain injuries on direct and indirect memory tests. Whereas damage to the hippocampus and surrounding brain structures often leads to severe impairments on direct memory tasks, performance on indirect measures of memory remains intact (Graf, Squire, & Mandler, 1984; Shimamura, 1986; Warrington & Weiskrantz, 1968, 1970). Crafting a satisfactory theoretical explanation of the striking dissociations that are found in performance on direct and indirect tasks has proved to be both a major challenge and controversy for memory theorists (see Foster & Jelicic, 1999 for a book on this topic).

## Research Methods Used to Study Forgetting

A full understanding of human memory must include an account of why we are at times unable to retrieve an event that was experienced in the past. In many cases, theories of forgetting can be easily derived from research conducted on other aspects of memory. For example, research investigating the effect of different encoding processes has demonstrated that memory depends critically on the way in which stimuli are studied. Generally speaking, forgetting is less likely to occur when stimuli are repeated (e.g., Ebbinghaus [1885] 1964), processed deeply (e.g., Craik & Tulving, 1975), generated from an incomplete cue (e.g., Slamecka & Graf, 1978), or are distinctive in some way (e.g., Einstein, McDaniel, & Lackey, 1989; Hunt & Lamb, 2001). Similarly, research investigating the interaction between encoding and retrieval processes has convincingly demonstrated that forgetting is less likely to occur when there is a great deal of overlap between the cues available during encoding and those available during retrieval (e.g., Morris, Bransford, & Franks, 1977). In these cases, there are no special research methods that are used to study forgetting, per se. Rather, theories of forgetting fall out naturally from theories of memory. In other cases, specific research methodologies have been developed for the purpose of studying forgetting. Some of the more common methods used to study forgetting will be reviewed below.

One method that has been used to study forgetting over relatively short intervals is commonly called the *Brown–Peterson task* after the researchers who popularized the task (Brown, 1958; Peterson & Peterson, 1959). Participants in Peterson and Peterson's (1959) original experiments were presented with three consonants, which were followed immediately by a three-digit number. A participant's task was to use the three-digit number as a starting point to begin counting backward by threes. After 3, 6, 9, 12, 15, or 18 seconds of counting backwards, participants were cued to recall the consonants that were presented just prior to the three-digit number. When participants' performance across many trials at each time lag is considered, the finding that emerges is that memory for the consonants declines very quickly even with only brief periods of backward-counting, with recall performance dropping close to zero after 18 seconds. Originally, this finding was interpreted as evidence for a decay process in memory; that is, without rehearsal, information will be forgotten simply due to the passage of time. However, the decay interpretation of this data pattern has since been shown to be false (Baddeley & Scott, 1971; Keppel & Underwood, 1962), and the rapid forgetting found with the Brown–Peterson task has since been explained primarily as a result of the interference produced by other trials of the task (Keppel & Underwood, 1962).

Although the original decay interpretation of performance on the Brown–Peterson task turned out to be inaccurate, the task is still used to investigate forgetting across brief intervals. For example, a recent study by Sebastian, Menor, and Elosua (2001) used the performance on the Brown–Peterson task to compare the pattern of forgetting for individuals with Alzheimer's disease to the pattern found with participants in an elderly control group. Other recent research has used a modified version of the Brown–Peterson task to study memory for order (Nairne, Whiteman, & Kelley, 1999), and to make comparisons between "passive" short-term memory tasks, such as the Brown–Peterson task, and more complex working memory tasks (Tehan, Hendry, & Kocinski, 2001).

Another mechanism that has been implicated as a powerful source of forgetting is *interference* that is produced by the presence of other information in memory. Forgetting of a particular event may be the result of the interference produced by preceding events (*proactive interference*) and succeeding events (*retroactive interference*). Research on interference effects in memory was at one time so abundant that the period from 1900 to 1970 is sometimes referred to as the "classical interference era" (see Postman & Underwood, 1973 and Crowder, 1976 for thorough reviews of the work during this era as well as reviews of theoretical accounts of interference effects in memory). The role of interference in memory has been most commonly studied by using a paired-associate learning method that is commonly called an AB–AD design. With an AB–AD design, pairs of items are studied. For example, participants in an experiment investigating retroactive interference may be presented with a list of word pairs such as: ice–desk, pillow–frog, tree–lamp, and so forth. To maximize interference, participants study another list of paired items that consists of the first word from each pair presented with a different second word. For example, the second list may read: ice–barn, pillow–net, tree–shoe. Later, participants are given the first word of each pair and are asked to recall the word that it had been paired with on the first list. The canonical result is that the ability to recall ice–desk is typically quite poor relative to a control group that studied two lists of words that do not have any of the words repeated (e.g., McGeoch, 1942).

A variation of the AB–AD design has been used to study eyewitness memory. For example, in a study by Loftus, Miller, and Burns (1978), participants were shown a sequence of slides. One of the slides in the series depicted a car at a stop sign. Later, participants were given a questionnaire about the slide sequence that contained misinformation about some of the slides. For example, one of the questions mentioned that the car from the slide sequence was at a *yield* sign. Later, participants were given a forced choice recognition test for items from the original slide sequence. One of the questions asked participants whether the car in the slide sequence was at a stop sign or a yield sign. The results of the forced choice recognition test showed the same interference effect that was found with more conventional paired-associate word lists (e.g., McGeoch, 1942). Participants who were exposed to information about the car at the yield sign (analogous to an AD condition, with the car being the A term and the yield sign being the D term), were much more likely to incorrectly choose the yield sign on the recognition test, compared to a control group that was not exposed to postevent misinformation (59% vs. 25%).

Another method that is used to try to understand forgetting is based on the idea that retrieval failure may occur due to inhibition that is produced by the retrieval of other information from memory (Bjork, 1989). Researchers have used this view to explain the phenomenon of *part-set cueing inhibition* in semantic memory (see Nickerson, 1984; Roediger & Neely, 1982), and more recently to understand forgetting in episodic memory. One of the methods used to study inhibition in forgetting from episodic memory has been called the *retrieval-practice paradigm* (Anderson, Bjork, & Bjork, 2000; Anderson & Neely, 1996; Anderson & Spellman, 1995). The retrieval practice paradigm includes three phases. In the first phase, participants study words from several different semantic categories. Each category exemplar is presented with its category label, for example, "clothing–pajamas" and "clothing–slacks" may appear on a study list. In the second phase, participants are given practice retrieving a portion of the items from one of the categories on the study list. For example, the cue, "clothing–pa_____" might be presented as a cue to recall the word "pajamas." The third phase is a final recall test in which participants are given category names and are asked to recall all of the words from the study list. The results from studies using the retrieval-practice paradigm have shown that participants have very high levels of recall of the words that were practiced during the retrieval phase (e.g., pajamas), but very poor recall of the nonpracticed words from the same category (e.g., slacks). Anderson and colleagues have interpreted this result as evidence that the retrieval-practice phase makes nonpracticed items from the same category temporarily less accessible because they are suppressed during the retrieval-practice phase. In addition to the suppression of nonpracticed items from the same category, Anderson and Spellman (1995) also found that items from an entirely different category are also suppressed if they are similar to some of the items from the practiced category. For example, retrieval practice for some of the items in the clothing category also suppressed recall of the word "belt" when it was presented as a member of the "leather" category.

The retrieval practice paradigm has also been extended to the study of forgetting in the domains of eyewitness memory (Shaw, Bjork, & Handal, 1995) and social cognition (Macrae & MacLeod, 1999). However, Williams and Zacks (2001) reported some difficulty in replicating certain aspects of Anderson and Spellman's (1995) findings. Specifically, the finding that retrieval practice will impair memory for similar items from a different category was not found in the Williams and Zacks experiments. Therefore, the robustness of some of the results found with the retrieval practice paradigm remains to be seen.

## Concluding Comments

This chapter has dealt with some of the common methods that are used to investigate human memory from a cognitive perspective. We have attempted to take a broad approach to this topic to try to cover as many different aspects of memory research as space would permit. Nevertheless, many valuable techniques were omitted. For instance, this chapter did not include the many techniques that have been used to investigate immediate memory, nor did it include a discussion of the methods used to study semantic memory and knowledge.

There was also only a cursory treatment of the theoretical questions that inspired the methods described in this chapter. However, this feature was not due to space limitations. The sparseness of theoretical detail was meant to convey the versatility of the methods that are reviewed here. For instance, although the decay theory of forgetting that gave rise to the Brown–Peterson task fell from grace long ago, the task has appeared in several recent papers on different topics related to forgetting (e.g., Nairne et al., 1999; Sebastian et al., 2001). Similarly, the encoding manipulations that were inspired by Craik and Lockhart's (1972) article on levels of processing are now part of a common bag of tricks used by researchers to investigate many disparate topics related to human memory (to be persuaded on this point, see the following recent articles that have used levels of processing manipulations to investigate different topics: Hamilton & Rajaram, 2001; Lee, Cheung, & Wurm, 2000; Thapar & McDermott, 2001). Although there are theoretical questions that originally motivated each of the research techniques described here, the methods do not depend on the theories that inspired them. Rather, they are tools that, with minor modifications, can be used for many purposes.

# Note

1.  Ebbinghaus is generally credited as the first to study human memory experimentally. However, this attribution is unfair to Nipher, who actually deserves the credit. Nipher, a physicist, discovered the serial-position effect and published a report on the topic in 1878 (as cited a century later by Stigler, 1978).

# References

Anderson, M. C., Bjork, E. L., & Bjork, R. A. (2000). Retrieval-induced forgetting: Evidence for a recall-specific mechanism. *Psychonomic Bulletin and Review, 7*, 522–30.

Anderson, M. C., & Neely, J. H. (1996). Interference and inhibition in memory retrieval. In E. L. Bjork & R. A. Bjork (eds.), *Memory. Handbook of perception and cognition* (2nd edn.) (pp. 237–313). San Diego: Academic Press.

Anderson, M. C., & Spellman, B. A. (1995). On the status of inhibitory mechanisms in cognition: Memory retrieval as a model case. *Psychological Review, 102*, 68–100.

Atkinson, R. C., & Juola, J. F. (1973). Factors influencing speed and accuracy of word recognition. In S. Kornblum (ed.), *Attention and performance, IV* (pp. 583–612). New York: Academic Press.

Baddeley, A. D., & Scott, D. (1971). Short-term forgetting in the absence of proactive interference. *Quarterly Journal of Experimental Psychology, 23*, 275–83.

Bahrick, H. P., & Hall, L. K. (1991). Lifetime maintenance of high school mathematics content. *Journal of Experimental Psychology: General, 120*, 20–33.

Bahrick, H. P., Hall, L. K., & Berger, S. A. (1996). Accuracy and distortion in memory for high school grades. *Psychological Science, 7*, 265–71.

Bjork, R. A. (1989). Retrieval inhibition as an adaptive mechanism in human memory. In H. L. Roediger III & F. I. M. Craik (eds.), *Varieties of memory and consciousness: Essays in honour of Endel Tulving* (pp. 309–30). Hillsdale, NJ: Erlbaum.

Bousfield, W. A. (1953). The occurrence of clustering in the recall of randomly arranged associates. *Journal of General Psychology, 49*, 229–40.

Bower, G. H. (1981). Mood and memory. *American Psychologist, 36*, 129–48.

Bransford, J. D., & Johnson, M. K. (1972). Contextual prerequisites for understanding: Some investigations of comprehension and recall. *Journal of Verbal Learning and Verbal Behavior, 11*, 717–26.

Brown, J. (1958). Some tests of the decay theory of immediate memory. *Quarterly Journal of Experimental Psychology, 10*, 12–21.

Brown, R., & Kulik, J. (1977). Flashbulb memories. *Cognition, 5*, 73–99.

Casey, P. J., & Heath, R. A. (1983). Categorization reaction time, category structure, and category size in semantic memory using artificial categories. *Memory & Cognition, 11*, 228–36.

Clark, S. E., & Gronlund, S. D. (1996). Global matching models of recognition memory: How the models match the data. *Psychonomic Bulletin & Review, 3*, 37–60.

Cleary, A. M., & Greene, R. L. (2001). Memory for unidentified items: Evidence for the use of letter information in familiarity processes. *Memory & Cognition, 29*, 540–5.

Craik, F. I., & Lockhart, R. S. (1972). Levels of processing: A framework for memory research. *Journal of Verbal Learning and Verbal Behavior, 11*, 671–84.

Craik, F. I., & Tulving, E. (1975). Depth of processing and the retention of words in episodic memory. *Journal of Experimental Psychology: General, 104*, 268–94.

Crowder, R. G. (1976). *Principles of learning and memory*. Potomac, MD: Erlbaum.

Deese, J. (1959). On the prediction of occurrence of particular verbal intrusions in immediate recall. *Journal of Experimental Psychology, 58*, 17–22.

Ebbinghaus, H. ([1885] 1964). *Memory: A contribution to experimental psychology*. New York: Dover.

Eich, E. (1985). Context, memory, and integrated item/context imagery. *Journal of Experimental Psychology: Learning, Memory, and Cognition, 11*, 764–70.

Eich, E., & Metcalfe, J. (1989). Mood dependent memory for interval versus external events. *Journal of Experimental Psychology: Learning, Memory, and Cognition, 15*, 443–55.

Eich, J. E., Weingartner, H., Stillman, R. C., & Gillin, J. C. (1975). State-dependent accessibility of retrieval cues in the retention of a categorized list. *Journal of Verbal Learning and Verbal Behavior, 14*, 408–17.

Einstein, G. O., McDaniel, M. A., & Lackey, S. (1989). Bizarre imagery, interference, and distinctiveness. *Journal of Experimental Psychology: Learning, Memory, and Cognition, 15*, 137–46.

Fisher, R. P., & Craik, F. I. (1977). Interaction between encoding and retrieval operations in cued recall. *Journal of Experimental Psychology: Human Learning and Memory, 3*, 701–11.

Foster, J. K., & Jelicic, M. (eds.) (1999). *Memory: Systems, process, or function?* New York: Oxford University Press.

Galizio, M., Stewart, K. L., & Pilgrim, C. (2001). Clustering in artificial categories: An equivalence analysis. *Psychonomic Bulletin and Review, 8*, 609–14.

Gillund, G., & Shiffrin, R. M. (1984). A retrieval model for both recognition and recall. *Psychological Review, 91*, 1–67.

Godden, D. R., & Baddeley, A. D. (1975). Context-dependent memory in two natural environments: On land and underwater. *British Journal of Psychology, 66*, 325–31.

Graf, P., & Mandler, G. (1984). Activation makes words more accessible, but not necessarily more retrievable. *Journal of Verbal Learning and Verbal Behavior, 23*, 553–68.

Graf, P., Squire, L. R., & Mandler, G. (1984). The information that amnesic patients do not forget. *Journal of Experimental Psychology: Learning, Memory, and Cognition, 10*, 164–78.

Green, D. M., & Swets, J. A. (1966). *Signal detection theory and psychophysics*. New York: Wiley.

Greene, R. L. (1984). Incidental learning of event frequency. *Memory & Cognition, 12*, 90–5.

Greene, R. L. (1988). Generation effect in frequency judgment. *Journal of Experimental Psychology: Learning, Memory, and Cognition, 14*, 298–304.

Gronlund, S. D., & Ratcliff, R. (1989). Time course of item and associative information: Implications for global memory models. *Journal of Experimental Psychology: Learning, Memory, and Cognition, 15*, 846–58.

Guttentag, R. E., & Carroll, D. (1997). Recency judgments as a function of word frequency: A framing effect and frequency misattributions. *Psychonomic Bulletin and Review, 4*, 411–15.

Hamilton, M., & Rajaram, S. (2001). The concreteness effect in implicit and explicit memory tests. *Journal of Memory and Language, 44*, 96–117.

Hasher, L., Goldstein, D., & Toppino, T. (1977). Frequency and the conference of referential validity. *Journal of Verbal Learning and Verbal Behavior, 16*, 107–12.

Hintzman, D. L. (1988). Judgments of frequency and recognition memory in a multiple-trace model. *Psychological Review, 95*, 528–51.

Hintzman, D. L. (2001a). Similarity, global matching, and judgments of frequency. *Memory & Cognition, 29*, 547–56.

Hintzman, D. L. (2001b). Judgments of frequency and recency: How they relate to reports of subjective awareness. *Journal of Experimental Psychology: Learning, Memory, and Cognition, 27*, 1347–58.

Hintzman, D. L., & Block, R. A. (1971). Repetition and memory: Evidence for a multiple-trace hypothesis. *Journal of Experimental Psychology, 88,* 297–306.

Hintzman, D. L., Caulton, D. A., & Levitin, D. J. (1998). Retrieval dynamics in recognition and list discrimination: Further evidence of separate processes of familiarity and recall. *Memory & Cognition, 26,* 449–62.

Hintzman, D. L., & Curran, T. (1994). Retrieval dynamics of recognition and frequency judgments: Evidence for separate processes of familiarity and recall. *Journal of Memory and Language, 33,* 1–18.

Hunt, R. R., & Lamb, C. A. (2001). What causes the isolation effect? *Journal of Experimental Psychology: Learning, Memory, and Cognition, 27,* 1359–66.

Jacoby, L. L. (1983). Remembering the data: Analyzing interactive processes in reading. *Journal of Verbal Learning and Verbal Behavior, 22,* 485–508.

Jacoby, L. L. (1991). A process dissociation framework: Separating automatic from intentional uses of memory. *Journal of Memory and Language, 30,* 513–41.

Jacoby, L. L., & Dallas, M. (1981). On the relationship between autobiographical memory and perceptual learning. *Journal of Experimental Psychology: General, 110,* 306–40.

Jacoby, L. L., Kelley, C., Brown, J., & Jasechko, J. (1989). Becoming famous overnight: Limits on the ability to avoid unconscious influences of the past. *Journal of Personality and Social Psychology, 56,* 326–38.

Johnson, M. K., & Hasher, L. (1987). Human learning and memory. *Annual Review of Psychology, 38,* 631–68.

Johnson, M. K., Hashtroudi, S., & Lindsay, D. S. (1993). Source monitoring. *Psychological Bulletin, 114,* 3–28.

Keppel, G., & Underwood, B. J. (1962). Proactive inhibition in short-term retention of single items. *Journal of Verbal Learning and Verbal Behavior, 1,* 153–61,

Kolers, P. A. (1975). Memorial consequences of automatized encoding. *Journal of Experimental Psychology: Human, Learning, and Memory, 1,* 689–701.

Kolers, P. A., & Ostry, D. J. (1974). Time course of loss of information regarding pattern analyzing operations. *Journal of Verbal Learning and Verbal Behavior, 13,* 599–612.

Lee, Y. S., Cheung, Y. M., & Wurm, L. H. (2000). Levels-of-processing effects on Chinese character completion: The importance of lexical processing and test cue. *Memory & Cognition, 28,* 1398–405.

Lewis, M. B., & Ellis, H. D. (2000). The effects of massive repetition on speeded recognition of faces. *Quarterly Journal of Experimental Psychology: Human Experimental Psychology, 53A,* 1117–42.

Lockhart, R. S., & Craik, F. I. (1990). Levels of processing: A retrospective commentary on a framework for memory research. *Canadian Journal of Psychology, 44,* 87–112.

Loftus, E. F., Miller, D. G., & Burns, H. J. (1978). Semantic integration of verbal information into a visual memory. *Journal of Experimental Psychology: Human Learning and Memory, 4,* 19–31.

Macmillan, N. A., & Creelman, C. D. (1991). *Detection theory: A user's guide.* New York: Cambridge University Press.

Macrae, C. N., & MacLeod, M. D. (1999). On recollections lost: When practice makes imperfect. *Journal of Personality and Social Psychology, 77,* 463–73.

Mandler, G. (1980). Recognizing: The judgment of previous occurrence. *Psychological Review, 87,* 252–71.

Mandler, G. Nakamura, Y., & Van Zandt, B. J. (1987). Nonspecific effects of exposure on stimuli that cannot be recognized. *Journal of Experimental Psychology: Learning, Memory, and Cognition, 13,* 646–48.

McGeoch, J. A. (1942). *The psychology of human learning: An introduction.* New York: Longmans.

Morris, C. D., Bransford, J. D., & Franks, J. J. (1977). Levels of processing versus transfer appropriate processing. *Journal of Verbal Learning and Verbal Behavior, 16,* 519–33.

Mulligan, N. W. (2000). Perceptual interference and memory for order. *Journal of Memory and Language, 43,* 680–97.

Murphy, M. D., & Puff, R. (1982). Free recall: Basic methodology and analyses. In R. Puff (ed.), *Handbook of research methods in human memory and cognition* (pp. 92–128). New York: Academic Press.

Nairne, J. S. (1988). The mnemonic value of perceptual identification. *Journal of Experimental Psychology: Learning, Memory, and Cognition, 14,* 248–55.

Nairne, J. S., Pusen, C. P., & Widner, R. L. (1985). Representation in the mental lexicon: Implications for theories of the generation effect. *Memory & Cognition, 13,* 183–91.

Nairne, J. S., Whiteman, H. L., & Kelley, M. R. (1999). Short-term forgetting of order under conditions of reduced interference. *Quarterly Journal of Experimental Psychology: Human Experimental Psychology, 52A,* 241–51.

Nairne, J. S., & Widner, R. L. (1988). Familiarity and lexicality as determinants of the generation effect. *Journal of Experimental Psychology: Learning, Memory, and Cognition, 14,* 694–99.

Neisser, U. (1981). John Dean's memory: A case study. *Cognition, 9,* 1–22.

Neisser, U., & Harsch, N. (1993). Phantom flashbulbs: False recollections of hearing the news about Challenger. In E. Winograd & U. Neisser (eds.), *Affect and accuracy in recall: Studies of "flashbulb" memories* (pp. 9–31). New York: Cambridge University Press.

Nickerson, R. S. (1984). Retrieval inhibition from part-set cuing: A persisting enigma in memory research. *Memory and Cognition, 12,* 531–52.

Pellegrino, J. W., & Hubert, L. J. (1982). The analysis of organization and structure in free recall. In R. Puff (ed.), *Handbook of research methods in human memory and cognition* (pp. 129–72). New York: Academic Press.

Peterson, L. R., & Peterson, M. R. (1959). Short-term retention of individual verbal items. *Journal of Experimental Psychology, 58,* 193–8.

Postman, L., & Underwood, B. J. (1973). Critical issues in interference theory. *Memory & Cognition, 1,* 19–40.

Richardson-Klavehn, A., & Bjork, R. A. (1988). Measures of memory. *Annual Review of Psychology, 39,* 475–543.

Roediger, H. L. III, & McDermott, K. B. (1995). Creating false memories: Remembering words not presented in lists. *Journal of Experimental Psychology: Learning, Memory, and Cognition, 21,* 803–14.

Roediger, H. L., & Neely, J. H. (1982). Retrieval blocks in episodic and semantic memory. *Canadian Journal of Psychology, 36,* 213–42.

Roenker, D. L., Thompson, C. P., & Brown, S. C. (1971). Comparison of measures for the estimation of clustering in free recall. *Psychological Bulletin, 76,* 45–8.

Rotello, C. M., Macmillan, N. A., & Van Tassel, G. (2000). Recall-to-reject in recognition: Evidence from ROC curves. *Journal of Memory and Language, 43,* 67–88.

Rubin, D. C. (2000). The distribution of early childhood memories. *Memory, 8,* 265–9.

Schab, F. R. (1990). Odors and the remembrance of things past. *Journal of Experimental Psychology: Learning, Memory, and Cognition, 16,* 648–55.

Schacter, D. L., Harbluk, J. L., & McLachlan, D. R. (1984). Retrieval without recollection: An experimental analysis of source amnesia. *Journal of Verbal Learning and Verbal Behavior, 23,* 593–611.

Schacter, D. L., & Tulving, E. (1994). What are the memory systems of 1994? In D. L. Schacter & E. Tulving (eds.), *The memory systems of 1994* (pp. 1–38). Cambridge, MA: MIT Press.

Sebastian, M. V., Menor, J., & Elosua, R. (2001). Patterns of errors in short-term forgetting in AD and ageing. *Memory, 9,* 223–31.

Shaw, J. S., Bjork, R. A., & Handal, A. (1995). Retrieval-induced forgetting in an eyewitness-memory paradigm. *Psychonomic Bulletin and Review, 2,* 249–53.

Sheen, M., Kemp, S. & Rubin, D. (2001). Twins dispute memory ownership: A new false memory phenomenon. *Memory and Cognition, 29,* 779–88.

Shepard, R., & Teghtsoonian, M. (1961). Retention of information under conditions approaching a steady state. *Journal of Experimental Psychology, 62,* 302–9.

Shiffrin, R. M., & Steyvers, M. (1997). A model for recognition memory: REM – retrieving effectively from memory. *Psychonomic Bulletin and Review, 4,* 145–66.

Shimamura, A. P. (1986). Priming effects in amnesia: Evidence for a dissociable memory function. *Quarterly Journal of Experimental Psychology: Human Experimental Psychology, 38,* 619–44.

Slamecka, N. J. (1985). Ebbinghaus: Some associations. *Journal of Experimental Psychology: Learning, Memory, and Cognition, 11,* 414–35.

Slamecka, N. J., & Graf, P. (1978). The generation effect: delineation of a phenomenon. *Journal of Experimental Psychology: Human Learning and Memory, 4,* 592–604.

Smith, S. M., Glenberg, A. M., & Bjork, R. A. (1978). Environmental context and human memory. *Memory & Cognition, 6,* 342–53.

Snodgrass, J. G., & Corwin, J. G. (1988). Pragmatics of measuring recognition memory: Applications to dementia and amnesia. *Journal of Experimental Psychology: General, 117,* 34–50.

Sommers, M. S., & Lewis, B. R. (1999). Who really lives next door? Creating false memories with phonological neighbors. *Journal of Memory and Language, 40,* 83–108.

Sperling, G. (1960). The information available in brief visual presentations. *Psychological Monographs, 74* (Whole no. #11).

Squire, L. R. (1992). Memory and the hippocampus: A synthesis from findings with rats, monkeys, and humans. *Psychological Review, 99,* 195–231.

Stigler, S. M. (1978). Some forgotten work on memory. *Journal of Experimental Psychology: Human Learning and Memory, 4,* 1–4.

Tehan, G., Hendry, L., & Kocinski, D. (2001). Word length and phonological similarity effects in simple, complex, and delayed serial recall tasks: Implications for working memory. *Memory, 9,* 333–48.

Thapar, A., & McDermott, K. B. (2001). False recall and false recognition induced by presentation of associated words: Effects of retention interval and level of processing. *Memory & Cognition, 29,* 424–32.

Thomson, D. M., & Tulving, E. (1970). Associative encoding and retrieval: Weak and strong cues. *Journal of Experimental Psychology, 86,* 255–62.

Tulving, E. (1983). *Elements of episodic memory.* New York: Oxford University Press.

Tulving, E., & Osler, S. (1968). Effectiveness of retrieval cues in memory for words. *Journal of Experimental Psychology, 77,* 593–601.

Tulving, E., Schacter, D. L., & Stark, H. A. (1982). Priming effects in word-fragment completion are independent of recognition memory. *Journal of Experimental Psychology: Learning, Memory & Cognition, 8,* 336–42.

Warrington, E., & Weiskrantz, L. (1968). A study of learning and retention in amnesic patients. *Neuropsychologia, 6,* 283–91.

Warrington, E., & Weiskrantz, L. (1970). A study of forgetting in amnesic patients. *Neuropsychologia, 8,* 281–8.

Westerman, D. L. (2001). The role of familiarity in item-recognition, associative-recognition, and plurality recognition on self-paced and speeded tests. *Journal of Experimental Psychology: Learning, Memory and Cognition, 27,* 723–32.

Westerman, D. L., & Greene, R. L. (1997). The effects of visual masking on recognition: Similarities to the generation effect. *Journal of Memory and Language, 37,* 584–96.

Whitten, W. B., & Bjork, R. A. (1977). Learning from tests: Effects of spacing. *Journal of Verbal Learning and Verbal Behavior, 16,* 465–78.

Whittlesea, B. W. A., & Price, J. R. (2001). Implicit/explicit memory versus analytic/nonanalytic processing: Rethinking the mere exposure effect. *Memory and Cognition, 29,* 234–46.

Williams, C. C., & Zacks, R. T. (2001). Is retrieval-induced forgetting an inhibitory process? *American Journal of Psychology, 114,* 329–54.

Yonelinas, A. P. (1997). Recognition memory ROCs for item and associative information: The contribution of recollection and familiarity. *Memory & Cognition, 25,* 747–63.

Zajonc, R. B. (1968). Attitudinal effects of mere exposure. *Journal of Personality and Social Psychology, 9,* 1–27.

# CHAPTER SEVENTEEN

# Research Methods in Cognition

## David G. Payne and Deanne L. Westerman

Generally speaking, the study of human cognition involves specifying the structure and organization of knowledge (Anderson, 1985), and the processes that utilize this knowledge, to allow people to perceive, attend to events, read, learn, solve problems, and so forth (Payne & Wenger, 1998). Although the study of the mind was banished from mainstream psychology during the 1920s to 1950s when the behaviorist tradition was in vogue, the study of cognition is now a major area in psychology. Psychologists now appreciate that cognition plays a critical role in areas such as developmental psychology, social psychology, educational psychology, clinical psychology, and organizational psychology, to name but a few.

A moment's reflection on the nature of cognition will reveal one of the fundamental challenges facing cognitive researchers: the knowledge and processes that are presumed to underlie cognition are not directly observable, which makes studying them rather tricky. Because the focus of cognitive research is on unobservable phenomena, cognitive researchers must employ clever research techniques to study these phenomena. As we will see, cognitive researchers now have quite an extensive "tool kit" of research techniques at their disposal to study cognition, and in recent years there have been tremendous advances in our understanding of the processes underlying the human mind.

The remainder of this chapter is organized as follows. In the first section we review some of the important assumptions shared by cognitive researchers. It is important to be aware of these assumptions because, without this knowledge, much of the research reported in the scientific literature can be confusing and it is difficult to see how this work relates to the study of the mind. The second section reviews some general strategies employed by cognitive researchers. After discussing these assumptions and the logic underlying modern approaches to studying cognition, we present several representative behavioral techniques used to study cognition. In the fourth section we summarize several research techniques in neuroscience that have contributed to our understanding of cognitive processes.

## Three Metatheoretical Assumptions Shared by Cognitive Researchers

Although cognitive psychologists vary considerably in the approaches they take toward studying human mental processes and in the theories they embrace, they share three basic assumptions that serve to unite them and to differentiate the cognitive approach from other approaches in psychology (e.g., behaviorism). These three assumptions are so central that they are never explicitly stated in any of our theories (Lachman, Lachman, & Butterfield, 1979; Payne & Wenger, 1998) but rather they are implicitly accepted as valid by cognitive psychologists. Assumptions that have this status are referred to as *metatheoretical assumptions*, or assumptions that go beyond the specifics of any individual theory.

The first theoretical assumption is that humans and other animals store information in an organized manner in their memory systems. The second assumption holds that there are mental processes that utilize the information stored in memory, along with information perceived from the external environment, to allow us to think and behave intelligently. The third metatheoretical assumption is that these organized systems of information and the mental processes that underlie thinking and intelligent behavior are appropriate subject matter for scientific investigation. Let us now consider the first two assumptions in more detail. The third assumption is borne out in the techniques we review later in the chapter.

### Organized knowledge

It is easy to demonstrate that knowledge is organized – simply ask someone to recite the alphabet forwards and backwards and see how long it takes them and how many errors they make. This demonstration is useful in making our general point and it also highlights two of the primary types of measures used by cognitive psychologists, namely reaction times and patterns of correct and incorrect responses. It is assumed that mental processes take time to be completed and that by carefully examining the patterns of reaction times across various conditions we can discern the nature of the mental processes involved in performing the task. In addition, the patterns of participants' responses can provide valuable insights into the knowledge and cognitive processes operating in various situations.

Researchers have developed analytical tools that shed light on the organization of knowledge. For example, they have investigated the extent to which mental images are processed in a manner analogous to pictures. Processing images (e.g., scanning or rotating them) is analogous to applying the same processes to physical representations (for a review, see Finke and Shepherd, 1986). In other domains researchers have shown that presenting a word (e.g., doctor) that is related to a second word (e.g., nurse) speeds responding to the second word (e.g., Neely, 1977). These effects presumably occur because the two items are closely associated in lexical memory, or our memory for words. Later we will discuss these and other tasks that have also been used to study the organization of information and how this information is processed.

*Humans as active information processors*

Whereas the early behaviorists viewed humans as largely passive organisms who respond to the environment as a consequence of prior conditioning, cognitive psychologists assume that humans are active information processors. One simple yet elegant demonstration of the active role mental processes play in cognitive tasks is provided by the phenomenon of *subjective organization*, the process by which people organize lists of items that are presented to them in different random orders on each trial (Tulving, 1962). Subjective organization is demonstrated by presenting people with multiple opportunities to study a list of words. Despite the facts that there is no requirement to organize the list and the list is presented in a new order each time, people tend to recall the items in a similar order on each test. The list organization differs from person to person, hence the term *subjective* organization. Other studies have shown that subjective organization occurs even when participants have only a single opportunity to study a list of items. In these studies (e.g., Madigan & O'Hara, 1992; Payne & Wenger, 1994) participants have several successive recall tests with no intervening study opportunities. When subjective organization is measured across the repeated tests the results show that organization increases, despite the fact that there is no task requirement or instruction informing participants to attempt to organize their retrieval.

Another domain that clearly illustrates the active nature of cognitive processes is reading. As we read we have the impression that our eyes are moving smoothly across the text; this impression is entirely an illusion. The reality is that our eyes come to rest at one location for short periods known as fixations. Between fixations the eyes make rapid ballistic movements known as *saccades*. With sophisticated eye-tracking equipment researchers have examined a host of factors (e.g., word length, reading skill) that affect our eye movements during reading, and it is now clear that eye movements reflect an active effort on the part of the brain and visual system to focus on and encode (i.e., take in) visual information that will aid comprehension (Rayner & Pollatsek, 1989). We will review some of the research techniques that support this conclusion later in the chapter.

*Further assumptions regarding the cognitive system*

In addition to these three primary metatheoretical assumptions, cognitive psychologists have also embraced several other more specific assumptions that affect research in a number of different areas. These assumptions are not metatheoretical assumptions that are not questioned. Rather, each assumption is supported by a great deal of empirical evidence; what is important to stress here is that these assumptions underlie many research techniques and yet they are typically not stated in research reports. In a way, these assumptions reflect the working knowledge of researchers in the field.

The first of these assumptions is that processing information takes time. This is why cognitive psychologists utilize reaction times. An assumption that underlies the use of reaction time is that the length of time it takes to complete a task can be used to draw conclusions regarding the nature of the information-processing demands of the task. For example, Shepherd and Metzler (1971) presented participants with letters or numbers that were either in the normal form or a reversed mirror-image form. The participant's task was to decide whether the items were presented in the normal or reversed format. The items were spatially rotated when they were presented to participants (i.e., the items were not always in their normal upright positions). The primary finding from the study was that the further the stimulus item was rotated away from the standard upright position, the longer it took participants to make their decisions. The general interpretation of these results is that participants "mentally rotated" the items before making their decisions, and the further the item had to be rotated, the longer this process took and hence the longer the reaction time.

The final general assumption is that there are fundamental and functional differences in the memory systems that support retention over short versus long intervals. This assumption is embodied in the short-term memory versus long-term memory distinction (e.g., Atkinson & Shiffrin, 1968) and also the more current working memory model (Baddeley & Hitch, 1974) that emphasizes both processing and storage aspects of memory. These assumptions are reflected in many research areas in cognitive psychology.

## General Strategies for Studying Unobservable Knowledge and Cognitive Processes

Broadly speaking, cognitive researchers are restricted to making observations about human behavior and the events that preceded these behaviors. The behaviors here may range from recordings of the activities of specific brain structures, to the responses made by individual participants in controlled laboratory studies, to the performance of groups trying to perform some task. Cognitive researchers are generally not interested in the behavior per se of the participants in their studies. Rather, the researchers hope to draw inferences from these behaviors by noting the relations between behaviors and antecedent events and the (unobservable) knowledge structures and mental processes that could have produced these observed behaviors.

In order to test hypotheses concerning unobservable knowledge structures and mental processes, researchers who employ the experimental approach generally attempt to set up conditions in which they can manipulate one or more aspects of the experimental setting that they presume to be related to the unobservable mental processes. Because the mental processes are themselves unobservable, the researcher needs to be cautious in drawing simple conclusions about how the conditions varied in the experiment and how the behavioral measures collected relate to these processes.

Independent variables are factors controlled or manipulated by the researcher and dependent variables are measures of performance collected during the study. The third class of variables, and the one that is central to cognitive research, involves entities not directly observed but rather inferred. This class is made up of two subclasses of variables known as *intervening variables* and *hypothetical constructs*. An intervening variable is a variable used to summarize several related concepts conveniently using a single term.

MacCorquodale and Meehl (1948) suggested that these variables be distinguished from other theoretical concepts in which the theoretical terms imply something more "real." For example, if we use the term "memory" to refer simply to retention of information over time without assuming that memory presumes any specific sort of underlying brain structure or manner of representing information, then in this sense memory is an *intervening variable*; presumably there are a variety of processes that are responsible for allowing you to remember a telephone number long enough to dial it. In contrast, if by "memory" the researcher is referring to, say, a specific memory system that is presumed to store all of our knowledge about the words of the language(s) that we can speak, then in this case memory is being used as a hypothetical construct. A hypothetical construct is a concept involving an unobservable factor or variable that is able to account for existing data (or knowledge) as well as providing implications for new observations. Presumably the researcher using "memory" in this latter case is making certain assumptions about the nature and operation of this word-information memory system.

## Operational definitions and converging operations

Because cognitive psychologists are interested in unobservable events, they need to be very careful in how they measure and characterize these events. Two widely used approaches for dealing with this problem involve the use of *operational definitions* and *converging operations*. Cognitive psychology borrowed the concept of operational definitions from the behaviorist tradition, but modified it so as to allow for the possibility of cognitive processes. Operationism is a concept that was introduced to psychology by the physicist Bridgman (1945). In its strongest version operationism is the idea that scientific concepts are defined in terms of the experimental manipulations/operations used to produce or assess them. Thus hunger may be defined in terms of hours of deprivation. Taken literally, a strict operationist view of psychological concepts (e.g., perception, memory) does not allow for internal processes or knowledge. According to this view, psychology should limit itself to studying the operations performed by the experimenter and the behaviors exhibited by participants.

Garner, Hake, and Eriksen (1956) made a tremendous contribution to the study of perceptual and cognitive processes by introducing the notion of converging operations as a method for identifying and characterizing unobservable phenomena. According to Garner et al., "converging operations can be thought of as any set of two or more experimental operations which allow the selection or elimination of alternative hypotheses or concepts which could explain an experimental result" (pp. 150–1).

The value of converging operations can be illustrated by considering one of the classic studies in cognitive psychology. Sperling (1960) was interested in the question of how much information people can extract from the environment in a brief period. Early experiments reported that when participants were presented with displays containing a large number of items they could usually report only four or five items (e.g., Whipple, 1914). The number of items participants could report was termed the span of apprehension (Averbach & Sperling, 1960) and researchers thought this measure reflected the amount of information that a person could take in (or "apprehend") in a single glance.

Note, however, that the displays were very brief and that it takes time to identify and then report the items.

Sperling (1960) reasoned that the results from the span of apprehension studies might reflect what persons are able to remember and report as opposed to what they perceived. He reasoned that if we could ask people to report only a subset of the items from the display then this procedure should decrease both the number of items participants have to remember as well as the length of time they spent reporting items. He tested this notion using two main conditions. In the *whole report* condition participants reported all the letters from the display. In the second condition, known as a *partial report* condition, after the visual display ended a tone was presented that signaled to the participant which row of the display they were to report (high frequency signaled report top row, middle frequency indicated report middle row, low frequency signaled bottom row). Sperling assumed that whatever percentage of the target row of letters the participants could report represented an estimate of the number of letters available for report from the whole display soon after the display was presented.

Replicating the earlier span of apprehension studies, Sperling found that his participants reported about 4.3 letters in the whole report condition. In the partial report condition Sperling used the number of items that participants could report from one row to estimate the total number of items available for report. For example, if participants could report three items from a display of three rows of four items each, this number was multiplied by the number of rows in the display to give the total number of items available for report, in this case about nine items. These data suggest that about 75 percent of the items in the display (9 of 12 items) were available after the initial display. According to this logic the difference between the partial and whole report conditions reflects a difference in the number of items *perceived* from the display (as indicated by the partial report data) versus the number of items that participants *remember* from the entire display (whole report data).

Before we accept this interpretation of Sperling's results, however, we need to rule out an alternative explanation for the differences between the partial and whole report conditions. This alternative explanation is based on a phenomenon known as output interference (Tulving & Arbuckle, 1963). When people recall items from memory, the more items they recall the less likely they are to be able to recall additional items. Because there are more items that need to be recalled in the whole report condition than in the partial report condition, any observed differences between these two conditions could be due to differences in output interference.

Sperling tested between the output interference interpretation and the rapid forgetting view by setting up conditions in which the two explanations make opposing predictions. He did this by varying the time interval between when the display ended and when the participant was signaled as to which row to report. If the difference between the partial report estimate and the whole report data is due to rapid forgetting affecting performance in the whole report condition more than in the partial report condition, then with an increasing interval between display offset and signal onset the partial report superiority effect should disappear. In contrast, the output interference hypothesis predicts that the partial report superiority should be unaffected by the delay of the signal because, regardless of when the signal is presented, there are still fewer items to report in the partial report condition than in the whole report conditions. Sperling's results showed that, as predicted by the rapid forgetting hypothesis, there was a decrease in the partial report superiority as the interval between the display offset and signal onset was increased. These findings provide converging evidence in favor of the rapid forgetting view and against the output interference explanation.

## Dissociations

Another widely used strategy in cognitive research is to look for situations in which performance on one cognitive task is uncorrelated with, or dissociated from, performance on another cognitive task. The logic here is that if factors affect different conditions, participant populations, and so forth, differently, then these differences point to functional differences between the conditions, cognitive processes, participants, and so forth. One early demonstration of the benefit of looking for dissociations is a study by Warrington and Weiskrantz (1970, Experiment 2). They presented amnesics and matched controls who had no memory problems with a list of common words presented three times before giving them one of several types of memory tasks. These tests included (1) a free recall test in which participants recalled all the words they remembered from the list, (2) a yes/no recognition test that required participants to decide whether the test items had or had not appeared in the study list, and (3) a word fragment task in which participants identified words when given word fragments in which individual letters had been visually degraded. As you might expect, results showed that the amnesics performed much more poorly than the control participants on the recall and recognition tests. More importantly, the two groups performed equally well in identifying previously studied items on the word fragment completion test. These results showed that the amnesics' performance on the word fragment completion test was dissociated from their performance on the recall recognition tests (see Shimamura, 1986, for a review of similar studies).

Roediger (1990) has provided a theoretical framework that can account for these and many other dissociations in a wide variety of tasks. This framework, known as transfer-appropriate processing, assumes that performance in any task will reflect the extent to which the processes required to perform the task are the same as or similar to those processes that were involved in encoding the items initially. According to the transfer-appropriate processing framework there are two general types of cognitive processes, conceptually driven processes and data-driven or perceptually driven processes. Conceptually driven processes can be thought of as those processes that involve analyzing the meaning or semantic information in an item. Data-driven processes involve the analysis of perceptual or surface features of an item. According to this framework the reason that amnesics perform poorly on recall and recognition tests is that these tests primarily depend upon conceptually driven processing, which is impaired in these participants. In contrast, the word fragment completion test is largely dependent upon data-driven processes, which are largely intact in the amnesic participants.

Researchers have also used dissociations to study cognitive processes in normal participants, and the transfer-appropriate processing framework can account for much of these

data. For example, Jacoby (1983) demonstrated dissociations on various retention measures as a function of the manner in which participants had initially processed a list of
stimulus items. In the first phase of these experiments participants either read or generated a target word in one of three conditions. In the No-context condition participants
saw a neutral stimulus followed by a target word (e.g., XXX – *cold*) that they were
instructed to read aloud. In the Context condition the target word was preceded by an
antonym (e.g., HOT – *cold*). Finally, in the Generate condition participants produced
the target item in response to the antonym cue (e.g., HOT – XXX).

Following this initial phase participants completed either a recognition memory test
or a perceptual identification test that required identifying rapidly presented words.
Recognition memory performance was very good in the Context and Generate conditions but was quite poor in the No-context condition. In contrast, performance on
the perceptual identification task was best in the No-context condition. Jacoby (1983)
interpreted these results as indicating that recognition memory tests mainly involve
conceptual processes whereas performance in perceptual identification tasks depends
upon perceptual processes.

## Research Methods Used to Study Cognition

In this section we will review some of the many research methods used to study cognition. These methods illustrate the diversity of approaches employed and they also will
make clear how the assumptions made by cognitive researchers are reflected in their
methods.

### Direct and indirect measures

Cognitive researchers have developed a host of tasks that can be divided into the general
categories of either direct or indirect measures. In the memory domain these tasks are
referred to as explicit and implicit tests, respectively. Explicit memory tests involve
conscious recollection. Standard free recall and recognition tests are explicit tests because
participants are required to base their responses on their conscious recollection of having
previously experienced the items during an encoding phase. Implicit memory tests do
not require conscious recollection. Tests such as the word fragment completion test used
by Warrington and Weiskrantz (1970) and the perceptual identification task used by
Jacoby (1983) are examples of implicit tests. In other domains the term direct refers to
situations in which the researcher directly measures performance in the task of interest,
and thus recall is a direct measure of memory. In contrast, indirect measures allow the
researcher to make inferences about cognitive processes from some measure(s) of performance. Direct and indirect measures such as those used in the studies described next
frequently reveal fundamental dissociations between tasks that can be quite revealing.

McCloskey (1983) examined people's understanding of the principle that objects
move in straight lines in the absence of external forces. To assess this knowledge McCloskey

asked participants to draw the expected trajectories of objects when they are released from curved enclosures or when they are released from a continuous rotation (e.g., as when a ball is attached to a string and rotated around a person and then the string suddenly breaks). McCloskey found that many participants drew curved pathways indicating that they believed that an object forced to travel in a curved path (e.g., a ball attached to a string) acquires a force or momentum that causes it to continue in curvilinear motion. McCloskey referred to these beliefs as "naive physics," or the implicit theories that people have developed over their lifetimes regarding the motion of physical objects.

Results such as these raise a host of interesting questions. For example, would these demonstrations of "naive physics" be obtained if the participants were students who had taken a course or two in physics? Also, to what extent do these demonstrations of naive physics depend upon the type of test that is given to participants? Recent research by Kozhevnikov and Hegarty (2001) provided insight into both of these questions. These researchers gave their participants two different types of performance measures: one was a type of indirect measure and the second was a more direct type of measure. The indirect measure they used involved a representational momentum (RM) paradigm in which participants view an object that is moving in a given direction and at a specific velocity. At some point the object suddenly disappears from view and the participant is asked to indicate the object's final location. A common finding in this paradigm is that participants' memory for the object's final position is shifted forward in the direction of the movement of the object.

Kozhevnikov and Hegarty (2001) presented subjects with large and small objects and found that the magnitude of the RM effects differed as a function of the size of the object in a manner that is inconsistent with Newtonian principles. These results are similar to those of McCloskey (1983). Importantly, Kozhevnikov and Hegarty also found that participants' responses on a paper and pencil questionnaire test elicited correct Newtonian-based responses. This dissociation between the results obtained with the indirect RM measure and the more direct questionnaire measure demonstrates a common principle in cognitive research, namely that the pattern of responses obtained in a study can vary tremendously depending upon many factors.

## Priming

The priming technique involves presenting participants with items/events and then observing the effects of these items/events upon subjects' responses to later items/events. MacKay (1973) used priming in a study that involved speech shadowing. In a speech-shadowing task participants are presented with two passages aurally, via headphones (e.g, a story about baseball and a story about a trip to the zoo), and they are required to repeat aloud one of these passages that is designated the attended passage. In the MacKay study some of the sentences presented in the attended passage had a word with two meanings, e.g., "They were standing near the bank." In the unattended passage, MacKay presented either the word *money*, or *river*. Participants interpreted the word *bank* as either a "river bank" or a "financial bank" dependent upon which word was presented in the unattended passage. This shows that participants must have understood whether money or river was presented in the unattended ear. If the meaning of an item is accessed, then clearly these items could not have been filtered out before perceptual processing as the early selection models suggested.

MacKay's results represent a priming effect. In this case *river* or *money* were primes and *bank* was the target stimulus. Many researchers have reported priming of attended target items by unattended primes. Balota (1983) and Marcel (1983a, 1983b) presented words visually at rates that were so rapid that the participants were not able to identify the words. These briefly presented items primed participants' responses to target items. Eich (1984) used a selective listening task in which participants heard words presented over either the left or right earphone. They were instructed to listen to items in one earphone and ignored the word pairs presented in the other earphone. The unattended items consisted of word pairs in which the first word provided a context for interpreting the second word (e.g., taxi – fare). After the listening task participants spelled various words as they were spoken, including the words from the unattended word pairs. They spelled the words more often in the manner consistent with how they had been pre-sented in the unattended channel (e.g., fare vs fair). Importantly, this bias in spelling the word consistently with the context word was larger when participants attended to the word pairs. This finding suggests that the processing of the word pairs in the attended condition was more complete when participants attended to these pairs.

There are many examples of what is referred to as positive priming, that is, situations in which a stimulus is responded to more quickly when it is preceded by an item that is similar, for example in meaning or sound, to the target item. Dual-process models of selective attention account for these results by assuming there are two separate mech-anisms, a *facilitatory* mechanism that works to process attended stimuli and an *inhibitory* mechanism that serves to block the representations of ignored stimuli. Recent research supports the notion of an inhibitory mechanism in selective attention. The critical question in these experiments is whether the prime will facilitate or inhibit the process-ing of the target stimuli.

Tipper and Driver (1988) presented participants with a series of trials each containing a prime display and a target display. On each trial there were two stimuli, a prime item presented in green and a target item presented in red. Of interest here was how reaction times to target items varied depending upon the nature of the primes and targets in the displays. Tipper and Driver measured how long it took participants to name the items in red from the target displays. They found that when the attended-to items were the same on two successive displays participants were faster to name the target item than when the attended-to items in two trials were unrelated. This result is a positive priming effect and it is a well-documented finding. A similar positive priming effect was obtained when the attended to items in successive displays were semantically related (e.g., CAT and DOG). The novel finding from this study concerns the trials on which the item that is *ignored* in one display was the same as or related to the attended item in the next display. Under these conditions participants were actually slower to name the target item than they were in the control condition. This slower response rate is called negative priming and it has been interpreted as indicating that the unattended-to prime was not simply ignored but was actively inhibited.

## Divided attention paradigms

As we discussed earlier, many cognitive theories assume that humans are limited in the amount of information they can process per unit of time (e.g., Broadbent, 1958; Kahneman, 1973). A closely related assumption involves the notion of "cognitive resources" (e.g., Wickens, 1980), or the idea that there are different systems that are involved with processing different types of stimuli (e.g., verbal vs. pictorial) or different stages of information processing (e.g., encoding, memory, response selection/response execution). Based on theories that assume that there are limits on either attentional capacity or processing resources a researcher can make some very general and straightforward predictions. Generally speaking, whenever the amount of attentional capacity or processing resources available to perform a task is less than the amount required for optimal performance there should be a performance deficit relative to a condition in which there is adequate capacity or resources available.

One technique that is frequently used to test predictions such as these is the dual-task, or divided attention, technique. In a dual-task experiment participants perform two tasks, both singly and in conjunction, with performance being compared in the single-task and dual-task conditions. The single-task conditions provide us with a baseline measure of performance against which we can compare the dual-task performance to determine whether the two tasks selectively interfere with one another. In divided attention experiments performance is generally compared under two conditions, a full attention condition in which participants can attend fully to the primary task of interest and a divided attention condition in which participants are required to perform two tasks simultaneously. Here again, the question of interest is whether performance will differ in the full versus divided attention conditions.

Mulligan (1998) used the divided attention technique to test predictions derived from Roediger's (1990) transfer-appropriate processing framework. Mulligan also compared performance in both explicit and implicit memory tests. Mulligan (1998) employed eight perceptual and conceptual tests and compared performance under full versus divided attention. As predicted by the transfer-appropriate processing framework, divided attention affected performance on conceptual tests involving explicit memory but had no effects on perceptual tests involving implicit memory. Note that these findings do not make it clear whether the critical distinction is the explicit/implicit test difference or the perceptual/conceptual processing difference. To resolve this issue, Mulligan used two explicit perceptual tests, both of which involved nonwords that resembled real words (e.g., "cheetohs" resembles "cheetahs"). In the graphemic cued recall test participants had to recall list words (e.g., cheetohs might cue the participant to recall the list work cheetahs). In the graphemic recognition tests participants had to recognize which nonwords were similar in appearance to list words. Although both of these tests involve perceptual processing, there was a significant effect of full versus divided attention for both test types. That is, for both the graphemic cued recall and the graphemic recognition tests performance in the full attention condition was significantly better than in the divided attention condition. Mulligan concluded that performance on explicit tests is dependent on attention at encoding, regardless of whether the test involves conceptual or perceptual processing.

Two studies that examined dual-task performance involving an auditory task demonstrate the generality of the dual-task technique. Payne et al. (1994) asked whether changes in level of speech intelligibility in an auditory task would affect performance in a concurrent visual task. Speech intelligibility refers to the extent to which a listener can understand a spoken message. Payne et al. conducted four experiments in which participants performed both an auditory and a visual task under both single-task and dual-task conditions. They predicted that changes in speech intelligibility level would affect performance in visual tasks that required a great deal of "central" cognitive resources (e.g., memory, decision making) but not in visual tasks that did not require significant central resources. The tasks they chose were intended to mimic some of the perceptual, cognitive, and motor processes required for real world tasks such as driving or making decisions while navigating. Their results showed that, as predicted, performance in a largely perceptual task similar to driving was unaffected by changes in speech intelligibility level. In contrast, visual tasks that required decision making and reasoning were severely affected by changes in speech intelligibility level. One implication of these results is that although a person in the real world may be able to drive reasonably well while listening to a degraded auditory communication, the same person may not be able to make decisions effectively while listening to this message.

Strayer and Johnston (2001) reported a dual-task study that assessed the effects of cellular phone conversations on performance on a simulated driving task. Participants in this experiment performed a simulated driving task both singly and in conjunction with a secondary auditory task. There were four secondary auditory task conditions, a hand-held cellphone condition, a hands-free cellphone condition, one control condition in which participants listened to the radio, and a second control condition in which participants listened to a passage from a book on tape. Results showed that there was no difference in performance on the simulating driving task for the hand-held cellphone and hands-free cellphone conditions. More importantly, participants in the two cellphone conditions were more than twice as likely to fail to detect a simulated traffic signal as compared to participants in the two control conditions. Participants in the cellphone conditions were also slower in their reactions to those signals that they did detect. Strayer and Johnston concluded that cellphone use results in poor driving performance because cellphone use diverts attention to an engaging cognitive task (i.e., carrying on a conversation) and away from the perceptual, cognitive, and motor demands associated with driving.

## Implicit learning

Seger (1994) defined implicit learning as "learning complex information without complete verbalisable knowledge of what is learned" (p. 63). Although, as Seger and others have noted, there is no distinct line between implicit learning and implicit memory, the research techniques used to study these phenomena are quite different. One frequently used task to study implicit learning is artificial grammar learning, which involves presenting participants with a series of letter strings that have been produced according to the rules of an artificial grammar. The "grammar" here really refers simply to the probabilities by which specific letters may follow other letters. During the grammar-learning phase of these experiments participants view a series of letter strings produced according to the rules of the grammar. It is not critical that the participants perform any tasks with these letter strings; they simply need to observe the letter strings as they are presented (Reber, 1989).

After viewing the series of letter strings, participants are then presented with a second set of letter strings, some of which are legal letter strings according to the grammar and others of which violate the rules of the artificial grammar. The participants' primary task is to identify those strings that are legal according to the grammar versus those that violate the grammar. A well-documented finding in studies using artificial grammar learning is that participants perform at above chance levels at this grammaticality judgment task, even when they cannot reliably discriminate between letter strings that had been presented during the first phase of the experiment versus those that are new. Another important finding from these studies is that participants are typically not able to verbalize either the rules they are using for making these grammaticality judgments or the rules that make up the artificial grammar (Berry & Broadbent, 1984; Reber, 1989).

Another test used to study implicit learning involves presenting participants with a series of stimuli such as characters in various locations on a computer screen to be responded to by pressing a key that corresponds to that location. The position of these characters over trials is governed by a complex rule that is not described to the participants. The participants are instructed simply to respond by pressing the appropriate key as quickly as possible. Participants in the studies show clear evidence of learning the pattern as evidenced by the fact that their reaction times become faster and faster as learning progresses. This speed up in reaction time is greater than what would be expected simply on the basis of becoming familiar with the key-pressing task, and this result shows that participants have learned something about the order in which items are presented. When the same participants are asked to describe the pattern of these stimuli they are unable to do so. Similarly, when they are asked to predict where the next stimulus will appear, their performance is typically at the chance levels (e.g., Howard & Howard, 1992).

Finally, there is another very interesting demonstration of what may be viewed as either implicit learning, implicit memory, or very long-term priming. Kolers (1976) had participants read passages of text in which the characters were spatially transformed (e.g., a mirror image of normal text). One year after participants had read these texts, Kolers retested them by asking them to read passages that they had read a year previously as well as new passages. When the participants decided which texts they had read a year previously, results showed that, not surprisingly, participants did very poorly on this recognition task. However, when the reading speeds were compared for new passages versus previously read passages there was a speed advantage for the previously read passages. These results show a very nice dissociation between an explicit measure of memory (recognition) and an implicit measure of memory or learning.

## Methods for studying reading

Reading researchers have developed a number of very sensitive methods for studying the perceptual and cognitive processes involved in reading. One particularly sensitive method is the moving-window techniques introduced by McConkie and Rayner (1975). In this task participants' eye movements are recorded as they read text from a computer display. The "window" in this technique refers to that segment of text that is presented normally during reading. As the eyes move across the line of text the eye-tracking equipment records where the person is looking and, depending upon the size of the window, a specified number of characters to left and right of the current fixation are presented. Any characters of text outside this window are replaced with meaningless symbols (e.g., XXX). When the eyes move from one fixation point to another the computer changes the text display and the "window" moves along with the person's fixation. McConkie and Rayner and their colleagues have documented some very intriguing facts regarding reading using this technique. For example, the length of a reader's saccades vary depending upon the size of the moving window. With a window size of 31 characters (including spaces), subjects are able to read at normal speed and with normal comprehension. With window sizes smaller than 31 characters saccade size decreases and reading speed declines.

The finding that the perceptual span is approximately 31 characters has been replicated in other studies (e.g., Rayner & Bertera, 1979) and we have also learned more about the nature of this perceptual span. For example, McConkie and Rayner (1975) showed that for readers of English the perceptual span is asymmetric to the right and left. When participants are reading English they extract far more information from characters to the right of the fixation point than they do from characters to the left. Interestingly, the asymmetry of the perceptual span depends upon the language being read. Pollatsek, Bolozky, Well, and Rayner (1981) found that for participants who were reading Hebrew (which is read from right to left) their perceptual span was asymmetric to the left of the fixation point, but when the same participants read English their perceptual span was asymmetric to the right. These findings demonstrate that the ways in which the cognitive and perceptual systems extract information from the environment depend on the specific task demands. This is a very clear and compelling demonstration of how the cognitive system plays an active role in our interactions with the environment. It is also important to note that these results demonstrate that characteristics of the cognitive system are not entirely "hard wired" – if the perceptual span were a function of the makeup of the visual system and the brain, then we would not expect to see the differences in perceptual span when reading Hebrew versus English. Here again a dissociation, this time caused by the language being read, provides valuable insights into the cognitive processes of interest.

Researchers also use eye-tracking equipment to record where readers fixate as they read normal text presented on a computer screen. In the laboratory these detailed records of eye movement patterns can be used in many ways including testing theories of reading comprehension, studying the programming of eye movements during reading, determining how syntax and semantics affects comprehension on movements, and so forth (see Rayner and Pollatsek, 1989, for an excellent review). Another on-line method used by reading researchers involves recording people reading aloud. This method allows the researcher to examine the types of errors participants make when reading, when pauses occurred during reading, and so forth. Researchers can also examine the effects of manipulations to the text passage such as misspellings or anomalous words inserted in the passage (Danks & Hill, 1981). One major limitation of this technique is that it is very unnatural for adults to read aloud and therefore a person may question the extent to which performance in this type of task corresponds to actual silent reading.

Another group of research techniques identified by Rayner and Pollatsek (1989) are word identification techniques. The general approach here is to have people read text and then at some point during the reading task stop them and require a specific response to a given word. Two frequently used word identification techniques are the lexical decision task and the naming task. In the lexical decision task participants are required to decide whether a string of letters is a word or a nonword, while in the naming task participants are required to read the word aloud as quickly as possible. For both tasks the primary dependent measure is the participant's reaction time. These techniques may be used to assess the extent to which a word has been activated by the text that preceded it, with the assumption being that a word that is activated will be responded to more quickly than a word that has not been activated.

Because reading involves processing at many different levels (e.g., letter identification, word identification, mapping spelling to sound, comprehension) a researcher needs to be careful when interpreting the results from tasks such as lexical decision in naming. Balota, Paul, and Spieler (1999) have reviewed the evidence that leads them to conclude that different reading tasks vary in the extent to which they reflect processing at these various levels. Here again, converging operations are very helpful in providing the information needed for appropriate interpretation of results.

## Metacognition

Metacognition refers to cognition about one's own cognitions. There are many everyday examples of metacognitive processes, such as students deciding how to allocate their study time, grade school students deciding what approach to take when presented with a problem-solving task, or elderly individuals deciding what strategies to use to remember to take their medications at the appropriate time. Nelson and Narens (1990) have developed a theoretical framework that is quite useful for considering the various aspects of metacognitive processes and especially metamemory. Nelson and Narens outline several types of monitoring that people employ when presented with memory tasks. These monitoring activities cover all three of the standard stages of memory, that is, encoding, retention, and retrieval. People make ease-of-learning judgments when they decide how easy a set of materials will be to memorize before they get started or while they are in the process of memorizing these items. Judgments of learning involve people's assessment of how adequately they have mastered a set of materials, and feeling-of-knowing judgments correspond to the extent to which people feel that they have learned or remembered something. Finally, confidence in the accuracy of retrieved information is an example of metacognition during the retrieval process.

The prototypical way of assessing metacognitive processes is to present participants with a specific task to complete and then provide them with a scale to assess their metacognitive judgments. For example, as a set of items is being presented to a participant for memorization, the participants could rate on a 1 to 7 scale how well they believe they have learned each individual item. Alternatively, if participants are unable to recall an item they may be asked to indicate their confidence that they would be able to recognize the item if it was presented to them (i.e., a feeling-of knowing-judgment).

There are many tasks in which participants' metacognitive judgments are quite accurate. For example, Underwood (1966) showed that participants' ease-of-learning judgments were an accurate predictor of the rate of learning during subsequent experimenter-paced study trials. Similarly, Nelson and Leonesio (1988) showed that ease-of-learning judgments are related to the matter of study time allocated to individual items during self-paced study trials. There are also instances, however, in which participants' metacognitive judgments do not correlate well with performance in related tasks. For example, confidence is often not correlated with recognition accuracy (e.g., Chandler, 1994; Neisser & Harsch, 1992).

*Phenomenological measures*

Another cognitive domain that has received a great deal of attention recently concerns people's phenomenological experiences as they perform various types of tasks. Although this work has largely centered on memory process, the techniques used and the findings from this work have important implications for our understanding of the mind. The source-monitoring framework (SMF) developed by Johnson and her colleagues (Johnson, Hashtroudi, & Lindsay, 1993) has guided much of the research in this area. This framework is intended to characterize the qualitative characteristics of memories (both true and false) from various sources (e.g., hearing, seeing, imagining). The framework also attempts to identify those factors that determine when accurate and inaccurate source attributions occur (e.g., "Did I see it or did I only imagine it?").

Researchers have used several different measures to assess people's experiences when they recollect previous events. The general approach taken to assess a person's phenomenological experiences of a memory is to provide the person with a rating scale along with a description of the characteristics of the memory to be rated. Confidence ratings are widely used measures that can be employed with both recall and recognition tests. After participants recall or recognize an item they rate their confidence that this item was one that they experienced earlier (e.g., Sporer, 1992; Sporer, Penrod, Read, & Cutler, 1995). Research in the eyewitness memory domain has indicated that there is a complex relation between confidence and accuracy in eyewitness identification (Sporer et al., 1995), with confidence often not correlated with accuracy.

Another popular memory assessment technique is the Remember/Know measure (Tulving, 1985). This technique is typically used in conjunction with a recognition test. For each item that the participant indicates that they recognize as having appeared in a study list the participant is required to make a Remember/Know judgment. Participants label an item as a "remember" response if they can consciously recollect details of the actual occurrence of the item during the study phase, and use a "know" response when they recognize the item as having been presented in the study phase but cannot consciously recollect anything specific about its presentation (Rajaram, 1993). Research has shown that when participants falsely recognize an unrelated lure item presented on a recognition test, these items are predominately given a "know" response (Rajaram, 1993). Interestingly, a number of false memory experiments have shown that under certain circumstances people will label many false memories with "remember" responses (e.g., Payne, Elie, Blackwell, & Neuschatz, 1996; Roediger & McDermott, 1995), suggesting that these people actually believe that they can consciously recollect an event that never occurred.

Finally, an even more detailed assessment of a person's memories is provided by the memory characteristics questionnaire (MCQ; Johnson, Foley, Suengas, & Raye, 1988). The MCQ assesses subjective ratings of specific characteristics of memories including confidence, perceptual detail, emotional feelings or reactions experienced when the item was presented, and the number of associations the person had to each item as it was presented. Mather, Henkel and Johnson (1997) used the MCQ to assess the character- istics of veridical and false memories and found that false memories had less auditory detail and less remembered feelings and emotional reactions than memories for actually studied items.

Taken together, these and other assessment techniques are providing researchers with a much more detailed view of participants' memories than would be provided simply by measures such as recall or recognition. Examinations of the characteristics of memory have also brought together the issues of memory and beliefs about memory (e.g., "Do I believe that this really happened?") and this work promises to have important applica- tions for many real world domains including eyewitness memory, psychotherapy, and personality assessment.

Overall, the study of metacognitive processes has proven to be a fruitful area of inquiry and has contributed significantly to our theoretical understanding of cognitive processes. For example, Neisser and Harsch (1992) examined people's memories of the Challenger disaster and found that over time there were significant changes in their memory for the episode in which they first learned of the Challenger disaster. That is, when participants' reports collected the day after the Challenger disaster were compared with their reports collected three years later, in many cases there were significant changes in what the participants reported. Nonetheless, many participants were very confident in these changed recollections reported three years later. Researchers' efforts to determine the conditions under which metacognitive reports can and cannot be used as accurate indices of the state of the cognitive system will depend on future laboratory and real world research.

## Research Methods in Cognitive Neuroscience

With the advent of modern techniques for recording the activities of the brain and nervous system, neuroscience has provided cognitive researchers with an important set of tools for observing how people's brains and nervous systems react to various types of stimuli, tasks, and so forth. Although an in-depth review of the cognitive neuroscience literature is beyond the scope of this chapter, we will review briefly some of the primary brain imaging techniques (see also Chapter 15 by Brenda Anderson et al. in this volume) that are currently being employed to study cognitive processes. It is important to note that, in many respects, behavioral and brain imaging research on cognitive processes are proceeding in parallel and the findings from one level of analysis (e.g., behavior) provide a form of converging evidence for research in the other domain.

## Scalp electroencephalography

Because the brain is composed of billions of neurons that communicate through various changes in electrical charges it is possible to measure the electrical potentials of these cells at the scalp on the surface of the skull. The collective electrical activity of large groups of cells can be measured with an electroencephalogram (EEG), which provides an overall measure of the electrical activity of the brain. Researchers use several different types of EEG measures, one of which is of greatest use to cognitive researchers. This type of EEG is known as event-related potentials (ERPs). In the ERP technique each participant is presented with a given type of stimulus many times and the EEG is recorded for each of these stimulus presentations. By averaging the EEGs across many repetitions of the stimulus presentation, the background noise averages out, and what is left is a representation of the average response of the brain to the external stimulus.

ERPs have been used successfully in studying a wide variety of cognitive processes. The basic approach is to present the participant with a specific type of stimulus and take an EEG recording each time the stimulus is presented. For example, on each trial a participant might be asked to read a sentence stem (e.g., "The pizza was too hot to") followed by a single word. On some trials the word given after the sentence stem fits the sentence (e.g., "eat") and on others it does not fit in the sentence frame (e.g., "cry").

By carefully varying the types of stimuli and instructions given to participants, researchers can correlate certain aspects of the ERP wave with perceptual and cognitive processes. For example, there is a large negative waveform obtained at about 400 msecs when the stimulus is incongruous in meaning, as in presenting "cry" after "The pizza was too hot to" (Kutas & Van Petten, 1988). ERP data such as these provide valuable information regarding the time course of the brain's response to specific stimuli, tasks, instructions, and so forth.

## Magnetic resonance imaging

Another useful imaging technique is magnetic resonance imaging (MRI). An MRI scanner produces an extremely strong magnetic field. When tissue (e.g., a human head) is placed in a strong magnetic field, the nuclei of some molecules in the tissue spin in a particular spatial orientation. The MRI procedure takes advantage of the fact that hydrogen atoms will emit energy at a specific frequency when activated by radio frequency waves in the magnetic field produced by the MRI. Because the concentration of hydrogen atoms varies considerably and predictably in different neural structures, the MRI procedure produces an image of the brain that is of much higher spatial resolution than that yielded by the CAT (computerized axial tomography) scan procedure.

Recent technological advances have allowed researchers to use the MRI procedure to also examine the *activity levels* within given brain structures. In one procedure, known as *functional MRI* (or fMRI), the MRI works indirectly by detecting blood flow. As blood cells give up their oxygen to active brain cells the MRI traces this process. Because of the way the vascular system works, active areas of the brain have a much greater level of oxygenated blood than do inactive areas. The fMRI technique allows researchers to determine the relative activation levels in different regions of the brain while people perform various tasks.

## Positron emission tomography

Another valuable technique for determining activity levels in the brain is the positron emission tomography (PET) scan. In the most common type of PET scan procedure, the patient is first injected with a radioactive substance similar to glucose. Communication within and between neurons requires considerable energy that must be supplied through the blood system. Glucose is the primary source of energy for neural tissue and, as a consequence, the radioactive substance injected into the patient is taken up by the most active neurons in the patient's brain. As the radioactive material decays, it emits subatomic particles known as positrons, and these positrons are measured by detectors in the PET scanner. Data from the PET scanner are analyzed by computer to produce an image of the human brain that represents the relative activity level of various regions within the brain.

PET scans and fMRI measures are quite useful because they allow researchers to investigate dynamic processes that take place in real time. By varying the stimuli and tasks given to people and then examining which regions of the brain increase (or decrease) in activity levels, we can determine which areas are involved in performing the various tasks. Let us consider how PET scans have been used to study the activity you are engaged in right now – reading.

In reading, very small differences in the physical stimulus can signal important information about the intended meaning of the letter strings. For example, "bead" and "head" differ only slightly in terms of the physical stimulus and yet these items are perceived by readers of English to mean quite different things. These differences clearly are learned, which means that there must be some way in which the nervous system has acquired the ability to differentiate small differences, including the fact that some letter strings correspond to meaningful words in a given language whereas others (e.g., xrtuzq) do not.

Peterson, Fox, Posner, Mintum, and Raichle (1988) began with the assumption that as visual stimuli, words could be represented by four different types of codes or internal representations. First, words are made up of combinations of connected lines and curves in various spatial arrangements; these codes are called *visual features*. Second, there is a subset of all possible visual features that make up the 26 letters of the alphabet used in the English language. This set of features corresponds to the *letter* codes for English. Third, there are rules within the English language that determine the permissible orders in which the 26 letters can be arranged to make pronounceable letter strings. These rules represent the *orthographic* codes for the language. Finally, there are the specific meanings of words that are understood by speakers of the language – these can be referred to as the *word meaning* codes. Given this set of four codes, how can we identify which parts of the nervous system are responsible for processing each code? If we were to present a participant with English words and measure the brain's response to these words, this response should be the response to all four codes.

Peterson and his colleagues were interested in whether different areas are responsible for, say, visual feature processing versus word meaning processing. To answer this question they presented various types of visual stimuli to their participants and monitored brain activity using a PET scan procedure. In order to separate the entire response of the nervous system to English words they used four sets of stimuli that were created such that each higher level set included all the codes of the lower set plus one additional code.

Peterson et al. conducted PET scans of a group of normal English-speaking adults as they were passively observing these four types of stimuli. Results from the PET scan showed that the nervous system responds in a very different manner to these four classes of stimuli. By combining appropriate experimental methodology with powerful brain imaging techniques Peterson et al. demonstrated that the brain responds in very discernible ways to stimuli possessing different characteristics. Subsequent research along these lines has expanded this methodology by requiring participants to actively process the visual items as they are presented.

## Concluding Comments: A Useful Conceptual Framework and a Cautionary Note

This chapter has presented some of the assumptions made by cognitive researchers, several major approaches to studying cognition, and a brief review of some specific techniques used to study cognitive processes. We have also attempted to convey a sense of the range of research techniques by describing both behavioral and brain imaging techniques. In this final section we would like to consider a useful conceptual framework for research in cognition as well as an important cautionary note.

Jenkins (1979) proposed a simple model that serves as a very useful heuristic for characterizing memory research. The model proposes that memory research can be placed within a tetrahedron in which the four vertices correspond to four major aspects of memory research. These four categories comprise participant variables (e.g., interests, knowledge), encoding tasks (e.g., instructions, activities), materials factors (e.g., pictures vs. words, organization of materials), and criterial tasks (e.g., recall, recognition). Jenkins argued that memory researchers typically focus on one or two of these vertices, for example, comparing recall versus recognition with pictures versus words. He astutely noted that most interesting memory research involves interactions among these four classes of variables.

We propose that it is useful for readers interested in cognition to keep these four classes of variables in mind as they consider cognitive research. We would, however, make the following changes to this model to make it more appropriate to cognition in general, as opposed to just memory research. First, we would change encoding tasks to any cognitive task, for example, problem solving or divided attention. Second, we would change criterial tasks to simply performance measures; this change allows the researcher to consider implicit versus explicit tasks, behavioral versus brain imaging techniques, and so forth. Finally, we would add the critical dimension of "context" to this model as a fifth category of variables. There is a host of research that indicates that performance measures vary tremendously depending upon the context within which the tasks are performed (for a review see Ceci, Rosenblum, & DeBruyn, 1999). Considering these five categories of variables will allow the reader to ask questions regarding possible future directions for research, to generalize ability of a specific pattern of results, and so forth.

The cautionary note we would raise here regarding research in cognition echoes observations made by Tulving (1989). Tulving discussed the relation between three aspects of memory – behavior, knowledge, and conscious experience – and he noted that many memory researchers tend to focus on memory behavior and use the data they obtain to construct models of recall and recognition performance (as well as perform-ance and other tasks such as priming). These models are fine scientific accounts of *memory performance* but they do not necessarily reflect that individuals remember *con-scious experience*; they have memories for previous episodes in their lives. We would argue that this concern for conscious experience needs to be extended to cognitive processes overall. Thus the cautionary note we would share with the reader is that, as you consider research on cognition, always keep in mind that cognitive process are not necessarily synonymous with conscious experience. Keeping this in mind will help tremendously as the reader continues to study the mind.

# References

Anderson, J. R. (1985). *Cognitive psychology and its implications*. New York: W.H. Freeman.

Atkinson, R. C., & Shiffrin, R. M. (1968). Human memory: A proposed system and its control processes. In K. W. Spence & J. T. Spence (eds.), *Advances in the psychology of learning and motivation: Research and theory* (vol. 2, pp. 89–95). New York: Academic Press.

Averbach, E., & Sperling, G. (1960). Short-term storage of information in vision. In C. Cherry (ed.), *Information theory* (pp. 196–211). London: Butterworth.

Baddeley, A. D., & Hitch, G. J. (1974). Working memory. In G. H. Bower (ed.), *The psychology of learning and motivation* (vol. 8, pp. 47–89). New York: Academic Press.

Balota, D. A. (1983). Automatic semantic activation and episodic memory encoding. *Journal of Verbal Learning and Verbal Behavior, 22*, 88–104.

Balota, D. A., Paul, S., & Spieler, D. (1999). Attentional control of lexical processing pathways during word recognition and reading. In S. Garrod & M. J. Pickering (eds.), *Language Process-ing* (pp. 15–57). Hove, UK: Psychology Press.

Berry, D. C., & Broadbent, D. E. (1984). On the relationship between task performance and associated verbalisable knowledge. *Quarterly Journal of Experimental Psychology, 36A*, 209–31.

Bridgman, P. W. (1945). Some general principles of operational analysis. *Psychological Review, 52*, 246–9.

Broadbent, D. E. (1958). *Perception and communication*. London: Pergamon Press.

Ceci, S. J., Rosenblum, T. B., & DeBruyn, E. (1999). Laboratory field approaches to cognition. In R. J. Sternberg (ed.), *The nature of cognition* (pp. 385–408). Cambridge, MA: MIT. Press.

Chandler, C. C. (1994). Studying related pictures can reduce accuracy, but increase confidence, in modified recognition tests. *Memory & Cognition, 22*, 145–74.

Danks, J. H., & Hill, G. O. (1981). An interactive analysis of oral reading. In A. M. Lesgold & C. A. Perfetti (eds.), *Interactive process in reading* (pp. 131–53). Hillsdale, NJ: Erlbaum.

Eich, E. (1984). Memory for unattended events: Remembering with and without awareness. *Memory & Cognition, 12*, 105–11.

Finke, R. A., & Shepherd, R. N. (1986). Visual functions of mental imagery. In K. K. Boff, L. Kaufman, & J. P. Thomas (eds.), *Handbook of perception and human performance* (Vol. 2, pp. 1–55). New York: Wiley-InterScience.

Garner, W. R., Hake, H. W., & Eriksen, C. W. (1956). Operationism and the concept of perception. *Psychological Review, 63*, 149–59.

Howard, D. V., & Howard, J. H. (1992). Adult age differences in the rate of learning serial patterns: Evidence from direct and indirect tests. *Psychology & Aging, 7*, 232–41.

Jacoby, L. L. (1983). Remembering the data: Analyzing interactive processes in reading. *Journal of Verbal Learning and Verbal Behavior, 22*, 485–508.

Jenkins, J. J. (1979). Four points to remember: A tetrahedral model of memory experiments. In L. S. Cermak and F. I. M. Craik (eds.), *Levels of processing in human memory* (pp. 429–46). Hillsdale, NJ: Lawrence Erlbaum Associates.

Johnson, M. K., Foley, M. A., Suengas, A. G., & Raye, C. L. (1988). Phenomenal characteristics of memories for perceived and imagined autobiographical events. *Journal of Experimental Psychology: General, 117*, 371–6.

Johnson, M. K., Hashtroudi, S., & Lindsay, D. S. (1993). Source monitoring. *Psychological Bulletin, 114*, 3–28.

Kahneman, D. (1973). *Attention and effort.* Englewood Cliffs, NJ: Prentice Hall.

Kolers, P. (1976). Reading a year later. *Journal of Experimental Psychology: Human Learning and Memory, 2*, 554–65.

Kozhevnikov, M., & Hegarty, M. (2001). Impetus beliefs as default heuristic: Dissociation between explicit and implicit knowledge about motion. *Psychonomic Bulletin and Review, 8*, 439–53.

Kutas, M., & Van Petten, C. (1988). Event-related brain potential studies of language. In P. Ackles, J. R. Jennings, & M. Coles (eds.), *Advances in psychophysiology* (pp. 139–87). Greenwich, CT: JAI Press.

Lachman, R., Lachman, J. L., & Butterfield, E. C. (1979). *Cognitive psychology and information processing: An introduction.* Hillsdale, NJ: Lawrence Erlbaum Associates.

MacCorquodale, K., & Meehl, P. E. (1948). On a distinction between hypothetical constructs and intervening variables. *Psychological Review, 55*, 95–107.

MacKay, D. G. (1973). Aspects of a theory of comprehension, memory and attention. *Quarterly Journal of Experimental Psychology, 25*, 22–40.

Madigan, S., & O'Hara, R. (1992). Initial recall, reminiscence, and hypermnesia. *Journal of Experimental Psychology: Learning, Memory and Cognition, 18*, 421–5.

Marcel, A. J. (1983a). Conscious and unconscious perception: Experiments on visual masking and word recognition. *Cognitive Psychology, 15*, 197–237.

Marcel, A. J. (1983b). Conscious and unconscious perception: An approach to the relation between phenomenal and perceptual processes. *Cognitive Psychology, 15*, 238–300.

Mather, M., Henkel, L. A., & Johnson, M. K. (1997). Evaluating characteristics of false memories: Remember/know judgments and memory characteristics questionnaire compared. *Memory & Cognition, 25*, 826–37.

McCloskey, M. (1983). Intuitive physics. *Scientific American, 24*, 122–30.

McConkie, G. W., & Rayner, K. (1975). The span of an effective stimulus during a fixation in reading. *Perception & Psychophysics, 17*, 578–86.

Mulligan, N. W. (1998). The role of attention during encoding in implicit and explicit memory. *Journal of Experimental Psychology: Learning, Memory & Cognition, 24*, 27–47.

Neely, J. H. (1977). Semantic priming and retrieval from lexical memory: Roles of inhibitionless spreading activation and limited-capacity attention. *Journal of Experimental Psychology: General, 106*, 226–54.

Neisser, U., & Harsch, N. (1992). Phantom flashbulbs: False recollections of hearing the news about Challenger. In E. Winograd and U. Neisser (eds.), *Affect and accuracy in recall: Studies and "flash bulb" memories* ( pp. 9–31). New York: Cambridge University Press.

Nelson, T. O., & Leonesio, R. J. (1988). Allocation of self-paced study time and the "labor-in-vain effect." *Journal of Experimental Psychology: Learning, Memory & Cognition, 14*, 676–86.

Nelson, T. O., & Narens, L. (1990). Metamemory: A theoretical framework and new findings. In G. H. Bower (ed.), *The psychology of learning and motivation* (vol. 26, pp. 125–41). New York: Academic Press.

Payne, D. G., Elie, C. J., Blackwell, J. M., & Neuschatz, J. S. (1996). Memory illusions: Recalling, recognizing, and recollecting events that never occurred. *Journal of Memory and Language, 35*, 261–85.

Payne, D. G., Peters, L. J., Birkmire, D. P., Bonto, M. A., Anastasi, J. S., & Wenger, M. J. (1994). The effects of speech intelligibility level on concurrent visual task performance. *Human Factors, 36*, 441–75.

Payne, D. G., & Wenger, M. J. (1994). Initial recall, reminiscence, and hypermnesia: Comment on Madigan and O'Hara (1992). *Journal of Experimental Psychology: Learning, Memory and Cognition, 20*, 229–35.

Payne, D. G., & Wenger, M. J. (1998). *Cognitive psychology.* Boston, MA: Houghton Mifflin.

Peterson, S. E., Fox, P. T., Posner, M. I., Mintum, M., & Raichle, M. E. (1988). Positron emission tomographic studies of the cortical anatomy of single-word processing *Nature, 331*, 585–9.

Pollatsek, A., Bolozky, S., Well, A. D., & Rayner, K. (1981). Asymmetries in the perceptual span for Israeli readers. *Brain and Language, 14*, 174–80.

Rajaram, S. (1993). Remembering and knowing: Two means of access to the personal past. *Memory & Cognition, 21*, 89–102.

Rayner, K., & Bertera, J. H. (1979). Reading without a fovea. *Science, 206*, 468–9.

Rayner, K., & Pollatsek, A. (1989). *The psychology of reading.* Englewood Cliffs, NJ: Prentice-Hall.

Reber, A. S. (1989). Implicit learning and tacit knowledge. *Journal of Experimental Psychology: General, 118*, 219–35.

Roediger, H. L. (1990). Implicit memory: Retention without remembering. *American Psychologist, 45*, 1043–56.

Roediger, H. L., & McDermott, K. B. (1995). Creating false memories: Remembering words not presented in lists. *Journal of Experimental Psychology: Learning, Memory, & Cognition, 21*, 803–14.

Seger, C. A. (1994). Implicit learning. *Psychological Bulletin, 115*, 163–96.

Shepherd, R. N., & Metzler, J. (1971). Mental rotation of three-dimensional objects. *Science, 191*, 701–3.

Shimamura, A. P. (1986). Priming effects in amnesia: Evidence for a dissociable memory function. *Quarterly Journal of Experimental Psychology, 38A*, 619–44.

Sperling, G. (1960). The information that is available in brief visual presentations. *Psychological Monographs, 74* (Whole no. #498), 1–29.

Sporer, S. L. (1992). Post-dicting eyewitness accuracy: Confidence, decision-times and person descriptions of choosers and non-choosers. *European Journal of Social Psychology, 22*, 157–80.

Sporer, S. L., Penrod, S., Read, D., & Cutler, B. (1995). Choosing, confidence, and accuracy: A meta-analysis of the confidence-accuracy relation in eyewitness identification studies. *Psychological Bulletin, 118*, 315–27.

Strayer, D. L., & Johnston, W. A. (2001). Driven to distraction: Dual-task studies of simulated driving and conversing on a cellular telephone. *Psychological Science, 12*, 462–6.

Tipper, S. P., & Driver, J. (1988). Negative priming between pictures and words: Evidence for semantic analysis of ignored stimuli. *Memory & Cognition, 16*, 64–70.

Tulving, E. (1962). Subjective organization in free recall of "unrelated" words. *Psychological Review, 69*, 344–54.

Tulving, E. (1985). Memory and consciousness. *Canadian Psychology, 26*, 1–12.

Tulving, E. (1989). Memory: Performance, knowledge, and experience. *European Journal of Cognitive Psychology, 1*, 3–26.

Tulving, E., & Arbuckle, T. Y. (1963). Sources of intratrial interference in immediate recall of paired associates. *Journal of Verbal Learning and Verbal Behavior, 1*, 321–34.

Underwood, G. (1966). Individual and group predictions of item difficulty for free learning. *Journal of Experimental Psychology, 71*, 673–9.

Warrington, E., & Weiskrantz, L. (1970). Amnesia: Consolidation or retrieval? *Nature, 228*, 628–30.

Whipple, G. M. (1914). *Manual of mental and physical tests. Part I: Simpler processes*. Baltimore, MD: Warwick & York.

Wickens, C. D. (1980). The structure of attentional resources. In R. Nickerson (ed.), *Attention and performance, VIII* (pp. 239–57). Hillsdale, NJ: Erlbaum.

# CHAPTER EIGHTEEN

## Motivation

### Melissa Burns

*Tessa lifted a final forkful of pasta to her mouth. She really wasn't hungry any longer but the sauce was so delectable that she simply couldn't resist eating it all. She let the morsel linger in her mouth for a few seconds, savoring every nuance of the flavor, then swallowed. Almost simultaneous with setting her fork on the plate, the perky waitress appeared at the side of the table. "Could I interest anyone in dessert or coffee?" asked the waitress. "Absolutely!" said Brian, Tessa's boss. "You have to try one of the desserts. This restaurant is famous for its desserts." The thought of eating more food was not at all appealing to Tessa. However, she had been trying to make a good impression on Brian all week. Annual evaluations were coming up soon and Tessa knew that Brian would be making a decision about promotions. She tried to reason with herself, "A piece of cake is not going to make me regional manager." Plus, she had been trying to lose a few pounds before her 10-year high school reunion next month so was planning to skip dessert. But she didn't want to risk offending Brian. "Sounds great!" she said eagerly as she grabbed the dessert menu off the table. All of the desserts sounded delicious. Just the thought of the triple chocolate fudge cake topped with caramel was enough to make her mouth water. But instead, she selected the dessert that she thought had the fewest calories, a lemon tart. A few minutes later, with her stomach still full from the large pasta dinner, she smiled broadly at Brian then lifted the fork to her mouth once again.*

With just a superficial glance at behavior, one may conclude that identifying motives is just common sense. You stop eating when you are satiated. You socialize because you are lonely. You start eating when you are hungry. However, a comprehensive look at behavior reveals that motivation is not that simple. Why do you eat when you are not hungry? Why do you seek to please some individuals but not others? Why do you deny your body food when you are hungry? To answer questions like these, a much deeper look into the human psyche is necessary, and motivation is revealed to spring not from a single source but rather from an elaborate tapestry woven with threads of biology, experience, and cognition.

Like many psychological constructs, it is impossible to measure motivation directly; rather one has to take an indirect approach to assess the source, the type, even the degree of motivation. Many great minds have risen to this challenge, and all utilized what was believed to be the best source of knowledge at the time. As the preferred means of acquiring knowledge changed across the centuries, so have the methods of investigating motivation. Each new method brought a new perspective, often generating new theories that conflicted with and criticized older ideas. In some cases, conflicts and criticisms have been so severe that the older theory was abandoned. However, a few concepts survived such slings and arrows, often morphing shapes but maintaining the basic idea. The persistence of these motivational concepts for hundreds or even thousands of years makes them worth discussing, not only for what they have told us about motivation, but also for experimental research. This chapter will present many different methods that have been used to investigate motivation, and discuss how these methods led to the development, and in some cases abandonment, of theories of motivation.

## Early Philosophers

### Methods of the ancient philosophers

The concept of motivation has its roots in the philosophical work of the ancient Greeks. More than 2,400 years ago, scholars formulated a theory about forces that guide behavior. Armed only with logic, common sense, and a bit of intuition, the philosophers of this era based their theory on nonsystematic observations of animals (including humans), their own personal experiences, and the experiences of others around them.

### Hedonism

Democritus (460–370 BC) was one of the earliest philosophers to propose a theory of motivation. Based on his observations of human behavior and on his own experiences, Democritus concluded that motivation stemmed from a simple desire to pursue objects and activities that helped him to attain pleasure and to avoid pain. This explanation, known as *hedonism*, is the oldest and most persistent theme in the study of motivation. Even though many theorists after Democritus (e.g., Epicurus, Thomas Hobbes, Sigmund Freud) based motivation on this fundamental desire for attaining pleasure and avoiding pain, it is not absolutely clear what constitutes pleasure and what constitutes pain for any given person. The sensations of "pain" and "pleasure" are very subjective events. What is pleasurable for one individual may be painful for another. For instance, some people are motivated to run 26.2 miles for the satisfaction of completing a marathon whereas other people find running very aversive and avoid it whenever possible. Democritus made pain/pleasure distinctions on a case-by-case basis, depending on a person's behavior. Something was pleasurable if an individual strived for it, and something was painful if an individual avoided it. Implicit in his definition is the idea that the source of motivation lies in the external environment in the form of objects or situations that are either sought or avoided.

Although most philosophers of the time agreed with the general principles of hedonism, there was debate over whether all behavior was essentially selfish or if some behavior was motivated by a desire to influence another individual's pleasure or pain. Thrasymachus (late fifth century BC) proposed that people were motivated solely by self-interest, acting only in ways that would benefit themselves directly or indirectly. Any appearance of altruism or sympathy is based solely on calculated, long-term self-interest. Socrates (470–399 BC) disagreed with this notion of selfishness. Socrates noticed that people tend to agree on how to behave in a particular situation, that is, what behavior is "right." Similarly, people are also able to identify behavior that is "wrong." This concurrence on appropriate behavior is not consistent with Thrasymachus' idea of self-interest. If humans were motivated to behave in ways that only benefited themselves, then there would be no agreement about what acts are right and what acts are wrong because one person's self-interest is not always the same as another individual's self-interest. Rather, people seem to have a common standard for rightness and wrongness and are innately motivated to do what is right. Thus, unlike the other ancient philosophers, Socrates felt that motivation was rooted in judgment about which behaviors were appropriate and would lead to pleasure. In other words, motivation for behavior was not found in the external environment, but rather in the internal environment – the conscience.

Although the ancient philosophers generally agreed that behavior was motivated by hedonistic tendencies, they initiated a controversy debated for many centuries: is behavior motivated by external stimuli as proposed by Democritus or is it guided by an internal source as proposed by Socrates?

## Methods in the Middle Ages

Like the philosophers before them, philosophers in the Middle Ages had to rely on nonscientific methods of acquiring knowledge. During this time, authority, power, and information were under the primary control of the church. Philosophers of the Middle Ages preferred a more refined cognitive approach to explain motivation to the ancient philosophers' behavioral approach. The church taught that humans were created in the image of God. As Godlike creatures, humans were thought to have more sophisticated control over their behavior than other animals.

## Volition

By the third century AD, scholars began turning away from ancient philosophies and religions. These classics were replaced with a single authority: the Christian church. During the fifth century, the influential teachings of Saint Augustine (354–430) claimed that humans, unlike other creatures, have free and conscious control over all thoughts and behavior. Thus motivation was exclusively internal. Good Christians were expected to exercise their volition, or free will, to deprive the body of that which it desires in order that their eternal souls could be saved. Surrendering to physical temptations, that is, behaving as a hedonist, would condemn the soul to eternal damnation. Thus, present behavior was motivated by a long-term goal – spending eternity in heaven and avoiding hell – which is an intangible concept that resides inside one's mind rather than taking a physical form in the external environment. This religion-based doctrine of deprivation and volition became the prevailing view of human motivation throughout the Middle Ages. The idea of enduring immediate pain/discomfort in the short term in anticipation of greater reward has been echoed throughout history.

The theory of volition represented the intersection between the physical and nonphysical world. It proposed that an intangible force moved matter. This is another point of contention in the history of motivation theory. Should behavior be attributed to physical or cognitive sources?

## Weaknesses of early philosophers

The ancient philosophers provided a solid foundation for the study of motivation. Their ideas were remarkably accurate despite the methods they used. However, relying solely on nonscientific methods of investigation leads to inherently weak theories. Democritus, Thrasymachus, and Socrates all relied, at least in part, on common sense to make judgments about the source of behavior. Commonsense explanations may provide what feels like an accurate account for a given situation but often such explanations do not generalize well to other situations. For instance, Democritus' and Thrasymachus' hedonism cannot account for altruistic behavior that is commonly seen in humans and other animals. Socrates' hedonism fails to explain why people sometimes behave selfishly.

The ancient philosophers relied heavily on logic to make inferences about the workings of the world. Logic is an indispensable tool for the intellect. However, the ancient philosophers fell into the logical trap of circular reasoning. Democritus recognized pain and pleasure as subjective concepts that vary from person to person. To increase generalizability of his theory, it was necessary to objectify these concepts so that they would apply to everyone in the same way. His solution was clever on the surface but problematic when used in a logical argument. He defined motivation (approach pleasure or avoid pain) based on the behavior of the individual. But then he explained the behavior as being a product of motivation.

Although authority can be helpful in gathering knowledge, it is not a faultless source. For instance, confidence in authority is tied to subjective biases toward certain types of personalities. Speakers who seem more prestigious, respectable, and trustworthy are more likely to be believed than speakers who do not possess such qualities. Thus decisions to believe information are based on the quality of the speaker rather than the quality of the information. Any source of knowledge that does not incorporate a means of sorting accurate from inaccurate information is likely to produce incorrect information at some point.

Sir Francis Bacon (1561–1626) provided us with an excellent example of the extent to which this reliance on authority extended. In 1432, a group of monks engaged in an intellectual debate over the number of teeth in a horse's mouth. All the ancient books and chronicles were brought out and arguments were made with hearty enthusiasm. After 13 days without reaching a consensus, a young friar asked his learned superiors for permission to join the debate. When given the opportunity to speak, the young friar suggested that the best way to answer this hotly debated question was to look into the open mouth of a horse. Uproar ensued. The other monks were appalled that the neophyte would suggest such an unholy and unheard-of way of finding truth, contrary to all the teachings of the fathers. Their dignity being hurt, they attacked the young friar with their fists and accusations of satanic possession. The dispute was finally resolved when one man declared the problem to be an everlasting mystery because of the lack of historical and theological evidence (Mees, 1934).

## The Scientific Revolution

### Methods of the first scientists

During the early days of scientific experimentation, the scientific method was used primarily as a means of medical exploration. As a result, researchers made great strides in understanding physiology. The details of the anatomy and functioning of the nervous system and its role in behavior were revealed, for example, Descartes defined the reflex and Galvani discovered that a frog's leg would twitch when the muscle was connected to a primitive battery (Boring, 1950). Although the scientific method was not yet used outside of medicine and physiology, scholars soon began looking at the world with a critical and objective eye. This new perspective brought some old ideas about motivation back into favor and generated many new ideas as well.

### The behavioral approach

*Hedonism* The scientific revolution brought a movement toward *empiricism*, the belief that experience is the basis of knowledge. John Locke used a simple metaphor to capture the philosophy: *tabula rasa* – we are born with minds blank like a sheet of paper upon which our experiences will be written. The empiricists of the day accounted for motivation in the same way they accounted for knowledge: both motivation and knowledge result from experience. The ultimate basis for why we do some things and not others lies in our experiences and the consequences of our behavior. Only by doing something first can we ascertain what effect the behavior will have. Then, based on these experiences, we behave in ways that brought pleasure in the past, and we avoid behaving in ways that brought us pain. In this way, the hedonic approach to human motivation came back into the mainstream after its long exile.

There was a problem, however, with the theory of hedonism that had not been addressed by ancient philosophers: if we are motivated to approach or avoid external stimuli, how can behavior have the foresightful, forward-looking character that it has?

How can we take account of future events and not just respond to present ones? This problem was addressed by Thomas Hobbes in the seventeenth century.

*Incentive motivation* In his writings on motivation, Thomas Hobbes (1588–1679) addressed an inherent weakness of hedonic theory. Ancient philosophers were aware that postponing immediate reward or suffering immediate discomfort could be beneficial in the long run. However, they failed to explain how an individual could avoid a pleasurable stimulus or approach an aversive stimulus. Hobbes explained this behavior in terms of anticipation of future events, or *incentive*. The incentive theory differs from hedonism in that it places the source of motivation inside the brain rather than in the external environment. Furthermore, Hobbes provided a mechanism for antihedonistic behavior using the concept of *materialism*.

Materialism is the notion that all matter, including the bodies of humans and animals, moves in accordance with the principles of mechanics. If the mind is responsible for activating behavior, the mind must consist of physical matter. Hobbes thought that information entering the nervous system causes movement of particles in the brain. When two units of information enter the brain at the same time, the moving particles become linked with one another such that activating one will activate the other. For instance, consider hearing a new acquaintance say your name while you are looking at him. When the image of the man's face and the sound of his voice enter the brain together, the particles become linked to one another. Then, as one of the ideas occurs, the other is likely to occur as well (e.g., when you hear his voice on the telephone, you are likely to engender images of his face as well). The concept of linking sensations together is known as *association* and is the foundation of learning. By forming associations, an individual could anticipate future pains or pleasures that were associated with stimuli rather than reacting solely to the immediate consequences. This association allows the individual to behave in a way that would maximize the pleasurable events and minimize the painful outcomes, even when that requires enduring discomfort in the present. Thus approach to an aversive stimulus (e.g., physical exertion and smelly chemicals) could ultimately lead to a great deal of pleasure (e.g., a clean house). Similarly, avoidance of a pleasurable stimulus (e.g., cheesecake) could minimize pain (e.g., obesity-induced diabetes) in the long run.

## The biological approach: dualism

Like the early hedonists, René Descartes (1596–1650) believed that animals, including humans, were machines ruled by the laws of mechanics. Behavior, therefore, could be analyzed like the workings of a machine. Using this approach, Descartes developed the concept of the reflex as a basic unit of behavior. Although the mechanics were wrong, the idea was correct – a reflex is an involuntary behavior elicited by a stimulus. Descartes concluded the behavior of all "lower" animals could be attributed to the biologically based reflex. Due to his religious beliefs, however, he was not willing to place humans on the same plane as other animals. Humans surely exhibited a few reflexes like the lower animals (e.g., sucking in infants, withdrawing the hand from fire, the patellar knee jerk), but Descartes maintained that most of human behavior was controlled by free will. Not all behaviors have a physical observable cause. Rather some behaviors seem to originate from internal sources. Descartes referred to these actions as voluntary behaviors and claimed that only humans are capable of such behavior. Although some human behavior is reflexive, most is willed by the mind, which is not a part of the vast world-machine of matter and force. Because the mind is outside of the world of force, the laws of mechanics do not bind it; it stands outside the chain of mechanical causality. This approach is known as *dualism*.

## The cognitive approach: volition

Immanuel Kant (1724–1804) argued for the Socratic view of motivation. He believed that we know, without being taught, that there are right and wrong actions, and we know that we ought to do one and avoid the other. Therefore, contrary to the tabula rasa perspective, Kant believed that some aspects of the human mind are innate and those that are innate are by far the most important. Kant based his argument on the fact that there are concepts in our minds that sensory input cannot account for. For instance, the notion of causality – the idea that one event causes the other is simply not a part of the sensory input. We must bring certain concepts by which we interpret and organize the inputs from the sensory world. Kant argued that each person possesses a central self that is capable of understanding and acting on moral imperatives – that is, voluntarily making behavioral choices.

## Weaknesses of the first scientists

During the early days of the scientific revolution, the explanations for behavior became much more detailed. The theories of the ancient philosophers and the Middle Ages were expanded in order to explain a greater range of behaviors. However, these explanations were still primarily based on logic and common sense. Although the intellectuals of the time were considering the issue of motivation with a much more objective and critical eye, they were still not fully utilizing the scientific method to determine if their ideas had some degree of accuracy. It was not until the nineteenth century that we saw behavior investigated with the full-blown scientific process.

# The Birth of Psychology

## Methods of the first psychologists

During the nineteenth century, church authority was still influencing the scientific community but was slowly losing its status as a source of truth. The scientific method, in contrast, was gaining popularity. New findings about anatomy and physiology inspired an experimental approach to the investigation of behavior. This new approach to the study of behavior took a new name, *psychology*.

Using the precepts of science, early psychologists attempted to answer questions such as: how does motivation affect behavior? Although "behavior" is a concept that is overt, easy to define, and measurable, "motivation" is none of these things. Motivation, per se, cannot be measured directly. But it can be expressed indirectly in physiology (e.g., cardiovascular activity, ocular activity, electrodermal activity, and plasma activity), in behavior (e.g., effort, latency, choice, probability of response, facial expression, and bodily gestures), and verbally (e.g., self-report and case study) (Reeve, 2001). By focusing on specific aspects of these categories, researchers have drawn some insightful conclusions about motivation.

## The biological approach

*Instinct theory* With his innovative theory of evolution, Charles Darwin (1809–82) established physical relatedness between all animals, including humans. Similarly, the American philosopher and psychologist William James (1842–1910) sought to bridge the psychological gap between humans and other animals. Prior to this time, behavior of nonhuman animals was attributed to noncognitive responses, known as *instincts*. Humans, who were capable of rational thought and free will, had no need for instincts. James, however, disagreed. His idea of an instinct was virtually synonymous with a reflex: an impulse that is provoked by a specific stimulus. Much like Kant before him, James believed that humans intuitively know how to respond in different situations, and attributed this intuition to instinct. He recognized that humans react to certain stimuli (e.g., an infant's distress) with feelings of sympathy and actions of help or rescue without regard for their own gain, and without having been taught to do so. James proposed that the nervous system was sensitive to specific stimuli and reacted to such stimuli with a particular behavior. The form of the instinct behavior could then be shaped by experience with the stimulus in order to maximize the chance of a beneficial outcome. That is, instinct provided the clay from which learned behaviors were molded. James proposed a list of human instincts that included sucking, smiling, walking, anger, resentment, fear of strange men, fear of noise, fear of dark things, curiosity, secretiveness, shame, and parental love. (For review, see James, 1890.)

William McDougall (1871–1938) formed a theory for instinctive behavior based on his observations of several different species confronted with different types of challenges. For instance, mice and rats were placed in a water maze that had several different escape routes: runways located at the surface of the water or subterranean passageways accessible only by diving. Sometimes use of a particular passageway resulted in electrical shock to the feet so the subject had to discriminate between the safe and dangerous options (e.g., McDougall, 1927; McDougall, 1938). McDougall also used puzzle boxes, requiring mice (McDougall & McDougall, 1927) and raccoons (McDougall & McDougall, 1931) to open several latches to access food inside the box. The results of these and other experiments led McDougall to conclude that much of animal behavior is of an unlearned, instinctual nature.

Unlike James's simple instinct, McDougall's instinct could be described in terms of cognitive (i.e., knowing which object can satisfy the instinct), affective (a feeling toward the object), and conative (a sense of purpose to move toward or away from the object) aspects. It was the notion of purpose that made McDougall's theory particularly noteworthy.

McDougall felt that all behavior was guided by "prevision" of future events, a sense of purpose to achieve a particular goal. He did not limit "prevision" to humans but thought all animals were capable of anticipating future events, then acting in such a way to make them happen or not happen. Like Hobbes, McDougall argued that behavior is motivated by the anticipated outcome. Attributing "prevision" to nonhuman animals was a point of weakness for McDougall's theory because it was an anthropomorphic interpretation that could not be tested or verified scientifically. However, the idea of using future events as an incentive for behavior persisted long after McDougall's instinct theory had been dismissed. (For review, see McDougall, 1970.)

Instinct theory did not stay in favor because of several practical problems. First, several theorists each derived unique lists of instincts. Some lists were short whereas other lists were long enough to classify every possible behavior as a discrete instinct. Second, instinct theorists were guilty of the same mistake made by the hedonists – circular logic. An instinct was defined as an elicited behavior. The behavior, in turn, was explained as being an instinct. "Instinct" is merely a descriptive term that labels a behavior but cannot explain the causes of it. It was generally agreed that focusing on instincts as motivation for behavior was futile.

*Biological drive theory* As instinct theory was losing favor in the scientific community, a new theory was making itself known. Drive theory was a logical replacement for instinct theory as an explanation of motivation because it shared the same strengths but not the same weaknesses as instinct theory. Both theories asserted that motivation originated from the individual's biology. However, a drive had a distinct physiological etiology whereas an instinct did not.

Drive theory was based on the concept of homeostasis developed by Walter B. Cannon (1871–1945). Homeostasis is the idea that there are certain ideal physiological levels within the body. For instance, the ideal body temperature for humans is around 98.6° F and for dogs around 103° F. Any deviation away from this ideal temperature will result in discomfort and a need, or drive, to eliminate the discrepancy. Drive was understood as an energizing or activating force that initiates and intensifies activity. Behavior engendered by the drive is geared toward returning to homeostasis. Responses that are successful in achieving this goal will be repeated in similar situations in the future whereas behaviors that do not reduce drive will not be repeated. Although the general precept of the various drive theories was the same, they differed in terms of the details.

Cannon also developed the "local theory" of motivation. In a unique experiment, a colleague of Cannon's, A. L. Washburn, swallowed a balloon that was attached to a pneumatic recording system. With such an arrangement, a marking pen could record movements of the stomach on a piece of moving paper. Washburn's subjective sensation of hunger coincided with his stomach contractions. Based on this data, Cannon and Washburn assumed that stomach contractions were the basis of hunger signals and, as a result, of eating (Cannon & Washburn, 1912). According to the local theory of motivation, signals that control motives such as hunger and thirst are produced in the peripheral organs of the body.

Clark Hull (1884–1952) investigated motivation by training food- and/or water-deprived rats to press a bar to receive a pellet of food or access to water. Hull varied the type and degree of deprivation and measured how the change in the drive (and presumably motivation) was reflected in the subject's behavior, such as the effort and persistence with which the rat pressed the bar.

Hull developed the concept of a single generalized drive state that was the impetus for all behavior. When a physiological level deviated from the ideal level, a need was created, activating a generalized drive state. Activation of the drive energizes the animal and it becomes very active, performing random behaviors. The animal will serendipitously discover that one of these behaviors recovers the homeostatic level, thereby reducing the drive. Reduction of the drive is reinforcing for the animal, thus increasing the probability that the behavior will occur again when the drive returns. (For a review, see Amsel & Rashotte, 1984.)

Hull's drive theory soon fell out of favor with the scientific community due to several shortcomings. First, evidence indicated that a single source of drive that motivated all behavior was very unlikely. Rats that are deprived of both food and water will not press a bar that delivers food more often than rats that are only deprived of food. Second, Hull's theory failed to explain why rats would work for a reinforcer that did not reduce any biological need. Sheffield and Roby (1950) found that rats that were reinforced with saccharine (a sweet-tasting chemical containing no nutrients and no calories) ran faster down a runway than rats not reinforced with saccharine even though no need, thus drive, was being reduced with the reinforcement. Similarly, monkeys would press a lever in order to gain visual access to other monkeys (Butler, 1957) or to illuminate a dark chamber (Fox, 1962). Thus performance seemed to be dependent on preference for the reinforcer rather than the extent to which it satisfied a physical need. These problems led theorists to postulate motivational drives that included psychological needs in addition to biological needs.

Sigmund Freud (1856–1939) relied on case studies of individual patients to investigate motivation. He began his famous career by hypnotizing patients during clinical sessions, but soon came to believe that hypnosis was not necessary to gain access to the underpinnings of the human psyche. Most of Freud's data were collected using a method called *free association* in which the patients conveyed their free-flowing thoughts while Freud listened. With this method, Freud identified how thoughts and memories were linked in the patient's mind, and then inferred the patient's motives.

Freud concluded that motivation was seated in the biological drive to secure pleasure and avoid discomfort (i.e., hedonism). He referred to this as the *pleasure principle*. This goal is achieved through a system of physical and psychological drives that result from physical stimulation of the body (e.g., hunger pains, sleepiness, sexual arousal) and the mental representation of such stimulation. Freud proposed two distinct categories of drives: self-preservative and sexual. The self-preservative drive was based on homeostatic mechanisms. The sexual drive is more complex than biological drives. Sexual stimulation can emanate from many different sources. Originally each source is independent, but eventually the sources come to work in concert with each other. The physical stimulation and associated mental stimulation result in an uncomfortable tension, which the individual attempts to reduce. Unlike self-preservative drives, however, the object used to reduce the tension is variable. Freud considered the sexual drive to be much more important to mental functioning than self-preservative drives because sexual drives could become suppressed, leading to mental psychoses and neuroses. (For a review, see Freud, 1949.)

Freud's theory could explain virtually any behavior after the fact (post hoc explanations) but is virtually useless in making predictions about behaviors before they occur (a priori predictions). Furthermore, psychoanalytical theory failed to generate many testable hypotheses. Thus, Freud's theory cannot be subjected to the scientific process of testing under controlled conditions.

## The behavioral approach

Edward Thorndike's (1874–1949) most influential work was conducted with cats. He would place a hungry cat in a puzzle box. A plate of food was located just outside the puzzle box. The cat had to push a lever and/or pull a loop in order to escape from the puzzle box and gain access to the food. As a cat's experience with the puzzle box increased, it was able to escape from the box faster and faster. Thorndike measured motivation in terms of the probability that an appropriate response would occur and the latency to that response would decrease.

Thorndike investigated motivation from a new perspective. He de-emphasized all variables that could not be directly observed or measured (e.g., mental representations, instincts, and purpose). Thorndike focused instead on the way behavior changes as a function of consequences. Based on his research with puzzle boxes and hungry cats, Thorndike formulated his law of effect. The law of effect is a theory of learning, but also one of motivation. It states that responses that are followed by satisfaction to the animal will be more likely to recur, whereas responses that are followed by annoyance will be less likely to recur (Thorndike, 1911). Thorndike was careful in his choice of words to describe the potential outcome of events. For instance, "pleasant" and "unpleasant" were not selected because it is not possible to measure pleasantness directly for a species that cannot talk. He also avoided "favorable" and "unfavorable" as descriptions of potential outcomes because not all satisfying events are favorable and vice versa. Overeating and intoxication can be satisfying but not necessarily favorable for one's health and survival. Although based on hedonistic principles, Thorndike's law of effect favors an objective approach to motivation – some stimuli increase behavior and other stimuli decrease behavior based on past experience – over the more subjective hedonist principle of simple pursuit of pleasure and avoidance of pain. (For a review, see Thorndike, 1913.)

Although Thorndike's theory of motivation is strong in many ways, an inherent weakness of the theory is its inability to explain why an individual would approach an aversive stimulus or avoid a pleasant stimulus. That is to say, Thorndike's theory of motivation does not allow for expectancies of outcomes or incentive affects. Edward Tolman, however, was concerned with this issue.

## The cognitive approach

*Purposive behavior* Edward Tolman's (1886–1959) theory of motivation was primarily based on experiments in which rats ran through a maze in order to receive a food reward. Some mazes were rather simple, such as the shape of a cross, while others were complex patterns. The experimenters manipulated variables such as the degree of food deprivation and the amount or type of food reward, and then measured the time it took the rat to run from the start box to the food box (e.g., Tolman, Ritchie, & Kalish, 1946).

Based on his own findings and the work of several other researchers (e.g., Simmons, 1924; Tinklepaugh, 1928), Tolman concluded that drive alone was insufficient to fully explain motivation. Often, behaviors occur and persist, that is, habits develop, in the absence of a biologically important consequence. Tolman confirmed this with a series of experiments that demonstrated what he called *latent learning*. In a typical latent learning experiment, one group of rats always received a food reward at the end of the maze. These rats eventually learned to find the end of the maze quickly. Another group never received a reward for completion of the maze. The rats in this group were typically quite slow in reaching the finish box. A final group was not rewarded for reaching the finish box on the first 10 trials but was rewarded on the last 10 trials. These rats were very slow to finish each trial on the first 10 trials but once rewards were instated, they learned to find the goal box at a rate that was much faster than the group of rats that received reinforcement from the beginning of the experiment. These results indicated that it is possible for animals to learn about a situation without reinforcement and without overtly expressing what they have learned. Thus learning is not just a function of the consequences of behavior. Rather, learned behaviors can develop without any satisfying or annoying outcomes. However, the behavior is typically not expressed unless there is reinforcement or incentive involved.

Incentives contribute to behavior in the way of value and expectation. Incentives control behavior when experienced enough times that a cognitive expectation builds up. A behavior, then, is the product of the expectation that a particular reward will follow the behavior. The effects of the reward on the behavior depend on the value of the particular incentive for the organism. The value of a reward depends on the individual's psychological or physiological state. Goals that have high value, such as a large amount of food or a highly preferred food, will engender more motivation and thus more vigorous behavior leading to the reward. Low value rewards will elicit comparatively less vigorous behavior. Thus motivation is due to incentive and expectation, which direct behavior toward a certain goal, rather than the strengthening of stimulus–response connections. (For a review, see Tolman, 1932.)

The primary complaints about Tolman's theory of motivation came from behavioral theorists who opposed the cognitive aspects of the theory. They argued that there was no clear description of how cognition would lead to action. Other theorists, however, embraced the idea of a cognitive source of motivation.

Kurt Lewin (1890–1947) studied the behavior of children and adults by making detailed observation of subjects' responses to a particular situation. In one experiment, subjects were asked to complete a task such as grabbing a flower without moving their feet from a certain location marked on the floor, which, unbeknown to the subject, was impossible. The experiment, which often lasted several hours, or resumed two or three days in succession, was designed to induce anger (Lewin & Dembo, 1931). In another experiment, it was noted whether subjects would resume working on a task that had been interrupted (Lewin, 1928). These and other experiments allowed Lewin to formulate the concept of *psychological force*, which bridges external and internal sources of motivation. According to the theory, unfulfilled physiological or psychological needs create tension in an individual. The presence of the tension instills valence on relevant stimuli in the environment. Objects or activities that will reduce the tension by reducing the need will have a positive valence that attracts the individual. If, however, an object or activity increases tension, it has a negative valence and will be avoided. Also, incentives that are more appealing (e.g., a piece of chocolate cake versus a carrot) will create a stronger psychological force, and incentives that arrive sooner and are closer are more desired than more distant incentives. (For a review, see Lewin, 1938.)

Eric Klinger (b.1933) used physiological measures as well as behavior to investigate cognitive aspects of motivation. He operationally defined a change in motivation as a change in electrodermal activity of his human subjects. One way Klinger tested his theory of motivation was by testing subjects on a dichotic listening task in which one ear heard a narrative relevant to the subject's current goals while the other ear heard a goal-irrelevant narrative. Subjects were able to recall more details from the goal-related narrative than the irrelevant one (Klinger, 1977). In another experiment, subjects listened to a word list that contained both goal-related and goal-unrelated words. Words associated with goals elicited greater increases in the galvanic skin response than did unrelated words (Nikula, Klinger, & Larson-Gutman, 1993).

Unlike Tolman and Lewin, Klinger believed goals rather than incentives were important in motivating human behavior. Goals are larger and more important than incentives, potentially affecting a person's entire life rather than just a few minutes of the day. Klinger went so far as to say that when people are deprived of important goals, life becomes meaningless. To select a goal, a person evaluates the worth of each potential outcome, then chooses the one that is emotionally important. The person will then formulate the necessary plans to achieve the goal. Klinger used the term "current concern" for the force, or psychic tension, that drives humans to complete goals. A person persists in trying to reach a goal until the goal has been achieved, the original goal has been displaced by another goal, or the goal has been abandoned. Achieving a goal has a reinforcing value. Not achieving a goal is aversive. (For a review, see Klinger, 1975.)

*Psychological drives* Henry Murray (1893–1988) used several methods for assessing the motivational force, which he called "nonconscious" tendencies, but he is probably best known for the development of the Thematic Apperception Test (TAT). The procedure involved showing an illustration of an ambiguous scene to the subject and asking the subject to create a story describing the scene. The idea was that the nonconscious needs, or motivation, of the individual would make themselves evident in the story that was told. The story is assessed for evidence of specific needs. For example, if investigators were interested in the subject's need to achieve, the story would be scored based on references to competition with a standard of excellence, a unique accomplishment, or long-term involvement (Murray, 1936).

Although biological drive theorists thought motivation was derived from physical needs, Murray devised a motivation theory in which behavior was directed by a few basic psychological needs. Murray defined a need as a recurrent concern for a goal state. A need is both a directional and an energizing force that results in approach to or avoidance of stimuli associated with the need. Murray's list of psychological needs that drive behavior included achievement, affiliation, aggression, autonomy, deference, dominance, exhibition, harm avoidance, nurturance, order, play, rejection, sex, and understanding. Some of these needs are innate but others are acquired with experience. (For a review, see Murray, 1938.)

Research has shown that Murray's need theory is inadequate to explain behavior thoroughly. For instance, two different people with the same basic psychological need do not expend the same amount of energy in order to achieve a goal. Most of the psychological needs described by Murray are no longer studied; however, three have survived and are the focus of some motivational research today – the need for achievement, affiliation, and power.

Abraham Maslow (1908–1970) took the radical view that if you wanted to understand human psychology, you should study mentally healthy humans. He took this approach to an extreme, arguing that in order accurately to assess the potential for good mental health, we should limit our attention to the most moral, ethical, or saintly people. Maslow selected qualified subjects from among his friends, acquaintances, public, and historical figures such as Abraham Lincoln and Thomas Jefferson. Maslow's theory of motivation is based on these case studies.

Maslow, like Murray, believed that humans had basic physiological and psychological needs. Unlike Murray, however, Maslow thought that needs were arranged in a specific hierarchy. Physiological needs (e.g., food, water, thermoregulation, excretion) were located at the bottom of the hierarchy. These needs were essential to the survival of the individual and therefore were the most important. Only after all of the physiological needs had been met would higher-order needs be activated. Next in the hierarchy was the need for physical safety. Safety needs can be seen in preferences for familiar surroundings, secure jobs, and adequate savings accounts. If a person feels safe, then a need for love or belongingness presides. According to Maslow, humans need to feel accepted as part of a group in order to achieve fulfillment. Next in the hierarchy is esteem, both self-esteem and the esteem of others. We must be proud of ourselves and have others admire us in order to reach the next level of need. Maslow referred to the first four needs as a source of "deprivation motivation." Behavior related to the first four need categories is motivated by a deprivation of those things necessary for full development. The final need is a need for self-actualization. Humans are energized to achieve self-actualization by "being motivation." Self-actualization is a higher level of consciousness, intelligence, awareness, and acceptance that is achieved by very few people because most people get stuck trying to meet the first four needs. (For a review, see Maslow, 1943.)

There have been many criticisms of Maslow's methods. Because many of his subjects preferred to remain anonymous, other researchers could not replicate or verify his findings. Although written accounts of historic figures were readily available, the information was

often by a third party describing the prominent individual from his or her own perspective. If the written information was autobiographical, it was often self-serving. Thus
Maslow was not necessarily basing his conclusions on an accurate depiction of the
individual's behavior. The generalization of the theory is also questionable because so
few people successfully self-actualize. Subsequent researchers attempted to test Maslow's
hierarchy by asking subjects about the importance of various needs. They found that
steps can be skipped by some individuals. Maslow loosened the theory, thereby weaken-
ing it considerably, to account for any deviation from the hierarchy in terms of flexibility of the system. Overall, little support for Maslow's theory has been found in such
data.

## Current Theories of Motivation

All past efforts have proven wholly inadequate to explain more than a small subsection
of behavior. Increasingly it appeared that motivation was multiply determined; some
behaviors are programmed into the organism's biology, whereas other behaviors are
acquired through experience with the environment or depend on social interaction.
Psychologists accordingly abandoned efforts to explain motivation with a single, all-
encompassing theory, and now acknowledge that many motivated behaviors are the
product of a combination of these factors.

### The behavioral approach

*Hedonism*  Although the theory of hedonism does not currently generate much research,
it continues to generate much debate from a philosophical perspective. For instance,
it has recently been proposed that there is insufficient psychological evidence and philosophical argument to justify rejecting hedonism as a source of motivation but it is
unlikely that natural selection would have led to such an individual-oriented outlook
(Sober & Wilson, 1998). Others are not convinced by this viewpoint (Harman, 2000;
Laland, Odling-Smee, & Feldman, 2000); unfortunately, the theory fails to generate
any testable hypotheses when one considers hedonism strictly at the behavioral level.
Without hypotheses, the theory of hedonism cannot stand up to the rigors of the
scientific method, and thus will never have the support of convincing evidence nor be
ruled out as a motivational theory. However, it does not remain solely in the realm of
intellectual pondering, but has been incorporated into other theories of motivation.

Researchers have tried to reduce the sensation of pleasure and pain to the hedonistic
character of individual neurons in the brain. Olds and Milner (1954) documented that
certain areas of the rat brain, when stimulated with an electric current, created the
sensation of pleasure. Rats learned to press the bar to receive electrical stimulation of the
hypothalamus in an operant chamber. Some response rates were as high as 7,000 presses
per hour. One rat averaged 2,000 responses per hour for 26 consecutive hours (Olds,
1958).

Following the initial discovery of reward centers in the rat brain, neuroscientists began mapping the location of these centers in great detail (Wise, 1996; Wise & Rompre, 1989). The limbic system is involved in providing pleasures and rewards, as well as playing a role in thirst, hunger, sex, and emotions. By injecting rats with a dopamine antagonist, researchers were able to determine that dopamine is the neurotransmitter involved in the pleasurable effects of natural rewards such as food, water, and sex (Wise & Rompre, 1989). Blocking dopamine receptors resulted in anhedonia – a lack of pleasure from hedonic stimuli in general (Smith, 1995; Lopez & Ettenberg, 2001) and therefore a decrease in hunger, thirst, and sexually motivated behaviors.

*Incentive motivation*  Incentive motivation continues to be an important theoretical approach to understanding motivation. Incentive motivation is found in any situation that has the potential of a reward or punisher following behavior. The reward or punisher acts as a consequence of behavior, thereby determining which behavior is most likely to occur based on previous experiences. The anticipation of the reward or punishment, in contrast, is the incentive, which actually energizes behavior. The details of how incentives affect motivation are still being worked out with unique and innovative research methods. For instance, Biner, Huffman, Curran, and Long (1998) manipulated the level of food deprivation by having one group of human subjects go without breakfast or lunch and another group eat both meals prior to a 1 p.m. experiment. The subjects then rated how attractive they thought a hamburger was. Deprived participants rated the hamburger as much more attractive than nondeprived subjects. Additionally, the value of an incentive is determined relative to past reinforcements, and this is known as a *contrast effect*. Rats that were previously reinforced with a large food reward will run slower for a small food reward than rats that received only the small food reward throughout training. The incentive to run for the small reward was smaller for the shifted rats because of the history with the larger reward (Pellegrini & Mustaca, 2000). Logue (1998) manipulated incentive by having subjects choose between a small immediate reward and a large delayed reward in order to assess self-control and impulsiveness. Evidence suggests that incentives play a role in sexual attraction. Characteristics of the potential sex partner act as incentive motivators for sexual attraction (Symons, 1979). Incentive value, effects of incentive delay, preference reversals, incentive utility, and primary versus secondary incentives are some of the aspects of incentive motivation that are currently under investigation.

## The biological approach

*Instinct theory*  Although psychologists today agree that instincts alone cannot explain all behavior, they generally agree that evolution is an important factor in the behavior of all animals. Instinct theory is rooted in the idea that certain behaviors evolved because they aided an individual, and thus a species, in survival. Today there are two different approaches to studying instinct as a source of motivation: ethology and evolutionary psychology. Ethologists have developed several concepts to help us to understand how some behaviors are motivated by genetically controlled programs. According to the ethologist's approach, key stimuli in the environment act as releasing mechanisms. When such a stimulus is encountered, the stimulus automatically elicits an unlearned stereotypical behavior. Evolutionary psychologists examine behavior from a life history perspective in an attempt to determine what direct or indirect survival motives underlie specific behaviors.

Evolutionary psychology is a relatively new field that attempts to understand human behavior by relating it to our evolutionary past. For example, by looking at the basic needs and the reproductive biology of our ancestors, David Buss has developed an explanation for the sexual motivation of humans today (e.g., Buss, 1998; Buss & Schmitt, 1993). Much like modern women, ancestral women had limited reproductive opportunity: they could only produce a limited number of offspring due to a long gestation (nine months), followed by an even longer lactation (up to several years), and then still had a small child to care for. Unlike modern women, however, the ancestral woman was very dependent on her mate to provide enough resources for her survival and the survival of the child. Making a poor mate choice would jeopardize the survival of her young and thus her reproductive fitness. By choosing men with qualities such as a high economic capacity, high social status, industriousness, ambition, dependability, stability, and intelligence, a woman could ensure that her mate could provide for her and her children. Modern women also show a strong preference for these qualities when making mate choices even though they are no longer dependent on their mates for survival (Buss, 1994).

Men, in contrast, enter the mating game from a different corner. For men, sex is biologically cheap. Sperm are plentiful and replaced quickly. Whereas a woman's minimal time commitment to a successful sexual encounter is at least five years (before the child is somewhat less dependent on her), a man's minimal time commitment to the same encounter that produces an offspring could be as short as a few minutes. Women can increase their reproductive success (number of reproducing offspring) by investing their time and energy into just a few offspring. However, men can increase their reproductive fitness by impregnating as many different women as possible. Thus what a man looks for in a woman is not telltale signs of her behavior in the future, but rather what her reproductive condition is in the present. Reproductively successful ancestral men would have had sex with many different young, healthy, fertile women. These are precisely the qualities that attract modern men. Modern men look for youth, physical beauty (a marker of good health), body shape (a marker of reproductive condition and health), and novelty (Buss, 1994). Thus looking back at the evolutionary history of a species can help explain why certain unlearned motivations exist.

*Biological drive theory*   Cannon's research revealed the role of local stimuli in motivation but was insufficient to explain motivation in full. For example, severing the vagus nerve of rats caused stomach contractions to cease but did not eliminate the experience of hunger (Grossman & Stein, 1948), nor did it eliminate food intake (Morgan & Morgan, 1940). This finding suggests that changes in the periphery of the body are unnecessary for the experience of hunger. Therefore, scientists began looking at the internal state of the body for cues to motivation, and are currently mapping out the biological mechanisms of hunger, thirst, and sexual motivation.

There is not a single cue for biological needs but rather several mechanisms designed to achieve the same end through different means. Investigators have identified several internal stimuli that can trigger a biological drive. A drop in availability of blood glucose (Smith & Epstein, 1969; Thompson & Campbell, 1977) or fatty acids (Ritter & Taylor, 1990) is accompanied by hunger and ravenous feeding. Other internal stimuli, such as full stomach (Kraly & Smith, 1978; Deutsch, Young, & Kalogeris, 1978) and the presence of food in the intestines (Smith & Gibbs, 1994) signal satiety, the offset of motivation.

Unlike early researchers, however, current investigators have recognized the important role that external stimuli play in motivation to carry out biological functions. Behavior isn't just motivated by a desire to reduce a biological need or maintain a homeostatic state. Rather, biologically unimportant factors such as taste can increase or decrease the consumption of food or water. Rats that have not been deprived of food or water will drink copious amounts of nonnutritious but sweet-tasting water (Ernits & Corbit, 1973). A variety of stimuli will increase feeding and sexual activity. In one experiment, human subjects ate more cooked pasta if it was offered in a variety of shapes (spaghetti, hoops, and bow-ties) than when offered as a single form, even though nutritional value was identical (Rolls, Rowe, & Rolls, 1982). In another experiment, rams that were repeatedly offered the same ewe as a sexual partner were slower and slower to resume mating. Rams that were repeatedly offered a novel sexual partner, however, copulated immediately on every occasion, showing no signs of a decrease in sexual motivation (Bermant, 1976).

Internal and external stimuli work together in determining motivation. Internal states of the body affect how an individual responds to external stimuli. For example, the nutritional status of the body affects the pleasantness of sweet solutions. After human subjects had swallowed appreciable amounts of a sweet solution, the ratings, which were originally high, reversed such that the sweet solution was rated as tasting worse than an unsweetened solution. This change in perception is called *alliesthesia*. If the subjects rinsed their mouth with the solution and spat it out again there was no such effect (Cabanac, 1971). Similarly, as a person continues to eat one food, its pleasantness rating drops, but the pleasantness of other food, not yet eaten, may change less or not at all (Rolls, 1990).

The needs of the body have a significant effect on how an individual will behave. However, biological drives can be overridden by other motivational factors, such as goals and incentives. This effect is evident in individuals who restrict their diet in order to lose weight. Dieters attempt to ignore their biological drive to eat by not eating whenever they get hungry and ending a meal before satiation. For successful dieters, the goal of achieving a more appealing body shape is stronger than the desire to satisfy an immediate biological need. This behavior has been taken to an extreme in individuals suffering from anorexia nervosa, who will actually starve themselves to death in order to achieve a distorted version of an "ideal" body shape.

## The cognitive approach

*Psychological drives* Cognitive theorists propose that people's internal goals and standards for success motivate them to act in specific ways. Motivation revolves around the accomplishment of certain goals, with such goals influencing both the choices people make and the consequences they find reinforcing. For instance, goal difficulty motivates people to produce more effort and makes that goal more valuable to the person (Brehm & Self, 1989). Attainment of goals leads to higher standards for future performance (Bandura, 1986, 1989). Goals are only beneficial to the extent that they are accomplishable; if they are unrealistically high, the consistent failure to achieve them may result in excessive stress or depression.

Contemporary achievement motivation researchers seek to understand why people adopt either mastery-oriented or performance-oriented goals. Before reaching school age, children seem to focus primarily on mastery goals, which are designed to develop or improve competence (Ames & Archer, 1988). Infants, for instance, seek out experiences that are likely to increase mastery of the environment, and they derive genuine pleasure from new accomplishments (Dweck & Elliot, 1983). When children enter school, they are surrounded by peers to whom they can compare their own behavior; as a result, some may begin to define success more in terms of performance goals, that is, demonstrations of competence by doing better than their classmates, than in terms of task mastery. These individuals may stay away from some tasks because of their challenging nature. Failure on the task would lead to embarrassment and thus aversion. Some people choose mastery goals over performance goals fairly consistently. These people can be thought of as having a strong motivation to learn. For these individuals, failure on a task is not an aversive condition but rather a necessary step for achieving the goal of mastery.

Expectancies and values also influence the choices people make (Feather, 1982; Wigfield, 1994; Wigfield & Eccles, 1992). Both factors must be present for motivated behavior to occur. People must have an expectancy, or belief, that they can succeed when setting a goal. Expectancies are probably the result of prior successes and failures at a related task. Dweck, Goetz, and Strauss (1980) found that after repeatedly failing to complete the task of carefully drawing 10 Chinese characters in less than one minute, subjects formed increasingly lower expectations. Other factors that are involved in expectancy of success include perceived difficulty of task, general work habits, environmental resources, quality of instruction, and anticipated effort needed (Dweck & Elliot, 1983; Wigfield & Eccles, 1992; Zimmerman, Bandura, & Martinez-Pons, 1992).

Motivation to achieve a goal will only occur if the goal has value in the form of direct or indirect benefits in performing a task. Activities are valued because they are associated with certain personal qualities, are seen as a means to achieve a desired goal, or bring pleasure and enjoyment.

In general, motivation to achieve a goal occurs when people are confident that they can perform the activity successfully with a reasonable amount of effort (high expectancy) or learn from their failure (mastery) that the activity or its outcome is worthwhile (high value). In most cases, this need to achieve can override other sources of motivation such as hedonism, biological drives, and social pressures.

*The social influence*  Not all behavior has a direct, observable benefit for the actor. Rather, some behaviors seem to be exclusively for the benefit of another individual, not for the actor. Some researchers suggest that this class of behavior, altruism, is the result of an unselfish concern for others. After reviewing the biological and psychological evidence,

Hoffman (1981) concluded that altruism is a part of our makeup and can generate helping behavior. Babies tend to cry when they hear another baby crying. Neither audio recording of its own cries nor a computer-simulated cry has the same effect (Hoffman, 1981) suggesting that the baby feels an innate empathy for another individual in distress. Batson and colleagues have presented evidence that altruistic motivation is triggered by empathetic emotions. By manipulating empathy feeling, Coke, Batson, and McDavis (1978) found that subjects who experience the most empathy also offered the most help to someone in need. Spontaneous "giving" in young children (e.g., Hoffman, 1981; Murray, 1979; Wallach & Wallach, 1983) also supports the claim that people can behave in a truly selfless manner.

Other researchers, however, maintain that all behavior is hedonistic – even behaviors that may appear to be altruistic. According to the hedonistic explanation of altruistic behavior, seeing another individual upset causes an unpleasant state of tension. Any acts to help the distressed individual are primarily intended to relieve the tension of the actor by reducing the distress of the recipient. For instance, a baby is upset by crying (and thus cries as well) but cannot act to terminate the source of its distress. When the infant gets older, however, cries could motivate the child to take action to remove the distress. There is evidence of this sequence of events in slightly older children. Children as young as 15 months will try to comfort younger children in distress (Rheingold, Hay, & West, 1976). Toi and Batson (1982) designed an experiment in which hedonistic helping could be tested against altruistic helping. Their subjects in the low-empathy condition helped less if escape from the situation was easy than if escape was difficult, suggesting that these subjects engaged in helping behavior hedonistically to reduce their own distress. Subjects in the high-empathy condition, on the other hand, exhibited large amounts of helping regardless of the ease of escape, suggesting that their behavior was motivated altruistically.

Some researchers have a more liberal definition of altruism: if the only reward a person receives for helping another person is feeling good, then we are justified in calling the action altruistic (Mook, 1991). It seems likely that helping behavior is sometimes motivated by hedonistic needs and sometimes by altruism. Either may lead to helping behavior, and we can assume that helping behavior sometimes results from a combination of concern for others and a reduction of one's own distress.

## Conclusion

If we revisit Tessa from the beginning of the chapter, we now have a better idea of why she behaves the way she does. Even a behavior as simple as eating a piece of lemon tart cannot be explained by any one theory of motivation. Rather, motivation is multiply determined. The pleasant taste and the variety of the food, the desire to impress her employer, the need to achieve the position of regional manager, the goal of losing weight and looking good in front of her old high school friends, and the food in her digestive system are just a few of the factors that will have an effect on a decision even as mundane as eating a piece of lemon tart.

In conclusion, we have seen that early approaches to explain motivation with a single mechanism were ineffective. Motivation is much more complicated than early theorists realized. Early philosophers and researchers were successful in identifying some of the individual threads of motivation: hedonism, physiological needs of the body, experiences with the consequences of behavior, anticipation of future events, goals, reflexes and instincts, psychological needs, social influences, and many more. These themes were more thoroughly investigated during the first century of psychology. Such investigations have provided a detailed description of how these individual factors affect motivation. Only recently are we beginning to recognize the ways in which these threads are woven together to create the intricate tapestry of motivation. Much of the complex interactions between the various factors remain to be worked out.

## References

Ames, C., & Archer, J. (1988). Achievement goals in the classroom: Students' learning strategies and motivation processes. *Journal of Educational Psychology, 80,* 260–7.

Amsel, A., & Rashotte, M. E. (1984). *Mechanisms of adaptive behavior: Clark L. Hull's theoretical papers, with commentary.* New York: Columbia University Press.

Bandura, A. (1986). *Social foundations of thought and action: A social cognitive theory.* Englewood Cliffs, NJ: Prentice Hall.

Bandura, A. (1989). Human agency in social cognitive theory. *American Psychologist, 44,* 1175–84.

Bermant, G. (1976). Sexual behavior: Hard times with the Coolidge effect. In M. H. Siegel and H. P. Zielger (eds.), *Psychological research: The inside story* (pp. 76–103). New York: Harper & Row.

Biner, P. M., Huffman, M. L., Curran, M. A., & Long, K. L. (1998). Illusory control as a function of motivation for a specific outcome in a chance-based situation. *Motivation and Emotion, 22,* 277–91.

Boring, E. G. (1950). *A history of experimental psychology* (2nd edn.). New York: Appleton-Century-Crofts.

Brehm, J. W., & Self, E. A. (1989). The intensity of motivation. *Annual Review of Psychology, 40,* 109–31.

Buss, D. M. (1994). *The evolution of desire.* New York: BasicBooks.

Buss, D. M. (1998). Sexual strategies theory: Historical origins and current status. *The Journal of Sex Research, 35,* 19–31.

Buss, D. M., & Schmitt, D. P. (1993). Sexual strategies theory: An evolutionary perspective on human mating. *Psychological Review, 100,* 204–32.

Butler, R. A. (1957). The effect of deprivation of visual incentives on visual exploration motivation in monkeys. *Journal of Comparative and Physiological Psychology, 50,* 177–9.

Cabanac, M. (1971). Physiological role of pleasure. *Science, 173,* 1103–7.

Cannon, W. B., & Washburn, A. L. (1912). An explanation of hunger. *American Journal of Physiology, 29,* 444–54.

Coke, J. S., Batson, C. D., & McDavis, K. (1978). Empathic mediation of helping: A two-stage model. *Journal of Personality and Social Psychology, 36,* 752–66.

Deutsch, J. A., Young, W. G., & Kalogeris, T. J. (1978). The stomach signals satiety. *Science, 201,* 165–7.

Dweck, C. S., & Elliot, E. S. (1983). Achievement motivation. In E. M. Hetherington (ed.), *Handbook of child psychology: Vol. 4. Socialization, personality, and social development* (4th edn.) (pp. 643–91). New York: Wiley.

Dweck, C. S., Goetz, T. E., & Strauss, N. L. (1980). Sex differences in learned helplessness: IV. An experimental and naturalistic study of failure generalization and its mediators. *Journal of Personality and Social Psychology, 38*, 441–52.

Ernits, T., & Corbit, J. D. (1973). Taste as a dipsogenic stimulus. *Journal of Comparative and Physiological Psychology, 83*, 27–31.

Feather, N. T. (1982). *Expectations and actions: Expectancy-value models in psychology.* Hillsdale, NJ: Erlbaum.

Fox, S. S. (1962). Self-maintained sensory input and sensory deprivation in monkeys: A behavioral and neuropharmacological study. *Journal of Comparative and Physiological Psychology, 55*, 438–44.

Freud, S. (1949). Formulations regarding the two principles of mental functioning. In *Collected papers of Sigmund Freud* (vol. 4). London: Hogarth Press.

Grossman, M. I., & Stein, I. F., Jr. (1948). Vagotomy and the hunger producing action of insulin in man. *Journal of Applied Physiology, 1*, 263–9.

Harman, G. (2000). Can evolutionary theory provide evidence against psychological hedonism? *Journal of Consciousness Studies, 7*, 219–21.

Hoffman, M. L. (1981). Is altruism part of human nature? *Journal of Personality and Social Psychology, 40*, 121–37.

James, W. (1890). *Principles of psychology.* New York: Holt.

Klinger, E. (1975). Consequences of commitment to and disengagement from incentives. *Psychological Review, 82*, 1–25.

Klinger, E. (1977). *Meaning and void.* Minneapolis: University of Minnesota Press.

Kraly, F. S., & Smith, G. P. (1978). Combined pregastric and gastric stimulation by food is sufficient for normal meal size. *Physiology and Behavior, 21*, 405–8.

Laland, K. N., Odling-Smee, F. J., & Feldman, M. W. (2000). Group selection: A niche construction perspective. *Journal of Consciousness Studies, 7*, 221–5.

Lewin, K. (1928). Investigations on the psychology of action and affection. VI. The resumption of interrupted acts. *Psychologische-Forschung, 11*, 302–89.

Lewin, K. (1938). *The conceptual representation and the measurement of psychological forces.* Durham, NC: Duke University Press.

Lewin, K., & Dembo, T. (1931). Investigations in the psychology of action and affection. X. Anger as a dynamic problem. *Psychologische-Forschung, 15*, 1–144.

Logue, A. W. (1998). Laboratory research on self-control: Applications to administration. *Review of General Psychology, 2*, 221–38.

Lopez, H. H., & Ettenberg, A. (2001). Dopamine antagonism attenuates the unconditioned incentive value of estrous female cues. *Pharmacology, Biochemistry, and Behavior, 68*, 411–16.

Maslow, A. H. (1943). A theory of human motivation. *Psychological Review, 50*, 370–96.

McDougall, K. D., & McDougall, W. (1931). Insight and foresight in various animals – monkey, raccoon, rat, and wasp. *Journal of Comparative Psychology, 11*, 237–73.

McDougall, W. (1927). An experiment for testing the hypothesis of Lamark. *British Journal of Psychology, 17*, 267–304.

McDougall, W. (1938). Fourth report on Lamarckian experiment. *British Journal of Psychology, 28*, 321–45.

McDougall, W. (1970). The nature of instincts and their place in the constitution of the human mind. In W. A. Russell (ed.), *Milestones in motivation* (pp. 18–33). New York: Appleton-Century-Crofts.

McDougall, W., & McDougall, K. D. (1927). Notes on instincts and intelligence in rats and cats. *Journal of Comparative Psychology, 7*, 145–75.

Mees, C. E. K. (1934). Scientific thought and social reconstruction. *Sigma Xi Quarterly, 22*, 13–24.

Mook, D. G. (1991). Why can't altruism be selfish? *Psychological Inquiry, 2*, 139–41.

Morgan, C. T., & Morgan, J. T. (1940). Studies in hunger: II. The relation of gastric denervation and dietary sugar to the effect of insulin upon food-intake in the rat. *Journal of Genetic Psychology, 57*, 153–63.

Murray, A. D. (1979). Infant crying as an elicitor of parent behavior: An examination of two models. *Psychological Bulletin, 86*, 191–215.

Murray, H. A. (1936). Techniques for a systematic investigation of fantasy. *Journal of Psychology, 3*, 115–43.

Murray, H. A. (1938). *Explorations in personality*. New York: Oxford University Press.

Nikula, R., Klinger, E., & Larson-Gutman, M. K. (1993). Current concerns and electrodermal reactivity: Responses to words and thoughts. *Journal of Personality, 61*, 63–84.

Olds, J. (1958). Self-stimulation of the brain. *Science, 127*, 315–24.

Olds, J., & Milner, P. (1954). Positive reinforcement produced by electrical stimulation of the septal area and other regions of the rat brain. *Journal of Comparative and Physiological Psychology, 47*, 419–27.

Pellegrini, S., & Mustaca, A. (2000). Consummatory successive negative contrasts with solid food. *Learning and Motivation, 31*, 200–9.

Reeve, J. (2001). *Understanding motivation and emotion* (3rd edn.). Fort Worth, TX: Harcourt College Publishers.

Rheingold, H. L., Hay, D. F., & West, M. J. (1976). Sharing in the second year of life. *Child Development, 47*, 1148–58.

Ritter, S., & Taylor, J. S. (1990). Vagal sensory neurons are required for lipoprivic but not glucoprivic feeding in rats. *American Journal of Physiology, 258*, R1395–1401.

Rolls, B. J. (1990). The role of sensory-specific satiety in food intake and food selection. In E. J. Capaldi and T. L. Powley (eds.), *Taste, experience, and feeding* (pp. 197–209). Washington, DC: American Psychological Association.

Rolls, B. J., Rowe, E. T., & Rolls, E. T. (1982). How sensory properties of food affect human feeding behavior. *Physiology and Behavior, 29*, 409–17.

Sheffield, F. D., & Roby, T. B. (1950). Reward value of a non-nutritive sweet taste. *Journal of Comparative and Physiological Psychology, 43*, 471–81.

Simmons, R. (1924). The relative effectiveness of certain incentives in animal learning. *Comparative Psychology Monographs, 2*, 7.

Smith, G. P. (1995). Dopamine and food reward. In S. J. Fluharty, J. M. Sprague, A. R. Morrison, & E. Stellar (eds.), *Progress in psychobiology and physiological psychology* (vol. 16, pp. 83–144). San Diego, CA: Academic Press.

Smith, G. P., & Epstein, A. N. (1969). Increased feeding in response to decreased glucose utilization in the rat and monkey. *American Journal of Physiology, 217*, 236–41.

Smith, G. P., & Gibbs, J. (1994). Satiating effects of cholecystokinin. *Annals of the New York Academy of Sciences, 713*, 236–41.

Sober, E., & Wilson, D. S. (1998). *Unto Others*. Cambridge, MA: Harvard University Press.

Symons, D. (1979). *The evolution of human sexuality*. New York: Oxford University Press.

Thompson, D. A., & Campbell, R. G. (1977). Hunger in humans induced by 2-deoxy-D-glucose: Glucoprivic control of taste preference and food intake. *Science, 198*, 1065–8.

Thorndike, E. L. (1911). *Animal intelligence*. New York: Macmillan.

Thorndike, E. L. (1913). *Educational psychology: The psychology of learning* (vol. 2). New York: Teachers College Press.

Tinklepaugh, O. (1928). An experimental study of representative factors in monkeys. *Journal of Comparative Psychology*, *8*, 197–236.

Toi, M., & Batson, C. D. (1982). More evidence that empathy is a source of altruistic motivation. *Journal of Personality and Social Psychology*, *43*, 281–92.

Tolman, E. C. (1932). *Purposive behavior in animals and men*. New York: Appleton-Century.

Tolman, E. C., Ritchie, B. F., & Kalish, D. (1946). Studies in spatial learning: II. Place learning versus response learning. *Journal of Experimental Psychology*, *36*, 221–9.

Wallach, M. A., & Wallach, L. (1983). *Psychology's sanction for selfishness: The error of egoism in theory and therapy*. San Francisco: Freeman.

Wigfield, A. (1994). Expectancy-value theory of achievement motivation: A developmental perspective. *Educational Psychology Review*, *6*, 49–78.

Wigfield, A., & Eccles, J. (1992). The development of achievement task values: A theoretical analysis. *Developmental Review*, *12*, 265–310.

Wise, R. A. (1996). Addictive drugs and brain stimulation reward. *Annual Review of Neuroscience*, *19*, 319–40

Wise, R. A., & Rompre, P. P. (1989). Brain dopamine and reward. *Annual Review of Neuroscience*, *40*, 191–225.

Zimmerman, B. J., Bandura, A., & Martinez-Pons, M. (1992). Self-motivation for academic attainment: The role of self-efficacy beliefs and personal goal setting. *American Educational Research Journal*, *29*, 663–76.

# CHAPTER NINETEEN

# Audition

## Henry E. Heffner and Rickye S. Heffner

## Introduction

Fifty years ago, a general review of auditory research could be accomplished in four chapters (Stevens, 1951); today, one review has grown to 14 volumes with more on the way (*Springer Handbook of Auditory Research*, R. R. Fay and A. N. Popper, series editors). The growth of auditory research has come about because more areas of neuroscience have been applying their techniques to understanding the neurological basis of hearing. Although a complete understanding requires a multidisciplinary approach, it is often the case that researchers know little about important issues in closely related disciplines – a problem that is becoming widespread in neuroscience (Cahill, McGaugh, & Weinberger, 2001). This problem has been compounded by an emphasis on recent research, giving those new to the field the impression that there is little to be learned from older work (e.g., Moore, Rothholtz, & King, 2001).

One area of auditory research that impinges on all others is the behavioral study of hearing in animals. Because all anatomical and physiological models of auditory processing must eventually be related to behavior, and because virtually all such models are based on animal research, it is obviously necessary to know the hearing abilities of animals. Furthermore, it should be possible to test the validity of such models by studying the effects of central nervous system lesions on hearing, that is, ablation/behavior experiments.

The purpose of this chapter is to describe two lines of behavioral research. The first is the comparative study of mammalian hearing, that is, the determination of *what* mammals hear and *why* they hear as they do. The second is the study of the auditory cortex using the ablation/behavior approach. In doing so, we will highlight issues to be considered when interpreting and applying this research.

We thank G. Koay and I. Harrington for their useful comments on a previous draft of this chapter.

## Comparative Study of Mammalian Hearing

The first comparative studies of hearing were conducted in the nineteenth century by Francis Galton, who used specially constructed whistles to determine the unconditioned responses of animals to high-frequency sounds (Galton, 1883). Galton made several discoveries that have since been supported by modern research, such as that cats have particularly good high frequency hearing and that human high-frequency hearing ability declines with age. However, he incorrectly concluded that large dogs could not hear high frequencies, because, unlike small dogs, they showed no reaction to his whistles (H. E. Heffner, 1983). Thus he was unable to distinguish the inability to hear a sound from the failure to respond to it, although he was well aware of such a possibility. This is the problem with using a simple startle reaction as a test of hearing.

Modern comparative studies of mammalian hearing have focused on the basic auditory abilities of detection, localization, and frequency discrimination. (Interest in the ability to perform more complex auditory discriminations is growing, e.g., Dooling & Hulse, 1989.) Before turning to what we know about these basic abilities, it is important to consider how they are measured.

### Behavioral measurement of hearing

A number of behavioral procedures for determining the sensory abilities of animals were available by the late 1960s (e.g., Stebbins, 1970). These procedures, along with the use of precision instruments for presenting and measuring sound, made it possible to use conditioning techniques to determine the behavioral hearing abilities not only of mammals, but birds and fish as well (Klump, Dooling, Fay, & Stebbins, 1995). Reptiles, on the other hand, have proven virtually impossible to condition to sound (for an exception, see Patterson, 1966), although they readily learn to make visual discriminations (e.g., Burghardt, 1977). Similarly, no conditioning procedures have been developed for amphibians, although the use of startle reflex modification techniques and the natural tendency of females during mating season to approach the sound of a male have been used to study some aspects of frog hearing (e.g., Klump et al., 1995). The fact that amphibians and reptiles do not readily learn to respond to sound suggests that they may lack the neurological mechanisms for doing so.

Some conditioning procedures are better than others. The better ones not only reward an animal for correctly responding to a sound, but they also have good control over responses in the absence of that sound. In the language of signal detection theory, this fact means that "hits" are sufficiently rewarded and "false positives" are kept under control. A good procedure should also be easy for an animal to learn and should allow their heads to be fixed in the sound field so that the stimulus reaching their ears can be specified with some precision. One procedure that meets these requirements is "conditioned suppression," in which an animal is trained to place its mouth on a spout in order to receive water (or food), and to break contact with that spout whenever a stimulus is presented that signals impending shock (H. E. Heffner & Heffner, 1995a).

By carefully adjusting the reward rate and shock intensity, it is possible to optimize an animal's performance – that is, to maximize its hit rate and minimize its false positive rate. Animals are capable of learning the basic avoidance response within a session or two and the response of placing its mouth on a spout fixes the animal's head within the sound field. Although procedures that use positive reward with a delay or "error time out" as a punisher may work well in some cases, comparisons have shown that shock is a more effective punisher and the combined use of positive reward and shock generally gives better results (e.g., H. E. Heffner & Heffner, 1984).

In a hearing test, sounds are presented to an animal either from a loudspeaker or through headphones. Although headphones make it possible to test each ear separately, problems may arise in calibrating the sound (e.g., Pfingst, Hienz, & Miller, 1975; Zhou & Green, 1995). Moreover, headphones bypass the external ear and thus will not reflect the contribution of the pinnae to hearing. Thus, for comparative studies, sounds are best presented from a loudspeaker located in front of the animal in an acoustic environment that minimizes sound reflections, that is, a free field (Larsen, 1995).

In measuring an animal's performance, it is necessary to correct its hit rate for false positives (e.g., H. E. Heffner & Heffner, 1985, 1995a). One way to do this is to reduce the hit rate in proportion to the false positive rate using the formula: "Corrected Hit rate = Hit rate – (Hit rate × False Positive rate);" this formula is sometimes expressed as "Hit Rate × (1 – False Positive rate)." Another way to correct for false positives is to calculate an animal's percentage correct using the formula: "(Hit rate + (1 – False Positive rate))/2"; note that 1 – False Positive rate is known as the "correct rejection rate." The threshold for a particular discrimination is then defined as the stimulus that gives a corrected hit rate of 0.50 or a percentage correct of 75 percent. Experience has shown that thresholds defined in this way remain stable over a range of false positive rates.

Although it has been claimed that performance should be specified using a signal detection measure such as $d'$ or $A'$ (e.g., Penner, 1995), there are at least two reasons for avoiding such measures when working with animals. First, the values generated by these calculations are nonintuitive and cannot be interpreted without additional information. For example, a corrected hit rate of 50 percent means that the animal is capable of detecting a signal half of the time and conveys more information than the statement that its $d'$ is 2.33 or 1.64 (which are the $d'$ values for a 50% hit rate with 1% and 5% false alarm rate, respectively). Second, it is sometimes assumed that a researcher can use such measures to obtain useful information when an animal has a high false positive rate. However, a high false positive rate (e.g., > 25%) may indicate that the animal is not carefully attending to the stimulus and is attempting to perform the task by guessing, a situation in which signal detection measures do poorly (Green, 1995).

## Detection of sound

The most basic measure of hearing is an animal's *behaviorally determined* sensitivity to pure tones throughout its hearing range, that is, its audiogram. Although electrophysiological estimates of absolute sensitivity may be of interest in their own right, they do not accurately reflect behavioral sensitivity. This applies to such electrophysiological measures

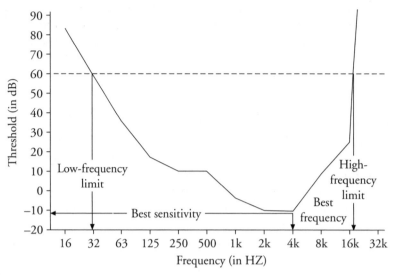

**Figure 19.1**   Human audiogram illustrating the 60-dB high- and low-frequency hearing limits, best frequency, and best sensitivity.

*Source*: Adapted from H. E. Heffner & R. S. Heffner (1992), with permission.

as the cochlear microphonic, thresholds of inferior colliculus neurons, and the auditory brainstem response (see below).

The audiograms of animals are compared on the basis of the following features: high- and low-frequency hearing limits, frequency of best hearing, and best sensitivity (see Figure 19.1). Of these measures, the high- and low-frequency hearing limits have proven to be the most interesting. Note that these limits are defined as the highest and lowest frequencies audible at a particular intensity level.

*High-frequency hearing*   Mammals differ from other vertebrates in that virtually all of them hear well above 10 kHz, which is the upper limit for birds. Reptiles, amphibians, and fish (with some exceptions) do not hear above 5 kHz (H. E. Heffner & Heffner, 1998). Those few mammals that do not hear above 10 kHz (i.e., subterranean mammals) are considered to have degenerate hearing (R. S. Heffner & Heffner, 1993).

High-frequency hearing ability varies between different species of mammals – the 60-dB high-frequency hearing limit ranges from 5.9 kHz for the blind mole-rat (a subterranean rodent) to over 100 kHz for some bats and porpoises, a range of more than 4.5 octaves (H. E. Heffner & Heffner, 1998). There is substantial evidence that high-frequency hearing evolved in mammals primarily for the purpose of localizing sound; although some species also use high-frequency communication calls, and bats also use their high-frequency hearing for echolocation, these uses appear to be secondary adaptations.

The existence of variation in the high-frequency hearing of mammals came to the attention of the late R. Bruce Masterton in 1967 when he noticed that smaller mammals generally had better high-frequency hearing than larger ones. Because he was studying sound localization at the time, he realized that this observation had implications for the use of the two binaural sound-localization cues: the difference in the time of arrival of a sound at the two ears ($\Delta t$) and the difference in the frequency-intensity spectra of the sound reaching the two ears ($\Delta f i$). Noting that the magnitude of the $\Delta t$ cue decreases with the size of an animal's head, he suggested that the smaller an animal's head, the more dependent it would be on the $\Delta f i$ cue (Masterton, Heffner, & Ravizza, 1969). However, for an animal to use the $\Delta f i$ cue, it would need to hear frequencies high enough to be effectively shadowed by its head and pinnae because small heads do not block lower frequencies as effectively as large heads. Therefore, the smaller an animal's *maximum* $\Delta t$ (the time it takes for sound to travel around the head from one ear to the other), the higher it must hear to adequately localize sound.

The relation between maximum $\Delta t$ (sometimes called functional head size) and high frequency hearing has proven to be robust ($r = -0.79$, $p < 0.001$) and has been shown to hold for over 60 animals (R. S. Heffner, Koay, & Heffner, 2001a). The only modification to this theory has been the realization of the importance of high-frequency hearing for pinna cues as well as for $\Delta f i$. Over the years, the work of Bob Butler and others has demonstrated that the directionality of the pinna not only provides effective cues for localizing sound in the horizontal plane, but it also provides the primary cues for vertical localization and for preventing front–back confusions (e.g., Butler, 1975; Musicant & Butler, 1984). For pinna cues to be effective in humans, the sounds must contain frequencies above 4 kHz and even sounds as high as 15 kHz have been shown to be necessary for optimal localization performance. Thus, the upper two octaves of human hearing (from 4 to 16 kHz) appear to be used primarily, if not exclusively, for sound localization as they are not necessary for the perception of speech. As with the $\Delta f i$ cue, the smaller the pinnae, the higher an animal must hear in order to extract pinnae cues for sound localization.

The importance of high-frequency hearing for sound localization is also supported by two lines of experimental evidence. First, filtering out high frequencies from a signal has been shown to degrade sound localization performance in monkeys, humans, horses, chinchillas, and mice (Brown, 1994; Butler, 1975; H. E. Heffner & Heffner, 1983; R. S. Heffner, Heffner, & Koay, 1995; R. S. Heffner, Koay, & Heffner, 2001b). Thus mammals require high-frequency hearing to localize sound using either the $\Delta f i$ locus cue, pinna cues, or both. Second, it appears that subterranean animals that are adapted to the one-dimensional world of an underground habitat have little use for sound localization and are therefore released from the selective pressure to hear high frequencies. Thus, the pocket gopher, naked mole-rat, and blind mole-rat do not localize sound and have lost their high-frequency hearing as well as their pinnae (R. S. Heffner & Heffner, 1990, 1992b, 1993). In short, sound localization and high-frequency hearing go hand-in-hand in mammals. Mammals cannot adequately localize sound without high frequencies and those that relinquish the ability to localize sound also give up their high frequency hearing.

*Low-frequency hearing*  The variation in mammalian low-frequency hearing is even greater than that for high-frequency hearing. Indeed, the 60 dB low-frequency limit for mammals extends from 17 Hz (the Indian elephant) to 10.3 kHz (the little brown bat), a range of over nine octaves. Analysis of this variation has resulted in two findings. First, mammals appear to fall into two groups: those that hear below 125 Hz and those that do not. Second, low-frequency hearing varies with high-frequency hearing (R. S. Heffner et al., 2001a).

Figure 19.2 shows the distribution of 60 dB low-frequency hearing limits for mammals (underwater audiograms have been excluded because of the difficulty in equating air and water thresholds). Of the 59 species, 38 have low-frequency hearing limits below 125 Hz whereas 20 species have low-frequency hearing limits above 500 Hz. Only one species falls within the two-octave gap from 125 to 500 Hz, the subterranean pocket gopher (an animal with degenerate hearing).

We have suggested that the two groups may differ in the mechanisms they use to perceive the pitch of a sound (R. S. Heffner et al., 2001a). Briefly, there are two different neural mechanisms that may underlie the perception of pitch (for a recent description, see Moore, 1993). In one mechanism, frequency is encoded by temporal mechanisms based on phase locking of auditory nerve fibers; this mechanism is limited to low frequencies because phase locking declines as frequency increases. In the second mechanism, higher frequencies are encoded by a place mechanism in which tones of different frequencies excite hair cells and nerve fibers at different locations along the basilar membrane. However, the actual frequencies over which either the temporal or the place mechanism is dominant are not agreed upon. Some observations suggest that the upper limit of the temporal mechanism for the perception of pitch is around 4–5 kHz (e.g., Moore, 1993). However, other observations, such as studies of the perception of the pitch of click trains and psychophysical studies of patients with cochlear implants, suggests that temporal coding extends up to only about 300 Hz (Flanagan & Guttman, 1960; Shannon, 1983). Because this latter upper limit corresponds to the 125–500 Hz gap in mammalian low-frequency limits, it suggests that the animals that do not hear below 500 Hz are not using temporal coding for pitch perception. Thus, animals that hear below 125 Hz may be using both temporal and place mechanisms, whereas those that do not hear below 500 Hz may be using only the place mechanism.

Various factors, such as body size, phyletic lineage, and lifestyle have been examined in an attempt to explain the variation in low-frequency hearing. So far, the only factor found to be reliably correlated with low-frequency hearing is high-frequency hearing – that is, animals with good high-frequency hearing generally have poor low-frequency hearing (R. S. Heffner et al., 2001a). The degree to which high- and low-frequency hearing are related differs for the two groups of mammals: among those that do not hear below 500 Hz, $r = 0.691$ ($p = 0.0015$), whereas for those that hear below 125 Hz, $r = 0.567$ ($p = 0.0006$). In either case, high-frequency hearing accounts for considerable variance in low frequency hearing for both groups, suggesting that it may provide a clue for understanding some of the variation in low-frequency hearing.

The existence of such a relationship suggests that good high- and low-frequency hearing are incompatible. One possibility is that there is some anatomical limitation that prevents the mammalian ear from encoding both high and low frequencies. However, there are several species with good high- and low-frequency hearing, including the chipmunk (39 Hz to 52 kHz), least weasel (50 Hz to 60 kHz), bushbaby (92 Hz to

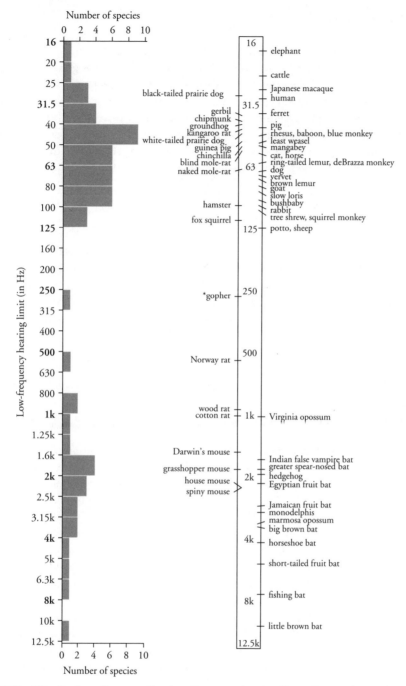

**Figure 19.2** Distribution of mammalian low-frequency hearing limits (lowest frequency audible at 60 dB). Note that low-frequency hearing limits fall into two distinct groups with a gap between them at 125 to 500 Hz. Rodents (shown on the left side of the bar) are the only order with members in both groups.

\* Note that only the subterranean gopher, which has vestigial hearing, falls into the gap between 125 and 500 Hz. Bin width of the histogram is 1/3 octave.

*Source*: Data from R. S. Heffner et al. (2001a).

65 kHz), and domestic cat (55 Hz to 79 kHz), suggesting that any anatomical constraints that might exist can be overcome. Another possibility is that good low-frequency hearing could be disadvantageous in situations where low-frequency sounds interfere with the analysis of high-frequency sounds. For example, we have noted that animals often localize high-frequency noise slightly more accurately than broadband noise (R. S. Heffner et al., 1995). This finding suggests that mammals may restrict their low-frequency hearing to prevent the low-frequency component of sounds from interfering with the analysis of the high frequency components needed for sound localization.

## Localization of sound

At one time it was believed that all mammals were under selective pressure to localize sound as accurately as possible, and that the only factor limiting their accuracy was the availability of the locus cues (as determined by head size). However, it is now clear that animals localize sound only as accurately as is necessary to direct their eyes to the source of a sound. Moreover, an animal may relinquish one or more of the sound localization cues, or even the entire ability to localize sound, if it is not needed for survival.

*Measuring sound localization ability* There are two ways to measure sound localization ability. One is to have the subject point in the direction from which a sound appeared to come and measure the *accuracy* of pointing. The other is to have the subject discriminate between two sound sources, bringing the sources closer together until they can no longer be discriminated, a procedure that measures localization *acuity*.

Accuracy of sound localization can be measured by training an animal to orient its head toward the source of a sound. This procedure is commonly used with owls as they have a strong natural orientation response to sound that can be maintained with food reward (e.g., Wagner, 1995). Among mammals, only cats have been successfully trained to orient to the source of a sound (e.g., Populin & Yin, 1998). Most mammals do not reliably point their head to a sound source and there are several reasons why this may be: first, their visual fields may be so broad that they do not need to turn their heads much to see the sound source; second, they may be able to turn their eyes instead of their head; and finally, their natural response to an unexpected sound may be to freeze.

One way to measure localization acuity is to train an animal to discriminate between two sound sources by walking to the source of a sound to receive a reward (e.g., Neff, Diamond, & Casseday, 1975; Thompson, Heffner, & Masterton, 1974). Another common method is to have the animal discriminate between two sound sources by responding when a sound comes from one location but not another (e.g., Brown, 1994; H. E. Heffner & Heffner, 1984). Using the conditioned suppression task, an animal can be trained to maintain contact with a water spout to receive water while a sound is presented from one location, and to break contact to avoid a mild electric shock when the sound comes from a different location. In either case, the angle of separation between the two sound sources is then reduced until the animal is no longer able to discriminate between the two sources.

Both accuracy (pointing) and acuity (discrimination) measures give essentially the same results. However, fine-grain comparisons of the two procedures are complicated because accuracy is measured in terms of how much the subject's estimate of location differs from true location whereas acuity is measured in terms of "minimum audible angle," that is, the smallest angle that can be discriminated (for a recent comparison of the two procedures, see Recanzone, Makhamra, & Guard, 1998). However, minimum audible angle is a better comparative measure of sensory ability because it is not confounded by species differences in the ability to point.

The most common sound-localization measure is the minimum audible angle for a left–right discrimination, in which the animal is trained to discriminate two sound sources located in front of, and centered on, its midline. The standard stimulus is a 100 ms broadband noise burst, which is too brief to be tracked or scanned, but contains both high and low frequencies, thus permitting the use of all three sound-localization cues: binaural time difference ($\Delta t$), binaural frequency-intensity spectral difference ($\Delta fi$), and pinna cues.

In addition to determining acuity around midline, minimum audible angle can be determined for locations off to the side, including centering the sound sources on the interaural axis (i.e., front–back localization) and for vertically separated sound sources (elevation). Both the front–back and vertical-localization tests measure the ability of an animal to localize in situations where the pinnae provide the primary cues for discriminating locus.

In testing an animal's ability to discriminate two sound sources, it can be difficult to obtain loudspeakers that are perfectly matched for broadband noise. As a result, an animal may shift from discriminating locus to discriminating the quality differences in loudspeakers when the angle of separation is too small to distinguish locus. This problem can be avoided by using several pairs of loudspeakers during a session, by randomizing the intensity of the sound, and by not testing at subthreshold angles for extended periods. However, the crucial test of whether an animal is discriminating sounds on the basis of locus, as opposed to speaker quality, is to demonstrate that there is some small angle at which the animal performs at chance – it is not sufficient to assume that performance would fall to chance if both speakers were placed at 0°.

*Variation in sound localization acuity* When early sound-localization studies showed that humans and elephants have better sound-localization acuity than cats and dogs, which in turn have better acuity than rats, it was naturally assumed that the large binaural cues generated by large heads were necessary for good localization. This belief was abandoned when it was subsequently discovered that horses and cattle have poorer acuity than rats (R. S. Heffner & Heffner, 1992a).

Midline sound localization thresholds have been obtained for over 30 different species of mammals, from mice to elephants (H. E. Heffner & Heffner, 1998; R. S. Heffner, Koay, & Heffner, 2001b). Thresholds range from about 1° for humans and elephants to more than 20° for horses and cattle, and over 30° for house mice with the subterranean rodents (gopher, blind mole-rat, and naked mole-rat) being unable to localize brief sounds (see Table 19.1).

**Table 19.1**   Sound localization acuity and use of binaural cues in mammals

| Species | Midline acuity | Binaural phase cue | Binaural intensity cue |
| --- | --- | --- | --- |
| Indian elephant | 1.2° | yes | yes* |
| Human | 1.3° | yes | yes |
| Harbor seal | 3.2° | — | — |
| Domestic pig | 4.5° | yes | no |
| Virginia opossum | 4.6° | — | — |
| Domestic cat | 5.2° | yes | yes |
| Squirrel monkey | 5.9° | — | — |
| Japanese macaque | 6.8° | yes | yes |
| Dog | 8.0° | — | — |
| Sea lion | 8.8°** | — | — |
| Jamaican fruit bat | 9.9° | yes | yes |
| Greater spear-nosed bat | 10° | no | yes |
| Egyptian fruit bat | 11.6° | yes | yes |
| Ferret | 11.8° | — | — |
| Least weasel | 12° | yes | yes |
| Wild Norway rat | 12.2° | yes | yes |
| Fox squirrel | 14° | yes | yes |
| Big brown bat | 14° | no | yes |
| African pigmy hedgehog | 14.3° | no | yes |
| Short-tailed fruit bat | 14.5° | no | yes |
| Chinchilla | 17.5° | yes | yes |
| Domestic goat | 18° | yes | yes* |
| Hamster | 18.8° | — | — |
| Spiny mouse | 18.9° | no | yes |
| Desert hedgehog | 19° | no | yes |
| Wood rat | 19° | — | — |
| Grasshopper mouse | 19.3° | no | yes |
| Domestic rabbit | 22.3° | — | — |
| Horse | 25° | yes | no |
| Cottontail rabbit | 27° | — | — |
| Gerbil | 27° | yes | yes |
| Merriam's kangaroo rat | 27°** | yes | yes |
| Groundhog | 27.8° | yes | yes |
| Cattle | 30° | yes | no |
| Black-tailed Prairie dog | 32.8° | yes | yes |
| Eastern chipmunk | 33° | yes | yes |
| House mouse | 33° | no | yes |

Dashes indicate no data.
* Unable to use binaural intensity cue in the upper octaves of its hearing range.
** Localization tested with clicks. For all other animals, the stimulus was broadband noise.

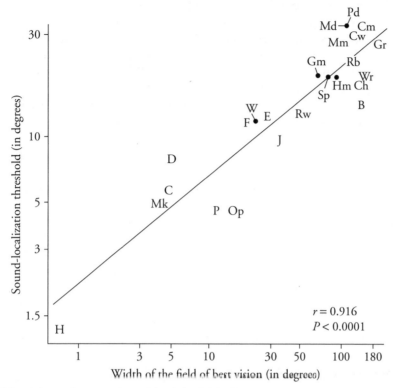

**Figure 19.3**   Relation between the width of the field of best vision and sound-localization threshold. The field of best vision is defined anatomically as the area of the retina containing ganglion-cell densities at least 75% of maximum. Species with narrow fields of best vision have better localization acuity (smaller thresholds) than species with broad fields of best vision. **B**, big brown bat; **C**, domestic cat; **Ch**, chinchilla; **Cm**, chipmunk; **Cw**, cow; **D**, dog; **E**, Egyptian fruit bat; **F**, ferret; **Gm**, grasshopper mouse; **Gr**, gerbil; **H**, human; **Hm**, hamster; **J**, Jamaican fruit bat; **Md**, domestic mouse; **Mk**, Japanese macaque; **Mm**, marmot; **Op**, Virginia opossum; **P**, domestic pig; **Pd**, prairie dog; **Rb**, domestic rabbit; **Rw**, wild normal rat; **Sp**, spiny mouse; **W**, least weasel; **Wr**, wood rat.
*Source*: Data from R. S. Heffner et al. (2001c).

The explanation for the variation in mammalian sound localization acuity lies in the fact that the primary function of sound localization is to direct the eyes to the source of a sound (R. S. Heffner & Heffner, 1992c). Just how accurate sound localization must be to direct the eyes depends on the width of an animal's field of best vision. Animals with narrow fields of best vision, such as humans, require good sound-localization acuity to direct their gaze so that the image of the sound source falls upon their field of best vision (e.g., the human fovea), whereas animals with broad fields, such as those with visual streaks, do not require as high a degree of sound-localization acuity to direct their gaze.

The relation between the width of the field of best vision (estimated from retinal ganglion cell densities) and sound-localization acuity is shown in Figure 19.3. This figure illustrates that mammals with narrow fields of best vision are more accurate localizers than mammals with broader fields ($r = 0.916$). The close relation between vision and sound localization is further supported by the observation that the subterranean rodents, which are adapted to living in dark burrows where visual scrutiny of sound sources is not possible, have lost virtually all of their ability to localize sound.

*Use of binaural locus cues* Mammals vary not only in sound localization acuity, but also in their use of binaural time ($\Delta t$) and binaural spectral ($\Delta f i$) locus cues. Whereas most mammals use both binaural cues, some use only one or the other. Animals that differ in their use of these cues should show corresponding differences in the physiology of their auditory systems.

The ability to use $\Delta t$ and $\Delta f i$ to localize sound can be determined two ways (e.g., R. S. Heffner & Heffner, 1992a). The first is to use headphones to present sounds separately to each ear and varying the relative time of arrival or intensity of the sound at the two ears. However, this test can only be used with animals that can be fitted with headphones. The second method is to present pure tones from two loudspeakers located in front of the animal at a fixed angle of separation and determine its ability to localize low- and high-frequency pure tones. This test can be used with any animal and is based on the fact that low-frequency pure tones are localized using binaural time-difference cues whereas high frequencies are localized using binaural intensity-difference cues. Briefly, low-frequency pure tones that bend around the head with little or no attenuation can only be localized by comparing the time of arrival of the phase of each cycle of the tone at the two ears, the binaural phase difference cue being a subset of $\Delta t$. However, the phase-difference cue becomes ambiguous for pure tones at high frequencies when successive cycles arrive too quickly for the nervous system to match the arrival of the same cycle at the two ears. The exact "frequency of ambiguity" depends on an animal's head size and the angle of the sound source relative to its midline – it is higher for smaller heads and sound sources closer midline (e.g., R. S. Heffner et al., 2001c). Pure tones above the frequency of ambiguity, then, must be localized using the binaural intensity-difference cue, a subset of $\Delta f i$. Thus, the ability of an animal to use the two binaural cues can be measured by determining the ability to localize pure tones above and below the frequency of ambiguity.

Most studies of the use of binaural cues have determined an animal's ability to localize pure tones presented from loudspeakers placed 30° to the left and right of its midline. The results of these studies have shown that the majority of mammals are able to localize both low- and high-frequency pure tones, indicating that they can use both binaural phase- and binaural intensity-difference cues. However, some animals can use only one of these cues (see Table 19.1). For example, horses and cattle can use binaural time, but not binaural intensity, whereas house mice and big brown bats use binaural intensity, but not binaural time. Finally, a few animals, such as the goat and Indian elephant, use both cues, but are unable to use binaural intensity differences for frequencies in the upper octaves of their hearing ranges.

Another aspect of sound localization for which mammals show systematic differences is in the upper frequency limit for use of the binaural phase cue. As shown in Figure 19.4,

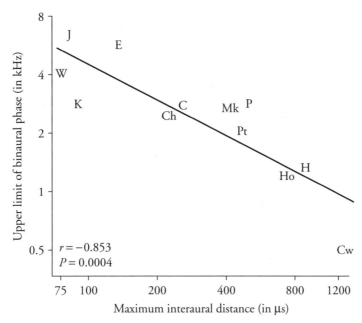

**Figure 19.4** Relation between maximum interaural distance and the highest frequency at which the use of the binaural phase-difference cue has been observed. Although the binaural phase-difference cue is physically available at higher frequencies for animals with smaller heads, the limits shown here represent an animal's behavioral upper limit, not physical availability. C, domestic cat; **Ch**, chinchilla; **Cw**, cow; **E**, Egyptian fruit bat; **H**, human; **HO**, horse; **J**, Jamaican fruit bat; **K**, kangaroo rat; **Mk**, Japanese macaque; **P**, domestic pig; **Pt**, pig-tailed macaque; **W**, least weasel.
*Source*: Data from R. S. Heffner, et al. (2001c).

the upper frequency limit for the use of binaural phase spans a range of more than three octaves from the 500 Hz upper limit of cattle to the 6.3 kHz upper limit of the Jamaican fruit bat. Specifically, animals with small heads (small interaural distances) are able to use the binaural phase cue at higher frequencies than animals with larger heads. Although this relation seems obvious because the phase-difference cue is physically available at higher frequencies for animals with smaller heads, it should be noted that the upper limits shown in Figure 19.4 are, in most cases, well below the frequency of ambiguity. Thus they represent the ability of the animals' auditory systems to extract the binaural phase cue. Because using the binaural phase cue requires that auditory neurons fire in synchrony with the phase of the sine wave (i.e., phase lock), the variation in the upper limit for using binaural phase suggests that there is also variation in the upper limit of phase locking. Interestingly, the Jamaican fruit bat appears capable of phase locking up to at least 6.3 kHz, which is higher than the 5 kHz commonly listed as the upper limit for phase locking in the mammalian auditory system (R. S. Heffner et al., 2001c; Moore, 1997).

## Discrimination of frequency

The ability to discriminate frequency has been determined for a small number of species (Fay, 1988). The most common procedure for obtaining frequency discrimination thresholds is to train an animal to discriminate between a standard tone and a comparison tone of higher frequency and then reducing the frequency of the comparison tone until the animal can no longer discriminate between the two. Frequency discrimination thresholds are then obtained at frequencies throughout the animal's hearing range.

So far, comparison of the abilities of different species to discriminate frequency has not yielded any theoretical insight (e.g., Fay, 1992). A possible explanation for this result may be that the way in which frequency-difference thresholds are obtained does not always yield an accurate estimate of an animal's ability. Some time ago we noticed that some animals appeared to have unusual difficulty performing frequency discriminations, as compared to their performance on detection and localization tasks. Indeed, even an animal as intelligent and as cooperative as the Indian elephant showed poorer asymptotic performance when discriminating frequency (R. S. Heffner & Heffner, 1982). It is possible that the difficulty some animals have in performing a frequency discrimination is due to the way in which the stimuli are presented. That is, it is often easier to train an animal to detect when a tone is changing in frequency than it is to train it to discriminate between discrete tones that differ in frequency. Moreover, there are a number of natural sounds in which the direction of a frequency change is a significant parameter (e.g., communication calls), suggesting that animals may naturally be more experienced in detecting such changes. Thus, a more appropriate test of the ability to discriminate frequency may be to determine an animal's ability to detect frequency changes, such as frequency sweeps and frequency-modulated tones.

## Final considerations regarding mammalian hearing

It is necessary to emphasize both the importance of knowing what animals hear and that such information must be obtained behaviorally.

*General relevance of species differences in hearing* Given the differences in mammalian hearing ranges, sounds that are clearly audible to one species may be completely inaudible to another. An extreme example is the Indian elephant, which hears up to 11.8 kHz, and the little brown bat, which hears down to 10.3 kHz – their hearing ranges show such little overlap that they hear virtually no sounds in common (H. E. Heffner & Heffner, 1998). However, even common laboratory species can have very different hearing abilities, a situation that can lead to problems if not taken into consideration. One such case is a series of studies that concluded that laboratory rats were superior to cebus monkeys in discriminating melodies (D'Amato, 1988). However, inspection of the auditory stimuli reveals that some of the melodies contained frequencies below 500 Hz, which, although clearly audible to monkeys, are beyond the hearing range of rats. As a result, the monkeys had to discriminate between two clearly audible, but different tunes, whereas the rats had to discriminate between a tune they could hear well and one that contained many inaudible notes. Thus, the results of this study are more likely a demonstration of sensory, rather than cognitive, differences between monkeys and rats. Clearly, it is important not to assume that what is audible to one species is equally audible to another.

Acknowledging species differences is also important for the meaningful interpretation of physiological results, especially as it is not uncommon for physiological data from animals to be compared with behavioral data from humans. In such cases, it appears that there is an underlying assumption that auditory neurons in a particular nucleus have the same general properties regardless of the species in which they are found – indeed, a study may even fail to state what species was being studied (e.g., Skottun, 1998). This situation leads to the construction of auditory models that are composites of different creatures – auditory chimeras – although, because many are half human and half beast, the term "auditory sphinx" might be more appropriate. Such a composite can have interesting results. For example, it has been claimed that single auditory thalamic neurons are able to "distinguish" interaural time differences with the same acuity as human observers (about 10 $\mu$s), suggesting that a handful of neurons may account for human localization acuity (Skottun, 1998). However, it turns out that the auditory neurons in question were located in the thalamus of the domestic rabbit, an animal with extremely poor sound localization acuity (~22° vs the ~1° acuity of humans). Thus, although physiologists can detect neural changes to binaural time differences in the rabbit as small as 10 $\mu$s, the rabbit can at best detect differences of about 30 $\mu$s, assuming that it is relying solely on the time differences available to it at its threshold with no help from spectral cues, which is by no means certain. In short, physiological results must be compared with behavioral results obtained in the same species for the conclusions to be meaningful.

*Electrophysiological measures of hearing* Because behavioral tests of hearing are difficult and time-consuming, measures of neural responses are often used to estimate what an animal can hear. Some common physiological measures are the cochlear microphonic, thresholds of units in the inferior colliculus, and the auditory brainstem response (ABR). Although such measures cannot help but reflect some aspect of hearing, they are imperfect estimates of actual hearing ability. Moreover, the degree to which they correspond to behavioral thresholds is generally unknown, as few studies have attempted to determine the correspondence between behavioral and electrophysiological thresholds (for an exception, see Szymanski et al., 1999).

An example of the difference between behavioral and electrophysiological results can be seen in the comparison of the behavioral audiogram and ABR thresholds of C57BL/6J × C3HeB/FeJ mice (Koay, Harrington, Heffner, & Heffner, unpublished observations). As shown in Figure 19.5, the ABR generally reflects the behavioral audiogram, even to the extent of indicating the animals' best frequency. However, the ABR thresholds overestimate low-frequency hearing while underestimating high-frequency hearing and best sensitivity. Such a discrepancy is not surprising and there are at least two reasons why one would expect the two estimates of hearing to diverge (Szymanski et al., 1999). First, the tones used to generate the ABR are not pure tones because they

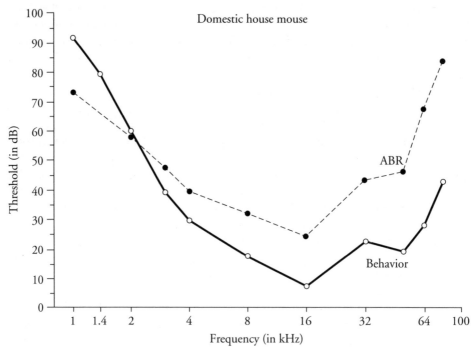

**Figure 19.5**   Behavioral audiogram and auditory brainstem response (ABR) thresholds of C57BL/6J × C3HeB/FeJ mice. Note that the ABR overestimates low-frequency sensitivity and underestimates high-frequency sensitivity.

have rapid onsets that cause "spectral splatter," whereas the tones used in behavioral audiograms have slow onsets to keep the signal pure. Second, the ABR procedure uses very brief tones with effective durations of 2 ms, whereas behavioral audiograms use much longer tone durations of 400 ms or more. However, detection thresholds depend on the duration of a sound, with sensitivity (in humans) improving as the duration of the stimulus increases up to about 200 ms, a process known as temporal integration (e.g., Moore, 1997). Thus, the difference in the purity and duration of the stimuli alone are sufficient to suggest that the ABR will be an imperfect estimate of behavioral sensitivity.

## Role of the Auditory Cortex in Hearing

The search for the functions of different areas of cortex began during the late part of the nineteenth century following the discovery of the motor cortex in the dog by Fritsch and Hitzig (1870). One of the principal localizationists involved in this search was David Ferrier, a British physician who studied the cortex of various mammals using electrical stimulation and ablation techniques. By observing that stimulation of the temporal lobe of monkeys resulted in an acoustic startle reaction, Ferrier correctly placed the auditory cortex in the upper two thirds of the superior temporal gyrus (Ferrier & Yeo, 1885). His subsequent demonstration that removal of this area abolished all responsiveness to sound was then taken as conclusive evidence that he had successfully identified the auditory cortex. However, ablation studies conducted by other researchers failed to replicate his findings, with the result that William James concluded that Ferrier was most likely wrong (James, 1890). But, as we shall see, Ferrier was essentially correct in both the location of the auditory cortex and the effect of its ablation (H. E. Heffner, 1987).

Although it is currently fashionable to infer the function of an auditory center from the response properties of its neurons, historically it has been the results of ablation/ behavior studies that have carried the most weight (Neff et al., 1975). Although experimental lesions have been made in all auditory centers, only auditory cortex has been studied extensively. The following sections review the effect of auditory cortex lesions on the detection and localization of sound as well as on the discrimination of frequency, including tone patterns and frequency sweeps. The results are presented by species, as the role of the auditory cortex can vary greatly from one species to the next.

## Making and assessing the effects of cortical lesions

*Making cortical lesions* There are two basic methods for making cortical lesions. To date, virtually all experimental lesions of the auditory cortex have been permanent lesions made by subpial aspiration. However, it is also possible to make reversible lesions, that is, to temporarily inactivate the cortex either by cooling it or by the application of chemicals (Lomber, 1999), a technique that is bound to yield new insights into the role of auditory cortex.

*Assessing the effects of cortical lesions* The effects of cortical lesions have been assessed with various behavioral techniques, including the conditioned suppression technique in which an animal is trained to associate a sound with a mild shock. However, studies on the neural mechanisms of fear conditioning have suggested that disruption of auditory input to the amygdala could reduce or eliminate the response of an animal to a sound that has been paired with shock (e.g., LeDoux, Sakaguchi, & Reis, 1984). Thus the question arises as to whether any of the cortical deficits about to be described could be attributed to reduced fear conditioning rather than to a strictly auditory deficit. The answer to the question is no. Most ablation/behavior studies include control tests to demonstrate that an observed deficit is not due to any attention, motivation, cognitive, or motor disorder. For example, when an animal is unable to discriminate sounds, a routine control test is to use the same procedure to demonstrate that it retains the ability to detect the sounds. Moreover, the loss of the ability to localize sound following cortical lesions can be demonstrated with a pure reward procedure as well as with a shock procedure (e.g., H. E. Heffner & Heffner, 1990b). Thus a reduction in fear conditioning cannot serve as an alternative explanation of the effects of cortical lesions on hearing.

On the other hand, the possibility that the reduced fear response observed following lesions of the amygdala (and other sites) may be due to a hearing loss has never been ruled out. Not only has the possibility that such lesions themselves may cause a hearing loss never been investigated, but the lesions are made stereotaxically and the earbars used to position an animal's head in a stereotaxic device are known to rupture an animal's eardrums. Thus, although a reduction in fear conditioning cannot account for the cortical deficits in hearing, it is not possible to rule out hearing loss as an alternative explanation of the results of fear-conditioning studies, especially those obtained using stereotaxically placed lesions.

## Detection of sound

Ablation of the auditory cortex has a dramatic effect on absolute sensitivity in monkeys and humans, a small effect in carnivores, and little or no effect in other species that have been tested.

*Primates* The effect of both unilateral and bilateral auditory cortex ablation on absolute thresholds has been studied in some detail in macaque monkeys (H. E. Heffner & Heffner, 1986, 1989, 1990a). Unilateral ablation of the auditory cortex results in a substantial hearing loss in the ear opposite the lesion (the contralateral ear) with no effect on thresholds in the ear on the same side as the lesion (the ipsilateral ear). The hearing loss is greatest immediately after ablation with pure-tone thresholds improving over a period of a few months to near normal levels. The residual hearing loss is small and best demonstrated by comparing preoperative and postoperative thresholds.

Unilateral damage to the auditory cortex in humans undoubtedly results in a contralateral hearing loss (e.g., Karp, Belmont, & Birch, 1969). However, because the residual hearing loss is small, especially when part of the auditory cortex is spared, and because premorbid audiograms of brain damaged patients are rarely available for comparison, the existence of such a hearing loss has been controversial.

Bilateral ablation of the auditory cortex in Japanese macaques results in a profound hearing loss. Initially, there may be total deafness lasting for a few days to a few months after surgery. Pure-tone thresholds show substantial recovery during the first two months, with more gradual recovery thereafter, but the animals continue to show a substantial hearing loss several years after surgery. Thus Ferrier was correct – lesions of the posterior two-thirds of the superior temporal gyrus in monkeys do result in a profound hearing loss. The failure of his contemporaries to replicate his results was most likely because their lesions did not extend far enough into the depths of the Sylvian fissure and were therefore incomplete (H. E. Heffner, 1987).

Although bilateral damage to the auditory cortex in humans is rare, there have been cases showing a hearing loss similar to that observed in macaques. That is, the patient reports a sudden inability to hear any sound followed by gradual, but incomplete, recovery (Jerger, Weikers, Sharbrough, & Jerger, 1969; for a review, see H. E. Heffner & Heffner, 1986).

This pattern of the cortical hearing loss – deafness followed by substantial but incomplete recovery – suggests that the detection of sound is primarily mediated by subcortical structures that receive input from the auditory cortex. The removal of the cortex, then, results in deafness due to the shock of the sudden loss of cortical input (i.e., diaschisis). This condition is followed by partial recovery as the subcortical areas adjust to the loss of the cortex. There is currently no evidence that the recovery of hearing is mediated by other cortical areas.

*Nonprimates* The possibility of a cortical hearing loss has been examined in a few other species, none of which have shown the dramatic hearing loss that occurs in primates. Bilateral ablation of all neocortex in the Virginia opossum has no noticeable effect on absolute thresholds, whereas bilateral auditory cortex lesions in rats, cats, dogs, and ferrets result in small, but detectable hearing losses (for a review, see H. E. Heffner & Heffner, 1986).

On the other hand, a recent study found that rats were initially unresponsive to sound following temporary inactivation of auditory cortex using muscimol, a GABA-A agonist with an inhibitory effect on neurons (Talwar, Musial, & Gerstein, 2001). However, no control tests were conducted to determine whether the effect was due to a general unresponsiveness to sensory stimuli, and no conclusion can be drawn as to whether such inactivation of the auditory cortex in rats causes a hearing loss.

## Localization of sound

The discovery that auditory cortex ablation in cats results in a sound localization deficit was made over half a century ago by W. D. Neff and his colleagues (Neff, Fisher, Diamond, & Yela, 1956; Neff & Yela, 1948). As with the cortical hearing loss, this deficit is found in some species (primates and carnivores), but not others (rodents).

*Primates* Unilateral lesions of the auditory cortex result in a complete inability to discriminate the locus of a sound in the hemifield opposite the lesion (the contralesional hemifield), an effect that has been demonstrated in both macaques and squirrel monkeys (H. E. Heffner, 1997; Thompson & Cortez, 1983). The animals retain both the normal ability to localize sound in the ipsilesional hemifield and the ability to distinguish sounds arising in the one hemifield from sounds arising in the other. There is also some residual ability to localize sound in the contralesional hemifield when the source is close to midline (e.g., within 15° of midline), which may be mediated by the intact hemisphere. In short, unilateral ablation results in a "collapse" of auditory space in the contralesional hemifield.

Bilateral ablation of the auditory cortex appears to be the sum of two unilateral lesions – auditory space collapses in both hemifields (H. E. Heffner, 1997; H. E. Heffner & Heffner, 1990b). Although a macaque with a bilateral lesion can be trained to distinguish left *sounds* from right *sounds*, it shows no awareness of the location of the sound *source*. This result is demonstrated by the great difficulty the animals have in learning to approach the source of a continuous sound, which they eventually do by using a tracking strategy (i.e., move to where the sound is loudest). Some operated animals eventually learn to go left or right when the sound is brief, but they appear to be learning to associate a spatial response with an arbitrary sound that has no spatial locus. However, the animals are completely unable to distinguish sounds coming from two locations within the same hemifield. Thus, bilateral auditory cortex lesions appear to result in the total collapse of the left and right auditory hemifields leaving only a residual ability to discriminate between left and right sounds that are devoid of spatial meaning.

The effect of bilateral lesions has also been studied in the bushbaby (*Galago senegalensis*), a prosimian (Ravizza & Diamond, 1974). Although the results suggested that their sound localization ability is only moderately affected by auditory cortex lesions, only preliminary results were presented, and it is not known whether the remaining ability represents a species difference or if the lesions were incomplete.

Most studies indicate that unilateral lesions in humans result in a sound-localization deficit in the hemifield contralateral to the lesion, just as they do in macaques (for reviews, see H. E. Heffner & Heffner, 1990b; Neff et al., 1975). However, the observed deficits do not appear to be as severe as those found in macaques, even for patients in which one hemisphere has been entirely removed (Lessard, Lepore, Poirier, Villemagne, & Lassonde, 2000). One possible explanation is that such patients typically sustained cortical damage early in life, allowing for greater function compensation than occurred in the macaques, all of which were adults at the time of surgery. Surprisingly, a recent study has suggested that sound localization in humans is lateralized such that lesions of right, but not left, auditory cortex result in a sound localization deficit (Zatorre & Penhune, 2001). However, these results rest on the premise that partial lesions of the auditory cortex that include primary auditory cortex, AI, are sufficient to produce the classic sound localization deficit – but this premise may not be correct. In macaques, partial lesions of the auditory cortex, even if they include substantial portions of primary auditory cortex, do not result in a total collapse of the contralateral auditory field (Harrington & Heffner, 2002). Thus the results of the study by Zatorre and Penhune (2001) should be reevaluated with regard to the location and completeness of the lesions.

The effects of bilateral lesions in humans on sound localization are not clear owing to the rarity of cases with complete bilateral auditory cortex lesions. Indeed, given the severe hearing loss that accompanies such lesions, the patients would be difficult to examine. However, we expect that bilateral lesions in humans, as in macaques, would result in a complete inability to localize sound.

*Carnivores* The effect of cortical lesions on sound localization has been studied in cats, dogs, and ferrets (see H. E. Heffner & Heffner, 1990b for a review). All species appear to show the same sound-localization deficit as macaques. Specifically, unilateral lesions in cats and ferrets result in a sound-localization deficit in the hemifield contralateral to the lesion, and bilateral lesions in cats, dogs, and ferrets result in a deficit in both hemifields. In addition, a study using cats indicated that restricting the lesion to a particular frequency representation in primary auditory cortex affects the ability to localize those specific frequencies (Jenkins & Merzenich, 1984). However, this finding deserves further study in light of the finding that cats experience a mild hearing loss following cortical lesions and because lesions restricted to primary auditory cortex in monkeys do not appear to result in the classic sound-localization deficit (see above).

*Rodents* In contrast to primates and carnivores, bilateral ablation of the auditory cortex in the Norway rat, as well as in the wild wood rat (*Neotoma floridana*), does not abolish the ability to localize sound – at most it may result in a slight increase in threshold (e.g., H. E. Heffner & Heffner, 1990b; Kavanagh & Kelly, 1986).

*Other species* Two other species that have been examined are the hedgehog, an insectivore, and the Virginia opossum, a marsupial (Ravizza & Diamond, 1974; Ravizza & Masterton, 1972). In both cases, cortical ablation appears to result in increased thresholds for left–right discriminations. However, neither study examined the possibility that, in spite of the animals' ability to perform a left–right discrimination, the lesions may have resulted in a collapse of auditory space within each hemifield. Thus the complete effect of cortical lesions on sound localization in these species is not known.

## The discrimination of frequency

Early electrophysiological studies indicated that frequency was mapped on the auditory cortex in an orderly manner (tonotopic maps), giving rise to the idea that the cortex is necessary for frequency discrimination (Neff et al., 1975). Once it was discovered that cortical ablation did not totally abolish the ability of the animals to discriminate one frequency from another, testing moved on to the discrimination of tone patterns and frequency sweeps.

*Discrimination of discrete frequencies* Studies of the effect of auditory cortex lesions on the ability of macaques to discriminate tones of different frequency have established that auditory cortex lesions result in a small but reliable increase in thresholds (e.g., Massopust, Wolin, & Frost, 1970). For example, the average frequency increment needed to discriminate a 625 Hz tone from higher frequencies was shown to increase from 7.5 Hz to 27.5 Hz (Harrington, Heffner, & Heffner, 2001). Thus, although the auditory cortex is not necessary for frequency discrimination per se, its loss does result in an increase in thresholds.

   Although an initial study indicated that bilateral auditory cortex lesions in cats abolished the ability to discriminate frequency (Meyer & Woolsey, 1952), a subsequent study failed to find a deficit (Butler, Diamond, & Neff, 1957). However, the two studies used different methods of stimulus presentation, giving rise to the idea that although operated animals could detect a *change* in the frequency of an ongoing train of tone pips, they could not discriminate tones of two different frequencies if the presentation of the tones was separated by a long silent interval – that is, they could make a "relative," but not an "absolute," frequency discrimination (Thompson, 1960). However, it has since been demonstrated that cats with auditory cortex lesions retain the ability to make absolute judgments of frequency (Cranford, 1978) and the current view is that such lesions have at most only a small effect on the ability of cats to discriminate frequency.

Although it was established long ago that removal of cortex has no effect on frequency discrimination in the Norway rat (J. B. Kelly, unpublished doctoral dissertation), a recent study has suggested that the chemical inactivation by the application of muscimol to the auditory cortex results in a temporary inability to discriminate frequency (Talwar et al., 2001). The implication of this finding is that the auditory cortex in rats (and other mammals) is normally involved in the discrimination of frequency. However, no control tests were conducted to rule out alternative explanations of the failure of the rats to respond to a difference in frequency. Thus we do not know at this time if the results were due to an auditory deficit per se, or to an attentional, cognitive, or motor deficit. Indeed, it is conceivable that the application of muscimol to the auditory cortex results in the perception of phantom sound that distracts the animal from external auditory stimuli.

*Tone pattern discrimination* Once it was found that cortical lesions did not abolish the ability to discriminate frequency, researchers moved on to determine the role of the cortex in discriminating changes in temporal patterns of tones. The tone patterns were typically sequences of three tone pips of a high or low frequency, such as Low–High–Low, High–Low–High, Low–Low–Low, and High–High–High. By using such stimuli, researchers hoped to discover how the cortex processed patterns of stimuli that were analogous to the spatial patterns used in visual and somatosensory studies. However, because many of the discriminations proved difficult even for normal animals to learn, the resulting deficits may have been cognitive rather than perceptual in nature. Thus the significance of this line of research is unclear (for reviews, see Elliott & Trahiotis, 1972; Neff et al., 1975).

*Frequency sweeps* The discovery that some auditory cortex neurons in cats are selective for the direction of a frequency change (Whitfield & Evans, 1965) was the motivation for investigating the effect of auditory cortex lesions on the discrimination of frequency sweeps. The results of these studies indicated that bilateral auditory cortex lesions impaired, but did not abolish, the ability to discriminate a rising from a falling frequency sweep (Kelly & Whitfield, 1971).

The motivation for determining the effect of cortical lesions on the discrimination of frequency sweeps by macaques was different. Specifically, Japanese macaques lose the ability to discriminate between different forms of their coo call following auditory cortex lesions (H. E. Heffner & Heffner, 1986, 1994, 1995b). Although this result suggested that the animals had an aphasia-like deficit, in that they were no longer able to interpret their vocal communications, the possibility existed that it might be part of a general sensory deficit. Because the coos used in those studies were tonal calls that either rose or fell in frequency, it was necessary to determine whether auditory cortex lesions affected the ability to discriminate frequency sweeps. The results indicated that although the animals could discriminate a rising from a falling frequency sweep, they did so on the basis of absolute frequency differences, for example, comparing the initial frequency of each sweep, rather than responding to the direction of frequency change. When they were prevented from using that strategy, by randomizing the frequency of the stimuli, their performance fell to chance. Thus, auditory cortex ablation in macaques abolishes the ability to determine whether a sound is *changing* in frequency (Harrington et al., 2001). This result demonstrates that the inability of macaques to discriminate their coo vocalizations is part of a broader sensory deficit. It also raises the question of whether a similar deficit underlies sensory aphasia in humans.

Recent studies have found that cortical lesions impair the performance of gerbils in discriminating rising from falling frequency sweeps (Ohl, Wetzel, Wagner, Rech, & Scheich, 1999; Wetzel, Ohl, Wagner, & Scheich, 1998). However, the group data presented in these studies (no individual data were shown) showed relatively large variance, suggesting that not all of the operated animals were impaired. It has long been the rule that a lesion must consistently result in a deficit before the ablated area can be considered essential for a function (James, 1890). Thus, without knowledge of individual results, no definite conclusion can be reached regarding the role of auditory cortex in gerbils on the discrimination of frequency sweeps.

## Final considerations regarding the auditory cortex

The auditory cortex has been described as being functionally unilateral, with each hemisphere processing sound arising from the contralateral hemifield (Glendenning & Masterton, 1983). This view is based on the observation that the majority of neurons in the auditory cortex respond best to sounds in the contralateral sound field, that ipsilateral input is usually inhibitory, and that unilateral damage to the auditory cortex results in sound-localization deficits confined to the hemifield contralateral to the lesion. Although this view may be valid for sound localization, it does not necessarily apply to other auditory abilities, such as sound detection and discrimination. For these abilities, the auditory cortex may be more appropriately characterized as being asymmetrically bilateral with each hemisphere having a greater involvement in processing information from the contralateral *ear* as opposed to the contralateral hemifield.

With regard to the detection of sound, a unilateral auditory cortex lesion in a macaque results in a hearing loss in the ear contralateral to the lesion, with thresholds in the other ear completely unaffected. This means that sounds arising from the contralesional hemifield, even if inaudible in the ear on that side because of the unilateral hearing loss, will be detected as long as the sound can reach the other ear (H. E. Heffner & Heffner, 1989). The same applies to the discrimination of frequency change, which is impaired for sounds presented to the contralesional *ear* and not for sounds presented in the contralesional *hemifield* that reaches both ears (H. E. Heffner and Heffner, 1994). In neither case, however, is the deficit as severe as that resulting from a bilateral lesion, demonstrating that each hemisphere plays a role in processing sounds from both ears with the opposite hemisphere having a greater role. Thus, although unilateral lesions abolish sound localization in the contralateral hemifield, they affect the detection and discrimination of sounds in the contralateral ear.

It should be noted that the above results are species-specific – they apply to macaques, but not necessarily to other mammals, and particularly not to rodents. There is currently no explanation for why some species should show a deficit when others do not. It may be noted that rats have smooth (lissencephalic) brains, whereas carnivores and primates have highly convoluted (gyrencephalic) brains, and that rats normally have poorer sound localization acuity than primates and carnivores. Whether either factor is related to the observed species differences in cortical function is not known. However, it should be clear that a person cannot speak of the function of "the auditory cortex" without also stating the species from which the functions have been inferred.

## References

Brown, C. H. (1994). Sound localization (pp. 57–96). In R. R. Fay & A. N. Popper (eds.), *Comparative hearing: Mammals*. New York: Springer-Verlag.

Burghardt, G. M. (1977). Learning processes in reptiles. In C. Gans (ed.), *Biology of the reptilia, Vol. 7: Ecology and behavior* (pp. 555–681). New York: Academic Press.

Butler, R. A. (1975). The influence of the external and middle ear on auditory discriminations. In W. D. Keidel & W. D. Neff (eds.), *Handbook of sensory physiology: Auditory system* (Vol. V/2, pp. 247–60). New York: Springer.

Butler, R. A., Diamond, I. T., & Neff, W. D. (1957). Role of auditory cortex in discrimination of changes in frequency. *Journal of Neurophysiology, 20*, 108–20.

Cahill, L., McGaugh, J. L., & Weinberger, N. M. (2001). The neurobiology of learning and memory: Some reminders to remember. *Trends in Neuroscience, 24*, 578–81.

Cranford, J. L. (1978). Polysensory cortex lesions and auditory frequency discrimination in the cat. *Brain Research, 148*, 499–503.

D'Amato, M. R. (1988). A search for tonal pattern perception in cebus monkeys: Why monkeys can't hum a tune. *Music Perception, 5*, 453–80.

Dooling, R. J., & Hulse, S. (eds.) (1989). *The comparative psychology of audition: Perceiving complex sounds*. New York: Lawrence Erlbaum Associates.

Elliott, D. N., & Trahiotis, C. (1972). Cortical lesions and auditory discrimination. *Psychological Bulletin, 77*, 198–222.

Fay, R. R. (1988). *Hearing in vertebrates: A psychophysics databook*. Worcester, MA: Heffernan Press.

Fay, R. R. (1992). Structure and function in sound discrimination among vertebrates. In D. B. Webster, R. R. Fay, & A. N. Popper (eds.), *The evolutionary biology of hearing* (pp. 229–63). New York: Springer-Verlag.

Ferrier, D., & Yeo, G. (1885). A record of experiments on the effects of lesion of different regions of the cerebral hemispheres. *Philosophical Transactions of the Royal Society of London, Biology, 175*, 479–564.

Flanagan, J. L., & Guttman, N. (1960). On the pitch of periodic pulses. *Journal of the Acoustical Society of America, 32*, 1308–19.

Fritsch, G., & Hitzig, E. (1870). Über die elektrische Erregbarkeit des Grosshirns. *Archives für Anatomie Physiologie und Wissenshaftlicke Medicin, 37*, 300–32.

Galton, F. (1883). *Inquiries into human faculty and its development*. J.M. Dent & Sons: London.

Glendenning, K. K., & Masterton, R. B. (1983). Acoustic chiasm: Efferent projections of the lateral superior olive. *Journal of Neuroscience, 3*, 1521–37.

Green, D. M. (1995). Maximum-likelihood procedures and the inattentive observer. *Journal of the Acoustical Society of America, 97*, 3749–60.

Harrington, I. A., & Heffner, H. E. (2002). A behavioral investigation of "separate processing streams" within macaque auditory cortex. *Abstracts of the 25th Annual Midwinter Research Meeting of the Association for Research in Otolaryngology, 25*, 120.

Harrington, I. A., Heffner, R. S., & Heffner, H. E. (2001). An investigation of sensory deficits underlying the aphasia-like behavior of macaques with auditory cortex lesions. *Neuroreports*, *12*, 1217–21.

Heffner, H. E. (1983). Hearing in large and small dogs: Absolute thresholds and size of the tympanic membrane. *Behavioral Neuroscience*, *97*, 310–18.

Heffner, H. E. (1987). Ferrier and the study of auditory cortex. *Archives of Neurology*, *44*, 218–21.

Heffner, H. E. (1997). The role of macaque auditory cortex in sound localization. *Acta Oto-Laryngologica Supplement*, *532*, 22–7.

Heffner, H. E., & Heffner, R. S. (1983). Sound localization and high-frequency hearing in horses. *Journal of the Acoustical Society of America*, *93*, S42.

Heffner, H. E., & Heffner, R. S. (1984). Sound localization in large mammals: Localization of complex sounds by horses. *Behavioral Neuroscience*, *98*, 541–55.

Heffner, H. E., & Heffner, R. S. (1985). Hearing in two cricetid rodents: Wood rat (*Neotoma floridana*) and grasshopper mouse (*Onychomys leucogaster*). *Journal of Comparative Psychology*, *99*, 275–88.

Heffner, H. E., & Heffner, R. S. (1986). Effect of unilateral and bilateral auditory cortex lesions on the discrimination of vocalizations by Japanese macaques. *Journal of Neurophysiology*, *56*, 683–701.

Heffner, H. E., & Heffner, R. S. (1989). Unilateral auditory cortex ablation in macaques results in a contralateral hearing loss. *Journal of Neurophysiology*, *62*, 789–801.

Heffner, H. E., & Heffner, R. S. (1990a). Effect of bilateral auditory cortex lesions on absolute thresholds in Japanese macaques. *Journal of Neurophysiology*, *64*, 191–205.

Heffner, H. E., & Heffner, R. S. (1990b). Effect of bilateral auditory cortex lesions on sound localization in Japanese macaques. *Journal of Neurophysiology*, *64*, 915–31.

Heffner, H. E., & Heffner, R. S. (1994). Lateralization of the perception of communicative vocalizations in Japanese macaques. In J. R. Anderson, J. J. Roeder, B. Thierry, & N. Herrenschmidt (eds.), *Current primatology, Vol. III, behavioural neuroscience, physiology and reproduction* (pp. 1–8). Strasbourg: Université Louis Pasteur.

Heffner, H. E., & Heffner, R. S. (1995a). Conditioned avoidance. In G. M. Klump, R. J. Dooling, R. R. Fay, & W. C. Stebbins (eds.), *Methods in comparative psychoacoustics* (pp. 73–87). Basel: Birkhäuser.

Heffner, H. E., & Heffner, R. S. (1995b). Role of auditory cortex in the perception of communicative vocalizations by Japanese macaques. In E. Zimmermann, J. Newman, & U. Juergens (eds.), *Current topics in primate communication* (pp. 207–19). Plenum: New York.

Heffner, H. E., & Heffner, R. S. (1998). Hearing. In G. Greenberg & M. M. Haraway (eds.), *Comparative psychology: A handbook* (pp. 290–303). New York: Garland.

Heffner, R. S., & Heffner, H. E. (1982). Hearing in the elephant: Absolute sensitivity, frequency discrimination, and sound localization. *Journal of Comparative and Physiological Psychology*, *96*, 926–44.

Heffner, R. S., & Heffner, H. E. (1990). Vestigial hearing in a fossorial mammal, the pocket gopher, (*Geomys bursarius*). *Hearing Research*, *46*, 239–52.

Heffner, R. S., & Heffner, H. E. (1992a). Evolution of sound localization in mammals. In D. B. Webster, R. R. Fay, & A. N. Popper (eds.), *The evolutionary biology of hearing* (pp. 691–715). New York: Springer-Verlag.

Heffner, R. S., & Heffner, H. E. (1992b). Hearing and sound localization in blind mole rats. *Hearing Research*, *62*, 206–16.

Heffner, R. S., & Heffner, H. E. (1992c). Visual factors in sound localization in mammals. *Journal of Comparative Neurology*, *317*, 219–32.

Heffner, R. S., & Heffner, H. E. (1993). Degenerate hearing and sound localization in naked mole rats (*Heterocephalus glaber*), with an overview of central auditory structures. *Journal of Comparative Neurology*, 331, 418–33.

Heffner, R. S., Heffner, H. E., & Koay, G. (1995). Sound localization in chinchillas, II: Front/back and vertical localization. *Hearing Research*, 88, 190–8.

Heffner, R. S., Koay, G., & Heffner, H. E. (2001a). Audiograms of five species of rodents: Implications for the evolution of hearing and the encoding of pitch. *Hearing Research*, 157, 138–52.

Heffner, R. S., Koay, G., & Heffner, H. E. (2001b). Sound-localization acuity changes with age in C57BL/6J mice. In: J. F. Willott (ed.), *Handbook of mouse auditory research: From behavior to molecular biology* (pp. 31–5). Boca Raton, FL: CRC Press.

Heffner, R. S., Koay, G., & Heffner, H. E. (2001c). Sound localization in a new-world frugivorous bat, *Artibeus jamaicensis*: Acuity, use of binaural cues, and its relationship to vision. *Journal of the Acoustical Society of America*, 109, 412–21.

Jackson, L. L., Heffner, R. S., & Heffner, H. E. (1999). Free-field audiogram of the Japanese macaque (*Macaca fuscata*). *Journal of the Acoustical Society of America*, 106, 3017–23.

James, W. (1890). *Principles of psychology*. New York: Holt.

Jenkins, W. M., & Merzenich, M. M. (1984). Role of cat primary auditory cortex for sound-localization behavior. *Journal of Neurophysiology*, 52, 819–47.

Jerger, J., Weikers, N. J., Sharbrough, F. W. III, & Jerger, S. (1969). Bilateral lesions of the temporal lobe: A case study. *Acta Otol-Laryngologica Supplement*, 258, 1–51.

Karp, E., Belmont, I., & Birch, H. G. (1969). Unilateral hearing loss in hemiplegic patients. *Journal of Nervous and Mental Disorders*, 148, 83–6.

Kavanagh, G. L., & Kelly, J. B. (1986). Midline and lateral field sound localization in the albino rat (*Rattus norvegicus*). *Behavioral Neuroscience*, 100, 200–5.

Kelly, J. B., & Whitfield, I. C. (1971). Effects of auditory cortical lesions on discriminations of rising and falling frequency-modulated tones. *Journal of Neurophysiology*, 34, 802–16.

Klump, G. M., Dooling, R. J., Fay, R. R., & Stebbins, W. C. (eds.) (1995). *Methods in comparative psychoacoustics*. Basel: Birkhäuser.

Larsen, O. N. (1995). Acoustic equipment and sound field calibration. In G. M. Klump, R. J. Dooling, R. R. Fay, & W. C. Stebbins (eds.), *Methods in comparative psychoacoustics* (pp. 31–45). Basel: Birkhäuser.

LeDoux, J. E., Sakaguchi, A., & Reis, D. J. (1984). Subcortical efferent projections of the medial geniculate nucleus mediate emotional responses conditioned to acoustic stimuli. *Journal of Neuroscience*, 4, 683–98.

Lessard, N., Lepore, F., Poirier, P., Villemagne, J., & Lassonde, M. (2000). Sound localization in hemispherectomized subjects: The contribution of crossed and uncrossed cortical afferents. *Experimental Brain Research*, 134, 344–52.

Lomber, S. G. (1999). The advantages and limitations of permanent or reversible deactivation techniques in the assessment of neural function. *Journal of Neuroscience Methods*, 86, 109–17.

Massopust, L. C., Jr., Wolin, L. R., & Frost, V. (1970). Increases in auditory middle frequency discrimination threshold after cortical ablations. *Experimental Neurology*, 28, 299–305.

Masterton, B., Heffner, H., & Ravizza, R. (1969). The evolution of human hearing. *Journal of the Acoustical Society of America*, 45, 966–85.

Meyer, D. R., & Woolsey, C. N. (1952). Effects of localized cortical destruction on auditory discriminative conditioning in cat. *Journal of Neurophysiology*, 16, 149–62.

Moore, B. C. J. (1993). Frequency analysis and pitch perception. In W. A. Yost, A. N. Popper, & R. R. Fay (eds.), *Human psychophysics* (pp. 56–115). New York: Springer.

Moore, B. C. J. (1997). *An introduction to the psychology of hearing* (4th edn.) London: Academic Press.

Moore, D. R., Rothholtz, V., & King, A. J. (2001). Hearing: Cortical activation does matter. *Current Biology*, *11*, R782–4.

Musicant, A. D., & Butler, R. A. (1984). The influence of pinnae-based spectral cues on sound localization. *Journal of the Acoustical Society of American*, *75*, 1195–2100.

Neff, W. D., Diamond, I. T., & Casseday, J. H. (1975). Behavioral studies of auditory discrimination: Central nervous system. In: W. D. Keidel & W. D. Neff (eds.), *Handbook of sensory physiology. Auditory system, Vol. V/2* (pp. 307–400). New York: Springer-Verlag.

Neff, W. D., Fisher, J. F., Diamond, I. T., & Yela, M. (1956). Role of auditory cortex in discrimination requiring localization of sound in space. *Journal of Neurophysiology*, *19*, 500–12.

Neff, W. D., & Yela, M. (1948). Function of the auditory cortex: The localization of sound in space. *American Psychologists*, *3*, 243.

Ohl, F. W., Wetzel, W., Wagner, T., Rech, A., & Scheich, H. (1999). Bilateral ablation of auditory cortex in Mongolian Gerbil affects discrimination of frequency modulated but not of pure tones. *Learning & Memory*, *6*, 347–62.

Patterson, W. C. (1966). Hearing in the turtle. *Journal of Auditory Research*, *6*, 453–64.

Penner, M. J. (1995). Psychophysical methods. In G. M. Klump, R. J. Dooling, R. R. Fay, & W. C. Stebbins (eds.), *Methods in comparative psychoacoustics* (pp. 47–57). Basel: Birkhäuser.

Pfingst, B. E., Hienz, R., & Miller, J. (1975). Reaction-time procedure for measurement of hearing. II. Threshold functions. *Journal of the Acoustical Society of America*, *57*, 431–6.

Populin, L. C., & Yin, T. C. T. (1998). Behavioral studies of sound localization in the cat. *Journal of Neuroscience*, *18*, 2147–60.

Ravizza, R. J., & Diamond, I. T. (1974). Role of auditory cortex in sound localization: A comparative ablation study of hedgehog and bushbaby. *Federation Proceedings*, *33*, 1917–19.

Ravizza, R. J., & Masterson, R. B. (1972). Contribution of neocortex to sound localization in the opossum (*Didelphis virginiana*). *Journal of Neurophysiology*, *35*, 344–56.

Recanzone, G. H., Makhamra, S. D. D. R., & Guard, D. C. (1998). Comparison of relative and absolute sound localization ability in humans. *Journal of the Acoustical Society of America*, *103*, 1085–97.

Shannon, R. V. (1983). Multichannel electrical stimulation of the auditory nerve in man. I. Basic psychophysics. *Hearing Research*, *11*, 157–89.

Skottun, B. C. (1998). Sound localization and neurons. *Nature*, *393*, 531.

Stebbins, W. C. (ed.) (1970). *Animal psychophysics: The design and conduct of sensory experiments*. New York: Appleton-Century-Crofts.

Stevens, S. S. (1951). *Handbook of experimental psychology*. New York: Wiley.

Szymanski, M. D., Bain, D. E., Kiehl, K., Pennington, S., Wong, S., & Henry K. R. (1999). Killer whale (*Orcinus orca*) hearing: Auditory brainstem response and behavioral audiograms. *Journal of the Acoustical Society of America*, *106*, 1134–41.

Talwar, S. K., Musial, P. G., & Gerstein, G. L. (2001). Role of mammalian auditory cortex in the perception of elementary sound properties. *Journal of Neurophysiology*, *85*, 2350–8.

Thompson, G. C., & Cortez, A. M. (1983). The inability of squirrel monkeys to localize sound after unilateral ablation of auditory cortex. *Behavioral Brain Research*, *8*, 211–16.

Thompson, G., Heffner, H., & Masterton, B. (1974). An automated localization chamber. *Behavior Research Methods and Instrumentation*, *6*, 550–2.

Thompson, R. F. (1960). Function of auditory cortex of cat in frequency discrimination. *Journal of Neurophysiology*, *23*, 321–34.

Wagner, H. (1995). Sound-localization experiments in owls. In G. M. Klump, R. J. Dooling, R. R. Fay, & W. C. Stebbins (eds.), *Methods in comparative psychoacoustics* (pp. 183–94). Basel: Birkhäuser.

Wetzel, W., Ohl, F. W., Wagner, T., & Scheich, H. (1998). Right auditory cortex lesion in Mongolian gerbils impairs discrimination of rising and falling frequency-modulated tones. *Neuroscience Letters, 252,* 115–18.

Whitfield, I. C., & Evans, E. F. (1965). Responses of auditory cortical neurones to stimuli of changing frequency. *Journal of Neurophysiology, 28,* 655–72.

Zatorre, R. J., & Penhune, V. B. (2001). Spatial localization after excision of human auditory cortex. *Journal of Neuroscience, 21,* 6321–8.

Zhou, B., & Green, D. M. (1995). Reliability of pure-tone thresholds at high frequencies. *Journal of the Acoustical Society of America, 98,* 828–36.

# CHAPTER TWENTY

# Psychophysics

## H. R. Schiffman

As earlier chapters have indicated, physical energy from the environment is transformed into electrochemical messages that affect the nervous system and give rise to psychological experience. The goal of this chapter is to describe the key features of the major methods and techniques that experimental psychologists employ to establish quantitative relations between physical stimulation and sensory and perceptual experience. Collectively, these methods provide an essential tool called *psychophysics*. Specifically, psychophysics is the study of the quantitative relation between environmental stimulation (the physical dimension) and sensory-perceptual experience (the psychological dimension).

Among the basic issues and questions of psychophysics are those questions concerning the detection of very weak or *threshold* levels of stimulation. For example, what is the dimmest light that can be seen, the softest sound that can be heard, the weakest touch that can be felt? The general detection or threshold question is this: what is the minimum amount of physical energy for a particular sensory system that can just produce a sensation? There is also the related psychophysical question of the *difference threshold*, or the least difference between stimuli that can be detected: what is the smallest intensity difference or change between two stimuli that can just be detected? To answer such questions, this chapter will outline the traditional *psychophysical methods*. It will also examine an alternative approach, called *signal detection theory (SDT)*.

The final section of this chapter will examine ways to measure sensory experience and attempt to answer this fundamental psychophysical question: if environmental stimulation is varied, what is the corresponding effect on sensory or perceptual experience? That is, what is the quantitative relation between changes in the physical dimension and resultant changes in the psychological or experiential dimension?

Consider the challenge involved in this task of psychophysics. Although it is clear that features of the physical environment – such as sounds, lights, chemicals, and pressures – can be readily measured and quantified, it is also clear that the resulting psychological effects – sensations and perceptions – are private, unobservable experiences, which are not easily quantified. However, as we shall see, psychophysical methods and techniques make it possible to express the relation between the physical environment and its psychological effects.

Many of the general concerns of psychophysics are among the oldest in psychology. Historically, measuring sensory experience has often been tied to such central philosophical issues as the nature and meaning of conscious sensory experience, as well as the continuing enigma of the relation between the mind and the body (generally referred to as the mind–body problem). Although we will not focus on these issues here, it is obvious that psychophysics is crucial to the study of sensation and perception. Indeed, what psychophysics attempts to do is to link and quantify changes in our inner mental experience – our sensations and perceptions – to changes in external environmental stimulation. The first section introduces the problem of stimulus detection and the measurement of the detection or absolute threshold.

## Detection and the Absolute Threshold

One of the most fundamental experimental problems of psychophysics concerns the detection of very low intensity physical stimuli: what is the minimal amount of stimulus intensity required for detection? That is, how intense must a stimulus be for an observer to reliably detect its presence? Clearly, no organism is responsive to *all* portions of the possible range of physical energies. Instead, the potentially detectable stimulus must be of sufficient intensity to cause the degree of neural activation required in order to sense it.

The minimum stimulus magnitude necessary for detection is generally known as the absolute threshold or *absolute limen* (*limen* is Latin for threshold). Traditionally, absolute threshold stimulus values approximate the lower limit of the observer's absolute sensitivity. If the stimulus is too weak, not producing a reliable detection response, its magnitude is said to be subthreshold or subliminal. Some approximate absolute threshold values are shown in Table 20.1 (however, based on the means of computing them, they should not be taken too seriously in their present form).

**Table 20.1**   Approximate values of absolute thresholds expressed in everyday terms[a]

| Sense | Threshold |
| --- | --- |
| Vision | A candle flame seen at 30 miles on a dark, clear night |
| Hearing | The tick of a watch under quiet conditions at 20 feet |
| Taste | One teaspoon of sugar in two gallons of water |
| Smell | One drop of perfume diffused into the entire volume of a three-room apartment |
| Touch | The wing of a bee falling on your cheek from a distance of one centimeter |

*Source*: From Galanter (1962).
[a] These values apply under ideal conditions and will vary from individual to individual and from time to time for the same individual.

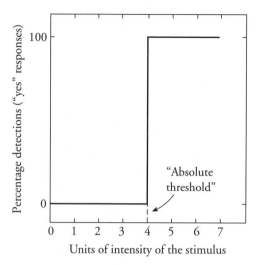

**Figure 20.1** A hypothetical absolute threshold curve. The vertical axis plots the proportion of trials on which the observer detects the stimulus. As shown, the threshold value is four units of stimulus intensity. This means that below four units of intensity the stimulus is not detected, whereas for four units and above, the stimulus is detected 100 percent of the time.

Strictly speaking, the concept of an absolute threshold assumes that there is a precise magnitude or stimulus point on the intensity or energy dimension that, when reached, becomes just detectable to the typical observer. It follows, then, that a stimulus one unit weaker will not be detected. If this were, in fact, the case, then some form of the hypothetical curve, such as that shown in Figure 20.1, would be the result. As Figure 20.1 illustrates, the observer will not detect the stimulus until a certain energy level is reached (i.e., four units in the figure), at which point (and beyond), the stimulus will be detected 100 percent of the time. In short, the absolute threshold is the stimulus magnitude that lies at the transition point in intensity between being undetectable and detectable. For the absolute threshold for tones, for example, either a sound will be heard or complete silence results. However, this is rarely the case. Instead, empirical laboratory investigations of the absolute threshold typically yield gradual empirical or *S-shaped* curves like that shown in Figure 20.2, suggesting that there may be no fixed or absolute stimulus magnitude separating the energy levels that never yield a detection response from those that always do (this point will be elaborated in a following section). However, for an approximation of the threshold value, psychologists have adopted a statistical concept. By convention, the absolute threshold value is assumed to correspond to that stimulus intensity or magnitude that elicits a detection response on *half* of its test trials, that is, the absolute threshold is specified by a particular magnitude that is detected 50 percent of the time. This statistically defined value is indicated by the dotted line in Figure 20.2.

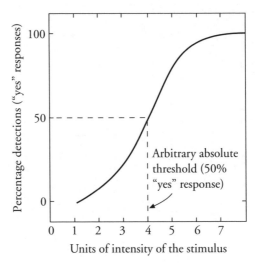

**Figure 20.2**   A typical empirical threshold function. By convention the absolute threshold is defined as the intensity at which the stimulus is detected on 50 percent of the trials.

## Psychophysical Methods

The methods traditionally used to determine the absolute threshold were devised by the nineteenth-century physicist and philosopher, Gustav Theodor Fechner (1801–87), who is generally regarded as the founder of psychophysics. Fechner's general interest was in examining the relation between physical stimulation and inner, mental experience and in order to study the detection problem he devised three main methods that enable a quantitative expression of the absolute threshold (Fechner [1860] 1966).

### *Method of limits (method of minimal change)*

One of Fechner's simplest methods is the *method of limits* or the *method of minimal change*. For example, to determine the absolute threshold for the detection of light, we might start with a light sufficiently intense to be easily perceived by an observer and then systematically reduce its intensity in small, gradual increments with a device such as a light dimmer until a point is reached where the observer reports that the light is no longer detectable. We record that intensity level and then show the light at a still dimmer setting, but now gradually increase its intensity level until the observer reports that the light is just perceptible. After a number of *descending* and *ascending* series of trials, we compute an average based on the energy levels at which the stimulus just crosses the boundary between being undetectable and detectable. In other words, we compute a numerical estimate of the absolute threshold by taking the average of the stimulus intensities reached when the observer reaches a "limit" or makes a response shift for the ascending and for the descending series of stimuli. This average serves as the

**Table 20.2**  Use of method of limits to determine the detection threshold for a visual stimulus

|                                   | *Observer's Response* |      |      |      |      |      |
| --------------------------------- | --- | --- | --- | --- | --- | --- |
|                                   | *Series* |  |  |  |  |  |
| *Light intensity (arbitrary units)* | *1* | *2* | *3* | *4* | *5* | *6* |
| 10 | YES |     |     |     |     |     |
| 9  | YES |     | YES |     |     |     |
| 8  | YES | <u>YES</u> | YES |     | YES |     |
| 7  | <u>YES</u> | NO | YES | <u>YES</u> | YES | <u>YES</u> |
| 6  | NO  | NO  | <u>YES</u> | NO | <u>YES</u> | NO |
| 5  |     | NO  | NO  | NO  | NO  | NO  |
| 4  |     |     |     | NO  |     | NO  |
| 3  |     |     |     |     |     | NO  |
| 2  |     |     |     |     |     |     |
| 1  |     |     |     |     |     |     |
| Limit value | 6.5 | 7.5 | 5.5 | 6.5 | 5.5 | 6.5 |

In the results of the three descending series of trials alternated with the three ascending series illustrated, the YES responses mean that on a given trial the stimulus is detected, and the NO responses mean that it is not detected. The horizontal bar in each series column represents the stimulus value of the "limit" in which a transition from detection to no detection, or vice versa, occurs. Typical of this method is some variation in the limit obtained for each series, which in this example ranges between 5.5 and 7.5. The threshold value is computed as the average of the limits obtained for each series, or $(6.5 + 7.5 + 5.5 + 6.5 + 5.5 + 6.5)/6 = 6.333$. That is, the threshold value for the detection of the light is 6.333 intensity.

statistical measure of the threshold for that observer under the general experimental conditions of testing. Table 20.2 presents an example of computing the absolute threshold using the method of limits.

Although very useful, the method of limits is open to various sources of bias and error. One drawback of its basic form is that generally the change in stimulus intensity (increase, ascending or decrease, descending) is orderly and regular so that over a series of trials the incremental stimulus changes may become somewhat predictable by the observer. Consequently, the observer's expectation that each successive stimulus is increasing or decreasing may bias the response. Another similar source of bias is the error of *habituation*, the tendency to keep responding that the stimulus is detected in a descending series and that it is not detected in an ascending series. In other words, observers make the same response in successive trials in a given series because they "habituate," or become used to, a particular response, continuing to give it even after the detection threshold is reached. To counteract these and other related sources of bias and error, modifications of the method of limits are commonly used. In one form, called the *staircase* method (Cornsweet, 1962), the experimenter initially presents an intensity level below the assumed threshold value, yielding an undetectable "No" response, and increases it until the observer detects it (i.e., a "Yes" response). As soon as the report changes from "No" to "Yes," the direction of the magnitude of the stimulus is reversed. Now the experimenter decreases the stimulus values until the response changes again; that is, when the observer reports "No," the intensity increases again. In a typical staircase method, the threshold is thus calculated as the average of all stimuli values at which the observer's response changes. Variations on this simple form of the staircase method are also often employed.

## Method of constant stimuli

Another method of determining the absolute threshold is the method of constant stimuli. This method requires a series of forced-choice trials. A fixed number of stimuli of different intensities, extending over a relatively wide range, are singly presented many times in an irregular or random order that ensures that each stimulus intensity occurs equally often. On each presentation the observer must make a detection response – either "Yes" (detection) or "No" (no detection). For each stimulus intensity, the percentage of trials in which the stimulus value is detected is computed. The intensity of the stimulus value detected on 50 percent of the trials is generally used as the measure of the absolute threshold. Although the method of constant stimuli is somewhat involved and laborious, it tends to yield the least variable and most accurate absolute threshold values.

## Method of adjustment (method of average error)

Lastly, there is the method of adjustment (or method of average error). Here the intensity of the stimulus is under the observer's control; that is, the observer is required to adjust the intensity to a *just detectable* level. Once the observer adjusts the stimulus intensity until it is just detectable, the value of that intensity level defines the threshold. However, although this method is quick and direct, it is generally the least accurate. Its major drawback is that it yields somewhat variable threshold values, probably because observers vary significantly in the precision and care with which they do their adjusting in a typical detection task.

## Signal Detection Theory (SDT)

In the empirically derived detection values for the absolute threshold plotted in Figure 20.2, there is a range of stimulus intensity levels over which an observer sometimes responds that the stimulus is detected and sometimes that it is not detected. That is, the *same* stimulus magnitude may sometimes be detected and sometimes not. This variation in the detection response to the same stimulus intensity implies that the absolute threshold may not be an absolute or fixed magnitude. This aspect, of course, poses a serious challenge to the traditional all-or-none notion of a sensory threshold, namely, that there is a precise stimulus intensity value separating stimuli that are detectable from those stimuli that are not.

To appreciate this threshold problem, we should note that in many real-life situations we are often unsure whether we have crossed the sensory threshold – that is, whether we accurately detected a weak or marginal stimulus. Clearly, we confront many stimulus conditions that are ambiguous from a sensory point of view, yet generally we make decisions concerning them. Do we really see that faint star in the night sky? Do we really hear the phone ring when in the shower?

In such real-life situations, decisions concerning the presence of weak stimuli pose special problems for the traditional threshold notion. Are our decisions based exclusively on the sensory effects of the stimuli or are there psychological *biases* within us that influence our decisions? This section presents an approach to assessing situations in which psychological factors may predispose us toward making certain decisions – the sorts of factors that the traditional threshold notion does not take into account.

## Sensitivity versus response bias

Because the magnitude of the stimulus required for a threshold or detection response varies, especially under weak or marginal conditions of stimulation, factors in addition to the observer's detection abilities, or the observer's sensitivity, may play a role in the task of detecting a weak stimulus (or signal, as it is called in this context). These factors may include the level of the observer's attention to the stimulus, the motivation for performing the detection task, the expectation that a stimulus is present, and other such *nonsensory* factors – collectively referred to as response bias – that may affect the observer's decision as to whether a signal is present or absent. Hence, during a detection task, when the observer sometimes responds "Yes" and at other times "No" to a constant signal or stimulus intensity, we do not know for sure whether this is a result of some change in the observer's sensitivity or whether it is merely the effect of nonsensory response factors such as fluctuations in the observer's attention or motivation. Indeed, observers may even sometimes say that they detect a stimulus when actually they are uncertain.

## Detection and noise

Why does the detection of a weak stimulus show such variability? That is, why is a weak or marginal constant stimulus sometimes detected and other times not detected? Consider what happens to the sensory system when any weak environmental signal occurs, such as a dim light or a faint sound. If it is sufficiently intense, sensory receptors at the neural level may register action potentials that can influence neural activity in the brain. This activity signals to the observer's nervous system that a light or a sound has occurred. However, spontaneous neural activity occurs continuously in the sensory systems and the brain, even in the total absence of external stimulation. This spontaneous sensory-neural activity is due, in part, to random patterns of neural firing – like static heard on AM radio or "snow" seen on TV – and is considered a form of extraneous background noise ($N$) in the sensory system (note that *noise* in this context is in no way restricted to the auditory sense). In addition to spontaneous sensory-neural activity, neural noise may include such factors as the unpredictable random effects of fatigue, and the effects of nonsensory response biases such as the observer's fluctuating level of attention, expectations, and motivation to the detection task.

Although noise is not part of the environmental stimulus (or signal) to be detected, when it occurs in an ambiguous situation, it can significantly influence the detection of a weak signal. In fact, what an observer tries to do on each presentation or trial of a typical signal detection experiment is to decide whether the sensory effects experienced – the sensations – are due to background noise ($N$) alone or to the signal heard against the background noises (i.e., the signal plus noise, or $SN$).

The distribution of the sensory effects of noise on the observer's sensory system is outlined in Figure 20.3. The familiar bell-shaped curve of Figure 20.3($a$) shows that the level of sensory activity attributed to noise alone in the sensory system varies considerably. The $x$-axis gives the level (low to moderate to high) of sensory activity, and the $y$-axis plots the frequency (rare to frequent) of different levels of sensory activity. Sometimes the noise *level* is minimal and sometimes it is extreme, but most frequently it is of moderate or average intensity, labeled $X_n$. However, when an environmental event (e.g., a sound or light) stimulates a sensory receptor, it produces sensory activity (a *signal*) that is added to the effects of the background noise. Specifically, if a signal of *constant* intensity is added to all possible levels of the randomly varying background noise, the composite effect on sensory activity caused by the signal plus noise ($SN$) will appear as in the normal distribution, or bell-shape curve, of Figure 20.3($b$). As was noted with the effects of $N$ alone, the level of sensory activity of $SN$ also varies, sometimes high, sometimes low, but it hovers around an average value (labeled $X_{s+n}$).

Figure 20.3($c$) shows that the average level of $SN$ is clearly higher than the average level of $N$ alone (i.e., $X_{s+n}$ is displaced to the right of $X_n$). However, as Figure 20.3($c$) also shows, the sensory effects of $N$ alone and $SN$ overlap each other. That is, they produce some common effects on the sensory system so that, when attempting to determine whether a weak stimulus is present or not, the observer must decide if the particular level of activity in his or her sensory system is due to the effects of $N$ alone – that is, to extraneous or irrelevant background activity – or to the effects of $SN$.

## The criterion

The observer's task in the typical signal detection experiment is to decide whether the sensation experienced on a given trial (based on the level of sensory activity) came from a signal ($SN$) or from noise alone ($N$). According to SDT, observers typically adopt some cutoff point, or internal criterion in overall sensory activity, in deciding whether a signal is present (the criterion measure is symbolized by the Greek letter beta, or $\beta$). One such criterion level is indicated on the $x$-axis of Figure 20.4. According to the criterion, the observer will respond "Yes" (affirming the presence of a signal) when the level of sensory activity shown on the $x$-axis exceeds that point, and "No" (denying the presence of a signal) when the sensory effect is less. Note that in both instances the observer may

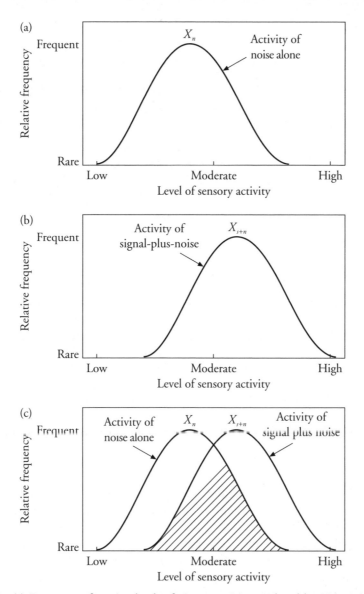

**Figure 20.3**    (a) Frequency of varying levels of sensory activity produced by *N* (noise) alone on the sensory system. The frequencies vary from rare to frequent. As shown, the most frequently occurring level of sensory activity is a moderate one that hovers around a midpoint at $X_n$. (b) Frequency of different levels of sensory activity produced by *SN* (signal plus noise) on the sensory system. The frequency of sensory effects when a stimulus or signal is added to all values of *N* given in (*a*) is shown.
(c) Frequency of various levels of sensory activity produced by distributions of *N* and *SN* on the sensory system. The average sensory-neural effect of *SN* is greater than the average effect of *N* due to addition of the *SN* to the *N* effects. However, the sensory effects of *N* alone and *SN* overlap and produce some sensory effects in common. That is, there is a range of sensory effects – shown in the shaded area – that could come from *either* the *N* or the *SN* distribution.
*Source*: Based on Schiffman (2001).

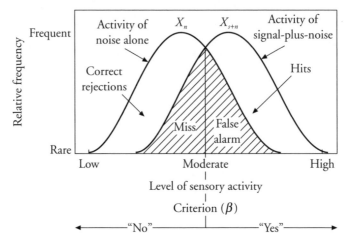

**Figure 20.4**    Frequency of sensory effects produced by *N* and by *SN* related to the observer's criterion value. The *x*-axis shows a hypothetical decision point or criterion value ($\beta$) at which the observer decides whether to report "Yes" or "No" regarding the presence of a signal on a given trial. Any number of criterion values could be adopted. In this hypothetical one, all signals whose effects lie below the criterion sensory level (i.e., to its left) take a "No" response; all signals whose effects lie above the criterion level (i.e., to its right) take a "Yes" response. Also shown for the hypothetical criterion are the regions of sensory activity for correct rejections and hits.
*Source*: Based on Schiffman (2001).

be in error. The observer can respond that a signal was present when in fact the sensory effect came only from the *N* distribution, that is, from noise alone (shown on the figure as a false alarm); likewise, the observer could respond that a signal was not present when actually one did occur (i.e., a miss). This follows because, as was noted in Figure 20.3(*c*), the sensory effects of the *SN* and *N* distributions overlap, making it impossible for an observer to set a sensory criterion that permits a correct response on *every* presentation of the signal. In fact, the shape of the overlap of the *SN* and *N* distributions in Figures 20.3(*c*) and 20.4 shows the possibility that on some *SN* trials (in which the signal actually occurs), the sensory effects on the observer may be less than those resulting from noise alone.

*Outcome matrix*

As noted in describing Figure 20.4, on a given signal detection trial the observer must decide whether the sensory activity is produced by the *SN* or the *N* effects, and the decision is determined by the criterion measure adopted at the moment. If the level of sensory activity is below the observer's criterion, he or she will respond "No"; if the level of sensory activity is above this criterion, he or she will respond "Yes."

**Table 20.3**   Stimulus–response outcome matrix for the observer responding either "yes" or "no" on each trial of a signal detection experiment

| Stimulus alternatives | *Response alternatives* | |
|---|---|---|
| | *"Yes, signal is present."* | *"No, signal is absent."* |
| Signal + noise | Probability of a positive response when the signal is present **Hit** | Probability of a negative response when the signal is present **Miss** |
| Noise response | Probability of a positive response when *no* signal is present **False Alarm** | Probability of a negative response when *no* signal is present **Correct Rejection** |

These responses result in one of four possible outcomes, as shown in Table 20.3. A hit results when the observer reports "Yes," and correctly detects the presence of a stimulus. As was noted, a false alarm occurs when the observer reports "Yes," that a stimulus is present when actually it is not, and a miss occurs when the observer reports "No," that a stimulus is not present when in fact it is. Finally, a correct rejection occurs when the observer correctly reports "No," a stimulus is not present, when in fact it is absent. Of course, as shown in Figure 20.4, false alarms and misses are errors due to the overlap of the sensory effects from the *SN* and *N* distributions and their relation to the criterion set by the observer for deciding whether a stimulus is present or not.

## Criteria effects: expectation and motivation

According to SDT, the ability to detect a weak stimulus varies from moment to moment because several relatively independent sources affect the observer's performance. One factor, of course, is that the level of noise itself in the sensory system varies. That is, the sensory effects from varying background noise, or from a constant signal plus varying background noise, from presentation to presentation, give rise to variations in the ability to detect a marginal stimulus. This point was illustrated in the bell-shaped curves of Figure 20.3.

Another factor that affects the performance is the observer's *expectation* about the presence of a signal. Unlike the traditional psychophysical methods in which the signal occurs on *every* trial, in a typical signal detection experiment the probability that a signal will be present on a given trial can be varied. Varying the frequency of the signal creates within the observer a source of *nonsensory response bias* – expectation – that affects the setting of the observer's criterion ($\beta$) level, and it can be created during the course of the experiment.

In other words, the expectation that a signal will be present on a given trial can be made to change by varying the probability or frequency of the signal over the trials of the experiment. If the signal occurs on almost every trial, then the observer may almost

**Table 20.4**   Response proportions for a signal presented on 90% of the trials and no signal on 10%

|                 | Response |      |
|-----------------|----------|------|
|                 | *Yes*    | *No* |
| Signal present  | 0.95     | 0.05 |
| Signal absent   | 0.78     | 0.22 |

**Table 20.5**   Response proportions for a signal presented on 10% of the trials and no signal on 90%

|                 | Response |      |
|-----------------|----------|------|
|                 | *Yes*    | *No* |
| Signal present  | 0.28     | 0.72 |
| Signal absent   | 0.04     | 0.96 |

always expect a signal to be presented. As a result, the observer will adopt a relatively generous or liberal criterion (a shift of the criterion to the left in Figure 20.4). The result is a tendency by the observer to respond "Yes" even when no signal is present. The result, of course, will be a high probability of hits, but due to the observer's positive expectation and the resulting tendency of the observer to report, "Yes," the probability of false alarms will be higher than if no such expectation was created. In contrast, if the signal is rarely present, the observer will adopt a relatively conservative criterion (a shift of the criterion to the right in Figure 20.4) with a tendency to respond "No," even when the signal is present. The result in this case is fewer false alarms but also more misses.

Table 20.4 presents some reported response proportions for the case when the signal is presented on 90 percent of the trials and not presented on 10 percent (note that trials in which no signal is presented are typically referred to as catch trials in signal detection research). Table 20.5 shows the response proportions for the case when the same signal is presented on 10 percent of the trials and no signal is presented on 90 percent. The difference between the two tables for the *same* signal magnitude shows that the difference in the proportion of signal presentations (and catch trials) alone markedly affects the expectations, and hence the performance, of the observer; the result is systematic changes in the proportion of hits and false alarms. In other words, variations in the proportion of hits and false alarms are attributable to variation of the observer's criterion $\beta$ (in this case due to expectation) in reaction to the change in the proportion of catch trials. It should be stressed that the differences in the response proportions between Tables 20.4 and 20.5 indicate that changes occur in detection performance to a constant stimulus, with no corresponding change in stimulus intensity. Specifically, in this case, detection performance varies due to changes in the observer's *expectation* that a stimulus will occur, not to any change in the stimulus magnitude itself.

Another nonsensory response bias factor that affects the criterion ($\beta$) level is the *motivation* to detect a specific outcome, that is, the observer's concern with the consequences of the detection response. For instance, if the observer is highly motivated to detect the signal – trying never to miss it – he or she will likely lower the criterion or $\beta$ level for reporting its presence, thereby increasing the number of "Yes" responses and hits (again, a shift of the criterion to the left in Figure 20.4). Increasing the number of "Yes" responses will also raise the number of false alarms. On the other hand, the use of a more restrictive, conservative criterion (i.e., moving the $\beta$ level in Figure 20.4 to the right) increases the number of "No" responses. Although this strategy may yield fewer false alarms, it also results in fewer hits.

An experimental task in which $\beta$ is intentionally manipulated shows how an observer's motivation may affect the proportion of hits and false alarms. Suppose that you are an observer in the following signal detection experiment. You are instructed that on each trial you may or may not hear a very faint tone. Accordingly, after each trial you are to respond "Yes" or "No," depending on whether or not you heard a tone. Moreover, your response has certain monetary consequences. Consider three different outcome or payoff conditions:

1. For each hit, you win $1. You will tend to respond "Yes" on almost every trial, even when you are unsure if you heard a tone.
2. Similarly, for each hit you win $1, but you are also penalized 50 cents for a false alarm. You will still tend to respond "Yes" when you are unsure, although more reluctantly than in condition (1), where there was no penalty for a false alarm.
3. In contrast to the payoff conditions in (1) and (2), you receive 50 cents for each hit but are also penalized $1 for a false alarm. With this payoff condition you will tend to respond cautiously, answering "Yes" only when you are certain.

A summary of some observed response proportions of hits and false alarms appropriate to these three payoff conditions is given in Table 20.6.

**Table 20.6**   Proportion of hits and false alarms for three payoff conditions[a]

| | Response proportion made by observer | |
|---|---|---|
| *Payoff Condition* | *Hits* | *False alarms* |
| Observer gets: | | |
| 1. $1 for hit | 0.95 | 0.95 |
| 2. $1 for hit and 50-cent penalty for false alarm | 0.85 | 0.70 |
| 3. 50 cents for hit and $1 penalty for false alarm | 0.40 | 0.10 |

[a] Varying the outcome or payoff produces variation in the proportion of hits and false alarms for the same stimuli.

What has been described is a change in the criterion or $\beta$ and the corresponding variation in the proportion of hits and false alarms due to the payoff of the response. The same stimuli may elicit a "Yes" or a "No" response, depending on the consequences – the rewards and penalties – independent of the observer's sensitivity to the stimuli. Thus, even in a relatively simple psychophysical task like deciding whether a faint signal is present or not, the observer's performance may be significantly affected by nonsensory factors, that is, by response bias. This consideration should make it clear that there is no simply observed absolute threshold value. Rather, the observer adjusts the response criterion to both the intensity of the signal and to certain nonsensory variables, such as motivation to the task and the expectation of the signal's occurrence.

## ROC curves

SDT holds that we cannot extract an absolute threshold value. However, we can obtain a measure of an observer's *sensitivity* to the presentation of a stimulus and his or her decision criterion or $\beta$ level at the same time. The separate effects of the observer's sensitivity in detecting the signal and the effects of a shifting criterion ($\beta$ is derived by analyzing the relation between the proportion of hits and the proportion of false alarms – a relation, as noted, that shifts as the criterion is varied). Typically, the proportion of hits (saying "Yes" to *SN* activity) is plotted on the *y*-axis and the proportion of false alarms (saying "Yes" to *N* activity alone) is plotted on the *x*-axis. The resultant curves, called receiver operating characteristic (ROC) curves, graphically display the relation between the proportions of hits and false alarms for a constant stimulus intensity (see Figure 20.5 for an example of an ROC curve, whose derivation is described below).

The term *ROC* refers to the idea that the curve measures and describes the operating or sensitivity characteristics of the receiver (i.e., the observer) in detecting signals. Consider how an ROC curve may describe an observer's sensitivity measure for a particular signal, whose intensity level is held constant. Table 20.7 illustrates how the probability of a signal affects the proportion of hits and false alarms for a hypothetical experiment in which the signal intensity is held constant (some of these signal proportions are taken from Tables 20.4 and 20.5). Thus, if the signal is almost always present in the trials of a signal detection experiment (e.g., 90 percent in Table 20.7), the observer tends to increase the probability of saying "Yes." The result is an increase in the proportion of hits (0.95 for this example), with a corresponding increase in the proportion of false alarms (0.78). In contrast, when the signal is presented on only 10 percent of the trials (i.e., 90 percent catch trials), for the *same signal intensity*, the proportion of hits is 0.28 and the proportion of false alarms is 0.04. Clearly, when the signal is infrequent – actually present in only 10 percent of the trials – the observer tends to say "No." As a result, although the proportion of false alarms is quite small (0.04), the proportion of hits is also relatively low (0.28). Figure 20.5 is an ROC curve based on these values. Note, for example, that the top value is for the condition in which 90 percent of the trials had a signal. Referring to the table, we note that the hit rate plotted on the

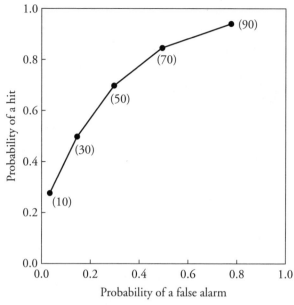

**Figure 20.5** ROC curve for the data of Table 20.7. The probability of a hit (*y*-axis) is plotted against the probability of a false alarm (*x*-axis). Each point plotted represents the hits and false alarms for a different percentage of signal presentations (shown in parentheses). (Note that the curve is fitted by eye.)
*Source:* Based on Schiffman (2001).

**Table 20.7** Proportion of hits and false alarms for different percentages of signal presentations (hypothetical data)[a]

| Percentage of trials containing a signal | Proportion of: | |
|---|---|---|
| | Hits | False alarms |
| 90 | 0.95 | 0.78 |
| 70 | 0.85 | 0.50 |
| 50 | 0.70 | 0.30 |
| 30 | 0.50 | 0.15 |
| 10 | 0.28 | 0.04 |

[a] These proportions are derived from presentation of a signal of constant intensity. Hence, the differences in the proportions of hits and false alarms reflect the effects of differences in criteria, or $\beta$, produced by varying the percentage of signals and catch trials (10% to 90%) over the course of many trials.

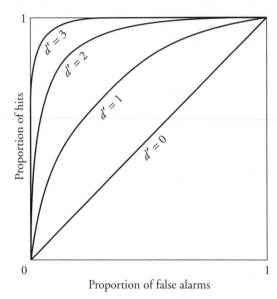

**Figure 20.6**    ROC curves for three signals that are detectable to different degrees.
The proportion of hits (*y*-axis) is plotted against the proportion of false alarms (*x*-axis).
Each curve expresses a specific value of sensitivity to a specific signal intensity. (The *d′*
value represents a numerical measure of the observer's sensitivity, described in the text.)
*Source*: Based on Schiffman (2001).

*y*-axis is 0.95 and the false alarm rate plotted on the *x*-axis is 0.78. When all the data
points of Table 20.7 are plotted, an obvious trend emerges: The data points appear to lie
on a symmetrical curve bowed to the left. If more trials were administered, using the
same *stimulus intensity* but with probabilities of signals to catch trials different from
those plotted here, their hit and false alarm proportions would no doubt differ from
those in Table 20.7 – reflecting the effect of a shifting criterion – but when plotted on
Figure 20.5, they would lie somewhere *on* the curve. That is, a given ROC curve reflects
the observer's detection performance for a single stimulus intensity. Thus, for a given
ROC curve, the observer's sensitivity is constant for all points along the curve. The
signal intensity and the observer's sensory ability do not change. What does change is
the proportion of hits and false alarms due to variations in the observer's criterion or
*β* level.

It has been stressed that the points plotted in Figure 20.5 are for a signal of constant
intensity. When the signal is more intense, it becomes more detectable and a different
ROC curve is generated. For a weaker, less detectable signal, still another ROC curve is
derived (examples of different ROC curves are given in Figure 20.6). Thus an ROC
curve illustrates how varying the observer's *β* level (in this case, by varying the *expectation* of a signal) affects the proportion of hits and false alarms for a fixed signal intensity.
Each ROC curve graphically shows the effect of the observer's sensitivity to a constant
signal intensity *plus* the effects of the observer's *β* level.

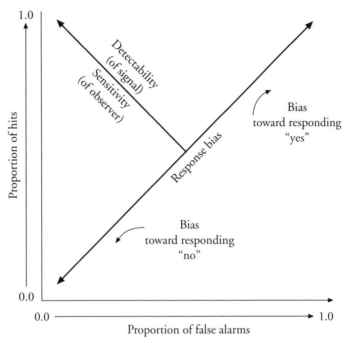

**Figure 20.7** The features of a ROC curve. The 45° diagonal response bias line represents chance performance. In this case the hit rate equals the observer's false alarm rate.
Source: Based on Schiffman (2001).

*Sensitivity: d'*

As an aid to visualization, the general features of an ROC curve are given in Figure 20.7, showing how the curvature of the ROC curve represents the observer's sensitivity to the signal and his or her response bias or criterion effects. As noted, when the signal is made more intense, it becomes more detectable and, as indicated earlier in Figure 20.6, the ROC curve is bowed higher to the left; when the signal is weaker, the ROC curve lies closer to the 45° diagonal (the diagonal line represents the observer's chance perform-ance, that is, where the hit and false alarm rates are equal). In short, the bow of the ROC curve to the left, that is, away from the 45° line, is determined by the intensity of the signal and is independent of the observer's response bias.

A measure of the bowing or curvature of the ROC curve, called *d'*, can be calculated. It is based on the hit and false alarm rates and serves as a statistical measure of the observer's sensory capacity or sensitivity to a particular signal intensity. In practice, the value of *d'* is estimated by the linear distance of a given ROC curve from the 45° diagonal chance line. Figure 20.6 gives ROC curves for values of *d'* ranging from 0 to 3. Note that the higher the *d'* value (and the more bowed the curve), the higher the hit rate and the lower the rate of false alarms. Thus the greater the *d'* value, the more sensitive is the observer to the particular signal intensity and the greater is the detectability of the signal. In graphic terms, the degree of bowing in the ROC curve serves as a measure of the observer's sensitivity to a signal of constant intensity. Note also that differences in $d'$ between individuals for a constant signal intensity reflect individual differences in sensitivity.

The procedure for computing $d'$ is beyond the scope of this chapter (there are published tables that researchers use to compute values of $d'$ from hit and false alarm rates; e.g., Green & Swets, 1966). However, it is important to understand that $d'$ serves as a measure of the observer's sensitivity to the signal's intensity independent of his or her response bias effects ($\beta$). This can be visualized by graphing the sensory effects from which the ROC curves of Figure 20.6 are derived. Observe that $d'$ represents the linear distance between the two sensory distributions introduced at the beginning of the discussion of SDT, namely, the $N$ and $SN$ distributions (see Figure 20.8). With increasing signal intensity, the $SN$ distribution moves farther to the right of the $N$ distribution. In contrast, if the intensity of the signal is very weak, the $N$ and $SN$ distributions lie very close together. For example, for $d' = 1$, the distributions of $N$ and $SN$ lie relatively close together; the signal is moderately weak, and therefore it is somewhat difficult to detect (incidentally, the $d'$ value for the data of Table 20.7 plotted in Figure 20.5 is 1). In contrast, for $d' = 3$, the signal is relatively intense and its effect on the sensory system is quite easy to detect from the effect of noise. Thus, with increasing signal intensity, the $SN$ distribution is displaced farther from the $N$ distribution, resulting in a larger value of $d'$. In short, a high $d'$ value means that the signal is intense (and/or that the observer is sensitive to the particular signal). Thus the $d'$ value provides a measure of sensitivity to the signal independent of such nonsensory factors as the observer's expectations and other decision-making strategies. In short, $d'$ reflects the detectability of a signal intensity based only upon an observer's sensitivity or sensory capacity.

What SDT points out about the detection of weak stimuli is that even simple commonplace tasks, such as deciding whether a stimulus was present or not, is not nearly as precise as we might think. Moreover, SDT allows a researcher to do what the traditional approach to thresholds does not: to assess the role of nonsensory bias effects ($\beta$) on the observer's decision in a signal detection task. Clearly, as we have observed, the observer's decision as to the presence of a signal depends on the experiences that he or she brings to the task, as well as expectations, motives, attention factors, and probably other nonsensory psychological factors. Indeed, perhaps the most significant feature of SDT is that it allows researchers to isolate and evaluate the separate effects of the observer's sensory capacity apart from the observer's nonsensory response bias on his or her performance in marginal stimulus conditions.

The discussion of SDT questions the validity of a single absolute stimulus that represents the minimum value of a stimulus – a *threshold* level – for its detection. However, this is not to say that the sensory threshold notion should be discarded. Rather, it is reasonable to assume that the general notion of a threshold encompasses and describes a *range* of values whose expression is influenced by a variety of nonsensory environmental and observer effects. In fact, a threshold, as a statistical average, is a very useful concept that has widespread application. In terms of energy values, it provides an important approximation of the range and limits of the sensory system. It is thus necessary to interpret threshold statements cautiously; they serve as statistical approximations

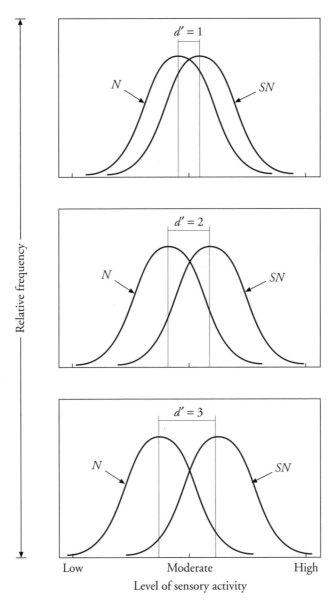

**Figure 20.8** A graphic representation of the distributions of *N* and *SN* for the three ROC curves of Figure 20.7. Here the value of *d'* is shown to vary with the sensory effects of the *SN* distribution relative to the effects of the *N* distribution. This is indicated by the distance between the average of the distributions of *N* and *SN*. Of course, for *d'* = 0 the distributions of *N* and *SN* fully overlap. The value of *d'*, then, represents a measure of signal intensity and the observer's sensitivity to the signal, independent of response bias.
*Source*: Based on Schiffman (2001).

suggesting an average magnitude and/or a range of magnitudes, rather than as a single energy value.

## The Difference Threshold

The difference threshold (or difference limen) is the smallest difference between two stimuli necessary to detect them as different. In other words, the difference threshold is the measure of the smallest detectable difference between two stimuli. Basically, it answers the psychophysical question: how different must two stimuli – say, two lights, two colors, two sounds, or two touches – be from each other in order to detect them as different stimuli?

In practice, the difference threshold, like the absolute threshold described at the beginning of this chapter, is a derived statistical measure: generally, it is the difference in magnitude between two stimuli, usually a standard and a comparison stimulus, that is detected 50 percent of the time (sometimes the difference threshold is based on a stimulus difference between the standard and the comparison that is detected 75 percent of the time). For instance, if two tones of the same intensity or nearly the same intensity are presented, one immediately following the other, the listener will generally report that they are equal in loudness. However, as we gradually increase the intensity difference between the two tones, a difference in intensity will be reached at which a different judgment will be reported on 50 percent of the trials. The magnitude of this difference in intensity specifies the difference threshold. Thus the difference threshold is the amount of *change* in a physical stimulus necessary to produce a just noticeable difference (JND) in sensation. As an example, if the magnitude of a physical stimulus – say, a sound, given in arbitrary units – is 100 units, and the sound has to be increased to 110 units to produce a *just noticeable change* in the sound, the difference threshold of 10 units (i.e., 110 minus 100) corresponds to one JND.

It should be clear that the difference threshold is a measure of the observer's ability to discriminate two stimulus magnitudes from each other; as such, it is measured in physical units. By contrast, the JND refers to the resultant psychological unit; that is, it represents the unit of subjective experience or sensory magnitude.

### Weber's fraction

The investigation of the difference threshold is a significant milestone in the history of the measurement of sensation. In 1834, Ernst Weber, a German physiologist, invest-igated the ability of observers to perform discrimination tasks. He observed that the amount of change – increase or decrease – in a stimulus necessary to detect it as different is proportional to the absolute magnitude of the stimulus. In short, he noted that discriminating between the magnitudes of two stimuli is a matter of relative rather than absolute judgment. For example, Weber found that although the addition of one candle to 60 lit ones resulted in the perception of a difference in brightness, one candle added to 120 did not. For a JND for the brightness of 120 candles, at least two candles were required (i.e., the brightness of 122 candles was just noticeably different from the brightness of 120 candles). Extending this example, the difference threshold for the brightness of 300 candles requires five or more lit candles; for 600 candles, 10 additional ones are required, and so on.

What Weber had observed more than 150 years ago is that regardless of their absolute physical magnitudes or intensities, two stimuli must differ by a constant *proportion* in order for their physical difference to be perceptible (i.e., to produce a JND). This general principle of the relativity of sensory experience – that the detection of a change in a stimulus is relative to the magnitude of the stimulus – makes intuitive sense. For instance, although a couple of drops of water will be easily detected when added to the contents of a small test tube, the same two drops will likely produce no discernable sensory effect when added to a gallon of water. Likewise, we readily perceive that 1 lb. is different from 2 lbs, but we find it difficult to distinguish between 50 lbs and 51 lbs, yet both pairs of weights differ by the same amount: 1 lb.

The discussion has focused on a fundamental principle of relative sensitivity referred to as Weber's fraction (or Weber's ratio), which is symbolized as follows:

$$\Delta I / I = k$$

where $I$ is the magnitude of the stimulus intensity at which the threshold is obtained; $\Delta I$ (read as "delta" $I$) is the difference threshold value or the increment of intensity that, when added to the stimulus intensity $I$, produces a JND (i.e., the increment of change in sensation); and $k$ is a constant that varies with the sensory system being measured.

The equation states that the smallest detectable increment ($\Delta I$) in the intensity continuum of a stimulus is a constant proportion ($k$) of the intensity of the original stimulus ($I$). Weber's fraction thus indicates the proportion by which a stimulus intensity must be changed in order to detect the change (i.e., produce a JND), and that $k$ is constant within a given stimulus dimension such as brightness, loudness, weight, and so on. In Weber's example of the brightness of candles, the $\Delta I$ values for 60, 120, 300, and 600 lit candles would be 1, 2, 5, and 10, and the respective Weber fractions would be 1/60, 2/120, 5/300, and 10/600, which all reduce to $k = 1/60$. Thus, in general, computing the proportion of a stimulus that must be changed in order to yield a JND solves the value of $k$.

Table 20.8 gives the representative Weber fractions for a variety of sensory dimensions. Observe that for these sensory dimensions, the Weber fractions vary from a high of 0.083 (8.3%) for salty taste to a low of 0.013 (1.3%) for electric shock. Using "heaviness" for a computational example, the Weber fraction is 0.02 or 2/100; this means that we must increase the weight of a stimulus by 0.02 or 2% to produce a JND. Thus 2 grams must be added to a 100-gram weight, 4 grams must be added to a 200-gram weight, and 20 grams must be added to a 1000-gram weight for a difference to be detected.

The size of the Weber fraction gives a measure of the overall sensitivity to detecting differences in stimulus intensity along a particular sensory dimension. Recall that the smaller the fraction, the smaller is the change in intensity necessary to produce a JND. Thus, the smaller the Weber fraction, the greater is the sensitivity to stimulus differences.

**Table 20.8**   Representative Weber fractions for different sensory dimensions

| Dimension | Weber value[a] |
| --- | --- |
| Taste (salt) | 0.083 |
| Brightness | 0.079 |
| Loudness | 0.048 |
| Vibration (at fingertip) | 0.036 |
| Line length | 0.029 |
| Heaviness | 0.020 |
| Electric shock | 0.013 |

*Source*: Based on Teghtsoonian (1971).
[a] Weber values are expressed in decimal form for ease in making computations. For example, Heaviness, 0.020, expressed as a fraction, is 1/50 (or 2%). The smaller the Weber value, the smaller the change in the intensity of a stimulus necessary to produce a JND.

With respect to the values given in Table 20.8, note that we are least sensitive to differences in taste and brightness – requiring an 8.3 percent and 7.9 percent change, respectively – whereas we are most sensitive to differences in electric shock and heaviness – requiring only a 1.3 percent and 2 percent change, respectively.

How accurate is Weber's fraction? In general, it is reasonably valid for a wide range of stimulus intensities, including most of our everyday experiences, but it tends to break down for very weak and very strong intensity levels along all sensory dimensions. It can be concluded that within a broad middle range of intensities, the Weber fraction provides a useful measure of the ability to discriminate between two stimuli. However, beyond practical considerations, Weber's fraction has played an important role in the measurement of sensation, and it stands as one of the broadest empirical generalizations in the history of experimental psychology. Moreover, it provided the groundwork for a quantitative analysis of the relationship between the physical stimulus and sensory experience, especially the analysis made by Fechner.

## Fechner's law

In 1860 Gustave Theodor Fechner published *The Elements of Psychophysics* (Fechner [1860] 1966), a monograph that had a profound effect on the measurement of sensation and perception. His basic premise was that mental experience – sensation – is quantitatively related to the physical stimulus. He attempted to derive an expression of the relation between the two, developing a numerical scale of sensation for a given sensory modality. Fechner's work led to an important equation relating the magnitude of sensation to the magnitude of the stimulus. More specifically, he proposed that the difference threshold ($\Delta I$) that produces the JND could be used as a standard unit to measure the subjective magnitude of sensation (recall that the difference threshold refers to the

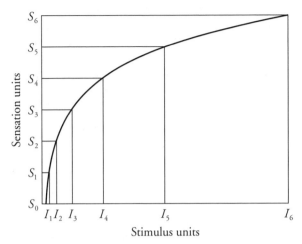

**Figure 20.9** The relation between the sensation continuum and the stimulus continuum according to Fechner's law. Notice that larger and larger differences between stimulus units ($I$) are required with increases in the stimulus continuum in order to maintain equal differences between sensation units ($S$) on the sensation continuum. That is, as the sensation increases in equal steps (arithmetically), the corresponding stimulus continuum increases in physically unequal but proportional steps (geometrically). The relation between an arithmetic and a geometric series is represented by a logarithmic function. Thus $S = k \log I$.
*Source*: Based on Schiffman (2001), revised from Guilford (1954).

incremental change in stimulus intensity that produces a JND). What Fechner attempted was a scale that linked subjective experience – sensations, in units of JND – to changes in stimulus intensity, in units of $\Delta I$. He began with the assumption that, for a given sensory system, all JNDs represent subjectively equal units of sensation. This proposition means that the subjective impression of the difference between two stimuli separated by a single JND is the same, regardless of the values of the two stimuli. That is, if you take two stimuli at the low end of the intensity scale that are separated by one JND, then the sensation of the difference between them is the same as it is for two stimuli separated by one JND taken from the high end of the intensity scale. In effect, according to Fechner's assumption, every JND, regardless of its location on the intensity scale, is equal to every other JND.

Recall that according to Weber's constant fraction, a given JND corresponds to a constant proportional increase in the stimulus (i.e., $\Delta I / I$ is a constant, so as $I$ increases, $\Delta I$ must increase correspondingly). This relation means that if the basic intensity is low, the increment of change necessary to produce a JND is correspondingly small; in contrast, if the initial intensity is high, the stimulus increment necessary for the JND is correspondingly large. In other words, at the low end of the intensity scale, two stimuli will be separated by one JND when they are physically close together, whereas at the high end of the intensity scale, two stimuli will be separated by one JND when they are widely separated physically. This relation between sensation and stimulation is illustrated in Figure 20.9. Under the assumption that all JNDs are psychologically equal, it follows that as the sensation scale (*y*-axis) increases in equal units, the stimulus intensity scale increases in progressively larger and larger units. As Figure 20.9 shows, larger and larger outputs in stimulus intensity are required to obtain corresponding effects in sensory experience. In more quantitative terms, as the number of sensation units (i.e., JNDs) grows arithmetically (*y*-axis), the stimulus intensity increases geometrically (*x*-axis).

Arithmetic increases in the sensory scale and geometric increases in the intensity scale express a logarithmic relationship. The arithmetic to geometric progression between sensation and intensity reduces mathematically to the logarithmic relation known as Fechner's law. That is, the magnitude of a sensation is a logarithmic function of the stimulus, or

$$S = k \log I$$

where *S* is the magnitude of the sensation, *I* is the logarithm of the physical intensity of the stimulus, and *k* is a constant that takes into account the Weber fraction of the specific sensory dimension examined. This logarithmic relation shows that sensation increases less rapidly than stimulus intensity; as stimulus intensity increases, a greater increase in intensity is necessary to produce the same sensory effect. So larger and larger steps in intensity are required to produce equal sensory effects.

How effective is Fechner's law in describing the relation between sensation and stimulus intensity? Like Weber's law, on which it is based, Fechner's law is reasonably accurate under many conditions, but it is limited, serving best as an approximation of the relationship of sensory magnitude to stimulus magnitude. In fact, the key assumption in Fechner's law that all JNDs are subjectively equal is questionable. For example, according to this assumption, a tone 20 JND units above the absolute threshold should sound twice as loud as one 10 JND units above the threshold (since one tone contains twice as many JND units as the other tone). In fact, however, the tone 20 JND units above the threshold sounds far more than twice as loud as one 10 JND units above the threshold. In short, all JNDs for a given sensory dimension do not produce equal sensory effects.

### Stevens's Power Law

Fechner devised a psychophysical scale of sensation based on the difference threshold and the constancy of Weber's fraction along a given sensory dimension. A different psychophysical scale, based on different assumptions, was devised by S. S. Stevens about 100 years after Fechner's work. Stevens proposed that the relation between sensory magnitude and stimulus magnitude is *not* logarithmic. In fact, one of Stevens's papers disputing Fechner's logarithmic equation is pointedly titled, "To honor Fechner and repeal his law" (Stevens, 1961a). Although recognizing that the relation between stimulus magnitude and sensory magnitude is not a simple one, Stevens argued that a researcher could obtain a direct estimation of an observer's sensory experience using several psychophysical methods in which observers directly translate estimates of their sensations into numbers.

When using the most frequently employed method, called *magnitude estimation*, the observer is presented with a standard stimulus, called a *modulus*, such as a light or a tone of moderate intensity, and is instructed to assign a numerical value to it, say 10 or 100. Then the observer is presented, one at a time, with a series of randomly ordered stimuli that vary along a single dimension, say physical intensity. For each stimulus, the observer gives a number that expresses his or her judgment of the stimulus relative to the standard (modulus). In essence, in a very direct way the observer is estimating the sensory impression of each stimulus with a number. For an example, using tones and a modulus value of 100, if the observer is presented with a tone that sounds twice as loud as the standard modulus, he or she will assign the number 200; a tone that the observer estimates to be half as loud as the modulus is assigned the number 50; a tone that sounds only one-fourth as loud as the standard modulus is rated 25, and so on. In short, the observer attempts to match the perceived intensity of each stimulus in the series with a number relative to the standard modulus number. When the task is completed, the physical intensities of the tones presented can be directly compared with the magnitude estimates made by the observers resulting in a scale of loudness.

Using such methods, Stevens and numerous other workers have found a mathematical relation between the magnitude of the stimulus dimension and the magnitude of sensation called the power law. According to the power law, sensory or subjective magnitude grows in proportion to the physical intensity of the stimulus raised to a power. In short, sensory magnitude is equal to physical intensity raised to a power. Stated as an equation,

$S = kIb$

where $S$ is sensation, $k$ is a constant (a scale factor that takes into account the choice of units used in a given sensory dimension, e.g., inches, grams, watts) in stimulus intensity, and $b$ is the exponent to which the intensity is raised (which is a constant for a given sensory dimension).

Two points should be stressed: (1) the exponent of the equation – $b$ – reflects the relation between sensory magnitude and stimulus magnitude, and (2) each sensory continuum or dimension – brightness, loudness, and so on – has its own exponent ($b$). Some of the sensory continuums that conform to a power law relation, along with their exponents, are shown in Table 20.9. Thus, by using a power law formulation, it is possible to show that the sensory dimensions for various perceptual tasks differ from each other in the extent to which the sensory magnitude changes with stimulus magnitude. For example, when the magnitude estimation method is used for the judged length of a line (cited as "Visual length" in Table 20.9), the exponent of the calculated power equation is very close to 1.00 and the equation reduces to $S = kI$. This relation means that apparent length grows in direct proportion to physical length. The relation between sensation (or psychological magnitude) and stimulus magnitude can be plotted as a curve called a power function. This relation is depicted in Figure 20.10 as a straight 45° line power function. This relation between sensation and stimulation for line length means, for example, that a line 10 inches long looks twice as long as one 5 inches long, and that a 10-inch line looks half as long as a 20-inch line. For the sensation of brightness, as derived by the direct method of magnitude estimation, the exponent is

**Table 20.9**   Representative exponents *(b)* of the power functions relating psychological magnitude to stimulus magnitude

| Continuum | Measured exponent (b) | Stimulus condition |
|---|---|---|
| Loudness | 0.6 | Both ears |
| Brightness | 0.33 | Small target in dark |
| Smell | 0.55 | Coffee |
| Taste | 1.3 | Sucrose |
| Taste | 0.8 | Saccharine |
| Taste | 1.3 | Salt |
| Temperature | 1.0 | Cold on arm |
| Temperature | 1.6 | Warmth on arm |
| Vibration | 0.95 | 60 Hz on finger |
| Duration | 1.1 | White noise stimuli |
| Pressure on palm | 1.1 | Static force on skin |
| Heaviness | 1.45 | Lifted weights |
| Force of handgrip | 1.7 | Hand dynamometer |
| Electric shock | 3.5 | Current through fingers |
| Tactual roughness | 1.5 | Rubbing emery cloths |
| Tactual hardness | 0.8 | Squeezing rubber |
| Visual length | 1.0 | Projected line |

about 0.33. When the relation between stimulus magnitude and sensory or psychological magnitude is plotted, as in Figure 20.10, the power function relation is a curve that is concave downward. This function means that brightness (the sensory dimension) increases much more slowly than light intensity – a *compression* of the sensory or response dimension. For example, to double the brightness sensation of a light, a considerable amount of light intensity – clearly in excess of the doubling of light intensity – must be expended.

In contrast to brightness, the exponent for electric shock applied to the finger is about 3.5. As shown in Figure 20.10, its power function is represented by a curve that is concave upward. Clearly, even a small amount of electric current applied to the finger tip (which may, of course, also signal pain) results in a significant sensory effect – in this case, an expansion of the sensory dimension. Indeed, a doubling of the electric current flow through one's finger tip results in considerably more than a doubling of sensation (more like a 10-fold increase), that is, *response expansion.*

In general, the exponent of the power function determines its curvature and indicates how sensory magnitude grows with stimulus magnitude. An exponent close to 1.00 results in a straight line. A power function with an exponent greater than 1.00 is represented by a curve that is concave upward, with a response expansion; if the exponent is less than 1.00, the curvature is concave downward, reflecting a response compression. However, a convenient property of power functions is that when stimulus intensity and sensory or psychological magnitude are plotted in log-log coordinates (i.e.,

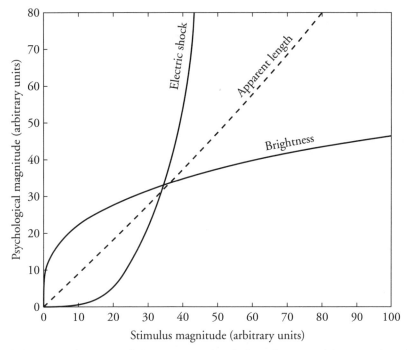

**Figure 20.10**   Power functions relating sensation (psychological magnitude) to stimulus intensity (stimulus magnitude). The shape of a power function is related to its exponent; a curve is concave upward when its exponent is greater than 1.0 and concave downward when its exponent is less than 1.0. Thus the sensory magnitudes of electric shock and brightness follow different growth curves because their power law exponents (*b*) are 3.5 and 0.33, respectively. The power function for apparent length is almost straight because its exponent is about 1.00. Here the scale units of the *x*- and *y*-axes have been chosen arbitrarily to show the relative form of the curves on a single graph.

*Source*: Based on Schiffman (2001), revised from Stevens (1961b).

logarithmic scales on both *x*- and *y*-axes, generally achieved by using special graph paper that has both axes stretched out logarithmically), the power law equation describes a straight line whose *slope* (or measure of steepness) is the exponent, *b*. This equation means that when both the sensory magnitude and stimulus magnitude are plotted on logarithmic scales, the curvature of the functions disappears and the slope of the result-ant straight line becomes a direct measure of the exponent of the power equation. Accordingly, as shown in Figure 20.11, when the power function curves of Figure 20.10 are replotted in log-log coordinates, differences in curvature become differences in slope. In log-log coordinates the high exponent for the sensation of electric shock gives a steep slope, brightness gives a relatively flat slope, and the linear function for perceived length results in a 45° line with a slope of about 1.00.

Stevens's power law has proved to be extremely useful in psychophysics because almost any sensory dimension – within which observers can reliably assign a numerical

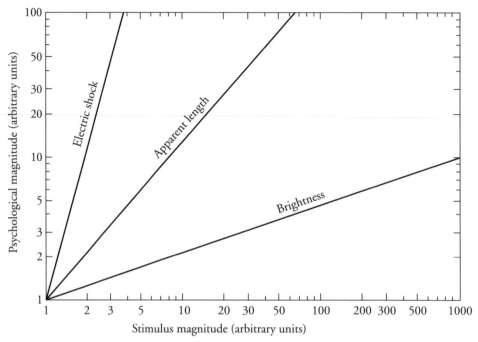

**Figure 20.11**   Power functions plotted in logarithmic coordinates. When the curves in Figure 20.10 are replotted in log-log coordinates, they become straight lines. The slope of the lines corresponds to the exponent of the power function governing the growth of the sensation (psychological magnitude).
*Source*: Based on Schiffman (2001), revised from Stevens (1961b).

value to their subjective impression or sensation – can be readily scaled. Indeed, there is general agreement that the power law provides a valid representation of the relation between subjective experience (sensation) and physical intensity.

## Summary

This chapter outlined some of the central topics of psychophysics, an area of sensation and perception that examines the relation between physical stimulation and subjective experience. The concepts of the absolute and difference threshold, including general techniques for their assessment, were described. The absolute threshold (or absolute limen) was defined as the minimum amount of energy required to detect a stimulus.

The topic of the absolute threshold was followed by a discussion of signal detection theory (SDT). SDT stresses that, when confronting marginal or very weak stimulus conditions, an observer's decision as to whether or not a stimulus (or signal) is present is affected by certain nonsensory response biases – such as the observer's attention, expectation, and motivation. The discussion noted that SDT makes it possible to isolate and evaluate the effects of sensory capacity and response bias on the observer's performance.

The difference threshold was introduced as the amount of change in stimulus energy necessary to produce a detectable difference between two stimuli. This was followed by a discussion of Weber's fraction, which states that the amount of change in a stimulus necessary to detect it as different is proportional to the magnitude of the stimulus. Fechner's extension of Weber's fraction was then described. Fechner formulated a mathematical equation linking sensation to stimulation. Fechner's equation states that the magnitude of a sensation is proportional to the logarithm of the physical intensity of the stimulus. Although the general validity of both Weber's fraction and especially Fechner's equation has been questioned, their impact on measurement in psychology has been significant.

Stevens's power law, an alternative to Fechner's law concerning scaling sensory experience, was then discussed. This law holds that for many kinds of sensory and perceptual phenomena, the relation between sensation and stimulation can be expressed by an exponential function; that is, sensation grows in proportion to the physical intensity of the stimulus raised to a power. This formulation expresses the relation between sensation and stimulation that has been applied effectively in many diverse domains of psychology.

## References

Cornsweet, T. N. (1962). The staircase-method in psychophysics. *American Journal of Psychology*, 75, 485 91.

Fechner, G. T. ([1860] 1966). *Elements of psychophysics*. New York: Holt, Rinehart & Winston.

Galanter, E. (1962). Contemporary psychophysics. In R. Brown, E. Galanter, E. H. Hess, & G. Mandler (eds.), *New directions in psychology* (pp. 89–156). New York: Holt, Rinehart and Winston.

Green, D. M., & Swets, J. A. (1966). *Signal detection theory and psychophysics*. New York: Wiley.

Guilford, J. P. (1954). *Psychometric methods*. New York: McGraw-Hill.

Schiffman, H. R. (2001). *Sensation and perception: An integrated approach*. New York: Wiley.

Stevens, S. S. (1961a). To honor Fechner and repeal his law. *Science*, 133, 80–6.

Stevens, S. S. (1961b). Psychophysics of sensory function. In W. A. Rosenblith (ed.), *Sensory communication* (pp. 1–33). Cambridge, MA: MIT Press.

Teghtsoonian, R. (1971). On the exponents in Stevens' law and the constant in Ekman's law. *Psychological Review*, 78, 71–80.

# Subject Index

# Name Index

Campbell, R. G.   406
Campos, A. C.   158
Candilis, P. J.   136, 137
Cannold, L.   131
Cannon, W. B.   397–8, 405
Canter, M. B.   116
Capaldi, E. J.   26, 27, 28, 32, 112, 303, 306, 307, 308
Capitanio, J. P.   228
Caplan, A. L.   129
Capron, A. M.   136
Carew, T. J.   165, 230
Carlsmith, J. M.   46, 63
Carlson, N. R.   120
Carpenter, W. T.   136, 137
Carr, H.   17–18
Carrasco, M.   263
Carroll, D.   354
Carroll, R. M.   92–3
Carroll, S. B.   234
Carsrud, A. L.   120
Cartee, G. D.   335
Carter, D. E.   254
Carver, R. P.   83, 85, 88
Casas, J. M.   133
Casey, P. J.   352
Casseday, J. H.   420
Castellan, N. J., Jr.   122
Cattell, J. M.   3, 4, 6–7, 8, 14–15, 108
Caulton, D. A.   354
Cavallaro, S.   165
Cavoto, B. R.   249, 251
Cavoto, K. K.   251, 256
Cechetto, D. F.   290
Ceci, S. J.   139, 385
Cerella, J.   256
Chalmers, A. F.   25, 32, 33, 35
Chamizo, V. D.   159
Champoux, M.   172, 175–6
Chandler, C. C.   380
Chappell, N. L.   137
Charney, D. S.   317
Chastain, G.   132
Chatzifotiou, S.   138
Chen, L.   165
Cheney, C.   116
Cheney, D. L.   170, 171, 174, 178, 228
Chennaoui, M.   341
Cheung, Y. M.   358

Choi, J.   327, 338
Chomsky, N.   324
Christensen, L.   133
Christie, B. R.   329
Church, R. M.   180, 181
Clark, M. M.   173, 177
Clark, R. E.   165
Clark, S. E.   353
Cleary, A. M.   354
Cleaveland, J. M.   157
Cobb, J. L. S.   173
Coburn-Litvak, P. S.   335
Coe, C. L.   228
Cohen, A.   128
Cohen, A. D.   167
Cohen, A. R.   56
Cohen, J.   83, 85, 86, 89, 90, 92, 98–9
Cohen, J. D.   273
Cohen, S. P.   51
Coke, J. S.   408
Collier, F. J.   220
Colombo, M.   253
Comery, T. A.   334, 335
Conley, R. R.   136, 137
Cook, R. G.   160, 249, 251, 252, 254, 256
Coomber, P.   165
Cooney, B. R.   120
Cooper, H.   90, 93
Cooper, J. O.   73
Cooper, M. A.   172, 175, 180
Cooper, R. M.   286
Copernicus, N.   34
Corbie-Smith, G.   128
Corbin, J.   114
Corbit, J. D.   406
Corl, K. G.   224
Cornelissen, P.   274
Cornsweet, T. N.   445
Cortez, A. M.   431
Cortina, J. M.   86
Corwin, J. G.   353
Costall, A.   16
Cotman, C.   327, 338, 340
Couvillon, P. A.   158, 161
Covinsky, K.   325
Cowles, M.   83
Cozby, P. C.   133
Craik, F. I.   348–9, 350, 355, 356, 358